HUMAN RESOURCES
MANAGEMENT

HUMAN RESOURCES
— MANAGEMENT —

*Perspectives, Context,
Functions, and Outcomes*

Third Edition

Gerald R. Ferris

*Institute of Labor and Industrial Relations
University of Illinois at Urbana-Champaign*

M. Ronald Buckley

*Department of Management
University of Oklahoma*

 Prentice-Hall, Englewood Cliffs, New Jersey 07632

Library of Congress Cataloging-in-Publication Data

Human resources management : perspectives, context, functions, and
   outcomes / [edited by] Gerald R. Ferris, M. Ronald Buckley. — 3rd
   ed.
  p. cm.
  Second ed. published as: Human resource management. c1990.
  Includes bibliographical references and index.
  ISBN 0-205-16377-7 (alk. paper)
 1. Personnel management. I. Ferris, Gerald L. II. Buckley, M.
Ronald. III. Human resource management.
 HF5549.H8735 1995
658.3—dc20   95-18154
                     CIP

Acquisitions Editor: Natalie Anderson
Production Management: Impressions, a Division of Edwards Brothers, Inc.
Project Manager: Cathi Profitko
Managing Editor: Joyce Turner
Buyer: Vincent Scelta
Associate Editor: Lisamarie Brassini
Editorial Assistant: Nancy Proyect
Production Assistant: Florrie Gadson

 © 1996 by Prentice-Hall, Inc.
A Simon & Schuster Company
Englewood Cliffs, New Jersey 07632

Printed in the United States of America

10 9 8 7 6 5 4 3 2 1

ISBN 0-205-16377-7

Prentice-Hall International (UK) Limited, *London*
Prentice-Hall of Australia Pty. Limited, *Sydney*
Prentice-Hall Canada Inc., *Toronto*
Prentice-Hall Hispanoamericana, S.A., *Mexico*
Prentice-Hall of India Private Limited, *New Delhi*
Prentice-Hall of Japan, Inc., *Tokyo*
Simon & Schuster Asia Pte. Ltd., *Singapore*
Editora Prentice-Hall do Brasil, Ltda., *Rio de Janeiro*

Contents

Preface

About 10 years ago we determined a need for a book of current readings in the field of personnel management with an applied orientation. At that time only a few books of such readings existed, and most of those were aimed at a reasonably high level, focusing on articles from scholarly journals. This was also a time when the field of personnel management was undergoing change. People were beginning to look upon the personnel function within organizations as one that made a difference. So, with a couple of colleagues, we published the first edition of *Current Issues in Personnel Management* in 1980.

In 1983 we published the second edition of *Current Issues,* continuing the focus on applied articles and reporting additional evidence concerning the transition of personnel management. The third edition was published in 1986, with a focus similar to that of the previous editions but also with some notable changes. Besides restructured content, the third edition of *Current Issues* incorporated the rapidly emerging new theme of strategic human resources management. This concept was and continues to be met with some skepticism concerning both its value and its viability. Our position has been more sympathetic and supportive. Rather than simply dismissing it as a passing fad, we prefer to regard strategic human resources management as a concept that is at an early stage in its evolution, with much need for development but also with much opportunity and potential for contribution.

In 1988, as a result of an evolution in our own thinking over the years about the issues our book addressed, we published an edition that reflected some changes in terminology and carried a more contemporary title—*Human Resources Management: Perspectives and Issues;* that volume, along with its second edition, continued the tradition and pursued the objectives we established initially.

In many respects, our mission and our objectives have not changed as we present the third edition of *Human Resources Management.* We continue to address the needs of undergraduate-, professional-, and graduate-level courses on personnel and human resources management. We have attempted to conceptualize, identify, and articulate what we consider the important contemporary perspectives and issues in the field and then to assemble a set of current readings that address these perspectives and issues with a decidedly applied, rather than scholarly, orientation. However, this edition has been modified somewhat in both organization and content to reflect the new and different issues that have been brought to bear on human resources management in recent years.

The third edition of *Human Resources Management* contains fifty-two articles. Of the fifty-two, 80 percent are new and different from the readings used in the last edition. Furthermore, twenty of the readings (38 percent) were prepared especially for this volume. One of the goals we have had since the preparation of our book's very first edition has been to increase the number of original papers included. The twenty papers in this volume represent a 33 percent increase, since the previous edition, in the number of specially prepared papers.

Instead of perpetuating the eight-chapter structure of the second edition, the third edition expands and updates the coverage of material and organizes the articles into six major parts and sixteen chapters. Users of the earlier editions will find the functional issues and activities still covered in at least as much depth as before. Moreover, this edition addresses a number of new issues concerning perspectives on the field, internal and external environmental influences, and outcomes of human resources management. Following is an overview of the book's structure and contents.

Part 1, "The Field of Human Resources Management," offers an introduction to and overview of the field; the material is organized into two chapters. The first, "Overview of Human Resources Management," provides a historical view of the field and its evolution, as well as a discussion of the meaning of this evolution for the development of future human resources professionals. Chapter 2, "Perspectives on Human Resources Management," treats three important perspectives on the field (i.e., strategic, political, and international) and demonstrates both the opportunities and challenges that these perspectives pose for human resources management.

Part 2, "The External Context of Human Resources Management," identifies certain features of the external environment or context that have impact on human resources activities. Chapter 3, "The Legal Environment," representatively reflects the strong influence of federal legislation and case law on human resources issues in organizations. Chapter 4, "The Labor Market and the Changing Work Force," deals with some key labor market characteristics and challenges and examines what diversity in the work force means for organizations. Chapter 5, "Organizational Restructuring," reveals how organizational responses to environmental events (in the form of downsizing, redesign, and restructuring) have significant implications for human resources management.

Part 3, "Functions of Human Resources Management," provides thorough coverage of the various activities and functions of human resources management, although reorganized a bit since the previous edition of this book. Chapter 6, "Human Resources Planning and Staffing," includes all of the material that is traditionally found in separate chapters devoted to human resources planning, recruitment and selection, career planning and development, and promotion and succession processes. The grouping of these various issues in a single chapter is intended to reflect their natural relatedness and the need to view them in an integrated way in organizations. Chapter 7, "Performance Appraisal," addresses the performance appraisal process, outlining some of the problems encountered and suggesting possible solutions. The articles in Chapter 8, "Compensation and Reward Systems," are concerned with the importance of the compensation function in organizations; they include examinations of compensation strategy, performance-based pay, and comparable worth. Chapter 9, "Training and Development," addresses a number of issues related to the building of work force skills at various levels and the need to link training and development efforts with business strategy.

Part 4, "Management of the Employment Relationship," is, we believe, a contemporary title that reflects the encompassing nature of the work force governance issues facing organizations today and in the future. Chapter 10, "Union-Management Relations," presents some traditional material regarding unions but, more important, discusses new and different ways in which unions and management might interact in the future. An increasingly important topic in work force governance is represented in the title of Chapter 11, "Employee Participation and Empowerment." Involving workers in organizational decisions can be useful and effective for a number of reasons, but it needs to be part of an overall strategy, not simply an ad hoc action.

Part 5, "The Internal Context of Human Resources Management," examines features of the internal organizational environment or context that have impact on human resources management. Chapter 12, "Accountability in Human Resources Systems," discusses the importance of making people in organizations answerable for their decisions and actions and highlights the problems that can result from a lack of accountability. In Chapter 13, a number of issues are examined under the title "Work Environment Stressors, Support, and Health." The authors investigate job stress, sexual harassment, and invasion of privacy as sources of stress, and they examine employee assistance programs and health issues.

The book concludes with Part 6, "Outcomes of Human Resources Management," which comprises three chapters. Chapter 14, "Employee Attitudes," emphasizes the importance of the way employees view their work, management, and the organization; it stresses the potential dysfunctional consequences of negative attitudes. "Organizational Exit," the title of Chapter 15, reflects the broad range of processes through which employees can depart from an organization. The legitimacy and effectiveness of decisions about which employees to terminate under specific conditions are examined, as are the topics of turnover, absenteeism, and outplacement. Finally, Chapter 16, "Performance and Effectiveness," treats what may be the ultimate criteria for human resources management. Topics examined include the influence and effectiveness of the human resources department as well as performance improvement, cost containment, and competitiveness as resulting from effective human resources practices.

Thus, the third edition of *Human Resources Management: Perspectives, Context, Functions, and Outcomes* reflects some reorganization, updating, and considerable coverage of the multitude of issues confronting human resources management today and in the future. With its organization and comprehensive coverage, this edition can serve as a stand-alone text for a course in human resources management or as an effective supplement to a conventional textbook that will allow the student to transcend the boundaries established by traditional treatment of the subject matter and explore some new issues.

Acknowledgments

We gratefully acknowledge the assistance and support provided by several people who helped make the third edition of *Human Resources Management* possible. First and foremost, we would like to extend a personal expression of appreciation to our editor at Prentice Hall, Natalie E. Anderson.

Second, we would like to thank our colleagues who gave unselfishly of their time to contribute original papers for this book: Jim Austin (Ohio State), Dharm Bhawuk (Hawaii), Terry Beehr (Central Michigan), Philip Benson (New Mexico State), Don Fedor (Georgia Tech), Kristofer Fenlason (Central Michigan), Jeffrey Hornsby (Ball State), Tom Kolenko (Kennesaw State), Toni Locklear (Boeing), Nancy Napier (Boise State), Ron Sims (William and Mary), Becky Thacker (Ohio), John Veres (Auburn–Montgomery), Pete Villanova (Appalachian State), Pat Wright (Texas A&M), Tom Reed (Wayne State), Joe Martocchio (Illinois), Denise Chachere (Illinois), Dwight Frink (Mississippi), Carmen Galang (Victoria), Matt Stollak (Ohio), Jack Howard (Western Illinois), Greg Bergin (Compaq), Tom Urban (ARCO), and Jeff Bender (ARCO), Brian Peach (West Florida), Harry Triandis (Illinois), John Keiser (Massachusetts), Amelia Prewett (Auburn–Montgomery), and David Gudanowski (Central Michigan).

PART 1

The Field of Human Resources Management

Our intention in Part 1 is to provide an introduction and overview of human resources management. This field is a dynamic discipline. Many of the truisms that were helpful in the past are no longer useful in facilitating the effective use of the human resources component of organizations. As all managers are managers of human resources, it is crucial that all managers have an accurate view of the human resources component. This overview will put the history and future of our field in proper perspective.

To accomplish this, we have chosen, for Chapter 1, a pair of articles that provide a historical overview of the field. These articles also treat the evolution of the field and the implications of this evolution for current practitioners. Further, these articles raise important implications for the development of future professionals in the field of human resources management.

The articles in Chapter 2 present a number of different perspectives (strategic, political, international) on human resources management. Significantly, these articles outline the challenges that face human resources professionals and, at the same time, demonstrate the opportunities that exist for those who see the importance of the human resources function. By reading the articles in this part, you will gain an appreciation of the complexity of the field of human resources, along with an optimism concerning the challenges and opportunities awaiting those who have as their goal the effective use of human resources in organizations.

CHAPTER 1

Overview of Human Resources Management

Although the history of human resources management has been relatively short, it has included a number of important advances. The field has developed greatly since the early stages of the Army Alpha and Beta Classification tests and the Hawthorne studies. Personnel clerks have been replaced by personnel managers who have, in turn, been replaced by human resources professionals. Whereas personnel was once handled by clerical staff, human resources management is now handled by professionally educated and trained staff. We have realized that human resources are the spark that turns the organization engine. Because organizations have such a large investment in their human resources, it only makes sense that they exert a sincere effort to excel at human resources. Failure to do so can have a negative effect upon organizational profitability.

With respect to human resources management, three questions need to be raised: Where are we now? Where have we been? Where should we go from here? The answers to these questions are pivotal if we are to accept the challenge of international competition. Much research and practitioner thought go toward addressing these issues. Many questions concerning human resources have been satisfactorily resolved; many more remain. The challenge is to continue to develop novel approaches to the implementation of the science of human resources management.

The authors of the articles in this chapter confront a number of the aforementioned issues. Wright and Ferris outline the historical developments in the field of human resources management. They tell where the field has been and where they believe it is headed. They offer some scenarios that should be heeded by researchers, students, and practitioners of human resources management. The second article, by Bender, Urban, Galang, Frink, and Ferris, is important because it outlines the plans of ARCO Oil and Gas Company in developing human resources professionals. ARCO has a novel approach that synthesizes a number of the important issues confronting front-line practitioners of human resources management. The authors provide a valuable template that can be used to develop human resources professionals in any organization. ARCO has a successful human resources program that can easily be emulated.

Suggestions for Further Reading

Brown, D. (1993). Centralized control or decentralized diversity: A guide for matching compensation with company strategy and structure. *Compensation & Benefits Review, 25,* 47–52.

Conner, D. (1993, Autumn). Managing change: A business imperative. *Business Quarterly,* pp. 88–92.

Fyock, C. (1993, Winter). Diversity: Passing fad, or here to stay? *Human Resources Professional,* pp. 10–12.

Kemmerer, B., & Arnold, V. (1993, Winter/Spring). The growing use of benchmarking in managing cultural diversity. *Business Forum,* pp. 38–40.

Micolo, A. (1993, September). Suggestions for achieving a strategic partnership. *HR Focus,* p. 22.

Mirvis, P. (1993, September). Is human resources out of it? *Across the Board,* pp. 50–51.

Optimism for workforce growth varies among regions. (1993, September). *HR Focus,* p. 2.

Overman, S. (1993, September). Learning system serves many HR needs. *HR Magazine,* pp. 68–69.

Overman, S. (1989). The total business partner. *Personnel Administrator, 34,* 50–53.

Stright, J., Jr. (1993). Strategic goals guide HRMS development. *Personnel Journal, 72,* 68–78.

Human Resources Management: Past, Present, and Future

Patrick M. Wright and Gerald R. Ferris

In the new information society, human capital has replaced dollar capital as the strategic resource. People and profits are inexorably linked.

Naisbitt and Aburdene,
Re-inventing the Corporation

Introduction

An increasing number of authors and managers are recognizing the critical role that human resources play in corporate success or failure. Books such as *The One-Minute Manager, In Search of Excellence, Passion for Excellence,* and *The Next American Frontier* emphasize that, without proper management of the organization's human resources, maximum productivity, profitability, and achievement in the competitive marketplace are impossible. The human resources management (HRM) function is concerned with effectively using the assets of human resources for the attainment of organizational goals and the continued viability and success of the organization.

Human resources management includes such activities as recruiting and selecting qualified individuals, training them and motivating them through performance appraisal and pay systems, negotiating union contracts, and ensuring that all of these activities are performed within the requirements of the applicable legal systems.

To provide an overview of the field, we examine the HRM function from several perspectives. First, a historical perspective on the evolution of the HRM function provides an understanding of the forces that have molded and defined present activities. Second, an environmental perspective sheds light on the external forces that continually pressure and constrain these activities. Third, a strategic perspective illuminates the role of the HRM function in the strategy of the organization. Fourth, a political perspective shows how both supervisors and subordinates may use human resources systems to maximize their own self-interests, which may not reflect the interests of the organization. Fifth, an international perspective highlights the problems and opportunities that face the HRM function in what is fast becoming a global marketplace. Finally, an evaluation perspective reveals the ways in which human resources activities can be evaluated as to their usefulness in attaining organizational goals.

A Historical Perspective on Human Resources Management

To understand the present HRM function in the United States, one first needs to understand its historical evolution. With each succeeding generation, other organizational functions have tended to view HRM as a weak stepsister, a necessary evil that must be dealt with. And during each generation, HRM professionals have sought to justify their existence in a variety of ways.

Early Developments

Industrial expansion and the emergence of labor unions, which characterized the early 1900s, necessitated an organizational function designed to deal with labor unions and the union environment. In response to these developments, personnel departments were created. These departments emphasized "welfare capitalism" as a means of convincing employees that unions were unnecessary. The

4

next few decades saw added responsibilities for the HRM function. Conditioned by the existence of a tight labor market during World War I and stimulated by the work of several industrial psychologists (Munsterberg, 1913), the function began to engage in such personnel activities as employment testing, training, and performance appraisal. Whereas past activities had focused only on keeping unions out of the workplace or negotiating with existing unions over wages, hours, and the terms and conditions of employment, human resources activities now reflected a more proactive orientation aimed at promoting greater productivity.

From this emphasis on using human resources activities to increase productivity, and based especially on the work of two Harvard University professors, Mayo and Roethlisberger (Roethlisberger & Dickson, 1939), came an awareness of the impact of social factors on employee satisfaction and productivity. In a sense, this awareness resulted in a revival of welfare capitalism, now resurfacing under a new name: the human relations movement. This movement's basic assumption was that a satisfied employee was a productive employee. The human relations movement, which saw an unprecedented amount of government-sponsored research in personnel-related areas such as groups, motivation, morale, and leadership, flourished from World War II until the 1960s.

Recent Trends

As an increasing amount of research began to cast doubt on the idea that job satisfaction and productivity are strongly related, the role of the HRM function was again called into question. However, with the civil rights movement of the 1960s, it found a needed and critical place among organizational functions. The civil rights movement produced a good deal of legislation bearing on the employment relationship, such as the Equal Pay Act of 1963, which forbade pay discrimination based on sex, and the Civil Rights Act of 1964, which outlawed discrimination in any employment

decision on the basis of race, religion, color, sex, or national origin. The increase in discrimination-based litigation during the 1970s boosted the legitimacy of the HRM function in organizations.

Although all of the aforementioned developments enhanced the status of the HRM function in the United States, it is the rise of international competition in a global market that may finally liberate human resources management from second-class status. As American corporations continue to be bested in both foreign and domestic markets by international competitors such as Swedish, German, Japanese, and Korean firms, the critical need for using employees as a competitive resource has become increasingly evident. This international competition has led to four conceptual trends in the HRM function: (1) the need to link human resources to the strategic management process; (2) the need to select, train, and compensate individuals to function in an international marketplace; (3) the need to understand the political dynamics that undermine rational HRM decision-making processes; and (4) the need to provide quantitative estimates of the dollar value contributions made by the human resources department. Before discussing these issues, however, we must explore the environment in which the HRM function exists.

An Environmental Perspective on Human Resources Management

Reactions to major developments in the external environment are often transformed through the legal environment into federal laws. In a sense, the legal environment serves as the filter and as the ultimate mechanism for merging fact and value in society. The federal laws bearing on the employment relationship enacted before 1960 are quite different from those enacted during the 1960s and 1970s.

Legislation enacted during the human relations movement dealt extensively with wages and work hours and with union-management relations within the organization and the policing of those relations—that is, the rights of employees to organize and bargain collectively vis-à-vis the rights of the employer and the union. Among these earlier laws are the Fair Labor Standards (Wages and Hours) Act of 1938, the National Labor Relations (Wagner) Act of 1935, the Labor-Management Relations (Taft-Hartley) Act of 1947, and the Labor-Management Reporting and Disclosure (Landrum-Griffin) Act of 1959. Although these laws are still in force, the federal laws enacted during the 1960s and 1970s dealt more directly with the rights of the individual (or of classes of individuals, such as minorities and women) in a wide range of issues concerning employer rights. The most basic and important federal laws bearing on the employment relationship enacted during the 1960s and 1970s are the Civil Rights Act of 1964 (Title VII), as noted earlier; the Occupational Safety and Health Act of 1970; and the Employee Retirement Income Security Act of 1974.

Most recently the personnel/HRM function has had to deal with the increase in regulatory action stemming from the Americans with Disabilities Act of 1990, the Civil Rights Act of 1991, and the Family and Medical Leave Act of 1993. The first two acts have resulted in a substantial increase in the number of discrimination complaints filed with the Equal Employment Opportunity Commission. In fact, in the first three quarters of 1993, the EEOC reported an increase of over 24 percent in the number of complaints filed.

Organizations as Open Systems

To indicate that the environment has a major impact on organizations implies the acceptance of a few related premises. One of these is that organizations, as proposed by Katz and Kahn (1978), are open systems—*open* in that they are responsive to external pressures and *systems* in that a response by one element in the organization/environment relationship usually leads to a variety of other responses by the same element or other elements in that relationship. Another premise is that, because of

the flood of federal legislation during the past few decades concerning many broad organization-to-society issues, most organizations are more permeable to external pressures than ever before. Never, it seems, has the environment been closer to or more involved with the core technology of organizations (Thompson, 1967). What could be closer to the inner workings of organizations than legislation regarding the ways in which organizations should manage their human resources? Finally, not only is the organization more permeable to environmental pressures, but the environment itself also continues to change at a rapid pace.

Buffering Strategies as an Organizational Response

How can managers begin adequately to plan, organize, and control? Thompson (1967) offers a conceptual answer to this question at the organization/environment level: He suggests that organizations develop a number of strategies—including forecasting and buffering—to deal with the uncertainty created by the environment. Forecasting represents an attempt to anticipate change before it occurs. Buffering, on the other hand, is associated with the design of structural devices (such as larger or more specialized organizational units) and technological work-flow devices (such as new or more complex procedures). These buffering devices serve in both proactive and reactive ways to shield the organization from the pressures of the environment and to give managers a little time to try to make sense of them. Once the strength or potential impact of these pressures is reasonably understood and resources for coping with them are reallocated or secured, the nature of the buffering devices (especially the reactive ones) may change from one of initial defensiveness to one of compromise or confrontation. There is the subsequent danger, of course, that once these devices are designed and in place, they will become inflexible to further change and represent a nonproductive drain on resources.

The notion of buffering is particularly appealing. A close look suggests that many organizations have apparently used this strategy in responding to actual or potential pressures of the legal environment. Legal requirements concerning the rights of employees in the employment relationship are addressed by larger, more specialized human resources departments involved in an ever-widening range of activities. In addition, the legal or public relations departments of organizations are often engaged in boundary-spanning activities (Aldrich, 1979) to supplement and support the activities of the human resources department and facilitate the overall buffering process. This process may include more proactive political activities, such as joining industry or association lobbying efforts and supporting selected candidates for public office, or more direct economic activities, such as entering into joint ventures or mergers (Pfeffer & Salancik, 1978).

Designing buffering devices for the HRM function (or any other function) in turn draws on the resources of the organization and places greater responsibility on that function to meet its organizational obligations. For the HRM function this means protecting or shielding the organization from errors of commission or omission in the management of its human resources. This obligation carries with it increased visibility and risk for the function. No wonder human resources professionals have been seen at times as heroes and at other times as traitors and have designed a few internal buffering devices of their own. Janger (1977), for example, indicates that one way to attempt to control the "uncontrollables," and thereby reduce the risk of errors, is to centralize human resources policy-making and planning activities at the corporate level while continuing to support decentralized decision making at the unit level, where more sensitivity to, and information regarding, critical interpersonal and intergroup relationships presumably exist.

A Model of the Organization/Environment Relationship

A model of the organization/environment relationship is presented in Figure 1. It is an adaptation of a model proposed by Leavitt (1965) for approaching intraorganizational change. This model, a fairly simple one, includes four interdependent variables: task, structure, technology, and people. Leavitt proposes that one must account for and reasonably balance the interdependencies of these variables to avoid or reduce negative consequences for the organization. When the variable *task* is interpreted to mean the task of the organization, it is replaced with the variable *mission,* which connotes a primary organizational goal or set of goals. This permits consideration (and to some extent, assessment) of the condition of the ongoing relationship between the organization and its external environment (i.e., its effectiveness) as well as the condition of the organization itself (i.e., its efficiency). Finally, to accommodate Leavitt's task (job) variable, we incorporate it into the technology (work flow/equipment) variable.

Borrowing once again from Thompson (1967), we have used the concept of *task environment.* Task environments are viewed as elements of the larger environment, but they are more immediately critical to the organization's well-being. They affect the day-to-day decisions of managers and serve to define the organization structurally, establish its mission, and determine its domain or boundaries. For illustrative purposes only, five critical task environments are identified: customers and clients, competitors, regulators, suppliers, and influential others.

In general, people in the external environment (i.e., the general public), with values, needs, information, and resources, act as initiators and organizers of inputs to the creation and control of the organization. Rules and procedures for the interpretation and use of such inputs are developed within the legal environment in the form of laws. These laws

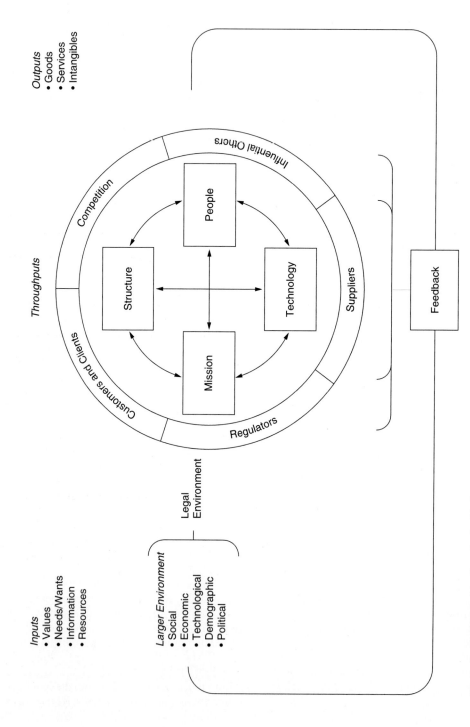

Figure 1. A Model of the Organization/Environment Relationship (From "Perspectives on Personnel Management" by K. M. Rowland and G. R. Ferris, eds., in *Personnel Management* [Boston: Allyn and Bacon, 1982].)

8

prescribe the content and process of relationships in the throughput milieu—relationships among the task environments and between the task environments and components of the organization. The outputs, as goods, services, and intangibles, are fed back to the environment as potential contributions to the wellbeing of the general public. Within this context, coalitions of individuals, including managers (entrepreneurs), seek opportunities for self-expression and fulfillment.

A Strategic Perspective on Human Resources Management

Environmental pressures such as those previously mentioned have mandated recognition of the need to link human resources activities to the organization's strategy. For example, in the early 1980s, the industrial United States was faced with an urgent sense of competition. Foreign corporations began to export their products to the United States at lower prices than U.S. companies could offer. Their cost advantage stemmed from lower labor costs and a strong dollar and made it nearly impossible for American corporations to pass on increased raw material and labor costs to the consumer. This in turn caused American corporations to look for more efficient and ef-

fective ways to use the resources available to them. The ensuing effort gave rise to the concept of *strategic human resources management,* defined as "the pattern of planned human resource deployments and activities intended to enable an organization to achieve its objectives" (Wright & McMahan, 1992, p. 298).

Galbraith and Nathanson (1978) were among the first organization theorists to discuss explicitly the concept of human resources strategies in the context of strategic management. They recognized the need to fit human resources into the strategy implementation process. In their discussion of the role of human resources in the implementation of organizational strategy, they outlined four basic HRM subfunctions or strategies: selection, appraisal, rewards, and development. A general model of the HRM function, showing the interdependencies of the four major subfunctions, is shown in Figure 2. Subsequent writers in the area of human resources strategy have adopted this same basic breakdown (Ferris, Schellenberg, & Zammuto, 1985; Fombrun, Tichy, & Devanna, 1984; Pucik, 1985; Schuler & MacMillan, 1985; Schuler & Jackson, 1987).

Recently, writers such as Baird and Meshoulam (1988) and Lengnick-Hall and

Figure 2. A Model of the Human Resources Management Function (Reprinted from "Strategic Human Resource Management," by Noel M. Tichy, *Sloan Management Review,* Winter 1982, pp. 47–61, by permission of the publisher. Copyright © 1982 by the Sloan Management Review Association. All rights reserved.)

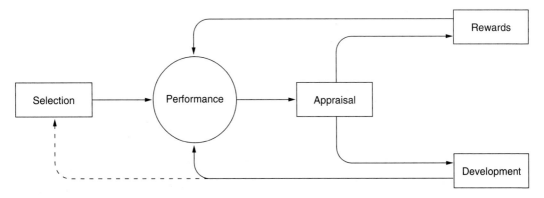

Lengnick-Hall (1988) reviewed the literature on human resources strategy and found that three approaches have been used: (1) matching managerial style or human resources activities with strategies; (2) forecasting human resources requirements, given certain strategic objectives or environmental conditions; and (3) presenting means for integrating the management of human resources into the overall effort to match strategy and structure. Their conclusion is that each of these approaches is deficient because the two types of strategy (human resources and organizational) are reciprocally interdependent. A more effective way of viewing the two types of strategy would recognize that each is an input to and a constraint on the other.

Baird and Meshoulam (1988) discussed the need for human resources strategies to manage both the external fit (relating strategies to the stage of the organization) and the internal fit (managing the various human resources components to support one another). They presented five stages of HRM growth (initiation, functional growth, controlled growth, functional integration, and strategic integration) and six strategic components of HRM (manager awareness, management of the function, portfolio of programs, personnel skills, information technology, and awareness of the environment). From this they developed a matrix for managing both external fit and internal fit.

The notion of fit is central to an understanding of the role of human resources in organizations from an open systems perspective. Zedeck and Cascio (1984) noted that "HRM issues are part of an open system, and research is theoretically bankrupt unless placed in the broader context of organizations" (p. 463). Wright and Snell (1991) have used open systems theory (Katz & Kahn, 1978) as a means of integrating the two types of strategy from a systems view of organizations. Wright and Snell described an open systems model of the human resources system and developed human resources strategies from this perspective. According to these

authors, the inputs to the human resources system are the knowledge, skills, abilities, and other characteristics of the individuals in the organization. Following McKelvey (1982), they referred to these inputs as *competencies* or simply *comps.* They viewed the throughput component of the system as comprising the behaviors of individuals in the organization. Finally, they referred to two types of outcomes from the system: affective outcomes and performance outcomes. Affective outcomes are the feelings of the employees within the system about being part of the system itself. Performance outcomes are the products or services that the organization produces.

From this model of the human resources system, Wright and Snell (1991) stated that the HRM function consists of two basic tasks: managing the competencies of the system and managing the behaviors of the system. Within each of these tasks, generic strategies could be discussed. Competency management strategies include competency acquisition (acquiring the skills the system needs through selection, training, etc.), competency utilization (utilizing the competencies of the system through quality of work life programs, etc.), and competency displacement (ridding the system of obsolete competencies through firings, early retirements, etc.). Behavior management strategies include behavior control (eliciting certain behaviors from individuals through behavior performance appraisal, etc.) and behavior coordination (coordinating the behaviors of individuals to achieve effective group performance through such means as group bonuses, organization development techniques, etc.).

Snell (1992) expands upon the open systems concept, proposing a "control theory" model of strategic human resources management. According to this model, firms seek to control the inputs, throughputs, and outputs of human resources. Inputs are controlled through rigorous selection, training, and socialization processes. Firms control throughputs by specifying, appraising, and rewarding individuals' behaviors. Finally, they control outputs by specifying, appraising, and rewarding the objective results attributable to individuals and work groups.

A recent focus of attention within the field of strategic human resources management is on understanding the role of human resources in sustaining competitive advantage. Using the resource-based view of the firm (Barney, 1991; Wernerfelt, 1984), Wright, McMahan, and McWilliams (in press) have demonstrated that a firm's human resources constitute one resource that fulfills the four criteria for being a potential source of sustained competitive advantage: High-quality human resources are valuable, rare, difficult to imitate, and not subject to substitution. This finding underscores the fact that human resources, if managed effectively, are a firm's most valuable asset. Thus, firms seeking competitive advantage in today's global competition need to invest wisely in these strategic assets.

A Political Perspective on Human Resources Management

The strategic perspective, as previously discussed, focuses on the rational decision making aimed at aligning HRM practices with the organization's strategic goals. However, as anyone in organizations knows, not all decisions are rational, and many have very little to do with achieving organizational goals. Recent writers in HRM have suggested that influence and politics are a significant part of the HRM function, or at least that they strongly affect that function.

The notion of politics seems to imply effort on the part of individuals or groups to exert influence over others for purposes and in ways that are not sanctioned by the organization (Mintzberg, 1983). Influence need not be limited to simply prevailing through the promise of reward or the threat of punishment but can often entail proactively seeking to manage how others interpret events and symbolic actions. In fact, Ferris and Judge (1991) define politics as "the management of shared meaning by individuals, groups, or organizations" (p. 450). It is this view of politics that allows us to better understand the role of influence in HRM, particularly with regard to personnel selection, performance appraisal, and promotion/reward systems.

A strategic perspective on personnel selection assumes a rational decision-making process entailing an effort to identify the skills required in a job and then to assess the extent to which various applicants possess those skills and hire the individual who provides the best match. It is in the notion of fit between applicant skills and job skill requirements that the potential for political influence appears. In the real world of HRM, it is not easy to identify perfectly the skill requirements of a particular job or to assess perfectly an applicant's level of each of the various skills. It is the inability to assess fit perfectly in an objective manner that lets politics enter the decision-making process.

Because there is no objective standard for assessing fit, selection decisions often revolve around the perceived similarity of an applicant's skills with the standard. Thus, managing the perceptions of the decision maker can allow the applicant an opportunity to influence the decision-making process in a political manner. More specifically, the process of "impression management" in the employment interview is an example of politics in HRM. Applicants typically conduct research on a company in part to assess the "type of employee" that the organization seeks. An applicant interviewing with an organization that publicizes its aggressive, market-oriented strategy will attempt to come across as quite aggressive in the interview. The same applicant interviewing with a firm that promotes its team atmosphere and group cohesiveness is likely to act significantly less aggressively in an effort to appear to fit that organization (Ferris & Judge, 1991).

Recent research has demonstrated that attempts to bring influence to bear on the employment interview do, in fact, affect decision outcomes. For example, it appears that interviewees who exhibit controlling tactics such as self-promotion and efforts to dominate the interview prove more successful than those who act passive or submissive (Kacmar, Delery, & Ferris, 1990; Tullar, 1989).

Another area of HRM that is particularly fertile ground for political influence is performance evaluation. In spite of the fact that a sacred principle of performance evaluation is to evaluate performance itself rather than the person in the abstract, in most jobs it is difficult to define and measure all relevant aspects of performance objectively. In fact, in many situations it appears that the performance evaluation process is almost entirely subjective, as evaluators form generalized impressions regarding employees' contributions to the organization. As a result of this absence or ambiguity of objective performance standards, evaluations are influenced by the people being evaluated. An employee's behaviors, as well as beliefs, values, and level of effort— all of which can be easily manipulated—influence these generalized impressions. Thus, the political perspective on HRM focuses attention on the fact that a discrepancy often exists between an individual's performance and performance evaluation and notes that this difference stems from political influence.

Not only does the employee have incentive to engage in political influence, but the supervisor conducting the rating often has reason to be political as well. For example, a manager who rates employees low may be perceived by others as not doing his or her job. In addition, to assign low ratings and then have to deliver those ratings in feedback sessions is somewhat disconcerting. Thus, the evaluator may have ample incentive not to appraise performance accurately but rather to manipulate the ratings to achieve his or her own goals.

Finally, promotion/succession systems are similarly subject to the dynamics of political influence. These systems often represent a combination of selection and appraisal systems. Firms may prefer to fill open managerial positions from within the ranks as a way of providing motivation at lower levels. Such a promotion can be seen as a reward for a job well done. In an effort to assess the fit, the firm must rely in part on past performance evaluations as well as on additional information gathered through interviews and other means. We have already discussed how each of these processes is susceptible to political influence. Add to this the fact that firms generally can use these processes to promote and perpetuate homogeneity in beliefs and values, and it becomes obvious how political influence processes often permeate these systems.

The political influence perspective focuses attention on aspects of HRM decision making that most in the profession want to deny the existence of, at worst, and at best simply ignore. These attitudes stem from the fact that political influence processes undermine the rational legitimacy of the HRM function. However, anecdotal and empirical data demonstrate quite convincingly that these processes are a very real part of organizational life, and thus to ignore them is extremely shortsighted.

An International Perspective on Human Resources Management

The past decade has brought ever-increasing international competition to the United States. The realization that most American corporations are now functioning in a global economy has triggered a revolution in management practices. New management techniques and increased emphasis on quality of work life (QWL) issues have infiltrated many American corporations. The need to compete internationally has also caused American corporations to establish new overseas facilities and services, at times through joint ventures and partnerships. This development has resulted in two general concerns that organizations and academics have begun to address. First, how does one manage American citizens working overseas? Second, how do organizational management policies and practices in other cultures differ from those in the United States?

With reference to the first concern, the expansion of production facilities outside U.S. borders provides a number of challenges and opportunities for the HRM function. For example, in spite of his repeated calls for protectionist legislation to help the American automobile industry compete, Lee Iacocca turned more and more to setting up plants in other countries as a means of reducing production costs. (Chrysler Corporation was certainly not alone in this trend.) In fact, in 1993 Iacocca led the fight for the passage of the North American Free Trade Agreement (NAFTA). This agreement created the world's largest free trade zone by virtually eliminating trade barriers among Canada, Mexico, and the United States. U.S. firms will now have even more latitude in capitalizing on Mexico's lower labor costs by building production and assembly facilities there.

When a firm goes overseas, foremost among the challenges is the need to select and train individuals who are able to work in a foreign culture. This need has inflated the value of international management schools as training grounds for managers who have the skills required to work in a foreign country. Also, some undergraduate and graduate degree programs in the United States, including those in business schools, require students to study at least one foreign language to fulfill their degree requirements. Emphasis is also placed on cross-cultural training.

Related to the problem of selection and training is the problem of adequate compensation for overseas workers. The volatility of the U.S. dollar relative to other foreign currencies has exacerbated this problem. What may have been a high-paying job before the drop of the dollar may now seem to offer a pauper's wage. Corporations have attempted to meet this challenge through tax equalization allowances, housing allowances, education and training allowances, and cost-of-living adjustments.

The second general concern—the influence of culture on human resources policies and practices—has created more awareness among researchers of the need to explore the types of policies and practices that are current in other countries. This need stems from the fact that, in the quest for more competitiveness both at home and abroad, many American corporations have entered into joint ventures and partnerships with foreign competitors. Whether the joint facilities are in the United States or in the partner's country of origin, two relatively different cultures are being fused together; this requires a better reciprocal knowledge of the cultures.

Evidence of this concern comes from a 1987 conference on international personnel and human resources management held at the National University of Singapore. Academic researchers used a number of methods in various Pacific Rim countries (Japan, China, Taiwan, Korea, and so on) to learn how human resources practices in those countries compared with U.S. practices. The results proved to be quite interesting.

Steers (1989) noted the need to understand the way in which culture affects problem-definition, problem-solving, and problem-resolution strategies. Moore and IsHak (1989) reviewed and evaluated the organizational implications of Hofstedes's (1980) four metacultural dimensions (power distance, uncertainty avoidance, individualism versus collectivism, and masculinity versus femininity) for human resources practices and then compared these implications to observed recruiting and training practices in Korea. They found considerable variance with Hofstede on Korea's placement on the dimension of individualism versus collectivism and masculinity versus femininity. They concluded that although metaculture has an effect on human resources practices, corporate culture can also be a major determinant of these practices.

Latham and Napier (1989) examined training, selection, appraisal, motivation, and leadership practices in Hong Kong and Singapore. They concluded that the practices in training, motivation, and leadership set Hong Kong (especially) apart from the United States. In Hong Kong training is not government supported, but the culture encourages employees to learn constantly. Motivation was found to be based on legal compliance of prosocial behavior. Finally, leadership in corporations is characterized by a benign autocratic management style.

Von Glinow and Chung (1989) explored human resources practices in the United States, Korea, Japan, and the People's Republic of China. They found that the United States and Japan had the most elaborate human resources systems for integrating across all subsystems and activities. Korean human resources management was observed to be in the early stages of development, while the People's Republic of China had yet to articulate the need for integrating individual and organizational activities.

It should be noted that in spite of these efforts to gain a better understanding of human resources practices in Pacific Rim countries, the researchers' evaluations were essentially guided by an ethnocentric view of the world. For example, Latham and Napier (1989) tended to evaluate the effectiveness of selection and appraisal techniques using U.S. practices as a bench mark. Although certain practices have been found to be effective, it is too early to conclude that their effectiveness can be transferred across cultures.

Although cross-cultural partnerships present problems for organizations, they also provide opportunities for the HRM function. The geographic expansion of plants and offices will mean further reliance upon the HRM function to provide the necessary human resources to staff them. Adler and Bartholomew (1992) note that for a firm to be competitive in today's world, the firm's HRM function must be characterized by transnational scope, transnational representation, and transnational process. Transnational scope means going beyond a simple national or regional perspective and making human resources decisions with a global perspective. Transnational representation refers to the fact that globally competitive organizations must have multinational representation among their managerial employees. Finally, a transnational process is a decision-making process that involves representatives and ideas from a variety of cultures. As corporations continue to expand to include facilities outside the United States, a better understanding of the overseas cultures and the resulting human resources policies and practices is of utmost importance.

An Evaluation Perspective on Human Resources Management

We have now discussed the historical evolution of the HRM function, the ways in which external elements exert pressure on the function, the ways in which human resources activities are linked to the organization's strategy, the impact of influence and politics on HRM, and the problems and prospects that a globalized economy has for the function. It now seems logical to examine how HRM activities are evaluated within organizations.

The usual criteria for assessing the "goodness" of the HRM function are efficiency and effectiveness. In judging the effectiveness of human resources activities, we are usually concerned with whether or not the function is "doing the right things." Unfortunately, in the assessment of effectiveness, the matters of who conducts the assessment and what specific criteria are used (or should be used) are problematic (Cameron, 1978). As one might surmise, the idiosyncratic values of individuals and groups play a large role in determining what the "right" things are. As a result, the biases of special-interest groups vying for influence and power can render the reliability and validity of the results questionable at best. Efficiency, by contrast, is typically associated with an internal, value-free assessment of the function. Efficiency can be viewed as maximizing outputs relative to inputs and, in contrast to effectiveness, is concerned with "doing things right." The HRM function can be judged as efficient but ineffective, effective but inefficient, or inefficient and ineffective.

The effectiveness of the HRM function is often judged by the organization in terms of efficiency criteria. Were personnel requisitions promptly filled? Was the union contract settled with a minimum of new and costly benefits? Were the rates of absenteeism and turnover maintained or reduced? The long-run effectiveness of the HRM function, however, in terms of both the organization and the environment, often depends on its being somewhat inefficient, at least in the short run. For example, preparing job descriptions; conducting orientation meetings; providing career, retirement, and outplacement counseling; and processing complaints, grievances, and suggestions are essentially inefficient activities but are critical to long-run effectiveness. In most organizations there is a continual trade-off between efficiency and effectiveness. Both are necessary. The ongoing problem, of course, is to determine an optimal mix. The discussion here is analogous to the one concerning whether (and to what extent) an organization, as implied within the QWL philosophy, should emphasize a course of action that responds to the crisis of commitment or the crisis of adaptability.

Personnel Audits and Utility Analysis

Operationally, by what means is an assessment of the HRM function made? One popular approach is the personnel audit, which usually includes a procedural audit and a functional audit. The procedural audit focuses on the activities performed by members of the human resources department and the amount of time spent on each. The procedural audit is internal to the human resources department and thus represents a measure of the function's efficiency. The functional audit seeks to measure the function's effectiveness. It attempts to assess how well the function, as it performs its various activities, is serving the organization and helping it achieve its short-run and long-run goals.

Although these audits are helpful in evaluating the HRM function, they do not allow for demonstration of the value added in human resources activities. In the past, justifying human resources activities on financial grounds was almost impossible. This was due to the lack of data regarding the dollar value benefits that accrue to organizations as a result of human resources activities. However, Schmidt, Hunter, McKenzie, and Muldrow (1979) and more recently Boudreau (1983a) demonstrated how human resources activities can be subjected to "utility" analysis so the dollar value of these activities to the organization can be determined.

Schmidt et al. (1979) focused on what they referred to as the *standard deviation of performance in dollars*. This concept can be thought of as the dollar value to the organization of someone who is performing in the top 15 percent of all employees in a particular job versus an average employee. The researchers then demonstrated how certain human resources activities can raise the general performance level of all employees subject to those activities. They showed how their utility estimates could be applied to evaluation of the Programmer Aptitude Test (PAT) for selecting computer programmers in the U.S. government. Their analysis yielded an estimated gain in utility of $37.6 million.

Boudreau (1983a) pointed out some weaknesses of this approach from a financial perspective. He noted that the Schmidt et al. (1979) procedure ignored some important cost considerations, such as tax rate, discounted cash flow, and variable costs. He reanalyzed the Schmidt et al. data and observed a utility estimate of about one-third less than that reported by Schmidt and coauthors. Although Boudreau's finding revealed that the results by Schmidt et al. overestimated the value of the use of PAT for selecting computer programmers in terms of the real dollar value gain that accrued to the organization, it still showed that the use of the test would substantially add value to the organization. This conservative estimate, however, was then revised upward by Boudreau (1983b) when he included *employee flows*. This concept recognizes that if an organization hires a number of employees each year for a particular job, the skill level of the work force increases as the former poor performers leave and, through the selection system, are replaced by employees with greater skill. This reanalysis resulted in an observed utility of $105.01 million over a 25-year period.

Although the discussion so far has centered on selection activities, utility analysis can be applied to other human resources activities. Schmidt, Hunter, and Pearlman (1982) applied the Schmidt et al. (1979) formula to performance measurement and feedback. Their estimate for a 1-year period indicated a utility of $5.3 million.

Not only does the utility approach help human resources managers communicate the value of their programs to the organization, but these formulas can also serve as a proactive decision-making aid. The formulas can aid HRM decision makers in choosing the most valuable alternative program among a set of mutually exclusive programs (e.g., the most valuable selection system) as well as in choosing the optimal mix of HRM programs (e.g., how to determine adequate compensation levels given a particular recruiting and selection system). The result can be a more rational approach to decision making (Jones & Wright, 1992).

Although these refined utility formulas have made it possible to communicate the dollar value of human resources activities in financial language, it is not yet clear how effective they are for justifying the HRM function. Some financial managers have applauded the development and application of these formulas, but very little evidence exists to show the widespread use of these formulas in American industry.

At present, the major obstacle to the expansion of utility application lies in the estimation of the standard deviation of performance in dollar terms. Substantial research is currently being conducted to compare alternative techniques for estimating this value. In addition to the Schmidt et al. (1979) expert estimates, Schmidt and coauthors also recommended simply using 40 percent of the mean salary for the job as the standard deviation estimate. More recently, Cascio and Ramos (1986) developed what they refer to as the Cascio-Ramos estimate of performance in dollars (CREPID), which entails breaking the job into its principal work tasks, determining the significance of each task, assigning a proportional dollar value of annual salary to each principal work task, rating each incumbent's performance on each task, translating those evaluations into dollars, and computing the standard deviation of the resulting dollar-weighted performance ratings.

Although each technique may result in different estimates, estimates gained using all of the techniques still show substantial evidence that human resources activities make a large dollar value contribution to the organization. In spite of this, however, it seems that non–human resources managers are still suspicious of what they view as extremely subjective estimates. Thus, although the existing utility formulas present tremendous potential for increasing the HRM function's status as an organizational function, this potential has not yet been realized.

Conclusion

The history of the HRM function in the United States has been characterized by a continual striving for recognition as a legitimate organizational function—a striving that continues today. Pressures from the external environment have elevated the status of the function within organizations. At the same time, these environmental pressures have encroached upon the practices by which organizations have traditionally managed their human resources. Increased litigation stemming from Equal Employment Opportunity legislation and the recent trend away from the employment-at-will doctrine have made proper human resources management an imperative. In addition, the expansion of U.S. corporations into foreign markets and foreign corporations into U.S. markets has created a need to give adequate attention to managing human resources from an international viewpoint.

Further, the strategic and evaluation perspectives should greatly enhance the future status of the HRM function in organizations. Increasing recognition has been given to the importance of tying human resources to the strategy of the firm. Moreover, the political perspective suggests that we have developed an incomplete understanding of how HRM systems actually operate. Likewise, as the HRM function becomes more sophisticated in the ways it can evaluate human resources activities by communicating—both internally and externally—the actual dollar value gains attributable to these activities, the less likely it is that the legitimacy of the function will be questioned.

Although the strategic, political, and evaluation perspectives are receiving greatly increased attention in academic settings, as yet none of these perspectives has seen rapidly increasing application in industrial settings. The delay most likely stems from the relative newness of these topics and techniques. The next decade should provide a reasonable time frame for evaluating the value of human resources strategy and utility analysis in promoting the HRM function to a status equal to that of other organizational functions. This development, combined with the already recognized value of human resources in dealing with environmental pressures and international expansion, will lead to a recognition that the HRM function truly manages the organization's most important asset: people.

References

Adler, N., & Bartholomew, S. (1992). Managing globally competent people. *The Executive, 6,* 52–65.

Aldrich, H. E. (1979). *Organizations and environments.* Englewood Cliffs, NJ: Prentice Hall.

Baird, L., & Meshoulam, I. (1988). Managing two fits of strategic human resource management. *Academy of Management Review, 13,* 116–128.

Barney, J. (1991). Firm resources and sustained competitive advantage. *Journal of Management, 17,* 99–120.

Boudreau, J. (1983a). Economic considerations in estimating the utility of human resource productivity improvement programs. *Personnel Psychology, 36,* 551–576.

Boudreau, J. (1983b). Effects of employee flows on utility analysis of human resource productivity improvement programs. *Journal of Applied Psychology, 68,* 396–406.

Cameron, K. (1978). Measuring organizational effectiveness in institutions of higher education. *Administrative Science Quarterly, 23,* 604–632.

Cascio, W., & Ramos, R. (1986). Development and application of a new method for assessing job performance in behavioral economic terms. *Journal of Applied Psychology, 71,* 20–28.

Ferris, G. R., & Judge, T. A. (1991). Personnel/human resources management: A political influence perspective. *Journal of Management, 17,* 447–488.

Ferris, G., Schellenberg, D., & Zammuto, R. (1985). Human resource management strategies in declining industries. *Human Resources Management, 23,* 381–394.

Fombrun, C., Tichy, N., & Devanna, M. (1984). *Strategic human resource management.* New York: Wiley.

Galbraith, J., & Nathanson, R. (1978). *Strategy implementation: The role of structure and process.* St. Paul, MN: West.

Hofstede, G. (1980). *Cultural consequences.* Beverly Hills, CA: Sage.

Janger, A. R. (1977). *The personnel function: Changing objectives and organization* (Conference Board Report No. 712). New York: Conference Board.

Jones, G., & Wright, P. (1992). An economic approach to conceptualizing the utility of human resource management practices. In G. Ferris & K. Rowland (Eds.), *Research in personnel and human resources management* (Vol. 10, pp. 271–299). Greenwich, CT: JAI Press.

Kacmar, K. M., Delery, J., & Ferris, G. (1990). *The effectiveness of the use of impression management tactics by applicants on employment interview outcomes.* Paper presented at the meeting of the Southern Management Association, Orlando.

Katz, R., & Kahn, R. (1978). *The social psychology of organizations.* New York: Wiley.

Latham, G., & Napier, N. (1989). Chinese human resource management practices in Hong Kong and Singapore: An exploratory study. In A. Nedd, G. R. Ferris, & K. M. Rowland (Eds.), *International human resources management, Supplement volume 1, Research in personnel and human resources management* (pp. 173–99). Greenwich, CT: JAI Press.

Leavitt, H. J. (1965). Applied organizational change in industry. In J. G. March (Ed.), *Handbook on organizations.* Chicago: Rand McNally.

Lengnick-Hall, C., & Lengnick-Hall, M. (1988). Strategic human resources management: A review of the literature and a proposed typology. *Academy of Management Review, 13,* 454–470.

McKelvey, B. (1982). *Organizational systematics: Taxonomy, evolution, and classification.* Berkeley: University of California Press.

Mintzberg, H. (1983). *Power in and around organizations.* Englewood Cliffs, NJ: Prentice Hall.

Moore, R., & IsHak, S. (1989). The influence of culture on recruitment and training: Hofstede's cultural consequences as applied to the Asian Pacific and Korea. In A. Nedd, G. R. Ferris, & K. M. Rowland (Eds.), *International human resources management, Supplement volume 1, Research in personnel and human resources management* (pp. 277–300). Greenwich, CT: JAI Press.

Munsterberg, H. (1913). *The psychology of industrial efficiency.* Boston: Houghton Mifflin.

Pfeffer, J., & Salancik, G. R. (1978). *The external control of organizations.* New York: Harper and Row.

Pucik, V. (1985). White collar human resource management in large Japanese manufacturing firms. *Human Resource Management, 23,* 257–276.

Roethlisberger, F. J., & Dickson, W. J. (1939). *Management and the worker.* Cambridge, MA: Harvard University Press.

Schmidt, F., Hunter, J., McKenzie, R., & Muldrow, T. (1979). Impact of valid selection procedures on work-force productivity. *Journal of Applied Psychology, 64,* 609–626.

Schmidt, F., Hunter, J., & Pearlman, K. (1982). Assessing the economic impact of personnel programs on work force productivity. *Personnel Psychology, 35,* 333–347.

Schuler, R., & Jackson, S. (1987). Linking competitive strategies with human resources practices. *Academy of Management Executive, 1,* 207–220.

Schuler, R., & MacMillan, I. (1985). Gaining competitive advantage through human resource practices. *Human Resource Management, 23,* 241–256.

Snell, S. (1992). Control theory in strategic human resource management: The mediating effect of administrative information. *Academy of Management Journal, 35,* 292–327.

Steers, R. (1989). The cultural imperative in HRM research. In A. Nedd, G. R. Ferris, & K. M. Rowland (Eds.), *International human resources management, Supplement volume 1, Research in personnel and human resources management* (pp. 23–32). Greenwich, CT: JAI Press.

Thompson, J. D. (1967). *Organizations in action.* New York: McGraw-Hill.

Tullar, W. (1989). Relational control in the employment interview. *Journal of Applied Psychology, 74,* 971–977.

Von Glinow, M. A., & Chung, B. J. (1989). Comparative human resource management practices in the United States, Japan, Korea, and the People's Republic of China. In A. Nedd, G. R. Ferris, & K. M. Rowland (Eds.), *International human resources management, Supplement Volume 1, Research in personnel and human resources management* (pp. 153–171). Greenwich, CT: JAI Press.

Wernerfelt, B. (1984). A resource-based view of the firm. *Strategic Management Journal, 5,* 171–180.

Wright, P., & McMahan, G. (1992). Theoretical perspectives for strategic human resource management. *Journal of Management, 18,* 295–320.

Wright, P., McMahan, G., & McWilliams, A. (in press). Human resources and sustained competitive advantage: A resource-based perspective. *International Journal of Human Resource Management.*

Wright, P., & Snell, S. (1991). Toward an integrative view of strategic human resource management. *Human Resource Management Review, 1,* 203–225.

Zedeck, S., & Cascio, W. (1984). Psychological issues in personnel decisions. *Annual Review of Psychology, 35,* 461–519.

Developing Human Resources Professionals at ARCO Oil and Gas Company

*Jeffrey M. Bender, Thomas F. Urban, Maria Carmen Galang,
Dwight D. Frink, and Gerald R. Ferris*

Organizational America has witnessed a transformation of considerable proportion with regard to the human resources management (HRM) function. The field and profession of HRM have evolved from a largely maintenance function, focused on record keeping and forms processing, to a function widely regarded as providing bottom-line impact. This change in the image and status of the HRM function brings with it both opportunity and challenge. HRM professionals are becoming involved in organizational activities of strategic importance and finally are receiving the respect that they feel they deserve. So indeed this is a time of opportunity. However, a major challenge for the profession is to articulate more precisely the knowledge, skills, and abilities—or core competencies—of HRM jobs in order to specify accountabilities and to design valid and effective development and evaluation systems.

The purpose of this article is to help sharpen the focus on the HRM profession by presenting the progressive efforts being made in this area at ARCO Oil and Gas Company (AOGC). At AOGC the foundation is the precise articulation of HRM core competencies, which then serve as a basis for an informed understanding of the accountabilities, performance dimensions, and key results areas as well as for the design of multifaceted development and skill-building experiences to ensure individual effectiveness. Also discussed is the issue of what role, or roles, the HRM function should play in organizations and how AOGC has addressed this important issue.

Historical Antecedents of the Human Resources Function

Human resources management emerged as a viable function and subject area around 1920. This emergence was underscored by the offering of the first university personnel course at Columbia in 1920. The issues addressed in the field that was to be known as personnel administration (PA) were essentially, as the name states, administrative issues. The issues facing the PA staff often concerned the employment aspects of a collective bargaining agreement. These included administration of medical care benefits for work injuries, selection, placement, entrance and exit processing, pay administration, and other duties stemming from the application of workplace engineering and technology. Because the PA staff often found themselves in the middle of a conflict of interests between management and production personnel, the seeds were sown for a future role of confidant and conflict resolution intermediary.

A pervasive influence in the PA field was the fallout from the 1939 studies at the Hawthorne facility of Western Electric (Roethlisberger & Dickson, 1939). The impact of these studies came from the finding that, in spite of the researchers' efforts to examine the effects of changes in work conditions, the influence of social factors was strong enough to outweigh the workplace environmental factors. The result was a dramatic shift from primary concern with the workplace and job engineering to a concern with the human element and psychological and sociological variables.

From that platform the American industrial complex entered World War II, and the challenges for industry, and for the PA function, were unprecedented. With millions of members of the labor force sent overseas, a national priority became maximization of the productivity of the remaining work force, many of whom were new entrants with no prior production experience (i.e., wives and mothers). Two central issues in this effort were (1) training and development of new entrants and (2) employment stability with clear labor markets. The means used combined the historical approaches of industrial engineering with the new social-psychological approach featuring motivation, goal setting, and other contributions from industrial and organizational psychology. Another major concern of the federal government at this time was assessment of personnel for appropriate work, especially for very sensitive and intensive jobs, such as covert operations. Classification batteries and assessment centers were developed and became the basis for later widespread industrial and commercial use (Katzell & Austin, 1992).

Another major outcome of the war effort would have indelible and increasing effects on the PA function, effects that are still felt today. This outcome was the explosion of technology. The major impact was to be seen many years later, but the snowball effect has since permeated every aspect of commerce and industry. Probably the most notable areas of influence are transportation, communication, and information processing.

In the postwar era the restructured global environment left the United States in the position of political and economic hegemony. Among the benefits of such a position are consistent growth in markets and productivity. In this context the importance of the PA function diminished in relation to other factors in development and growth, such as marketing, engineering, finance, and operations. PA departments often attempted to legitimize

their diminished activities through centralization and bureaucratization of their functions (Baron, Dobbin, & Jennings, 1986). This tendency reflected the overall tendency of organizations to formalize, bureaucratize, and centralize to achieve increased control and legitimacy (Selznick, 1957).

The 1960s witnessed the beginnings of social reformation that transformed PA functions. Until this point the major areas of expertise developed by PA staffs had included record keeping, administration, employment, classification, and training (Desatnick, 1979). With the passage of the Equal Pay Act of 1963 and the Civil Rights Act of 1964, expertise in these areas was needed (1) to meet federal requirements for record keeping and compliance and (2) to assist in implementation through recruitment, evaluation, compensation analysis, training, and compliance monitoring. These legislative events provided opportunities for PA staffs to elevate their identity and functional position within the organization, although they still possessed the characteristics of problem people, addressing the problems associated with employing people.

In the 1970s and 1980s, the technological explosion and social reforms together prompted reforms in PA functions and roles. Improvements in information processing, communication, and transportation effectively reduced the globe to a single marketplace for major producers and their clientele. This change resulted in intensified competition in the context of a changing work force. The successes of the Japanese economic recovery emphasized the importance of the firm's human resources to its viability and profitability. Especially notable were firms like Matsushita, with a lifetime employment policy and a 500-year business plan.

As the status of the firm's human resources was elevated, the PA status rose as well. This development was reflected in a change in department title, first from *personnel administration* to *industrial relations,* as union-management relations became more critical. Then the term *employee relations* was used to reflect the increased focus on people and their importance. Finally, the term *human resources* emerged and continues to be used to the present. Human resources (HR) reflects the valuation of employees and the perception of employees as assets instead of costs. The continued development of functional expertise involved skills in compensation planning, conflict resolution, organization manpower planning, human resources searches and selection, work design, labor law, equity issue resolution, and performance measurement. The elevation in status was evidenced by the organizational elevation in many firms of the chief HR officer to the level of vice president (VP), frequently reporting directly to the chief executive officer.

The elevation of the HR function to business partner and VP status also signaled the realization that the HR function was moving beyond the reactive people-problem mentality to a proactive planning and consulting mentality. Continued success stemming from the attention given to human resources places the HR function at the threshold of the next higher step in the organization, that of strategic business partner. The movement from systems and operations planning to a strategic role in the organization is a significant step for firms that have implemented it. The shift has given the HR department a mandate to possess expertise in psychology, sociology, the business of work, and employment relations. It signals a new paradigm for the HR function and a new set of roles in the organization with a new set of required competencies.

The Roles of Human Resources Management

In addition to examining the evolution of the HRM function over time, it is useful to observe the various roles that the function has served. The terms that have been used to label the function succinctly capture such roles: paper processor, repository of files and information, employee advocate, law enforcer, do-gooder, and the more unflattering terms like management meddler and dumping ground for ineffective employees (Briscoe, 1982; Desatnick, 1979; Fitz-enz, 1990; Rowland & Ferris, 1986). In general, the HRM function was perceived negatively and thus was accorded a low, peripheral status in organizations. In addition, such roles have resulted in line managers' finding ways to circumvent personnel policies or abdicating their responsibility for human resources (Briscoe, 1982; Desatnick, 1979).

By the mid-70s, things had begun to change. External pressures from the economic, political, social, and technological environment made it imperative for organizations to respond more effectively in order to survive and remain competitive (Beer, Spector, Lawrence, Mills, & Walton, 1986; Fitz-enz, 1990; Rowland & Ferris, 1986). Many of these challenges faced by organizations involved or affected human resources (Fitz-enz, 1990)—for example, increased diversity in terms of demography as well as values and expectations of the work force, rapid technological innovations requiring different skills and abilities, and federal legislation regarding employment practices. Thus the firm's human resources began to be recognized as a key resource in its competitive efforts. With this recognition came the need to improve the effectiveness of the human resources function, which meant contributing to organizational performance (Heneman, Schwab, Fossum, & Dyer, 1989; Miller & Burack, 1979).

Changing Perspectives on HRM Jobs

Improving the effectiveness of the HRM function is important not only to line executives and other employees but to HR practitioners as well. It has been recognized that even among HR practitioners, the old orientations still exist and must be changed. For example, Fitz-enz (1990) urged HR departments to "adopt a new self-perception" in order to respond more effectively to the new demands and opportunities, and Stockard (1980) wrote of a "confused identity" that contributes to HRM's being a "profession in trouble."

Nevertheless, changes in the role of HRM have already been initiated in some firms. Beer and Spector (1985) conducted an in-depth field study of six companies and reported on dramatic changes in the role and status of the HR function, which require new competencies indicative of the shift toward viewing human resources as assets rather than as costs. In particular the HR function was being redefined in terms of human resource development rather than labor relations. In a survey of 224 large firms (i.e., with more than 1,000 employees), Mills and Balbaky (1985) reported that only 15 percent did "little or no people planning," while the majority engaged in human resources planning, varying in degree of integration into the long-range business planning process.

In summary, the transformation of the HR function can be characterized by three major changes: (1) viewing people as assets rather than costs; (2) being proactive rather than reactive; and (3) recognizing multiple constituencies, or balancing employee interests and organizational concerns (Beer & Spector, 1985; Fitz-enz, 1990; Giblin, 1986; Miller & Burack, 1979; Mills & Balbaky, 1985; Tsui, 1987). One can glean such transformations from some of the new labels given to the function: "business effectiveness agent" (Desatnick, 1979) or "consultant to management" (Briscoe, 1982).

The first fundamental change is in the realization of the importance of the firm's human resources, triggered perhaps by the tremendous changes in the nature of the labor market. With a change in values and in expectations of the work force, together with increasing costs involved in attracting and retaining workers, motivation of employees to perform and contribute more productively to the organization has gained importance. Furthermore, organizations are increasingly becoming aware that effective management and utilization of their human resources can be to their competitive advantage.

A second change in the role of HRM entails being more proactive than reactive. A proactive orientation requires a more integrated HR function, as well as a linking of the HR function to the business strategy of the organization (Rowland & Ferris, 1986). Where the HR functions were previously uncoordinated and segregated, a need emerged for the integration of various activities, where "HR systems and programs fit together, complement and reinforce each other as building blocks of a larger HR plan that is developed in relation to the overall strategic business plan of the company" (Mills & Balbaky, 1985, p. 265). Being proactive required linkage with the organization's business plan at the top management levels. Such a proactive role for HRM has been recognized under the term *strategic human resource management* (SHRM). Anthony, Perrewe, and Kacmar (1993) identified six key elements of SHRM: explicit recognition of the influence of the external environment, recognition of labor market features, long-range focus, focus on choice and decision making, consideration of all personnel, and integration with overall corporate strategy and functional strategies.

A third change is in the constituencies being served by the HR function. From initially serving the interests of management alone, to being an employee advocate concerned only with employee welfare even to the extent of being adversarial to the organization's interests, HRM has evolved into a new role that calls for balancing the interests of the employees with those of the organization (Fitz-enz, 1990). Tsui (1987) identified eight constituencies whose needs and expectations must be satisfied by the HR department as a basis for the effectiveness of the HR function. Along with the employees and the line managers, she includes union officers, academic HR experts, and other HR managers at various levels.

Implications for the Practice of HRM

The new role of HRM calls for changes in the scope of HRM activities as well as new competencies for the HR practitioner.

Scope and Function of HRM

Implementation of SHRM.   Butler, Ferris, and Smith-Cook (1988) identified three approaches for implementing strategic human resource management, varying in the extent of involvement in the overall strategic management of the firm. At the lowest level of involvement, HRM merely responds to and accommodates the organization's strategic goals. A higher level entails a more interactive role: HRM has input in the formulation of strategies, particularly with respect to implementation issues. At the third level, that of full integration, HRM is linked to the strategic planning group, and the various HR activities are linked as well.

Dyer (1986) likewise identified specific contributions that HRM can make in strategy formulation—in particular, involvement in the assessment of various strategic alternatives in terms of feasibility and desirability. The HR function can provide input concerning the availability of the required human resources (e.g., quantity, quality, and skill mix) and the costs of acquiring, retaining, developing, and motivating such resources. HRM's potential contributions to the assessment of desirability would be in representing concerns and conveying the likely reactions of employees to whatever decisions are reached. Dyer also identified the various ways in which HRM can be linked to formal strategic planning in the organization: parallel or sequential linkage, inclusion, participation, and review.

Other conceptual models prescribe various approaches to linking HRM with the strategic planning of the organization and even recommend higher levels of integration. Buller (1989) empirically investigated the linkage of HRM and strategic planning in eight high-performing firms (e.g., Digital Equipment, JC Penney, Mary Kay Cosmetics) and concluded that the level of integration depends on the fit of HRM with its environment. Lower levels of linkage may be sufficient where the environment is stable and predictable. The Buller study also reported other factors that shape the type of linkage: organizational history and culture, strategy, structure, incumbent executives' values and skills, work force values and skills, and management systems.

Expanded activities.   HRM's new role implies not only improvement in the quality of the traditional personnel or HR activities (Dyer, 1986; Stockard, 1980) but also an expanded scope of activities. Tsui (1987) reported on the expectations of 805 managers and other employees as to the HR departments' activities. A factor analysis of 73 activities on the strategy implementation or operating level yielded eight dimensions: staffing/HR planning, organization/employee development, compensation/employee relations, employee support, legal compliance, labor/union relations, policy adherence, and administrative services. Fitz-enz (1990) presented a diagram of the job of HR with the objective of helping managers improve their productivity, quality, and effectiveness. Together with traditional spheres of activity such as labor relations, compensation and benefits, and training, newer responsibilities of strategic planning, management consulting, and organization development have been included. One additional activity that HRM must undertake to implement strategic human resource management entails environmental scanning (Odiorne, 1986; Anthony et al., 1993) to identify appropriate strategies and plans.

A frequent theme is the need to evaluate the HR department's effectiveness or contribution to organizational performance. Just as other sectors are required to show proof of their value to the organization faced with tremendous external competitive pressures, it has become necessary to provide a more objective basis for HRM's contributions to the bottom line (Briscoe, 1982; Fitz-enz, 1990). Tsui (1987) has provided empirically derived criteria for evaluating HR performance using responses of various constituencies. The criteria, which concern responsiveness, management of costs and negative performance, proactivity and innovativeness, training and development, and affirmative action accomplishments, further support the recognition of a new role for HRM. Fitz-enz (1990) likewise has proposed a method for measuring HRM.

The notion that HRM impacts on organizational performance is now generally accepted, although it is rare to find hard evidence of this impact. The few studies that have been done include Kravetz's (1988) survey of 150 companies, which concluded that various criteria for financial success (sales, profits, dividends, etc.) were strongly related to human resources progressiveness, measured by items pertaining to such elements as degree of emphasis on people in the company culture and so forth. Fitz-enz (1990) cited an unpublished doctoral dissertation that shows the relationship between HR department performance and organizational performance. Such efforts to evaluate and document the impact of HRM are in fact part of the new role being defined for the function.

With the need to improve the quality of traditional services, as well as to implement additional activities expected of the HR department, HR staff need growth and development not only to effectively perform their jobs but also to provide an example for human resource development for the rest of the organization (Stockard, 1980). Indeed, in its recent efforts to enhance HR and organizational effectiveness, Amoco increased its HR staff by 100 percent, from about 320 people in 1986 (in a company of 55,000) to around 700 (Keller & Campbell, 1992).

Required knowledge, skills, abilities, and orientation.   Several authors have proposed the new competencies that are or should be required for the HR practitioner (Baird & Meshoulam, 1984; Briscoe, 1982; Desatnick, 1979; Keller & Campbell, 1992; Miller & Burack, 1979; Stockard, 1980). In addition, Ulrich, Brockbank, and Yeung (1989) surveyed 8,900 HR associates concerning perceived competencies for the HR professional; the results strongly suggested three main areas of competency: in addition to func-

tional specialization, business knowledge and management of change now are important components. Another survey, among 306 members of the American Society for Personnel Administration (now called the Society for Human Resources Management) (Harper & Stephens, 1982), focused on appropriate education. In terms of academic preparation, an M.B.A. with personnel/labor specialization seems to be more favored than a general M.B.A. or an M.A./M.S. degree; in terms of curriculum content, broader, more general courses such as management of human resources, in contrast to specific technical ones such as psychological testing, seem to be preferred.

The various authors generally agree that aside from specialization in the personnel function, business knowledge is required for the new role of HRM: As a member of management, the HR professional is expected to have a business/profit orientation as much as the rest of the management team. In terms of skills, technical and human relations skills are no longer sufficient; the HR professional must have management and research skills as well. In addition he or she must develop consultation skills because the new role entails not merely solving problems already identified by other managers but also working together with line managers to identify problems and pinpoint opportunities to optimize the use of human resources toward the achievement of goals. These new competencies suggest a major departure from skills previously believed necessary to perform HRM jobs.

The ARCO Oil and Gas Company Case

In light of the evolution and considerable change in the very nature, image, and status of the HRM function, we might reasonably ask how organizations are responding to the challenges and opportunities posed by such change. In this section we will discuss some interesting and progressive efforts undertaken by ARCO Oil and Gas Company (AOGC). We hope that this case will suggest ways for other organizations to translate the new HRM role into practice because it has been observed that although organizations realize the need to do so, they often do not know where to begin (Dyer, 1986).

The AOGC Human Resources Department

AOGC, an operating company of Atlantic Richfield, is responsible for the exploration, production, and marketing of crude oil, natural gas, and natural gas liquids in the lower forty-eight states. Headquartered in Dallas, AOGC has major operation and production facilities primarily in Texas, Louisiana, Oklahoma, and California.

The evolution of the HR function in AOGC to that of strategic business partner paralleled the evolution of the field and the profession as discussed earlier. However, several specific developments were crucial in the evolution of HR at AOGC. First, the economics of the oil industry helped shape that evolution. The energy industry is heavily capital intensive, in contrast with other industries (particularly the growing service industries) that are highly labor intensive. However, international competition confers the necessity in a mature commodity market, such as oil and gas, to be a low-cost producer because it is really not possible to differentiate the product as a source of competitive advantage. Thus human resources become more prominent.

Second, the energy industry has over the past decade experienced considerable downsizing, which has resulted in increased emphasis on the development and utilization of the employees remaining in the organization. In 1985 oil prices dropped from $30 per barrel to around $9 per barrel; of course, the drop tremendously affected organizations' profitability. The resulting downsizing of districts, elimination of layers in the organizational hierarchy, and so forth meant greater reliance on remaining employees, which led to greater emphasis on training and development of those survivors. In 1991 gas prices dropped 40 to 50 percent; again, the result was work process redesign and downsizing and, again, added reliance on survivors to help the organization operate effectively.

A third factor that helped shape the evolution of the HR function at AOGC was organizational change. The downsizing and organizational redesign efforts resulted in an organization that had fewer layers or hierarchical levels and broader spans of control for managers. This redesign produced greater decentralization and called for more empowerment and self-management/control of existing human resources.

The fourth factor that influenced HR function development at AOGC was client feedback. Up to this point the HR department had been seen by its internal organizational clients (e.g., line managers) as capable of administering human resources policies and procedures—but only in a reactive posture. In fact, clients were looking for more proactive efforts from the HR function, which had bottom-line impact, but they did not feel that current HR staff had the skills and competencies necessary to satisfy these client needs. Because of feedback concerning these views and needs, the HR department made staffing changes to address the limitations noted. Specifically, the department began recruiting its own staff both among graduates of programs (i.e., M.B.A. and M.A.) at top universities and among experienced people from other functions in the organization, such as geology, quality control, and finance. Thus we began to see the importance of HR core competencies emerge as a concern of AOGC, with the organization's executive and line management serving as the primary driving force behind the further development of the HR function. They wanted HR to expand its reach and take a more proactive position, playing a more pivotal role in the effectiveness of the entire organization. However, executive and line management saw deficiencies that needed to be addressed in areas like business and financial knowledge, influence, and change leadership if HR was to develop as they wished.

Another key event that facilitated the evolution and development of the HR function at AOGC was the appointment of John Kelly as

Table 1
Organization Vision

Following is the vision for the AOGC Human Resources Department. Boldfaced words highlight attributes that constitute the organization characteristics in the diagram of the HR Department as a strategic business partner.

A viable human resources organization in AOGC is a strategic business partner whose actions, advice, and recommendations significantly and positively impact the successful implementation of AOGC's strategies.

We must evolve into an organization that is consistently sought out for **guidance,** not just approval. We must be a close-knit **team** that integrates a high level of functional expertise (depth) with a variety of learning experiences (breadth) to help our clients recognize and take advantage of ongoing change in our industry.

We must exhibit **balance** in representing employees and supervisors, AOGC and ARCO, and business needs and proper control. The department must inspire **trust** in and from our employees, our management, our stakeholders, and one another.

It is a department that people want to work in because they take **pride** in what they contribute. We must provide answers to complex, ambiguous, and leveraging human resources issues within the company. It is a work unit that values and reinforces good **judgment** in assessing people, resolving conflict, and applying new ideas.

The Human Resources Department is a highly **professional** organization that is clearly regarded as the best in ARCO—one that creates a standard of excellence within the business community.

vice president of human resources. John developed a vision of HR as a strategic business partner (see Table 1), and he directed a task force to focus on articulating the core competencies necessary to implement that vision. Interestingly, as Keller and Campbell (1992) discussed the development of, and new initiatives in, the HR function at Amoco, a key factor they noted as contributing to the progressive steps taken was the appointment of Wayne Anderson as the new vice president of human resources. It appears that Kelly at AOGC and Anderson at Amoco both had considerable impact on moving their HR functions in important new directions, toward fully realizing the role of strategic business partner.

The stage was thus set for the establishment of a program to develop HR competencies. Top HR management had issued a strong case for such a program, supported by feedback from line management. Furthermore, the implementation of new staffing initiatives by the HR function resulted in some unevenness in the distribution of core HR skills. New college graduates were well versed in HR functional skills but not in business operation and dealings with client groups. They also fell short of the requisite level of change leadership skills. At the same time, experienced people entering the HR function from other parts of AOGC possessed good knowledge of the business and were experienced in change management and influence; however, they tended to have little knowledge of functional HR issues. Thus a systematic effort to develop HR professionals and ensure the acquisition of core competencies was needed at AOGC in order for the HR function to realize its new role as strategic business partner.

Development of the HR Staff

AOGC has developed a program that effectively integrates a precise articulation of the core competencies of HR jobs with systematic efforts to develop and evaluate HR skills. This staff development program reflects the roles and contributions of HRM in today's organizations.

Guided by AOGC's business statement, "Our strength is in our people," the department expresses its philosophy in such key phrases as "an organization sought for guidance, not approval," "significantly and positively impact successful implementation of AOGC's strategies," and "balance in representing employees and managers" (from a cover letter by ARCO Vice President of Human Resources John H. Kelly). This orientation is embodied in the role of strategic business partner defined for the HR department; it requires continual improvement on the part of its staff. The department has thus formulated a development program, providing numerous opportunities for self-development and urging its employees to take advantage of those opportunities.

Figure 1 illustrates AOGC's program for HR as a strategic business partner. The program's three components include organization characteristics, individual characteristics, and employee development. The organization characteristics—guidance, teamwork, trust, judgment, balance, professionalism, and pride—are the key elements outlined in the "Organization Vision" (Table 1). The individual characteristics—strategic/business perspective, technical expertise, resourcefulness,

Figure 1. Human Resources Department: A Strategic Business Partner

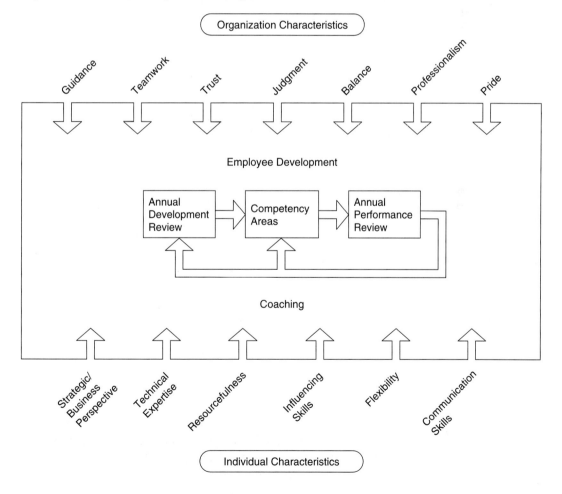

influencing skills, flexibility, and communication skills—are defined in Table 2.

Employee development represents the primary focus of the development guide in AOGC's Human Resources Department. Although the development process includes an annual performance review, the development guide concentrates on competency areas, coaching, and the annual development review. These developmental efforts are linked with organizational characteristics, which are key elements of AOGC's organizational vision (see Table 1), and individual characteristics, the qualifications required for AOGC HR employees (see Table 2).

Human Resources Department employees in AOGC become strategic business partners by developing competency in three areas: business knowledge, functional knowledge, and change leadership. Formulated from research at the University of Michigan and customized for AOGC by the HR Development Task Force, these areas are represented in Figure 2.

Competencies are complex, but these interrelated areas are essential to the develop-ment of strategic business partners. An understanding of employees' profiles—that is, where they are in their experience—will help them use these competency areas in their development plans. As human resources employees progress in their development, through the entry, intermediate, and advanced phases of their careers, they encounter a hierarchy of expectations. A close examination of each of the competency areas will provide a clear understanding of how it fits into the overall picture of HR jobs.

Business knowledge competency. Understanding AOGC's business environment is one of the initial stages of development of a strategic business partner. Business knowledge competency equips HR employees to develop and demonstrate understanding of the financial, strategic, and technological capabilities of their employer and of its client groups. Development in this competency is based on the individual characteristic of strategic/business perspective. Development patterns and potential development resources for the entry, inter-

Table 2
Individual Characteristics

The following characteristics are derived from "Essential Criteria for Human Resources" in the *AOGC Human Resources Recruitment Manual* prepared by Medina & Thompson, Inc., in 1990. The descriptions provide examples of the characteristics of an individual that are conducive to becoming a strategic business partner.

Strategic/Business Perspective: Identifies alternative courses of action and makes appropriate choices while maintaining objectivity, balance, and a strategic focus on business objectives.

Influencing Skills: Anticipates the motivations, interests, and needs of others and uses that understanding to build and maintain relationships. Affects people and the course of events by exhibiting a standard of excellence and integrity that produces respect, creates visions, and enlists constructive support. Recognizes conflict situations and brings them to productive resolution.

Technical Expertise: Demonstrates a high degree of HR functional knowledge. Integrates, synthesizes, and analyzes diverse and current information and concepts to provide sound counsel for problem resolution.

Flexibility: Operates constructively in a changing environment; deals effectively with uncertainty, multiple priorities, and new assignments. Uses initiative and adaptability to achieve desired objectives.

Resourcefulness: Initiates and sustains focused actions toward short- and long-term results. Generates innovative and practical solutions by identifying resources and drawing from them appropriately.

Communication Skills: Is an active listener. Constructively organizes thoughts and shares them effectively in conversations, presentations, and writing.

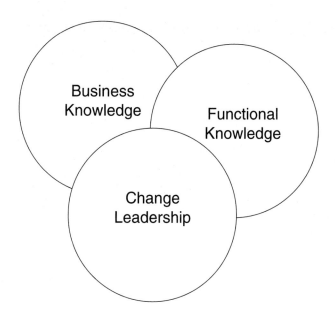

Figure 2.   Key Human Resources Competencies

mediate, and advanced level HR employee have been clearly specified.

At the entry level HR employees become familiar with the firm's basic structure and organization and the general nature of the oil industry, via general information sources and staff functions. Intermediate-level employees build on that general understanding with more specific knowledge of the value added by the HR function, the interrelationships of the HR function with other divisions and business units, and the organizational influences on HR decisions. This level of expertise can be reached through training programs and self-study. Moving to the advanced level, HR employees are expected to demonstrate competency in initiating and evaluating HR strategies and their impact, conducting broad-based business analysis, and counseling senior management, as well as to display a broad yet thorough understanding of the business implications of the HR function. Resources for this level include in-house training, staff functions, and external information sources.

Functional knowledge competency.   In addition to business knowledge competency,

HR professionals must understand the functional areas of human resources. Unless they can demonstrate competency in those areas, they will not be in a position to exert positive impact on the business activity in AOGC.

Human resources employees who develop functional knowledge competency are able to analyze, integrate, and implement diverse and current information and concepts. These employees are also able to provide sound functional advice, counsel, and recommendations to clients. Development in this competency is based on the individual characteristic of technical expertise. The AOGC HR development program characterizes human resource professionals who have developed functional knowledge competency at various levels as it relates to job scope, job knowledge, and client scope.

At the entry level, HR employees demonstrate competency in the area of job scope by means of task and assignment completion. Job knowledge competency at this level is associated with knowledge of HR principles and the technical aspects of the HR functions. The client scope competency is demonstrated via interactions with and inputs to HR clients.

At the intermediate level employees are given more responsibility for self-direction concerning job scope competency. The job knowledge emphasis is on proficiency in analyzing HR issues, implementing solutions, and integrating the HR function with other resources. Client scope concerns at this level involve assisting HR clients with diagnoses and recommendations. Advanced level employees build on these competencies via independent analysis and problem solving, with only conceptual direction from organizational leadership for job scope issues. Job knowledge concerns at this level include thorough knowledge of HR operations and the proactive application of that knowledge toward implementing leadership and change. Client scope concerns reflect a broad perspective on applying HR functions across client groups, offering expertise as well as training less experienced HR employees.

Change leadership competency.   Change leadership is the most critical competency for development of a strategic business partner, yet it is the most difficult to define, illustrate, and demonstrate. The core competencies of business knowledge and functional knowledge are necessary for human resources employees to be effective, but they are not sufficient for the development of strategic business partners. The essential components of change leadership competency may be implemented through the individual characteristics of resourcefulness, flexibility, communication skills, and influencing skills.

Entry-level skills in this area include increasing usefulness as a resource to clients by understanding their roles and their abilities. Flexibility at this level includes working with clients on problem definition and analysis, including familiarity with likely outcomes and innovative approaches. Communication skills are developed for several contexts, including presentations, counseling, listening, and small group facilitation. Intermediate-level issues involve the higher-level skills of evaluation, project management, and innovation. Em-

ployees are expected to demonstrate deeper insight and finer discernment concerning client issues, along with the ability to see these insights through to implementation. Change leadership skills at the advanced level assume a perspective on and understanding of resources and issues beyond the organization itself and the ability to integrate these resources and issues strategically into practice. Leadership is important at this level, as are training others and effectively conceptualizing and managing emerging issues in the organization.

In summary, across all these areas of HR competency, the basic issues for the entry level center around task and assignment skills, with a view toward being able to take more initiative. The central issues for the intermediate level include broadening one's perspective on the HR function from the HR group as a unit to the HR group as a subunit of the larger organization and adding evaluative and diagnostic skills with a view toward becoming more proactively oriented. At the advanced level, the basic issues concern broadening the perspective beyond the organization to the industry as well as understanding HR practices, trends, resources, and issues in general in the business community. This strategic, organizational level development of HR policy and function is added as part of the larger development of organizational policy and strategy, as well as part of the business community at large.

HR Skill Development

In addition to the skill development opportunities and mechanisms just described, the HR department has identified other developmental resources such as training programs, reading materials, and additional learning opportunities (e.g., professional affiliations, work-related discussions with supervisors, company committees, and community service activities) of which employees may avail themselves to facilitate skill acquisition.

The development program likewise provides support for individuals' independent efforts at self-improvement through its formalized coaching activities—specifically, the annual development review and annual performance review. The distinction between these two reviews addresses the common problem of conflicts that arise when these two activities are done jointly. AOGC's HR department maintains the distinction by observing different implementation schedules as well as by clearly differentiating the processes in terms of focus, orientation, objective, roles of the supervisor and employee, communication, climate, relation to salary and promotion, and acceptance of critical feedback. Furthermore, to enable both supervisor and employee to take full advantage of the coaching experience, guidelines have been provided for the participation of each in the process.

Assessment of Performance

Performance evaluation poses a number of challenges for organizations; most of these arise from the difficulties of dealing effectively with subjective measures. However, there are ways to specify subjective criteria more clearly, tying them to the key dimensions of the job, and also to define them in terms of observable behaviors. In the AOGC program, the assessment of performance is the final system component, which logically relates back to the program areas of job definition, core competencies, and skill development. We saw that HR jobs are defined in terms of core skill competencies, which then serve as the basis for skill development efforts. The next step is to translate the core competencies into key performance dimensions and results areas, which serve as the basis of the performance evaluation system. The advantage is that performance areas are clearly and specifically defined, permitting greater accuracy in the assessment of key results areas. Furthermore, the performance areas are logically related to the most important aspects of the job; this results in a valid assessment of only job-relevant dimensions and reduces the extent to which irrelevant features find their way onto the performance evaluation form.

Conclusion

The HRM field, profession, and function have changed considerably in recent years thanks to forces and influences both inside organizations and in the external environment. That's the good news. The bad news is that unless we account for the effects of such changes in HR jobs by precisely articulating core competencies and skill development areas and integrate them with systematic skill development and performance evaluation efforts, the newfound importance of the HRM function could quite easily erode. Some organizations are taking progressive steps to address these challenges actively and, in the process, to position the HRM function strongly for the next decade and beyond. In this paper we have presented the progressive efforts being made by ARCO Oil and Gas Company in the HRM area. We believe that such efforts will continue to enhance the importance of this function and clarify its contribution to overall organizational effectiveness, thereby solidifying HR's role as a strategic business partner.

References

Anthony, W. P., Perrewe, P. L., & Kacmar, K. M. (1993). *Strategic human resource management.* Orlando: Harcourt Brace Jovanovich.

Baird, L., & Meshoulam, I. (1984). Strategic human resource management: Implications for training human resource professionals. *Training and Development Journal, 38,* 76–78.

Baron, J. N., Dobbin, F. R., & Jennings, P. D. (1986). War and peace: The evolution of modern personnel administration in U.S. industry. *American Journal of Sociology, 92,* 350–383.

Beer, M., & Spector, B. (1985). Corporatewide transformations in human resource management. In R. E. Walton & P. R. Lawrence (Eds.), *HRM trends and challenges* (pp. 219–253). Boston: Harvard University Press.

Beer, M., Spector, B., Lawrence, P. R., Mills, D. Q., & Walton, R. (1986). Managing human assets: A general manager's perspective. In K. M. Rowland & G. R. Ferris (Eds.), *Current issues in personnel management* (pp. 10–14). Boston: Allyn and Bacon.

Briscoe, D. R. (1982). Human resource management has come of age. *Personnel Administrator, 27,* 75–83.

Buller, P. F. (1989). Successful partnerships: HR and strategic planning at eight top firms. *Organizational Dynamics, 17,* 27–43.

Butler, J. E., Ferris, G. R., & Smith-Cook, D. S. (1988). Exploring some critical dimensions of strategic human resource management. In R. S. Schuler, S. A. Youngblood, & V. L. Huber (Eds.), *Readings in personnel/human resource management* (pp. 3–13). St. Paul: West.

Desatnick, R. L. (1979). *The expanding role of the human resources manager.* New York: AMA-COM.

Dyer, L. D. (1986). Bring human resources into the strategy formulation process. In H. G. Heneman & D. P. Schwab (Eds.), *Perspectives on personnel/human resource management* (pp. 16–27). Homewood, IL: Richard D. Irwin.

Fitz-enz, J. (1990). *Human value management: The value-adding human resource management strategy for the 1990s.* San Francisco: Jossey-Bass.

Giblin, E. J. (1986). The challenge facing human resources. In H. G. Heneman & D. P. Schwab (Eds.), *Perspectives on personnel/human resource management* (pp. 11–16). Homewood, IL: Richard D. Irwin.

Harper, E., & Stephens, D. B. (1982). Personnel and labor relations master's degrees for the '80s and '90s. *Personnel Administrator, 27,* 53–56.

Heneman H. G., III, Schwab, D. P., Fossum, J. A., & Dyer, L. D. (1989). *Personnel/human resource management.* Homewood, IL: Irwin.

Katzell, R. A., & Austin, J. T. (1992). From then to now: The development of industrial-organizational psychology in the United States. *Journal of Applied Psychology, 77,* 803–835.

Keller, D. A., & Campbell, J. F. (1992). Building human resource capability. *Human Resource Management, 31,* 109–126.

Kravetz, D. J. (1988). *The human resources revolution: Implementing progressive management practices for bottom-line success.* San Francisco: Jossey-Bass.

Miller, E. L., & Burack, E. (1979). The emerging personnel function. In R. B. Peterson, L. Tracey, & A. Cabelly (Eds.), *Readings in systematic management of human resources* (pp. 521–529). Reading, MA: Addison-Wesley.

Mills, D. Q., & Balbaky, M. L. (1985). Planning for morale and culture. In R. E. Walton & P. R. Lawrence (Eds.), *HRM trends and challenges* (pp. 255–283). Boston: Harvard University Press.

Odiorne, G. S. (1986). Human resources strategies for the 90s. In K. M. Rowland & G. R. Ferris (Eds.), *Current issues in personnel management* (pp. 4–9). Boston: Allyn and Bacon.

Roethlisberger, F. J., & Dickson, W. J. (1939). *Management and the worker.* Cambridge, MA: Harvard University Press.

Rowland, K. M., & Ferris, G. R. (1986). *Current issues in personnel management.* Boston: Allyn and Bacon.

Selznick, P. (1957). *Leadership in administration: A sociological interpretation.* New York: Harper.

Stockard, J. G. (1980). *Rethinking people management: A new look at the human resources function.* New York: AMACOM.

Tsui, A. S. (1987). Defining the activities and effectiveness of the HR department: A multiple constituency approach. *Human Resource Management, 26,* 35–69.

Ulrich, D., Brockbank, W., & Yeung, A. (1989). *Human resource competencies in the 1990s: An empirical assessment.* University of Michigan working paper.

CHAPTER 2

Perspectives on Human Resources Management

Although the field of human resources management has been with us for nearly 70 years, only recently has there been major redirection in thought concerning its importance to the effectiveness of organizations. For many years human resources management was viewed as a maintenance function for the organization, a repository of files and information but not a function that had any noticeable impact on the bottom line.

During the mid- to late 1960s and the 1970s, a different perspective began to emerge that elevated the importance and status of human resources management. A number of factors contributed to this changing perspective on the field and the practice of personnel/human resources management (PHRM) in organizations. Perhaps the most critical factor was the enactment of considerable federal legislation, particularly with respect to fair employment practices. As a result the personnel function gained more visibility and influence by acquiring responsibility for a variety of critical interactions with powerful federal regulatory agencies such as the Equal Employment Opportunity Commission, the Occupational Safety and Health Administration, and the Internal Revenue Service, which carefully monitored—and continue to monitor—the employment practices of organizations with respect to fairness, health and safety, and retirement income security.

Other factors that have led over the years to an increase in the importance and status of PHRM include the focus on productivity and the changing nature and demographics of the U.S. work force. All of these factors, when placed in the context of significant economic and political changes in the rest of the world, have created the need for a newer, more business-focused perspective on the field.

The newer perspective is that of strategic human resources management. This perspective takes a broader, more integrated view of the personnel function; seeks to link the personnel function with the longer-term strategies of the organization; and asks how the personnel function can facilitate the implementation of those strategies. In this environment the importance and status of PHRM will continue to increase as the field responds to changing requirements and expectations.

We have divided this chapter into three areas dealing with strategic perspective, political perspective, and international perspective. This division reflects the notion, proffered in Chapter 1, that human resources management is expanding into a number of different areas involving a number of important organizational variables. In the strategic perspective section, Napier focuses on the integration of strategic management, human resources management, and organizational effectiveness and discusses the relevant issues and research evidence available to date. Napier then proposes a framework that illustrates how the three foregoing components influence one another as a basis for potential integrative actions. In the political perspective section, Ferris and King report that politics is an important variable in the human resources management process. They suggest a number of steps that can minimize the impact of political behaviors in the selection process. Addressing the international perspective, Corey outlines the challenges that occur when human resources are spread among a number of international locations. Different issues arise when an organization decides to compete and locate in different countries.

Suggestions for Further Reading

Strategic Perspective

Boudreau, J., & Berman, R. (1991). Using performance measurement to evaluate strategic human resource management decisions: Kodak's experience with profit-sharing. *Human Resource Management, 30,* 393–410.

Guest, D. (1989). Personnel and HRM: Can you tell the difference? *Personnel Management, 21,* 48–51.

Holden, L., & Livian, Y. (1992). Does strategic training policy exist? Some evidence from ten European countries. *Personnel Review, 21,* 12–23.

Teagarden, M., Butler, M., & Von Glinow, M. (1992). Mexico's Maquiladora industry: Where strategic human resource management makes a difference. *Organizational Dynamics, 20,* 34–47.

Political Perspective

Forsberg, M. (1993). Childhood affects office politics. *Personnel Journal, 72,* 29–32.

Kacmar, K., & Ferris, G. (1993). Politics at work: Sharpening the focus of political behavior in organizations. *Business Horizons, 36,* 70–74.

Lenzner, D. (1993, June). Food for thought: Eight keys to success and growth. *HR Focus,* p. 17.

International Perspective

Oddou, G., & Mendenhall, M. (1991). Succession planning for the 21st century: How well are we grooming our future business leaders? *Business Horizons, 34,* 26–34.

Shumsky, N. (1993). Keeping track of global managers. *Human Resources Professional, 5,* 6–9.

Torrington, D., & Holden, N. (1992). Human resource management and the international challenge of change. *Personnel Review, 21,* 19–30.

Strategy, Human Resources Management, and Organizational Outcomes: Coming Out from between the Cracks

Nancy K. Napier

For many years researchers and managers have examined and discussed specific aspects of strategic management (e.g., strategy types, planning, implementation, and evaluation), human resources management (e.g., employee selection, appraisal, and training), and organizational outcomes (e.g., company performance and effectiveness). Because research that tries to investigate relationships among these elements does not fit neatly into a single discipline, it may tend to fall between the cracks. Indeed, only recently have research and practice begun to pull together those disciplines into more integrated approaches (e.g., Butler, Ferris, & Napier, 1991).

There are several reasons why researchers and managers should want to integrate these three areas. First, to increase our understanding of the way organizations should (and perhaps do) operate, we must examine a more comprehensive set of issues. Second, because top managers are often forced to think outside of a single discipline, research should help them decide what types of human resources practices fit their firms' chosen strategies. Finally, managers are seeking guidance and creative thinking on how to integrate strategy, human resources issues, and organizational outcomes. We see evidence of this from the number of business best-sellers in recent years.

Integrating strategy, human resources management (HRM), and organizational outcomes should help to guide and contribute to more effective use of—and decisions about—human resources. If managers understand the links between strategy and compensation, for instance, they can better design programs that will motivate and reward employees as firms alter their strategies over time.

A model linking these elements is useful for understanding how each element affects the others. Figure 1 shows how managers and researchers can study pairs of elements (i.e., strategy-HRM; HRM-outcomes) or all three together. Managers must realize that human resources practices can be either *influenced* (by strategy) or *influencers* (of organizational outcomes) (Butler, 1988). For example, a firm pursuing a growth strategy may design a compensation system to reward managers who bring in new business rather than those who simply maintain existing accounts. In this case the human resources practices are influenced by strategy. Such a compensation practice could in turn be an influencer if it in some way affected firm performance.

It is also possible that human resources practices can influence strategy selection and planning (Butler, Ferris, & Smith Cook, 1988). For example, the types of employees (i.e., their skills and abilities) in an organization may affect the choice among different kinds of strategies, such as whether to grow by developing internally or by acquiring other firms. Likewise, it may be true that human re-

I'm grateful to Kathie McClannahan for her help in updating this article.

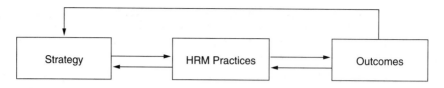

Figure 1.   Role of HRM in Linkages

sources practices are affected by outcomes: An organization that performs better may be more likely to increase its emphasis or spending on HRM activities.

The overall approach of examining links among strategy, human resources management, and organizational outcomes is in an early stage of research development. There is much speculation, but there are few firm conclusions. We simply do not yet know what causes what.

What We Do Know about the Links

Although an integrated approach to the links among business strategy, human resources management practices, and outcomes is still in its infancy, we do have information about those links. This section reviews some of that information.

Strategy-HRM Links

At present the available information about the link between strategy and human resources practices is both conceptual (theory oriented) and empirical (data based). This link is the one we know most about in terms of the effect strategy seems to have on human resources activities. Even so, much of the writing about it has been based on speculation concerning what should occur rather than on what actually occurs.

The theory-oriented writings have been useful for human resources researchers and managers. First, the writings show that people *outside* the functions of personnel and human resources, such as senior managers, think that HRM issues are indeed important and contribute to effective implementation of an organization's strategy (Beer, Spector, Mills, &

Walton, 1985; Henn, 1985). If *others* believe this, then it is easier for the human resources manager to convince all managers of the importance of people issues. In addition to people *inside* firms, people and institutions *outside* of firms (e.g., legal/governmental groups) may influence HRM (Florkowski & Nath, 1990).

Second, researchers keep raising the same elements as being particularly important in HRM, elements such as performance and reward systems (Galbraith & Nathanson, 1978; Kerr, 1985; Stonich, 1981). As more information on these frequently mentioned issues becomes available, we will have greater confidence in whether—and how—they are related to strategy. Finally, more researchers are suggesting *how* to go about discovering or examining the potential links. In other words, rather than just saying that strategy *should* relate to human resources practices, they are gathering facts about the actual relationships as well as ideas about how to study those links in greater depth. In particular, researchers are developing ways to measure important variables like strategy and human resources practices (Buller & Napier, 1993). In addition, there has been more guidance about how to conduct research to answer questions about the links (Olian & Rynes, 1984).

The existing empirical knowledge, or that based on collecting and analyzing data from firms, has focused on links between strategy, structure, industry and technology, and such human resources functions as compensation, management transfer patterns, and career patterns (Jackson, Schuler, & Rivero, 1989). The general conclusion is that there are differences in certain compensation components (e.g., bonus size and the way it is decided) among firms pursuing different strategies. Firms with different growth strategies vary in the method of payment to managers (e.g., salary versus bonus), the type of performance criteria used, and the comparison groups for manager performance (Napier & Smith, 1987; Pitts, 1974, 1977). For instance, a firm that wants to grow by acquiring new firms may evaluate a manager's performance on the ease with which a new firm is integrated into the existing one, taking into account the expectation that neither firm may perform as well financially as before the merger. Another example concerns firms that pursue different diversification strategies. When firms diversify, or grow by getting into new product areas, they tend to reward managers with bonuses. The greater the diversification (i.e., the more unrelated the products), the higher the bonus tends to be (Napier & Smith, 1987). In other words, firms pursuing different strategies are likely to structure human resources practices, such as pay or performance evaluation, to support their strategies.

There are several problems with the existing research on strategy and HRM. First, we still have little information about what happens with a number of different strategies. Most of the data-based knowledge has come from research on generic strategies or growth strategies. More recently, however, researchers have begun examining newer challenges such as managing innovation, downsizing, and mergers and acquisitions and their effects on selection, pay, performance, and the like under new conditions (Cameron, 1991; White, 1992). Another area gaining attention involves strategy-HRM links in international contexts (Pennings, 1993; Schuler, Dowling, & De Cieri, in press), whether in multinational firms or in domestic firms where different cultures must be managed. Thus, as firms become more sophisticated in formulating strategy, the existing research may be too general to help managers.

A second problem is that we have little sense of how strategy affects the full range of HRM activities (e.g., training, staffing, re-

cruiting). Because much of the research has focused on compensation, performance criteria, and transfer patterns, other human resources areas have been neglected. In addition, we know very little about how organizations design HRM practices to be consistent with one another while supporting a given strategy. For example, in a high-growth-strategy firm, a major human resources practice may be to reward managers who develop new product markets. In addition to a reward practice to support the strategy, the firm may also need to provide training to experienced managers who need it and to those who are newly hired. The training must help managers gain the ability to develop new markets and thus be consistent with the reward practices.

Another limitation of existing research is that it has focused on HRM practices for very specific and thus limited groups of employees, usually middle managers or managers at the strategic business unit (SBU) level. One reason for the focus on these managers is that computer databases of financial and market information exist for certain units (e.g., SBUs) within firms. The SBU level has been a popular one for researchers to investigate because it is discrete and because it is possible to identify managers at that level. There is less information about managers at levels for which no readily available databases exist.

One final difficulty with current knowledge about strategy-HRM issues concerns our belief that integrating strategy and HRM will lead to good outcomes (e.g., financial performance). Unfortunately, that belief has yet to be confirmed. Several popular books—even those over 10 years old!—such as *In Search of Excellence* (Peters & Waterman, 1982) present anecdotal evidence to support such links, but as yet we have little firm empirical data in that regard.

HRM-Outcomes Links

Our knowledge about HRM-outcomes links seems to answer at least two questions: (1) How effective are the human resources functions and the department? and (2) What is the overall contribution of HRM activities to the organization?

Researchers and managers have assessed the effectiveness, costs, and benefits of specific human resources management activities. The focus has been on three general areas: (1) ways to assess the *costs* of specific human resources activities, such as selection, training, or benefits (Cascio, 1982); (2) methods to evaluate the *effectiveness* of human resources activities, such as the pre/post evaluation of training programs (Hall, 1984; Wexley & Latham, 1981); and (3) general approaches to the *audit* of the strengths and weaknesses of the overall human resources activities (Devanna, Fombrun, & Tichy, 1981). Each of the three categories is relatively well developed. For instance, Cascio (1982) proposes models, some of them very complex, for assessing the costs of human resources activities. In assessing the cost of selecting a bank teller, for example, a firm would consider the costs of a newspaper ad, time spent screening and interviewing candidates, training time, and loss of productivity while the new employee is learning the job. Unfortunately, these costs typically are not tied to firm performance. Also, the models do not often address ways to attach monetary values to benefits.

The methods used to assess the effectiveness of programs (e.g., training) usually involve evaluating employee attitudes about the programs. For example, a training program is commonly evaluated on the basis of trainees' reactions to the program right after its completion; less common is an assessment of employee performance. Napier and Deller (1984) evaluated mistakes made by bank tellers before and after a training program and suggested that tellers of highly trained and untrained supervisors performed better than tellers of moderately trained supervisors, raising the question of whether "a little training is a dangerous thing." As with the cost assessment literature, though, there is rarely any evidence that program effectiveness is linked to firm performance. This is partly because of the difficulty of isolating the impact of a single factor such as a training program on the performance of a large unit such as a bank branch or firm.

Finally, personnel department audits are often used to justify departmental activities and determine areas for future focus. Again, our knowledge in this area is limited.

The second stream of research in the area of HRM-outcomes links has examined differences between high- and low-performing organizations and the nature of the human resources practices in each (Buller & Napier, 1993). Again, we have no firm conclusions about whether good HRM practices are related to high performance. The research on the topic seems to suggest that it does, but we are still gathering information.

Putting It All Together: Strategy-HRM-Outcomes

All three elements together—strategy, HRM, and outcomes—have been examined in only a limited way. Several case studies describe organizations' attempts to link strategic planning with HRM issues, such as planning, compensation, development, and firm performance. For example, Misa and Stein (1983) examined whether and how HRM concerns were included in strategic decisions in high-performing and low-performing firms. They found that high-performing firms had more human resources department participation in business decisions and strategic planning than did poorer performers. Also, Horovitz and Thiebault (1982) found that high-performing firms pursuing the same strategy had similar management systems.

Others have argued that a better match between strategy and HRM issues is associated with better firm performance or effectiveness. For example, Tichy, Fombrun, and Devanna (1982) have discussed how firms that appear to match strategic business unit level strategy, type of manager, and human resource practices seem to have better performance.

Our knowledge about how to integrate strategy, HRM, and organizational outcomes is still limited. A major problem for the study of this integration is that few organizations have actually successfully linked the three elements; thus it is difficult to find firms to examine. However, it is encouraging that researchers show increasing interest in examining these relationships (Butler et al., 1991; White, 1992). Although there is much current interest in the strategy-HRM links, it is critical for managers to consider the linkages among the three elements and the possible benefits of integrating them.

An Illustrative Framework

Managers can view the three elements (strategy, HRM, outcomes) on a three-dimensional matrix (Figure 2) to consider how each may affect the others. In addition to these three main elements, a fourth is critical: the type or level of employee affected by the other three factors. For example, many firms find that the approaches to selection or pay vary, depending upon whether the employee is a line worker, a middle manager, and so on.

Figure 2.   A Working Matrix

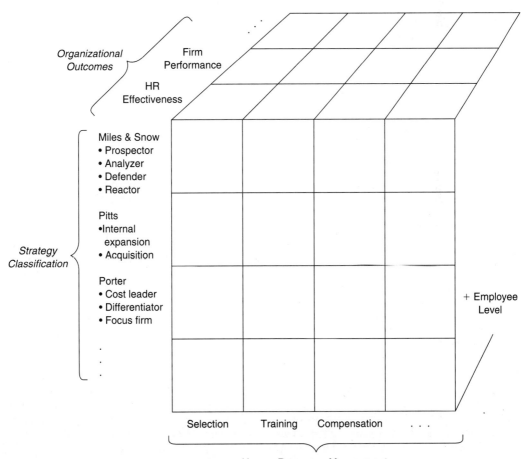

The vertical axis of the matrix identifies overall strategy classification. Any given firm might employ a single strategy within one classification. Several strategy classification schemes are proposed in the literature (Galbraith & Nathanson, 1978; Miles & Snow, 1978; Pitts, 1974; Porter, 1981; Rumelt, 1974). For example, the Miles and Snow typology refers to four general stances a firm may take in its industry: defender, prospector, reactor, and analyzer. A defender firm seeks to protect its current market share and concentrates on maintaining the status quo. A prospector, on the other hand, aggressively pursues new markets, new product ideas, and the like. A reactor responds to what happens in the market and takes advantage of such occurrences whenever possible. An analyzer combines strategies, acting as a prospector in some markets and a defender in others.

Rumelt (1974) proposes a strategy classification based on the extent of product diversity in a firm. Product diversity refers to the range of products a firm offers and the degree to which those products are related to one another (e.g., through use of similar technology or market channels). According to Rumelt's classification, firms that produce only one product—that is, firms that generate all revenues from a single product—are called single-business firms. Firms that rely on a few similar products—that is, firms that receive 70 percent of revenue from those products—are called dominant-product firms. Firms producing many widely diverse products are unrelated firms.

Porter (1981) classifies firms into three groups: cost leadership firms (firms that pursue a strategy of having relatively lower costs than competitors), differentiators (firms providing products or services that distinguish them from competitors in some way, for example, through more luxury or better service), and focus firms (those concentrating on selling to specific market groups).

The HRM dimension of the matrix, shown on the horizontal axis in Figure 2, emphasizes the set of personnel activities related to managing employees: acquiring (human resource planning, recruitment, selection), allocating (placement, orientation, socialization), developing (training, development, career management), managing performance (performance appraisal, compensation, discipline), and maintaining (benefits, health/safety). Within each activity are specific types of actions or stages that would apply to each kind of employee. For example, acquiring practices vary widely for different levels of employees and different organizations. For firms with a policy of promoting from within, the selection process would probably focus more on past employee performance within the firm rather than on education or other types of experience. Likewise, some firms may seek new hires for certain types of jobs (e.g., research and development, marketing) to acquire new ideas. Thus, some of the factors to consider under the selection activity might include the source of new employees (i.e., inside/outside the firm), the selection criteria used (e.g., within-firm performance, evaluation), and the goal of selecting a new employee (e.g., to gain new ideas, to learn about a competitor, to reward the employee).

The third matrix element—organizational outcomes—refers to ways we tell how well a firm is doing in terms of meeting goals (effectiveness) or achieving financial, marketing, or other types of performance standards.

The fourth element—level of employee—includes the common categories of top-, middle-, and first-line levels of management as well as nonmanagement employees. The level of employee is important because HRM functions differ significantly by level. For example, most firms typically have much more specific job descriptions or responsibility lists for nonmanagement and lower-level managers than for top managers. Similarly, the recruitment techniques may vary markedly. Use of executive search firms or the "old-boy network" is more common at top levels; at lower levels, advertisements in media (newspapers, newsletters) or other methods, such as walk-ins, are more common.

The matrix can help managers consider what types of human resources activities relate to different strategy classifications. The following discussion relates different growth strategies to different ways of designing the human resources selection function for top management.

Let us assume that a firm pursues a growth strategy either by internal expansion or by acquisition of other firms. From earlier research we know that there are indeed links between growth strategy and incentive compensation, manager transfer patterns, and the size of the corporate-level technological staff (Pitts, 1974, 1977). It follows, then, that selection of top managers may also vary, given emphasis on different criteria or talents needed in managers responsible for different approaches to growth (Gerstein & Reisman, 1983). In particular, firms that expand internally tend to use mainly subjective (nonquantifiable) performance criteria, with fewer objective, quantifiable ways to assess performance. Therefore, we would expect that these firms might also use more subjective selection criteria in choosing candidates for top management positions. In firms that grow by expanding internally (e.g., developing and marketing their own new products), the existing management pool is well known to the evaluators selecting candidates. Thus, in addition to specific objective criteria (e.g., the performance of the manager's unit in a specified time period), the criteria may also concern the promoted manager's "fit" with top management, suggesting more emphasis on a subjective assessment of personality traits.

In the case of a firm that grows by acquiring other firms, the candidate pool in the acquired firm will be less well known because the firm is buying new units. In this situation top management may base selection decisions on more objective criteria—for instance, years of experience or examples of achievement in previous organizations.

It also seems reasonable that firms that grow through internal expansion will use transfers to promote managers to top management positions, whereas firms that acquire others to grow will tend to draw upon managers from units being purchased ("new" insiders) or from other organizations altogether ("outsiders").

In addition, we expect internal growth firms to use more subjective methods of selection (e.g., gut feeling of evaluators through interviews), whereas acquiring firms would tend to use more objective methods (e.g., external assessment by a psychologist or some type of assessment facility) in addition to interviews.

Summary and Conclusions

Managers need to understand the importance of integrating strategy, human resources management, and organizational outcomes. The 1980s saw growing interest in understanding the links between these elements as well as developing evidence in research and practice that should further clarify the links. Such understanding can only increase in the 1990s.

Even with the limitations mentioned here, managers can—and should—use what we do know in linking the elements together. This means that human resources as well as other functional areas and top management must recognize the importance of the links and know how to use them. It is critical that human resources managers understand their firms' strategies and be involved in forming and implementing the strategies. For too long human resources departments and managers have focused on specific personnel activities without understanding their role in the firm at large. It is up to these managers to show top management the importance of human resources issues in determining and achieving the firm's strategy and in contributing to organizational outcomes. Conversely, top managers need to learn more about how human resources issues may contribute to strategy implementation and firm performance.

References

Beer, M., Spector, P. R., Mills, D. Q., & Walton, R. E. (1985). Managing human assets, part 1: A general manager's perspective. *Personnel Administrator, 30,* 60–69.

Buller, P. F., & Napier, N. K. (1993). Strategy and human resource management integration in fast-growth versus other mid-sized firms. *British Journal of Management, 4,* 77–90.

Butler, J. E. (1988). Human resource management as a driving force in business strategy. *Journal of General Management, 13(4),* 88–102.

Butler, J. E., Ferris, G. R., & Napier, N. K. (1991). *Strategic human resources management.* Cincinnati: Southwestern.

Butler, J. E., Ferris, G. R., & Smith Cook, D. A. (1988). Exploring some critical dimensions of strategic human resources management. In R. S. Schuler, S. A. Youngblood, & V. L. Huber (Eds.), *Readings in personnel and human resource management* (3rd ed., pp. 3–13). St. Paul: West.

Cameron, K. (1991). Downsizing can be hazardous to your future. *HRMagazine, 36(7),* 85, 96.

Cascio, W. F. (1982). *Costing human resources: The financial impact of behavior in organizations.* Boston: Kent.

Devanna, M. A., Fombrun, C. J., & Tichy, N. M. (1981). Human resource management: A strategic perspective. *Organizational Dynamics, 9,* 51–67.

Florkowski, G. W., & Nath, R. (1990). MNC responses to the legal environment of international human resource management. *International Journal of Human Resource Management, 4(2),* 303–324.

Galbraith, J. R., & Nathanson, D. A. (1978). *Strategy implementation: The role of structure and process.* St. Paul: West.

Gerstein, M., & Reisman, H. (1983). Strategic selection: Matching executives to business conditions. *Sloan Management Review, 24,* 33–49.

Hall, D. T. (1984). Human resource development and organizational effectiveness. In C. J. Fombrun, N. M. Tichy, & M. Devanna (Eds.), *Strategic human resource management* (pp. 159–182). New York: Wiley.

Henn, W. R. (1985). What the strategist asks from human resources. *Human Resource Planning, 8,* 193–220.

Horovitz, J. H., & Thiebault, R. A. (1982). Strategy, management design, and firm performance. *Strategic Management Journal, 3,* 67–76.

Jackson, S. E., Schuler, R. S., & Rivero, J. C. (1989). Organizational characteristics as predictors of personnel practices. *Personnel Psychology, 42(4),* 727–786.

Kerr, J. L. (1985). Diversification strategies and managerial rewards. *Academy of Management Journal, 28,* 155–179.

Miles, R. E., & Snow, C. C. (1978). *Organizational strategy, structure, and process.* New York: McGraw-Hill.

Misa, K. F., & Stein, T. (1983). Strategic HRM and the bottom line. *Personnel Administrator, 28,* 27–30.

Napier, N. K., & Deller, J. (1984, February). Train right or don't train. *Training and Development Journal,* pp. 90–94.

Napier, N. K., & Smith, M. (1987). Product diversification, performance criteria, and compensation at the corporate manager level. *Strategic Management Journal, 8,* 195–201.

Olian, J. D., & Rynes, S. L. (1984). Organizational staffing: Integrating practice with strategy. *Industrial Relations, 23,* 170–183.

Pennings, J. M. (1993). Executive reward systems: A cross-national comparison. *Journal of Management Studies, 30(2),* 261–280.

Peters, T. J., & Waterman, R. W. (1982). *In search of excellence.* New York: Harper and Row.

Pitts, R. A. (1974). Incentive compensation and organization design. *Personnel Journal, 53,* 338–348.

Pitts, R. A. (1977). Strategies and structures for diversification. *Academy of Management Journal, 20,* 197–208.

Porter, M. E. (1981). *Competitive strategy: Techniques for analyzing industries and competitors.* New York: Free Press.

Rumelt, R. (1974). *Strategy, structure, and economic performance.* Boston: Harvard Business School, Division of Research.

Schuler, R. S., Dowling, P. J., & De Cieri, H. (in press). An integrative framework of strategic international human resource management. *International Journal of Human Resource Management.*

Stonich, P. J. (1981). Using rewards in implementing strategy. *Strategy Management Journal, 2,* 345–352.

Tichy, N. M., Fombrun, C. J., & Devanna, M. A. (1982). Strategic human resource management. *Sloan Management Review, 23,* 47–61.

Wexley, K. N., & Latham, G. P. (1981). *Developing and training human resources in organizations.* Glenview, IL: Scott, Foresman.

White, A. F. (1992). Organizational transformation at BP: An interview with Chairman and CEO Robert Horton. *Human Resource Planning, 15(1),* 3–14.

Politics in Human Resources Decisions: A Walk on the Dark Side

Gerald R. Ferris and Thomas R. King

Although many experts have developed a fascination for the so-called rational model of organizations, the political model, despite the complexity (and perhaps cynicism) it introduces, deserves study—especially as it relates to human resources.

Perhaps the organizational function that still labors under implicit assumptions of rationality is human resources. Yet anecdotal evidence suggests that political considerations frequently enter into decisions concerning, for example, whom to hire and how an employee's performance is evaluated.

As part of our effort to examine closely the effect of politics on organizations, we draw here upon results from a program of research the first author has been conducting for nearly ten years, in addition to the work of others in this area. We propose to develop a clearer understanding of how politics emerges and influences decisions made in human resources by focusing on personnel selection and performance evaluation systems.

The Nature of Political Behavior

In modern American society, the organization is most often compared to a machine. There are inputs (physical, financial, and human resources), outputs, and throughput. Individuals serve as moving parts in the transformation process and maintain the machine's smooth operations. People are oriented either toward conducting routine operations or toward solving problems (breakdowns, repairs, replacements). Efficiency is the standard, and control underlies the methods for effective operations.

Much more than a standard, however, efficiency has become the most important shared value in modern society. To some extent this may stem partially from our language. The root of the word *organization* comes from the Greek *organon,* which means tool or instrument. Nearly every textbook on management and organizations suggests that organizing is the instrument that allows for individual goal attainment. Alternatively, the Chinese characters for organization mean "grouping" and "weaving." This places emphasis on groups and patterned activity, and moves away from individual activity. However, it lacks the connotation of manipulation that is present in the English term.

A popular alternative perspective, organization as culture, suggests that organizations never work according to the simplistic means implied in the machine metaphor. After all, the reasoning goes, human beings are so unmachinelike. They do not work as efficient, functional units. Rather, they work according to their own self-motivation—which is (unfortunately from the standpoint of machine-logic) not always congruent with the goals of others in the organization, not even management. Organizations are diffused, complex, heterogeneous, and rife with ambiguity and, therefore, cannot be managed by any particular design. They are composed of many stakeholders with multiple, often conflicting values and attitudes—all applying pressure at the same time. Even if we were presumptuous enough to suggest that human resources management (HRM)—or indeed, the field of management and organizations as a whole—

needs a new metaphor, simply replacing one dominant metaphor with another would be just as limiting. Rather, we can use the metaphors (organization as machine and organization as culture) to help us carve out an alternative understanding of politics in its larger sense.

Simply stated, politics is what takes place in the space between the perfect workings of the rational model (efficiency) and the messiness of human interaction. The greater the gap, the more political behavior becomes necessary. Likewise, the more an organizational system holds up the efficiency of the machine as the model for emulation, and uses the congruence as the standard for determining the worth of human individuals, the more the individuals within that system must create the impression that they actually have attained that congruence.

In the area of performance evaluation, politics is what has to occur to make the reality of messy human practice fit the myth of performance. The assumptions are that we know the exact meaning of "performance" in all cases, that it can be precisely measured, and that it will be objectively assessed for all individuals in the organization. In such an organization, politics acts as the slippage, the play in the system that the efficiency of the machine will not tolerate. Hence, from a machine-logic point of view, politics is something bad that needs to be eradicated.

But how does this logic work around opportunistic behavior? It seems that opportunism is a function of the shared values within the culture. If the values of greed, the win-at-all-costs mentality, and the glorification of the individual pervade a culture, that culture is more likely to be characterized by dysfunctional opportunistic behavior. Organizations desire the positive, motivational outcomes associated with the acceptance of these values, but we do not want people to get the wrong message and use organizational resources for their own purposes. At the same time, individuals would not be in the organization unless it was serving their own purposes. Where, then, do we draw the line between opportunism and altruism?

The major problem appears to be that because we require individuals to conform to a standard they cannot possibly achieve, these individuals place primary importance on making it appear as if they do. Form is far more critical than substance in these organizational systems. Thus, rather than focus on political or even opportunistic behavior, we choose instead to focus on behaviors that are geared toward form or the perceived need to manufacture an appearance of machinelike efficiency. We view this subset as the "dark side" of political behavior. For lack of a better term, we refer to these as influence behaviors or tactics and define them as behaviors geared toward influencing by creating the impression that the individual conforms to the machine-like performance standards valued by the organization.

Politics in Human Resources Systems

Human resources management has never received more attention and recognition than today for its role in the effective functioning of organizations. Perhaps the two most critical aspects of HRM are the hiring of employees and the systematic evaluation of their performance. Both systems are typically designed to include a methodical series of steps. They involve certain assumptions about the intentions and behaviors of both the job candidate or employee and the decision maker. Most important, they both assume an objective reality that is knowable and identifiable. These issues pertain to both personnel selection and performance evaluation decisions and the emergence of influence behavior. But before discussing the emergence of influence behavior, we need to briefly depict the nature and characteristics of work environments.

Ambiguity in Work Environments

The most central characteristic of work environments that serves to permit and even facilitate political behavior is ambiguity. The ambiguous nature of organizational environments is fertile ground on which political behaviors flourish. As we move up the organizational hierarchy, objectives become more ambiguous and conflicting, as do the work and performance expectations of employees. Also, the nature of work and its outcomes become increasingly nebulous until evaluation criteria become unclear. When such lack of clarity occurs with regard to evaluation criteria, organizations tend to rely less on measurable results and more on employee effort, perceived potential, personal characteristics, attitudes, and values, all of which could be changed through deliberate manipulation.

Ambiguity emerges in the personnel selection process as well. For example, many employment interviews are conducted by interviewers who have little experience and limited information about the job for which they are evaluating candidates. In light of such uncertainties, there seems to be ample opportunity for an astute, enterprising interviewee to capitalize on this ambiguity by contriving an impression of competence.

Although we see how ambiguity in the work environment can create opportunities for political behavior to emerge and be successful, we still need to see how this ambiguity affects decision makers. For one thing, ambiguity in the work environment contributes to uniformity in beliefs since individuals tend to seek consensus in their opinions when receiving ambiguous stimuli. Thus, decision makers in such contexts would seem to be particularly susceptible to influence by others in an effort to create the impression of shared meaning. Moreover, we know from extensive research on interpersonal attraction that similarity (perceived or actual) leads to attraction because it reduces ambiguity by increasing our confidence that our beliefs, opinions, and so forth are correct. Thus, to reduce ambiguity in the hiring process, managers may tend to rely on similarity (i.e., between candidate and evaluator) in personal characteristics and attitudes as selection criteria.

We now turn to personnel selection systems and more specifically investigate how politics plays out to affect selection decisions.

Politics in Personnel Selection

Personnel selection systems are designed to enumerate several logical and systematic steps through which decision makers proceed in order to ensure the hiring of the most suitable job candidates. The implicit assumption is that we can accurately measure both the demands of the job and the job-relevant qualities of candidates; thus, the task for decision makers is quite simply to hire those individuals who reflect the best match between the two pieces of information.

We might legitimately ask at this point, "What constitutes the 'best match'?" What we tend to find is that organizations and selection decision makers increasingly hire on the basis of "fit"; that is, they hire those "right types" who reflect the proper "chemistry" and thus fit well with the organizational environment and culture.

But the notion of fit seems to be a rather vague and largely undefined concept, which allows it to take a number of forms. It also permits job candidates to play upon the ambiguity and exercise a greater degree of influence over the selection process and outcomes. If fit manifests itself as attitude, belief, or value similarities to that of the decision maker, the job candidate can effectively create impressions of these. One way this could be done is through the opportunistic reflection or articulation of particular views that happen to coincide with those of the selection decision maker.

The reason the term "fit" is crucial in the human resources lexicon is because it is a machine term and, therefore, consistent with the prevailing philosophy of the field. Given the assumptions of human resource managers, an individual "fits" into the position or slot in the same way that a new part fits into the machine, replacing one that has worn out, has become defective, or has simply become obsolete. In the machine, however, there is no tolerance, no slippage, no play; the "fit" is as perfect as technology allows. Any ambiguity in the mechanical system and the machine breaks down. But attempts to achieve such perfection always stultify human creativity and innovation.

The notion of fit captures the congruence with the perfection of the machine; thus, fit also might take the form of how congruent or similar the job candidate behavior is with what the selection decision maker considers to be appropriate in a particular situation. Some of our research on politics in organizations has begun to investigate this notion. In a recent study of political behavior of applicants in the employment interview, we examined the effectiveness of two different types of influence tactics on interviewer ratings of candidate suitability. Candidates using the controlling, self-promoting types of tactics were rated as significantly more suitable for the job than those employing more submissive behaviors. These results may appear to be counterintuitive at first, given conventional expectations about how people react to self-promoting behavior. Generally, self-promotion tends to be perceived as egotistical, and people usually react negatively to one who engages in such behavior. However, the employment interview is a unique situation in which a positive flow of information is expected in both directions. Interviewers are expected to promote the positive features of the job and company, and the job candidate is expected to expound upon his or her superior qualifications. Humble behavior, although perhaps valued, appreciated, and even rewarded in other situations, is actually punished in a job interview; the interviewer may view the candidate as too subservient.

Politics also emerges in the selection process due to active efforts on the part of decision makers to maximize their own self-interest. Much internal organizational politics involves not just interpersonal influence but also coalition building. Operating managers may seek to become actively involved in the personnel selection process as a means of hiring people who think like they do in order to form a homogeneous internal constituency—and thus build their own power base.

Influence Behavior in Performance Evaluation

There is no human resources system more central and integrated with others than performance evaluation. It represents an area of enormous dissatisfaction among managers, who feel that no performance measurement works the way it is intended. Among the reasons for this dissatisfaction, the most prevalent is the frequently potent influence of politics in performance evaluation decisions.

Like personnel selection, performance evaluation systems are designed with a process and outcome in mind. Several systematic steps are defined that involve the observation and measurement of job performance, with the outcome being the most accurate evaluation of "true" performance over some period of time (usually one year). An implicit assumption in the process is that job performance is an objective reality that can easily be identified and measured. But as we saw in our earlier discussion of ambiguity in the work environment, this assumption may prove problematic. Particularly as we move upward in the organizational hierarchy, the very nature of job performance becomes ambiguous. When performance outcomes are less easily measured objectively, we tend to focus on employee behavior rather than actual results. In addition to a focus on behavior, we tend to evaluate people on the basis of beliefs, values, and effort, all of which can be easily manipulated. In other words, we can unwittingly create conditions that reward form over substance, with individuals quite rationally responding accordingly.

Because the evaluation of performance in many jobs is not amenable to objective assessment and quantification, we find that subjective performance ratings by supervisors typically incorporate a variety of nonperformance factors, leading to a violation of the most sacred principle of performance evaluation—that we are evaluating performance, not the person in the abstract. The violation of this fundamental principle suggests that factors such as liking; perceived similarity in values, beliefs, and attitudes; and "fit" may well explain much of the content of performance ratings in organizations.

A recent study we conducted demonstrates this to be the case. We found that influence tactics of employees contributed to being liked by the supervisor, which led the supervisor to rate the employee's job performance more favorably. However, this did not work for all types of influence tactics. Supervisors tended to like their employees more and give them higher performance ratings when the employees demonstrated ingratiating behaviors such as doing favors, offering extra help, and showing an interest in the supervisor's personal life. On the other hand, employees that engaged in self-promoting behaviors for enhancements (making more of one's accomplishments than was warranted) and entitlement (taking responsibility for positive events or outcomes even if not justified in doing so) were liked less by their supervisors and received considerably lower performance ratings.

These results, within the context of performance evaluation, are exactly opposite of those reported above in our discussion of behaviors associated with personnel selection. There, recall that self-promotion behaviors led to rewards, while ingratiating (submissive) behaviors were punished. In the context of performance evaluation, however, self-promotion behaviors led to less positive outcomes than did ingratiation. This is likely the result of different expectations concerning what is situationally appropriate behavior.

As we have seen, employees can effectively exercise their influence over the performance evaluation process and decisions through the political behaviors they exhibit. The evaluators, however, can behave politically as well, also contributing to distortion,

error, and inaccuracy in performance evaluation decisions. Our traditional assumption that an evaluator's main objective is to provide the most accurate possible evaluation of performance is perhaps naive. There may exist many more reasons to rate inaccurately than accurately. For example, as a manager, I may be evaluated on how effectively my work unit is performing, which is determined by my ratings of the performance of all employees in that work unit. Thus, we should not be terribly surprised to see inflated ratings as a result.

It seems, then, that ambiguity in the work environment provides fertile ground for the emergence and effectiveness of political behavior, particularly as it affects personnel selection and performance evaluation decisions. Furthermore, whether organizations do so consciously or unconsciously, the systems they design actually may reward influence behavior and thus perpetuate and increase the nature of environments likely to be characterized by such behaviors. Of course, just because the conditions permit influence behavior to flourish, it does not mean that all individuals possess the skill and motivation to engage in such behavior. There tend to be individual differences with respect to both one's ability to read situations and identify opportunities to exercise influence and one's natural tendency to be manipulative. Obviously, the people with the influence skills and the propensity to exhibit those behaviors in organizations in order to gain some advantage are the "political animals" that we need to examine and understand.

The political dynamics in human resources systems and decisions, then, appear to be driven largely by the opportunity to influence, which is presented through ambiguity in the decision context for both personnel selection and performance evaluation. This process is illustrated in Exhibit 1.

Form versus Substance in Organizations

The feigning of attitudes, values, beliefs, and emotions in purely opportunistic fashion pre-

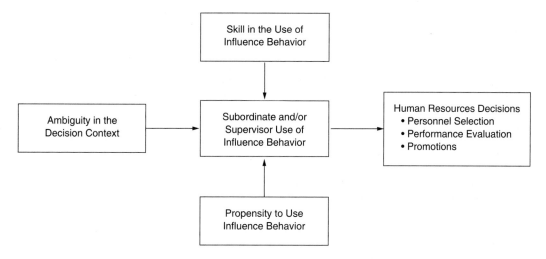

Exhibit 1. Politics in Human Resources Decisions

sents a fairly complex picture of organizational life. It becomes, in fact, difficult to distinguish the genuine from the superficial, the form from the substance. And form or image appears to be quite important in organizations today. As noted by former U.S. Secretary of State Alexander Haig, "The rule used to be 'What am I saying?' Now it is 'How do I appear?' " This observation may have arisen from General Haig's experience with a military practice referred to as "ticket-punching," or earning credit for appearing to do the right thing as opposed to actually doing a good job. This has become absolutely critical to survival in organizations.

An indication of the importance of style and image in today's society comes from *Esquire* magazine. In each issue there is a section entitled "Man at His Best. A Gentleman's Guide to Quality and Style." In this section one can learn (ostensibly) where to live, what to wear, what to eat, where to travel and where to stay, what to listen to, and what to do if one wishes to be successful. It is important to note what is not said in these articles. They imply that they are the things to be done to *be seen as successful,* not to *be successful.* But in such a context the boundaries invariably blur, and being seen as successful and being successful have become the same.

Is it the case, then, that in organizations today, form has replaced substance, and that it is not what you are, but what you appear to be? The evidence certainly seems to point in that direction. Studies in the area of procedural justice in organizations have recently reported some quite interesting findings regarding the issue of form versus substance. In one, it was found that managers are not nearly so concerned with "being fair" as they are with "looking fair."

We operate on the basis of our perceptions of reality, not reality *per se.* In that sense, perhaps Tom Peters was right when he made the statement: "Perception is all there is. There ain't no such thing as steak, sad to say—just the sizzle." From this, we might suggest that "competence" of employees (in any kind of objective sense) becomes an irrelevant issue, and is replaced by one's ability to socially construct a reality of competence—a "cosmetic competence" if you will—through political acumen. This seems no better portrayed than in the motion picture *Broadcast News,* which contrasts form and substance quite effectively through the characters portrayed by William Hurt and Albert Brooks. The skillful image managed by the TV news anchorman played by Hurt is a classic example of "cosmetic competence." The focus of his attention is not on the content and controversies inherent in the news he reports, but rather on the shade of his makeup or the "line" of his coat. Despite his own occasional misgivings about this, he knows that he will be well rewarded for his political skills and ability to construct an image of something he is not. In contrast, the character played by Brooks is as substantive as the Hurt character is superficial. More important, both characters know this. Like the Brooks character, competent employees are often frustrated when they see organizational politicians practice their craft with precision, and reap the riches of prestigious promotions and hefty pay increases.

Implications

Despite our observations in the foregoing discussion, we would not be so cynical as to suggest that this "form over substance" is the primary interest of all employees in all organizations. But there is ample evidence to indicate that form or image certainly is the concern of many.

The dedicated and committed "organization man" of the 1950s appears to have taken a back seat to a variety of creatures who roam the corridors of organizational America today. Included among those creatures are Hirsch's "Free-Agent Manager" (*Pack Your Own Parachute,* Addison-Wesley, 1987), Maccoby's "Gamesman" (*The Gamesman,* Bantam Books, 1978), Kelly's "Destructive Achiever" (*The Destructive Achiever: Power and Ethics in the American Corporation,* Addison-Wesley, 1988), and Kanter and Mirvis's "Articulate Player" (*The Cynical Americans: Living and Working in an Age of Discontent and Disillusion,* Jossey-Bass, 1989).

We believe that contemporary personnel selection and performance evaluation systems are encouraging the development of yet a different creature, one we might dub the "organization chameleon" because fitting or blending in becomes the all-important result of one's image-management efforts. This clever

and skillful politician would gain entry to organizations by effectively managing the impression of "fit," a criterion that seems to be increasingly popular with personnel selection decision makers. Once in the system, this opportunistic character will ensure favorable performance reviews and rapid upward mobility by reflecting the proper norms, beliefs, values, and effort, and by demonstrating highly visible and organizationally valued behaviors at strategically appropriate times.

Yes, the organization chameleon will get ahead by becoming exactly what it is the company is looking for and as such, proves a formidable opponent. These characters should not be taken lightly; they are shrewd, calculating, and quite difficult to detect. Those who have honed their political skills to perfection can construct their image so carefully and precisely that they easily pass undetected through the most sensitive monitoring devices. But to go back to our earlier point, the problem is that these monitoring devices are not sensitive enough. Their failure to screen effectively allows our skilled chameleon to work the system with smoke and mirrors.

Fortunately, though, there are some ways that organizations can improve their personnel selection and performance evaluation systems and render them at least somewhat less prone to job applicant and employee manipulation.

Improving Human Resources Practices

Following are some recommendations we have outlined for improving personnel selection and performance evaluation systems on the basis of our work in organizational politics:

Define "fit." We will probably never convince organizations not to hire on the basis of "fit." But we can recommend that "fit" be as precisely defined as possible for each job to which it is being applied. For example, if "fit" in one context is found to involve a certain type of personal style that is congruent with the particular work environment or culture, selection decision makers may be able to assess that attribute using a personality inventory, or at least formulate a line of questioning in the interview that is designed to tap that dimension. We would also suggest that it is potentially dangerous for organizations if they neglect to explain what they mean by "fit." For example, a vague notion of "fit" serving as the impetus for hiring decisions may result in disproportionately larger numbers of women and minorities denied entry. This potentially places the organization in the precarious position of trying to defend its personnel selection practices against charges of employment discrimination.

Prepare decision makers for the selection task. All too frequently, organizations fail to ensure that the personnel selection decision makers are adequately prepared to perform effectively the task at hand. One source of concern is the quality and quantity of information given to these decision makers regarding precisely what the job involves—and therefore the types of knowledge, skills, abilities, and experience that represent necessary job-relevant qualities candidates need to possess. When this information is sketchy, it places the decision maker in the position of not having a clear idea of exactly what he or she is looking for. As the quality of the information improves, it changes the focus and structure of the decision task by reducing ambiguity and rendering political influence attempts of candidates less effective.

Derive specific, job-relevant performance criteria. Our earlier discussion suggested that ambiguity surrounding job performance for many types of jobs allows job incumbents to create impressions of "doing the right things," thus perhaps effectively diverting attention away from a focus on outcomes and toward a focus on the evaluation of effort, and even on the beliefs and values the employee reflects. Although it may pose some difficulty (more so for some jobs than for others), key results areas and critical performance criteria can and should be specified for each job. The performance criteria for a particular job should

be documented and communicated to both supervisor and employee so there is shared and common understanding concerning the criteria on which the employee will be evaluated. This serves to reduce some of the ambiguity and closes off some of the opportunities for employees to influence the outcomes.

Objectify an inherently subjective system through documentation. For most of the types of jobs with which we regularly deal, job performance is not amenable to quantification and objective assessment. Instead, performance is judged subjectively, usually by one's immediate supervisor. Such subjectivity allows for error to enter the performance rating process in several ways. First, there may be unintentional errors due to the rater's information-processing approach, and relevant information could be forgotten. Second, there may be intentional rating errors introduced when a supervisor lets his or her own personal agenda drive the rating process. And, third, there are errors in rating introduced through the active influence efforts of employees who seek to exercise control over the evaluations they receive.

A recommendation that can help to reduce the incidence of these rating errors is to require documentation to accompany the performance ratings. Specific documentation of events, incidents, and actual employee behaviors to justify or substantiate a particular rating on some performance criteria adds more definition to the resulting performance ratings. And as more and more organizations consider additional sources of evaluation, and begin to incorporate self-evaluation along with supervisor evaluation, the documentation requirement imposed on both parties presumably should lead to more effective performance review sessions.

Revise your "fast track" philosophy. A characteristic of organizational life that compounds our problem of designing effective performance evaluation systems is the expectation of rapid movement within the organization, usually in an upward direction. Typically referred to as the "fast track," such a philosophy involves hiring high-potential people and allowing them to move quickly upward through a series of positions, with no time-in-grade requirement for any particular position. Such a philosophy can potentially be dysfunctional for several reasons. First, such rapid movement creates even more ambiguity for the accurate assessment of job performance. In fact, it has the potential to create an environment in which form, not substance, is rewarded and employees are actually encouraged to display their influence talents. John Younger, manager of training and organization development for Exxon, was quoted in *The Wall Street Journal* (March 24, 1986) as saying "form becomes a whole lot more important than substance." As a result, Younger claimed, many fast-trackers will initiate "a couple of things that have a lot of flash and create a lot of noise but may not make a heck of a lot of substantive difference." This is evident, for example, when a fast-tracker dramatically slashes a department's budget to show instant results.

Second, when a person spends such little time in a position, how can the true nature of his or her performance contributions be accurately assessed? In fact, we must question precisely the yardsticks on which we are basing our favorable evaluations of each employee's performance. Are the "contributions" merely quite visible but superficial behaviors? And, third, the developmental experiences and skill acquisition one gains on a job are lost. In light of these issues, organizations might be better served by rethinking the "fast track" philosophy and moving toward a slower and more careful evaluation and promotion system. Such a move, it seems, could only help to improve the quality of resulting performance evaluation and promotion decisions that are made.

Rethinking Our Assumptions

Another direction leads to reexamining our assumptions and giving up our reliance on the rational model—that is, developing organizational systems and practices that more closely mirror the messy, ambiguous human side of the continuum. This does not necessarily have to conjure up images of hordes of "loose cannons" running amok in the halls of corporate America. It may involve no more than loosening up on some elements while tightening up others. In terms of performance evaluation, the key appears to be to downplay the importance of form or image in the performance equation.

As instructors, we recognize that we will never be good enough to uncover all of those people in our classes who turn form into an art. The only way to weed them out is to create classroom experiences that force them to *use* the skills we teach, rather than tell us what they have learned. This seems simplistic, but it is at the center of the form and substance issue. If people have jobs in which they can tell others how good they are, from the standpoint of machine-logic, it is much more efficient and effective to do so. Therefore, as simple as it seems, we need to create systems in which such telling is irrelevant.

The cultural approach suggests putting people together and making them interdependent. This is indeed what appears to be happening in many organizations as they experiment with superteams. Although this has been used primarily in manufacturing and for lower-level positions, it is now spreading to service industries and to higher levels in many other industries.

Another way to set up performance systems that emphasize substance rather than form for middle- and upper-level managers comes from the work of W. Edwards Deming, the American credited with teaching management to the Japanese. In Deming's system, most managers exist to give lower-level employees the information they need to do their jobs and to remove barriers for them. This more directly ties managers' performance to the overall performance of the group, team, or department and, for our purposes, reduces the emphasis on form over substance.

Discussions of organizational influence behavior, and how it affects critical systems and decisions in companies, present—in some people's view—an unduly cynical perspective on organizational dynamics. We would agree that to consider these kinds of behavior universally, as being prominent in the thoughts of all employees, is overly cynical and inaccurate. We would hasten to add, however, that to refuse to acknowledge the existence of organizational influence behavior is naive. We need to be realistic. Political behavior will probably always exist in organizations. Thus for managers the most appropriate perspective would seem to be to develop a better understanding of politics and how it affects human resources decisions so that its dysfunctional consequences can be prevented.

Ensuring Strength in Each Country: A Challenge for Corporate Headquarters Global Human Resource Executives

Anne V. Corey

The most valuable long-term contribution a corporate or headquarters-based international human resource (HR) executive can make to the success of the business (and to his or her career) is to ensure that each country operation is supported by its own professional HR function. For compelling business reasons at various organizational levels, country operations must be able effectively to manage:

1. organization planning/succession planning
2. employee training/development
3. recruitment/selection
4. compensation/benefits
5. HR information systems
6. industrial relations/employee relations
7. employee relocations
8. employee services/facilities management

Whether an enterprise is part of an organizational structure which is traditional or matrix, centralized or decentralized, it must have an appropriately sized and staffed HR function: one professional, supported by a clerical assistant, for every 100 to 125 employees.

This article reviews a structure—used in 18 years of actual experience primarily outside the U.S.—for defining the HR function, convincing management at various organizational levels to allocate required resources, and helping country operations to make it happen.

Defining the Function: But we already have a personnel department!

The list of major components above was developed to help country operations envision the scope of support that could be realized from their own on-the-ground, professional HR management function. The structure resembles a "domestic" HR function and would look pretty much the same in country operations around the world. The HR management function must be strong at the country level *and* at each higher organizational level to achieve the organization's strategic and operating objectives.

The way in which issues are addressed, however, does vary from country to country. To illustrate, following is an outline of a presentation I gave in Mexico and Egypt to managers for Latin America and the Middle East, respectively, and to an International HR Management class at American University. I have added comments at the end of each section to highlight the "international" nuances.

I. **Organization planning/succession planning**

  A. must be carried out by top management in each country to ensure the most effective organizational structure and continuity of professional management

Reprinted with permission of The Human Resource Planning Society from *Human Resource Planning 14:1* (1991): 1–8.

B. HR in each country must be an integral member of the management team for strategic and operational planning purposes

C. includes:
1. present and future organization (including time frame)
2. succession positions to be reviewed
3. elements of/requirements for each position
4. data about incumbents:
   a. time in present job
   b. current performance
   c. future potential
5. planned replacements (including contingency or emergency replacements)
6. development plans (for incumbents and successors in current and future jobs)

Comment: Organization planning/succession planning is *not* an activity carried out exclusively at headquarters. It must be managed effectively at every organizational level down to, and including, country operations. It is especially important for operations which cannot support depth in the management ranks and where each succession position is, therefore, absolutely critical to the success of the enterprise. Also, in developing viable organization/succession plans, practical considerations such as language and immigration requirements must be included. For instance, if an individual is not fluent in a required language or cannot obtain authorization to work in a particular country, his or her other qualifications for a position become less relevant.

II. Employee training/development

A. must be done for *all* employees; must be linked to succession plan for employees in and/or identified for succession positions
B. needs a performance management system that includes:
1. objectives/responsibilities
2. performance development (current position)
3. career development (future positions)
4. achievement appraisal
5. skills appraisal
6. manager and subordinate participation in process

C. identifies the need for/objectives of training and development programs

D. allocates necessary resources (budget for employee training and development)

E. tailors programs for different levels/categories of employees

F. should include varied approaches:
1. external/internal courses
2. on-the-job training
3. committee/task-force assignments
4. rotational assignments (lateral moves are okay)
5. technical/skills training (remember language skills)

Comment: Training and development is a perfect example of a joint venture with the parties being (1) each employee and (2) his or her supervisor. Responsibility for success rests on both parties. Within global organizations, supervisors and subordinates frequently are located in different countries and possess different cultural backgrounds. However, mutual dedication to the principles of employee appraisal and development, combined with proper logistical planning, should eliminate concerns based on geography, culture, customs, or language. For example, a General Manager in Australia reporting to a Regional Vice President in Hong Kong or New York might take the initiative and request time to discuss performance and career development plans with his or her boss well in advance of corporate succession planning, performance appraisals, and/or remuneration recommendation deadlines so as to ensure adequate and relaxed time for these important discussions.

III. Recruitment/selection

A. must include current position descriptions

B. *planning* should include the following considerations:
1. what is needed?
2. when?
3. where is the vacancy located?
4. how will you find the best internal/external candidates? (cast your net wide)
5. what is each candidate's potential for higher-level positions?
6. why should someone join your organization?
7. why should he or she stay?

C. *process* must be in compliance with legal requirements

D. Remember: it is much easier to hire than to fire—recruit and select carefully

Comment: In international recruitment and selection, the best candidates may be anywhere in the world. You must first consider where they might be and direct your search accordingly. In selecting search firms, in addition to the usual criteria, consider their capabilities for a particular geographic location. Think about migration patterns: Where do people move from and where do they resettle? Final candidates for key positions often must be interviewed by decision makers in other countries, so budget time and expenses accordingly. Also, final candidates for positions reporting to country General Managers and above must be fluent in the language of the country in which the organization is headquartered. Otherwise, they will not be able to participate effectively in the management of the business.

IV. Compensation/benefits

A. determine country-specific ways of delivering cash and noncash remuneration: what are *all* the components in the total remuneration package?

B. ensure compliance with mandatory/statutory requirements in each country

C. be competitive:
1. know where you want to rank in the marketplace for employees
2. know where you rank now
3. determine actions required to close gap—know cost and timetable

D. pay for performance—link appraisal and reward programs

E. "market" compensation and benefit programs to employees

F. be vigilant in maintaining your standing in the market

Comment: The most frequent question asked of international HR executives by corporate executives is: "Why are we doing that? We don't do it *here.*" Although the principle of paying for performance is universal, the number of ways in which compensation and benefits are delivered is equal to the number of countries in the world. The best approach is to (1) understand *thoroughly* how remuneration is delivered in each country in which you have employees, (2) keep up-to-date as changes occur, (3) avoid comparisons between countries which may be interesting but often irrelevant, (4) obtain appropriate corporate approvals of remuneration plans, and (5) minimize the use of global standards. Leading-edge companies insist on competitive, *country-specific* remuneration systems developed, communicated, implemented, and maintained by competent HR professionals in *each* country.

V. HR information systems

A. automate!

B. ensure compatibility throughout the organization worldwide (systems must be able to talk to each other)

C. essential contents include:
1. legal requirements

2. company requirements
3. biographical data—the individual's:
   a. education
   b. experience
   c. career goals and desires

Comment: A truly global HR information system must be flexible. It must contain these essential components for each and every country. Enhancements can always be added to meet needs in larger, more complex, more mature operations and to accommodate growth in smaller and younger markets. From the headquarters' perspective, country operations around the world should not be burdened by data requests for files. This wastes valuable time which could be used more productively and is disheartening for those involved. From the individual country's perspective, it is essential to take the initiative to implement automated, compatible, expandable, useful HR information systems. From *all* perspectives, think of HR information systems as an available bank, not as a guarded museum.

VI. Industrial relations/employee relations

A. is needed whether or not employees are represented by an enterprise, industry, national, or international labor organization
B. balances interests by considering rights and responsibilities of employers and employees
C. performs many roles as:
   1. mediator of differences
   2. supporter/interpreter of policies, programs, and procedures
   3. social director for celebrations
   4. messenger of good and bad news
   5. listener in confidence

Comment: The need for industrial relations/employee relations at the country affiliate/subsidiary level is not much different from that need at other organizational levels. However, the way in which disputes, grievances, and communications are handled varies dramatically from country to country; corporate "umbrellas" are not useful here. This component needs to be managed on-the-ground in each country by HR professionals who speak the language (literally and figuratively). For example, a personnel policy manual developed for employees in the U.S. cannot be exported to an organization's operations around the world; operations in each country need to develop their own personnel policy manuals.

VII. Employee relocations

The following outline could serve as a table of contents for an international assignments policy:
A. General
   1. types of relocations
      a. long-term but temporary (bona fide expatriates)
      b. short-term but temporary (long business trip)
      c. permanent transfer
   2. objectives and scope of relocations
   3. definitions: for example, *base country for remuneration purposes* (is it country of birth or nationality, last, current, or next work location?) or *compensation* and *benefits* (how many elements comprise the total package?)
   4. selection of candidates for international assignments
   5. responsibility for development, approval, communication, implementation, and administration of relocation and remuneration packages
   6. responsibility for costs
   7. currency focus and method of payment
   8. repatriation to base country or transfer to another host country

9. adjustment of status

B. compensation
   1. annual base salary
   2. incentive compensation
   3. mobility premium
   4. hardship allowance
   5. cost-of-living allowance
   6. housing
   7. education of children
   8. income tax equalization

C. employee benefits
   1. mandatory/legislated programs
   2. company-provided programs
   3. major hazards of:
      a. illness
      b. disability
      c. death
   4. retirement income
   5. personal property and liability insurance

D. personnel practices
   1. orienting international assignees before and after transfer
   2. immigration requirements in host country
   3. medical examinations
   4. pretransfer visit to host country
   5. shipment/storage of personal and household possessions
   6. transportation to host country: employee, accompanying dependents, pets
   7. interim living expenses
   8. settling-in allowance
   9. language training
   10. automobiles
   11. annual vacation/home leave
   12. periodic rest-and-relaxation leave
   13. emergency leave
   14. completion of assignment
       a. repatriation
       b. reassignment
       c. retirement
       d. termination of employment

Comment: Truly global organizations must have international-assignments policies, programs, and procedures managed from corporate headquarters. Responsibility for developing, communicating, implementing, administering, and *updating* international-assignments policies is a full-time job for an experienced international HR professional. In addition, expatriates in each country cannot be the only ones familiar with this policy; at a minimum, the country's General Manager, Finance Manager, and HR Manager must be knowledgeable about this policy. Days, weeks, and months could be (and have been) spent discussing an organization's international assignment policy. My recommendations are: (1) Spend whatever time it takes to keep the policy current and competitive, (2) adhere to the existing policy, (3) be fair and consistent, (4) maintain a sense of humor, (5) get to know the *people* who are moving between countries, and (6) remember that the policy exists to serve the needs of the business *and* the needs of relocating employees and families.

VIII. Employee services/facilities management
   A. is often thought of as an integral part of "Personnel" or of "HR" since it meets the daily needs of employees
   B. but each major component calls for specific skills
   C. therefore, if Employee Services/Facilities Management is part of HR, it should be a separate department within the total function

Comment: Once when I was visiting an affiliate for the purpose of reviewing and evaluating their HR function, I noticed that the Employee Training and Development Manager was in charge of the day-care center which, at that time, had a population of about 27 preschool children! There certainly was a lot of training and development going on, but not of employees. Needless to say, we restructured to ensure that both needs were met—but not by the same manager.

Convincing Management: Okay, okay, we get the picture! But there's no money in the budget this year!

As a senior international HR executive, you may find the following arguments and strategies persuasive in convincing management to allocate the required resources:

1. The company is not paying the General Manager or the Finance Manager (who typically "take care" of personnel issues in the absence of a professional function) to function as HR Managers; these managers need to concentrate on managing the business and the finances, respectively.

2. The need to respond promptly and professionally to directives and requests from corporate headquarters is real, even if occasionally these are perceived as unnecessary. These demands will not stop just because an operation is not staffed to handle them. Also, if the organization has a leading-edge HR function, many policies, programs, and procedures will be global in scope and headquarters will expect support and implementation right down to the individual country level.

3. Without a designated HR Manager, each department head will assume that role—but in his or her way. This is not desirable. In one instance, the regional marketing manager and the country marketing manager in the same location separately engaged the same search firm to identify candidates for staff vacancies and then began bidding against each other for the best candidates, creating salary structures and benefit plans as they went along! The candidates thought it was terrific, but discontent with remuneration arrangements among the existing employees

rose to an all-time high. Today the company's regional and country operations each have professional HR Managers who coordinate policies, programs, and procedures for the benefit of the total workforce in the country.

4. Management worldwide has a mandate to communicate and implement the corporation's values statement. Many corporate values statements claim commitment to employees as their most valuable assets. Members of internal and external constituent groups will not be able to reconcile claims of commitment to employees with the absence of professional HR management functions. ("If they don't care about the function, how can they care about the people?") Trying to "globalize" a corporate values statement does much to drive home the need to establish an HR function.

5. Remember that General Managers want to be viewed favorably by their peers. Trying to persuade a General Manager who could not see the need to spend the money to establish an HR function and recruit a real professional to manage it, we shared with him reliable survey information which showed that his was the only operation without an HR function. That got his attention! As a result, the operation now has a splendid function supported by the General Manager.

6. It is important that each country operation be well represented at the organization's periodic HR conferences (held to introduce new global HR management policies, programs, and procedures and to share information and experiences). An HR professional is the best person to do this.

7. Remember that country General Managers normally want to be self-sufficient in terms of day-to-day HR management, but were to consult generalists and specialists at higher organizational levels for guidance and assistance with communicating and implement-

ing global, corporatewide, strategic HR policies, programs, and procedures. Having an HR function provides this resource. Conversely, as a senior international HR executive, you need to have professional counterparts in each country to advise and keep you current on the local labor situation: You do not want to spend your time flying from headquarters to country operations around the world to fill the local personnel manager role. Ensuring the existence of professional, country-level HR functions serves both the General Manager and your own objectives.

Helping to Make It Happen: Okay, okay, we get the picture and we're convinced! Now what?

Just to make sure you will be ready to help implement an HR function, following is a recommended checklist to share with your General Manager and his management team. The approach is fairly universal. However, you may discover that local management wants to move *too* quickly once the decision is made to establish an HR function. In one instance, the country General Manager wanted to promote his secretary to the top HR position because "she handles the confidential payroll anyway." This is not to say that individual employees within the organization cannot be trained for HR, but the top HR executive on the management team within an operation must be an HR professional. Here is where you may have to redefine a professional HR function for the General Manager and his management team.

Checklist

1. What is going on right now? Take the time to find out what is being done, who is doing it, what is working fine, what needs strengthening, and what is *not* being done. Consult with those who have been doing personnel (if not HR) management in each country; include them in the planning process. Those

who were doing all that was being done will be invaluable and often can continue in key roles in the new function.

2. Design the structure of your HR function not just for now but to support your long-term or strategic business plan. Identify each and every professional and support position needed. Prepare new and/or revise existing position descriptions (remember to include language skills). Make sure the senior HR position reports directly to the General Manager and that the proposed structure of the HR function is compatible with that of other departments such as Marketing, Sales, Finance, Manufacturing, and Research and Development in the country *and* in the region. Country operations within geographic regions often share characteristics which can be helpful here.

3. Develop remuneration packages that will eventually be offered to the final candidate for each position. Make sure they are internally equitable and externally competitive. Allocate adequate resources for quality. Be prepared to bear relocation expenses for the right candidates.

4. Develop a timetable and obtain the necessary management approvals to proceed with the proposed plan.

5. Begin the recruitment/selection process to fill the senior HR position; the successful candidate should recruit to fill other staff vacancies. Look within the company and the country; look outside the company and the country. If necessary, engage an international search firm: You never know where in the world the best candidates are. Be sure to involve each member of your management team in the interview process. Consider arranging for the No. 1 candidate to be interviewed by line and staff executives at higher organizational levels prior to employment. (Some organizations with matrix structures require this.)

6. Once the operation's senior HR executive has been employed, the General Manager should work with him or her to accomplish four specific tasks on a priority basis:
   a. recruitment and selection to fill remaining vacancies in the HR department
   b. completion of an in-depth orientation program within the HR function at higher organizational levels such as regional, international, and/or corporate to learn global HR strategies/objectives
   c. completion of an in-depth orientation program within the local operation and with the full involvement of the other management team members
   d. development of specific objectives for the balance of the business year. This should involve the General Manager and the other members of the management team and reflect the corporate and local priorities discussed during the orientation programs.

One Last Point

You absolutely cannot accomplish all this from your office at corporate headquarters. You must spend time with the operations: Tour the manufacturing plants, work with the sales representatives, hang around the office. Let me illustrate with one last anecdote: In planning a trip to Indonesia (*before* the firm had an HR function), I asked for a list of what the firm wanted me to concentrate on during my visit. Included in the list was the entry: "Scooter Policy." I had never been to Indonesia before, but what a Scooter policy was became crystal clear during my first trip from the hotel to the facility: We were surrounded by people moving about Jakarta on scooters! It was an essential means of transportation for many workers. So a competitive scooter policy was important in attracting and retaining qualified employees for the local operation.

You never know what will turn up on your list as you start to ensure strength in each country operation. But remember: there are as many similarities as differences among people.

The most valuable long-term contribution a corporate or headquarters-based international HR executive can make to the success of the business (and to his or her career) is to ensure that each country operation is supported by its own professional HR function. You accomplish this by *defining* the function, by *convincing* management at various organizational levels of the need to allocate the required resources, and by *helping* country operations around the world to make it happen.

PART 2

The External Context of Human Resources Management

If organizations were insular entities and had little contact with the external environment, concern with external issues could be minimal. But organizations exist in dynamic, complex environments. In fact, many of our activities concerning the management of human resources are directly related to addressing external constraints. The external environment in which an organization operates does have a significant impact on human resources activities. Ignorance of these environmental constraints would significantly dilute the effectiveness of human resources management.

Part 2 is mostly concerned with a number of the features of the external environment that have impact upon the human resources management function. The articles in Chapter 3 reflect the significant influence of federal legislation on the operation of an organization. Throughout the book are numerous articles concerning these legal issues. In this chapter the emphasis is on what a human resources manager can do to comply with the vast amount of case law and legislation affecting human resources.

The work force is changing, and a successful human resources program must keep abreast of these demographic changes. The Chapter 4 articles examine some of the key labor market characteristics that will pose a challenge for human resources. Creating diversity in the workplace is a goal of many organizations. What impact will this have on human resources? The articles in this chapter identify the challenges and opportunities that diversity will bring to the human resources function.

Organizations must respond to changes in the external environment. So far, the decade of the 1990s has seen environmental events dictating human resources policies in many organizations. When environments demand downsizing, redesign, or restructuring, or when mergers and acquisitions occur, human resources are significantly affected. The article in Chapter 5 offers a number of suggestions for reducing the ambiguity associated with these organizational interventions, while presenting the challenges that accompany these changes.

CHAPTER 3

The Legal Environment

Federal legislation with respect to fair employment practices has had a major influence on personnel and human resources management over the past 25 years. To move toward a greater sense of fair treatment for all, Title VII of the Civil Rights Act of 1964 made it a violation to discriminate on the basis of race, color, religion, sex, or national origin in the employment relationship. Subsequent legislation and court decisions moved the pendulum away from blatant discrimination toward equality for all. Some would argue that, in recent years, the pendulum has swung too far to the other side and that we are seeing evidence of reverse discrimination, which clearly was not the intention of those working to promote civil rights. Additional legislation, such as the Age Discrimination in Employment Act of 1967 and a 1978 amendment that disallows mandatory retirement before age 70, expanded the application of fair employment practices to all activities in the processing of people *through* and *out of* organizations as well. Examples include promotion and transfer activities, training and development, compensation, and termination.

The use of personnel testing as an aid to employment decisions declined after the passage of the Civil Rights Act. It has increased since then, however, as companies have begun to realize that it is not tests per se that are discriminatory but the ways and the situations in which the tests are used.

Although the last Republican administrations did not make major cuts in the budgets of federal regulatory agencies that oversee compliance with the law in regard to the employment relationship, they at least relegated these agencies to a lower level of visibility and generally deemphasized the issues they address. Counterforces to this federal posture are emerging, however. Many state and local governments are creating their own laws and ordinances to protect employee rights.

Legal issues pervade all that occurs in the human resources management function. For that reason many of the subsequent articles in this book are concerned with legal issues. Some of the writing concerns the legal defensibility of performance appraisal. Further, the issue of affirmative action serves as the basis of the desire of many organizations to create diversity in the work force. Professionals in human resources management must be aware of the legal standards that guide the implementation of many human resources initiatives.

Niculescu, in the first article in this chapter, outlines the recent legislative events that have had an effect upon the selection process. The author examines a number of important issues and presents her belief in the necessity of job-specific tests customized for each position in an organization. Buckley, Miceli, Purvis, and Gross discuss some of the potential unintended consequences of legislation. They point out how the implementation of the Americans with Disabilities Act may result in some subsequent difficulties with employee motivation. In addition, the reader is referred to other chapters of this book (e.g., Chapter 7) where legal issues in human resources are discussed.

Suggestions for Further Reading

Colbert, C., III, & Wofford, J. (1993). Sexual orientation in the workplace: The strategic challenge. *Compensation & Benefits Management, 9,* 1–18.

Hughes, P., & Grote, R. (1993, June). Peer review places trust with employees. *HR Magazine,* pp. 57–62.

The in box. (1993). *Supervisory Management, 38,* 4–5.

Laabs, J. (1993). Insurance coverage must be clearly defined. *Personnel Journal, 72,* 30–32.

Marshall, R. (1993). A clause too far in the employment bill? *Personnel Management, 25,* 6.

Matthes, K. (1993, July). ADA update: The first year in review. *HR Focus,* p. 3.

Peters, S. (1993). Word-of-mouth recruitment can be risky. *Personnel Journal, 72,* 92–93.

Pusker, H. (1989). Leased employees and qualified plans. *Compensation & Benefits Management, 5,* 125–131.

Rappaport, A. (1989). After MCCA: Plan design for postemployment benefits. *Compensation & Benefits Management, 5,* 153–159.

SHRM information center. (1993). *Employment Relations Today, 20,* 235–242.

Legal Developments Affecting the Selection Process

Debbie Eide Niculescu

As employers who hire from a population with numerous risk factors, sales managers and retailers have to ensure they are fully aware of legislation and court actions which could have a serious impact on their recruitment and selection process. To that end, you need to know about recent legal decisions. Specifically we are talking about Negligent Hiring suits, the Civil Rights Act of 1991, Discriminatory Interviewing Practices and the need for validation of each step of the employee selection process.

Negligent Hiring Suits

There is a growing body of lawsuits brought to court in which an employer was sued by a person unrelated to the business because an employee, whether on the job or during off hours, caused damage or harm to the customer or his possessions. In these cases the courts found employers liable if it can be proven they did not do everything within their power to ensure that there was nothing in the employees' background which indicated he/she could intentionally put another person at risk. This included having a thorough selection process and ongoing performance appraisal system.

For instance, in one case, a resident of an apartment complex was assaulted by a maintenance person when the employee was not on duty. The resident sued the management company which employed the maintenance worker, and the court ruled in favor of the resident, citing that the management company did not do a thorough screening which could have determined the maintenance worker might present future problems and eliminate that person from consideration for hire.

There are steps an employer or manager can take to reduce this risk. Chief among these is the use of Employment Tests which measure job-related personality traits and integrity as these tests are often the most objective means available for identifying potential problems. Many times sales managers and retailers fall into the trap of believing that tests are too expensive for use with front-line employees such as salespeople, customer service representatives or office staff. One company estimates a savings of $60,000 annually because they use honesty and aptitude tests in the selection process. Other organizations we work with use honesty tests to reduce the likelihood of fraudulent worker's compensation claims.

It is also important for employers to go through the process of reference checks, even though they may only get "name, rank and serial number." When this step is documented, it is additional proof that the employer sought to obtain the most information possible to make an informed hiring decision. It might also be wise to consider background or TRW checks, depending on the position for which the applicant is being considered.

Civil Rights Act Of 1991

In an effort to conform with EEOC and Affirmative Action guidelines, many Employment Test Publishers have subtly shifted points on their tests to give minorities and females a better opportunity to succeed. This practice is called "racial norming."

As of December 12, 1991, former President Bush called for an immediate cessation of "racial norming" on all tests used to hire a public service worker. Employers in the private sector who utilized employment tests were to comply shortly thereafter by ensuring pre- and postemployment tests measured all test takers by the same standards, with no point separations between races or sexes.

Soroka vs. Dayton Hudson

As California often leads the way in new legal trends, it behooves the rest of the country to take note of a recent finding. In this case, the Target store chain was sued by three employees because of its use of the MMPI/CPI Multiphasic tests. Questions on these tests were deemed an invasion of privacy and, as such, discriminatory under California's statutes.

However, the same court ruled that use of other testing instruments, which were job-specific, was entirely appropriate. The key point to remember is that the MMPI/CPI measures aberrant behavior and cannot be related directly to jobs as it was designed for clinical use and are not industrially validated. Instruments such as the Personality Profile and our Honesty Test already give employers job-specific information and meet the criterion specified by the courts.

Discriminatory Interviewing Practices and Validation of the Selection Process

Employers have long been under the impression that employment tests are the only part of the selection process which need to be validated. This is not true. Employers need to make sure that each step of the hiring process is valid and can be proven job specific. To that end, employment tests are often the easiest and best tool to use in objectively measuring an individual's ability to handle a position's demands, but the other steps of the selection process need to be validated as well.

The Supreme Court has ruled that employers who discriminate during the interview, even unintentionally, are subject to substantial fines. This means not only discrimination against race, sex, age, national origin, color, marital status, and sexual preferences, but now, with the American Disabilities Act, the Disabled.

It is imperative that questions not be asked during the interview regarding the following areas: personal finances, religious preferences, whether single or married, age, race, previous residences (which might point to a particular racial, ethnic, or economic status), ability to speak a foreign language unless it is directly related to the position's needs, child-care arrangements, car ownership, questions concerning previous claims for worker's compensation or arrests. Never ask about union membership or even an opinion about labor unions. It is even inappropriate to ask about membership to political groups or voluntary organizations.

It is a good practice to have applicants sign a waiver allowing the employer to inquiry previous employers and gather personal references. Make sure all references and background checks are fully documented. Asking for references from previous employers via letter can serve as a means of documentation and if legal, job specific questions are asked, might elicit more information than a simple phone call.

Increasingly, interviews and performance appraisal procedures are being subjected to the need for validation procedures. To ensure conformance to the legal standards, make sure each task in a position is job relevant. Questions in an interview must be job-specific as well. And again, employment tests must be job-specific. A select few tests have been validated and can be customized for the exact position in the organization. This is one of the best tools an employer can make use of.

Each step of the recruitment process must be as valid and objective as possible. This includes the development of accurate and thorough job descriptions (which, if written correctly, can also help deter fraudulent worker's compensation claims). A job description must be explicit. It is better to say "Must be able to operate a Personal Computer using the DOS environment and WordPerfect 5.0 program" than to say "Must be able to use a computer." Background checks, TRW checks, medical exams, and drug tests need to be job specific and valid to the position's needs.

Concluding Remarks

Each of these areas: the Civil Rights Act of 1991, Negligent Hiring and Retention, Discriminatory Interviewing and Selection Procedures, and the *Soroka vs. Dayton Hudson* decision are complex in nature. If an organi-

zation does not have access to an in-house expert, they might be best served by hiring an experienced, knowledgeable Management Consultant who is well versed in these areas. Family businesses and retailers are already stretched thin by numerous responsibilities and are generally too busy to keep up with the volumes of literature surrounding legal decisions and trends. A Management Consultant can work with an employer to assess the current selection and appraisal processes, to minimize the chance of ever facing the liabilities and costs involved in suits brought forth because of these issues.

Some Unintended Consequences Associated with the Implementation of the Americans with Disabilities Act

M. Ronald Buckley, N. S. Miceli,
Elaine Purvis, and D. Leigh Gross

Public policy decisions typically have consequences going beyond the effects envisioned by the bodies enacting legislation. In the area of civil rights, equal employment opportunity and affirmative action laws have required human resource managers to ensure that the staffing function is performed without adverse impact. Although this is an obvious consequence of such legislation, the secondary effects related to increasing diversity in the workplace could not have been as easily predicted. It would be useful at this time to anticipate some of the effects of the Americans with Disabilities Act (ADA).

The promulgation of the ADA was a major step forward in terms of integrating physically challenged workers into the labor force. As such workers are absorbed into the work force, human resource professionals must be concerned with the changes that ADA implementation may require. The ancillary impact of this legislation on various human resource functions is relatively unknown. Dealing with this impact is the challenge that ADA poses for human resource professionals.

This challenge will be especially acute in the area of performance appraisal, a pivotal concern of human resource management. Performance appraisals are tied to many individual and organizational outcomes—for example, pay and promotion. ADA's implementation will have an effect on the way performance appraisals are conducted in organizations. To determine the extent of this effect, we need to refer to ADA and define a number of important factors. ADA protects all "qualified individuals with a disability (QUID)." The Equal Employment Opportunity Commission decided to write its own definition of QUID rather than use the definition provided by Congress (Snyder, 1993):

> Qualified individuals with a disability means an individual with a disability who satisfies the requisite skill, experience, education, and other job-related requirements of the position such individual hold or desires, and who, with or without reasonable accommodations can perform the essential functions of such position. (Section 1630.2 of the ADA)

A QUID must be able to perform the essential job functions of a position, which are defined as the fundamental job duties of the given position. Thus, if disabled individuals can perform the fundamental duties of a job, with or without accommodation, they are considered qualified for that position. Further, such people are not required to perform marginal job functions if their disabilities make that impossible.

The nondiscrimination provisions of the ADA are interpreted to mean that employers must evaluate job performance solely on the basis of whether the job candidate or incumbent can perform the essential functions of the job, defined as the tasks actually necessary to complete the job as performed in the workplace. In addition, although employers need not lower performance standards for any job, they must make reasonable accommodations for people with disabilities. It is clear that managers must scrutinize the rules or heuristics used to evaluate performance as well as the way in which information is used to prevent discrimination, both against those ADA is designed to protect and employees currently working for the organization.

Performance appraisal is an important process. Cleveland, Murphy, and Williams (1989) have identified 20 different uses for the information gathered during that process. ADA will significantly affect the areas classified by Cleveland and colleagues as within-person evaluation and between-person development. We also believe that ADA will have a substantial effect upon participant perceptions of the fairness of the performance appraisal process.

The nature and extent of ADA's impact on performance appraisal are as yet unknown. Employers must hold disabled and nondisabled employees to the same standards of performance for essential job functions. In addition, uniform standards can be applied for marginal job functions unless a disability interferes with performance. Finally, a disabled employee who requires some kind of accommodation should always be evaluated on the ability to perform job functions with reasonable accommodations already in place.

The first important issue concerning the performance appraisal process is the possible impact of stereotypes and prejudices on evaluations. An evaluation does not occur in a vacuum. It is based on the observations, attitudes, and judgments of the rater, and consequently some subjective biases may be introduced. One of the fundamental purposes of ADA is to bring more physically or emotionally challenged people into the labor force. Many raters who currently have little experience with the population covered by the ADA will at some time be asked to evaluate the job performance of disabled individuals. This may cause problems if the raters are unaware—as many people are—of their own impressions and prejudices concerning individuals with disabilities.

When Minskoff, Sautter, Hoffmann, and Hawks (1987) studied employer attitudes to-

ward hiring of people with disabilities, they found that 18 percent of the employers surveyed were not willing to accommodate those with disabilities. Giving multiple reasons for their unwillingness, 100 percent of those respondents perceived accommodation as unfair to other workers; 45 percent believed that accommodation would be too costly. One-third of the respondents were not willing to hire learning-disabled workers, who were the focus of the survey. This last finding could be conservative because 16 percent of the respondents did not answer that question.

These attitudes may be rooted in discomfort from interacting with disabled individuals. This discomfort can result in a performance appraisal that fails to approximate the reality of an individual's performance level. A sympathetic or paternalistic/maternalistic attitude toward disabled individuals may also distort the appraisal process.

Generally, attitudes toward disabled persons (ATDP) in the workplace are negative. McDonough (1992) and Noel (1990) have summarized ATDP as follows. Compared with nondisabled workers, those with disabilities are viewed negatively as regards performance levels and skills, work ethic, accident and illness rates, insurance and benefit costs, absenteeism, and productivity. All of these beliefs have not stood up under empirical scrutiny. Unfortunately and predictably, these attitudes can distort the perception of an individual's performance level. Managers who evaluate disabled employees must be made aware of their own prejudices and stereotypes toward people with disabilities. Compliance with ADA seems to dictate that organizations train managers in methods that may facilitate the management and accurate evaluation of disabled employees. This in turn will make performance appraisals more fair and ensure greater compliance with ADA.

ADA requires employers to make reasonable accommodation for individuals with disabilities. Reasonable accommodation varies according to the nature of the position and the disability in question. Examples of these accommodations include the provision of access ramps, the redesign of entire work stations, and the provision of special equipment or interpreters. Surveys (Maslen, 1992; Noel, 1990) have indicated that approximately 70 to 80 percent of accommodations cost less than $500, and only 1 percent cost more than $5,000.

Although ADA requires equal standards for all employees on essential job functions, it is clear that reasonable accommodation may have some serious implications for the performance appraisal process. The accommodation itself may change the basic nature of the job. Job restructuring may include elimination of certain job duties or at least modification of the way essential job functions are performed. In other words, modifications have commensurate complications.

Initially, the employer and the disabled employee need to develop the means and standards that can be used to evaluate performance because that person's job duties may differ from those of other workers. Marginal job duties that are eliminated will not be included in the appraisal. If other marginal duties are assigned to replace those removed, the new job duties need to be incorporated into the evaluation system. This requires communication and coordination between the manager and the employee at the start of the employment relationship. If reasonable accommodation is necessary, it should be noted both in the employee's written job description and in the specific standards used to evaluate job performance.

The process of defining and documenting duties and standards may entail extra work for a supervisor. There is some danger that the supervisor may consider this work as a burden and see it as unfair to employees who are not accommodated. This may cause the supervisor to feel resentment, which may later be manifested in malicious behavior toward the accommodated individual.

A side effect of the performance appraisal process that is of major concern is its effect on the perceptions of nondisabled employees. When job restructuring or accommodation occurs, perceptions of inequitable treatment may arise. Other employees may feel that the disabled employee is the recipient of special, unfair treatment. A situation in which a disabled worker has been relieved of marginal job functions may be particularly conducive to feelings of inequitable treatment. Adding to this frustration is the reality that the other workers may be required to perform those job duties as well as their own. In addition, work schedule modification, which may be required to accommodate a disabled individual, may be an especially problematic issue, as coworkers may covet the modified work schedule. Thus, accommodation may result in serious morale problems and a growing feeling among other employees that the disabled worker is "getting a free ride" (Hodge & Crampton, 1993).

According to a study conducted by the Bureau of National Affairs (To accommodate workers with disabilities, 1992), 52 percent of workers surveyed believed it was fair to have their work schedules or job duties changed to accommodate disabled coworkers. However, 33 percent felt that such accommodation would be unfair, and 16 percent of the respondents indicated that they felt so strongly about the perceived inequity that they would protest the situation. If this survey accurately reflects the feelings of the American labor force, it is clear that there will be a significant number of resentful workers when reasonable accommodations are made under the ADA.

The aforementioned perceived inequities may result in some motivational deficiencies. Equity theory, developed by Adams (1963, 1965), provides a theoretical background for the belief that perception of inequity may have a debilitating effect upon the motivation of workers in situations where accommodations are implemented. Equity theory posits that people make social comparisons between themselves and others concerning their inputs and outcomes in a particular situation. Inputs could be factors such as abilities, skills, traits, experience, output, or effort; basically, they are the characteristics that a worker contributes to the work environment. Outcomes are best described as the set of rewards associated with task performance; they can include raises, promotions, better assignments, better scheduling, or praise. People compare the ratios of their own inputs/outputs to the ratios of others' inputs/outputs. These comparisons can result in one of three outcomes: overpayment, underpayment, or equitable payment.

In situations other than equitable payment, workers will find ways to restore equity to the situation. The reality is that when a disabled worker joins a workplace, there may be problems with perceptions of inequity. Some nondisabled workers may allow their prejudices to distort reality, or some inequity may in reality exist. Guilt may also develop in disabled workers who perceive that they are the recipients of unfair advantage (Austin, 1977; Goodman, 1977).

Later researchers (Cosier and Dalton, 1983) dispute the propensity of typical workers to feel guilt for overpayment. It should be noted that if workers with disabilities did not feel guilt for perceived overpayment, they would not differ significantly from the rest of the population. Other researchers (Peters, 1989) characterize workers with disabilities as having a strong internal locus of control orientation regarding barriers in the workplace; they believe that it is their responsibility to perform so that barriers are not significant obstacles. From Peters's account it would be difficult to infer greater opportunism among disabled workers than in the general population. Noel's (1990) findings reveal higher levels of concern for performance and work quality compared with the general population; these findings also support the inference that the disabled would perform at high levels and would not desire more than "a fair deal" in the workplace.

Nondisabled workers may perceive differences in either input or outputs. In terms of inputs, co-workers may be unwilling to credit a physically challenged individual with the capability of performing work to the standard met by nondisabled workers. Perceptions of

handicapped workers as "more trouble than they are worth" have increased since Minskoff et al.'s (1987) results indicated high levels of concern about accommodation costs.

Further, with ADA now in place, co-workers might think that a disabled person was hired for the sole purpose of compliance with the law. This belief might lead them to perceive a lower level of inputs on the part of the disabled worker, who in their opinion lacked the necessary skills or motivation for the job.

In fact, when extensive accommodations are made, there can be actual differences between the inputs of nondisabled and disabled workers. Job restructuring may allow a disabled worker to sit alongside co-workers yet not be required to complete the same set of tasks. Both disabled and nondisabled workers may find the situation inequitable.

Perceptions of outcomes can similarly be a problem when accommodations are made. Accommodation in the spirit of ADA compliance may lead to perceptions that a disabled worker is enjoying better outcomes. In most jobs the granting of time off or a flexible work schedule would be seen as a reward for superior past performance. Yet a patient on renal dialysis would be given these opportunities in order to receive medical treatment, regardless of quality of performance.

Behavioral reactions to perceptions of inequity can be many and varied. Workers who perceive overpayment may increase their inputs. Workers who perceive underpayment may simply decrease their inputs through reduced efforts or lackluster performance, which lead to negative organizational outcomes. Individuals who perceive that disabled workers are getting a "free ride" can easily rationalize a work slowdown.

These perceptions of inequity will have additional deleterious effects upon the performance appraisal system. Perceptions of unfairness will result when individuals place little trust in the integrity of that system. As Bernardin and Beatty (1984) report, a performance appraisal system characterized by a lack of trust between the appraised and the appraisers will be neither efficient nor effective. They suggest that before an appraisal system can work, all parties must trust the system, the participants, and the ability of the system to differentiate levels of performance. If participants perceive inequity, they may doubt the distributive justice inherent in the performance appraisal system. According to Greenberg (1990), distributive justice is the extent to which rewards are perceived as being related to performance. Bernardin and Beatty report that perceptions of fair treatment play a key role in employees' willingness to engage in organizational citizenship behavior. Further, it is difficult for employees to link pay with performance when perceptions of inequity exist.

The central thesis of our paper thus far has been that the implementation of ADA may unintentionally result in myriad problems in the performance appraisal process. The problems may be due to perceptions of inequity that correlate with accommodations resulting from ADA implementation. To minimize these problems we recommend the following activities, which we believe would minimize perceptions of inequity:

1. Train managers to understand the role of disabled individuals in the workplace. Employees with disabilities are really not receiving anything special. They are receiving accommodations that enable them to work at levels commensurate with their talents. Making reasonable accommodation for disabilities is no different from engineering the work area to improve or facilitate the performance of employees in general.

2. Educate workers about ADA requirements concerning specific treatment of disabilities. Have all employees participate in organizational efforts to comply with ADA. This will both educate employees and facilitate acceptance of ADA.

3. Educate workers concerning attitudinal perceptions of people with disabilities. Previously cited research (McDonough, 1992; Minskoff et al., 1987; Noel, 1990) has indicated that co-workers frequently harbor negative but demonstrably false beliefs about disabled workers. It must be stressed that those workers are not inherently better or worse employees; they are just different.

4. Apportion tasks in such a way that disabled workers are not isolated from nondisabled workers. This will serve a number of functions: It will educate all employees; it will help to integrate all employees; and it will result in greater tolerance by all, which in turn may reduce perceptions of inequity.

5. Distribute workload equitably. Accommodations for disabled workers should be made in a way that is fair to everyone. For example, when a job is restructured for a disabled worker, certain marginal functions may be reassigned to a nondisabled worker. To maintain equity, other marginal functions should be added to the responsibilities and duties of the disabled worker to keep all workloads as similar as possible.

6. Make sure that perceptions of inequity are not based in fact. If a worker leaves early one afternoon, that worker needs to arrive early or leave later on another day. If disabled workers are given the option of completing their work at home, management should consider whether it would be in the organization's best interest to extend that option to all employees. Although it may not be possible to achieve "eye of God" equity, this should certainly be management's goal. Perceptions of inequity will be extraordinarily difficult to overcome if they are based in fact.

7. Keep the appraisal process the same for all employees. Disabled workers should be held to the same standards as are other employees for job duties that are not affected by disability. When accommodations are made, standards that are fair and equitable, given the circumstances, should be developed.

8. Keep lines of communication open. Performance standards should be communicated to all employees. In addition, performance expectations, evaluation methodologies, and the determination of salary adjustments and raises should be communicated. Employees should be encouraged to express any misgivings, such as feelings of inequity, regarding the performance appraisal process.

Building on recommendations 7 and 8 is a final recommendation: Use more than one source of appraisal information for all workers. Besides the supervisor's evaluations, appraisals should include input from workers' peers and from workers themselves (Cascio, 1991). This approach will ensure a more informed evaluation of all workers' performances. At the same time, supervisors should be aware of potential biases in ratings, which may reflect attitudes toward people with disabilities.

Unfortunately, regardless of the steps taken to establish and maintain a fair appraisal system, some employees will still perceive unfairness. It is not possible for everything to be equal for all workers under ADA. The reality is that even without ADA, a perception of equality is difficult to achieve and maintain. Factoring in the misconceptions and prejudices toward individuals with disabilities further compounds the dilemma. Equity and fairness is always the goal in performance appraisal, but it is a goal that is infrequently achieved.

References

Adams, J. S. (1963). Toward an understanding of inequity. *Journal of Abnormal and Social Psychology, 67,* 422–436.

Adams, J. S. (1965). Inequity in social exchange. In L. Berkowitz (Ed.), *Advances in experimental social psychology* (Vol. 2, pp. 267–299). New York: Academic Press.

Austin, W. (1977). Equity theory and social comparison processes. In J. M. Suls & R. M. Miller (Eds.), *Social comparison processes* (pp. 279–301). Washington, DC: Hemisphere.

Bernardin, H. J., & Beatty, R. W. (1984). *Performance appraisal: Assessing human behavior at work.* Boston: PWS Kent.

Cascio, W. F. (1991). *Applied psychology in personnel management.* Englewood Cliffs, NJ: Prentice Hall.

Cleveland, J. N., Murphy, K. R., & Williams, R. E. (1989). Multiple uses of performance appraisal. *Journal of Applied Psychology, 73,* 130–135.

Cosier, R. A., & Dalton, D. R. (1983). Equity theory and time: A reformulation. *Academy of Management Review, 8,* 311–319.

Goodman, P. S. (1977). Social comparison processes in organizations. In B. M. Staw & G. R. Salancik (Eds.), *New directions in organizational behavior* (pp. 97–132). Chicago: St. Clair.

Greenberg, J. G. (1990). Organizational justice: Yesterday, today, and tomorrow. *Journal of Management, 16,* 399–432.

Hodge, J. W., & Crampton, S. M. (1993). ADA: Faster said than done. *Supervisory Management, 38,* 9–10.

Maslen, D. (1992). Accommodation: What is reasonable? *HR Focus, 69,* 3.

McDonough, H. (1992). Hiring people with disabilities. *Supervisory Management, 37,* 11–12.

Minskoff, E., Sautter, S., Hoffmann, F., & Hawks, R. (1987). Employer attitudes toward hiring the learning disabled. *Journal of Learning Disabilities, 20,* 53–57.

Noel, R. (1990). Employing the disabled: A how and why approach. *Training and Development Journal, 44,* 26–32.

Peters, J. (1989). How to bridge the hiring gap. *Personnel Administrator, 34,* 76–85.

Snyder, D. A. (1993). Qualified individuals with disabilities: Defining the ADA's protected class. *Labor Law Journal, 44,* 65–109.

To accommodate workers with disabilities. (1992). *HR Focus, 69,* 5.

CHAPTER 4

The Labor Market and the Changing Work Force

The work force consists of all people who are working, looking for work, or serving in the armed forces. The number of individuals in the work force has grown dramatically over the last few decades. This dramatic increase can be attributed to the growing numbers of women and minority group members who have recently been incorporated into the work force. The work force will continue to expand with higher than average growth in the participation rates for the African-American, Hispanic, and Asian populations. Further, workers are both living and working longer. The U.S. work force is aging. A number of organizations (e.g., McDonald's) have engaged in hiring seniors. This is both a sensible and a socially responsible action.

As the population becomes more diverse, organizations are becoming more interested in developing a work force that more accurately mirrors the population. Diversity is an asset. Inclusive hiring strategies will facilitate the expansion of a quality work force. During the 1970s and 1980s, affirmative action was seen as the way to include all individuals in the work force. The 1990s have seen the realization that diversity is a valued work force trait. Organizations are convinced that diversity will increase the knowledge, creativity, innovativeness, and competency base of the work force.

The changing work force has dictated additional emphasis in the strategies of human resources programs. Selection of a work force has always been driven by the choice of those who best fit in with organizational objectives. The most effective strategy with our evolving work force is to enlist the most competent and diverse population in order to increase coverage of potential and ideas. This shift toward diversity will necessitate greater sensitivity on the part of managers. The results of increasing diversity have thus far been quite positive. We predict that these positive outcomes will only increase.

In the first article in this chapter, Finney presents the results of a survey on recruitment practices. Recruitment is no longer an easy task, given changing demographics and demand for certain types of jobs. The article concludes with a series of suggestions that can be helpful for organizations that want to facilitate recruitment. In the following article Bhawuk and Triandis discuss the issue of diversity in the workplace. They outline current strategies of organizations that are attempting to diversify the work force. Many organizations value diversity simply because it is smart business. The authors present ways in which organizations are integrating the value of diversity into their strategic policies.

Suggestions for Further Reading

Cox, C. (1993). The ultimate downsize: A retailer's story. *Business Quarterly, 58,* 76–80.

Elliott, V. (1993, June). Competing for and with workforce 2000. *HR Focus,* pp. 3–4.

Freedman, E. (1993). Workers compensation: A process management approach. *Benefits & Compensation International, 23,* 33–38.

Fyock, C. (1993). Diversity: Passing fad, or here to stay? *Human Resources Professional, 5,* 10–12.

Galagan, P. (1989). Ronald E. Compton: Underwriting business with training. *Training & Development Journal, 43,* 30–35.

Kemmerer, B., & Arnold, V. (1993). The growing use of benchmarking in managing cultural diversity. *Business Forum, 18,* 38–40.

Lee, C. (1989). Industry report 1989: The 3 R's. *Training, 26,* 67–76.

Overman, S. (1989). The total business partner. *Personnel Administrator, 34,* 50–53.

Overman, S. (1993, June). Myths hinder hiring of older workers. *HR Magazine,* pp. 51–52.

Soderstrom, M., & Seppanen, R. (1993). An HRM role struggling for survival. *Personnel Management, 25,* 28–33.

The ASPA Labor Shortage Survey

Martha I. Finney

Recruitment is no longer a buyer's market in many parts of the country. Certain positions are increasingly difficult to fill, many school systems are not preparing their students for the needs of modern, private enterprise, and the cost of living in some areas is outpacing the salaries that companies can afford to offer.

To address the changing employment scene, human resource managers are looking at a variety of hiring alternatives, from offering in-house training to inventing new recruitment tools—whatever it takes to attract the right workers to get the job done.

The ASPA (American Society for Personnel Administration) Labor Shortage Survey has taken a nationwide snapshot of employer attitudes and experiences in recent hiring. Read on and find out where the workers are, what companies are doing to bring them in and what solutions human resource managers recommend for future recruitment crunches.

Are Traditional Recruitment Methods Still Valid?

Employee referrals, walk-ins, unsolicited resumés, and newspaper advertisements are traditional recruitment methods that, according to survey respondents, are used often because they work. Newspaper advertising and employee referrals are the top two recruitment methods, even though few companies indicated that they could rely on just two recruitment sources.

When asked what special recruitment strategies, if any, has their company adopted to address the labor shortage, the respondents indicated that *increased* use of want ads is a high priority. More than 73 percent reported that they have increased use of the help-wanted ads

and other forms of publicity. More than 80 percent of the respondents said their results were successful or somewhat successful.

Companies also have developed specialized recruitment alternatives—some involve perks for the new employee and some are just innovative ideas to attract the best candidates. Recruiting temporaries and part-time workers scored high as a recruitment tool, with 85 percent of the respondents reporting satisfaction.

Job fairs and career open houses (52 percent); an increased cooperation with education and training institutions (46 percent); relocation assistance (43 percent); and seasonal hiring patterns (41 percent) are the next favored recruiting alternatives.

The least used method specified in the survey was offering transportation assistance, which only 15 percent of the respondents use. Success was difficult to determine since 40 percent "didn't know" how the program worked, but 33 percent said it was at least somewhat successful.

Finding workers from abroad also received a 15 percent "use" rate. Forty-six percent of the respondents "didn't know" how well the tool had worked, and 43 percent were somewhat satisfied with the recruitment results.

Where the Jobs Are

Recruiters are hurting for qualified workers all over the country. Depending upon their competence, education, skill, and profession, employees have their pick of where to live. They can toast under the palm trees or roll in the snow.

Northeast: Economic growth, high cost of living and inadequate training have conspired to make the northeast region a tight labor market for employers. Respondents for this region report having "great/very great difficulty" recruiting executives (18 percent); professionals (26 percent); technical staff (35 percent); sales staff (12 percent); clerical staff (50 percent); skilled labor (62 percent); and unskilled labor (51 percent).

Southeast: This area, especially when compared with its strapped northern neighbor, is having an easier time—but not by a wide margin. It is having great/very great difficulty recruiting professionals (29 percent); technical staff (32 percent); office and clerical (27 percent); skilled labor (37 percent); unskilled labor (33 percent). Only 11 percent of responding southeast companies are having great/very great difficulty recruiting salespeople, and only 8 percent are having great/very great difficulty recruiting executives.

Midwest: This region is having the most trouble recruiting skilled labor at only 28 percent of the respondents reporting great/very great difficulty. Technical and professional employees (27 and 25 percent respectively) present the next most difficult category to find. Unskilled employees present great/very great difficulty to 21 percent of the responding employers; sales—17 percent; and office/clerical—12 percent.

South-central: At 32 percent, professional employees present the greatest difficulty for recruiters in the south-central region. Technical workers (28 percent) present the next greatest challenge. The other categories are executive (13 percent); sales (19 percent); office/clerical (14 percent); skilled (19 percent) and unskilled (12 percent).

West: According to the respondents, the west has the most difficulty hiring skilled labor (43 percent); technical (38 percent) and professional (35 percent). Only 15 percent of the companies report difficulty recruiting executives; salespeople (23 percent); office/clerical (20 percent) and unskilled (15 percent).

Northwest: In a region notorious among job seekers for its tight market, relatively few companies are having great/very great difficulty recruiting qualified workers. Executive-level employees present problems for only 4 percent of the responding companies; professionals—10 percent; technical workers—23 percent; salespeople—14 percent; office/clerical—4 percent; skilled labor—23 percent and unskilled labor—12 percent.

What Jobs Will Be in Greatest Demand Tomorrow?

Some sources believe trends in the availability of the American worker are expected to change dramatically by 1994—not a long time to prepare for new challenges and shortages down the road. To get a head start in preparing for tomorrow's changing employee requirements, ASPA asked the survey recipients what difficulties they expect within three to five years. The answer in a nutshell: same as today, only more so.

Executives: Except in the southwest, where 12 percent more companies expect to have great/very great difficulty recruiting executives, projected shortages are expected to remain about the same as today's.

Professionals: Once again, the southwest expects to be hit hardest, with almost half the respondents expecting to have great/very great difficulty hiring this level of employee. Throughout the rest of the regions, at least one-third of the respondents expect to have great/very great difficulty recruiting professionals in the near future.

Technical staff: The northwest respondents report a 15 percent increase in the number of companies expecting difficulty hiring this type of worker—38 percent in the future as compared with 23 percent of the employers today. But the west and the northeast will have the greatest trouble with almost half reporting projected difficulty (47 and 45 percent respectively).

Sales staff: The south-central is expecting to have less trouble recruiting salespeople, dropping from 19 percent of responding employers today to a projected 9 percent of tomorrow's employers. More companies in the northeast and northwest expect to have diffi-

Table 1

Extent of the Current Labor Shortage Problem

Occupational Classification	Degree of Difficulty Recruiting Qualified Applicants (Percent Responding)		
	Not at all/ Very Small	Moderate	Great/ Very Great
Executive/Administrative Managerial (n = 664)	57	32	11
Sales (n = 372)	56	28	16
Professional (n = 603)	46	29	25
Office/Clerical (n = 680)	50	23	27
Unskilled (n = 525)	53	19	28
Technical/Technical Support (n = 601)	34	35	31
Skilled/Craftsman (n = 437)	37	27	36

culties in five years than they do today—the two regions expecting the greatest increase in difficulty from 12 to 24 percent and 14 to 25 percent, respectively.

Office/clerical: The northeast, experiencing the greatest difficulty in hiring this level today, expects to experience the greatest difficulty tomorrow. Almost two-thirds of the northeastern respondents expect to have great difficulties in the future. But the southwest showed the greatest increase in expected difficulty, from 20 percent today to 40 percent of the respondents for the future.

Skilled: The northeast, with the greatest difficulty today hiring this employee, is expecting to have problems in the future. Of the survey's respondents from that region, 70 percent expect great/very great difficulties in the future. The west showed the greatest increase in expected difficulty, from 43 percent of the companies having trouble today to 60 percent of the companies expecting trouble tomorrow. Almost half of the southeastern respondents expect to have great/very great difficulties recruiting skilled employees.

Unskilled: Once again, the northeast and the southeast expect to have the greatest difficulty recruiting unskilled workers in the future. However, in the northwest, a 17 percent increase in companies expect to have trouble recruiting unskilled labor in the near future.

So, What's the Problem?

Throughout the quantifiable responses to the essay-type questions in the survey, the message was the same: The difficulty in recruiting is not so much population changes, but is the lack of quality education and training among employees (see Figure 1). For those workers who have been in the labor pool a long time, technology has generally outpaced them. For many others, basic skills and the lack of quality education is holding them back.

Half of the total respondents said that writing skills were the most lacking ability in their company's applicant pools. The next two missing are job specific/technical skills (43 percent) and verbal communication skills (42 percent).

"We're a specific industry—insurance— and we have to train our own specialists in the cities where we have offices," said one survey respondent from South Carolina. "Our worst problem is high school and college graduates who cannot communicate."

More than one-third of the companies (35 percent) said that English proficiency is lacking in applicants for whom English is not their native language.

Basic reading and math skills were reported lacking by just fewer than one-third of the responding companies. And 27 percent of the companies could not find computer skills

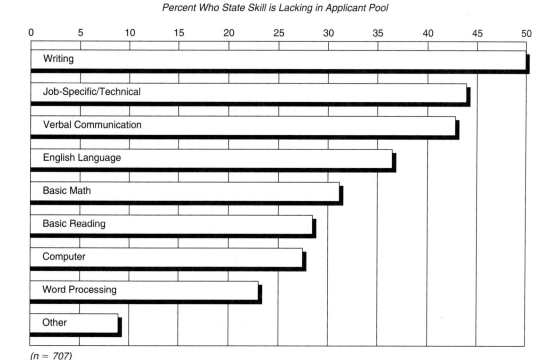

Percent Who State Skill is Lacking in Applicant Pool

(n = 707)

Figure 1. Types of Skill Shortages

in their applicants; 22 percent do not have word processing skills.

Half of the respondents said that they are trying to cope by offering training programs to employees already on the job. Of those who have such programs, 52 percent offer computer training, 40 percent offer word processing, and 35 percent offer training in communication skills. About 86 percent of the respondents reported that they have already introduced or enhanced training to maintain or upgrade job-specific and technical skills of their current employees; 68 percent offer such training for new employees, and 44 percent retrain current employees for other positions.

Training resources vary: 88 percent said they use in-house training; 58 percent use outside consultants; 51 percent tap into community colleges and universities. One-third use trade, commercial, or vocational schools. How-

ever, not all businesses feel they should be totally responsible for worker education.

"Secretaries who cannot spell, managers who cannot construct a clear, concise memo or employees who cannot calculate percentages are too numerous. Business cannot cure all that the schools have failed to do," said a California survey respondent.

It is also important to note that training was not the only culprit for reducing the numbers of qualified applicants. Several companies in the essay parts of the survey commented that local economic development priorities and the high cost of living in many areas have effectively reduced the numbers of people who can afford to take low-paying jobs.

"The problem is not labor shortage in our area," said a respondent from Vermont. "It's affordable housing for the employee and the family. The average per week gross income is $190.

Rents run $450 to $475. I find no problem hiring new people coming into the area, but I lose many because of the cost of living. This makes my hire rate equal to my termination rate."

Workers Where You Never Thought You'd Look

New problems require new solutions. But, even though companies have identified future problems in recruiting, many have not begun to develop innovative ways to reach new candidate pools to cope with projected shortages.

"Despite my urgings, the company is not responding to the future problems of labor shortages. This is typical of American industry in that too often we are overtaken by problems that could have been foreseen," said one respondent who has operations throughout the country.

Currently, students are the most used "nontraditional" applicants, with 53 percent of the responding companies recruiting them with the greatest amount of success (24 percent). The next popular group is retirees, with 43 percent of the responding companies cultivating them at 18 percent success. More than one-third of the responding companies recruit homemakers, with only a 14 percent success rate.

The least used nontraditional group is the mentally disabled, with 16 percent of the responding companies dipping into that pool with only a 5 percent success rate. Only 18 percent of the responding companies look to immigrants to help fill the staff positions.

While no companies report a thunderingly high success rate for any of the nontraditional groups, the "somewhat successful" rating was moderately respectable. The student population was highest in the "somewhat successful" rating (63 percent). Retirees and the disabled shared a 47 percent rating. The disadvantaged population yielded a "somewhat successful" rating, one point higher at 58 percent than the homemakers did.

Of course, many businesses still rely on a cranked-up version of the old community grapevine.

"When I hire a person for a management training position," said a Florida survey respondent, "I milk them for everyone they know at their previous company. And then I contact those people directly. I have also instituted a similar process for our unit managers when they are interviewing and hiring servers and cooks."

Ten Ways Business Can Help Alleviate the Worker Shortage

No one who returned the ASPA Labor Shortage Survey was without a strong opinion about what can be done to solve the problem. Here is a representative sampling of what they said:

- Move operations to areas with high unemployment.
- Expand on-the-job training.
- Provide training through local schools so that future workers will be employable.
- Subsidize education of health-care professionals.
- Participate in advisory groups in the community to gear the school curriculum toward skills needed by business.
- Use more flexible scheduling.
- Hire more entry level workers and train them.
- Provide benefits to part-time staff.
- Offer job sharing.
- Sponsor scholarships or provide loans to students that would be paid back with work after graduation.

Ten Ways the Government Can Help, Too

Businesses that responded to the survey have a few ideas for federal, state and local governments too . . .

- Provide paid higher education.
- Educate the illiterate.

- Establish meaningful incentives to offset expense of on-the-job training programs.
- Train people on welfare.
- Encourage and emphasize career planning and direction in high schools and colleges.
- Develop the work ethic as well as specific skills.

- Increase pay and quality of teachers to improve the quality of education offered to tomorrow's employees.
- Ease immigrant quotas.
- Stay out of it.
- Work more closely with business to determine labor needs.

Diversity in the Workplace:
Emerging Corporate Strategies

Dharm P. S. Bhawuk and Harry C. Triandis

In the future the workplace worldwide will become increasingly diverse, especially in the economically most developed countries. The reasons are many.

The populations of the industrialized countries are reaching a plateau while those of the developing countries are increasing. Thus, migration from the developing to the industrialized countries is likely to accelerate. This migration would be driven by the need of the migrants to improve their standard of living and of the people in the industrialized countries for the services that only the migrants would be willing to provide (George, 1993). In addition, because of the globalization of world business, professionals from the industrialized countries will interact increasingly with workers of the developing countries.

Environmental degradation is another factor that will create pressure for transnational migration. The United Nations expects 20 percent of the world's population to become environmental refugees by the year 2020 (George, 1993) because of deterioration of their physical environments, lack of water, and the like.

The design-production-distribution processes of the twenty-first century will involve extreme diversity. For example, the designing of a product might occur in Germany, financing might be obtained from Japan, execution of the plans might be directed from the United States, the clerical work might be done in Nepal, the manufacturing might take place in China, and the distribution might involve a universalist sales force. The interfaces among those activities would require highly diverse work places.

In the developed countries the shift from manufacturing to service and information economies will also require that the sales force

be as diverse as the customer populations. By the year 2000 only a minority of the new entries into the U.S. work force will be white males.

All these developments and more will make the workplaces of tomorrow very diverse. This article examines the issues that will be faced by future managers in these diverse workplaces. We begin with definitions of culture, race, ethnicity, and nationality and then examine the ways in which cultural differences can be operationalized. Next we will discuss two opposing philosophies of dealing with diversity, the melting pot view and multiculturalism. These sections provide the necessary conceptual framework for understanding diversity in the workplace.

In the next major section, we examine the consequences of intercultural interactions; an analysis of the workplace follows. Next, we focus on the U.S. work force and examine some of the major differences between the so-called mainstream and Asian-, African-, Hispanic-Americans, and we consider the issues that will emerge as more women, people of diverse sexual orientation, and people with physical disabilities enter the workplace. Finally, we discuss the reasons why U.S. corporations are concerned with diversity and outline the emerging strategies that are adopted by some of the large U.S. corporations.

Conceptual Framework for Understanding Diversity

Definitions

Culture is to society what memory is to individuals (Kluckhohn, 1954). It consists of ways of perceiving, thinking, and deciding that have worked in the past and have become institutionalized in standard operating procedures, customs, scripts, and unstated assumptions that guide behavior. Culture consists of both objective (tools, roads) and subjective (concepts, beliefs, attitudes, norms, roles, and values) elements (Triandis, 1972).

Culture is adaptive and functional; it allows a group of people who speak the same language to develop shared beliefs, attitudes, norms, roles, and values through transmission from generation to generation. Members of a culture have a common language so as to communicate the ideas that are later shared, and they live during the same period in areas that are geographically close enough to make communication possible. Thus, *language, time,* and *place* are three criteria that can be used to identify a culture (Triandis, 1994).

According to these criteria, there are about 10,000 cultures in the world (it is estimated that there are about 6,170 distinct languages; Moynihan, 1993). Given that the United Nations has fewer than 200 members, clearly most nations are multicultural. The need to address diversity is perhaps the most important national issue for most countries, and the United States is once again leading the world in developing ways to address these issues.

Having defined culture, it is easier to define race, ethnicity, and nationality. Race is not a scientific category but a social one. People respond differently to members of the same physical type (e.g., a race such as Caucasian, Negroid, or Mongoloid). People of the same descent (descending from particular common ancestors) or lineage are said to have the same ethnicity. Therefore, there are many ethnic groups within each race. Nationality refers to affiliation with a nation-state; in terms of culture, race, and ethnicity, nationality means little because in any one country there are people of many races and ethnic backgrounds. Race, ethnicity, residence in the same neighborhood, common gender, similar age, and so on provide opportunities to develop similar subjective cultures (concepts, beliefs, attitudes, norms, roles, and values), reflected in similar attitudes and the like.

Diversity is defined, by both researchers and practitioners, as difference in ethnicity, race, gender, religious beliefs, sexual orientation, (dis)ability, veteran status, age, national origin, and cultural and personal perspectives. Diversity refers to differences both in objective (demographic) variables and in subjective (behavior, attitudes, norms, and values) cultures.

Operationalizing Culture

Cultures differ among themselves along three dimensions: complexity versus simplicity, tightness versus looseness, and hierarchy versus equality. We will first discuss these constructs and then describe a summary dimension, individualism versus collectivism, that is useful in understanding cultural differences.

Complexity versus simplicity. The more a culture is characterized by role differentiation, stratification, and affluence, the more complex that culture is. Information societies are very complex; the "big seven" economies of the world provide examples of complex societies. In a complex society social behavior is based on exchanges (i.e., on profit and loss). Behavior in public settings has many of these attributes. The market provides a good metaphor for such relationships.

Folk societies (e.g., nomadic tribes, hunters and gatherers) are usually less complex in social organization, are less economically developed, and are characterized by simplicity. Usually every member of the society knows most other members, and much behavior occurs in private settings. The family is the best metaphor for such relationships.

Tightness versus looseness. The more homogeneous and isolated the culture is, the more agreement there is about the elements of subjective culture (e.g., clarity of norms), and thus the more definitively can the norms be imposed on members of the culture. The behavior of members of such cultures is tightly regulated. Even small deviations from "proper" behavior are punished. For example, in the tight Japanese culture, if one arrives even 2 minutes late for an appointment, there will be negative consequences.

In cultures that have evolved at the confluence of two or more unique cultures or that have more heterogeneous populations, norms are imposed only if there is a major deviation from accepted behavior patterns. These cultures show looseness (as opposed to tightness). Thailand and the United States are examples of such cultures. In Thailand an employee may simply walk away from a job without explanation and not be punished.

Hierarchy versus equality.   Hierarchy is present when people behave differently toward those at the top and bottom of the social structure relative to the way they behave toward people at their own level. Cultures vary on this dimension. Some societies are more hierarchical than others; for example, in Japan one cannot even speak correctly without knowing the rank of the other person relative to one's own.

In other societies (e.g., Iceland and Israel) status differences are downplayed, and equality is stressed. These cultures are less hierarchical.

A summary dimension.   Collectivism and individualism are contrasts that summarize the other three dimensions. Maximum collectivism occurs in simple, family-type relationships; in tight cultures; and where there is considerable emphasis on hierarchy. Maximum individualism occurs in complex societies that have market-type relationships, that are loose, and that favor equality.

Because a particular culture can be anywhere on the three basic dimensions, the final attributes of a culture involve some mixture of these dimensions. For example, Japan is complex, tight, and hierarchical; thus it is somewhat collectivist but not extremely so. Many folk societies are simple, tight, and equal; that makes them very collectivist. But there are folk societies with simple, tight, and hierarchical profiles. The United States is complex (with emphasis on public relations), loose, and moderate in hierarchy. Thus, collectivism versus in-

dividualism is a complex dimension, which can be analyzed into the three basic dimensions of complexity, tightness, and hierarchy.

In collectivist cultures the self is defined as an aspect of the collective—the family, caste, tribe, work group, village, or country. Each culture has its own profile of the relative importance of each collective. In individualistic cultures the self is independent of groups (Markus & Kitayama, 1991).

Brewer (1991) has argued that each human strives for "optimal distinctiveness," which is a balance between the forces toward assimilation and merging with groups and the forces toward differentiation from groups. The optimal point depends on the culture. This finding has important implications for diversity management: It can be predicted that people are unlikely to assimilate totally, as the melting pot philosophy assumes.

When cultures come in contact, the locations of the cultures on the three basic dimensions is a factor that determines, in part, their cultural distance. (Other barriers to good relationships are differences in economic status and language and past history of intergroup conflict.) The more different the cultures are on the basic dimensions, the more distance there is between them. People from cultures that are very distant have more difficulty interacting with and adjusting to each other and are more likely to experience communication breakdowns when they come in contact (Triandis, Kurowski, & Gelfand, 1993).

Two Conflicting Philosophies for Dealing with Diversity

Two points of view have been proposed to deal with diversity. On the one hand there is the melting pot conception (Zangwill, 1914), which argues that the best country has a single homogeneous culture. People of different cultures are encouraged to surrender their differences in favor of a mainstream language, norm, work ethic, and so on—that is, to form one culture.

For a long time the United States embodied the melting pot philosophy as people of different European descents adopted English as their language. Other countries maintain homogeneity by shutting out people who are different from their own. For example, Japan has refused to receive migrants on the ground that they would undermine the quality of life in Japanese society; in the 1970s Germany (then West Germany) returned to their countries thousands of "guest workers" who had lived in that country for decades.

Contrasting with the melting pot philosophy is the concept of multiculturalism, which assumes that each cultural group can preserve much of its original culture without interfering with the smooth functioning of the society. Canada has an official multicultural policy. The multiculturalist orientation requires, ideally, that each individual develop a good understanding of the viewpoints of members of the other cultures and learn to make attributions concerning the causes of behavior of members of the other culture that are more or less like the attributes that these members make in explaining their own behavior (Triandis, 1975).

The current diversity movement in the United States is causing a shift away from the melting pot metaphor to the multiculturalist view or what can be termed the "salad bowl" metaphor—every ingredient in the salad bowl retains its distinctive quality.

Consequences of Intercultural Interactions

Each culture emerges in its own ecology, in ways that favor adjustment to that ecology (Berry, 1967, 1976). People's experiences in particular ecologies result in unique ways of perceiving their social environments (Triandis, 1972). The level of people's adaptation (Helson, 1964) in making judgments depends on their experiences. For example, if a person has experienced wealth, that person has a much higher level of adaptation concerning compensation than a person who has experienced poverty.

Most humans are ethnocentric, that is, they judge other cultures as good to the extent that those cultures are similar to their own. That is inevitable because we all grow up in specific cultures and view those cultures as providing the only "correct" answers to the problems of existence (Triandis, 1994). As we encounter other cultures we may become less ethnocentric, but it is only by rejecting our own culture that we can become nonethnocentric, and that is relatively rare.

When people from different cultures work together, their ethnocentrism is likely to lead to misunderstandings and low levels of interpersonal attraction. The greater the cultural distance, the smaller the rewards experienced from working together. If the behavior of the other people in the workplace does not make sense because the attributions people make are too different, one experiences a loss of control. Such loss of control results in depression (Langer, 1983), culture shock (Oberg, 1954, 1960), and dislike of the other culture's members.

The more the interactions with these members are intergroup (emphasizing their membership in groups), the more the cultural differences will be emphasized. If the interactions become interpersonal (paying attention only to the personal attributions of the other and ignoring the cultural aspects of the other's behavior), it is possible to like the member in spite of the cultural distance (Tajfel, 1982). However, there are some necessary conditions: Contact must lead to the perception of similarity. This can be achieved if there is no history of conflict between the two cultures, if the person knows enough about the other culture to anticipate the culturally determined behaviors of the other, if the person knows the other's language, and if they have common friends and common goals (Triandis et al., 1993).

In the absence of these conditions, there is usually considerable social distance, which becomes greater the more insecure and anxious the perceiver is (Triandis & Triandis, 1960). If there is conflict, stereotyping becomes very negative (Avigdor, 1953), and interpersonal attraction is low or negative. However, if these conditions do exist, there can be attraction, minimal negative stereotyping, and little social distance. In our opinion, even where there has been conflict between certain groups, other factors like common organizational goals, common friends, knowledge of the other's language, and so on can lead to the perception of similarity in the workplace and improve interpersonal interactions.

Analysis of the Workplace

In the nineteenth century managers thought of the work force as an undifferentiated mass composed of identical individuals. Typical of this thinking was Taylor's notion of scientific management, which was popular early in this century. All workers were to be motivated, trained, and rewarded in the same way. These assumptions worked as long as workers had little education and power. But today's workers are more educated, have more power, and demand to be treated as individuals. Treating workers as individuals often includes showing special respect for their culture. This means that managers must become more sensitive to cultural differences; they can no longer assume that universalistic theories of management, which ignore culture, are applicable (Erez & Earley, 1993).

If the workplace is to be diverse, what should we expect? There will be some advantages and some disadvantages (Jackson & Alvarez, 1992). On the positive side there is evidence of greater creativity in heterogeneous work groups, as well as the capability to screen for decisions that would offend particular cultural groups. For instance, General Motors would not have had so much trouble selling the Nova in South America if someone had detected that *no va* (does not go) is not the best name for a car in that part of the world. On the negative side, cultural distance results in low attraction, poor communication, lack of coordination, and stress.

Characteristics of Significant U.S. Populations

Following is a brief outline of general ways in which significant U.S. populations differ from the "mainstream." A more complete discussion can be found in Triandis et al. (1993). Each relationship—African–Asian-Americans, African–Latin-Americans, and so on—is different and must be studied separately and examined in detail.

Asian-Americans. Asian-Americans are a very heterogeneous group, but they tend to be more collectivist and less assertive than the mainstream. They pay more attention to the context of social behavior than do mainstream Americans, who tend to depend entirely on the content of verbal exchanges. This difference can result in misunderstandings.

African-Americans. African-Americans are also very heterogeneous, especially because social class plays an enormous role in creating differences within that group (Triandis, 1976). On the whole this population is much more expressive and depends more on movement and sound than do members of the mainstream. African-Americans without jobs often develop a "cool" pose (Gordon & Majors, 1993) marked by an appearance of toughness, a willingness to use violence, and a display of sexual promiscuity, a pose that may produce adjustment problems in both family life and work life.

Hispanics. Hispanics are likewise a heterogeneous population, with roots in many different countries and influenced by Iberian, African, and American-Indian cultural patterns in different mixtures. One apparently common element is that they are collectivists in terms of family and hold high expectations that other people will treat them well, not criticize them, and try to be *simpático* (nice, pleasant, noncritical) when interacting with them (Triandis, Marin, Lisansky, & Betancourt, 1984). Thus, they feel that mainstream Americans behave quite inappropriately in not trying to be *simpático.*

Women. With women now representing almost half the work force, their special problems are of great interest. For example, the so-called glass ceiling, reflecting lack of promotion to higher managerial ranks, may be due in part to women's difficulties in finding suitable mentors. They are often confronted with old-boy networks that exclude them from access to important information. Sexual harassment is an additional issue that could merit a whole chapter. The threshold for its perception is lower for women than for men.

People of diverse sexual orientations.   A major question surrounding sexual orientation is whether to be open about it or to follow a "don't ask, don't tell" policy.

People with disabilities.   One of the issues emerging from research with this population concerns the attitudes evoked by people with disabilities, such as anxiety and an inability to handle the ambiguity of social situations.

Considering the diversity of populations present in the United States and knowing that this country adopted the melting pot philosophy to assimilate its diverse population both in society and in the workplace, we find it natural to ask, Why are U.S. corporations changing their way of handling human resources in the nineties? What has led the corporate world into the diversity movement? We found that organizations offered a number of reasons for investing in diversity management (Bhawuk & Triandis, 1993). The following sections, which concern diversity management in U.S. corporations, are based on the findings of a study that is currently in progress.

Diversity Management in U.S. Corporations

Reasons for Managing Diversity

Diversity management in the corporate world comes partly in response to demographic trends: By the year 2000 women and minorities will constitute 62 percent of the U.S. work force and 80 percent of the new entrants. By the year 2000 one-third of all workers will be age 50 or older. Competition for highly skilled, qualified employees will intensify in the coming years; only companies whose cultures support diversity will be able to retain the best talent necessary to remain competitive.

Following are some further reasons commonly offered by organizations for involving themselves in diversity management:

- To improve community and public support for the company's business agenda
- To position the company as an employer of "choice" in the recruitment of talented women and minorities
- To position the company as a leader in the marketplace for customers, vendors, potential employees, and shareholders
- To meet the diverse needs of the growing ethnic segments of the U.S. market
- To show commitment to the principles and practices of equal opportunity
- To address the legal requirements associated with Title VII of the Civil Rights Act of 1964, the Americans with Disabilities Act (ADA), guidelines concerning sexual harassment,[1] and the like

It is clear that organizations want both to hire the most talented people and to retain the people they hire. Because women and minorities will constitute the majority of people entering the work force 10 years from now, it is important for organizations to lure them into their folds. It is felt that if organizations do not have a fair representation of minorities and women in management, they may not be able to attract others from those ranks. Further, customers, vendors, and shareholders may ostracize such organizations. It is also

---

[1]Title VII of the Civil Rights Act of 1964 prohibits employment discrimination on the basis of race, color, religion, national origin, and sex. There is no mention of sexual harassment in the law or its legislative history. However, in accordance with court rulings (e.g., *William v. Saxbe,* 1976; *Barnes v. Costle,* 1977) and the 1980 guidelines from the Equal Employment Opportunity Commission (EEOC), the agency that enforces Title VII, sexual harassment is interpreted as sexual discrimination under Title VII.

clear that Title VII, ADA, and other legal requirements are still a driving force behind organizations' attention to the diversity issues. The costs of litigation related to alleged instances of sexual harassment, inadequate accommodation for disability, discrimination in promotion, and so on are so exorbitant that organizations are better off addressing these issues proactively. The emerging strategies adopted by many U.S. corporations for managing diversity are discussed next.

Emerging Diversity Strategies

Because organizations function in different environments, they must adopt different approaches to diversity management; also, they have different needs, which result in different policies. Organizations can be ranged on a continuum from "not doing anything" to "having a full-blown diversity strategy," with most falling in the middle, carrying out only awareness training programs or mandatory AA/EEO (affirmative action/equal employment opportunity) activities.

Organizations that have developed strategies for diversity management approach the issues from more than one perspective. Their approach is inclusive, encompassing AA/EEO activities, awareness and other training programs, and more. The points on the continuum are not discrete and exclusive; rather they are more like evolutionary phases for organizations going through different styles of diversity management. It is likely that most organizations will fall somewhere on this continuum.

The following three approaches to diversity management can be identified.

1. AA/EEO activities only. Every organization must deal at some level with the legal requirements of AA/EEO. Organizations that are involved in mandatory AA/EEO activities are sensitive to the Title VII rights of employees and make an effort to avoid lawsuits. Organizations that are limited to these activities consider dealing with minorities a legal aspect or a cost of doing business. Most organizations have gone through this phase. Those

that have no diversity programs may still fall in this category because AA/EEO requirements cannot be avoided.

All organizations disseminate legal information to managers and supervisors who are responsible for selection, training, promotion, and the like—that is, the areas that are affected by AA/EEO. Currently this is an important human resource (HR) function. Sexual harassment and the Americans with Disabilities Act are prominent topics of current discussion.

A disadvantage of doing only what is required under AA/EEO laws is that the mainstream employees feel rejected in the course of the implementation of AA/EEO activities. Even if organizations cannot identify the benefits of a diversity policy and do not have a pressing need for diversity activities, they often feel a need for an awareness program that allows the inclusion of mainstream employees.

2. Awareness training. When organizations realize that there is value in expanding their AA/EEO activities to exploit the benefits of diversity, they usually start conducting diversity awareness programs for their managers and salaried employees. However, these programs are usually not extended to grass-roots workers. Awareness programs can be classified into the following three categories.

The first category is based on films designed to increase employee awareness of diversity issues. Some of the popular films used are *Valuing Diversity* (by Griggs Productions Inc.), *Harness the Rainbow* (by Determan Marketing Corporation), and *Bridges: Skills for Managing a Diverse Work Force* (by BNA Communications). Usually a discussion session follows the film. This type of program is easy to conduct and relatively inexpensive, with internal human resource experts generally facilitating the discussion.

Second, most organizations invite experts in the area of diversity to conduct group discussions. The experts have their own approaches to handling diversity, and they promote these approaches in their discussion programs. It is difficult to estimate the effectiveness of these programs because they are of short duration and usually do not (and cannot due to time limitations) use a behavior modification approach.

Third, many organizations offer one-, two-, or three-day awareness training programs that aim at giving managers and other employees who must deal with a diverse work force the skills to build effective, culturally diverse teams. These training programs usually focus on topics such as cultural and gender differences, stereotypes, socialization processes, differences in communication style, legal aspects of AA/EEO, and so on. Again, group discussion led by experts is the popular vehicle for this training. Experiential exercises like Bafa-Bafa (Shirts, 1973), Albatross (Gochenour, 1977), and the like are seldom used. Also, discussions seldom offer theoretical explanations for differences in behavior or misunderstandings that arise in the workplace. We believe a theory-driven approach would improve the process of building intercultural communication skills.

We think HR managers and diversity trainers have a lot to learn from the rich cross-cultural training literature. Numerous methods of cultural training are available (see Bhawuk, 1990, for a succinct summary), and among the most important responses to diversity is to use them. Following are brief descriptions of the main types of training; interested readers are directed to the *Handbook of Intercultural Training* (Landis & Brislin, 1983).

(a) Self-insight training. People can understand how culture influences their own behavior by interacting with actors who have been trained to behave in the opposite way from the way members of the trainees' culture behave. Follow-up discussions about the trainees' reactions to these interactions can clarify the meaning of culture and elucidate its influence on behavior. This method can be particularly useful to raise awareness of ethnic differences in work ethics, interpersonal interaction styles, approaches to handling conflict, and so on, in a way that motivates employees to improve their interpersonal skills.

(b) Attribution training. Attribution training (also called a culture assimilator) uses a programmed learning curriculum based on episodes of social interaction (critical incidents) involving members of one's own and the other culture. After reading or viewing each episode, the trainee makes judgments about the causes of the behavior of the member of the other culture. Each judgment is followed by feedback that criticizes or supports it. This process shapes the trainee to make attributions matching the attributions that members of the other culture make when viewing the same episodes.

Culture assimilators, as the most extensively researched intercultural training method, are appropriate for diversity training. Culture assimilators are available for use in preparing people to interact with African-Americans and Hispanics. Considering the effectiveness of this method, it would be worthwhile to develop assimilators addressing the issues of sexual orientation, age, and so on. This method should also be effective for training people to reduce sexual harassment in the workplace.

(c) Behavior modification. In the behavior modification method, the trainee receives feedback while behaving in role-play situations toward members of the other culture. When the behavior is inappropriate (e.g., offensive to members of the other culture), the feedback directs the trainee to change and to substitute behaviors that are considered desirable in the other culture. This method is likely to be effective in training people to prevent sexual harassment in the workplace because new, acceptable behaviors are needed to replace old, unacceptable ones. Diversity managers and professionals have yet to take advantage of this method.

Diversity training programs seem to be more effective when they focus on particular issues like sexual harassment or problems surrounding disability, rather than when they discuss abstract ideas like stereotypes and communication styles. When training is issue focused, both the negative and the suggested replacement behaviors can be identified and discussed. For example, sexually harassing behaviors can be classified as verbal, physical, or visual, and an example of unacceptable and acceptable behaviors in each category can be offered and discussed. Similarly, in a program focused on dealing with disabilities, it is easy to point out how people inadvertently stereotype by using phrases like "John, a hard-working retarded person . . ." (implying that disabled people are not usually hard-working). Consideration of concrete behaviors helps people shape their own behaviors in the workplace.

Diversity programs are evaluated mostly by qualitative methods. A human resource manager commented that investment in diversity programs is like investment in advertising—one does not know what is useful and what is not. Feedback from participants is still the most prevalent evaluation method. However, opinion surveys and focus group analysis are also used.

3. *Fully developed diversity strategy.* Organizations that have fully developed diversity strategies have been experimenting with diversity for at least 3 years and are now ready to incorporate diversity in their daily business activities. This does not, however, mean that they have already achieved their long-term diversity goals. Indeed, it will be quite some time before they can fully realize those goals.

Organizations with fully developed diversity strategies typically do commit significant resources to deal systematically with diversity. Next we describe two unique diversity strategies, developed by organizations in our study.

(a) An integrated diversity strategy. An integrated strategy integrates the formal efforts of the organization at both corporate and business unit levels with the informal efforts of employees at the grass-roots level.

At the corporate level a demographically and functionally diverse employee panel is formed to monitor and oversee the diversity activities. This corporate body is known by various names—Diversity Forum, Chair's Af-

firmative Action Committee, Corporate Diversity Advisory Council, Corporate EEO Committee, Pluralism Council, and the like. The panel usually includes 15 to 20 people, among them the vice-president of human resources or diversity and a representative sample of line and staff managers. In other words, the corporate-level diversity forum is modeled after a diverse organization and conceptually drives the diversity activities.

At the business unit level, the impact of diversity issues on various business activities is analyzed, and diversity policies are integrated with the daily business activities, in coordination with the corporate diversity forum and grass-roots advocacy groups.

At the grass-roots level, employees form advocacy groups, which are independent, informal organizations of various minority populations within the company, as a vehicle for providing information about the issues that concern them. The advocacy groups convey issues and concerns of employees in the organization to both the corporate diversity forum and the business units.

The diversity forum, advocacy groups, and business units generally act in coordination, communicating and sharing information both as dyads and in a triad. This arrangement is illustrated in Figure 1.

The diversity forum usually serves the following objectives:

- It facilitates sustained attention on diversity issues.

- It heightens senior management's awareness of and sensitivity to the diversity issues.

- It examines the impact of new HR policies on various groups of employees.

- It shares information about both successful and unsuccessful diversity programs.

- It discusses urgent concerns related to diversity.

When organizations take this integrated approach, solving diversity problems is categori-

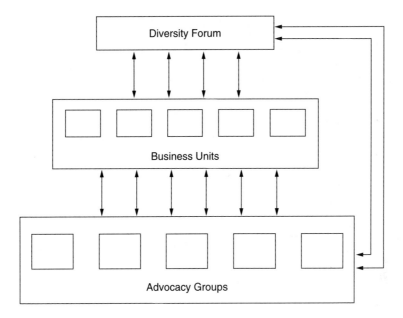

Figure 1.   An Integrated Diversity Strategy

cally stated to be the task of business units; the forum is only a platform for the discussion of issues and the development of policies. The corporate office provides broad strategies, policies, and training resources, but the business units are accountable for the management of diversity. Organizations apparently are concerned that diversity may become a staff function and hence lose some impetus, so they make efforts to delegate the handling of diversity issues to the business units, thus treating diversity strictly as a business issue.

Similarly, the advocacy groups (for African-Americans, women, Hispanics, Filipinos, etc.) do not implement diversity measures but rather serve as sources of information and channels of communication to both the forum and the business units. These groups also help internal organizations to network and communicate effectively with minority organizations and interest groups in the community.

(b) A top-down diversity strategy. Some organizations reject the integrated approach in favor of a top-down diversity strategy. In these organizations, usually, the champion of diversity management is the CEO.

This strategy takes a "changing corporate culture" or "organizational development" approach to managing diversity. The belief is that because the work force is diverse, management also should be diverse. A diverse management, it is hoped, will experience fewer problems handling a diverse work force. In the top-down approach, diversity management is operationalized through succession planning, and the focus is on breaking the "glass ceiling." This strategy is illustrated in Figure 2.

In the top-down approach the corporate office is responsible for formulating the strategy, which is communicated to the business units. In the first phase of the diversity effort, the CEO communicates "management accountability," telling presidents of the business units what is to be done, why it is to be done, and how the presidents are accountable. In formulating the strategy, the CEO is assisted by the vice-president of diversity.

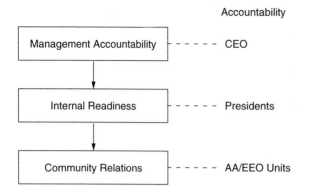

Figure 2.   A Top-Down Diversity Strategy

In the second phase, the business unit presidents are accountable for "internal readiness." They are responsible for finding out where the barriers to diversity are in their units, what strategy is needed to eliminate those barriers, how they should communicate about this with others in their units, and how they can make clear that diversity is a strategic and not a tactical issue. In short, the presidents are responsible for preparing their units to handle diversity issues effectively by breaking the glass ceiling.

The third phase involves managing "community relations." The organization strives to build a strong partnership with community organizations like the Urban League, La Raza, Catalyst (a women's advocacy organization), and the like. This allows the organization to gain the confidence of different communities.

Each business unit has an EEO/AA unit, and the vice-president of diversity meets with that unit twice a year. This group, called the Chair's AA Committee, helps keep open the communication lines between the corporate office and the business units.

The business units and their presidents are made accountable for the implementation of the diversity efforts, including the reaching of parity goals. Annual and long-term goals are given to the presidents. Because there are few minority individuals at the vice-president

level, the goal of promoting a minimum number of women and minority individuals (say, three women and two minority individuals) to the position of vice-president each year is set.

The business unit presidents are responsible for identifying, from among minorities, capable individuals, including women, who can become vice-presidents and then grooming them to assume those positions in about 3 years. It is important that the increase in minorities at the vice-president level not be limited to the traditional areas of human resource management; it should also occur in critical functional areas.

For directorial, managerial, and beginner positions, a reasonable goal is to match the national census—to have, in specific functional areas, proportions of managers and directors that correspond to the average national percentages of the ethnic groups in question.

Conclusion

Organizations are becoming aware of the growing diversity of the workplace and are searching for ways of managing that diversity. However, the major emphasis of diversity management is on the acceptance of demographic and ethnic differences; very little attention is paid to focusing on similarities.

Most human resource specialists recommend open communication in diversity management. It seems that diversity issues are forcing management to become more participatory, at least with respect to human resource management. One wonders if there was a lack of open communication in U.S. organizations in the past. If so, diversity is making a definite contribution by promoting participatory management in organizations.

Organizations are becoming sensitive to the use of languages other than English in the workplace. Knowledge of another language, especially Spanish, is considered an advantage, especially by organizations that have frequent interaction with Spanish-speaking clients. Some organizations have even started communicating with Filipino, Chinese, and Japanese customers in the clients' languages. Neither organizations nor other units of the society are paying enough attention to the implications of using more than one language in business activities.

Organizations are more willing than they were in the past to accept minority organizations and interest groups, both within the organization and in the community. They frequently communicate with those groups to deal with diversity issues. Also, organizations are clearly concerned about the glass ceiling phenomenon and are finding ways of grooming women and minorities for promotion to middle- and upper-management positions. EEO/AA is still an important consideration for companies doing business in the United States, and diversity management provides the umbrella under which these issues can be handled beyond legal requirements.

Will organizations develop comprehensive strategies along the lines discussed here, or will they just meet the challenges of the diverse work force halfway by merely protecting themselves from lawsuits? Will a multicultural society emerge in the end, or will the melting pot be victorious? We do not want to bet our money on any outcome now, but we are confident that the foundation of a society that will be just and open to differences is being laid and that U.S. corporations are taking a lead in finding ways to manage people with differences in their objective (demo-graphic variables) and subjective (attitude, norms, values, beliefs, etc.) cultures.

References

Avigdor, R. (1953). Etudes expérimentales de la genèse des stéréotypes. *Cahiers Internationaux de Sociologie, 5,* 154–168.

Berry, J. W. (1967). Independence and conformity in subsistence level societies. *Journal of Personality and Social Psychology, 7,* 415–418.

Berry, J. W. (1976). *Human ecology and cognitive style.* Beverly Hills, CA: Sage.

Bhawuk, D. P. S. (1990). Cross-cultural orientation programs. In R. W. Brislin (Ed.), *Applied cross-cultural psychology.* Beverly Hills, CA: Sage.

Bhawuk, D. P. S., & Triandis, H. C. (1993). *Bridging the gap between theory and practice: Comparative study of current diversity programs* (University of Illinois Center for Human Resource Management Working Paper Series, No. 2).

Brewer, M. B. (1991). The social self: On being the same and different at the same time. *Personality and Social Psychology Bulletin, 17,* 475–485.

Erez, M., & Earley, C. (1993). *Culture, self-identity, and work.* New York: Oxford University Press.

George, S. (1993). One-third in, two-thirds out. *New Perspectives Quarterly, 10,* 53–55.

Gochenour, T. (1977). The owl and the albatross. In D. Batchelder & E. G. Warner (Eds.), *Beyond experience.* Brattleboro, VT: Experiment Press.

Gordon, J., & Majors, R. (1993). *The black male: His present status and his future.* Chicago: Nelson-Hall.

Helson, H. (1964). *Adaptation level theory.* New York: Harper and Row.

Jackson, S. E., & Alvarez, E. B. (1992). Working through diversity as a strategic imperative. In S. E. Jackson & Associates (Eds.), *Diversity in the work place: Human resources initiatives* (pp. 13–36). New York: Guilford.

Kluckhohn, C. (1954). Culture and behavior. In G. Lindzey (Ed.), *Handbook of social psychology* (Vol. 2., pp. 921–976). Cambridge, MA: Addison-Wesley.

Landis, D., & Brislin, R. (1983). *Handbook of intercultural training* (Vols. 1–3). New York: Pergamon.

Langer, E. J. (1983). *The psychology of control.* Beverly Hills, CA: Sage.

Markus, H., & Kitayama, S. (1991). Culture and self: Implications for cognition, emotion and motivation. *Psychological Review, 98,* 224–253.

Moynihan, D. P. (1993). *Pandaemonium.* Oxford, England: Oxford University Press.

Oberg, K. (1954). *Culture shock* (The Bobbs-Merrill Reprint Series, No. A-329).

Oberg, K. (1960). Culture shock: Adjustment to new cultural environments. *Practical Anthropology, 7,* 177–182.

Shirts, G. (1973). *BAFA-BAFA: A cross-cultural simulation.* Del Mar, CA: Smile 11.

Tajfel, H. (1982). *Social identity and intergroup relations.* New York: Cambridge University Press.

Triandis, H. C. (1972). *The analysis of subjective culture.* New York: Wiley.

Triandis, H. C. (1975). Cultural training, cognitive complexity, and interpersonal attitudes. In R. W. Brislin, S. Bochner, & W. J. Lonner (Eds.), *Cross-cultural perspectives on learning.* Beverly Hills, CA: Sage.

Triandis, H. C. (1976). *Variations in black and white perceptions of the social environment.* Urbana: University of Illinois Press.

Triandis, H. C. (1994). *Culture and social behavior.* New York: McGraw-Hill.

Triandis, H. C., Kurowski, L. L., & Gelfand, M. J. (1993). Workplace diversity. In H. C. Triandis, M. Dunnette, & L. Hough (Eds.), *Handbook of industrial and organizational psychology* (pp. 769–827). Palo Alto, CA: Consulting Psychologists Press.

Triandis, H. C., Marin, G., Lisansky, J., & Betancourt, H. (1984). *Simpatia* as a cultural script of Hispanics. *Journal of Personality and Social Psychology, 47,* 1363–1375.

Triandis, H. C., & Triandis, L. M. (1960). Race, social class, religion, and nationality as determinants of social distance. *Journal of Abnormal and Social Psychology, 61,* 110–118.

Zangwill, I. (1914). *The melting pot: Drama in four acts.* New York: Macmillan.

CHAPTER 5

Organizational Restructuring

Organizations follow change strategies in the belief that proposed changes are in their own best interests. There are many ways to change. A number of organizations have decided that it is in their best interest to engage in downsizing. A major purpose of downsizing is to achieve a quick reduction in labor costs that have become excessive because current human resources have not been used effectively. Downsizing is associated with numerous negative human resources outcomes. For example, downsizing often reduces company morale to the point where individuals lose any sense of commitment or dedication to the success of the organization.

From a human resources perspective, these changes are complex. Change is typically a long and arduous process requiring time and patience, which are often in short supply in downsizing situations. Human resource professionals must develop ways to increase the effectiveness of human resources programs and the ability to adapt rapidly to change.

The Keiser and Urban article is concerned with the issue of downsizing in organizations. The authors suggest a number of important ways to minimize threats to organizational vitality.

Suggestions for Further Reading

Cox, C. (1993). The ultimate downsize: A retailer's story. *Business Quarterly, 58,* 76–80.

Ford, R., & Perrewe, P. (1993). After the layoff: Closing the barn door before all the horses are gone. *Business Horizons, 36,* 34–40.

Greenberg, E. (1989). The latest AMA survey on downsizing. *Personnel, 66,* 38–44.

Hyde, A., & Rosenbloom, D. (1993, Summer). Design of federal personnel management. *Public Manager,* pp. 9–14.

Overman, S. (1993, September). Under HR umbrella, career development pays dividends. *HR Magazine,* pp. 67–68.

Restaffing cuts jobs when early exits don't. (1993). *Employee Benefit Plan Review, 48,* 53–54.

Schay, B. (1993, Summer). Broad-banding in the federal government. *Public Manager,* pp. 28–31.

Schine, E. (1993, August 16). Take the money and run—Or take your chances. *Business Week,* pp. 28–29.

Schultz, J., & Crawford, A. (1993, June 1). When a plant shuts down: The psychology of decommissioning. *Public Utilities Fortnightly,* pp. 14–20.

Yates, M. (1993). The bright side of a merger: A refined compensation plan and new spirit. *Human Resources Professional, 5,* 47–51.

Approaches and Alternatives to Downsizing: A Discussion and Case Study

John D. Keiser and Thomas F. Urban

Attempting to become leaner and more competitive, business organizations have adopted downsizing as the prevalent strategy during the late 1980s and early 1990s. Downsizing, which implies reducing the work force through forced measures, was once considered a last-breath effort of a failing company. Currently it seems to be the fashion among American business concerns regardless of their financial performance. According to some estimates, 85 percent of the *Fortune* 1000 firms either have eliminated workers or are planning to do so in the foreseeable future (Cascio, 1993). Companies as reputationally sound as Kodak, Sears, and AT&T have reduced their work forces considerably (Cameron et al., 1992), and companies enjoying record performance, such as Wal-Mart, are also planning on decreasing organizational employment levels (Uchitelle, 1993). Even IBM, which not long ago championed its lifelong employment policy as a competitive advantage (Bolt, 1985), is paring its payrolls at a rapid rate in an effort to reduce overhead and overcome the poor financial performance of the past several years.

What has happened so that organizations of all descriptions are pursuing measures as drastic as laying off workers? Perhaps this question would be easier to answer if the success rate of companies pursuing downsizing strategies were high. However, it is not! Research in the area of downsizing shows that most companies that attempt downsizing through layoffs do not experience improved financial performance. Frequently their performance suffers after the implementation of downsizing (Cascio, 1993).

To date, what we have learned about the effects of downsizing is far outweighed by the uncertainties of implementing such a bold strategy. As a result managers contemplating downsizing face a formidable task in identifying exactly where, and how deep, to make cuts in an organization's work force. Or are there alternatives to downsizing that may achieve the desired effects? Ironically, as common as downsizing strategies have become, there are no generally accepted rules for work force reductions. So, even though an organization may be following the leads of thousands of other companies by downsizing, the true results are too ambiguous to predict.

We will attempt to integrate the current knowledge of downsizing to analyze the reasons why organizations pursue downsizing in favor of other labor cost reduction strategies and to identify different types of downsizing implementations. To illustrate our discussion, we will describe the alternatives ARCO Oil and Gas Company considered when they sought to reduce their overhead expenses. This article is divided into six sections. The first defines downsizing and outlines the reasons why organizations would want to pursue this strategy. The second section follows with descriptions of common downsizing approaches. The third section focuses on the reasons why our knowledge about downsizing is limited despite its prevalence. A brief review of the growing literature on the costs and benefits of downsizing makes up the fourth section. The fifth section identifies alternatives to downsizing as well as different approaches to downsizing. The case study of the considerations ARCO Oil and Gas Company faced in implementing its downsizing strategy is in section six. A wrap-up and discussion conclude the article.

Downsizing Defined

Before discussing different approaches to downsizing, we must first establish a clear understanding of what qualifies as downsizing. For our purposes downsizing is a set of activities designed to make an organization more efficient, productive, and/or competitive (Cameron, Mishra, & Freeman, 1992) through the planned elimination of positions or jobs (Cascio, 1993). Several elements of this definition deserve special attention. First, underlying the downsizing decision is the distinct intention to improve the organization's position in the market. Second, implementing a downsizing strategy requires eliminating a portion of the work force. This elimination can occur through voluntary means, such as enhanced retirement plans and employee buy-outs, or through involuntary means such as terminations or permanent layoffs. Either approach suggests a planned effort to eliminate workers. Finally, implementing a downsizing strategy requires more than reducing the number of workers; it demands organizational adaptation to a smaller work force.

The required organizational restructuring might eliminate functions or departments, reconfigure channels of authority or communication, or redesign the work to accommodate fewer individuals. In any event, downsizing is not synonymous with a simple work force reduction, which merely suggests that the organization attempts to do things the same way as before except with fewer workers. In downsizing the organization attempts to improve its performance by doing things differently with fewer people. Frequently the term *downsizing* is used interchangeably with related terms like *work force reduction, rightsizing, layoffs,* or *organizational decline.* For the sake of clarity, it is important that we distinguish our definition of downsizing from these other notions.

Work force reduction is similar to downsizing because both are aimed at improving an organization's competitive position and both depend upon eliminating workers. However, reducing the work force is only one aspect of downsizing. As mentioned in the previous paragraph, downsizing is a set of activities that also includes adapting the organization to accommodate fewer workers. Used alone, work force reduction does not necessarily suggest an organizational adaptation.

A layoff is a work force reduction that results from a drop in demand. One frequently observes layoffs in the industrial sector, such as in automobile manufacturing. When buyer demand for cars decreases, auto workers are laid off. By comparison, downsizing is not necessarily spurred by a drop in consumer demand. Also, in layoffs, once the demand increases, the organization will frequently rehire laid off employees or find replacement workers. Downsizing is not intended to be a temporary solution to overstaffing. Instead, the organization attempts to maintain its operations with fewer permanent employees.

Organizational decline is also used interchangeably with *downsizing* because the two frequently occur simultaneously. As an organization struggles to meet its expenses, eliminating workers may be a practical remedy during tough times. Similarly, if a company or industry recognizes that the demand for its products is falling with little hope of ever recapturing past sales levels, maintaining former peak work force levels would be foolish. However, decline is not a prerequisite for downsizing, as evidenced by the growing number of comparatively healthy companies reducing their work forces to be more competitive (Uchitelle, 1993).

Along with work force reductions, layoffs, and decline, there is the misleading assumption that downsizing as a phenomenon is simply the opposite, or reverse, of organizational growth. Even though it seems logical that an organization going through downsizing would want to "undo" what it had done during times of expansion, this is not necessarily the case. Disproving this misconception are the concepts of expanding and contracting markets. Although a company may seek to expand its markets during times of growth, it would not necessarily seek to shrink those markets in times of decline. If, however, the company downsizes by selling off one or more product lines, thereby decreasing its markets intentionally, the analogy to growth in reverse may be appropriate.

Approaches to Downsizing

According to the definition we have established, downsizing commonly takes a number of different forms. The organization can rid itself of excess employees through a variety of methods, some of which allow employees to leave voluntarily or through systematic elimination. Because eliminating workers through involuntary means is painful for everyone involved and can be detrimental to the organization's reputation as an employer, encouraging workers to leave voluntarily is an attractive alternative.

Voluntary eliminations are typically efforts on the part of the company to make resignation or retirement desirable for existing workers through financial incentives. Such incentives, known as buyouts, are compensation packages awarded to workers for resigning or retiring. Depending upon the magnitude of the packages, they can provide an effective means for eliminating workers without having to fire them. But this strategy conceals a double-edged sword: Its effectiveness is dependent upon the generosity of the packages, which is directly related to its costliness. It is not uncommon for companies to offer in their buyout packages all unused sick and vacation time, as well as several weeks' pay for every year of service. It is also common for companies to provide continuation of insurance benefits. For employees who are older or have greater seniority, a commonly used incentive is an enhanced pension plan to encourage early retirement. Such an incentive package generally requires the company to increase its contribu-

tions to people's retirement packages or reduce the number of years they must work before they can take advantage of the pension plan.

Voluntary downsizing efforts often precede involuntary efforts in the hope of minimizing the unpleasant task of eliminating workers involuntarily. The decisions concerning which employees to dismiss may be based on several criteria. Whichever means the organization uses to make these decisions, it must be certain that its method complies with EEO (Equal Employment Opportunity) guidelines by not unfairly affecting any class of workers protected under civil rights legislation. Because employees' livelihoods are at stake, the determination of who will stay and who will leave is a painful exercise for the decision makers as well as the workers affected. Following are some commonly utilized criteria for such decisions.

Divestiture of product or function: Occasionally the restructuring associated with downsizing involves the organization's eliminating a product or service or a departmental function. For example, Hartmarx, Inc., an apparel manufacturer and retailer, restructured by selling much of its retail network to concentrate on its manufacturing strengths (Strom, 1992). The majority of those terminated were affiliated with the divested properties.

Reduction of organizational or hierarchical layers: Attempting to become more lean and less bureaucratic, some organizations have eliminated entire layers of their organizational hierarchies. The most recent downsizing trend is unique because many of its downsizing efforts are aimed at middle management, a sector of the work force that had largely been immune from previous reductions. Eliminating entire organizational levels allows a firm to reduce its work force in a relatively quick process. One potential drawback to elimination of layers is that it redefines traditional career paths to allow fewer opportunities for promotion.

Elimination of specific jobs in the organization: If organizational changes cause certain jobs to become obsolete, one approach to downsizing is eliminating the incumbents in those jobs. The drawback to this approach is that the organization may lose good people simply because they have held the less essential jobs. To counteract this negative effect, companies try to keep the best people by transferring them to other jobs that will survive the downsizing.

Recognition of seniority: Retaining the most senior workers and eliminating those with the shortest tenure makes for a relatively easy decision. However, the resulting work force may not be ideal. In making such a decision, the organization risks losing its best younger workers while retaining some less able workers with seniority.

Recognition of merit: If, during downsizing, the company's goal is to retain only the best workers, basing the decisions on merit is the most logical approach. This is also described as "high-grading" or the "best players play" strategy, where management compares the workers against one another to determine who stays. If job performance is easily and accurately measurable (as in the case of sales records), this is a highly appropriate means for decision making. Unfortunately, for many jobs, evaluating performance is more subjective, so determining the best and worst workers can be difficult. Using past performance reviews as criteria is acceptable, but the organization must have confidence in the reliability of those reviews in distinguishing levels of performance. Interestingly, this approach raises some questions regarding the validity of using past performance to predict future performance in a post-downsizing organization. If the restructuring involved in downsizing is significant, it is conceivable that the skills that were necessary in the old organization will be obsolete in the new one. In this case old performance reviews might not be very helpful in determining the best employees to keep.

Whichever form of decision making the organization uses in determining who will stay and who will leave, the process is agonizing because careers and livelihoods are at stake.

Although use of voluntary processes eliminates some of the trauma, it does not ensure that the best individuals will still be with the company after the downsizing. Likewise, systematic approaches such as eliminating layers, using seniority, or getting rid of jobs cannot guarantee the quality of the surviving work force, although the decisions are readily understood and perceived as fair. The most difficult form of decision making is one in which the organization chooses individually the employees who are expected to be most productive after the downsizing. Because there is significant subjectivity in such decisions, the company risks choosing people who may not actually be qualified or choosing people for reasons other than merit, such as personal bias, organizational politics, and so on. In major downsizing efforts companies frequently utilize multiple downsizing methods. In any event, the company must weigh the benefits of each type of decision and select the method or methods that will yield a fair process for retaining the workers with the most to offer in the post-downsizing organization.

Limited Knowledge about Downsizing

It is ironic that, as popular a strategy as downsizing has become, not much is known about its effects and consequences. This situation reflects on the fundamental premise regarding American business that success is synonymous with growth. Perhaps the premise has roots in the postwar boom of the 1950s and 1960s, which was also the era when management education and research increased dramatically. Growth was the goal, and the best American companies were readily achieving it.

Perhaps the lessons learned then were not so much the consequences of good management practices but instead the result of the United States' being the predominant developed country not devastated by World War II. Japan and much of Europe were destroyed by the war, and this situation provided new markets for American products. These new markets and the void in international competition were catalysts for American business to undergo unprecedented expansion. Companies were experiencing record performance and growth in profits, sales, and markets, as well as in numbers of workers. During this period William H. Whyte (1956) documented life in large American firms in his book *The Organization Man,* which describes the managerial careers and bureaucratic mechanisms that were becoming increasingly vital features of the corporate landscape. Scores of professional managers, while adding to the overhead costs of running a business, were simultaneously accompanying the unprecedented wave of success. From this it is easy to see how growth—market and bureaucratic—were so intimately correlated with success.

Not until the 1960s and 1970s were foreign competitors such as West Germany and Japan able to mount viable threats to the American lead in international industry. From the lessons learned since the war, American businesses took up the challenge by replicating the practices that had made American industry so successful a generation earlier. They sought more growth. If, however, profits or product demand decreased, a company would typically reduce its blue-collar work force until demand or profits rebounded sufficiently to justify rehiring. During challenging times the blue-collar—or industrial—work force was typically the buffer protecting the jobs and careers of an organization's administrative and white-collar workers, who were becoming a proportionately larger segment of the organization's work force.

Only recently have we realized that the success occurring after World War II was not a direct consequence of management practices emphasizing expansion. Instead, the success was probably more a result of increased demand and limited competition. But because growth and success happened simultaneously, the correlation between the two was understandably exaggerated. As America's lead has decreased substantially (and in some industries been bypassed, as with Japanese elec-

tronics), we are faced with reevaluating our practices and divorcing ourselves from what was once conventional wisdom. This takes time, and people are hesitant to drop old theories without tested new ones to replace them.

Besides the "bigger is better" philosophy in business, one reason why our knowledge regarding downsizing is limited lies in the inherent difficulty of learning from failures. A company's ability to learn is dependent upon its organizational memory, much of which relies on the memories of the participants. Because businesses embellish and embrace their successes, failures are often forgotten. This is especially true when individuals who were involved with unsuccessful efforts are transferred or replaced, leaving fewer people to remember the lessons learned from the failures. As mentioned earlier, downsizing is perceived as a consequence of an inability to succeed. Therefore, an organization having gone through downsizing is less likely to have benefited from the experience because of its selective learning.

Industry is not wholly responsible for the dearth of knowledge about downsizing. Academicians have been equally slow in addressing this trend. Fortunately this is changing, and during the last few years there has been a growing literature on what we have learned about the antecedents and effects of downsizing. Researchers in the human resources field have contributed significantly in this area (Cook & Ferris, 1986; Ferris, Schellenberg, & Zammuto, 1984; Lengnick-Hall & Lengnick-Hall, 1988; Perry, 1984; Price & D'Aunno, 1983; Ropp, 1987; Schuler & Jackson, 1987). In the next section we will provide an overview of significant research.

What We Know

From an accounting perspective we know that an organization can decrease expenditures significantly by eliminating portions of its work force. Payroll is often a company's largest operating expense, and when combined with overhead costs such as insurance and pensions, the compensation and benefits expenses constitute highly significant portions of a firm's overhead. Reducing these expenses can change a company's financial statements considerably. However, the savings associated with downsizing are not as obvious as simply subtracting the payroll and benefits of terminated workers. There are costs, some anticipated and many unanticipated, involved in downsizing efforts.

Anticipated Costs

Anticipated costs of downsizing consist of expenditures the company will make to decrease its work force. Such costs include buyouts of unused vacation and sick time, enhanced retirement packages to entice workers to retire or resign voluntarily, and other forms of severance pay for terminated workers. Depending upon the degree of its benevolence, the organization may offer outplacement services, including financial and psychological counseling and assistance in finding new jobs. Combined, these costs are considerable though—to a certain degree—expected. When announcing downsizing strategies, companies frequently state their anticipated costs by declaring charges on future accounting periods. For example, in September 1993, Chemical Waste Management, Inc., a subsidiary of WMX Technologies, Inc., announced a plan to cut 1,200 jobs by the end of 1994. It also announced that it would take a $363 million charge during the third quarter of 1994 (Bukro, 1993). This equates to an expense of over $300,000 for every displaced employee! Even with such an enormous charge, it is evident that Chemical Waste Management expects in the long run to save money—an expectation that testifies to the potential savings associated with downsizing.

Unanticipated Costs

Unfortunately, the charges that companies announce reflect only the planned expenses of downsizing and neglect the unanticipated costs. Only recently have researchers been able to identify these costs, but not all of them

can be represented in dollar figures. Following are some nonmonetary costs of downsizing.

Threat to morale.   American workers have become accustomed to an implicit contract of employment whereby the workers agree to perform what is expected of them and, in return, the organization agrees to provide employment security. When this contract is broken, the results are troubling, not only to those who lose their jobs but also to those who survive the downsizing. Watching good employees lose their jobs is unsettling and often raises the question, If it happened to them, who's to say it won't happen to me? After a downsizing, employees can no longer expect their employer to provide security. As a result their commitment to the company may suffer. This weakening of commitment may lead employees to seek other jobs that they believe are more secure. Especially when difficult financial performance is the determining factor behind downsizing, there is a perception of floating on a "sinking ship" (Perry, 1984). Bailing out becomes an attractive alternative to staying on board. Even if the downsizing was not prompted solely by poor performance, the prevailing attitudes might spur employees to reconsider career options outside the organization.

On a more personal level, the loss of co-workers and friends is a painful experience that can affect the morale of the surviving workers. Some might argue that surviving a downsizing should be a morale booster, a reprieve and an opportunity to work hard to show appreciation for being retained. Also, knowing that a downsizing can occur any time, surviving workers may be expected to work harder to protect themselves in the event of future cutbacks. However, research suggests that survivors' feelings are more complicated than this. Surviving workers are faced with an array of emotions: sadness for their unemployed friends and co-workers, uncertainty based on the possibility of future cutbacks, frustration caused by having more work to do, and—less obvious—a sense of guilt at having been selected to stay while others were forced to leave. Surprisingly, there might even be an additional feeling of envy. Downsizing often leads to more downsizing, and survivors have nagging concerns about the future viability of the organization. Buy-out plans often become skimpier with each new round. After a layoff or downsizing, work increases, career paths become uncertain, opportunities for promotion decline, merit increases decrease (or disappear), new reporting channels require adaptation, information networks evaporate, and so on. The workers leaving the organization have the actual opportunity to be reemployed, and the finality of being terminated invites closure. For survivors, on the other hand, there are still high levels of ambiguity. Combined, these phenomena have come to be known as "survivor syndrome" (Brockner, Grover, Reed, DeWitt, & O'Malley, 1987; Krantz, 1985). The emotions associated with survivor syndrome do not even include those directed toward management. The latter often include anger for favoring the interests of the shareholders over the livelihoods of the workers and distrust for breaking the implied contract of employment. If there is a sense of unfairness surrounding the decisions regarding who stays and who leaves, the emotions toward management can be especially negative. As one can conclude, the emotional toll on survivors is enormous and can weigh heavily on their morale.

Loss of expertise. Besides the emotional costs involved, there is inevitably a loss in expertise associated with downsizing. This is especially evident when downsizing efforts include voluntary forms of work force reduction. When voluntary measures are used, the organization risks losing some of its most experienced and talented employees. Downsizing attempts in the academic arena document this scenario well. Budget deficits in many states during the late 1980s and early 1990s created significant decreases in university funding. In response, schools in these states attempted to trim their payrolls by offering enhanced pension packages to faculty members as an incentive to retire early. As a result many senior professors and other faculty retired at relatively young ages, creating voids in expertise and experience. This came to be known as "brain drain," and the universities' reputations were diminished by the exodus of well-respected faculty. The universities suffered further when many of their retired faculty, who were too young to retire completely, took positions with other schools, often taking with them future research funding opportunities.

The U.S. government may experience some similar problems in its attempts at reducing the military. Many believe that the military personnel most interested in leaving voluntarily are those who have the best opportunities for employment in the private sector, and these would be the most talented individuals. There is a fear that the military's best and brightest will leave to seek what are often more lucrative jobs in industry, leaving those who are less able (or unable to find outside work) in the military. Obviously this is an extreme prediction, but it provides an example of this unanticipated cost of downsizing.

Costs of adapting. A common reason many organizations pursue downsizing strategies is to become more efficient, to get rid of excess "fat." Yet if the individuals in the organization are used to doing work in a certain way, adapting to a more efficient structure—although desirable—may be troublesome. There is typically a transition period during which the "old" way of doing things is still followed while, simultaneously, new procedures are being installed. During this transition period more is asked of surviving workers, who not only are required to perform their normal duties but are also required to make up for the work that was previously performed by eliminated workers. Additionally, training in the new procedures is often required for the surviving workers, who find themselves at the low end of a learning curve. Not only can these training costs get expensive, they may pale in comparison to the expenses incurred through losses in productivity. Because employees are faced with continuing their "old" work, doing the work of their eliminated colleagues, learning new procedures, and eventually implementing the new ways of doing their jobs, workers during the transition period can easily feel overwhelmed and inadequate to the tasks at hand. Their frustration may intensify the previously mentioned morale conundrum, which can significantly affect an individual's productivity. To compensate for this difficulty, some organizations find themselves temporarily rehiring eliminated workers as consultants to perform the work they used to do. As a result the company ends up paying someone a severance or buyout, only to turn around and pay the person contractor's fees (often higher than the previous wage) to perform the same work. In a related scenario, a company may offer an attractive buyout or severance package, prompting individuals to leave voluntarily. However, the jobs those individuals held were vital to the organization, so that the company, after paying attractive buyouts, ends up hiring new people to do the same jobs. Meanwhile, new hires entail the additional costs of recruiting, selection, and placement.

Yet another cost of downsizing frequently occurs when an organization attempts to lower overhead simply by reducing head count—an action that tends to reduce lower-level workers (support staff, secretaries, nonexempts) more than executives, managers, or professionals. Inefficiencies can result as high-wage workers are left to perform lower-wage work, such as engineers doing their own typing or managers having to wait for the copy machine.

What we have discussed are the costs of downsizing when eliminating workers is the prevailing strategy. However, a company can reduce its payroll costs by other means. In the following section we will address the costs of pursuing alternatives to downsizing.

Alternatives to Downsizing

Because the costs of eliminating employees are so significant in terms of financial expenditure, morale, productivity, reputation, and adaptability, companies may pursue other methods of reducing expenses while retaining existing employees. The following paragraphs describe these alternative means and discuss their effectiveness.

Pay cuts. Pay cuts are most frequently associated with organized labor: Union members agree to sacrifice a portion of their pay in return for a promise that no layoffs will occur. Theoretically, pay cuts allow the company to maintain consistent levels of productivity because the amount of labor does not change. There are some well-known examples of pay reduction in lieu of downsizing; for example, during the 1970s Hewlett-Packard workers agreed to pay cuts so that all workers could keep their jobs (von Werssowetz & Beer, 1985). As a result, the company believes, its morale actually increased because the employees' esprit de corps helped Hewlett-Packard weather the recession better than many of its competitors without sacrificing jobs.

Pay freezes. Pay freezes are less dramatic than pay cuts, but they have the same intent. Because workers expect to receive occasional increases in their earnings through cost-of-living adjustments or merit increases, pay freezes save money in subsequent years' payrolls. For this reason, pay freezes are a relatively slow way to accumulate payroll savings. Also, issues of equity and worth may cause employees to seek employment elsewhere.

Reduced hours. As with pay cuts and freezes, the employees bear the sacrifice of lower income. However, a reduced-hour strategy allows employees to keep their same total wages, although they work fewer hours. This approach means that total productivity for the organization will decrease because it is utilizing fewer labor hours. So, when facing declining product demand, companies may prefer reduced-hour strategies over pay cuts. Reducing hours also raises the issue of part-time versus full-time status. Many organizations have nonwage benefit packages for full-time employees only, so if reduced-hour plans go into effect, formerly full-time employees may find themselves without the benefits they previously had. One major complaint about reduced-hour plans is that they not only decrease total output because fewer hours are worked but also decrease productivity per shift. Whenever a worker begins and ends the workday, there are set-up time and take-down time. Set-up time may involve gathering materials and preparing equipment. Take-down time includes cleaning up work stations and putting tools and materials away. Suppose it takes one half-hour to set up and another half-hour to take down each day. During a typical 8-hour day, the individual actually works just 7 hours (87.5 percent of the shift) because 1 hour (12.5 percent) is spent setting up and taking down. Now, if there were a reduced-hour plan in effect with the individual only working 6-hour shifts, the individual would only work 5 hours because he or she would still need an hour to set up and take down. As a result, the ratio of productive time to total time would decrease from 87.5 percent to 83.3 percent of the shift.

Job sharing.   Similar to reduced hours, job sharing entails fewer hours, but it also necessitates the coordination of multiple workers. Imagine that a company hires two accountants but then, because of restructuring, needs only one of the positions. Rather than eliminate one of the individuals, job sharing allows both to work by sharing the responsibilities of the single job. Each worker would work fewer hours than previously, but at least both would still be employed. Job sharing also allows for flexibility in coverage. If, for example, one sharer is ill or on vacation, the other can cover for him or her during the absence.

Talent pools.   Talent pools are frequently used for clerical workers who were habitually assigned to a specific function or individual. In a talent pool the workers are not assigned to anyone or anyplace in particular; they are used on an "as needed" basis throughout the organization. The argument for talent pools is that they distribute work more evenly and eliminate the need for temporary workers.

Hiring freezes.   Hiring freezes are a way to reduce the number of employees without resorting to eliminating workers. Using ordinary attrition—or the exit rate of workers who quit, retire, or are terminated for cause under normal circumstances—the organization decreases its labor force by not filling the vacancies caused by the departures. Although a hiring freeze eliminates the need to fire workers, comparatively it is a very slow means of paring down a work force. For example, if a downsizing plan calls for a 20 percent reduction in workers and there is normally a 10 percent annual attrition rate, it would take 2 years to reach the desired employment level (assuming that attrition occurs at the targeted job functions). Additionally, if the downsizing efforts fall during slow economic periods such as the most recent trend, attrition rates tend to fall because there are fewer jobs available to workers outside their organizations. In such a case, reaching the desired employment levels would take even longer.

Outplacement services.   Outplacement services are normally associated with workers who have been dismissed in downsizing efforts, but they can be used as a means to "push" employees out of the organization. Such services commonly include job and skills training that equip displaced workers to find jobs outside the organization after they have been dismissed. However, when the services are offered to incumbent employees, the newly acquired skills could encourage them to seek employment elsewhere.

Employment contracts.   For jobs that will be necessary for a finite period after the downsizing is implemented, employment contracts are a good way of ensuring that the work gets done without committing the organization to an unnecessarily long employment relationship. At the time of downsizing, the employee agrees to continue, via a contract, with the organization for a designated period or until the work is completed. As an incentive for such employees to completely fulfill their agreements, firms often provide a bonus upon completion of a contract.

Leaves of absence. Another strategy is to offer leaves of absence at reduced or no pay with the understanding that the employee will still have a job at the end of the absence. The purpose is to encourage workers to leave the organization, at least temporarily. The time could be spent in education, travel, or pursuit of personal interests. Not surprisingly, companies that encourage educational leaves of absence may do so in the expectation that the employee may seek other employment after the additional schooling. In such cases employees resign voluntarily, saving the company the unpleasant task of dismissing them.

Transfers. Transferring workers to other parts of the company that are not experiencing downsizing is a way to reduce payroll without losing workers completely. Unfortunately, this strategy can normally accommodate only a small proportion of the displaced workers and is dependent on the staffing requirements of other business units.

Unpaid time off. The last category of alternatives is unpaid time off, where firms do not pay for vacation, sick, or personal time.

It is interesting to note that despite the many alternatives to downsizing, reducing head count is still the preeminent strategy. To illustrate, in two surveys conducted by Right Associates of over 2,000 companies, 6 percent of the firms attempted cutting pay, 9 percent shortened work weeks, and 9 percent offered vacations without pay (Cascio, 1993). In truth, eliminating employees is a much faster method and maximizes financial savings. Whereas the alternatives concentrate on payroll reductions, decreasing head count also reduces nonwage benefits (i.e., insurance, pensions, and FICA contributions). Also, work force reductions are attempts at permanent solutions; the alternatives may suggest temporary remedies, which are not the intent of downsizing. In the following section we will discuss one company's considerations in determining its downsizing strategy.

Case Study: ARCO Oil and Gas Company

Historically, one industry that was seemingly immune from economic fluctuations was the oil industry. Major oil companies were perceived to be big and profitable, the type of organization in which individuals could establish themselves in satisfying careers. The oil companies paid well, offered attractive benefits and perks, and were committed to their employees. In return oil company employees were hard-working and loyal to their companies. Some say there is a unique quality associated with oil people. Frequently they are the descendants of other oil people; they go to school to prepare for careers in the industry; and, unlike many other professionals, they spend their entire careers in a single industry—oil. They claim to have "oil running through their veins."

The ARCO Oil and Gas Company (AOGC), which is part of the Atlantic Richfield Company, typified a major oil company by participating in all aspects of the industry in the lower forty-eight states: exploration, production, and marketing of crude oil, natural gas, and natural gas liquids. AOGC was large and profitable, and it was known as an excellent place to work. Being an industry leader, it could afford to be selective in hiring new members. AOGC hired bright and dedicated young people who were expected to work hard, remain committed, and eventually retire from the organization. Working at AOGC meant a good job, good wages, and job security. Employees often referred to the organization as "Uncle ARCO," the one who would always watch out for them.

In the mid-1980s, the once-stable oil industry was thrown into turmoil by an overabundance of cheap foreign oil. The foreign oil was so cheap that domestic companies could not justify the exploration and production of crude oil. As a result, several of AOGC's internal functions were deemed unnecessary, and the company began its first-ever downsizing effort. As it did so, the initial reductions in personnel were largely voluntary, with efforts targeted primarily at those nearing retirement age. The combination of employment security and a loyal work force had provided AOGC with a large population of employees who had logged several decades of service and were fully vested in the company's pension plans. Eliminating these individuals significantly reduced AOGC's overhead and put it in a better position to compete with foreign oil. However, not all eliminations were voluntary, as the company took the opportunity to downsize in those functions and locations that were nonleveraging and least competitive. Because retirements are a time for celebration and reducing costs was a prudent business decision, AOGC survived its first downsizing effort relatively unscathed. The surviving workers remained committed, and the organization continued to prosper.

Several years later an industry analysis was conducted by an external benchmarking firm. AOGC was surprised to discover that its overhead costs, stated in terms of overhead expenses per barrel of oil, were very high, among the highest in the industry. One reason for the surprise was that AOGC's operation and leasehold expenses were, by comparison, very low. Although the company was still profitable, AOGC management recognized the need to bring its overhead costs to a more competitive level. Moreover, this was the impetus for AOGC to pursue one of the more ambitious restructuring efforts in the energy industry. AOGC owned and operated oil fields throughout the country, but it was evident that a minority of the fields were producing the majority of the oil. Therefore, AOGC decided to sell a majority of the less productive fields and concentrate on the minority of highly productive properties. With fewer properties, AOGC was left with an overstaffed headquarters in Dallas, as well as two comparably overstaffed field offices in Houston and

Midland. In order for AOGC to reduce its overhead, it had to downsize. AOGC was given a target: reducing labor costs by $35.7 million.

Downsizing in any organization is difficult, but downsizing in one that has practiced lifelong employment is especially hard to comprehend. Even though AOGC had eliminated some workers in 1986, few people were ready for the extent of downsizing that was to occur with the restructuring. Moreover, AOGC was the first big oil company to pursue such a plan, so there was no precedent within the industry. There were no examples from other firms nor lessons learned from others' experiences.

The following figures will help one realize what $35.7 million meant for AOGC at the time. In 1991 AOGC had 3,627 employees, with annual payroll costs totaling $259 million. Approximately 30 percent of the workers were hourly, with their combined incomes totaling $55 million (21.3 percent of total payroll). The average hourly worker earned $53,033 in wages and benefits per year. Of the salaried workers, 567 (16 percent of the total work force) were nonexempt from Fair Labor Standards Act wage and hour requirements, and their payroll totaled $26 million (10 percent of total payroll). On average a nonexempt salaried worker earned a total of $44,659 in salary and benefits. The remaining 2,028 workers (56 percent of the work force) were salaried and exempt from wage and hour laws. The average annual package for each such worker was $88,101, for a total of $178 million (68.7 percent of total payroll). The $35.7 million target represented nearly 14 percent of AOGC's annual payroll budget in 1991.

The human resources management function of AOGC was assigned to propose a set of alternatives for reducing payroll without necessitating layoffs. In carrying out that task, they realized that various alternatives were better suited to some employees than to others. In response they developed a two-by-two matrix that provided a template for evaluating

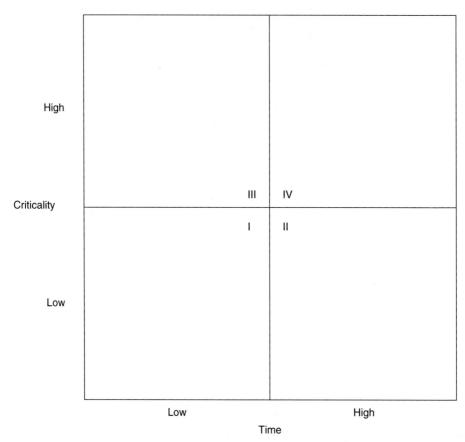

Criticality:
Individual to AOGC/ARCO; how important is it to retain the individual within AOGC and/or ARCO?

Time:
Minimal length of time the individual will be committed to the project (except in unusual cases, low is anticipated to be less than 1 year; high, more than 1 year).

Figure 1.   Alternatives: Overall Categories

the alternatives in relation to the employees. The two dimensions of the matrix were (1) individual criticality and (2) expected time commitment of the individual (see Figure 1). Each alternative approach to downsizing was seen as a project to which the affected employees would be assigned. Individual criticality asks, How important is it to retain the individual within AOGC or its parent, The Atlantic Richfield Company (ARCO)? Individ-

uals ranked high in criticality were those who had unique skills and experience, possessed a broad range of applicable business skills, possessed outstanding managerial/supervisory skills, had high potential with the organization, or would be difficult to replace. In the absence of those criteria, an employee was ranked low in criticality. The time commitment dimension was the minimal time that an individual would be committed to a project.

Anticipated high time commitment was greater than 1 year, whereas anticipated low commitment was less than 1 year.

For each of the quadrants in the matrix, a set of projects or alternatives was developed to suit the characteristics of the workers as identified by their criticality and time commitment (see Figure 2). In the following paragraphs we will describe the categories related to the quadrants and the alternatives identified as appropriate for the individuals categorized in terms of criticality and time commitment. We will also discuss the concerns AOGC had about the implementation of such projects. Many of the alternatives have been

mentioned previously in this chapter because of their familiarity in downsizing efforts, so they will not be described in further detail here. Others, however, are less common or were unique to AOGC; we will explain them as they occur.

Category I—low criticality, low time. For employees who were categorized as less vital and less suitable for a long-term commitment, AOGC identified alternatives marked by fewer hours and shared responsibility—job sharing, reduced hours, and talent pools. Also, they recognized that employment contracts would be applicable to projects in this category because of their short-term nature.

Figure 2.   Pay Cuts/Pay Freezes

For these jobs the most affected work force would be nonexempt employees. Advantages to these plans would include their limited effect on overall productivity and their allowance for flexibility to respond to work flow fluctuations. The most difficult aspect of the plans would be deciding which workers would participate. With estimates that approximately 200 employees would be involved with Category I plans in the 2-year period after implementation, AOGC projected overhead savings of $6.4 million.

Category II—low criticality, high time. Primarily focused on exempt employees, the projects in this category would partially remove individuals from AOGC, allowing them to pursue outside interests as loaned employees or with seed projects. Loaned employees are individuals who, although technically still employed, share their time with other organizations. Employees in such situations would be allowed time to work for nonprofit organizations (like the United Way's Loaned Executive Program) or other Atlantic Richfield companies. Working for a nonprofit is an expression of good corporate citizenship, and working for another ARCO company could offer good experience and provide a convenient way to split the salary. Seed projects would be for workers interested in maintaining long-term relationships with AOGC as independent contractors, but their work could be beneficial to other ARCO companies as well. The work they would perform for AOGC would be the "seed" for the future work with the other ARCO companies, and these companies could assist in paying the individuals. Concerns surrounding Category II plans focused on the difficulties of identifying the most appropriate individuals and coordinating efforts with other organizations. Also, the loaned employee program would imply that AOGC would guarantee positions for the individuals when their loan periods were completed. One other significant concern was the issue of divided loyalty that arises when someone works for more than one organization. Projected savings of Category II plans during the first 2 years of implementation were $881,000, comparable to the salaries of ten exempt workers.

Category III—high criticality, low time. Aimed at exempt workers and others with especially high potential, Category III plans were designed to allow the workers further to develop their skills, either within the parent organization as members of external task forces or outside the organization through leaves of absence. External task forces could be administered by the parent company (ARCO) to provide specialized assistance to critical projects on a short-term basis (e.g., an ARCO "SWAT Team"). ARCO and its other companies would help defray the salaries of the individuals involved. Meanwhile, the task forces could potentially save ARCO what it would otherwise spend on external consultants. Leaves of absence are frequently associated with returning to school, but this would not have to be the case. Also, a leave of absence could be either paid or unpaid, depending upon how beneficial the developmental experience would be to AOGC upon the employee's return. The advantage of Category III plans was that they would allow the retention of critical employees who could develop away from AOGC. Problems would occur if the critical employees found they preferred to work outside of AOGC. Additionally, such a plan could accommodate only a small portion of workers, and deciding who would participate could be problematic. Assuming that 100 workers would participate in the 2-year period, predicted savings for that time would be approximately $4 million.

Category IV—high criticality, high time. Category IV plans were aimed at all critical AOGC employees, who would be retained on a long-term basis. The two plans in this category involved implementing transfers and reducing labor costs through pay cuts or pay freezes. Transfers would allow critical employees to stay within the parent company while eliminating the payroll burden to AOGC. Although Category IV plans would be effective and relatively easy to implement, pay freezes and (especially) pay cuts would be unpopular among the workers. High performers who knew their worth outside of AOGC could be tempted to leave, more so than low performers. During the 2-year period of the forecasts, Category IV plans were predicted to save $13.2 million on the basis of pay cuts of 12.9 percent in the first year and 5.6 percent in the second year.

Combined, the alternative plans in the four-quadrant matrix would have saved $24.7 million during the first 2 years of implementation. To achieve the target of $35.7 million, the plans would have needed to be in effect nearly 3 years. The alternative to the matrix was to dismiss permanently 500 workers (hourly, nonexempt, and exempt) through an employee reduction plan. By all accounts the employee reduction plan was generous to the displaced employees. AOGC proposed a special termination package, which included a severance of 48 to 75 percent of a person's annual salary (depending upon years of service), 60 days' notice, extended insurance for 1 year, and outplacement assistance budgeted at $2,000 per employee. With the number of employees reduced by 500, and with the generous special termination package factored in, meeting the targeted goal of $35.7 million would have taken less than 2 years, approximately 1 year less than the alternative plans identified in the matrix.

Choosing between the matrix plan and the employee reduction plan was not an easy proposition. The matrix plan allowed for workers to keep their jobs and the company to retain the skills, abilities, and contributions of its work force while reaching the desired target in 3 years. However, implementation of such a plan would be challenging, with its success dependent upon the willingness of the employees, the parent company, and other outside organizations. Moreover, because the energy industry was relatively inexperienced in the implementation of such strategies, the level of uncertainty was high.

A work force reduction, in contrast, would be easier to implement because it would re-quire less coordination with other entities. Savings would be achieved 1 year sooner. Unfortunately, it would introduce to AOGC the unpleasant reality that lifetime employment security would no longer be fully implied. There were uncertainties with this plan as well, mostly related to how the organization would decide which employees would stay and which would be asked to leave. Also, no one could predict the effects of downsizing on the surviving employees and their job performance. Everyone knew that restructuring was inevitable, yet there were few actual blueprints detailing how the new AOGC would look.

AOGC's decision was to pursue the employment reduction plan. Because it was divesting so many of its properties, permanent reduction of the work force was the most feasible alternative. In deciding which employees to keep, AOGC aimed at retaining only those who would be best suited to the restructured environment. Therefore, the decisions were based on merit, which is typically the least objective (and thus most problematic) criterion for retaining employees. Interestingly, because the company wanted to make decisions based on future performance in a downsized organization, AOGC felt that old performance evaluations would need to be enhanced by the addition of supplemental predictors. AOGC identified two additional criteria that they felt would best predict future success in the restructured organization: (1) the ability to adapt to change and (2) the ability to work well with others and in teams. Other criteria such as general competence and technical expertise were assumed because everyone had shown these traits previously. After all, the company had deliberately hired the best people and had previously eliminated the workers whose skills were unnecessary.

Faced with such a difficult task and having no formal documentation or resources, AOGC took an innovative approach in deciding who the best workers would be in the post-downsizing organization. Senior and middle-level managers met outside of AOGC's offices to discuss every employee who might be affected by the downsizing. Each employee was known through direct interaction to at least one of the managers present at the decision meetings. The managers discussed their interactions and their evaluations of every employee, eventually deciding who would be most valuable to the organization. Although the exercise was seemingly highly subjective, the multiple input and consensual decision-making process provided equitable representation for each employee. Although the meetings were long and laborious and the decisions were difficult, the organization believes that this was the best way to select accurately and fairly those who would best contribute to AOGC in the future.

Conclusion

Few organizational strategies are as difficult and painful to implement as downsizing. Nevertheless, the strategy has become the prevalent antidote to gluttonous past expansion and recessionary times. Ironically, downsizing seems to contradict the business paradigm in which growth equals success. In this article we have defined the strategy and tried to explain why our knowledge in this area is still relatively limited. Additionally, we have identified different approaches for implementing downsizing attempts as well as alternatives to downsizing. The ARCO Oil and Gas case study provides some insights into one organization's decision whether to pursue downsizing or pursue alternative methods of reducing payroll. As evidenced by its popularity, downsizing is now perceived as a legitimate business practice. Companies are finding it increasingly necessary to maintain their competitive positioning by becoming leaner and quicker to react. Unfortunately, bureaucratic corporate institutions have difficulties making these changes without getting smaller—what Tom Peters calls "disorganizing." Therefore, companies will continue to downsize at a frenzied pace. What will eventually separate the successful companies from the unsuccessful ones will not be their decision to downsize. Instead it will be their ability to implement such a strategy effectively.

References

Bolt, J. F. (1985). Job security: Its time has come. In M. Beer & B. Spector (Eds.), *Readings in human resource management* (pp. 288–301). New York: Free Press.

Brockner, J., Grover, S., Reed, T., DeWitt, R., & O'Malley, M. (1987). Survivors' reactions to layoffs: We get by with a little help for our friends. *Administrative Science Quarterly, 32,* 526–541.

Bukro, R. (1993, October 13). WMX letter warns of streamlining possible job cuts. *The Chicago Tribune,* p. 3.

Cameron, K. S., Mishra, A., & Freeman, S. (1992). Organizational downsizing. In G. P. Huber & W. H. Glick (Eds.), *Organizational change and redesign.* New York: Oxford University Press.

Cascio, W. F. (1993). Downsizing: What do we know? What have we learned? *The Academy of Management Executive, 7(1),* 95–104.

Cook, D. S., & Ferris, G. R. (1986). Strategic human resource management and firm effectiveness in industries experiencing decline. *Human Resource Management, 25(3),* 441–458.

Ferris, G. R., Schellenberg, D. A., & Zammuto, R. F. (1984). Human resource management in declining industries. *Human Resource Management, 23(4),* 381–394.

Krantz, J. (1985). Group process under conditions of organizational decline. *Journal of Applied Behavioral Science, 21(1),* 1–17.

Lengnick-Hall, C. A., & Lengnick-Hall, M. L. (1988). Strategic human resources management: A review of the literature and a proposed typology. *Academy of Management Review, 13(3),* 454–470.

Perry, L. T. (1984). Key human resource strategies in an organization downturn. *Human Resource Management, 23(1),* 61–75.

Peters, T. (1992). *Liberation management: Necessary disorganization for the nanosecond nineties.* New York: Knopf.

Price, R. H., & D'Aunno, T. (1983). Managing work force reduction. *Human Resource Management, 22(4),* 413–430.

Ropp, K. (1987, February). Downsizing strategies. *Personnel Administrator,* pp. 61–64.

Schuler, R. S., & Jackson, S. E. (1987). Linking competitive strategies with human resource management practices. *The Academy of Management Executive, 1(3),* 207–219.

Strom, S. (1992, September 19). Hartmarx rids itself of retail unit. *The New York Times,* pp. 1, 3.

Uchitelle, L. (1993, July 26). Strong companies are joining trend to eliminate jobs. *The New York Times,* p. 1.

von Werssowetz, R. O., & Beer, M. (1985). Human resources at Hewlett-Packard. In M. Beer, B. Spector, P. Lawrence, D. Q. Mills, & R. E. Walton (Eds.), *Human resource management: A general manager's perspective* (pp. 711–747). New York: Free Press.

Whyte, W. H. (1956). *The organization man.* New York: Simon and Schuster.

PART 3

Functions of Human Resources Management

There are myriad activities with which human resources professionals need to be concerned. Managers confront and address these tasks on an ongoing basis. The effectiveness with which these tasks are accomplished can be translated directly into human resources effectiveness. Although many of these tasks are considered mundane and pedestrian, failure to accomplish them may result in great ineffectiveness from an organizational standpoint. Part 3 is directly concerned with the building blocks of organizational success that are the basis of the human resources functions. Successful managers cannot afford to ignore these foundations of human resources.

To reduce the impact of a dynamic environment on the human resources function, organizations need to collect information that will reduce ambiguity and facilitate the planning and staffing process. The articles in Chapter 6 indicate the necessity for extensive awareness of both individual and organizational needs. These needs must be integrated in such a way that they do not conflict. People (and organizations) don't plan to fail—they just fail to plan.

Individuals must be told where they stand in relation to the quality that managers expect. This is accomplished through appraisal. The articles in Chapter 7 outline the problems that pervade performance appraisal. The solutions that the authors suggest are valuable for helping to improve employees' understanding of their performance and their potential for improvement.

Once planning and staffing have occurred and performance appraisal procedures have been developed, a system of compensation must be implemented. The articles in Chapter 8 concern the myriad issues surrounding compensation. Compensation must be directly tied to organizational strategy and should be closely linked to the quality of individual performance.

Organizations have realized that they best serve their constituents through continuous training that builds the skills of the existing work force. Chapter 9 addresses the issues related to training and development of the work force. The authors point out that training is directly related to and a function of an organization's strategy.

CHAPTER 6

Human Resources Planning and Staffing

Personnel and human resources management is often viewed as a series of activities designed to process people into, through, and out of organizations. In this view, the first activity is human resources planning. Human resources planning seeks to determine the number and kinds of people the organization needs now and may need in the foreseeable future and seeks ways to satisfy those needs—perhaps even to anticipate them. With the growing interest in strategic human resources management and its link to strategic business planning, we will probably see attempts at more systematic human resources planning in the future.

The link between human resources planning and strategic business planning is important because, in the development of an informed forecast of the firm's human resources needs, it is necessary to have input concerning the direction the organization will be taking in the future: whether growth or decline is projected, what types of skills will be required, and so forth. It is also important to consider the current and potential availability or supply of human resources skills in the organization and the marketplace. Organizations establish human resources information systems to help keep track of such matters. Timely and accurate human resources information may, for example, enable an organization to postpone or implement a variety of recruitment and training activities or to capitalize on the availability of a given mix of skills to pursue a new venture.

Within a broader, more integrated view of the personnel function, career planning and development activities in organizations represent a logical component of human resources planning. Making sure that the right people with the right skills are at the right place at the right time is quite consistent with helping people plan their careers in organizations and establishing routes to take and time frames to meet.

The process of entry into the organization involves both recruitment and selection. Recruitment concerns itself with attracting as large a qualified pool of candidates as possible to apply for the organization's available openings. Selection then involves making the fine distinctions necessary to better match job requirements with personal skills and abilities.

A number of different personnel screening tools aid the organizational entry process. Despite its recognized lack of objectivity and validity, nearly every organization employs the interview in some phase of the entry process. Because it is unlikely that we will see a decline in the use of the interview, we need new ways to make it a more effective decision-making tool. Conducting multiple interviews or a structured interview, or using the interview only for evaluating the characteristics that it is good at measuring, might lead to improvement. Other selection devices include personnel tests, reference checks, weighted application blanks, and simulations or work samples.

The first section of this chapter is concerned with human resources information and planning issues. The first article, contributed by Veres, Locklear, Sims, and Prewett, reviews one of the most important pieces of organizational information, that collected through a job analysis. This article offers a current example of a methodology used to implement a job analysis system in the context of the legal requirements of any such system. Jackson and Schuler, in the next article, outline ways to use information for the purpose of developing human resources planning that is in line with organizational strategies. They make a strong case for the pivotal nature of human resources planning.

The second section of this chapter is an analysis of succession and mobility issues. In the first article Borwick presents eight criteria for determining whether an organization has an effective succession plan. In the other article in this section, Ferris, Buckley, and Allen report the results of a survey of the promotion practices used in a number of national organizations. Their analysis provides insight into the organizationally desired characteristics possessed by those competing for promotions.

Recruitment and selection is the topic of the last section of this chapter. Because these topics cover a multitude of issues, the selections in this section are quite diverse. In the first article Kolenko shatters a number of myths about the college recruiting process. Students and potential employees entertain a number of myths that are barriers to more effective recruiting at this level. An understanding of these myths may lead to better-prepared students and employers. Buckley and Eder analyze the interview process. Although the overwhelming majority of employers use interviews, few have appropriate expectations regarding interviews or knowledge of the most effective way to conduct them. Judge and Ferris expand upon this topic in terms of the difficulty of using the notion of organizational fit in the selection process. They further point out that we use a flawed process to gather data on a fit criterion that is not well developed. In the last article in this section, Solomon points out that employers should use job-specific tests that have no between-groups differences. She suggests that tests of written and verbal aptitude as well as personality and achievement tests may not yield reliable information when used with diverse groups.

Suggestions for Further Reading

Camuffo, A. (1993). Strategic human resource management—Italian style. *Sloan Management Review, 34,* 59–67.

Chiaramonte, P. (1993, Autumn). Coaching for high performance. *Business Quarterly,* pp. 81–87.

Eisenstat, R. (1993). Implementing strategy: Developing a partnership for change. *Planning Review, 21,* 33–36.

Greengard, S. (1993). How technology is advancing HR. *Personnel Journal, 72,* 80–90.

Herren, L. (1989). The new game of HR: Playing to win. *Personnel, 66,* 18–22.

Joseph, J. (1993, Autumn). Harnessing human resource technologies. *Business Quarterly,* pp. 71–75.

Overman, S. (1993, September). Under HR umbrella, career development pays dividends. *HR Magazine,* pp. 67–68.

Paul, R., & Townsend, J. (1993). Managing the older worker—Don't just rinse away the gray. *Executive, 7,* 67–74.

Peters, S. (1993). Word-of-mouth recruitment can be risky. *Personnel Journal, 72,* 92–93.

Wessel, J. (1993). The strategic human resource management process in practice. *Planning Review, 21,* 37–38.

Job Analysis in Human Resource Management Practice

John G. Veres III, Toni S. Locklear, Ronald R. Sims,
and Amelia J. Prewett

What is job analysis? Gatewood and Feild (1994) observed that there are probably as many different definitions of job analysis as there are writings on the topic. They suggested a definition that views job analysis as "a purposeful, systematic process for collecting information on the important work-related aspects of a job" (p. 285). Others have characterized job analysis as the collection and analysis of just about any type of job-related information by almost any method for any purpose (Tiffin & McCormick, 1965). One researcher has given us a definition bordering on the metaphysical, characterizing job analysis as a way to analyze reality (Levine, 1983). We prefer a definition that views job analysis as a systematic process for collecting, analyzing, and interpreting job-related information. The goal of this chapter is to get some handle on what is meant by job analysis and how we can use it.

Part of the problem in defining job analysis stems from a difficulty we have with the term *job*. Most of us seem to mean something fairly specific when we talk about a job. Ordinarily, we mean *the* job that we do on a day-to-day basis—the thing that results in a paycheck.

Experts in human resource management (HRM) do not use the term in the same way. The thing a given individual does is usually referred to as a *position* (Prien & Ronan, 1971). Position has been defined as a "group of related job functions performed by a single person . . . because each position is staffed by an unique person, it is different from any other position, even those bearing the same job title in the organization" (Lopez, 1988, p. 881). A job can then be defined as "a group of posi-

tions whose functions are so similar that their satisfactory performance requires an identical set of incumbent traits" (Lopez, 1988, p. 881). It is important to make this distinction because, to understand what is meant by job analysis, we must first understand that HRM specialists are talking about groups of positions whenever they use the term *job;* rarely are they talking about what one person does.

When we use the term *analysis,* most of us mean the separation of a whole into its component parts with the intent to examine and interpret those parts. Similarly, HRM specialists describe what is done in a job analysis as breaking down the component parts of a job so that we can achieve some better understanding of it. Bemis, Belenky, and Soder (1983) describe job analysis as "a systematic procedure for gathering, documenting and analyzing information about three basic aspects of a job: job content, job requirements, and the context in which the job is performed" (pp. 1–2).

Job content identifies and describes the activities of the job. Depending upon the particular job analysis method used, descriptions of job content may range from general statements of job activities through detailed descriptions of duties and tasks, or from more detailed statements of the steps or elements involved in a particular process to descriptions of motions needed to perform an activity.

In the past *job requirements* have included factors such as years of education and experience, degrees, licenses, and so forth—credentials assumed to be evidence that an individual possesses the qualifications for successful job performance. A more modern view of job requirements identifies the skills, abilities, areas of knowledge, and physical and other characteristics that a person must possess to perform the content of the job in a particular situation or context.

The *context* in which a job is performed generally includes factors such as its purpose, the degree of accountability or responsibility of the employee, the availability of guidelines, the extent of supervision received and/or exercised, the potential consequences of error, and the physical demands and working conditions of the job.

This definition is but one of many attempts to categorize the component parts of a job. Job analysis may be thought of as a process that attempts to reduce to words the things that people do in the world of work (Ash, 1988). The components into which the job is divided and the words that serve as labels for those components vary from one job analysis system to another. There are many different ways of analyzing jobs and many different uses for the information resulting from job analyses. As we shall see in the following sections, many researchers have adopted a variety of approaches for structuring information about jobs. Before we describe these approaches, it is important to think about why we should worry about conducting job analyses in the first place.

Why Conduct Job Analysis?

Job analysis has been described as a fundamental starting point for human resource management (Ghorpade & Atchison, 1980). Two major forces have contributed to this lofty description: competition and equal employment opportunity concerns (Holley & Jennings, 1983). Employers in the United States, faced with increased foreign and domestic competition, have a considerable interest in ensuring that their employees are working efficiently. Technology continually changes the way in which U.S. workers perform their jobs. Eliminating jobs that are no

longer necessary can streamline organizational functioning. Jobs that have changed in response to new technology create a somewhat different problem. Employers must find individuals with the requisite knowledge, skills, and abilities to perform adequately the activities required. Job analysis provides information that can help identify these individuals and thus ensure a competent pool of talent to an organization.

Bemis et al. (1983) have summarized ways in which job analysis information can be used in each phase of the human resource management cycle. Their list, which appears as Figure 1, includes job design, job classification and evaluation, recruitment, selection, training, performance appraisal, and performance management. Other researchers have categorized the application of job analysis techniques somewhat differently. Ash and Levine (1980) identified the following six major uses of job analysis information that contribute significantly to the organizational function:

1. Job description
2. Job requirements/specifications
3. Job classification
4. Job evaluation
5. Job design/restructuring
6. Performance appraisal

Major Uses of Job Analysis Information

Job description.   A job description is an account of the duties and activities associated with a particular job. Its purpose is to identify a job, define that job within established limits, and describe its content (Gael, 1988b). The job description is typically a one- or two-page summary of the basic tasks performed on a job and constitutes the role expectations relative to that job (French, 1982). Job descriptions have a number of important uses including development of job specifications, work force planning and recruitment, orientation of new employees, and development of performance appraisal systems.

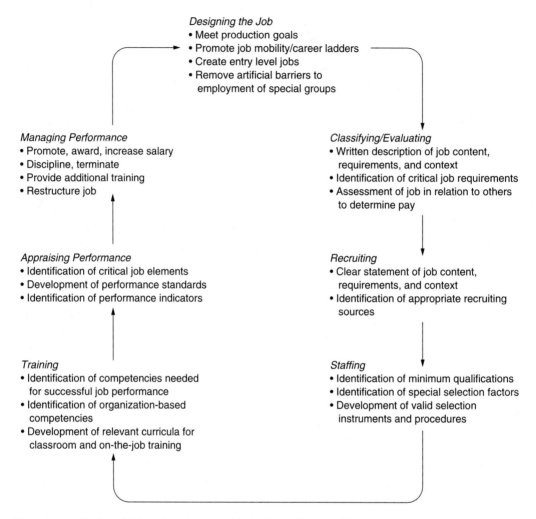

Figure 1. Applications of Job-Analysis Data. (Reprinted with permission "Exhibit 1, The Human Resource Management Cycle: Application of Job Analysis Data", from *Job Analysis: An Effective Management Tool,* by Stephen E. Bemis, Ann Holt Belenky, and Dee Ann Soder. Copyright ©1983 by The Bureau of National Affairs, Inc., Washington, DC 20037.)

Job specifications. Job specifications describe the characteristics needed to perform the job activities identified in the job description. They focus on the individuals doing the job rather than on the work itself. Job specifications may include information regarding the knowledge, skills, and abilities required to perform the job, as well as such items as the education, experience, and physical attributes needed for successful accomplishment of job tasks (Wernimont, 1988). Job specifications allow HRM specialists to identify persons with the skills they seek and help target efforts to recruit them.

Job classification and job evaluation. HRM specialists often mention job classification and job evaluation in the same breath. Classification means grouping similar positions into job classes and grouping job classes into job families. There are several good reasons to group jobs. One is simplicity. If HRM specialists (and managers) had to deal with each position individually, the sheer volume of paperwork would be overwhelming. Grouping positions into job classifications allows HRM specialists to deal with personnel functions at a more general level. One of the personnel functions that can be handled at this level is pay. Individuals employed in a particular job classification typically receive salaries within the pay range established for that classification.

The process of assigning a value (and a salary) to a given job classification is called job evaluation. There are two basic approaches to job evaluation. One involves comparing the target organization's pay practices to those of other organizations. This approach is often referred to as the market pricing method. The second approach involves rating jobs on the basis of factors that indicate the relative worth of different jobs within the organization. This approach has been called the factor comparison or point factor method. Both methods rely heavily on job analysis data.

Suppose that we want to apply the market pricing method. To compare our jobs to those in other organizations, we must be sure that our jobs are indeed comparable to the ones selected for comparison. Job analysis information on both jobs assures us that they are comparable. Next, suppose that we want to use the factor comparison method. Assessing the relative worth of jobs means analyzing them on a common set of criteria such as know-how, problem solving, accountability, working conditions, and complexity (Hay & Purves, 1954; U.S. Civil Service Commission, 1977). The factors selected for comparison may vary, but job analysis remains a foundation for job evaluation.

Job design.   Another use for job analysis data concerns the design of jobs. From the organization's viewpoint, jobs as performed must lead to efficient operations, quality products, and well-maintained equipment. From the workers' viewpoint, jobs must be meaningful and challenging, provide feedback on performance, and call on their decision-making skills (Davis & Wacker, 1988). HRM specialists design jobs that attempt to meet the needs of both employers and employees. Efficient job design allows organizations to take full advantage of technological breakthroughs without alienating the workers affected by change. Restructuring jobs allows companies to retain skilled workers while enhancing output.

Performance appraisal.   Finally, job analysis information is used to create performance appraisal instruments to evaluate employee performance. Job analysis identifies the "what" of evaluation: what activities should be assessed, what knowledge should be appraised, what organizational issues (i.e. tardiness, absenteeism) should be evaluated. Job analysis information can then determine the weights assigned to particular aspects of the job in order of importance (Bernardin & Beatty, 1984). The proper use of job analysis ensures that the appraisal instrument assesses what is *actually* being done on the job. A good match between the job and the performance appraisal assessment not only should improve organizational efficiency but should also enhance employee perceptions of fairness in the appraisal system. Performance evaluations not based on solid job analysis information risk being irrelevant to job performance and consequently demotivating employees.

The aforementioned uses for job analysis data represent only the tip of the iceberg in terms of organizational functions. For example, job analysis information forms the basis for assessment of training needs (Goldstein, 1993), which is an area of increasing importance in our changing environment. One recent publication on job analysis contains no fewer than sixteen chapters devoted to different applications of job analysis in organization administration and human resource management (Gael, 1988a). The uses of job analysis are many and can contribute substantially to an organization's competitiveness. As noted earlier, however, competition is not the only force acting to increase the importance of job analysis to business and industry.

Equal Employment Opportunity and Job Analysis

Despite the tremendous positive impact of job analysis on organizational functioning, perhaps the most profound factor increasing the use of job analysis techniques is equal employment opportunity legislation. Title VII of the Civil Rights Act of 1964, as amended; the Equal Pay Act of 1963; the Age Discrimination in Employment Act of 1967, as amended; the Americans with Disabilities Act of 1990; and other laws passed over the last 25 years have served to increase dramatically the use of job analysis as an integral part of establishing the job relatedness of employment practices. The large number of court cases involving allegations of employment discrimination has been highly instrumental in enhancing the importance of job analysis. One judge noted the following in an employment test validation case:

> The cornerstone of the construction of a content valid examination [an examination based on qualifications really needed in the job] is the job analysis. Without such an analysis to single out the critical knowledge, skills, and abilities required by the job, their importance to each other, and the level of proficiency demanded as to each attribute, a test constructor is aiming in the dark and can only hope to achieve job-relatedness by blind luck. (*Kirkland v. New York Department of Corrections,* 1974.)

It is hard to imagine a stronger endorsement of job analysis, particularly when we consider that the judge's words have the force of law.

In 1978 the federal agencies charged with enforcing equal employment opportunity laws issued the Uniform Guidelines on Employee Selection Procedures (Equal Employment Opportunity Commission, Civil Service Commission, Department of Labor, & Department of Justice, 1978), which confirm the place of job analysis as a fundamental prerequisite for proving employment practices to be free of discrimination (Holley & Jennings, 1983). The Guidelines make the following statement:

> There should be a job analysis which includes an analysis of the important work behavior(s) required for successful performance and their relative importance and, if the behavior results in work product(s), an analysis of work product(s). Any job analysis should focus on the work behavior(s) and the tasks associated with them. If work behavior(s) are not observable, the job analysis should identify and analyze those aspects of the behavior(s) that can be observed and the observed work product(s). The work behavior(s) selected for measurement should be critical work behavior(s) and/or important work behavior(s) constituting most of the job. (p. 38302)

The principle that job analysis should precede any HRM practice is thus well established in the federal Guidelines.

The courts have worked to define further the role of job analysis in demonstrating job relatedness. Thompson and Thompson (1982) reviewed a number of employment discrimination lawsuits to determine the criteria the federal courts use in assessing job analysis in the context of selection tests. The following were among their conclusions:

- Expert job analysts must perform the job analysis.
- The results of the analysis should be reduced to written form.
- The job analysis process employed must be described in detail.
- Data should be collected from a variety of sources (i.e., incumbents, supervisors, job experts).
- Information on tasks performed must be included in the job analysis.
- Knowledge, skills, and abilities should be clearly specified and must be operationally defined in terms of work performed.

More recently, Buckner (1989) reviewed 185 court cases from 1979 through 1987 dealing with hiring, promotion, reclassification, and training issues. Among her findings for content-related validation (job-relatedness) studies were that courts generally ruled for employers when the following conditions existed:

- Job content was well defined.
- Work behaviors were defined in behavioral terms.
- KSAs (knowledge, skills, and abilities) were operationally defined.
- Subject matter experts (i.e., incumbents and/or supervisors) rated KSA importance.

These findings, taken together with the Thompson and Thompson (1982) results and the language in the federal Uniform Guidelines, present a clear picture of the importance of job analysis in this context. The passage in 1990 of the Americans with Disabilities Act, discussed later in more detail, focused even more attention on job analysis outcomes. So long as equal employment opportunity laws remain on the books, job analysis is here to stay.

Collecting Job Data

As mentioned previously, job analysis is a systematic process for collecting, analyzing, and interpreting job-related information. Information involving job content, work method and approach, and expected outcome is collected and analyzed. In addition, the knowledge, skills, and abilities that workers need in order to perform their jobs may also be identified and analyzed. The individuals who collect, analyze, and interpret job data are generally referred to as job analysts. Although there is no such thing as a typical job analyst, preferred analysts are internal HRM specialists or external consultants trained to conduct job analysis. Sims and Veres (1985) and Siegel (1987) have emphasized the importance of training job analysts and made specific recommendations on a desired curriculum.

Sources of Data

In performing a comprehensive job survey, a job analyst may consult many diverse sources. Among these sources are documents such as technical manuals, organization studies, and training materials. Additional sources of information are job incumbents, supervisors, managers, engineers, and technical experts who provide information about the jobs being studied. The term *job agent* is generally used to refer to an individual who provides or collects the desired job information. In addition, the term *subject matter expert (SME)* is sometimes used to refer to a job agent who is familiar with the target job or possesses special expertise that is relevant to job activities. There are three classes of job agents typically employed to collect job analysis information: (1) job analysts, (2) job incumbents, and (3) job supervisors (McCormick, 1979).

Job analysts. Job analysts are specially trained individuals whose mission it is to collect and process job information. Formally trained job analysts should require less orientation to the job under study and less time to analyze it because they are already well versed in the method of job analysis being used (Gatewood & Feild, 1994). Gatewood and Feild also point out that job analysts should provide more objective, reliable, and accurate job data. However, there are some drawbacks associated with their use as job agents. Certain nuances and subtleties of a job may escape them because job analysts are less familiar with specific jobs than are incumbents or supervisors. Job analysts may rely on preexisting stereotypes of job content, particularly when they have prior experience with particular jobs or when commonly held jobs are studied (Harvey, 1991).

Job incumbents. An employee who performs a job should generally be in the best position to describe it. Incumbents are often best able to detail "what is *actually* done, rather than what *should* be done" (Gatewood & Feild, 1987, p. 187). Large numbers of employees may be available, allowing the job analyst to obtain differing perspectives on a given job. However, it should be noted that incumbents may have a vested interest in not portraying their jobs accurately. They may paint an inflated picture of their jobs if they believe it beneficial to do so (McCormick, 1979; Smith & Hakel, 1979). Another concern in using incumbents is adequacy of verbal skills because they must convey their impressions to job analysts in written or oral form.

Job supervisors.   Individuals who supervise incumbents performing the job under study can provide accurate job data because they observe the work being performed. Gatewood and Feild (1994) note that supervisory assessments assume that supervisors have worked closely enough with incumbents to possess "complete information about employees' jobs," an assumption that may not be correct. Researchers have observed a tendency for supervisors to describe subordinates' jobs on the basis of what *should* be done rather than what has been done in actuality (Sparks, 1979, 1981). Despite this limitation, supervisors *can* provide the analyst with an additional perspective on a given job. This perspective can be especially important when incumbents have limited verbal skills.

Cornelius (1988) reviewed the research pertaining to the choice of job agent and summarized that literature, with the following conclusion:

1. Supervisors and subordinates agree more about the tasks performed than they do about the personal characteristics necessary for job performance.
2. Incumbents and supervisors may provide higher ratings than analysts on job elements that are high in social desirability.
3. Supervisors and incumbents attach different meanings to various descriptions of work and may organize work activities differently.
4. Trained observers (i.e., job analysts) can give similar estimates of job characteristics.

Cornelius recommends that supervisors and subordinates be used to collect data on job ac-

tivities and that trained job analysts be used to collect data regarding the knowledge, skills, abilities, or other characteristics necessary to perform the job. Moreover, he suggests that the tendency of supervisors and incumbents to inflate their ratings of job characteristics high in social desirability prohibits their use as job agents in situations where job analysis data will be used in certain decisions (for example, salary decisions).

Although job incumbents and supervisors are typically the prime source of job analysis data, a good analyst will consult with multiple sources to collect the information he or she needs to understand the job in question and to complete the job analysis (Bemis et al., 1983). In choosing the sources of job data, a job analyst should be familiar with the research on the optimum source for obtaining job data. In cases in which job processes are extremely complex, it may be wise to add technical experts (e.g. production engineers, scientists) as job agents.

Data Collection Techniques

Not surprisingly, numerous techniques exist for collecting job information. HRM specialists tend to prefer different approaches in different situations. Jobs with substantial physical demands require different data collection techniques than those that call primarily on mental skills. Some jobs entail extensive documentation of task completion in the form of detailed paper trails, whereas others do not. Job characteristics play an important role in the selection of a specific technique. Some job analysis techniques include background research, performance of the job, site observations, individual interviews, group interviews, and job analysis questionnaires.

Background research.   Background research involves a review of job-relevant documents; it should be the first step in any job analysis process. Initially, the analyst should review the job analysis literature to identify previous job analyses or studies of the job in question. Literature might include the *Dictio-*

nary of Occupational Titles (U.S. Department of Labor, 1977); volume two of Sidney Gael's *Job Analysis Handbook for Business, Industry, and Government* (1988a); and professional publications such as the *Journal of Applied Psychology, Personnel Psychology,* and *Public Personnel Management.* This initial research serves to familiarize the analyst with the data collection and analytic techniques used by others, the problems they encountered, and their results (Gatewood & Feild, 1994). Familiarity with past research helps the analyst choose the most effective techniques for the analysis effort. The review of the professional literature should be followed by an examination of organization documents such as existing job descriptions, technical manuals, training materials, organization charts, and previous job analyses.

Job performance.   Performing the job may be an effective data collection technique when the job involves primarily either physical operations that can be learned readily or psychomotor skills. Performance-related data may prove very useful in cases where no substitute exists for actually performing the job. Equipment operation that demands hand-eye coordination or fine motor skills may require performing the task for full understanding. Generally, however, because of time constraints it is more efficient to rely on observation or interview techniques than to expend effort in training an analyst to perform the job.

Site observations.   Visiting incumbents at their work sites allows the job analyst to observe the specifics of task performance and determine the degree to which tasks are interrelated. Direct observation familiarizes the job analyst with the materials and equipment used on the job, the conditions under which work is performed, and the factors that trigger the performance of a given task. To minimize distortion, the analyst should explain the reasons for the visit and take care to be unobtrusive. Future job analysts should note that site observations may not be appropriate for jobs that involve primarily mental tasks, such as those of upper-level managers.

Individual interviews.   The interview is probably the most commonly used technique for collecting job data (Cascio, 1987; Van De Voort & Stalder, 1988). The job analyst questions experienced job incumbents or supervisors to determine the tasks that are performed on the job as well as the requirements workers must meet to carry out those tasks. Interviews may be structured or unstructured. However, structure is usually desirable to ensure that the analyst obtains the needed information. Interviews are sometimes conducted concurrently with the site visit so that the performance of job activities can be observed and discussed simultaneously.

Group interviews.   In the group interview technique, subject matter experts are convened to discuss the job in question. Typically, job incumbents or supervisors serve as subject matter experts. However, technical experts (such as design engineers or top management) are used to identify tasks when a new job is being created or an existing one updated. Like individual interviews, group sessions may be structured or unstructured. Typically, the job analyst directs the session and imposes structure upon the discussion to elicit the necessary information in the desired format.

Questionnaires.   A questionnaire presents a list of items that are assumed to be job related and asks subject matter experts to rate each item on its relevance to the job under study. SMEs identify, among the tasks listed on the inventory, the ones that job incumbents perform, and they rate each task on factors such as the importance to successful job performance and the frequency with which the task is performed. In addition, some questionnaires also require SMEs to identify the knowledge, skills, and abilities required for the job and to rate discrete KSAs on factors such as their importance to acceptable job performance and the extent to which their possession distinguishes between superior and adequate job performance. A commercially available questionnaire may be used, or one may be tailored to fit the job of interest. The items on tailor-made questionnaires can be developed on the basis of information derived from background research, job performance, site observations, individual interviews, or group interviews.

Job Analysis Methods

Job analysts commonly combine methods of data collection to achieve a comprehensive picture of the job under study. Most approaches to job analysis mix and match various job data sources and data collection techniques. The job analysis methods presented in this section offer systematic ways of formally applying the data collection techniques. By *formal* we mean that the data collection procedure, as well as the organization of the end product, is standardized. For example, in the individual interview, the job analyst is consistent in the questions asked of different subject matter experts. Furthermore, the data that emerges from the interview is generally structured into precise job statements that would be understandable to someone unfamiliar with the job. By *systematic* we mean that data collection techniques proceed in a set pattern. For example, several current approaches to job analysis progress from background research to individual interviews or observation, group interviews, and ultimately questionnaire administration.

As we have noted, a variety of systems have evolved for conducting job analyses and collecting job-related information. Not surprisingly, several systems for classifying job analysis methodology have also been suggested (e.g., Harvey, 1991). We have adopted the approach most commonly encountered—the distinction between *work-oriented* and *worker-oriented* methods. Work-oriented job analysis focuses on a description of the work activities performed on a job. Emphasis is on what is accomplished, including a description

of the tasks undertaken and the products or outcomes of those tasks. For example, a work-oriented analysis of a secretarial position might generate observable tasks such as "types letters" or "files documents." Other names for this approach include *task-oriented* and *activity-based* job analysis.

Worker-oriented analyses tend to examine the attributes or characteristics the worker must possess to perform job tasks. The primary products of work-oriented methods are the KSAs and other characteristics required for effective job performance. A worker-oriented analysis of a secretarial position might generate worker characteristics such as "skill in typing" or "knowledge of the organization's filing system." Until recently, worker-oriented approaches dominated the field to the extent that one writer, in a 1976 publication, described worker-oriented methods as "conventional job analysis procedures" (McCormick, 1976). Before we discuss the relative pros and cons of each approach, it may be beneficial to describe examples of each in a bit more detail.

Work-Oriented Approaches

Functional job analysis. Functional Job Analysis (FJA) (Fine & Wiley, 1971) provides an approach that takes into consideration the organization, its people, and its work. The FJA approach employs three data collection techniques, including a review by trained analysts of background and reference materials, interviews with employees and their supervisors, and on-site observations of employees. From this data collection, the purpose, goals, and objectives of the organization are identified. Once analysts have gained an understanding of the organization's work system, they develop task statements in consultation with SMEs. To ensure validity and reliability, analysts edit the task statements with the guidance of incumbents, supervisors, and other subject matter experts. From the task statements, worker functions are identified, primarily through inferences made by analysts. Finally, FJA attempts to place the individual job clearly in the context of the whole organization by focusing on the results of task performance and the way those results contribute to the attainment of organizational goals and objectives. Because FJA provides a means for assessing the level of each task by describing the employee's required level of involvement with other factors on the job, Fine, Holt, and Hutchinson (1974) recommended it for a broad range of applications.

The two most prominent features of FJA are its formal task statements and worker function scales. FJA's task statements include information on a variety of factors. Fine's (1988) illustration of an FJA task statement may prove instructive.

Behavior/Action is	-types/transcribes
Object of Action is	-form letter
Source of	-"standard" and
Information is	"information from records provided"
Nature of	-"standard form letter"
Instruction is	-"specified information"
	-"following SOP (Standard Operating Procedure) for form letter, but adjusting standard form as required for clarity and smoothness"
Machines, etc.	-typewriter and related desk equipment
Result	-letter for mailing
	(p. 1022)

The second feature, worker function scales, is probably the most widely applied of the two because of its adoption in the *Dictionary of Occupational Titles* published by the U.S. Department of Labor (1977). The worker function scales identify differing levels of complexity in three areas of task performance: things, data, and people. Tasks are assessed as to the degree of complexity involved in each of the three areas.

FJA is an important job analysis system in its own right. However, it is also important for its influence on subsequent systems. A careful review of a number of the methods described

in subsequent sections will reveal FJA concepts and techniques that other researchers have incorporated into their searches for the best job analysis approach.

Critical incidents technique.   Developed by John Flanagan (1954), the critical incidents technique (CIT) for job analysis relies on information from supervisors and others who are in a position to observe job behavior. Supervisors are asked to identify and classify those behaviors (critical incidents) that result in effective or ineffective job performance. Examples of particularly successful and unsuccessful job performance are used as guides for future performance. Critical incidents represent a high level of behavioral detail, focusing on the action of the worker, the context in which the behavior occurs, and the consequences of the behavior. CIT is widely applied in performance appraisal because of this specificity.

Perhaps the best way to understand the CIT approach is to examine a critical incident for the job of firefighter (Bownas & Bernardin, 1988):

> The firefighter studied two units of the "Red Book" during his daily training period for two weeks. At the end of the period, he couldn't perform the tasks outlined in the manuals, and he couldn't answer sample questions on the content. Because he hadn't picked up these skills, he could only be assigned as a helper to another firefighter at a fire scene. (p. 1123)

This example illustrates the characteristics of a good critical incident. It is specific; its focus is on observable behaviors, and the context in which the behavior occurred is described. Finally, it identifies the consequences of the firefighter's behavior.

As noted, the CIT has been used extensively to assess employee performance. Other suggested uses for the technique include training and job design (Bownas & Bernardin, 1988). One very interesting development noted by Gatewood and Feild (1994) is that CIT can prove useful in the development of structured oral interviews. They recommend conducting a traditional selection-oriented job analysis as a first step in determining interview content. Individual interview questions are then generated using CIT. A major advantage of this approach is the creation of more objective rating scales through the use of critical incidents as anchors for illustrating effective and ineffective responses.

Comprehensive occupational data analysis program.   The Task Inventory/Comprehensive Occupational Data Analysis Program (TI/CODAP) developed by Christal (1974) for application at Air Force installations consists of two basic components: a task inventory and a computer analysis package. Christal's task inventory is a questionnaire that requires subject matter experts to make judgments about the tasks constituting their job. A *task* is defined as a meaningful unit of work that can be readily identified by the employee. Task statements for the inventory are constructed by supervisors, incumbents, and other job experts. Once the task inventory has been developed, job incumbents rate the tasks on a 7-, 9-, or 11-point "relative time spent" scale and on other scales as deemed appropriate or applicable. The task inventory also collects background information such as work experience, education, race, sex, and use of equipment or tools as demanded by the job. These ratings are then analyzed through a series of interactive computer programs that organize the job information in a variety of forms.

CODAP programs exist to perform a number of important HRM functions, including describing work performed by individuals or groups, comparing work performed by specified groups, empirically identifying jobs in an occupational area, and analyzing task characteristics (Christal & Weissmuller, 1988). The programs that describe work performed can be used to produce group job descriptions and individual position descriptions. Other programs allow for job classification and evaluation. Christal and Weissmuller note that TI/CODAP has been applied to problems ranging from the study of job satisfaction to the fulfillment of equal employment opportunity requirements and even to the identification of job hazards. The breadth and flexibility of the programs has led to expanded use of TI/CODAP in business and industry.

Worker-Oriented Approaches

Position analysis questionnaire.   McCormick's Position Analysis Questionnaire (PAQ) (McCormick, Jeanneret, & Mecham, 1972) is a quantitative approach to job analysis that describes jobs in terms of worker activities. The PAQ is a structured questionnaire containing 187 items relating to worker activities. These items are organized into six categories, which are further broken down into job dimensions. The six categories include (1) information input, (2) mental processes, (3) work output, (4) job context, (5) interpersonal activities, and (6) other job characteristics. Examples of job dimensions contained in each of these categories include (1) use of written materials and use of pictorial materials, (2) level of reasoning and use of stored information, (3) use of keyboard devices and integrative manual activities, (4) physical working conditions and interpersonal conflict situations, (5) communications and personal contact, and (6) work schedules and job demands. Each PAQ item is rated on factors such as extent of use, essentiality, and applicability.

The PAQ is perhaps the most widely used job analysis approach. It has been described as one of the fifteen most significant milestones of personnel selection and classification research in the last 60 years (Dunnette & Borman, 1979). Like TI/CODAP, the PAQ is supported by an extensive array of computer programs that allow researchers to study a variety of HRM issues. McCormick, DeNisi, and Shaw (1979) found that the PAQ could be used to establish job aptitude requirements through the use of one computer program relating PAQ job analysis information directly to test data, making it possible to eliminate the need for conventional test validation procedures for each job.

Job element method. The Job Element Method developed by Primoff (1975) represents a unique approach to job analysis in that its focus is on worker characteristics rather than on job activities. The Job Element Method identifies skills, knowledge, inclinations, and other characteristics of employees in a particular job classification. This method typically relies not on job analysts to gather information but rather on a group of approximately six job incumbents, supervisors, or both who are familiar enough with the job under study to recognize easily characteristics of superior workers (Feild & Gatewood, 1989). These factors are organized into the following six broad categories of job elements (Primoff, 1975, p. 2):

- a knowledge, such as knowledge of accounting principles;
- a skill, such as skill with woodworking tools;
- an ability, such as ability to manage a program;
- a willingness, such as willingness to do simple tasks repetitively;
- an interest, such as an interest in learning new techniques; or
- a personal characteristic, such as reliability or dependability.

Once the job elements have been identified, the subject matter experts generate a corresponding list of subelements for each element. For example, having identified "knowledge of mathematics" as an element, SMEs might more clearly define the parameters of that knowledge by including "knowledge of addition of fractions" as a subelement. Subject matter experts then rate the job elements and subelements along a series of dimensions that are designed to measure the correlation between success on the job and possession of each job element. Through this correlation, the Job Element Method attempts to identify the characteristics that, if possessed by an individual, will probably result in superior job performance.

Primoff originally intended the Job Element Method for use in conducting job element rating sessions, preparing selection devices based on rating results, and testing and refining selection measures (Primoff, 1975). However, a drawback associated with this method was its inability to satisfy the federal Uniform Guidelines' requirements for content validation. The Guidelines require that a job analysis focus on work behaviors as well as knowledge, skills, and abilities. Later, however, Primoff began work to integrate the Job Element Method with FJA and CIT to meet content validity requirements (Bemis et al., 1983).

Threshold traits analysis. The Threshold Traits Analysis System (TTAS) is a job analysis approach first designed and implemented in 1971 (Lopez, 1986). TTAS differs from some other worker-oriented approaches in that it has identified thirty-three relatively enduring traits hypothesized to be related to the performance of a large number of different jobs. These traits are divided into two broad classes: ability and attitude. Ability-oriented traits are considered "can do" factors, whereas attitudinal traits are "willing to do" factors. Within TTAS, traits are assessed for six characteristics: level, practicality, weight, degree, criticality, and availability. Level refers to a trait's complexity. Practicality relates to the estimated proportion of job applicants thought to possess a given trait. Weight is an index of the impact of a particular trait on overall job performance. Degree represents a four-grade assessment of a person's possession of a trait, ranging from unacceptable to superior. Criticality, as the name implies, refers to the relationship between possession of a trait and overall job performance. Availability "describes the supply/demand ratio of each trait level in the employer's labor market" (Lopez, 1988, p. 884).

In TTAS the heart of the job analysis is the evaluation of traits. This technique demands that incumbents, supervisors, or other subject matter experts rate the relevance, level, and practicality of each of the thirty-three traits. These ratings are analyzed to produce a basic functional description of the job.

The functional job description then serves as the foundation for selection, training, performance evaluation, and compensation.

Other Approaches

The distinction between work- and worker-oriented approaches to job analysis became blurred as personnel consultants and human resource managers recognized the utility of collecting both types of information (Guion, 1978; McCormick, 1979; Prien, 1977). This development led to recommendations for the use of multiple job analysis systems, and new systems were developed in attempts to meet a variety of HRM needs. These so-called multi-method approaches employ data collection techniques that obtain both work- and worker-oriented information.

IMES variants.   The Iowa Merit Employment System (IMES) was an early attempt to incorporate both work- and worker-oriented job analysis data. The IMES approach is a systematic multistep process designed to aid in the development of content-valid selection devices (Menne, McCarthy, & Menne, 1976). IMES emphasizes the use of a group interview in which supervisors and incumbents work jointly to identify relevant job content. First, job tasks are identified. These tasks are then expanded into a standardized form that answers the following questions:

1. What is the action being performed?
2. To whom or what is the action directed?
3. Why is the action being performed?
4. How is the action done?

Once job tasks have been defined as formal task statements, the knowledge, skills, abilities, and personal characteristics (KSAPCs) needed to perform each of the job tasks are identified. Incumbents and supervisors then rate task statements on dimensions such as importance, time spent, and necessity at entry. The KSAPCs arising from the aforementioned group interview are also rated for their importance and linked to job tasks. The data provided by these ratings are analyzed, and a picture of the job task and job knowledge domain is obtained. Among the variants of the basic IMES approach are the Alabama Merit System Method (Elliott, Boyles, Hill, Palmer, Thomas, & Veres, 1980) and Integrated Job Analysis (Buckley, 1986).

Behavioral consistency method.   Schmidt, Caplan, Bemis, Dewir, Dunn, and Antone (1979) developed the Behavioral Consistency Method to identify competencies workers needed to perform mid-level government, professional, and managerial jobs. The method has since been used to identify competencies in private sector managerial and blue-collar jobs. Two basic principles underlie the Behavioral Consistency approach: (1) Applicants should be evaluated only on dimensions that clearly differentiate between superior and minimally acceptable performers, and (2) these dimensions must be determined through consultation with individuals who have known and observed superior and marginal performers. The Behavioral Consistency Method involves four major components: (1) the identification and description of job activities and tasks; (2) the identification of knowledge, abilities, skills, and other characteristics (KASOs) needed to perform the work; (3) the rating of KASOs by subject matter experts; and (4) the analysis of these ratings to evaluate KASOs.

Job agents independently rate each KASO on six scales. Scale 1 evaluates the importance of the KASO in preventing job failure. Scale 2 determines the percentage of current workers meeting minimum performance standards for each KASO. Scale 3 determines whether the KASO is necessary for all positions. Scale 4 evaluates the usefulness of the KASO in differentiating between superior and minimally acceptable workers. Scale 5 identifies the extent of variability of the KASO in the applicant pool. Scale 6 is used only when subspecialties are present in the occupation. The Behaviorial Consistency Method represents a significant breakthrough in reviewing the appropriateness of applicant qualifications. Its use has been limited primarily to this application.

VERJAS. A successor to the Behavioral Consistency Method is the Versatile Job Analysis System (VERJAS) developed by Bemis et al. (1983). VERJAS extends some of the principles underlying the Behaviorial Consistency Method to a wider variety of applications including job design, classification and evaluation, recruitment, selection, training, and performance appraisal. Important features of the approach include a detailed description of the context in which job tasks are performed as a prelude to identification of the basic competencies needed to perform those tasks. The detailed operational definitions of competencies and clear linkage of competencies back to important job tasks are two appealing features of VERJAS.

Bemis et al. (1983) identify five steps critical to the VERJAS process:

1. Write an overview of the job describing the purpose for which the job exists and the primary duties involved in accomplishing that purpose.
2. Describe the action, purpose, and result of each task involved in carrying out job duties, and then identify the training mode and rate its relative importance.
3. Describe the context of the job: its scope, effect, and environment.
4. Identify basic worker competencies needed for minimally acceptable performance of job tasks.
5. Identify the special worker competencies that make for successful job performance.
   (pp. 62–63)

These five steps also typify other multimethod approaches to job analysis, including Guidelines-Oriented Job Analysis (Biddle, 1976), the Health Services Mobility Study Method (Gilpatrick, 1977), and Integrated Job Analysis (Buckley, 1980).

Evaluation of Traditional Methods

Several factors have given rise to an increased preference for multimethod approaches to job analysis. Veres, Lahey, and Buckley (1987) enumerate some of the factors contributing to a rise in multimethod approaches, including level of task specificity, communicability, and the Uniform Guidelines' requirements. The Guidelines require that a validity study include a job analysis that generates the "important work behavior(s) required for successful performance" (p. 38302). The Guidelines define a selection procedure as "any measure, combination of measures, or procedure used as a basis for *any* employment decision" (Equal Employment Opportunity Commission et al., 1978, p. 38308). Given this definition, the Guidelines cover any measure or procedure that is used as the basis for a personnel decision. Thus, human resource professionals must consider the approach to job analysis that is used to construct each procedure, and worker-oriented techniques clearly do not conform to the Guidelines.

In addition, the courts have supported the Guidelines by endorsing a multimethod approach to job analysis. Courts have determined that a job analysis without task-oriented information does not comply with regulatory guidance and Title VII (Thompson & Thompson, 1982). They have also required demonstration of the ties between work behaviors (or tasks) and their companion KSAs (*United States v. State of New York, 1978*)—a goal that can be achieved only when both types of job information are collected.

Research on job analysis in this realm has been restricted largely to job analysts' evaluation of method effectiveness. Levine, Ash, Hall, and Sistrunk (1983) gathered evaluations on seven commonly employed job analysis methods. These evaluations were obtained by means of a questionnaire containing items regarding the effectiveness and practicality of each method. Ninety-three experienced job analysts completed the questionnaire. The researchers' findings, some of which are summarized in Table 1, produce no clear "winner" overall. However, particular systems were found to be superior for a given application.

Table 1

Evaluation of Selected Job Analysis Systems by Experienced Job Analysts

Purposes	Methods with highest effectiveness ratings[1]					
	FJA	CIT	TI/CODAP	PAQ	JEM	TTA
Job description	X		X			
Job classification	X		X	X		X
Job evaluation	X		X	X		
Job design	X		X			
Job specifications	X		X	X	X	X
Performance appraisal	X	X	X		X	
Worker training	X	X	X		X	
Efficiency/safety		X				
Work force planning	X		X			
Legal requirements	X		X	X		

[1]Average rating of 3 or higher on a 5-point scale.

Adapted from Table 1 in Levine, Ash, Hall, & Sistrunk (1983).

The effectiveness ratings revealed that the experienced job analysts preferred TI/CODAP and Functional Job Analysis for constructing job descriptions. For purposes of job classification, TI/CODAP, FJA, and the PAQ were rated highest, whereas the Critical Incident Technique was rated significantly lower than the other methods. The PAQ, FJA, and TI/CODAP were also rated highest for job evaluation. For job design purposes, TI/CODAP and FJA were rated higher than other methods. Only work- and worker-oriented methods were assessed in the 1983 study; no multimethod systems were considered.

Unfortunately, research has not yet answered the question of which job analysis system is the best (Bernardin & Beatty, 1984). Because research provides no definitive guidance on what system to use, the Guidelines' requirements and court opinions merit considerable weight. As mentioned previously, legal considerations would seem to favor multimethod approaches. Also, a number of researchers have advanced conceptual and measurement-oriented arguments for adopting multimethod approaches to job analysis (Guion, 1978; Prien, 1977). Others have argued that multimethod approaches should be preferred on more pragmatic grounds (Veres et al., 1987).

Recent Trends in Job Analysis

As noted previously, the passage of the Americans with Disabilities Act has placed new demands on human resource managers. Certain physical ability requirements long taken for granted, such as normal vision and hearing, can be applied only if an employer can document that an employee needs them to perform "essential job functions." The identification of the essential functions themselves must rely on a thorough task-oriented or multimethod job analysis. The linkage between essential functions and requisite knowledge, skills, mental abilities, and physical abilities can best be accomplished via a multimethod job analysis process. Obviously, job analysis methods that do not capture information salient to the essentiality of job functions and underlying mental and physical abilities must fail to protect employers from ADA-related law suits.

The need to produce ADA-sensitive job specifications has created renewed interest in the Fleishman Job Analysis System (F-JAS) (Fleishman & Reilly, 1992). The F-JAS is an approach to job analysis that has been researched and refined for a number of years and is based on a taxonomy of human abilities (Fleishman & Quaintance, 1984). F-JAS currently consists of seventy-two scales. There are four categories of abilities scales including Cognitive (1–21), Psychomotor (22–31), Physical (32–40), and Sensory/Perceptual (41–52). The other two scale categories, including Interactive/Social Scales (53–61) and Knowledges/Skills Scales (62–72), are currently being researched. Each scale consists of a definition of the ability to be rated; the difference between the ability to be rated on the scale and other, similar abilities; a behaviorally anchored rating scale; and the definition of the highest and lowest levels of the ability. F-JAS can serve as a useful method of job analysis, particularly as a tool to comply with the Americans with Disabilities Act. The inclusion of Cognitive, Psychomotor, Physical, and Sensory/Perceptual F-JAS scales can help analysts identify cognitive and physical aspects of work that are used to perform essential job functions. When F-JAS scales are linked to essential job functions, the analyst can use this information to determine abilities that are and are not essential to the job. Identification of requisite mental and physical abilities can indicate abilities that are likely to require consideration in the making of reasonable accommodations.

A second recent trend in job analysis methodology is a move toward increased specificity in descriptions of job tasks and of the knowledge, skills, and abilities (KSAs) needed on a job as a means of ensuring content validity in testing. Goldstein, Zedeck, and Schneider (1993) have articulated a central theme of this new movement, noting that a "test must be designed so that it calls forth the required KSAs (psychological fidelity) for the job regardless of whether physical fidelity is present." They go on to observe that

> since inferences about content validity are based on the degree to which a test reflects the critical job domains, clearly the job analysis itself is the most critical component. Two facets define the essence of an appropriate job analy-

sis procedure for deriving test content and format: the detailed task and KSA statements needed to approach physical, and thus psychological, fidelity and the judgmental process whereby individual KSAs are linked to tasks and task clusters and tests are linked back to KSAs. (p. 10)

A singular benefit of the Goldstein et al. approach is the explicit consideration of matching test format, as well as test content, to the job content domain. The increased specificity of task statements can also assist analysts in defining essential job functions for purposes of compliance with ADA, as well as providing input to the achievement of reasonable accommodations. The KSA domain's more explicit definition should also be of considerable help in ADA compliance.

Job analysis systems that emphasize increased specificity and take account of sensory and psychomotor abilities would seem to meet the job analysis needs of most organizations in the current regulatory and legal environment. New approaches introduced in the coming years should be expected to echo these two trends. In fact, a comparison of the following job analysis case study to the one presented in Veres, Locklear, and Sims (1988) will reveal the influences of both Fleishman and Reilly (1992) and Goldstein, Zedeck, and Schneider (1993).

A Job Analysis Case Study:
The Multimethod Approach in Action

We have examined the process of job analysis in some detail. However, we have not considered job analysis in context. A good way to convey a feeling for job analysis in the real world is with a case study that illustrates how job analysis fits into a program of test development and validation. We have chosen, as an example, a project that we completed for a large metropolitan police department in the southeast (the City Police Department). This case vividly illustrates two points that are sometimes overlooked when students are taught about job analysis: (1) Job analysis is performed with a particular purpose in mind—for example, selection or promotion; and (2) the organization and the jobs in question present distinctive circumstances that influence the way in which a job analysis is handled.

The City Police Department had a history of litigation involving past promotion procedures. As a result of an employment discrimination case, the police department had to make all future promotions in accordance with the instructions of the United States District Court. The court in this case issued an order banning race-conscious promotion decisions. This, in turn, led to a number of proceedings before the court on the issue of racial discrimination. Both black and white officers petitioned the court for changes in City Police promotion practices at various times. New promotion procedures were implemented without court challenge 2 years prior to the job analysis described herein. Thus, the job analysis studies described here were conducted in an atmosphere of considerable trust, in stark contrast to earlier efforts. Those involved were keenly aware of the past problems associated with the history of City Police promotions and took steps to reassure both management and job agents of the job analysis procedures' objectivity and lack of bias.

A job analysis study was undertaken as a first step in the development of new promotion procedures for the rank of police captain. The method used to analyze police ranks is an outgrowth of a number of the job analysis methods described earlier. The approach used defines both the work performed (in the form of work behaviors and tasks) and the attributes of the workers performing that work (in the form of knowledge, skills, and abilities). Additionally, the job analysis approach identifies the work conditions characteristic of the job. In the City Police Department case, data were collected from incumbents, supervisors, and upper-level management through a variety of techniques, including observation, individual interviews, group interviews, technical conferences, and a structured job analysis questionnaire. The study consisted of six operational phases: (1) review of background information, (2) site observations and individual interviews, (3) group interviews, (4) technical review and editing, (5) questionnaire administration and data analysis, and (6) final technical review.

Phase 1—Review of Background Information

During Phase 1 we began the job analysis process by familiarizing ourselves with departmental operations through the review of written materials such as organizational charts, existing job descriptions, and precinct and beat-configuration maps. In addition, we examined the results of previous job analysis efforts to obtain more specific information regarding the job duties of the rank being studied.

Phase 2—Site Observations and Individual Interviews

In Phase 2 and before the formal group interview sessions, we conducted site observations at the work sites of job incumbents at the rank of captain. We spent considerable time talking with and observing job incumbents. Though we always use a combination of direct observation and interviewing, some jobs are better understood through conversation with incumbents, and some are easier to understand through observation. We typically used more of an interview format with incumbents assigned to desk jobs because it is difficult to understand the requirements of less active jobs by simply observing. Incumbents assigned to field operations were observed and interviewed while they performed their jobs. For both types of jobs, we made sure to look at and note the types of forms they were required to complete, the types of equipment they used, and any reference materials that we had not reviewed in surveying background information.

We used site observations to familiarize ourselves with the work environment and the job content domain before the group interview sessions. In addition, the questions we asked incumbents during on-site interviews were designed to acquaint us with the knowledge, skills, and abilities that incumbents believed were important for successful job performance. We selected the locations for on-site observations in cooperation with the department so we would be exposed to incumbents in a variety of assignments and see a comprehensive picture of departmental operations. For example, we rode with captains from different precincts on different shifts, and we observed a captain from the Criminal Investigations Division serve a warrant on reputed drug dealers.

Phase 3—Group Interview Sessions

During Phase 3, group interviews, the job content domain was developed and defined through the pooled judgments of job incumbents working under our supervision. Job incumbents who participate in the job analysis effort are called subject matter experts, or SMEs, because of their familiarity with the target job. The department selected twelve SMEs for the rank in accordance with our policy for selection of group interview participants. Our practice is to select SMEs (1) who are representative by gender, race, shift, and duties performed of the job classification population; (2) who have at least 6 months' experience in the job classification under review; and (3) whose performance in that classification is at least satisfactory.

Development of work behavior and task statements. The group interview session began with SMEs brainstorming to generate, in short (two- or three-word) phrases, an exhaustive listing of all job-related activities performed by persons in their position. In the session SMEs provided phrases such as "attends meetings," "trains subordinates," and "processes crime scenes." After the brainstorming the job analyst chose work activities from the brainstorming list that he or she knew

were at the right level of specificity to be considered work behaviors. Work behaviors describe, in broad terms, the major work activities of the job. SMEs were then prompted to generate task statements for each of the work behaviors. Task statements describe the specific actions required to perform a work behavior. The purpose of this step was to specify the actions involved in each major work activity. For example, we asked SMEs to identify the actions involved in a work behavior such as "processes crime scenes." Some of the specific activities that they identified were securing the scene; providing assistance and first aid to injured victims; and taking notes documenting what occurred before, during, and after the crime. Task statements were written to include (1) what the worker does (action verb), (2) to what or whom it is done (object of the verb), (3) the reason for the task, (4) examples of the object for the purpose of clarification, and (5) how the work is performed. This procedure was followed until each of the activities identified during brainstorming was accounted for as either a work behavior or a task.

After our SMEs identified the appropriate task statements under a work behavior statement, we asked them to define the work behavior by telling us necessary details about tasks composing that work behavior. Thus, work behavior phrases were expanded to include (1) what the worker does (an action verb describing a specific observable action); (2) to what or to whom it is done (the object of the verb); (3) how it is done (a list of procedures, materials, tools, equipment used, instructions followed); and (4) why it is done (the reason for the task—the expected result, output, or product). Following was the complete work behavior statement for "processes crime scenes":

> **Processes crime scenes** using cameras, radios, fingerprint kits, and field notes following departmental policies and procedures, SOPs and GOs in order to preserve evidence located at the crime scene, identify possible suspects and plan follow-up investigations.

Development of knowledge, skill, and ability statements. After the work behavior statements were developed, we asked the SMEs to brainstorm for the knowledge, skills, and abilities (KSAs) they needed to perform their job duties. As in work behavior brainstorming, each KSA was described in a short (two- or three-word) phrase. For example, our captains generated the KSAs "knowledge of general crime prevention patrol procedures"; "ability to add, subtract, multiply, and divide"; and "knowledge of state traffic code." To ensure the identification of all KSAs, we compiled our brainstorming list by reviewing each work behavior statement and having SMEs name all the KSAs needed to perform the work behavior. Once the KSAs were identified, SMEs expanded KSA statements to describe (1) the extent to which each was needed by employees in the rank under study and (2) why each was needed. KSA statements were written in the following form:

> Skill in _____ to/with a score of _____
> as needed to _____.
> Knowledge of _____ to include _____
> as needed to _____.
> Ability to _____ to include (such as)
> _____ as needed to _____.

For example, the expanded KSA statement for knowledge of the general crime prevention patrol procedures was as follows:

> Knowledge of the general crime prevention procedures to include security checking, identification of stolen vehicles, and varying patrol routes as needed to reduce the likelihood crime will occur in the area.

Development of physical ability statements. Unlike the development of work behavior and KSA statements, development of physical ability statements did not start with brainstorming. Instead, we started with a prepared list of common physical abilities required for job performance. The list of physical abilities was a subset of those described by Fleishman

and Quaintance (1984). The description of the physical ability was used as a stem for the physical ability statement. This stem was augmented by (1) a list of activities requiring the physical ability and, when applicable, (2) information illustrating the level of the physical ability that was required for job performance. Following were the physical ability statements for the ability to run and the ability to climb:

> Ability to run short (up to 50 yards), moderate (50 yards to 1 mile), and long distances (over 1 mile) as needed to apprehend suspects and respond to incidents.

> Ability to climb objects or structures as needed to walk along the roofs of houses or buildings, climb over walls or chain-link fences, climb ladders, enter houses or buildings through windows, climb stairs in buildings, respond to incidents occurring in steep ravines or ditches, rappel down structures or climb on overturned vehicles.

Development of work condition statements. Work condition statements were generated in much the same way as physical ability statements. A list of common work conditions was adopted from the Stout Vocational Rehabilitation Institute's publication, *Physical Demands Job Analysis: A New Approach* (1974). Work conditions on the list were used as stems, and specific tasks requiring exposure to the working condition were added to each applicable stem. For example, a work condition statement would read, "Exposure to weather such as heat, cold, rain, sleet, snow, or wind as needed to assist motorists with disabled vehicles, direct traffic, walk through communities on foot patrol, and process crime scenes."

Phase 4—Technical Review and Editing

Following the group interviews, we edited the work behavior and KSA lists to ensure clarity and completeness. We corrected grammatical errors, changed the wording in some state-

Table 2
Work Behavior Ratings
Rank of Captain

Work behavior		Percent perform wk beh	Mean percent time	Mean impor rating	Percent nec entry
WB1	Assigns tasks and schedules	100	7.4	2.45	100
WB2	Monitors progress of assignmts	100	7.1	2.64	100
WB3	Evaluate subord work performance	100	6.1	2.45	100
WB4	Counsel, obtain feedbk fr subord	100	4.6	2.45	100
WB5	Perform administrative duties	100	10.9	2.45	82
WB6	Meet w/ inds outside chain comd	100	3.8	1.91	82
WB7	Manage physical resources	100	3.7	2.09	82
WB8	Provide police patrol & traffic serv	100	4.1	1.82	91
WB9	Process crime scenes	100	1.3	1.82	82
WB10	Collect and handle evidence	73	2.0	1.87	88
WB11	Interview witnesses & suspects	82	1.6	1.78	89
WB12	Conduct covert investigations	55	3.7	2.00	83
WB13	Respond to life-threat emerg	100	2.6	2.45	82
WB14	Respond to calls req srch, seiz, arr	91	3.2	1.90	90
WB15	Respond to law enforc situations	91	2.1	1.30	70
WB16	Interact with citizens	91	8.8	2.30	90
WB17	Admin discipline, investig alleg	100	5.4	2.45	100
WB18	Provide info to citizen groups	100	5.6	2.00	82
WB19	Maintain professional knowledge	100	4.3	1.91	73
WB20	Prepare and testify in court	64	1.6	1.57	100
WB21	Plan zone/section/unit goals	91	13.5	2.50	90
WB22	Conduct group training	82	2.8	1.78	56

N = 11

Note: Values for the mean percent time and mean importance are based on the responses of those SMEs who perform the work behavior.

Scale for importance ratings:

4 = *critical*

3 = *essential*

2 = *important*

1 = *somewhat important*

0 = *not important*

ments, and reorganized the list to ensure meaningful organization of job content and job requirements. The work behavior and KSA lists were then reviewed by a Technical Advisory Committee that consisted of the department's chief, three deputy chiefs, and a major. This committee was set up to review our lists and to tell us whether the SMEs had omitted an important work behavior or KSA. The committee's feedback was incorporated into the final version of the work behavior and KSA lists. The final work behaviors and task ratings for the rank of captain are listed in Tables 2 and 3.

Table 3
Sample Task Ratings
Rank of Captain

Task		Percent perform task	Mean freq	Mean impor rating	Percent nec entry
1	Plan patrol procedure	73	3.75	2.37	75
2	Assign radar sites/locations to prsnnl	36	1.75	0.75	25
3	Develop initial personnel roster	82	2.44	1.67	78
4	Prepare daily assignment sheets	55	1.67	1.33	67
5	Review requests for sched/roster modif	82	2.56	1.33	78
6	Develop work sched for special assignmts	73	3.12	1.87	75
7	Read subpoenas, spec orders, other docs	91	3.40	1.80	100
8	Talks w/ HQ, Zone, Sect Comm re spec req	91	3.80	2.00	90
9	Respond to scene of serious incidents	82	3.44	2.89	100
10	Keep record of comp time/hours worked	55	2.83	2.17	100
11	Notify subord of chgs in work sched	91	2.70	1.90	90
12	Mntn/rep data to sup re replacmt needs	91	3.00	2.00	70
13	Assign subord to follow-up investigations	82	2.89	1.89	89
14	Comm directions at crime scene	73	2.37	2.12	100
15	Coord preplanned emerg procedures	64	2.57	2.71	86
16	Discuss pendg work w/ super/subord	91	4.10	2.50	100
17	Monitor turn-arnd time on rep submit dates	100	4.64	2.55	100
18	Rev docs to determine work perf on shift	82	3.00	1.89	67
19	Rev logs to assure timely work completion	82	3.11	1.89	78
20	Rev sub timeshts to det accur of overtime	73	2.37	2.25	100
21	Inspect assigned area of responsibility	91	3.70	2.30	90
22	Instruct subord on pol/proc/job assignmt	100	3.55	2.27	82
23	Quest subord on mistakes/errors	91	3.40	2.40	90
24	Approve commitmt of staff/res to incid	91	3.60	2.30	80
.					
.					
.					
286	Monitor how well training follows schedule	36	1.50	1.25	50
287	Solicit feedback/recommendtn from trainees	64	1.86	1.57	71

N = 11

Note: All ratings except "percent performing task" are based on the responses of the SMEs who perform the task.

Scale for frequency ratings: Scale for importance ratings:

5 = *every day*   4 = *critical*

4 = *once/twice weekly*   3 = *essential*

3 = *once/twice montly*   2 = *important*

2 = *1 to 4 times a year*   1 = *somewhat important*

1 = *in unusual circumstances*   0 = *not important*

0 = *never*

Phase 5—Questionnaire Administration and Data Analysis

The job analysis phases just described provided us with a comprehensive picture of the rank under study. This picture, however, did not incorporate any information concerning the relative importance or frequency of the work behaviors and tasks, nor did it distinguish between those elements of the job that must be performed competently upon job entry and those that may be learned later. These questions were of great importance because our job analysis results would be used to develop job-related promotion procedures. In selecting officers for promotion into the rank under study, it is important to test for the knowledge, skills, and abilities that an employee needs to perform critical rather than trivial work activities. Thus, we administered a structured job analysis questionnaire (JAQ) to determine the critical aspects of the job performed by captains and the KSAs essential to the performance of those critical job activities. All available incumbents completed the questionnaire.

The incumbents completed the JAQ to describe how the work behaviors and KSAs related to their individual positions. It was emphasized that the appropriate frame of reference for a rater was his or her current job, not a hypothetical typical incumbent's job. The following three questions about tasks were asked of the SMEs:

1. How often do you perform this task in your current position? (on a scale from 0, never, to 5, continually)
2. How important is it for you to perform this task successfully? (on a scale from 0, not important, to 4, critical)
3. Must new employees be able to perform this task when they first start this job? (no or yes)

The following three questions about work behaviors were asked of the SMEs:

1. Indicate the percentage of time you spend performing this work behavior. Remember that the sum of this column must equal 100%.

2. How important is it for you to perform this work behavior successfully? (on a scale from 0, not important, to 4, critical)
3. Must new employees be able to perform this work behavior when they first start this job? (no or yes)

The following three questions concerning skills and abilities were asked of SMEs:

1. How important is this skill or ability to do your job successfully? (on a scale from 0, not important, to 4, critical)
2. Must new employees have this skill or ability when they first start this job? (no or yes)
3. Do workers who have more of this skill or ability do a better job than workers who have less of this skill or ability? (on a scale from 0, not at all, to 3, considerably)

The following four questions concerning knowledge were asked of SMEs:

1. How important is this knowledge to do your job successfully? (on a scale from 0, not important, to 4, critical)
2. Must new employees have this knowledge when they first start this job? (no or yes)
3. Do employees who have more of this knowledge do a better job than employees who have less of this knowledge? (on a scale from 0, not at all, to 3, considerably)
4. At what level do you have to remember this knowledge to do your job successfully? (on a scale from 0, no recall, to 3, full recall)

The following four questions concerning physical abilities were asked of SMEs:

1. How often do you use this physical ability when performing your job duties (WITHOUT HELP)? (on a scale from 0, never, to 5, continually)
2. How often do you use this physical ability when performing your job duties (WITH HELP)? (on a scale from 0, never, to 5, continually)

3. How important is this physical ability to do your job successfully? (on a scale from 0, not important, to 4, critical)
4. Must new employees have this physical ability when they first start this job? (no or yes)

Once all knowledge, skills, and abilities were rated, SMEs were asked to rank the top fifteen. We incorporated ranking in the job analysis questionnaire to help determine which of the KSAs and physical abilities were most central to the job. When only ratings of time spent and importance are requested, many of the KSAs and physical abilities are rated similarly, as important to the job. The ranking portion helps further differentiate the importance of KSAs and physical abilities.

The following section asked SMEs to rate work conditions. They were asked to rate each work condition by answering the question, "How often are you exposed to each working condition in your current position?" They responded by choosing a number from 0, never, to 6, hourly.

SMEs were finally asked to complete a matrix by rating the relationship of each KSA and physical ability with performance of each work behavior. The question concerning the relationship between work behaviors and KSAs was, "How important is this KSA when you perform each work behavior?" The answer to this question was based on a rating scale from 0, not important, to 3, essential.

Following questionnaire administration, incumbents' responses to each question concerning work behaviors and KSAs were computer analyzed to determine the critical components of the job content domain. Summaries of the incumbents' work behavior and task ratings are presented in Tables 2 and 3. Tables 4 and 5 contain summaries of SME ratings for KSAs and physical abilities. The critical components of the content and knowledge domains that emerged from the JAQ ratings, along with percent weights for those components, are listed in Tables 6 and 7.

The work behaviors listed in Table 6 met the following screens for inclusion:

1. They were performed by two-thirds of the SMEs.
2. They had mean importance ratings of at least 2.0.
3. They were rated as necessary upon entry to the job by 66 percent of all SMEs performing the work behavior and 50 percent of SMEs overall.

The KSAs listed in Table 7 met the following screens for inclusion:

1. They had ratings of at least 2.0 for mean importance and "extent distinguishes."
2. They were tied (mean work behavior–KSA relationship rating of at least 1.5) to at least one work behavior that met the previous three screens.
3. They were rated as necessary upon entry to the job by 60 percent of the SMEs.

For job analysis performed in an environment where the Americans with Disabilities Act is particularly important, these screens can be set at a somewhat higher level to identify essential job functions. We set the screens for importance ratings at 2.3 in order for the work behaviors, tasks, and KSAs and physical abilities to be identified as essential job functions.

Final Technical Review

The city's Technical Advisory Committee met with us for a second time following data analysis to review the outcomes of questionnaire administration and to discuss the implications of the job analysis outcomes for future testing. The committee supported the results of the job analysis and expressed their belief that the critical work behaviors and KSAs identified by the incumbents indeed accurately reflected the jobs currently performed by captains.

Table 4

Sample Knowledges, Skills, and Abilities Ratings

Rank of Captain

KSA description		Ranking factor	Mean import rating	Percent nec at entry	Extent dist rating	Recall level
Knowledge						
K1	K of geographical territory	1.98	2.00	64	1.82	1.55
K2	K of traffic control procedures	1.00	1.18	45	0.91	1.00
K3	K of vehicle stop procedures	1.00	1.64	73	1.27	1.55
K4	K of proc for resp to dom disp	1.00	1.45	64	1.18	1.18
K5	K of crime prev patrol proced	1.35	1.27	64	1.00	1.36
K6	K of radio signals and comm tech	1.18	2.27	91	1.82	2.00
K7	K of special evnts—public saf enf	1.38	2.36	82	1.73	1.64
K8	K of community issues/situations	2.84	2.18	82	1.64	1.55
K9	K of other law enf agencies/res	1.00	2.18	73	1.64	1.82
K10	K of use and maint of vehicles	1.00	1.64	73	1.00	1.27
K11	K of use and maint of radio	1.00	1.73	64	1.09	1.55
K12	K of current and impt events	2.98	2.18	82	1.55	1.55
K13	K of care and maint serv weap	1.40	2.27	82	1.45	1.91
K14	K of major areas of jurisdiction	1.51	1.73	64	1.27	1.64
K15	K of territorial areas of city	1.29	2.36	55	1.64	1.82
K16	K of proc coll/pres/transp evid	1.00	1.45	45	0.82	1.27
K17	K of proc for lifting fingerprints	1.00	1.00	45	0.64	1.00
K18	K of proc for cond backgrnd inves	1.33	0.73	18	0.27	0.45
K19	K of invest tech in drug cases	1.45	0.91	36	0.64	0.82
K20	K of dept proc for confid informts	1.76	1.09	55	0.73	1.00
K21	K of invest proc cri agst per/prop	1.16	1.45	73	1.09	1.36
K22	K of cap/limit of info fr lab/autopsy	1.00	1.09	45	0.73	1.00
K23	K of covert investigative tech	1.73	1.36	45	0.91	1.18
K24	K of cap/limit of wiretap/elec surv	1.64	0.91	27	0.64	0.82
K25	K of proc protct motor veh acc sc	1.44	1.18	55	0.64	1.09
K26	K of photo/meas mot veh acc sc	1.42	0.91	55	0.45	0.91
K27	K of accid scene invest techn	1.00	0.91	55	0.45	0.82
K28	K of dept proc complt acc repts	1.00	1.36	73	0.82	1.36
K29	K of proc detent/arrst suspects	1.42	1.45	64	0.82	1.36
K30	K of proc protct crime scene/inv	1.00	1.45	55	0.91	1.18
K31	K of proc for crime control	1.00	1.82	64	1.00	1.36
K32	K of proc for station surv/stakeout	1.29	1.18	45	0.64	0.91
K33	K of laws/pol regard physical force	1.00	2.55	82	1.64	2.00
.						
.						
.						
K70	K of Field Manual	1.85	2.55	100	2.00	1.91
K71	K of negotiation/calming tech	1.20	2.27	91	1.55	1.82
K72	K of EPAS - performc eval sys	3.02	2.27	91	1.73	1.91

Table 4 (continued)
Knowledges, Skills, and Abilities Ratings
Rank of Captain

KSA description		Ranking factor	Mean import rating	Percent nec at entry	Extent dist rating
Skills and Abilities					
A1	A to detect signs/efcts alcohol	1.47	1.64	82	0.82
A2	A to deal w/ mentally ill	1.00	1.27	73	0.73
A3	A to operate office equip	1.00	1.82	73	1.45
A4	S in oper motor vehicles	1.11	1.45	82	0.73
A5	A to ident char of com drugs	1.15	1.27	55	0.73
A6	A to interr criminal suspects	1.00	1.45	36	0.91
A7	A to use field drug/sobr test	1.00	0.82	27	0.55
A8	S in use of handguns	1.00	1.91	64	0.64
A9	A to decide meth invest cmplt	1.24	2.36	91	1.64
A10	A to get from pt A to pt B	1.00	1.82	55	1.00
A11	A to establish rapport w infrmt	1.00	1.27	27	0.73
A12	A to listen to all pts of view	2.11	2.36	91	1.91
A13	A to listen/resp to not aggrav sit	1.91	2.55	91	2.00
A14	A to obtain facts and info	2.96	2.00	82	1.73
A15	A to detect physical/vrbl resp	1.00	2.27	73	1.73
A16	A to negotiate a resolution	1.87	2.36	100	1.91
A17	A to use physical force	1.00	1.27	55	0.82
A18	A to recognize crim beh patt	1.00	1.91	45	1.27
A19	A to handle adolescent behav	1.58	1.64	64	1.27
A20	A to interact w/ pers diff bckgrnd	1.87	2.73	91	2.27
A21	A to interact in enf/nonenf sit	1.18	2.73	82	2.18
A22	A to mntn command prsnc at inc	1.33	2.55	100	1.82
.					
.					
.					
A95	A to mntn integrity/resist corrup	3.51	3.09	100	2.73
A96	A to rembr fact/det in ongng inv	1.47	2.73	82	2.45

N = 11

Scale for ranking factor:

1.0 = *not ranked*	4.2 = *ranked 15th*	6.4 = *ranked 4th*	
2.2 = *ranked 25th*	4.4 = *ranked 14th*	6.6 = *ranked 3rd*	
2.4 = *ranked 24th*	4.6 = *ranked 13th*	6.8 = *ranked 2nd*	
2.6 = *ranked 23rd*	4.8 = *ranked 12th*	7.0 = *ranked 1st*	
2.8 = *ranked 22nd*	5.0 = *ranked 11th*		
3.0 = *ranked 21st*	5.2 = *ranked 10th*		
3.2 = *ranked 20th*	5.4 = *ranked 9th*		
3.4 = *ranked 19th*	5.6 = *ranked 8th*		
3.6 = *ranked 18th*	5.8 = *ranked 7th*		
3.8 = *ranked 17th*	6.0 = *ranked 6th*		
4.0 = *ranked 16th*	6.2 = *ranked 5th*		

Scale for importance ratings:
4 = *critical*
3 = *essential*
2 = *extremely important*
1 = *somewhat important*
0 = *not important*

Scale for recall level:
3 = *full recall*
2 = *working knowledge*
1 = *general familiarity*
0 = *no recall*

Scale for extent distinguishing:
3 = *considerably*
2 = *moderately*
1 = *slightly*
0 = *not at all*

Table 5
Physical Ability Ratings
Rank of Captain

Physical ability		Mean ranking factor	Mean freq no help	Mean freq with help	Mean imp rating	Percent nec at entry
P1	A to lift/carry objects	1.00	1.27	1.36	0.82	45
P2	A to push	1.00	0.91	1.09	0.55	27
P3	A to pull objects	1.00	0.82	0.73	0.45	27
P4	A to run short/mod/long dist	1.00	0.73	0.64	0.36	27
P5	A to walk	1.00	1.09	0.73	0.64	36
P6	A to climb objects	1.00	1.00	0.55	0.45	27
P7	A to phys exrtn w/o short brth	1.00	0.91	0.64	0.55	45
P8	A to jump	1.00	0.73	0.73	0.45	36
P9	A to use muscle force	1.00	0.91	0.82	0.55	36
P10	A to coord mvmt of extrem	1.00	1.36	1.09	1.18	73
P11	A to stand for extnd time	1.00	1.91	1.27	0.91	64
P12	A to stoop/crouch/crawl	1.00	1.00	0.91	0.73	55
P13	A to bend/strch/twst/rch out	1.00	0.91	0.73	0.73	55
P14	A to keep/regain balance	1.00	0.45	0.36	0.36	27
P15	A to keep arm/hand steady	1.00	2.00	1.36	1.55	73
P16	A to rapid move fing/hnd/wrst	1.00	1.73	1.09	1.36	82
P17	A to move fing w/ skill/coord	1.00	3.00	2.09	1.82	82
P18	A to rspnd fast to sound/light	1.00	2.00	1.36	1.55	73
P19	A to adjust cntrls of mach/veh	1.00	3.91	2.73	2.18	82
P20	A to see close objects	1.00	3.82	2.91	2.18	82
P21	A to see distant objects	1.00	3.45	2.55	1.91	73
P22	A to match/distinguish colors	1.00	2.36	1.64	1.45	73
P23	A to see under low light	1.00	1.82	1.45	1.36	55
P24	A to dtct obj/mvmt in edg vis fld	1.00	3.18	2.18	2.00	73
P25	A to distngsh dist of sev obj	1.00	3.18	2.18	2.09	73
P26	A to focus on sngl sound/msg	1.00	4.36	3.18	2.73	100
P27	A to ident dirctn sound origin	1.00	2.09	1.55	1.82	73
P28	A to dtct dstngsh odor diff/sim	1.00	1.45	1.09	1.27	64
P29	A to sit for extnd per of time	1.00	3.00	2.00	1.91	73
P30	A to make sklfl/coord mvmt hand	1.00	2.00	1.36	1.91	73

N = 11

Scale for ranking factor:

1.0 = *not ranked*	4.2 = *ranked 15th*	6.4 = *ranked 4th*
2.2 = *ranked 25th*	4.4 = *ranked 14th*	6.6 = *ranked 3rd*
2.4 = *ranked 24th*	4.6 = *ranked 13th*	6.8 = *ranked 2nd*
2.6 = *ranked 23rd*	4.8 = *ranked 12th*	7.0 = *ranked 1st*
2.8 = *ranked 22nd*	5.0 = *ranked 11th*	
3.0 = *ranked 21st*	5.2 = *ranked 10th*	
3.2 = *ranked 20th*	5.4 = *ranked 9th*	
3.4 = *ranked 19th*	5.6 = *ranked 8th*	
3.6 = *ranked 18th*	5.8 = *ranked 7th*	
3.8 = *ranked 17th*	6.0 = *ranked 6th*	
4.0 = *ranked 16th*	6.2 = *ranked 5th*	

Scale for importance ratings:
4 = *critical*
3 = *essential*
2 = *extremely important*
1 = *somewhat important*
0 = *not important*

Scale for frequency ratings
(with or without help):
5 = *every day*
4 = *once/twice weekly*
4 = *once/twice montly*
2 = *1 to 4 times a year*
1 = *in unusual circumstances*
0 = *never*

Table 6
Percent Weights for Work Behaviors
Rank of Captain

Work behaviors were considered as *qualifying for the job content domain* if they met the following criteria:
1. They were performed by at least 66% of the SMEs.
2. They had a mean importance rating of at least 2.0.
Work behaviors were considered as *ADA qualifying* if they met the following criteria:
1. They were performed by at least 66% of the SMEs.
2. They had a mean importance rating of at least 2.3.
Work behaviors were considered *eligible for testing* if they met the following **additional** criterion:
1. They were rated as necessary at entry by at least 66% of the SMEs performing it and by at least 50% of all SMEs.

Work behavior		Qualifying for job content domain	ADA qualifying	Eligible for testing
WB1	Assign tasks and schedules	10.3	YES	10.3
WB2	Monitor progress of assignments	11.5	YES	11.5
WB3	Evaluate subord work performance	8.5	YES	8.5
WB4	Counsel, obtain feedback fr subord	6.5	YES	6.5
WB5	Perform administrative duties	15.3	YES	15.3
WB7	Manage physical resources	3.8	NO	3.8
WB13	Respond to life-threat emerg	3.7	YES	3.7
WB16	Interact with citizens	9.8	YES	9.8
WB17	Admin discipline, investig alleg	7.5	YES	7.5
WB18	Provide info to citizen groups	5.2	NO	5.2
WB21	Plan zone/section/unit goals	17.8	YES	17.8

N = 11

Note: The weight for a work behavior is computed as the product of the percentage of SMEs performing the work behavior multiplied by the mean percentage of time per SME spent on the work behavior multiplied by the square of the mean importance rating. These weights are then rescaled proportionately to sum 100 to provide percentage weights.

Table 7
Percent Weights for Knowledges, Skills, and Abilities
Rank of Captain

KSAs were considered as *qualifying for the job content domain* if they met the following criteria:
1. They had a mean importance rating of at least 2.0.
2. They were linked with a mean importance linkage rating of at least 1.5 to a qualifying work behavior.
KSAs were considered as *ADA qualifying* if they met the following criteria:
1. They had a mean importance rating of at least 2.3.
2. They were linked with a mean importance linkage rating of at least 1.5 to an ADA-qualifying work behavior.
KSAs were considered *eligible for testing* if they met the following **additional** criterion:
1. They were rated as necessary at entry by at least 60% of all SMEs.

KSA description		Qualifying for job content domain	ADA qualifying	Eligible for testing
A13	A to listen/resp to not aggrav sit	1.5	YES	1.6
A14	A to obtain facts and info	2.5	NO	2.5
A16	A to negotiate a resolution	1.3	YES	1.4
A23	A to exhibit interpersonal sensit	0.7	NO	0.8
A24	A to demonst approp patience	0.7	NO	0.9
A25	A to exhibit approp level firm	0.6	NO	0.8
A26	A to interact w/ subordinates	2.0	YES	2.0
A27	A to control one's emotion	0.9	YES	1.0
A28	A to detct beh chgs in subord	1.1	NO	1.2
A29	A to gather data for eval sub	0.9	NO	1.1
A32	A to counsel employee	0.8	YES	0.9
A33	A to rcmnd discip actn for subd	1.2	YES	1.3
A35	A to decide approp perf stds	2.2	YES	2.1
A36	A to confrnt others w/ perf def	1.5	YES	1.5
A37	A to undrst/use incent/pos reinf	1.7	YES	1.7
A38	A to identify perfmnc deficiency	0.9	NO	1.1
A40	A to manage time	3.3	YES	3.1
A41	A to delegate authority	3.2	YES	3.0
A45	A to organize people & equipmt	0.9	NO	1.0
A48	A to recgnz rel bet fact & situat	0.6	NO	0.7
A52	A to analyze facts	2.7	YES	2.6
A54	A to anal adv/disadv equip/supp	0.5	NO	0.0
A55	A to pick out patt/trnd num data	0.9	NO	1.0
A59	A to eval info dur interactions	1.0	YES	1.1
A62	A to read/undrstnd written mat	1.6	YES	1.6
A63	A to put aside pers feel/be obj	1.8	YES	1.9
A64	A to make timely decisions	3.7	YES	3.5

Table 7 (continued)
Percent Weights for Knowledges, Skills, and Abilities
Rank of Captain

KSA description		Qualifying for job content domain	ADA qualifying	Eligible for testing
A70	A to speak effectvly to a group	1.6	NO	1.5
A71	A to und what is being commun	0.8	YES	0.9
A74	A to adjust comm to diff bkgrnd	0.7	YES	0.8
A75	A to spk to audnc w/o prep	1.4	YES	1.4
A78	A to write w/ approp gramm/spell	1.8	YES	1.8
A79	A to exp oneslf accurtly in writing	1.4	YES	1.4
A80	A to write legibly	0.8	YES	0.9
A81	A to organize/present facts	2.3	YES	2.3
A82	A to present statist/numer info	1.0	YES	1.0
A83	A to simplify written mat/oral info	1.0	YES	1.1
A84	A to learn new knowledge	0.9	YES	0.9
A86	A to reduce data to percentages	0.5	NO	0.6
A87	A to read/understnd statist info	0.9	YES	1.0
A89	A to adjust managemt style	0.8	YES	0.9
A90	A to attnd to sev situatn simult	1.3	YES	1.3
A93	A to stick with a task	0.9	YES	1.0
A95	A to mntn integrity/resist corrup	2.7	YES	2.5
A96	A to rembr fact/det in ongng inv	1.6	YES	1.7
K1	K of geographical territory	1.7	NO	1.8
K6	K of radio signals and comm tech	0.6	NO	0.8
K7	K of special evnts—public saf enf	1.1	YES	1.2
K8	K of community issues/situations	2.5	NO	2.4
K12	K of current and impt events	3.3	NO	3.2
K15	K of territorial areas of city	1.3	YES	0.0
K33	K of laws/pol regard physical force	0.7	YES	0.9
K49	K of avail res for employee asst prg	0.8	YES	0.9
K52	K of prsnnl pol reg trnsf/leave/o.t.	2.3	YES	2.2
K53	K of dept disciplinary procedures	3.5	YES	3.2
K54	K of dept proc/laws reg empl rights	1.8	YES	1.8
K55	K of dpt pol/proc—inv sworn memb	2.7	YES	2.6
K59	K of depth pol—prov infor to media	1.1	NO	1.1
K60	K of dept chain of command	1.1	YES	1.2
K61	K of dept forms	0.7	NO	0.8
K63	K of proc hndlg work-rel injuries	0.7	NO	0.8
K68	K of SOPs, GOs, and SOs	4.0	YES	3.8
K69	K of Employee Work Rules	2.4	YES	2.4
K70	K of Field Manual	1.8	YES	1.8
K72	K of EPAS—performc eval sys	2.8	NO	2.7

N = 11

Note: The weight for a KSA/PA is computed by summing the product of its mean linkage ratings with the appropriate work behavior weights times the mean KSA/PA importance rating times the mean KSA/PA ranking factor. These weights are then scaled proportionately to sum 100 to give the percent weights.

Conclusions

We have attempted to convey a general idea of the practice of job analysis. As evidenced by the large number of studies cited in this article, much has been done in the way of job analysis research and application. However, at least one cautionary note bears repeating from our earlier paper (Veres, Locklear, & Sims, 1988). This concern is the effect of external influences on the practice of job analysis.

Job analysis research has been conducted for some 75 years, beginning with Hugo Munsterberg's (1913) study of streetcar operators. Progress has not been steady, however. Many of the accomplishments reported in these pages have occurred in the last 15 years. The federal courts have mandated that any personnel action that adversely affects minorities or women demonstrate its job relatedness. Job analysis has become the primary vehicle for making that demonstration. Although HRM specialists would like to assume smug self-satisfaction about milestones attained in job analysis research, external forces have worked to shape us, perhaps more than we have acted to shape them.

For example, Levine, Ash, and Bennett (1980) collected ratings from experienced job analysts on a number of job analysis methods. They found the Job Element Method (JEM) to be generally viewed as an exceptional job analysis approach. Levine, Ash, Hall, and Sistrunk's (1983) later study found markedly *lower* ratings for JEM. Why the difference? The most compelling argument centers around a federal court case involving state troopers in New York. In *United States v. State of New York* (1979), the judge ruled that JEM did *not* meet the requirements of the Uniform Guidelines. More recently the courts have weighed the opinions of professional organizations more heavily (e.g., *Watson v. Fort Worth Bank and Trust,* 1988), but all too often court decisions appear to drive professional practice, rather than the reverse.

Job analysis research has unquestionably come a long way. Sidney Gael's (1988a) sub-stantial work, *The Job Analysis Handbook for Business, Industry, and Government,* is a testament to the scope of job analysis research performed over the last three-quarters of a century. After five introductory chapters, Gael's text details six uses for job analysis results in organizational administration and nine uses for job analysis results in human resource management. Eleven chapters on methodological issues are included, and no fewer than thirty-seven chapters focus on specific job analysis methods. Harvey's (1991) chapter in the *Handbook of Industrial and Organizational Psychology* chronicles decades of research in the area and lays out a roadmap for future research. The enormous breadth of the research reported in these two handbooks can be taken as an indication that job analysis is indeed a fundamental starting point for human resource management.

References

Ash, R. A. (1988). Job analysis in the world of work. In S. Gael (Ed.), *The job analysis handbook for business, industry, and government* (Vol. 1, pp. 3–13). New York: Wiley.

Ash, R. A., & Levine, E. L. (1980). A framework for evaluating job analysis methods. *Personnel, 57,* 53–59.

Bemis, B. E., Belenky, A. H., & Soder, D. A. (1983). *Job analysis: An effective management tool.* Washington, DC: Bureau of National Affairs.

Bernardin, H. J., & Beatty, R. W. (1984). *Performance appraisal: Assessing human performance at work.* Boston: Kent.

Biddle, R. E. (1976). *Guidelines-oriented job analysis manual.* Sacramento, CA: Biddle & Associates.

Bownas, D. A., & Bernardin, H. J. (1988). Critical incident technique. In S. Gael (Ed.), *The job analysis handbook for business, industry, and government* (Vol. 2, pp. 1120–1137). New York: Wiley.

Buckley, R. (1980). *Integrated job analysis* (2nd ed.). Los Angeles: Psychological Services, Inc.

Buckley, R. (1986). *Integrated job analysis and selection.* Glendale, CA: Psychological Services, Inc.

Buckner, K. E. (1989). *A review and empirical analysis of court standards for employee selection.*

Unpublished doctoral dissertation, Auburn University, Auburn, AL.

Cascio, W. F. (1987). *Applied psychology in personnel management* (3rd ed.). Englewood Cliffs, NJ: Prentice Hall.

Christal, R. E. (1974). *The United States Air Force occupational research project.* Lackland Air Force Base, TX: Air Human Resources Laboratory.

Christal, R. E., & Weissmuller, J. J. (1988). Job-task inventory analysis. In S. Gael (Ed.), *The job analysis handbook for business, industry, and government* (Vol. 2, pp. 1036–1050). New York: Wiley.

Cornelius, E. T. (1988). Practical findings from job analysis research. In S. Gael (Ed.), *The job analysis handbook for business, industry, and government* (Vol. 1, pp. 48–68). New York: Wiley.

Davis, L. E., & Wacker, G. J. (1988). Job design. In S. Gael (Ed.), *The job analysis handbook for business, industry, and government* (Vol. 1, pp. 157–172). New York: Wiley.

Dunnette, M. D., & Borman, W. C. (1979). Personnel selection and classification systems. *Annual Review of Psychology, 30,* 477–525.

Elliott, R. H., Boyles, W. R., Hill, J. B., Palmer, C., Thomas, P., & Veres, J. G. (1980). *Content-oriented personnel selection procedures—A training manual.* Montgomery, AL: Auburn University at Montgomery, Center for Government and Public Affairs.

Equal Employment Opportunity Commission, Civil Service Commission, Department of Labor, & Department of Justice. (1978). Adoption by four agencies of uniform guidelines on employee selection procedures. *Federal Register, 43,* 38290–38315.

Feild, H. S., & Gatewood, R. D. (1989). Development of a selection interview: A job content strategy. In R. W. Eder & G. R. Ferris (Eds.), *The employment interview: Theory, research, and practice.* Beverly Hills, CA: Sage.

Fine, S. A. (1988). Functional job analysis. In S. Gael (Ed.), *The job analysis handbook for business, industry, and government* (Vol. 2, pp. 1019–1035). New York: Wiley.

Fine, S. A., Holt, A. M., & Hutchinson, M. F. (1974). *Functional job analysis: How to standardize task statements.* Kalamazoo, MI: W. E. Upjohn Institute for Employment Research.

Fine, S. A., & Wiley, W. W. (1971). *An introduction to functional job analysis: A scaling of selected tasks from the social welfare field.* Kalamazoo, MI: W. E. Upjohn Institute for Employment Research.

Flanagan, J. C. (1954). The critical incident technique. *Psychological Bulletin, 51,* 327–358.

Fleishman, E. A., & Quaintance, M. K. (1984). *Taxonomies of human performance: The description of human tasks.* Orlando, FL: Academic Press.

Fleishman, E. A., & Reilly, M. E. (1992). *Handbook of human abilities.* Palo Alto, CA: Consulting Psychologists Press, Inc.

French, W. L. (1982). *The personnel management process: Human resources administration and development.* Boston: Houghton-Mifflin.

Gael, S. (Ed.) (1988a). *The job analysis handbook for business, industry, and government* (Vols. 1–2). New York: Wiley.

Gael, S. (1988b). Job descriptions. In S. Gael (Ed.), *The job analysis handbook for business, industry, and government* (Vol. 1, pp. 71–89). New York: Wiley.

Gatewood, R. D., & Feild, H. S. (1987). *Human resource selection.* Hinsdale, IL: Dryden.

Gatewood, R. D., & Feild, H. S. (1994). *Human resource selection.* (2nd ed.). Hinsdale, IL: Dryden.

Ghorpade, J., & Atchison, T. J. (1980). The concept of job analysis: A review and some suggestions. *Public Personnel Management, 9,* 134–144.

Gilpatrick, E. (1977). *The health services mobility study method of task analysis and curriculum design basic tools: Concepts, task identification, skill scales and knowledge system.* Springfield, VA: National Technical Information Service.

Goldstein, I. L. (1993). *Training in organizations* (3rd ed.). Pacific Grove, CA: Brooks/Cole.

Goldstein, I. L., Zedeck, S., & Schneider, B. (1993). An exploration of the job analysis–content validity process. In N. Schmitt & W. C. Borman (Eds.), *Personnel selection in organizations* (pp. 3–32). San Francisco: Jossey-Bass.

Guion, R. M. (1978). Scoring of content domain sample: The problem of fairness. *Journal of Applied Psychology, 63,* 499–506.

Harvey, R. J. (1991). Job analysis. In M. Dunnette & L. M. Hough (Eds.), *Handbook of industrial and organizational psychology* (pp. 71–163). Palo Alto, CA: Consulting Psychologists Press.

Hay, E. N., & Purves, D. (1954). A new method of job evaluation: The guide chart-profile method. *Personnel, 31(7),* 72–80.

Holley, W. M., & Jennings, K. M. (1983). *Personnel management: Functions and issues.* Chicago: Dryden.

Kirkland v. New York Department of Corrections, 374 F. Supp. 1361 (S. D. NY 1974).

Levine, E. L. (1983). *Everything you always wanted to know about job analysis and more: A job analysis primer.* Tampa, FL: Mariner.

Levine, E. L., Ash, R. A., & Bennett, N. (1980). Exploratory comparative study of four job analysis methods. *Journal of Applied Psychology, 65,* 524–535.

Levine, E. L., Ash, R. A., Hall, H., & Sistrunk, F. (1983). Evaluation of job analysis methods by experienced job analysts. *Academy of Management Journal, 26,* 339–348.

Lopez, F. M. (1986). *The threshold traits analysis technical manual.* Port Washington, NY: Lopez and Associates.

Lopez, F. M. (1988). Threshold traits analysis system. In S. Gael (Ed.), *The job analysis handbook for business, industry, and government* (Vol. 2, pp. 880–901). New York: Wiley.

McCormick, E. J. (1976). Job and task analysis. In M. Dunnette (Ed.), *Handbook of industrial and organizational psychology.* Chicago: Rand McNally.

McCormick, E. J. (1979). *Job analysis: Methods and applications.* New York: American Management Association.

McCormick, E. J., DeNisi, A. S., & Shaw, J. B. (1979). Use of the Position Analysis Questionnaire for establishing the job component validity of tests. *Journal of Applied Psychology, 64,* 51–56.

McCormick, E. J., Jeanneret, P. R., & Mecham, R. C. (1972). A study of job characteristics and job dimensions as based on the Position Analysis Questionnaire (PAQ). *Journal of Applied Psychology, 56,* 347–368.

Menne, J. W., McCarthy, W., & Menne, J. (1976). A systems approach to the content validation of em-

ployee selection procedures. *Public Personnel Management, 5,* 387–396.

Munsterberg, H. (1913). *Psychology and industrial efficiency.* Boston: Houghton Mifflin.

Prien, E. P. (1977). The function of job analysis in content validation. *Personnel Psychology, 30,* 167–174.

Prien, E. P., & Ronan, W. W. (1971). Job analyses: A review of research findings. *Personnel Psychology, 24,* 371–396.

Primoff, E. S. (1975). *How to prepare and conduct job element examinations.* Washington, DC: U.S. Civil Service Commission, Personnel Research and Development Center.

Schmidt, F. L., Caplan, J. R., Bemis, S. E., Dewir, R., Dunn, L., & Antone, L. (1979). *The behavioral consistency method of unassembled examining.* Washington, DC: U.S. Office of Personnel Management.

Siegel, G. B. (1987). Education and training for the job analyst. *Personnel, 64(7),* 68–73.

Sims, R. R., & Veres, J. G. (1985). A practical program for training job analysts. *Public Personnel Management, 14,* 131–137.

Smith, J. E., & Hakel, M. D. (1979). Convergence among data sources, response bias, and reliability and validity of a structured job analysis questionnaire. *Personnel Psychology, 32,* 677–692.

Sparks, P. (1979). *Job analysis under the new Uniform Guidelines.* Houston, TX: Exxon Corporation, Personnel Research.

Sparks, P. (1981). Job analysis. In K. Rowland & G. Ferris (Eds.), *Personnel management* (pp. 78–100). Boston: Allyn and Bacon.

Stout Vocational Rehabilitation Institute, University of Wisconsin–Stout. (1974). *Physical demands job analysis: A new approach.* Menomonie, Wisconsin: Author.

Thompson, D. E., & Thompson, T. A. (1982). Court standards for job analysis in test validation. *Personnel Psychology, 35,* 865–874.

Tiffin, J., & McCormick, E. J. (1965). *Industrial psychology.* Englewood Cliffs, NJ: Prentice Hall.

U.S. Civil Service Commission. (1977). *Instructions for the factor evaluation system.* Washington, DC: U.S. Government Printing Office.

U.S. Department of Labor, Employment and Training Administration. (1977). *Dictionary of occupa-*

tional titles (4th ed.). Washington, DC: U.S. Government Printing Office.

United States v. State of New York, 82 FRD 2 (D. C. NY 1978) dec on merits, 475 F. Supp 1103 (D. C. NY 1979).

Van De Voort, D. M., & Stalder, B. K. (1988). Organizing for job analysis. In S. Gael (Ed.), *The job analysis handbook for business, industry, and government* (Vol. 1, pp. 315–328). New York: Wiley.

Veres, J. G., Lahey, M. A., & Buckley, R. (1987). A practical rationale for using multimethod job analyses. *Public Personnel Management, 16,* 153–157.

Veres, J. G., Locklear, T. S., & Sims, R. R. (1988). Organizational entry. In G. R. Ferris, K. M. Rowland, & M. R. Buckley (Eds.), *Human resource management* (pp. 79–103). Boston: Allyn and Bacon.

Watson v. Fort Worth Bank and Trust, 487 U.S. •••, 108 S.Ct. 2777 (1988).

Wernimont, P. F. (1988). Recruitment, selection, and placement. In S. Gael (Ed.), *The job analysis handbook for business, industry, and government* (Vol. 1, pp. 193–204). New York: Wiley.

Human Resource Planning

Susan E. Jackson and Randall S. Schuler

In an early treatment of the topic, Vetter (1967) defined human resource planning as

> the process by which management determines how the organization should move from its current manpower position to its desired position. Through planning, management strives to have the right number and the right kinds of people, at the right places, at the right time, doing things which result in both the organization and the individual receiving maximum long-run benefits. (p. 15)

Contemporary human resource planning occurs within the broad context of organizational and strategic business planning. It involves forecasting the organization's future human resource needs and planning for how those needs will be met. It includes establishing objectives and then developing and implementing programs (staffing, appraising, compensating, and training) to ensure that people are available with the appropriate characteristics and skills when and where the organization needs them. It may also involve developing and implementing programs to improve employee performance or to increase employee satisfaction and involvement in order to boost organizational productivity, quality,

or innovation (Mills, 1985b). Finally, human resource planning includes gathering data that can be used to evaluate the effectiveness of ongoing programs and inform planners when revisions in their forecasts and programs are needed.

Because a major objective of planning is facilitating an organization's effectiveness, it must be integrated with the organization's short-term and longer term business objectives and plans.[1] Increasingly this is being done in leading organizations, although in the past business needs usually defined personnel needs and human resource planning, which meant that planning became a reactive process. The reactive nature of the process went hand-in-hand with a short-term orientation. Now, major changes in business, economic, and social environments are creating uncertainties that are forcing organizations to integrate business planning with human resource planning and to adopt a longer term perspective. For example, according to Kathryn Connors, vice president of human resources at Liz Claiborne,

> Human resources is part of the strategic (business) planning process. It's part of policy development, line extension planning and the

[1]Throughout this article we use terms such as business objectives and business needs in a generic sense to refer to the bottom-line criteria against which an organization evaluates its performance. Our intention is to include the criteria considered by all types of employers, regardless of whether they are for-profit organizations.

We thank James Walker, two very helpful anonymous reviewers, and the special issue editors for their comments on previous drafts of this article. In addition, we thank Henry A. Goodstein, BMR, Inc., and Donald K. Brush, the Barden Corporation, for permitting us to quote our discussions with them, as well as Donald Laidlaw, the IBM Corporation, and Manuel London, AT&T, for their helpful insights.

Correspondence concerning this article should be addressed to Susan E. Jackson, Department of Psychology, 6 Washington Place, New York University, New York, NY 10003.

merger and acquisition processes. Little is done in the company that doesn't involve us in the planning, policy or finalization stages of any deal. (cited in Lawrence, 1989, p. 70)

John O'Brien, vice president of human resources at Digital Equipment Corporation, describes an integrated linkage between business and human resource plans as one by which human resource and line managers work jointly to develop business plans and determine human resource needs, analyze the work force profile in terms of future business strategies, review emerging human resource issues, and develop programs to address the issues and support the business plans. According to O'Brien, such joint efforts occur when human resource planners convince corporate business planners that "human resources represent a major competitive advantage" ("Planning with People," 1984, p. 7) that can increase profits when managed carefully. This article describes some of the activities that industrial/organizational (I/O) psychologists are engaged in as they seek to improve the competitiveness of organizations through effective human resource planning.

Factors Underlying Increased Interest in Human Resource Planning

Undoubtedly, there are many factors that account for the increased attention directed to human resource planning, but environmental forces—globalization, new technologies, economic conditions, and a changing work force—seem particularly potent (Dumaine, 1989; Dyer & Heyer, 1984; Greenhalgh, McKersie, & Gilkey, 1986). These create complexity and uncertainty for organizations. Uncertainty can interfere with efficient operations, so organizations typically attempt to reduce its impact; formal planning is one common tactic used by organizations to buffer themselves from environmental uncertainty (Thompson, 1967).

The changing characteristics of the work force, which is but one important environmental factor, make the need for planning ev-

ident. Between 1976 and 1980, the labor force grew an average of 2.8%, but between 1991 and 1995, the rate of growth will drop to 1.1%. Additionally, whereas more than 3 million people joined the labor force in 1978, less than 2 million people are projected to enter the labor force each year from 1987 to 1995. Comparatively, the proportion of younger people (aged 16 to 24) and older people (aged 55 and over) in the work force will decline. People aged 25 to 54 will constitute a greater percentage of the labor force, increasing from 61% in 1975 to 73% in 1995. The number of mothers in the work force with children under one year old increased from 42% in 1980 to 55% in 1989. The ethnic mix of the labor force is also changing. The Bureau of Labor Statistics estimates that ethnic minorities will account for 57% of the growth in the labor force between now and the year 2000. Of the approximately 25 million workers added to the work force between 1985 and 2000, 42% are expected to be native White women and only 15% are expected to be native White men. Fully 22% are expected to be immigrants (Glickman, 1982; Johnston & Packer, 1987; "Managing Now," 1988; "Needed," 1988; Nelton, 1988).

All of these demographic projections have significant implications for managing human resources, thereby increasing the importance of human resource planning (Coates, 1987; Davis & Associates, 1986). The changing demographics mean there will be fewer entry-level employees, so competition among employers will increase. In addition, the changing demographics signal changes in the abilities, skills, interests, and values of tomorrow's work force. For example, shortages of many types of skilled workers are imminent, including tool-and-die makers, bricklayers, shipbuilders, mechanics, machinists, and engineers ("Early Retirement," 1987). Even if organizations are willing to train new employees, the task may be difficult, as the U.S. Navy has found. At a time when many of its training manuals required 12th-grade reading skills, nearly one-fourth of the high school graduates who entered the Navy read below the 10th-grade level (National Alliance of Business, 1986). Such statistics are alarming when compared to projections indicating that the levels of various skills needed for new jobs are likely to increase in the future (see Johnston & Packer, 1987).

A consideration of how the values of workers who will soon make up the majority of the work force differ from those who will begin to leave it suggests additional changes on the horizon. There is already evidence of growing resistance from employees to relocation. Greater emphasis on self-evaluation and a reduction in loyalty and dedication to employers makes it more difficult for organizations to assume they can move employees around anywhere and anytime (Maccoby, 1988; Mills, 1987). A decline in organizational loyalty is occurring at the same time that workers are feeling insecure about their employment (Hay Group, 1988).

A recent study comparing the work values of those over 40 years old with those under 40 years old suggested other types of changes for which organizations must prepare. For example, employees from the younger generation, who grew up during the Vietnam war, do not trust authority as much as do members of the older generation, who are products of the World War II era. The younger generation thinks work should be fun, whereas the older generation sees work as a duty and vehicle for financial support. Younger employees believe people should advance as quickly as their competence permits, whereas older workers believe that experience is the necessary road to promotion. Finally, this study found that for the younger generation, "fairness" means allowing people to be different, but for the older generation it means treating people equally ("Work Attitudes," 1986).

Changes in the work force are just one aspect of the environment stimulating the need for human resource planning. The demographic changes are somewhat predictable, but when they are considered in combination with changing technology (see Davis & Asso-

ciates, 1986) and many of the other external changes described elsewhere in this issue (e.g., by Offermann & Gowing, pp. 95–108), they pose significant challenges for human resource planning and contribute to its changing status during the past two decades.

A Model for Describing Human Resource Planning

In the remainder of this article, we describe the activities engaged in by human resource planners in leading organizations. Throughout our discussion, we describe four phases of human resource planning: (a) gathering and analyzing data to forecast expected human resource demand, given business plans for the future, and to forecast future human resource supply; (b) establishing human resource objectives; (c) designing and implementing programs that will enable the organization to achieve its human resource objectives; and (d) monitoring and evaluating these programs (Burack, 1988; Odiorne, 1981). Activities related to the four phases of human resource planning are described for three different time horizons: short term (up to one year), intermediate term (two to three years), and long term (more than three years). These correspond to the typical time horizons for business planning. Using the same conventions that line managers use to distinguish between activities with differing time horizons is one step human resource planners can take to facilitate integration of their efforts with the needs of the business (Hennecke, 1984; Migliore, 1984, 1986; Walker, 1978).

Although the four phases of human resource planning are conceptually the same regardless of the time horizon, there are practical differences in the operationalization of the four phases as the time horizon is extended. Therefore, we describe the activities related to planning for each time horizon separately and in turn, beginning with short-term planning. We begin with the shorter term planning horizon because historically the activities of many I/O psychologists have been carried out for the purpose of achieving shorter term objectives. As organizations and I/O psychologists began to recognize the potential benefits of engaging in longer term planning, however, consideration of longer term issues became more common. As a result, as is described near the end of this article, many I/O psychologists are now engaged in activities designed to prepare organizations for the 21st century.

In separating our discussion of the phases of human resource planning activities according to three time horizons, we do not mean to suggest that organizations segregate their planning activities in this fashion. The reality is that organizations must integrate their activities across the four planning phases as well across all three time horizons, as is shown in Figure 1. As the feed-forward and feed-back arrows connecting the four phases of planning illustrate, planning activities within a time horizon are linked together into a dynamic system. Early phases (e.g., demand and supply forecasts) serve as inputs to later phases (e.g., setting objectives). Equally important, organizations can learn from the results generated during the evaluation phase and then apply what is learned to make adjustments in objectives and programs.

In addition to the arrows linking the four phases of planning within each time frame, Figure 1 includes arrows to illustrate (a) how longer term objectives can influence shorter term planning (dotted-line arrows), (b) how shorter term evaluation results can influence projections about future human resources and programs designed to meet future demands, and (c) how the results achieved through the implementation of human resource programs can influence business plans. The arrows connecting planning activities for different time horizons are important to note because they emphasize that planning for one time horizon typically has implications for another. For example, long-term planning almost always prompts the development of programs that need to be implemented in the short term and intermediate term. In addition, the evaluation results obtained for shorter term programs often lead to reevaluation of longer term projections about the availability of human resources, which in turn may prompt adjustments in programs designed to meet longer

Figure 1.   Dynamic Linkages among Components of a Fully Integrated System of Business and Human Resource Planning

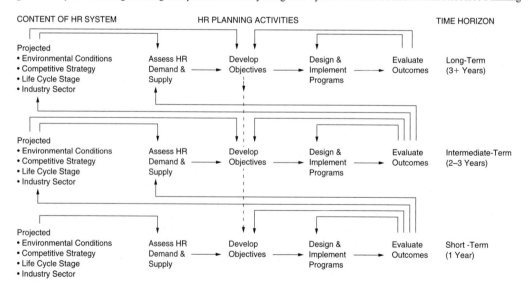

term needs. The ideal is to have full integration among all types of human resource planning activities as well as integration between human resource and business planning (Walker, 1988).

Short-Term Human Resource Planning

Many I/O psychologists work on activities related to designing and implementing programs (e.g., recruitment, selection systems, and training programs) to meet short-term organizational needs. Such activities generally involve an element of planning in that they are future-oriented to some extent. Even projects for which objectives are expected to be achieved in as little time as a few months have, ideally, been designed with an understanding of how the short-term objectives are linked to the achievement of longer term objectives. For example, an aeronautics company engaged in a recruitment campaign to hire 100 engineers should have a clear understanding of how this hiring goal will help the company achieve long-term goals such as becoming the world's most innovative company in that industry. This hypothetical company also might have a college recruiting drive designed to find 75 college graduates to enter a training program in recognition of the fact that a growing company needs to prepare for the middle managers it will need 5 to 7 years hence, as well as the top level managers it will need in 10 to 15 years. As this hypothetical example highlights, in order for a clear linkage to exist between human resource planning and strategic business planning, it is essential that an organization's top executives have a fully articulated vision for the future, which has been communicated and accepted by managers throughout the organization.

Forecasting Demand and Supply

In a short-term time horizon, demand and supply of human resources can be predicted with some certainty. Human resource objectives follow logically from consideration of any discrepancies between demand and supply. *De-mand* refers to the number and characteristics (e.g., skills, abilities, pay levels, or experience) of people needed for particular jobs at a given point in time and at a particular place. *Supply* refers to both the number and characteristics of people available for those particular jobs. Salient questions are "What jobs need to be filled (or vacated) during the next 12 months?" and "How and where will we get people to fill (or vacate) those jobs?"

What jobs need to be filled and vacated? Answering the demand question involves predicting who will leave jobs and create vacancies, which jobs will be eliminated, and which new jobs will be created. One method for predicting both vacancies and job growth is to project historical trends into the future. This is particularly relevant for organizations affected by regular, cyclical fluctuations in demand for their products or services. Behavioral theories of the causes of turnover (e.g., Mobley, Griffeth, Hand, & Meglino, 1979; Mowday, Porter, & Steers, 1982) combined with employee surveys designed to assess attitudinal predictors of turnover (e.g., job satisfaction) also help I/O psychologists and human resource planners predict how many currently filled positions are likely to become vacant. Such information can produce useful predictions when the organizational unit of interest is large, although making predictions about precisely which positions are likely to become vacant is less precise. Predictions about how many and what types of jobs will be eliminated or created in the short term generally follow directly from business plans submitted by line managers.

How and where will we get people to fill and vacate jobs? The first step in answering this question—the supply question—involves determining the desired characteristics of employees who fill (or vacate) the jobs of interest. Then the availability of those characteristics in the organization's current work force and in the external labor market must be assessed. The particular characteristics of current and potential employees that are inventoried and tracked by human resource planners are influenced by the nature of the organization and the environment in which it operates. For example, for human resource planners in growing organizations, simply finding people with the needed skills and abilities is likely to be a top priority. For planners in mature and declining organizations, the costs (e.g., salary level) associated with employees become more salient, especially if work-force reductions are needed. Thus it is important for the human resource planner to know the business needs and characteristics of the organization. This knowledge is gained by human resource planners meeting with line managers to discuss their business plans as well as their human resource needs. The process of discussion increases the accuracy of supply and demand forecasts and facilitates the establishment of human resource objectives (see Schuler, 1988).

Establishing Objectives

With a short-time horizon, objectives are often easy to state in quantifiable terms. Examples of short-term human resource objectives include increasing the number of people who are attracted to the organization and apply for jobs (increase the applicant pool); attracting a different mix of applicants (with different skills, in different locations, etc.); improving the qualifications of new hires; increasing the length of time that desirable employees stay with the organization; decreasing the length of time that undesirable employees stay with the organization; and helping current and newly hired employees quickly develop the skills needed by the organization. Such objectives can generally be achieved in a straightforward way by applying state-of-the-art human resource management techniques and working with line managers to ensure agreement with and understanding of the program objectives.

Design and Implementation of Short-Term Programs

The technical skills of I/O psychologists are often applied to short-term program design and implementation. For example, recruiting programs are used to influence the size and quality of the applicant pool. Selection programs are developed for making hiring decisions. Performance appraisal systems identify performance deficiencies to be corrected and competencies to be rewarded. Training programs emphasize developing skills for use in the near future. Compensation systems are designed to attract new employees, to motivate people to perform well, and to retain employees. Even when these activities are designed to achieve short-term objectives and are expected to have relatively immediate payoffs, they can serve to help an organization achieve its longer term goals.

Donald K. Brush, vice-president and general manager of the Barden Corporation, described how short-term human resource planning efforts helped his organization achieve its strategic goals (Brush, personal communication, March 8, 1989): Barden realized it had an opportunity to significantly increase its business, but to do so would require them to increase their hourly work force by a net of about 125 employees in one year, at a time when the local unemployment rate was only 2.5%. Past experiences had taught Barden that foreign immigrants often became excellent employees. Although there were many immigrants from a variety of different countries who were interested in employment, a major hurdle to their immediate success was their lack of fluency in English. Brush described the problem and the solution, like this:

> To begin to be functioning, qualified Barden employees, newcomers must not only master the basic "Barden" vocabulary, but they must be able to look up standard operating procedures, read Material Safety Data sheets, and they must also master basic shop mathematics, measurement processes and blueprint reading. . . . We asked Personnel to investigate how we might teach these people enough English to pay their way. The upshot was this: We retained Berlitz. A special intensive course was developed in cooperation with our training unit. . . .

All students are on our payroll and meet with a Berlitz instructor four hours a day for 15 consecutive work days during working hours. The effect has been electric. The confidence level of the students has soared as they have tried out their new language ability. Supervisors are impressed. And the word is getting out to the community with positive results. (Brush, personal communication, March 8, 1989)

This example illustrates a problem that organizations will face increasingly in the near future, namely, a shortage of qualified entry-level job applicants (Johnston & Packer, 1987). This demographic change is likely to mean that organizations will begin to shift the focus of their short-term human resource programs. During the past 20 years, the combined forces of equal employment opportunity (EEO) legislation and the abundant supply of new entrants into the labor force were congruent with human resource activities aimed at improving the ability of organizations to select employees on the basis of their job-related skills and abilities. Organizations benefited from investing in the design, validation, and use of selection "tests" of all sorts. This is because even tests with relatively low, but nonzero, validity can have economic utility when selection ratios are sufficiently low.

As the labor pool shrinks, however, selection ratios will tend to become larger. As a consequence, small marginal gains in test validity will have less economic utility, relative to the past. In order for investments in the development and use of sophisticated selection methods to yield economic returns, much more energy will have to be directed toward recruiting efforts to increase the number of job applicants because only by attracting a large pool of applicants can selection ratios be kept low. If small selection ratios cannot be maintained, organizations may conclude that their resources are better invested in training efforts designed to prepare those few who are available.

Examples of innovative recruiting programs are already plentiful. Giant Food, Inc.,

has a mobile recruiting office—a Winnebago van that is a self-contained recruitment center that seeks out job applicants by visiting schools, shopping centers, and so forth. Coopers & Lybrand employs successful minority business people in the community to help recruit minority applicants and to serve as mentors. McDonald's Corporation has emerged as a leader in the recruitment of older employees, which it does by using television commercials and formal relationships with senior citizen organizations. It is important to note that such efforts to broaden the pool of applicants often require coordinated, intermediate-term programs designed to ensure that nontraditional new hires are effective and can be retained.

Evaluating Short-Term Human Resource Programs

As is true for any type of program evaluation, this phase involves assessing how well objectives were achieved. Because short-term planning objectives are generally stated in terms that are relatively easy to quantify (e.g., numbers of applicants, numbers of hires, and performance levels of employees), systematic evaluation of human resource programs to meet short-term organizational needs is quite feasible, and some types of program evaluations are actually common in large organizations. For example, in part because numerous federal and state laws prohibit some forms of discrimination, selection programs in particular have been closely scrutinized to ensure that employers base their selection decisions on characteristics of applicants that are job related. Whether such scrutiny will continue is somewhat uncertain, however, given recent Supreme Court decisions (e.g., *Lorance v. AT&T,* 1989; *Martin v. Wilks,* 1989; *Patterson v. McLean Credit Union,* 1989; *Wards Cove Packing v. Atonia,* 1989).

Legal regulations have prompted many organizations, especially large ones, to assess empirically the relationship between an applicant's characteristics (e.g., abilities) and job performance. Such evaluation studies (validity studies) benefit employers because they serve to monitor the objective of getting the right people in the right job. Validity studies also serve a scientific function by providing valuable data to researchers interested in improving our understanding of the factors that influence human performance.

Until very recently, when programs for selection, training, and motivation were evaluated by I/O psychologists, the effectiveness criteria were almost exclusively behavioral (e.g., performance and turnover) or attitudinal (e.g., job satisfaction and commitment). Such criteria need no defense to be accepted by psychologists, but line management support for human resource programs can be difficult to achieve if the expected results of such programs are not translated into the language of business, that is, dollars. With continuing advancements in utility analysis techniques (e.g., Boudreau & Berger, 1985) and human resource cost assessment techniques (e.g., Cascio, 1986), it is becoming more feasible to build convincing economic arguments in support of human resource programs. Thus, rather than having to spend energy arguing for resources to conduct short-term programs, I/O psychologists in organizational settings are being freed to deal more extensively with intermediate-term and longer term human resource planning issues.

Intermediate-Term
Human Resource Planning

As we have noted, planning is used by organizations to buffer production or service delivery processes from sources of uncertainty. Human resource programs for the recruitment, selection, training, and motivation of employees help reduce uncertainty by ensuring that a sufficient number of people with the required characteristics and skills are available at all levels in the organizations. When the planning horizon is short, there is little uncertainty about which skills and how many people will be needed, and it is relatively easy to predict supply.

However, rapid and ongoing changes in today's business environment mean that the future cannot be easily anticipated by simply projecting past trends. As the focus of planning moves from short term to intermediate term, the question "What will we need?" is less easily answered and so becomes more dominant. For intermediate-term planning, there is also more uncertainty related to the question, "What will be available?" Consequently, human resource planning for the more distant future quickly raises the question, "How can we determine what will be needed and what will be available?" In other words, more technical attention must be given to the problem of forecasting. As in short-term human resource planning, the twin problems of forecasting demand and forecasting supply both must be addressed before objectives can be established and programs developed. With increased uncertainty, interaction between the human resource planner and line managers is even more critical for making accurate demand and supply forecasts.

Forecasting Intermediate-Term Demand

In order to forecast the numbers and qualities of people who will be needed to perform the jobs that will exist in the organization's intermediate-term future (in two to three years), strategic planners attempt to predict organizational outputs, such as expected production, volume, and sales levels. The outputs that an organization intends to produce or deliver, in combination with the technology that the organization intends to use to generate the outputs, dictate the human resource needs of the organization. Predicting outputs requires considering factors such as future demands from the marketplace for the products and services that the organization provides, the percentage of the market that the organization is likely to be able to serve, the availability and nature of new technologies that may affect the amounts and types of products or services that can be offered, and the different countries in which the organization expects to operate (Dumaine, 1989).

The task of formulating plans that specify the intended future outputs (in terms of quantity, type, and location) of the organization is usually the responsibility of middle-level line managers. Human resource planners must then translate these objectives for outputs into predictions about the amount and the nature of jobs that employees will need to perform in order to produce the desired outputs. Predicting future human resource demands requires (a) having an accurate model of the factors that will influence demand and (b) being able to predict the state of all the major variables in that model. Organizations operating in fairly stable environments may be able to construct models that include most of the major factors likely to determine demand for up to three years into the future. It is even possible for some organizations to quantify the expected values of variables in their models, which means they can use statistical forecasting techniques such as regression analysis, time-series analysis, and stochastic modeling to forecast human demand (e.g., see Charnes, Cooper, Lewis, & Niehaus, 1978). For firms operating in unstable environments, however, even three-year predictions are likely to be highly uncertain because both the variables and their expected values are difficult to specify accurately by relying on historical data.

Given the complexity of statistical forecasting, it is understandable that judgmental techniques are more commonly used than statistical techniques (Kahales, Pazer, Hoagland, & Leavitt, 1980; Milkovich, Dyer, & Mahoney, 1983). A simple type of judgmental forecasting is managerial estimation. Estimates of staffing needs are made by middle- and lower-level line managers who pass them up to top managers for further revisions to form an overall demand forecast (Walker, 1980). Increasingly, human resource planners are involved in these stages of estimation and revision to ensure an integrated approach to planning.

A more sophisticated method of judgmental forecasting is the Delphi technique, which is a decision-making method designed to maximize the benefits and minimize the dysfunctional aspects of group decision making. In a Delphi "meeting" (which need not be face-to-face), several experts take turns presenting their forecasts and assumptions. An intermediary passes each expert's forecast and assumptions to the others, who then make revisions in their own forecasts. This process continues until a viable composite forecast emerges. The composite may represent specific projections or a range of projections, depending on the experts' positions. The Delphi technique appears to be particularly useful for generating solutions to unstructured and complex questions, such as those that arise during human resource planning. It does have limitations, however. For example, when experts disagree, integrating their opinions to yield a final solution that all participants accept can be difficult (see Delbecq, Van de Ven, & Gustafson, 1975; Milkovich, Annoni, & Mahoney, 1972). Nonetheless, the human resource planner must integrate diverse predictions in order to establish human resource objectives and design programs to achieve those objectives, and line managers must accept the predictions as reasonable if they are to provide their support during the implementation phases of human resource programs.

Both managerial estimates and the Delphi technique typically focus on forecasting the number of employees that is likely to be needed. Less attention is usually paid to the issue of the qualities (e.g., skills and abilities) that future employees will need, primarily because techniques have not been widely available for predicting these (Goodstein, personal communication, February 9, 1989). When psychologists engage in short-term planning, job analysis is used to determine the qualities that employees need in order to perform currently existing jobs. Rapid technological changes mean jobs in the future are sure to differ from jobs in the present (Zuboff, 1988), however. As an indication of the fact that I/O psychologists are now more often dealing with problems of intermediate-term planning, research efforts are underway to develop procedures for conducting future-oriented ("strategic") job analyses (Arvey, Salas, & Gialluca, 1989; Schneider & Konz, 1989) and for identifying the managerial competencies that are necessary for effective performance in the future (DeLuca, 1988; Goodstein, personal communication, February 9, 1989). Because job analysis results are the foundation on which most human resource programs are built (Page & Van De Vroot, 1989), the development of sound future-oriented job analysis methodologies is a challenge that I/O psychologists must meet before they can realize their potential as contributors to the long-term effectiveness of organizations.

Forecasting Intermediate-Term Supply

Supply forecasts can be derived from both internal and external sources of information, but internal sources are generally most crucial and most available (Bechet & Maki, 1987; Miller, 1980). As with forecasting demand, two basic techniques help forecast internal labor supply—judgmental and statistical. One judgmental technique used to forecast supply is replacement planning. Replacement charts show the names of current position occupants and the names of likely replacements, providing a rough estimate of the "bench strength" of the organization. On the replacement chart the incumbents are listed directly under the job title. Those individuals likely to fill the potential vacancies are listed directly under the incumbent. Such lists can provide an organization with reasonable estimates of which positions are likely to become vacant, and they can indicate whether someone will be ready to fill the vacancy (Walker & Armes, 1979). Present performance levels, ages, and information about the loyalty of current employees can be used to predict future vacancies caused by raids of top talent, involuntary turnover, retirement, and employee-initiated job changes. Consistent with the spirit of integration, increasingly line managers and human resource planners jointly establish replacement charts for middle- and upper-level positions.

Less common techniques to forecast supply are statistical techniques, which include simple inventory models, Markov analysis, simulation (based on Markov analysis), renewal analysis, and goal programming (Dyer, 1982; Niehaus, 1979, 1980, 1988; Piskor & Dudding, 1978). Use of statistical methods for forecasting human resource supply involves two steps, regardless of the particular model used. The first step is generating an inventory of current supply (the number of people and their skills and abilities). The second step involves predicting how the supply is likely to change over time. Ideally, both steps consider both internal and external supply sources, although in practice it is often more difficult to estimate labor supplies external to the organization.

I/O psychologists have been studying the nature of human abilities and the nature of jobs for most of this century. Consequently, sophisticated techniques are available for directly assessing employees' skills and abilities (e.g., see Arvey & Faley, 1988; Schneider & Schmitt, 1986), or the supply of skills and abilities available in the organization's work force can be inferred from job analyses of the jobs that current employees are performing (see American Telegraph & Telephone, 1980; Arvey et al., 1989; Fleishman & Quaintance, 1984; Levine, 1983; McCormick, Jeanneret, & Mecham, 1972; U.S. Air Force, 1981). By assessing the extent to which the current work force possesses skills and abilities that can be transferred to aid their performance in jobs predicted to exist in the future, I/O psychologists can help organizations assess how much of a discrepancy exists between their current skills profile and the profile required to meet their strategic plan. Thus research by I/O psychologists clearly has contributed greatly to making it possible to inventory and forecast human resource supplies. At the same time, computer technology has increased the feasibility of keeping information provided from such inventories up-to-date (Murdick & Schuster, 1983). Furthermore, EEO requirements have led many organizations to view such inventories as highly desirable and perhaps necessary, so statistical models have been developed to deal specifically with this aspect of human resource planning (Bres, Niehaus, Schinnar, & Steinbuch, 1983; Krzystofiak, 1982; Ledvinka & La Forge, 1978).

For statistical forecasting, current supply information serves as a starting point. Figures describing the current work force, both within the organization and externally, are then transformed through statistical models to predictions of future supply levels. Such models require the human resource planner to provide information about how employees are likely to flow through the organization. Annual hiring levels, turnover rates, promotions, and within-firm transfers typically are considered. The result is a quantitative prediction of what the future work force would probably be like absent the implementation of programs designed to change the projected supply.

The accuracy of statistical techniques for forecasting future supply levels depends entirely on the accuracy of the user-supplied figures about how employees are likely to flow through the organization and the accuracy of the statistical model used to transform current supplies into predicted future supplies. Accurate estimates and accurate models of employee flows are most likely to be available in organizations that have extensive record-keeping procedures because these can be used to identify the typical movement patterns of employees in the past. The U.S. military is one example of such an organization, and much of the available research on statistical forecasting has been supported by the U.S. government. Extensive use has been made of a simple inventory model in the U.S. Navy's public shipyards in conjunction with the Naval Sea Systems Command (NAVSEA) efficiency study (Niehaus, Schinnar, & Walter, 1987). The Navy used goal programming models extensively in its work on downsizing the civilian work force after the Vietnam war and in incorporating EEO planning needs (Charnes, Cooper, Nelson, & Niehaus, 1982; Charnes,

Cooper, Lewis, & Niehaus, 1978). Other organizations that have successfully used statistical forecasting include IBM (Dyer & Heyer, 1984), Merck (Milkovich & Phillips, 1986), and Ontario Hydro (Rush & Borne, 1986).

Establishing Intermediate-Term Objectives

After projecting future human resource supplies and demands, intermediate-term objectives are set and action plans are developed to meet the objectives, through the joint efforts of the human resource planner and relevant managers throughout the organization. Differences in the types of objectives established for the short and intermediate term reflect differences in the types of changes that are feasible with two or three additional years of time. Thus, whereas short-term objectives include attracting, assessing, and assigning employees to jobs, intermediate-term objectives are more likely to include readjusting employees' skills, attitudes, and behaviors to fit major changes in the needs of the business, as well as adjusting human resource practices to fit changes in the needs of employees.

Intermediate-Term Programs to Help Employees Adjust to Changing Organizations

Training and retraining programs are often the method of choice for achieving intermediate-term objectives. The nature of training used to prepare for needs that will exist in two to three years can vary greatly. Programs include those designed to provide basic skills training to new hires, advanced education for existing employees, language training, internships and work-study programs, and public school partnerships (see Bolick & Nestleroth, 1988). The forces prompting organizations to develop such programs are many; they include changes in technology, a shift from a manufacturing-based to a service-based economy, and the failure of some public school systems to produce high school graduates who are competent to join the work force (Perry, 1988).

Changing technology creates the need for training. U.S. manufacturers are experiencing a revolution in technology. A century ago, the concept of assembly-line production created an industrial revolution; today computers are contributing to an electronic revolution. Blue-collar employees who previously were expected to perform routinized tasks hundreds of times a day are now being expected to operate the sophisticated robots that perform the routine work (Johnston & Packer, 1987). In addition, they are expected to use computers to monitor and evaluate, using statistical analyses, the flow of work through the plant. Learning skills such as these often means employees first must be trained in basic math and computer use. In addition, they may be taught, in effect, the logic of experimental design as a means for diagnosing the causes of problems that arise. For example, at Frost Inc., a small manufacturing company in Michigan, employees were taught how to determine whether a quality problem was being caused by a particular operator or by a particular machine. Such determinations were possible because extensive data were stored for each item produced. The data included information about which particular machines were used in each step of the process, who was operating the machines, and whether the final product met various quality standards. Thus, by applying the principles of analysis of variance, the cause of quality problems could be detected and corrected (Frost, personal communication, May 23, 1986). The retraining needed to provide these skills took approximately three years and was accomplished mostly on-the-job.

Service-related jobs require new management styles. Change in manufacturing technologies is a major stimulus for intensifying training at work, but it is not the only important stimulus. Another fundamental shift is the changing balance between goods-producing and service-related activities. Even within organizations that are primarily goods producing, the value of a service orientation is now being recognized by U.S. businesses. With more attention being directed toward service provision, the natural question that arises is whether different management practices are needed to manage service providers.

The delivery of services differs from the production of goods in three ways: products are intangible rather than tangible, customers are actively involved in the production of services, and the consumption of services occurs simultaneously with their production (Bowen & Schneider, 1988). The simultaneity of the production and consumption processes means that quality control cannot be achieved by the inspect-and-correct (or reject) method of performance monitoring traditionally used in manufacturing plants. Instead, quality control must occur at the point of service delivery. The service provider is responsible for ensuring the quality of service during each and every interaction with a client. To maintain control over quality, service organizations need to control the process of service production rather than to monitor the quality of outputs (Mills & Moberg, 1982). In other words, service providers must monitor and supervise their own behaviors.

Because employees who deliver services must engage in self-supervision, high levels of employee commitment and involvement are needed. Creating conditions supportive of such employee attitudes is complex; it requires careful planning and, in many cases, a willingness to change basic assumptions about how much power and information lower level employees should be given (see Hollander & Offermann, this issue; Lawler, 1986). I/O psychologists have already begun to study how various personnel practices affect the involvement and commitment levels of employees, so a foundation exists for experimenting with job redesign, use of participative management styles, and organizational structures built around small, stand-alone businesses instead of large hierarchical and bureaucratic enterprises.

Gaining cooperation with organizational changes such as those just noted is particularly challenging because managers' long-held beliefs about how to maximize employee performance are often brought into question.

Creating attitudinal and behavioral change is difficult under most conditions, but it is particularly difficult when there is uncertainty about the payoffs. Thus a significant task is convincing those top-level executives whose resources and support are needed that proposed human resource programs will be effective. This involves translating the scientific evidence into a form that is both understandable and convincing. Short of this, I/O psychologists can attempt to persuade organizational leaders to adopt the perspective that organizational learning is an objective worth pursuing in the interest of long-term survival (Guzzardi, 1989). Consistent with this perspective would be a willingness to implement programs on an experimental basis in anticipation of gaining knowledge that is valuable even if the program is ultimately not a complete success (see Staw, 1977).

A shortage of well-prepared new hires spurs outreach programs. In the past, employers generally relied on on-the-job training programs to teach new employees the specific job skills they needed, but a significant number of organizations now recognize that they can begin shaping their future work force while students are still in school. Time, Inc., brings disadvantaged students from nearby schools to their company headquarters in New York City weekly during the school year to receive tutoring in reading by employees in their offices. In 1982, American Express and Shearson Lehman Hutton began the Academy of Finance, which is a two-year program for juniors and seniors. In addition to their normal curriculum, Academy students take classes in economics and finance and attend seminars designed to socialize them into the culture of the financial services industry. Students then work as paid interns during the summer (Perry, 1988).

Honeywell, Inc., sponsors a summer Teacher Academy, where Minnesota high school math and science teachers team up with researchers to develop class projects (Ehrlich, 1988). General Electric invested $1 million in a program in a poor, Black, rural area of Lowndes County, Alabama. The program partly pays for tutoring sessions given by the faculty of Tuskegee Institute for students in secondary school (Teltsch, 1988). Arizona State University, armed with a $100,000 grant from AT&T, is trying to change the Hispanic cultural pattern that discourages college for women. Teams of mothers and their teenage daughters are brought to the college campus to impress them with the need for college training and to help the young women become eligible for entrance (Teltsch, 1988). Such educational programs are illustrative of a growing realization among employers that they must begin to attend to the general educational needs of the work force in order to ensure its future productivity. These programs are particularly striking because they represent large investments in people who are not yet, and may never be, employees of the sponsoring organizations.

Economic conditions force downsizing. A third major stimulus for intermediate-term human resource programs is organizational restructuring, including mergers and acquisitions and the work force reductions that often follow. From their experiences with massive layoffs in the past few years, organizations have become increasingly sensitive to the importance of planning programs for dealing with the effects of layoffs. Many organizations are trying to minimize the negative effects of layoffs through redundancy planning, outplacement counseling, buyouts, job skill retraining, creation of transfer opportunities, and promotion of early retirements ("Early Retirement," 1987).

Digital Equipment Corporation (DEC) is an example of one company that combined several of these activities with an intermediate-term planning horizon to effect a large-scale work force restructuring (see Kochan, MacDuffie, & Osterman, 1988). It is an excellent example of an integrated effort between human resource and line managers to solve an intermediate-term planning problem. During most of the 1970s and early 1980s, DEC grew rapidly, but a sudden and sharp stock price decline in October of 1983 dramatically signaled the beginning of a new era for the firm. DEC's senior line managers and the vice-president of human resources projected staffing needs for the next two years and determined they would need to go through a major transition (rapid layoffs were viewed as inconsistent with the company's organizational values). Top management gave responsibility for effecting the change to line managers at the plant level. A task force of line managers and human resource staff developed a strategy and general guidelines for the process, which ensured some uniformity across different units within the corporation. The task force established performance as the primary criterion to be used when making cuts, intentionally choosing not to rely on seniority. The decision not to emphasize seniority was at odds with the importance given traditionally to seniority by most unionized and nonunionized manufacturing firms as they downsize (McCune, Beatty, & Montagno, 1988). At DEC, the evaluation data collected to monitor the downsizing process revealed that seniority was a major criterion used by managers, despite the policy to emphasize performance-based decisions.

The task force also developed several training programs. One program was for counseling employees and teaching them career planning skills. Managers were trained to be supportive during the job search process. Retraining was offered to employees who could be transferred within the company rather than laid off. Transfer opportunities could be identified by using a computerized system for matching one's skills to available jobs, facilitating the reassignment of employees within the firm. (Interestingly, however, the system was underused because managers preferred to rely on their informal networks of contacts within the company.) In a two-year period, DEC's worldwide manufacturing work force was decreased by 5,598 employees.

Kochan et al.'s (1988) description of DEC's experiences with a work force reduction program raises a number of interesting issues for I/O psychologists. For example, DEC's experience with the computerized, but underused, job-matching system emphasizes the importance of developing technical supports that capitalize on, rather than ignore, interpersonal dynamics. Their experience with managers using seniority rather than performance as a criterion for targeting employees to be laid off emphasizes the importance of understanding perceptions of what constitutes "fair treatment." The DEC example illustrates that even the most conscientious planning does not guarantee that objectives will be met. Knowing this, experienced managers might be tempted to deemphasize the monitoring of outcomes in order to reduce the visibility of program failures. However, as the DEC example illustrates, by monitoring outcomes, significant opportunities are created for organizational learning.

Organizations must adapt to a diverse work force. The radical demographic transformation of the work force means that organizations need to develop competence in managing a work force that is more diverse on many dimensions, including age, ethnicity, family situation, educational background, country of origin, and the attitudes and values associated with each of these factors. As a consequence, there are an increasing number of training programs designed to sensitize supervisors and managers to the wide range of individual differences represented in the organization and the implications of such differences for organizational functioning. For example, Hewlett-Packard conducts training sessions for managers to teach them about different cultures and races and about their own gender biases and training needs (Nelson-Horchler, 1988). Procter & Gamble has implemented "valuing diversity" programs throughout the company. One example is their mentor program, which was designed to retain Black and female managers (Copeland, 1988). Examples of other programs include Equitable Life Assurance Society's support groups for minorities and women, which periodically meet with the chief executive officer to discuss problems in the company pertaining to them, and Avon's employee councils representing various groups, which inform and advise top management (Copeland, 1988). Programs such as these show that many organizations acknowledge the negative consequences of many of the inaccurate stereotypes common in our society. I/O psychologists working in such organizations now face the challenge of applying basic research findings on perception and attitude change to the design of interventions that will maximize the benefits of work-group diversity and minimize the conflicts that often arise. Another major challenge facing employers is the provision of conditions that permit employees to be fully productive at work, while at the same time meeting the needs of their families, including their parents, spouses, and children. Many of the programs used by organizations to facilitate these needs are described by Zedeck and Mosier (this issue, pp. 240–251).

Programs such as these are designed to facilitate the organization's effective adaptation to the diverse needs of employees. They are particularly interesting because they run counter to the normal tendency of organizations to manage individual differences through means such as normative pressure and sanctions intended to reduce the variance in employees' behaviors (see Katz & Kahn, 1978). Organizational attempts to manage diversity by pressuring employees to conform can be effective when (a) employees are able and willing to meet organizational demands, even when these conflict with the behaviors required to perform other, nonwork roles satisfactorily, and (b) the supply of potential human resources is sufficiently large that employers can afford to retain only employees who do conform.

The first condition was more easily met when the typical employee was a man married to a nonworking spouse who could attend to family needs. As the work force swells with people who are members of dual-career families and people who are single heads of households, both the ability and the willingness of employees to conform to rigid organizational demands are likely to decline. If, in addition, the total labor supply is relatively low, organizations will find themselves in the unfamiliar situation of seeking ways to relax pressures to conform and to assist employees in meeting their nonwork obligations as a strategy for increasing the organization's attractiveness to the scarce supply of labor. This will represent a change from using behavior control mechanisms to manage the uncertainty diversity creates to managing uncertainty by predicting variations in behavior and adapting the organization to them.

Evaluating Intermediate-Term Programs

I/O psychologists have spent less time evaluating intermediate-term human resource programs than evaluating short-term programs, partly because the intermediate time horizon encompasses more uncertainties and contingencies, as is illustrated in the example of DEC. Also, because intermediate-term programs are often larger in scope, the appropriate unit of analysis for evaluation is often the productivity level of an entire department or business unit. Although psychologists have sophisticated measurement methods for assessing the performance levels of individuals, our measurement techniques do not translate easily into measures of productivity (see Campbell & Campbell, 1988). Only recently have I/O psychologists begun to apply aggressively their measurement skills to developing measures appropriate for larger aggregates of employees within organizations (e.g., see Pritchard, Jones, Roth, Stuebing, & Ekeberg, 1988). Progress on this task should be particularly valuable for intermediate-term and long-term human resource planning.

Long-Term Human Resource Planning

Increasingly, long-term human resource planning (for beyond three years) is becoming critical to the effective functioning of organizations. The rapidly changing and highly competitive worldwide marketplace is causing firms to turn to their human resources for survival and competitiveness. Because there is a greater understanding that an organization's work force cannot be turned around on a dime, long-term human resource planning is gaining currency. It is an activity that demands integration of the skills and knowledge of the human resource planner and all the other executives responsible for strategic planning. Although there are many types of long-term planning efforts, we use succession planning as our primary example of the process.

Forecasting Demand and Supply: The Challenge of Succession Planning

More than ever, a major long-term business concern in organizations is "What types of managers do we need running the business into the 21st century, and how do we make sure we have them?" (Cowherd, 1986; London, personal communication, February 7, 1986). Consider this example: "Exxon is so far ahead in the succession planning game that it has already hired its CEO for the year 2010. Although it is not public knowledge who that person is, he or she is already being challenged, assessed and groomed for the top spot" (McManis & Leibman, 1988, p. 24). In describing how succession planning efforts differ now from the past, Goodstein (personal communication, February 9, 1989) pointed out that the turbulence and unpredictability of the current business environment has resulted in "a discernible trend" of substituting efforts to define more generic competencies for efforts to identify specific knowledge and skills in the specification of position requirements. H. A. Goodstein (personal communication, February 9, 1989) contrasted this with

> "the old" technology of management succession planning, which was largely an exercise in replacement planning. Organizations were planning within a model of minimal change in organization structure (internal environment) and a perceived static external environment. Position requirements could easily be extrapolated from the job descriptions of current in-

cumbents—factoring into these requirements those skills and abilities that the current incumbent lacked. Since position requirements were relatively stable and career paths reasonably well-defined, an effective performance appraisal system coupled with opportunities for key executives to observe candidates adequately served the selection process for many companies.

Succession planning programs are complex systems designed to safeguard the long-term health of the organization. The key activities in succession planning are identifying high-potential employees, identifying needed competencies, and providing learning experiences to develop these competencies (De-Luca, 1988). Well-developed programs include a variety of components: selection procedures, development plans, mentorships, frequent and systematic performance reviews, and career planning activities that involve employees in planning and monitoring their own development (e.g., see Hall & Associates, 1986; Leibowitz, 1988). Those programs known for their excellence, such as those sponsored by IBM, Exxon, Squibb, and General Electric, represent large investments in integrated human resource management systems (see Mahler & Drotter, 1986; Vancil, 1987). Such programs are examples of what can be done with respect to long-term human resource planning, given the state of our knowledge about human performance in organizational settings, a belief in the value of investing in human resources, and cooperation between the human resource planner and line management.

Staffing the upper echelons of organizations presents a number of unique challenges, particularly when a company practices a promotion-from-within policy. Because the planning horizon is so long, greater uncertainty exists when predicting both future demand and future supply. The uncertainty in predicting supply is compounded by the small numbers of people and jobs involved, which changes the prediction task from one of estimating the percentage of a pool of employees who are likely to be with the company x years into the future to one of estimating the probability that a few particular individuals will still be with the company x years into the future. Providing developmental experiences to a greater number of employees helps reduce the uncertainty of forecasted supply (Leibowitz, 1988), but orchestrating developmental experiences for large numbers of employees can be very difficult logistically because development is best accomplished by rotating employees through many key jobs throughout their careers (see McCall, 1988). Predicting who will be available and with what capabilities is only half of the problem, of course. Equally challenging is predicting the needs of the organization (DeLuca, 1988).

Organizations are dynamic systems embedded in dynamic environments. When planning for future needs, the only sure bet is that future needs will be different from current needs. Popular wisdom has long held that different types of leaders are effective under different business conditions (Campbell & Moses, 1986; Gerstein & Reisman, 1983). For example, the personal characteristics of managers that lead to success during the start-up and early growth phases of an organization's life cycle may inhibit their performance when the organization reaches the phase of maturity and stability (Gupta & Govindarajan, 1984). For companies currently in the early growth stages, this makes succession planning particularly difficult. Because the needs of the future are inconsistent with current needs, the challenge is to find ways to maximize the effectiveness of managers in the current organizational environment of rapid growth while at the same time providing experiences for these managers to help them develop the skills they will need in the mature-stage organizational environment of the future.

Another type of major change that an organization may experience during a several-year planning horizon is a modification of their competitive strategy. Like a change from rapid growth to mature stability, a change in competitive strategies may have significant implications for the types of managers needed. Competitive strategy refers to the means by which a firm competes for business in the marketplace (see Porter, 1985). Competitive strategies can differ along a number of dimensions, including the extent to which firms emphasize innovation, quality enhancement, or cost reduction (Schuler & Jackson, 1987). Briefly, the innovation strategy is used to develop products or services different from those of competitors; the primary focus is on continually offering something new and different. Enhancing product or service quality is the primary focus of the quality-enhancement strategy. In the cost-reduction strategy, firms typically attempt to gain competitive advantage by being the lowest-cost goods producer or service provider. (Although these three competitive strategies are described as pure types, in practice some overlap often occurs.)

It is likely that successful pursuit of these three different strategies requires employees to adopt different patterns of behavior. For example, organizations that pursue innovation as a strategy are likely to experience uncertainty because the path to innovation includes a mix of spurts in progress and unforeseen setbacks (Quinn, 1979). In addition, the innovation process depends heavily on individual expertise and creativity. Steep learning curves and the rapid speed at which knowledge is accumulated through experience make it difficult for organizations to codify procedures. This means that employee turnover can have disastrous consequences (Kanter, 1985). Furthermore, innovation often threatens the status quo, causing some natural resistance and a volatile political climate (Fast, 1976).

These organizational conditions suggest that the pursuit of innovation is likely to be successful only if employees behave in particular ways. A large literature on innovation suggests that some of the behaviors needed from employees in firms pursuing innovation include creativeness, cooperation, risk taking, flexibility, a long-term focus, and willingness to assume responsibility for outcomes. Many of these behaviors are quite unlike those needed when cost reduction is emphasized in an organization. When cost reduction is the focus, predictability is valued over creativity, risk taking is less appropriate, and a short-term focus usually predominates (see Schuler & Jackson, 1987).

The differences in needed employee behaviors associated with different strategies have significant implications for human resource planning. For example, a recent study compared firms pursuing an innovation strategy with firms for whom innovation was of little importance. Firms pursuing an innovation strategy were more likely than other firms to emphasize long-term needs in their training programs for managers and to offer training to more employees throughout the organization. Supporting the notion that innovative organizations need to encourage flexibility and creativity, managers in innovative companies had jobs that required the use of more diverse skills (Jackson, Schuler, & Rivero, 1989). Results such as these suggest that when organizations change competitive strategies in response to a changing business environment, they may need to significantly alter broad patterns of employee attitudes and behaviors in order to be successful in implementing a new competitive strategy. To do so, they may implement major changes in various aspects of their personnel systems. The decision to change strategies requires a long-term perspective, and its success depends in part on changing the work environment in order to support needed changes in employee behaviors, which also requires a long-term perspective. Clearly, when organizations attempt to change their competitive strategies, business and human resource planning should be fully integrated.

Program Design and Implementation

An early example of a company that used a psychological testing program to integrate its business needs and long-term human resource planning was Sears, Roebuck, & Company. In the early 1960s, Sears realized it would need managers with unique abilities to guide the organization through a period of rapid expansion and growth. Based on careful evaluation of the available talent and anticipated future business conditions, Sears concluded that it should begin developing a talent pool that would include people who had greater mental ability, who were psychologically compatible with the company's need for innovation and change, who were skilled administrators and effective decision makers, and who were emotionally stable yet aggressive (Bentz, 1968, 1983). To ensure that such people would be available and could be identified, Sears developed a battery of psychological tests for use in their selection process, a process aided by the joint efforts of line management and human resource planners. Such tests are now a general component of the long-range planning efforts of many organizations because they help identify high-potential employees early in their careers (Bentz, 1983).

For many organizations, succession planning and career development are tools for integrating diverse subgroups within a corporation (see Campbell, in press). For example, Sara Lee Corporation has acquired more than 40 companies during the past several years. The company uses succession planning to move talented employees through the different subsidiaries in order to build a consistent corporate culture and a sense of corporate unity (McManis & Leibman, 1988). The challenge of integrating diversity is even greater for IBM, which has operations in 132 countries. According to Donald Laidlaw, director of IBM's executive resources, succession planning systems at IBM are designed to cover human resource needs in all 132 countries (Laidlaw, personal communication, February 7, 1989). The size of IBM combined with the tremendous diversity of environments with which it must cope make predicting specific needs in the long term more or less impossible. This means effective leaders will be people who can deal well with ambiguity and who are broadly trained in all aspects of running a business. Developing such leaders is the objective of IBM's extensive succession planning and management development efforts. IBM's commitment to a general manager model of development led them to design a series of planned development positions that are used to test high-potential managers. Performance appraisals serve to continually revalidate initial judgments of future potential (and reduce executive management uncertainty).

Another company that has learned the value of having employees who can cope with ambiguity is AT&T, whose world was turned upside down in the early 1980s. In 1982, AT&T agreed to divest itself of its operating telephone companies. By 1984, more than 11,000 employees had chosen to leave AT&T rather than live with the massive changes that were about to take place as this former monolith was broken into eight different organizational units (Campbell & Moses, 1986). A leader in the design and use of assessment centers as a method for selecting managers for promotions, AT&T realized the need to begin proactively using assessment centers for developmental purposes. In addition to using assessment centers to develop managers' ability to cope with ambiguity, AT&T is trying to ensure that the organization as a whole is prepared for the future by developing two very different types of leaders—those with high levels of functional expertise and those with the broad expertise needed to be successful general managers (M. London, personal communication, February 7, 1989).

Although we have focused on succession planning in this article, it is important to note that other types of long-term human resource planning efforts are equally important. Space limitations prohibit us from discussing other types of efforts at length, but we offer one example to illustrate what can be accomplished when long-term human resource planning is used to its fullest extent to link competitive strategy and human resource practices. The example is Ford Motor Company's massive

quality improvement program (see Banas, 1988). In 1979, top management at Ford acknowledged the need to begin working to develop a new style of human resource management in order to achieve its goal of producing high-quality products at low cost ("At Ford, quality is job one"). Since 1979, Ford has actively and aggressively sought to increase employee involvement. Philip Caldwell, as president of the company in 1978, ushered in the new era at Ford when he announced to the top executives: "Our strategy for the years ahead will come to nothing unless we ask for greater participation of our workforce. Without motivated and concerned workers, we're not going to lower our costs as much as we need to— and we aren't going to get the quality product we need" (cited in Banas, 1988, p. 391). So began a major experiment in organizational change that included efforts to improve the quality of work life and the beginnings of an organizational restructuring. The experiment is revealing the limits of our knowledge about how to change an organization's approach to managing people, and at the same time it is contributing to our knowledge about how to manage change. It is also providing another excellent illustration of the integration of business needs and human resource planning. Most important, the description Banas has given of the change process is likely to serve as a stimulus to new research.

Evaluating Long-Term Programs

Presently most of our knowledge about how to develop and improve long-term human resource programs has been generated through trial and error rather than through systematic research. Nevertheless, much knowledge about individual behavior and development has been gained by analysis of the massive amounts of data generated by large-scale, ongoing management planning systems. The excellent studies conducted within AT&T are models for how the practice of I/O psychology can inform the science of psychology (Bray, Campbell, & Grant, 1974; Howard & Bray, 1988). These studies shed light on the question of how ability and personality factors contribute to managerial career success, and they also informed us about patterns of change over the life span and between generations.

Understandably, what rigorous researchers engaged in the evaluation of succession planning programs have emphasized is the ability to predict individual outcomes, such as career progress and satisfaction. It is also now appropriate to evaluate long-term programs using corporate outcomes such as share price, market share, receipt of industry awards, and so on. In the spirit of integrating business needs and human resource planning, such corporate indicators are legitimate criteria for evaluating success, in addition to individual outcomes. Doubtless there are many difficulties that complex, multifaceted interventions and long-term time horizons pose in drawing conclusions about cause-and-effect relationships; nonetheless, there are great opportunities for the I/O psychologist who adopts a long-term view and for human resource planners and line managers who coordinate their efforts to assess the long-term effectiveness of human resource programs in corporate and individual terms.

Conclusions

Because the purpose of human resource planning is to ensure that the right people are in the right place at the right time, it must be linked with the plans of the total organization. Traditionally, there has been a weak one-way linkage between business planning and human resource planning. Business plans, where they exist, have defined human resource needs, thereby making human resource planning a reactive exercise. A description of conditions in the 1970s was provided by Walker (1978) in the opening article of the inaugural issue of *Human Resource Planning:*

> Companies often give lip service to the importance of human resources in achievement of business objectives, but rarely is detailed,

thoughtful analysis performed. . . . Personnel professionals, even human resource planning specialists, often are not well informed regarding business planning processes (and rarely have any direct contact with business planners) and are thus ill-equipped to introduce linkages between human resource planning and business strategic planning. (p. 1)

This was the state of the art when the first professional association for human resource planners, the Human Resource Planning Society, was founded in 1977.

Many organizations now recognize that they can benefit from a two-way linkage between business and human resource planning. With a two-way linkage, business plans are considered somewhat malleable in that they are influenced by human resource considerations, such as the cost and availability of labor. Such organizations realize that profitability requires that business objectives be linked to people-planning activities. If the right people are unavailable, performance goals cannot be met. "A two-way linkage is evident when astute managers no longer assume that every plan is doable" (Mills, 1985a, p. 48).

Recently, some organizations have moved toward having a completely integrative linkage between business planning and human resource planning. In these organizations, organizational effectiveness is facilitated by a human resource executive who is a fully participating member of the top management team. In this case business plans can be substantially modified by the human resource executive, and business results can be substantially improved. For example, Don Rush, vice-president and chief executive officer of Weyerhaeuser Forest Product Company's Washington division, believes that "by integrating HR and business planning, we have 500 salaried people doing more than 1,200 did; we have improved teamwork, morale, commitment, and profitability" ("The HR Edge," 1988, p. 1). Such integration is likely to spread among the most competitive U.S. organizations. As this happens, the relationships that were illustrated in Figure 1 among human resource planning activities and those between human resource and business planning should become more common. Unfortunately, it is beyond the scope of this article to include a description of the management processes that organizations are using to achieve complete integration between their human resource and business planning activities, but interested readers are encouraged to read the discussions provided by Golden and Ramanujam (1985), Dyer (1986), Mirvis (1985), and Schuler (1988).

Human resource planning becomes more complex as the time horizon for planning stretches further into the future, so it is not surprising that companies become involved in longer term planning activities only after becoming proficient in shorter term planning activities. Mills (1985b) found support for this pattern in his study of the planning practices of 291 organizations. An evolutionary pattern, going from mastery of techniques for short-term planning to development of long-term planning capabilities, is also evident in the related technical and scientific literatures on planning. Much of the research conducted by I/O psychologists has been directed at improving short-term outcomes such as attracting applicants, maximizing performance, and minimizing dissatisfaction and stress in order to retain valued employees. Currently, there is a growing awareness that these activities need to be clearly and explicitly linked to improving organizational productivity, quality, innovation, and employee satisfaction and involvement (see Campbell & Campbell, 1988).

It seems clear that human resource management in general, and human resource planning in particular, will become more closely tied to the needs and strategies of organizations. As this occurs, human resource planning will be the thread that ties together all other human resource activities and integrates these with the rest of the organization. With the growing recognition that different types of organizations require different human resource practices (see, e.g., Kerr, 1982; Miles

& Snow, 1984; Schuler, 1987), human resource planners are being challenged to develop packages of practices that fit the unique needs of their organizations and contribute to effectiveness. Research that will assist planners in the development and implementation of integrated human resource systems is urgently needed.

Also needed is research on the change process. Organizations of the future are likely to be in a state of continuous change and uncertainty. Human resource planning is likely to be seen not only as the thread that ties together all human resource practices, but also as the instrument for establishing and signaling when and how practices should change. In other words, human resource planners are likely to take on the role of organizational change agents (Beer & Walton, 1987). To be effective in this role, they will need to adopt a systems perspective for understanding how the behaviors of individuals influence and are influenced by the larger organizational context.

As organizations change more quickly, so will the knowledge, skills, and behaviors needed from employees. This means that people working in organizations will be asked continually to adjust to new circumstances. Assessing and facilitating people's capacity for change are two activities that psychologists are likely to be called on to do, yet there is very little research available to consult for guidance. Whereas organizations are seeking changes from employees, employees will be demanding that organizations change to meet the needs of the increasingly diverse work force. Research designed to help us understand how organizations can establish and maintain employee flexibility and adaptability is likely to make an important contribution.

Thus a final challenge in human resource planning is balancing current needs—of organizations and their employees—with those of the future. The criterion against which this balancing act is measured is whether employees are currently at the right place doing the right things but yet are ready to adapt appropriately to different activities when organizational change is needed. Similarly, I/O psychologists involved in human resource planning can use the effectiveness of their current activities and their readiness to engage in the new activities needed to face the challenges of the future as the criteria against which they evaluate their own performance.

References

American Telephone & Telegraph Company. (1980). *Survey of business service center jobs: Technical supplement.* Basking Ridge, NJ: Author.

Arvey, R. D., & Faley, R. H. (1988). *Fairness in selecting employees* (2nd ed.). Reading, MA: Addison-Wesley.

Arvey, R. D., Salas, E., & Gialluca, K. A. (1989). *Using task inventories to forecast skills and abilities.* Unpublished manuscript, University of Minnesota, Industrial Relations Center, Minneapolis.

Banas, P. A. (1988). Employee involvement: A sustained labor/management initiative at the Ford Motor Company. In J. P. Campbell, R. J. Campbell, & Associates (Eds.), *Productivity in organizations* (pp. 388–416). San Francisco: Jossey-Bass.

Bechet, T. P., & Maki, W. R. (1987). Modeling and forecasting: Focusing on people as a strategic resource. *Human Resource Planning, 10,* 209–219.

Beer, M., & Walton, A. E. (1987). Organizational change and development. *Annual Review of Psychology, 38,* 339–367.

Bentz, V. J. (1968). The Sears experience in the investigation, description, and prediction of executive behavior. In J. A. Myers, Jr. (Ed.), *Predicting managerial success* (pp. 59–152). Ann Arbor, MI: Foundation on Research for Human Behavior.

Bentz, V. J. (1983, August). *Executive selection at Sears: An update.* Paper presented at the Fourth Annual Conference on Frontiers of Industrial Psychology, Virginia Polytechnic Institute, Blacksburg.

Bolick, C., & Nestleroth, S. (1988). *Opportunity 2000.* Washington, DC: U.S. Government Printing Office.

Boudreau, J. W., & Berger, C. J. (1985). Decision-theoretic utility analysis applied to employee separations and acquisitions. *Journal of Applied Psychology, 70,* 571–612.

Bowen, D. E., & Schneider, B. (1988). Services marketing and management: Implications for organization behavior. In B. M. Staw & L. L. Cummings (Eds.), *Research in organizational behavior* (pp. 43–80). Greenwich, CT: JAI Press.

Bray, D. W., Campbell, R. J., & Grant, D. L. (1974). *Formative years in business: A long-term AT&T study of managerial lives.* New York: Wiley.

Bres, E. S. III, Niehaus, R. J., Schinnar, A. P., & Steinbuch, P. (1983). Efficiency evaluation of EEO program management. *Human Resource Planning, 6,* 233–247.

Burack, E. H. (1988). A strategic planning and operational agenda for human resources. *Human Resource Planning, 11,* 63–68.

Campbell, R. J. (in press). Implementing human resource development strategies. In K. N. Wexley (Ed.), *Developing human resources.* Washington, DC: Bureau of National Affairs.

Campbell, J. P., Campbell, R. J., & Associates. (Eds.) (1988). *Productivity in organizations.* San Francisco: Jossey-Bass.

Campbell, R. J., & Moses, J. L. (1986). Careers from an organizational perspective. In D. T. Hall & Associates (Eds.), *Career development in organizations* (pp. 274–309). San Francisco: Jossey-Bass.

Cascio, W. F. (1986). *Costing human resources: The financial impact of behavior in organizations.* Boston: Kent.

Charnes, A., Cooper, W. W., Lewis, K. A., & Niehaus, R. J. (1978). A multi-level coherence model for EEO planning. In A. Charnes, W. W. Cooper, & R. J. Niehaus (Eds.), *Management science approaches to manpower planning and organization design.* New York: Elsevier North Holland.

Charnes, A., Cooper, W. W., Nelson, A., & Niehaus, R. J. (1982). Model extension and computation in goal-arc network approaches for EEO planning. *INFOR, 20*(4), 1–57.

Coates, J. F. (1987). An environmental scan: Projecting human resource trends. *Human Resource Planning, 10,* 209–219.

Copeland, L. (1988, July). Valuing diversity: 2. Pioneers and champions of change. *Personnel,* p. 48.

Cowherd, D. M. (1986). On executive succession: Conversation with Lester B. Korn. *Human Resource Management, 25,* 335–347.

Davis, D. D., & Associates. (Eds.) (1986). *Managing technological innovation.* San Francisco: Jossey-Bass.

Delbecq, A., Van de Ven, A. H., & Gustafson, D. (1975). *Group techniques for program planning.* Dallas: Scott.

DeLuca, J. R. (1988). Strategic career management in non-growing, volatile business environments. *Human Resource Planning, 11,* 49–62.

Dumaine, B. (1989, July 3). What the leaders of tomorrow see. *Fortune,* pp. 48–62.

Dyer, L. (1982). Human resource planning. In K. M. Rowland & G. R. Ferris (Eds.), *Personnel management* (pp. 31–47). Boston: Allyn & Bacon.

Dyer, L. (Ed.) (1986). *Human resource planning: Tested practices in five U.S. and Canadian companies.* New York: Random House.

Dyer, L., & Heyer, N. D. (1984). Human resource planning at IBM. *Human Resource Planning, 7,* 111–126.

Early retirement incentives: Two approaches. (1987, January 8). *Bulletin to Management,* p. 15.

Ehrlich, E. (1988, September 19). Business is becoming a substitute teacher. *Business Week,* p. 113.

Fast, N. D. (1976). The future of industrial new venture departments. *Industrial Marketing Management, 8,* 264–273.

Fleishman, E. A., & Quaintance, M. K. (1984). *Taxonomies of human performance.* New York: Academic Press.

Gerstein, M., & Reisman, H. (1983, Winter). Strategic selection: Matching executives to business conditions. *Sloan Management Review,* pp. 33–49.

Glickman, A. S. (Ed.) (1982). *The changing composition of the workforce: Implications for future research and its application.* New York: Plenum Press.

Golden, K. A., & Ramanujam, J. (1985). Between a dream and a nightmare: On the integration of the human resource management and strategic business planning processes. *Human Resource Management, 24*(4), 429–452.

Greenhalgh, L., McKersie, R. B., & Gilkey, R. W. (1986, Spring). Rebalancing the workforce at IBM: A case study of redeployment and revitalization. *Organizational Dynamic,* pp. 30–47.

Gupta, A. K., & Govindarajan, V. (1984). Business unit strategy, managerial characteristics, and business unit effectiveness at strategy implementation. *Academy of Management journal, 9,* 25–41.

Guzzardi, W. (1989, July 3). Wisdom from the giants of business. *Fortune,* pp. 78–88.

Hall, D. T., & Associates. (1986). *Career development in organizations.* San Francisco: Jossey-Bass.

Hay Group. (1988, April 3). *Forging a new workforce alliance: How to meet the broadened human resource needs of the 1990s.* Presentation given in New York City.

Hennecke, M. (1984). *Human resource planning: Strategy formulation and implementation.* Minnetonka, MN: Golle & Homes Consulting.

Hollander, E. P., & Offerman, L. R. (1990). Organizations of the future: Changes and challenges. *American Psychologist, 45,* 95–108.

Howard, A., & Bray, D. W. (1988). *Managerial lives in transition: Advancing age and changing times.* New York: Guilford Press.

The HR edge. (1988, September). *HR Reporter,* p. 1.

Jackson, S. E., Schuler, R. S., & Rivero, J. C. (1989). Organizational characteristics as predictors of personnel practices. *Personnel Psychology, 42,* 727–736.

Johnston, W. B., & Packer, A. H. (1987). *Workforce 2000.* Indianapolis, IN: Hudson Institute.

Kahales, H., Pazer, H. L., Hoagland, J. S., & Leavitt, A. (1980). Human resource planning activities in U.S. Firms. *Human Resource Planning, 3,* 53–66.

Kanter, R. (1985, Winter). Supporting innovation and venture development in established companies. *Journal of Business Venturing, 1,* 47–60.

Katz, D., & Kahn, R. L. (1978). *The social psychology of organizations* (2nd ed.). New York: Wiley.

Kerr, J. L. (1982). Assigning managers on the basis of the life cycle. *Journal of Business Strategy, 7,* 58–65.

Kochan, T. A., MacDuffie, J. P., & Osterman, P. (1988). Employment security at DEC: Sustaining values amid environmental change. *Human Resource Management, 27,* 121–144.

Krzystofiak, F. (1982). Estimating EEO liability. *Decision Sciences, 2,* 10–17.

Lawler, E. E. III. (1986). *High-involvement management.* San Francisco: Jossey-Bass.

Lawrence, S. (1989, April). Voice of HR experience. *Personnel Journal,* 61–75.

Ledvinka, J., & La Forge, R. L. (1978). A staffing model of affirmative action planning. *Human Resource Planning, 1,* 135–150.

Leibowitz, Z. B. (1988). Designing career development systems: Principles and practices. *Human Resource Planning, 11,* 195–207.

Levine, E. A. (1983). *Everything you always wanted to know about job analysis.* Tampa, FL: Mariner Publishing.

Lorance v. AT&T, 490 U.S., 1989.

Maccoby, M. (1988). *Why work: Leading the new generation.* New York: Simon & Schuster.

Mahler, W. R., & Drotter, S. J. (1986). *The succession planning handbook for the chief executive.* Midland Park, NJ: Mahler Publishing.

Managing now for the 1990s. (1988, September). *Fortune,* pp. 44–96.

Martin v. Wilks, 490 U.S. ___, 1989.

McCall, M. W., Jr. (1988). Developing executives through work experiences. *Human Resource Planning, 11,* 1–11.

McCormick, E. J., Jeanneret, P. R., & Mecham, R. C. (1972). A study of job characteristics and job dimensions based on the Position Analysis Questionnaire (PAQ). *Journal of Applied Psychology, 56,* 347–368.

McCune, J. T., Beatty, R. W., & Montagno, R. V. (1988). Downsizing: Practices in manufacturing firms. *Human Resource Management, 27,* 145–161.

McManis, G. L., & Leibman, M. S. (1988, August). Succession planners. *Personnel Administrator,* 24–30.

Migliore, R. (1984). *An MBO approach to long range planning.* Englewood Cliffs, NJ: Prentice-Hall.

Migliore, R. (1986). *Strategic long range planning* (rev. ed.). Tulsa, OK: Western Printing.

Miles, R. E., & Snow, C. C. (1984). Designing strategic human resource systems. *Organizational Dynamics, 12,* 36–52.

Milkovich, G., Annoni, A., & Mahoney, T. (1972, December). The use of Delphi procedures in manpower forecasting. *Management Science,* 381–388.

Milkovich, G. T., Dyer, L., & Mahoney, T. A. (1983). HRM planning. In S. J. Carroll & R. S. Schuler (Eds.), *Human resources management in the 1980s* (pp. 2-1–2-28). Washington, DC: Bureau of National Affairs.

Milkovich, G. T., & Phillips, J. D. (1986). Human resource planning: Merck. In L. Dyer (Ed.), *Human resource planning: Tested practices of five U.S. and Canadian companies* (pp. 2–20). New York: Random House.

Miller, G. E. (1980). A method for forecasting human resource needs against internal and external labor markets. *Human Resource Planning, 3,* 189–200.

Mills, D. Q. (1985a, August 8). Planning policies. *Bulletin to Management,* p. 48.

Mills, D. Q. (1985b, July–August). Planning with people in mind. *Harvard Business Review,* 97–105.

Mills, D. Q. (1987). *Not like our parents.* New York: Morrow.

Mills, P. K., & Moberg, D. J. (1982). Perspectives on the technology of service operations. *Academy of Management Review, 7,* 467–478.

Mirvis, P. H. (1985). Formulating and implementing human resource strategy: A model of how to do it, two examples of how it's done. *Human Resource Management, 24*(4), 385–412.

Mobley, W. H., Griffeth, R. W., Hand, H. H., & Meglino, B. M. (1979). Review and conceptual analysis of the employee turnover process. *Psychological Bulletin, 86,* 493–522.

Mowday, R. T., Porter, L. W., & Steers, R. M. (1982). *Employee-organization linkages: The psychology of commitment, absenteeism, and turnover.* New York: Academic Press.

Murdick, R. G., & Schuster, F. (1983). Computerized information support for the human resource function. *Human Resource Planning, 6,* 25–35.

National Alliance of Business. (1986). *Youth 2000: A call to action.* Washington, DC: Author.

Needed: Human capital. (1988, September 19). *Business Week,* pp. 110–141.

Nelson-Horchler, J. (1988, April 18). Demographics deliver a warning. *Industry Week,* p. 58.

Nelton, S. (1988, July). Meet your new work force. *Nation's Business,* pp. 14–21.

Niehaus, R. J. (1979). *Computer-assisted human resources planning.* New York: Wiley Inter-Science.

Niehaus, R. J. (1980). Human resource planning flow models. *Human Resource Planning, 3,* 177–187.

Niehaus, R. J. (1988). Models for human resource decisions. *Human Resource Planning, 11,* 95–108.

Niehaus, R. J., Schinnar, A. P., & Walter, L. C. (1987). Productivity and organizational economies of personnel services. In R. J. Niehaus (Ed.), *Strategic human resource planning applications* (pp. 111–138). New York: Plenum Press.

Odiorne, G. S. (1981, July). Developing a human resource strategy. *Personnel Journal, 534–536.*

Offermann, L. R., & Gowing, M. K. (1990). The changing face of corporate America: Themes and issues for psychologists working in organizations. *American Psychologist, 45,* 95–108.

Page, R. C., & Van De Vroot, D. M. (1989). Job analysis and HR planning. In W. F. Cascio (Ed.), *Human resource planning employment and placement.* Washington, DC: Bureau of National Affairs, Inc.

Patterson v. McLean Credit Union, 491 U.S. ___, 1989.

Perry, N. (1988, November 7). Saving the schools: How business can help. *Fortune,* pp. 42–52.

Piskor, W. G., & Dudding, R. C. (1978). A computer-assisted manpower planning model. In D. T. Bryant & R. J. Niehaus (Eds.), *Manpower planning and organization design* (pp. 145–154). New York: Plenum Press.

Planning with people. (1984, May 3). *Bulletin to Management,* pp. 2, 7.

Porter, M. E. (1985). *Competitive advantage.* New York: Free Press.

Pritchard, R. D., Jones, S. D., Roth, P. L., Stuebing, K. K., & Ekeberg, S. E. (1988). Effects of group feedback, goal setting, and incentives on organizational productivity. *Journal of Applied Psychology, 73,* 337–358.

Quinn, J. B. (1979, Spring). Technological innovation, entrepreneurship, and strategy. *Sloan Management Review.* 20–30.

Rush, J. C., & Borne, L. C. (1986). Human resource planning: Ontario Hydro. In L. Dyer (Ed.), *Human resource planning: Tested practices in five major U.S. and Canadian companies* (pp. 21–33). New York: Random House.

Schneider, B., & Konz, A. M. (1989). Strategic job analysis. *Human Resource Management, 38,* 51–64.

Schneider, B., & Schmitt, N. (1986). *Staffing organizations.* Glenview, IL: Scott, Foresman.

Schuler, R. S. (1987). Personnel and human resources management practice choices and organizational strategy. *Journal of Human Resource Planning, 10,* 1–21.

Schuler, R. S. (1988). A case study of the HR department at Swiss Bank Corporation: Customerization for organizational effectiveness. *Human Resource Planning, 11,* 241–253.

Schuler, R. S., & Jackson, S. E. (1987, August). Linking human resource practices with competitive strategies. *Academy of Management Executive,* 207–219.

Staw, B. M. (1977). The experimenting organization: Problems and prospects. In B. M. Staw (Ed.), *Psychological foundations of organizational behavior* (2nd ed., pp. 421–437). Santa Monica, CA: Goodyear.

Teltsch, K. (1988, December 4). Business sees aid to schools as a net gain. *The New York Times,* p. 1.

Thompson, J. D. (1967). *Organizations in action.* New York: McGraw-Hill.

U.S. Air Force Occupational Measurement Center. (1981). *Ground radio operator career ladder AFSC 293X3* (Rep. No. AFPT90-293-415). Randolph Air Force Base, TX: U.S. Air Force Occupational Measurement Center.

Vancil, R. F. (1987). *Passing the baton: Managing the process of CEO succession.* Boston: Harvard Business School Press.

Vetter, E. W. (1967). *Manpower planning for high talent personnel.* Ann Arbor: University of Michigan, Graduate School of Business, Bureau of Industrial Relations.

Walker, J. (1978). The role of human resource planning in corporate management. *Human Resource Planning, 1,* 39–44.

Walker, J. W. (1980). *Human resource planning.* New York: McGraw-Hill.

Walker, J. W. (1988). Managing human resources in flat, lean and flexible organizations: Trends for the 1990's. *Human Resource Planning, 11,* 125–132.

Walker, J. W., & Armes, R. (1979). Implementing management succession planning in diversified companies. *Human Resource Planning, 2,* 123–133.

Wards Cove Packing v. Atonia, 490 U.S. ___, 1989.

Work attitudes: Study reveals generation gap. (1986, October 2). *Bulletin to Management,* p. 326.

Zedeck, S., & Mosier, K. L. (1990). Work in the family and employing organization. *American Psychologist, 45,* 240–251.

Zuboff, S. (1988). *In the age of the smart machine: The future of work and power.* New York: Basic Books.

Eight Ways to Assess Succession Plans

Charles Borwick

Because succession planning is a strategic activity, it should be managed not on a year-round basis, but as a year-round guide. This process involves changing our understanding of succession planning in order to change our expectations. What most people expect is that succession planning is going to solve their day-to-day challenges in managing the flow of people through the organization. Indeed, the expectation (prior to the experience) is that when a key position opens, it will be filled by the chosen successor and things will proceed smoothly from there.

This is an unreasonable expectation because the succession plan is a plan. A plan is a set of intentions based on a set of assumptions at a given time. Over time, both the assumptions and the intentions may change, given new information. Actual succession decisions are made as the need arises based on the latest information that includes, but is not limited to, the succession plan.

Succession planning, like business planning, should provide a framework in which to make everyday decisions. It should not provide the absolute decisions.

With this understanding, managers can redefine their expectations of succession planning and conceive of it as a strategy. It is not the individual slated for the position that is the strategy, but rather the added value that one type of individual provides over another, that is, a marketing-oriented individual over a production-oriented individual. Succession planning does not simply boil down to a set of individual skills for a position, but requires an understanding of the business goals and the combined competencies of the team that will deliver them.

For example, at a review with the CEO of a *Fortune* 500 company, a manager presented his plan for the successor to the president of Latin American operations. The candidate met all the criteria one could expect for a regional president and was unarguably qualified. The CEO looked at the human resource chart projected on the wall and said: "Hey, there's a problem with that plan. We'll be releasing product X in Latin America next year and we'll need to have a person with a marketing background in that job. Our main problems won't be the usual production issues, they will involve introducing the new product."

The succession plan, in relation to the business plan and the team context, should not only communicate a potential candidate, but also the reasons why the candidate is preferable to other possible nominees—what value he or she adds. In this way, one can understand the strategy and adapt the tactics as the day-to-day business requires.

Steps to Improved Planning

There are eight areas in which the succession planning process is conceived and structured and in which problems could arise that would hinder the ongoing use of the plan. These areas are discussed next.

The Business Plan

If one fails to refer to the business plan, one ends up assuming an unchanging environment and plans succession solely for the maintenance of today's realities. Separation of succession planning from the business plan also leads to the creation of a "people process" that is mutually understood to be important, but quickly becomes a luxury when it comes time to "run the business"—hence, the isolation of the process. Succession planning is about running the business, and the process should reflect this truth.

An End in Itself

I always ask people the same question when working with them on succession planning: "If this process worked perfectly and everything happened that you would want to have happen, what would the results look like?" Most people answer the question in terms of the completeness of the plan or the data they can gather: "Every manager would have two listed successors and a development plan" or with the cliche: "We would always have the right person in the right place at the right time."

No one has ever told me: "Company revenues or profits or market share would increase." In fact no one has ever even said, "Succession would occur in a planned fashion" or "Our managers will be better developed" or "Our teams would function more effectively." It may seem as if this goes without saying—but it must be said. The succession planning process ends, and implementation never begins, because succession planning is seen as an end in itself.

Top-Down Communication

Succession planning is commonly referred to as a bottom-up process in which plans are created in the lower ranks and reviewed at increasingly higher levels of the organization. In this process the plans are reviewed, and approved, changed or scrapped where appropriate, and ultimately coalesce into a company-wide strategy. Because this is the most significant aspect of the process, in reality a "bottom-up" process is "top-down/bottom-up/top-down," where the process is initiated at the request of senior management (top-down), the process is carried out from the bottom-up, and change to the plans or their approval is communicated from the top-down.

In succession planning, the last top-down part of the cycle is missing. Thus, whether plans have been approved, changed, or scrapped is rarely, if ever, communicated to those who created the plan. This is often because managers do not want to communicate potential candidates' names. While the merits of communicating employee names can (and should) be debated, what does need to be communicated is the strategy related to filling the position. In other words, what "added value" is needed for a key position.

Secrets

Succession planning traditionally has been a secretive subject, which is often the reason that the final top-down part of the process does not occur. The topic of people moving into new or different jobs is probably the most sensitive in the company. It is sensitive for good reasons: It represents change, which is not only frightening, but can distract people from their current duties. It also can create expectations that managers are afraid they will not be able to meet.

Only a few companies have removed the secrecy to the degree that they will openly talk about candidates, and they would argue (as would I) that planning, without involving the person for which you have plans, has limited value. For example, the managers of a manufacturing organization initiated succession planning in response to losing a senior executive they had expected to be their next president. Faced with his resignation, they informed him of their intentions and the opportunity he would have at the company. His response was that he would have stayed had he known.

In fact, he would like to stay now that he knew, but unfortunately he had made commitments to his new employer that he could not back down from. At this point the company introduced succession planning and agreed that they would communicate their intentions (without obligation or commitment) to the individuals involved.

If succession planning is going to be totally secret, then it will never have a widespread impact on the organization. Again, this may require that the less sensitive issues of strategy be communicated and the more sensitive subject of specific candidates be confidential. By communicating the strategic plan for any position, the feedback problem can be overcome.

Readiness

Many succession plans do not contain a time frame. A plan without a time frame clearly falls under the category of "good intentions" as opposed to the kinds of plans that are implemented and, as Peter Drucker has said, "degenerate into work."

Readiness can take two forms in succession planning, and often both are used. The first is an assignment of general readiness to an employee—that is, an evaluation of when the individual will be ready to take on new responsibilities (not necessarily a promotion). The second form of readiness is known as specific or succession readiness, which is an evaluation of when an individual will be ready to take on a specific job for which he or she is a successor (a single individual may have multiple specific-readiness evaluations).

Readiness is the cornerstone of succession planning because it introduces the dimension of time to the plan. When time is introduced to the plan, there is a deadline. Although most managers are not fully aware of this, when a person is deemed ready to move within a year, he or she is likely to move within a year, even if moving necessitates going to another company. The deadline is real.

Layers

Succession planning, like business planning, is a line responsibility and as such is designed to pass up and down the organizational hierarchy. As with many other processes, the number of layers can impose limits on communication and effectiveness. In the case of succession planning, there is a clear correlation between the number of layers and the perceived value of the process—as the layers increase, satisfaction tends to decrease.

As a result, many corporations push responsibility for succession planning down the line and review only the most critical strategic moves at the highest levels of the corporation. This method leaves succession decisions closer to the business context in which they are made and has proved to be more effective.

Some companies have adapted their succession planning to conform to the growing trend of the team perspective. Just as performance evaluation may now include peer and subordinate reviews, so succession planning can be adapted to a more team-oriented approach.

Early efforts at this approach have allowed employees to nominate themselves for jobs. These self-nominations are reviewed by a committee (of cross-company representatives) that may suggest the individual as a candidate, or keep him or her on a more extensive slate of possible candidates. It is likely that these efforts, or ones like them, will play a more prominent role in succession planning in the future. It is an ongoing irony that an employee can apply for any job in any company except his or her own.

Problems, Not Pat Answers

To quote a management guru: "Managers solve the problems they know how to solve, not the problems that they have." This is not only true in succession planning, but it is encouraged by the way the process is conducted.

Succession planning is often defined in terms of the materials to be presented: "We will need you to complete a succession chart with two successors for each position and an employee profile for all successors and high potentials."

The suggestion behind the instructions is to choose successors whether they are available or not and whether they are competent or not. In other words the message is: "We want your solutions to this succession issue and this is the format we want it in." There is rarely anything which asks for the problems. Managers then fill out the forms as requested and often know that they are choosing successors who they would never put in the jobs.

The message is: "If you do not fill out the form, then you have not done your job." The message should be: "If you have not thought about the problem and are unaware of the potential issues that might arise, then you have not done your job." There may be no easy solution. The forms don't ask, or even allow, for the statement of problems—they simply want the answers. The review meetings then become a presentation of "pat answers," and real value is added only when someone detects a problem for discussion.

Information Quantity and Decision Making

There is a clear correlation between the amount of data used to make succession planning decisions and the impact of the process. Ironically, the more data that are used, the lower the impact. This is true because massive data collection creates a burden on the organization, reduces cooperation and quality, and makes timely data collection and management difficult.

In Summary

Succession planning should be conducted on an annual basis, in as brief a time as is necessary, to provide a strategic guide to managers for use in the everyday challenge of achieving results and accomplishing goals.

This can be achieved by:

- Setting expectations that are real and appropriate to a planning process.
- Tying the succession plan to the business plan and not seeing succession planning as an end in itself.
- Closing the feedback loop and ensuring "top-down" communication of strategy, particularly through removing the "cloak and dagger" view of the information.
- Ensuring that the plan has a time frame for implementation.
- Recognizing the effect that a multilayered management structure has on feedback and communication and pushing decision making down the line, closer to the context of the business.
- Providing other means, such as self-nomination, for considering candidates.
- Attempting to discover the obstacles to implementation at the time of planning instead of asking for "pat answers."
- Reducing the burdensome information gathering to those types of data that are pertinent to decision making.

Promotion Systems in Organizations

Gerald R. Ferris, M. Ronald Buckley, and Gillian M. Allen

Organizations have made dramatic changes in their structure and design in order to compete effectively in this increasingly global economy. Extensive downsizing and delayering efforts not only have changed the appearance of organizations, but also have seriously altered the opportunity structure for upward mobility. Virtually as long as work organizations have been in existence, employees have defined their career success in terms of upward mobility. The principal vehicle of upward mobility is the promotion system. Despite the importance of promotion systems, relatively little is known about them beyond the work done on CEO succession: a very specific promotion decision (e.g., Forbes and Piercy, 1991; Vancil, 1987a, 1987b). The research that has been conducted on promotion systems has tended to focus on the promotion decision itself, not on the characteristics of the system.

Thus, despite their importance as a principal vehicle of mobility in organizations and a mechanism for identification and control of talent and ability, we know surprisingly little about the mechanisms and causes of promotion systems in organizations. Unfortunately, this comes at a time when promotion decisions and systems are likely to receive increased scrutiny. Freiberg (1991) has argued that managerial incompetence has become a serious problem in organizations today, and that it may well have its roots in the way upward mobility decisions are made. Furthermore, Lublin (1991) cited the new federal civil rights law as a major reason why promotion systems will receive closer scrutiny. The Civil Rights Act of 1991 extends punitive damages and jury trials to those victimized by employment discrimination. There will need to be more legitimate substantiation of promotion decisions. Promoting in one's own image, which reflects an age-old pattern, may not be acceptable from a legal standpoint (Lublin, 1991). Furthermore, some research and anecdotal evidence have suggested that promotion decisions are the most "political" decisions in organizations. If politics in promotion decisions is bad and needs to be reduced, it is first necessary to better understand promotion systems and how it is that politics is allowed to have an influence. The purpose of the present study, then, was to develop better understanding of promotion systems. A model of the causes and outcomes of promotion systems was developed, and portions of that model were tested with data collected from a sample of organizations varying in industry, size, and other characteristics.

Promotion Systems Research

Mobility in organizations has been a topic of importance for quite some time, and it has been examined from diverse perspectives (e.g., Anderson, Milkovich, and Tsui, 1981; Markham, Harlan, and Hackett, 1987; Kanter, 1977; Rosenbaum, 1984). A considerable amount of research on mobility has tended to focus on mobility at the very top, or manager succession, which is indeed an important decision and worthy of investigation (e.g., Forbes and Piercy, 1991; Swinyard and Bond, 1980; Vancil, 1987a, 1987b). We know that intraorganizational movement goes on at other levels as well, but we know less about the nature and characteristics of the promotion process at other levels than the top one.

Reprinted with permission of The Human Resource Planning Society from *Human Resource Planning, 15:3* (1992): 47–68.

The published research that has been conducted on promotion systems, process, and decisions generally falls into about four categories, which are presented and briefly reviewed below.

Perceptions about Promotions

A body of research has focused on employee perceptions regarding the promotion process. Some of this work has focused on the criteria employees perceive to be used, and their perceptions regarding ways to obtain other jobs within the organization (Beehr and Juntunen, 1990; Beehr, Taber, and Walsh, 1980; Beyer, Stevens, and Trice, 1980; Heisler and Gemmill, 1978; Gemmill and DeSalvia, 1977). Other research on perceptions about promotions has examined the perceived opportunity for movement, and the factors affecting such employee perceptions (e.g., Landau and Hammer, 1986; White, 1974). A third area of perceptions research has investigated the issues of procedural justice on the perceived fairness of promotion practices (e.g., Folger and Greenberg, 1985; McEnrue, 1989). The research on perceptions then has tended to raise the issues of how much opportunity employees perceive for personal advancement, what criteria they perceive being used in the promotion process, and the fairness of both the procedures and outcomes of promotion systems.

Promotion Decisions

Another body of research has focused on the cognitive processes of decision makers who make promotion decisions, and on the effects of particular candidate characteristics on such decisions (e.g., London and Stumpf, 1983; Stumpf and London, 1981a, 1981b). Stumpf and London (1981b) developed a model that considered individual as well as organizational influences on the promotion decision process, including a focus on types of promotion decision criteria such as performance, potential, promotability, and so forth. In a later study, London and Stumpf (1983) found that the most prominent factor in managerial

promotion decisions was the rating of the candidate's potential. Other research has examined the role of other formal or informal evaluation criteria in promotion decisions, including seniority and ability (e.g., Halaby, 1978; Mills, 1985), performance (e.g., Taylor, 1975), and a number of demographic characteristics of candidates such as education, age, and sex (e.g., Markham et al., 1987).

It seems, then, that promotion criteria such as performance and potential are considered to be important inputs to promotion decisions. Yet, this still leaves unanswered the question of how we determine whether someone has potential. Perhaps the most well designed tool to measure management potential is the assessment center, and considerable evidence attests to its predictability over extended periods of time (Howard and Bray, 1988). Whereas the assessment center possesses a number of desirable characteristics (e.g., more objective evaluation), it has some deficiencies as well, including the way people are identified for the assessment center and potential effects of self-fulfilling prophecies (Forbes and Piercy, 1991).

Promotion System Characteristics

The research reviewed in the foregoing areas focused on individual employee perceptions and decision criteria used to make specific promotion decisions. The research on causes and characteristics of promotion systems raises the level of analysis to examine the nature and form of promotion systems, and how they operate. The Anderson et al. (1981) model included the effects of both external environmental (e.g., economic, legal, social) and organizational characteristics (e.g., size, structure, technology) on mobility in organizations. Also, although they did not consider promotion practices, Jackson, Schuler, and Rivero (1989) tested the effects of business strategy, technology, organization size, and unionization on personnel practices. Dimick and Murray (1978) conducted a study of predictors of personnel policies and practices in a sample of 20 companies that varied in size, industry, and location. They found that contextual factors (either economic or institutional) influenced the number of personnel practices, including the use of merit as a criterion for internal promotion and transfer decisions.

Three additional pieces of research have each dealt with promotion systems in an extensive manner, but in quite different ways. Friedman (1986) studied 230 *Fortune* 500 firms with regard to the rules and procedures that form the basis of their succession systems for the top echelon, defined as the top three levels below the CEO in the management hierarchy. The model tested in this research included the effects of contextual conditions (e.g., industry, size) and succession system characteristics (e.g., formalization, political criteria, technical criteria) on outcomes such as financial performance and succession system effectiveness.

Markham et al. (1987) developed a model of promotion opportunity in organizations which suggested that organization size, structure, and demography combine to affect the amount of promotion or advancement opportunity available to employees. They suggested that opportunity, in turn, is a scarce resource allocated by an administrative promotion system which includes a set of rules and procedures for processing candidates. It is the amount of opportunity and the nature of the administrative system which determine who receives promotions. They carefully analyzed the procedures used to identify candidates for promotion, the criteria used to evaluate candidates, and the procedures used to make final decisions.

Finally, Kanter (1977) conducted an extensive qualitative study of the employment practices of a particular organization, and a considerable portion of her analysis was devoted to promotion decisions and systems. She coined the term "homosocial reproduction systems" to characterize promotion systems whereby managers promote in their own image, thus highlighting the importance of political criteria instead of prior performance. Such systems, she argued, are particularly dis-

advantageous for women aspiring to higher levels in the organization when the promotion decision makers typically are men. This reference to political criteria in promotion systems effectively leads into the final category of research.

Politics in Promotion Systems

The role of politics in promotion decisions and systems has been recognized by several researchers (e.g., Friedman, 1986; Kanter, 1977; Markham et al., 1987; Stumpf and London, 1981b). Additionally, Gandz and Murray (1980) presented a number of organizational processes and practices to respondents, and asked them to indicate the extent to which politics influenced each. Promotions and transfers emerged as the second most political process, and the authors explained this as due to the fact that there are few established rules of standards and criteria, and the considerable ambiguity involved in the processes and practices. Other recent research has found politics to be associated with the promotion process (e.g., Ferris and Buckley, 1990; Riley, 1983), and in a very recent investigation of promotions, Ruderman (1991) reported evidence to support the notion that "it's who you know" and visibility that are strong determinants of promotion decisions.

The foregoing review allows us to assess the status of our knowledge base in this area, and identify limitations or gaps in our understanding that need to be addressed. One major need that emerges is the large-scale investigation of causes and outcomes of promotion system characteristics. With the exception of the Friedman (1986) study, which confined its focus to the three hierarchical levels below the CEO, there have been no known efforts to investigate promotion system characteristics in a comprehensive manner.

Another limitation or gap in our understanding of promotion systems relates to our need to integrate the macro- and micro-level studies by developing models of promotion systems which incorporate internal and external causes and organizational outcomes, as well as the intermediate linkages. That is, we need to know not only *what* factors affect promotion systems design, and *what* promotion system characteristics affect organizational performance, but also *how* these effects operate. It may well be the case that promotion system characteristics affect organizational effectiveness through their effects on employee attitudes and behavior. Such integrative and comprehensive theories have not been formulated or tested to date.

A Model of Promotion Systems

A model is proposed that depicts the factors which influence the characteristics of the organizations' promotion system, and also the consequences that the promotion system has for the performance of the organization. This model is presented in Exhibit 1.

A number of environmental, organizational, and job factors (1 in model) are believed to influence the nature, form, and characteristics of promotion systems (2 in model) present in the organization. The promotion system characteristics, then, are proposed to affect organizational performance (4 in model), but only indirectly through their effects on employee competence, attitudes, and behavior (3 in model). The nature of this model is consistent with a rather recent trend emerging in the human resources (HR) management field to investigate phenomena at the organizational level of analysis, in contrast to the individual-level research that historically has characterized this field. The unique feature of the present model is that it blends organizational-level and individual-level variables and, in the process, more precisely articulates the intermediate linkages between HR systems and firm performance and effectiveness. The purpose of the present study is to test portions of the model of promotion systems proposed in Exhibit 1, and begin to articulate more precisely the nature, characteristics, and processes of these most critical decisions in organizations.

Methodology

Research Sample and Procedure

Because the interest in this study was in identifying how promotion systems are designed and the factors that influence the form which they take, a sample of organizations was needed which had variability in industry, size, performance, and other key characteristics. Thus, in order to have enough companies within a particular industry to conduct meaningful analyses, the decision was made to select two manufacturing industries and two service industries and sample companies within each of these four industries. The four industries targeted and the number of firms in each, according to the U.S. Public Companies (June 1991) CD-ROM database, are listed below:

Manufacturing
Food Processing (N = 139)
Pharmaceuticals (N = 106)

Service
Health Service (N = 203)
Insurance (N = 294)

These numbers were reduced based on a number of criteria. Excluded from the samples were:

1. all companies with fewer than 100 employees. It was considered that smaller companies would be unlikely to have promotion systems in place.
2. all companies with head offices outside of the continental United States. Because of the time restraints on the study, it was thought that there would be insufficient time available to obtain responses from distant companies.
3. all companies for which current return on sales (ROS) figures were unavailable. Since ROS was our key index of performance of the companies, we excluded all companies for which these data were not found despite checking a number of sources of financial information.

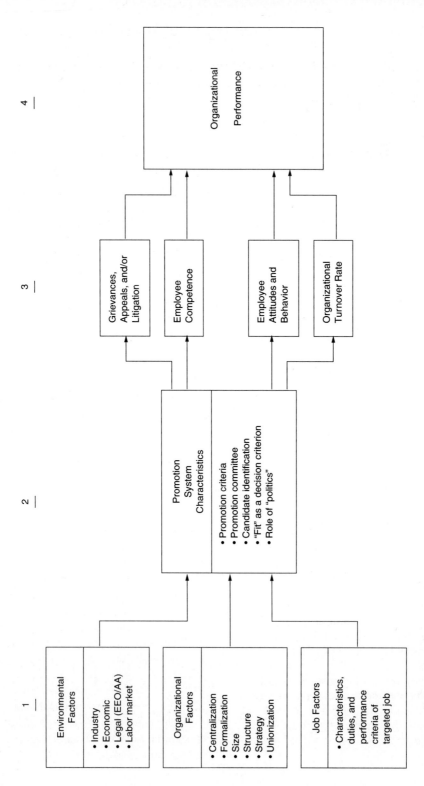

Exhibit 1. A Model of Promotional Systems

Questionnaires were sent to the HR managers or chief operating officers for the following sample of 347 companies:

Manufacturing
Food Processing (N = 92)
Pharmaceuticals (N = 97)

Service
Health Services (N = 63)
Insurance (N = 95)

The company manager was asked to complete the questionnaire and to return it to us in an enclosed postage-paid envelope. Instructions included with the questionnaire asked the managers to focus their attention on their promotion systems as applied to promotions into the middle management level of their company.

Additionally, on-site structured interviews were conducted at eleven of the organizations in order to pretest the instrument as well as to follow up on questions and to obtain more qualitative information and a more in-depth understanding of the promotion system dynamics. During these interviews, discussions were conducted to ensure that the areas which were included in our questionnaire were germane to our interests in promotion systems. In addition, we used this time to uncover any areas which we had overlooked in our initial questionnaire. We used this information to sharpen the focus of the questionnaire we eventually sent to all respondents.

Questionnaire

The survey instrument was divided into questions that related to three major groups of variables. The first group of questions was designed to obtain data on environmental and organizational factors that were believed to influence the characteristics of promotion systems. The second group of questions was designed to obtain descriptions of the promotion systems in place in the companies. The third group of questions was designed to obtain data on performance outcomes related to the promotion systems. The specific questions included in each of the three variables groups in the questionnaire are discussed below.

Environmental Factors

Industry. The companies were grouped according to their industry (Food Processing, Health Services, Insurance, or Pharmaceuticals, according to their classification in the U.S. Public Companies CD-ROM database). Also, participants were asked to identify their principal market: Regional, National, or International.

Affirmative action plan. Participants were asked if their companies had an affirmative action plan that influences promotions.

Organizational Factors

Centralization. The five-item scale developed by Dewar, Whetten, and Boje (1980) was used to measure centralization. Questions were answered by the respondents using the four-point scale: Definitely false, More false than true, More true than false, and Definitely true. The questions were:

1. There can be little action taken here until a supervisor approves a decision.
2. A person who wants to make his/her own decisions would be quickly discouraged.
3. Even small matters have to be referred to someone higher up for a final answer.
4. People around here have to ask their boss before they do almost anything.
5. Any decision someone makes in this organization has to have their boss's approval.

Formalization. The six-item scale developed by Oldham and Hackman (1981) was used to measure formalization. Questions answered by the respondents (using the five-point scale: Very inaccurate, Inaccurate, Uncertain, Accurate, Very accurate) were:

1. The organization has a very large number of written rules and policies.
2. A "rules and procedures" manual exists and is readily available within this organization.
3. Promotion procedures used in this organization are formal and well established.
4. There is a complete written job description for most jobs in this organization.
5. The organization keeps a written record of nearly everyone's job performance.
6. There is a formal orientation program for most new members of the organization.

Levels of hierarchy. Participants were asked how many hierarchical levels there are in their organizations.

Size. Participants were asked the number of full-time, paid employees in their organizations. The following ranges of numbers were used:

____ Less than 100	____ 1,001–5,000
____ 100–500	____ 5,001–10,000
____ 501–1,000	____ Over 10,000

These responses were treated as a continuous scale, representing a progression from the lowest to highest numbers of employees in the companies surveyed.

Strategy. Four questions relating to the promotion strategy of the companies were combined into a single scale. These were questions 3–6 in Section 3 of the questionnaire:

3. To what extent does your organization engage in formal strategic planning?
4. To what extent does your organization engage in systematic human resource planning?
5. To what extent does your organization have a career planning and development function in your human resource system?
6. To what extent does your organization engage in systematic succession planning?

Participants also completed an exercise that defined their companies as belonging in one of four strategic types of organizations. Question 1 of Section 3 of the questionnaire asked the managers to consider if their companies were:

Type 1   This type of organization attempts to locate and maintain a secure niche in a relatively stable product or service area. . . . Often this type of organization is not at the forefront of developments in the industry—it tends to ignore industry changes that have no direct influence on current areas of operation and concentrates instead on doing the best job possible in a limited area.

Type 2   This type of organization typically operates within a broad product-market domain that undergoes periodic redefinition. . . . The organization responds rapidly to early signals concerning areas of opportunity, and these responses often lead to a new round of competitive actions. . . .

Type 3   This type of organization attempts to maintain a stable, limited line of products or services, while at the same time moving out quickly to follow a carefully selected set of the more promising new developments in the industry. . . .

Type 4   No consistent product-market orientation. . . .

Unionization. Participants were asked for the percentage of employees in their work forces who belong to a union.

Promotion System Characteristics

Type of system. Four questions related to the type of promotion system in place in the companies. One question asked if the company has a "promotion-from-within" philosophy or if it tends to recruit outside the organization to fill managerial openings. Another asked if the company has a "fast track" system of mobility in the managerial ranks. A third question asked if there are formal or informal "time-in-grade" requirements for promotion. A fourth question asked if the company has a formal or informal *mentoring* program.

Method of system. Four questions related to the promotion methods in place in the companies. Question 1 asked how important job postings are as a source of candidates for promotion in the organization. Question 2 asked how important advance applications are as a source of candidates for promotion in the organization. Question 3 asked how important informal nomination by a higher level manager is as a source of candidates for promotion in the organization, and Question 4 asked if the criteria used for promotion decisions are well specified, common knowledge, and formally communicated to all concerned employees.

Candidate criteria. Respondents used a five-point scale (Unimportant, Of little importance, Of average importance, Somewhat important, Very important) to rate the importance of a number of different candidate criteria that can be used to make promotion decisions. They evaluated the importance of seniority, ability, prior performance, individual reputation, personality, fit, politics, and potential as promotion criteria in their companies.

Committee. Two questions were used to identify the committee processes involved in making promotion decisions. The first question asked if promotion decisions are made by promotion committees, or if one manager in the organization makes the decisions. The second question asked how many people are usually involved in making promotion decisions.

Role of fit. Seven questions were used to determine the role of fit in promotion decisions. The questions asked:

1. to what extent promotions are "wired."
2. to what extent the people who receive managerial promotions in the organization are just like their superiors in terms of having similar values.
3. to what extent the people who receive managerial promotions in the organization are just like their superiors in terms of having similar interests.
4. to what extent the people who receive managerial promotions in the organization are just like their superiors in terms of having similar backgrounds.
5. to what extent the candidate's particular functional area of experience affects his/her promotion chances to a managerial position.
6. to what extent career velocity affects promotion decisions.
7. to what extent losing out on an earlier promotion affects a candidate's chances in later promotion decisions in a negative manner.

Role of influence/politics. Two questions concerned the effects of influence and politics in the promotion decision-making process. One asked to what extent the label of "promotable" is based on being visible or having "gotten in good with" some influential manager. The other asked to what extent promotion decisions in the organization are political.

Performance Assessment

Turnover rates. A question was asked requesting the organization turnover rate for the most recent fiscal year.

Return on sales. Question ROS6 asked for the organization's ROS for the most recent fiscal year. We chose ROS as a more suitable measure of profitability than Earnings Per Share (EPS) based on the character of our sample. The U.S. Public Companies (June 1991) database did provide EPS data on the companies, but ROI, ROE, and ROS were considered to be more suitable measures of profitability because of the great variability in size of the companies surveyed. The Returns statistics could be considered to be more stable within industries, regardless of the size of individual companies, but it is less possible to compare companies of different sizes on the basis of EPS. On examining the reported financial information in the database, it was found that many more companies reported their ROS figures than their ROE figures, but ROI numbers were not included in the database. To have the largest possible sample with complete information, we decided to use the ROS figures from the database. Furthermore, the ROS measure has received considerable use in prior work.

Employee considerations. It was asked if the manager believed that everyone is well informed concerning what is required of them in order to be promoted.

Grievances concerning promotions. Respondents were asked to what extent grievances, appeals, or legal challenges to promotion decisions have been made in the organization in the last five years.

Data Analysis

Correlations were calculated between pairs of continuous variables in the study to test for significant relationships between those variables. Chi-squared statistics were calculated between pairs of nominal variables to test for significant relationships, and phi statistics were calculated as measures of association between those variables.

Because of the interest in applications, however, specific statistical tests are not reported here. Instead, the relationships that achieved statistical significance are presented and discussed without coefficients (a complete report of the statistical findings is available from the first author).

Results

The numbers of respondents represented in the four industries are shown in Exhibit 2. Be-

Exhibit 2
Response Rate by Industry (IND)

Industry:	Sent Out:	Returned/Rate:
Food Processing	92	11/11.96%
Health Services	63	8/8.25%
Insurance	95	12/12.63%
Pharmaceuticals	97	10/15.87%
Totals	347	41/11.82%

cause of the low response rates, this study must be viewed as exploratory, and results viewed as suggestive rather than definitive. Despite this, we believe that the information obtained will be useful in addressing a number of important questions. Additionally, these data will be beneficial in helping us to refine our thinking on the promotion process in organizations.

Environmental Factors– Promotion System Linkages

Industry. Industry was significantly related to the extent to which the fit between the functional areas of the candidates and the area of the promotional opportunities was considered. The health care industry considered functional area of more importance in their promotion systems than did the other industries.

The market served by the companies was significantly related to the extent to which similarity in background between the candidates and the promotion decision makers was considered. Companies in international markets were more likely to consider similarity in background as a promotion criterion. The market served by the companies was significantly related to the extent to which politics influenced promotions. Companies in national and international markets were more likely to think that politics influenced promotions.

Affirmative action plan. If companies had affirmative action plans, they also tended to have time-in-grade requirements for promotion. The managers thought that promotion criteria were common knowledge by employees, and that career velocity had less of an impact on promotion decisions.

Organizational Factors– Promotion System Linkages

Centralization. If companies were more centralized, the managers were more likely to think that promotion criteria were common knowledge by employees; the companies were less likely to use informal nominations by managers in making their promotion decisions; ability was a less important promotion criterion; managers thought promotions were more likely to be wired; and the managers thought career velocity was a less important promotion criterion than if the companies were less centralized.

Formalization. The greater the extent to which companies were formalized, the less likely they were to have time-in-grade requirements for promotion, the more likely they were to use job postings, the more likely they were to use advance applications, the more likely they were to consider potential as a promotion criterion, and the more likely it was that managers believed losing out on earlier promotions had an impact on promotion decisions.

Size. Larger companies were more likely to have a fast track for promotions. They were more likely to use informal nominations by managers for promotions; they were more likely to consider fit as a promotion criterion; they were more likely to consider similarity of values and interests between the candidates and the manager in making promotion decisions; and they were more likely to use career velocity as a promotion criterion.

Strategy. Companies which developed strategic planning processes in their promotion systems (i.e., the extent to which the organization engages in systematic HR planning which incorporates promotion and succession considerations) were less likely to use time-in-grade requirements in making promotion decisions and more likely to use informal nominations by managers in making promotion decisions. These companies had more people involved in making promotion decisions, were more likely to consider similarity in interests and background between the candidates and the manager in making promotion decisions, were more likely to consider career velocity in making promotion decisions, and were more likely to consider influence and politics in making promotion decisions. This suggests, on the surface, a counterintuitive finding; however, it is only counterintuitive if we expect that a formal planning process will necessarily be implemented through formal mechanisms or activities rather than informal or political means. Such an expectation may simply not reflect organizational reality.

Strategy within industry was significantly related to use of potential as a promotion criterion. Companies intending to remain stable within their industries were more likely to consider potential as a promotion criterion. Also, companies with a "second-in" strategy were more likely to involve more managers in making promotion decisions. Furthermore, managers in companies with a second-in strategy were more likely to believe promotions were wired in their companies.

Unionization. The more highly unionized the companies were, the less important were job postings as sources of candidates for promotion.

Relationships among Promotion System Characteristics

Type of system. If companies had fast track provisions, they also tended to have mentoring systems. They were also more likely to consider seniority as a promotion criterion, and they were more likely to consider potential as a promotion criterion.

If companies had time-in-grade restrictions, they were less likely to consider similarity in background between the candidates and manager in making promotion decisions. If companies had a mentoring system, they were less likely to consider potential as a promotion criterion.

Method of system.   If companies used informal nomination by managers, they were more likely to use fit as a promotion criterion.

Promotion System– Performance Assessment Linkages

The greater the extent to which informal nomination by a manager was used, the less informed the employees were believed to be about the requirements for promotion. Also, in companies earning higher return on sales, greater was the extent to which ability and prior performance were used as promotion criteria. Finally, it was found that if more managers were involved in promotion decision making, turnover rates were higher and numbers of grievances were increased.

Discussion

In this study, we attempted to provide a systematic and reasonably comprehensive examination of promotion systems in organizations. Without extensive research on the characteristics of promotion systems and process, speculation and anecdote tend to form the bases on which we form our impressions of the way these systems operate. And it is these bases that have led to the two extreme perspectives on promotion systems: the rational model and the political model. A rational model perspective would depict promotion systems as including clearly stated and widely communicated procedures for candidate identification and precise, job-relevant decision criteria, with all candidates processed uniformly. A political model would characterize the promotion process as a negotiated reality, where the outcome was explained more by connections and interpersonal influence strategies, and less by objective qualifications, performance, and competence.

The present results would suggest a compromise position that balances rational and political perspectives as the most accurate reflection of promotion systems and processes in organizations. A number of findings are particularly noteworthy. Organizational strategy appears to be the major variable which drives the promotion process. It has an effect upon (among many other factors) who is involved in the choosing, how the choice is made, what criteria are utilized, and who is chosen. This was our expectation from the inception of this research project. Although our sample size precludes a comprehensive strategy/promotion practices analysis, we are confident that our results are congruent with those reported by other researchers, namely that certain organizational strategies facilitate certain HR activities.

Interestingly, site interviews yielded mixed results among interviewees regarding the role of politics in the promotion process in their organization. The results of the questionnaire also produced mixed results. Many reported that the major factor responsible for judgments concerning suitability of promotion was ability. This is congruent with London and Stumpf's (1983) conclusion that ratings of candidate potential based upon perceptions of ability and past performance were the most prominent factors in the managerial promotion decision. Confirming the rational model, those organizations that reported using ability and prior performance as primary promotion criteria also earned higher ROS.

Many interviewees reported a strikingly different picture of the politics involved in the promotion process during the discussions. Although it is uncomfortable to affirm the existence of politics in organizations, perhaps due to the negative connotations associated with "politics," many of the activities which occur in this process are undeniably political. For example, many reported that similarity of values and interests, impression management, and ingratiation were important factors in this process. One manager summarized the process nicely: "We are looking for people with ability who can successfully navigate the politics of our organization. Who you know and who knows you is important. How well you fit in, in terms of interests and values, is important. . . ." Thus, based on prior research and experience, we can consider statements confirming the existence of politics to be underestimates due to social desirability bias.

We believe that political savvy is a necessary, but not sufficient condition for promotion. We agree with Kanter (1977) that political behavior can carry a candidate. We disagree with her in that political behavior will only carry an individual to a certain point at which ability and past performance are necessary in order to move further in an organization. One respondent stated that "pure organizational politicians will hit a promotion ceiling, which is well below the highest echelons of this organization." Basically, organizations are seeking political people with solid past performance and demonstrated ability. This appears to be a nice blending of the political and rational perspectives of managerial promotion. Furthermore, it suggests that politics does not have to be viewed as uniformly negative. Rather, some types of political behavior may be destructive while other types may represent necessary skills required to navigate turbulent organizational waters.

Although it is difficult to deny the political overtones associated with both affirmative action programs (both voluntary and involuntary) and mentoring programs, these programs appear to be mostly apolitical in their application. For example, these programs have specific time-in-grade requirements and well-communicated promotion criteria. By their design, they have relatively little degrees of managerial discretion built into their operation, which likely explains their relative freedom from political activity. On the record, interviewees expressed approval of these types of programs. Off the record, interviewees expressed disapproval, and expressed many

reservations concerning these programs in terms of managerial discretion, input into the program, and applicant quality.

Apparently, most of the respondents in this study subscribe to the notion of a generic manager. Functional area of expertise is, for the most part, not an important factor in consideration for promotion. Those in the health care industry attached more importance to functional expertise in their promotion systems. One respondent from the health care industry reported that "our product is now in such a state of instability that we are afraid to take many chances in our hiring and promotion. Our success is less people-driven than it is cost of technology driven." Their preference is to "stick to the knitting"—hiring functional managers until the industry stabilizes or the future of the industry becomes clearer. Surprisingly, other industry effects were minimal—type of industry does not appear to be a major factor in the promotion process.

The results confirmed our expectations that organizational size would be an important variable in terms of promotion systems. Larger companies were more likely to have a fast track; to use informal nomination by managers for promotions; and to consider similarity of interests, similarity of values, and fit in making promotion decisions. The larger an organization, the more difficult it is to obtain complete information concerning candidates for promotion. Thus, decision makers are compelled to utilize more nebulous promotion criteria, and the opportunity for politics becoming involved in the process increases dramatically. Similarly, the effects of both centralization and formalization were predictable in terms of their bureaucratic effect upon the promotion process. A number of the interviewees decried their lack of discretionary freedom to adapt the promotion process. Lastly, those organizations with a national/international market reported that promotion criteria were less likely to be communicated, similarity was used as a promotion criterion, and politics influenced the promotion process. Geographic spread has a disabling effect upon information dissemination—both ways. It is difficult to communicate with individuals over a great distance and it is likewise difficult for individuals to communicate their personal strengths, thus creating an opportunity for political behavior (e.g., impression management).

What do these results indicate to us concerning the need to revise Exhibit 1? (See Exhibit 3.) Most of what we have reported is concerned with parts 1 and 2 of Exhibit 1. Based on the evidence from the survey and our on-site interviews, we would feel uncomfortable removing any of the variables which are included in parts 1 and 2 of Exhibit 1. We would, though, be better able to prioritize the importance of the variables in the promotion process. For example, our respondents have indicated that both strategy and size of organization contribute relatively more to the method and outcome of the promotion process. In addition, the on-site interviews revealed that environmental factors have more of an effect than we had initially believed. Their effects are directly linked to each of the variables in parts 1 and 2 of Exhibit 1. Further, their effects upon organizational performance are unmediated by any of the variables in parts 1 and 2 of Exhibit 1.

Overall, our research suggests that the promotion process is quite complex, and we are confident that we have made an incremental advance in our understanding of this complex process. We believe we have a clearer idea of how these variables interact to yield a promotion decision. We are disappointed that we had such difficulty in eliciting responses from our target group. This is a difficulty which goes along with attempting to perform research in areas in which organizational decision makers are uncomfortable with divulging details. There is a need to move forward with this research. In addition, we feel as though the research base which has traditionally been followed in this area needs to be expanded. Relatively scant attention has been given to individual-level variables in this process. For example, what effect do employee attitudes or

employee competence have on the promotion process? Until these variables are included in promotion systems models, any speculation on this issue is, at best, incomplete, at worst, incorrect.

Implications for Practice

Previous research on promotion systems, the results of the present study, and observation and anecdote in organizations appear to have some interesting implications for practice. We first need to realize that whereas promotions represent one of the most highly valued rewards that can be given to employees, organizations are changing in form, resulting in fewer opportunities for advancement in the future. The extensive downsizing of American industry has produced organizations with "flat" organizational structures and far fewer employees. So, too, there are fewer people available to compete for promotions (but this issue is neutralized by the fact that there are fewer positions available to which to be promoted). The reality of the future, then, is that promotions will continue to be a highly valued reward, but an increasingly scarce one. This will serve to only magnify the importance of promotion decisions, and the careful scrutiny they receive in organizations. Evidence of such careful scrutiny is demonstrated by the employment discrimination charges filed with the Equal Employment Opportunity Commission. In 1990, nearly 61% of the bias charges filed focused on employee advancement/promotion and discharge decisions (Lublin, 1991). Lublin goes on to conclude that the 1991 Civil Rights Act, which allows for punitive damages and jury trials under certain categories of discrimination, dramatically raises the costs of making inaccurate or inappropriate HR decisions. For example, in October, 1991, Texaco was found guilty of sex discrimination for twice refusing to promote a female manager in favor of male candidates. The California court jury awarded the female manager approximately $17.7 million, which included $15 million in punitive damages.

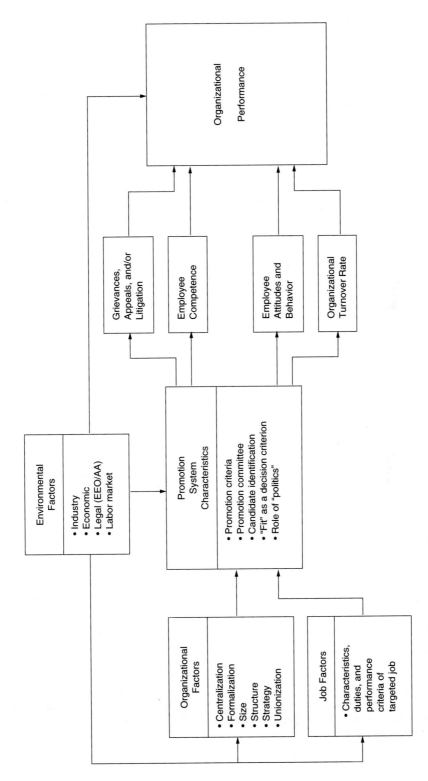

Exhibit 3. A Revised Model of Promotion Systems

In addition to the legal scrutiny that promotion decisions are likely to receive, organizations should be quite concerned about the skill and performance consequences of faulty upward mobility decisions. Freiberg (1991) has identified managerial competence as a quite serious problem in organizations, and suggests that this problem may well be the result of inappropriate procedures for making promotion decisions. Apparently, it is the subordinates of incompetent managers who pay the price with increased stress levels and greater supervisor-subordinate conflict. Nevertheless, it is the organization that ultimately feels the serious effects of such problems through increased costs due to absenteeism, more grievances filed, and lower productivity. The root of the problem, Freiberg suggests, lies in the way we assess people for staffing positions. The interview is the most frequently used tool for making selection and promotion decisions, and these assessment situations amount to "beauty contests. . . . People get hired on the basis of their charm, not on the basis of competence or talent for management" (Freiberg, 1991, p. 23). Also, the very people making the promotion decisions are typically the ones with whom the candidates have ingratiated themselves.

The seriousness of the foregoing issues suggests the need for action in the form of recommendations for how to improve promotion systems. One way to address the problem of incompetent managers being promoted based upon their skill at ingratiating themselves with the decision maker is to clearly specify the job-relevant promotion criteria, communicate it clearly to decision makers, and enforce those criteria and standards consistently. Additionally, this should involve implementation of accountability mechanisms which make the promotion decision maker answerable for his or her decisions. And third, alternative sources of promotion candidate assessment might be used to supplement the existing decision-making managers. Freiberg (1991) suggested that we go to the manager candidate's subordinates and solicit an evalu-

ation of the candidate. If a candidate for promotion devotes time and attention to managing impressions of others, those efforts are typically directed upward toward superiors. Subordinates, therefore, are often capable of providing a more realistic assessment of the manager's job-relevant skills and abilities, which abilities have not been obscured or inflated by charm and manipulation.

Organizational America is undergoing some rather dramatic changes, both in terms of how companies are structured and designed, as well as in the management systems that are implemented to operate the firm effectively. As we identify managerial talent as a critical need of effective organizations, we need to ensure that our promotion systems operate in a way that satisfy this need. This article has suggested some challenges regarding promotion systems, as well as some ways to improve their operation.

References

Anderson, J., Milkovich, G., and Tsui, A. "A Model of Intraorganizational Mobility." *Academy of Management Review, 6,* 1981, pp. 529–539.

Beehr, T. A., and Juntunen, D. L. "Promotions and Employees' Perceived Mobility Channels: The Effects of Employee Sex, Employee Group, and Initial Placement." *Human Relations, 43,* 1990, pp. 455–472.

Beehr, T. A., Taber, T. D., and Walsh, J. T. "Perceived Mobility Channels: Criteria For Intraorganizational Job Mobility." *Organizational Behavior and Human Performance, 26,* 1980, pp. 250–264.

Beyer, J., Stevens, J., and Trice, H. "Predicting How Federal Managers Perceive Criteria Used for Their Promotion." *Public Administration Review,* (January), 1980, pp. 55–66.

Dewar, R. D., Whetten, D. A., and Boje, D. "An Examination of the Reliability and Validity of the Aiken and Hage Scales of Centralization, Formalization, and Task Routineness." *Administrative Science Quarterly, 25,* 1980, pp. 120–128.

Dimick, D. E., and Murray, V. V. "Correlates of Substantive Policy Decisions in Organizations: The

Case of Human Resource Management." *Academy of Management Journal, 21,* 1978, pp. 611–623.

Ferris, G. R., and Buckley, M. R. "Performance Evaluation in High Technology Firms: Process and Politics." In L. R. Gomez-Mejia and M. W. Lawless (Eds.), *Organizational Issues in High Technology Management* (pp. 243–263). (JAI Press: Greenwich, CT, 1990).

Folger, R., and Greenberg, J. "Procedural Justice: An Interpretive Analysis of Personnel Systems." In K. M. Rowland and G. R. Ferris (Eds.), *Research in Personnel and Human Resources Management* (Vol. 3, pp. 141–183). (JAI Press: Greenwich, CT, 1985).

Forbes, J. B., and Piercy, J. E. *Corporate Mobility and Paths to the Top.* (Quorum Books: New York, 1991).

Freiberg, P. "Surprise—Most Bosses Are Incompetent." *APA Monitor,* (January), 22, 1991, p. 23.

Friedman, S. D. "Succession Systems in Large Corporations: Characteristics and Correlates of Performance." *Human Resource Management, 25,* 1986, pp. 191–213.

Gandz, J., and Murray, V. V. "The Experience of Workplace Politics." *Academy of Management Journal, 23,* 1980, pp. 237–251.

Gemmill, G., and DeSalvia, D. "The Promotion Beliefs of Managers as a Factor in Career Progress: An Exploratory Study." *Sloan Management Review,* 1977, pp. 75–81.

Halaby, C. N. "Bureaucratic Promotion Criteria." *Administrative Science Quarterly, 23,* 1978, pp. 466–484.

Heisler, W., and Gemmill, G. "Manager and MBA Student Views of Corporate Promotion Practices: A Structural Comparison." *Academy of Management Journal, 21,* 1978, pp. 731–737.

Howard, A., and Bray, D. W. *Managerial Lives in Transition: Advancing Age and Changing Times.* (Guilford: New York, 1988).

Jackson, S. E., Schuler, R. S., and Rivero, J. C. "Organizational Characteristics as Predictors of Personnel Practices." *Personnel Psychology, 42,* 1989, pp. 727–786.

Kanter, R. M. *Men and Women of the Corporation.* (Basic Books: New York, 1977).

Landau, J., and Hammer, T. "Clerical Employees' Perceptions of Intraorganizational Career Opportunities." *Academy of Management Journal, 29,* 1986, pp. 385–404.

London, M., and Stumpf, S. A. "Effects of Candidate Characteristics on Management Promotion Decisions: An Experimental Study." *Personnel Psychology, 36,* 1983, pp. 241–259.

Lublin, J. S. "Rights Laws to Spur Shifts in Promotions." *Wall Street Journal.* December 30, 1991, p. B1.

Markham, W., Harlan, S., and Hackett, E. "Promotional Opportunity in Organizations: Causes and Consequences." In K. M. Rowland and G. R. Ferris (Eds.), *Research in Personnel and Human Resources Management* (Vol. 5, pp. 223–287). (JAI Press: Greenwich, CT, 1987).

McEnrue, M. P. "The Perceived Fairness of Managerial Promotion Practices." *Human Relations, 42,* 1989, pp. 815–827.

Mills, D. Q. "Seniority Versus Ability in Promotion Decisions." *Industrial and Labor Relations Review, 38,* 1985, pp. 421–425.

Oldham, G. R., and Hackman, J. R. "Relationships Between Organizational Structure and Employee Reactions: Comparing Alternative Frameworks." *Administrative Science Quarterly, 26,* 1981, pp. 66–83.

Riley, P. "A Structurationist Account of Political Culture." *Administrative Science Quarterly, 28,* 1983, pp. 414–437.

Rosenbaum, J. *Career Mobility in a Corporate Hierarchy.* (Academic Press: New York, 1984).

Ruderman, M. N. "Promotion: Beliefs and Reality." *Issues & Observations* (Center for Creative Leadership), 11, 1991, pp. 4–6.

Snow, C. C., and Hrebiniak, L. G. "Strategy, Distinctive Competence, and Organizational Performance." *Administrative Science Quarterly, 25,* 1980, pp. 317–336.

Stumpf, S., and London, M. "Capturing Rater Policies in Evaluating Candidates for Promotion." *Academy of Management Journal, 24,* 1981a, pp. 752–766.

Stumpf, S., and London, M. "Management Promotion: Individual and Organizational Factors Influencing the Decision Process." *Academy of Management Review, 6,* 1981b, pp. 539–549.

Swinyard, A. W., and Bond, F. A. "Who Gets Promoted?" *Harvard Business Review, 58,* 1980, pp. 618.

Taylor, R. N. "Preferences of Industrial Managers for Information Sources in Making Promotion Decisions." *Journal of Applied Psychology, 60,* 1975, pp. 269–272.

Vancil, R. F. "A Look at CEO Succession." *Harvard Business Review, 87,* 1987a, pp. 107–117.

Vancil, R. F. *Passing the Baton: Managing the Process of CEO Succession.* (Harvard Business School Press: Boston, 1987b).

White, T. "Production Workers and Perceptions of Intraorganizational Mobility." *Sociological Inquiry, 44,* 1974, pp. 121–129.

College Recruitment: Realities and Guidelines for the 1990s

Thomas A. Kolenko

Organizations in the 1990s were projected to suffer critical shortages of qualified entry-level talent necessary for the demanding "high-tech" and "high-touch" leadership positions in today's competitive global marketplace. Low birth rates, an aging "baby boom" work force, and escalating skill demands were supposed to provide today's college graduates with abundant career opportunities, according to the *Workforce 2000* study (Johnston & Packer, 1987). Instead, today's college graduates face the poorest job market since World War II, compounded by a growing backlog of unemployed graduates from prior years (Lopez, 1993a). What has happened to the annual "mating ritual" between employer and college graduate that for so long has provided secure futures for both parties? Have the rules of "engagement" changed so quickly?

Employer downsizing, corporate reengineering programs, and a lingering recession have rewritten many employment relationships that had previously depended on regular infusions of fresh college graduates. In the period from 1988 to 1992, the number of graduating college seniors grew eleven times faster than the number of full-time nonfarm jobs, according to the Bureau of Labor Statistics (Rigdon, 1993). Consistent drops in the overall number of new college graduates hired by U.S. employers were also recorded for 1992 through 1993 (Scheetz, 1993). When these changes are coupled with the decidedly white-collar pattern of current job losses, which now account for 36 percent of the total unemployed workers in the U.S., college graduates have a right to worry about their career options. How has the college recruitment process changed to cope with the employment realities of the 1990s? What can today's college graduates do to keep from joining the ranks of the unemployed?

In spite of the discouraging statistics, the college recruitment function will remain a critically important human resource activity. Campus recruiting has for years provided a dedicated pool of technical, professional, and managerial talent for America's largest employers. College recruitment professionals continue to help fill engineering, information systems, secondary education, accounting, finance, law, and entry-level supervisory positions. This recruitment process, usually coordinated on campuses through college placement offices, often provides the first formal contact between novice job seekers and their future employers. Although job applicants now must practice proactive job search behaviors, employers are challenged by the need to attract and cull the best and the brightest from a huge applicant pool. Complicating matters is the employer's need to project hiring needs and agendas 9 to 11 months ahead before participating in the college recruiting cycle.

With the average cost of recruiting and hiring a new college graduate at $3,738, mistakes by recruiters can be costly (Scheetz, 1993). Budget accountability for the college recruitment function has risen dramatically for human resource professionals in these cost-sensitive times. With the stakes so high for both college graduates and employers, it is imperative that both parties manage their options using the best information available. This article tries to provide answers to the questions raised earlier. It is designed to furnish job seekers and employers with an overview of the processes, trends, and practices of effective college recruitment in the 1990s.

College recruitment can be conceptualized as encompassing all the organizational practices and decisions that affect the number and/or types of individuals who are willing to apply for, or accept, a given employer vacancy (Rynes, 1991). Locating, identifying, and attracting qualified college graduates capable of and interested in filling available job openings constitutes most of the college recruitment function. Clearly, the realities of the 1990s marketplace have suggested changes in strategy and practice for both employers and applicants. A shared understanding of the respective recruitment goals and objectives has the potential for increasing the efficiency and effectiveness of each party's decision making.

College seniors who are aware of the purpose and dynamics of the campus interview, corporate site visit, and job offer negotiations should have a competitive advantage in managing their reactions and behaviors in this often stressful process. Conversely, employers who understand student concerns, expectations, and behaviors can adapt their recruiting programs to support corporate human resource strategies. Overall, it is important to recognize that both parties have critical decisions to make that significantly affect their futures.

The objectives of this article are threefold. First, it reviews existing recruiting models and conceptual frameworks that attempt to explain and predict the actions of both applicant and employer. Second, the article strives to identify the significant forces, trends, and "realities" impacting the college recruitment process in this decade. Finally, guidelines are offered to help college graduates and employers better manage themselves throughout the recruitment process.

Recruiting Frameworks

In the past, few substantive theoretical or conceptual frameworks were available to guide the efforts of researchers examining recruitment behaviors and practices (Schwab, Rynes, & Aldag, 1987). Sound theoretical frameworks hold benefits for researchers, employers, and applicants alike. Such theories should be capable of explaining and predicting key relationships between critical recruiting factors and outcomes of interest to organizations and job seekers (e.g., organizational and job choice behavior, impacts of certain screening methods on work force productivity and employee satisfaction). The general focus to date, however, has been on narrow investigations of recruitment activities or student perceptions, with similarly narrow payoffs for employers and job seekers. (Some recent notable exceptions are Rynes, Bretz, & Gerhart, 1991, and Taylor & Bergmann, 1987.)

Although multiple theoretical perspectives addressing recruitment issues have been examined, the focus here is on college recruitment activities, behaviors, and responses. Existing recruiting models and conceptual frameworks have drawn freely from vocational counseling, motivational psychology, and decision sciences to provide partial explanations for organizational procedures and individual perceptions and behaviors. Often these efforts have been largely descriptive and rarely address organizational and individual perspectives simultaneously.

However, the recent effort by Taylor and Giannantonio (1993) presents one of the first comprehensive efforts at integrating individual and organizational perspectives across the total employment relationship. This ambitious effort reviews research published between 1988 and 1992 and constructs a framework for organizing the employment status activities in which individuals and work organizations form, adapt to, and terminate the employment relationship. It attempts to capture and integrate the following three conceptual frameworks across the whole employment relationship.

Comprehensive Matching or Fit Models

Dawis, Lofquist, and Weiss's (1968) Theory of Work Adjustment (TWA) has provided the foundation for several current efforts to describe the process of organizational entry (Wanous, 1992) and to structure the examination of major personnel activities such as recruitment. The richness of their model for recruitment purposes lies in its focus on optimizing the congruence or correspondence between individuals and their work environments in an effort to increase job performance, tenure, and employee satisfaction. Thus, organizational recruitment efforts that maximize the overall fit between applicant and job environment on multiple dimensions are hypothesized to influence critical personal and organizational outcomes.

Wanous (1992) has adopted the TWA logic in his Matching Model, which stresses that the matching of applicant needs and organizational environment is just as important as the efforts to fit applicant capabilities with job requirements. When recruits have inflated or unrealistic expectations of organizational life, as often occurs in first-job situations, the potential for mismatch increases. Conversely, when applicants overstate their qualifications on résumés or practice extensive impression management in recruiting interviews, optimal individual–job matching is distorted (Judge & Ferris, 1992). Studies by Chatman (1991) and Sheridan (1992) have identified the importance of a new hire's matching the employer's corporate culture and value orientation.

Critical consequences of mismatch for the new hire and the organization can result in low job satisfaction and commitment levels, voluntary new hire turnover, low job performance, and even employee termination decisions. Therefore, ethical commitment to honesty in the exchange of recruiting information is the joint responsibility of job seeker and employer if comprehensive matching models are to prove useful. In the absence of the candid exchange of such information, the diagnostic skills of the respective parties are strained to decipher critical information about the applicant and the employer. This becomes a difficult task indeed for the novice job seeker or the poorly trained recruiter.

Organizational Process Models

The organizational perspective on college recruitment has focused not on theory construction or model building but rather on the development of processes and procedures for culling requisite talent in a valid and reliable manner. The conceptual distinction between recruitment and selection is blurred in the eyes of many personnel researchers when final organization objectives are considered (Rynes & Barber, 1990). A breakdown in an organization's recruiting program can have far-reaching, costly implications for other human resource functions such as training and development, compensation, and the design of the work environment. Unfortunately, the effects of ineffective recruitment may not appear for years (Sheridan, 1992).

A sequential analysis of an organization's college recruitment activities is presented here to acquaint the novice job seeker with the extensive "unseen" efforts undertaken by corporations. Graduating students who are aware of the basic process will understand the objectives, practices, and sequencing of corporate recruiting actions and their role within these efforts. This overview is essentially descriptive, with critical comments and guidelines included later in the section on management.

Most large business organizations that experience recurring and predictable needs for specialized talent from college campuses have traditionally centralized the process into a formal college recruitment program. Although the number of steps or stages in the college recruitment process may vary, the sequence, goals, and methods employed are surprisingly similar. The college recruitment model described by Chicci and Knapp (1980) is representative of most large corporate efforts. The process typically begins in late spring with a recruiting needs analysis that seeks to estimate specific new talent requirements based on corporate business objectives and the firm's current human resources base for the upcoming year. Each new position request is formalized into an employee requisition, which describes the job's responsibilities and the skills and abilities one needs to perform it. Campus recruiters work from these requisitions. In early summer a formal recruiting program is developed; it covers the selection of appropriate schools and the formulation of the recruiting schedule.

The third stage consists of program implementation. Here, the typical sequence of activities includes fall and spring campus interviewing, initial screening decisions leading to site visit invitations, candidate evaluation and selection, job offer formulation and communication, and candidate follow-up. Finally, evaluation and control efforts are undertaken to assess the status of job vacancies, the quality of new hires, and the cost-effectiveness of the program. Recall that the formal recruitment process is year-long and often filled with midstream changes due to volatile business conditions or budgetary constraints. Late summer's staffing projections may not correspond at all with a spring scramble for additional candidates or a corporation-wide hiring freeze. Often graduating seniors acknowledge hiring freeze possibilities only when they experience them firsthand, yet today's corporate management has long recognized the utility of such an option.

Job Choice Models

Two sets of models of applicant job choice behavior have dominated the current literature. They represent decidedly different explanations for choice decisions because of basic differences in their underlying assumptions. The first set captures compensatory decision processes, where positive features on one job dimension compensate for merely acceptable features on other dimensions. The dominant model here is expectancy theory, which essentially suggests that applicants engage in rational, systematic searches for job attribute information on various prospective employers and are motivated to choose the jobs that offer the greatest likelihood of maximizing their satisfaction on their valued attributes.

The second set of job choice models to receive increased attention and interest captures an individual's noncompensatory decision processes and choice activities. Noncompensatory decision making describes the choice process in which one job characteristic or single criterion becomes so important to the job seeker that any available job failing to meet the person's standard on that characteristic will be ignored or rejected. Perhaps the best-known example is Soelberg's (1967) General Decision Process (GDP) model. This approach assumes that applicants are not driven to seek or use extensive information about potential employers in their decision making but rather use this data to rationalize or defend their choices *after* they have been made. Here, the job seeker becomes attached to a firm that is acceptable on one or two critical dimensions, develops an implicit organization choice based on those factors, and then engages in perceptual distortion to confirm the favorability of the implicit choice.

Image theory and signaling theory have emerged as two recent additions to the set of noncompensatory job search and choice models. Image theory (Beach, 1990; Stevens & Beach, 1992) posits that after identifying and investigating decision alternatives, the individual makes a choice by applying two tests, the first for compatibility with goals, the second for profitability. The final job choice comes from the selection of the best job from the set of employment alternatives passing the compatibility and subsequent profitability tests. Signaling theory (Rynes et al., 1991) assumes that because job choice decisions are made under conditions of imperfect and incomplete information, recruitment practices themselves can serve as signals of unobservable organizational characteristics capable of impacting job choice decisions. For example, subjecting the job applicant to a random drug testing program before a job offer is extended may signal the applicant that the organization does not trust employees or may violate their privacy in other areas. Taylor and Giannantonio (1993) report that expectancy models have been subjected to increasing scrutiny, with greater research interest in noncompensatory models such as Soelberg's (1967) GDP model and Beach's (1990) image theory.

A concern central to job choice decision making is the role of information. How does information overload, the kind generally experienced after campus interviews and site visits, affect the job choice decision? How do applicants acquire information on labor market conditions, and how does this information impact their job choice decisions? Some researchers have reported that, in general, job seekers make their choices on the basis of very little information about available job opportunities (Rynes, 1991). Why does the candidate who is initially attracted to a job sometimes distort or ignore negative information and focus only on the positives of the job (Greenhaus, 1987)? What are the optimal amounts, sources, and types of information that organizations need to communicate to job seekers to influence their choice behavior? Unfortunately, these questions remain essentially unanswered when examined against current research evidence about college recruiting.

Overall, the lack of integrated theoretical frameworks for understanding recruitment activities and their impact on the choice behavior of both organizations and individuals has handicapped the development of an integrated body of knowledge in this area. Researchers and practitioners are then left with the task of linking the available but often disjointed evidence into useful prescriptions for action. Taylor and Giannantonio's (1993) comprehensive examination of the total employment relationship may provide the blueprint for more effective recruitment research in the future. Their pioneering effort seeks to integrate the formative, adaptive, and termination activities of the employment relationship from both individual and organizational perspectives. Similar theory construction efforts could do much to advance our understanding of the recruitment activity; such efforts are to be encouraged.

Recruitment Realities

Marketplace realities are the most important factors in an understanding of today's job opportunities for new college graduates (Shingleton, 1993). Past job markets supported a specific set of assumptions and beliefs about what was appropriate and useful recruiting behavior for graduating seniors and employers alike. Many of these prior employment assumptions must be questioned and discarded in light of the radical transformation occurring in today's marketplace.

What are some of the new "realities" facing college graduates entering the work force in the 1990s? How will these realities impact their behavioral options and job choices? It is hoped that understanding the new realities will help college students better prepare for and direct their job search efforts. A review of seven job market realities is offered to help college graduates conduct a more successful job search.

Reality #1. Fewer entry-level jobs for new college graduates exist. A cursory comparison of labor supply and demand (viz., available graduates versus job openings) finds a very competitive employment situation for most college graduates in the 1990s. For example, the total number of bachelor's degrees granted in 1994 was projected to be about 35,000 more than the year before (Shingleton, 1993). Employers are also visiting fewer campuses than in the past. In 1986 the average number of corporate recruiters visiting most college campuses was forty-two, but the current average number of visits has dwindled to twenty-three, according to the College Placement Council. Demand for college graduates across most academic disciplines has eroded, with starting salaries also suffering (Lopez, 1993a).

Reality #2. Employers have focused their recruiting efforts and targeted specific applicant pools. The general "cattle call" campus recruitment practices used by employers in the past have all but disappeared. Recruitment efforts are increasingly being tied to strategic business plans (Walker, 1992). General Electric, in support of its global expansion efforts, reported that 30 percent of its 1992 college hires spoke at least one foreign language, while more than 80 percent of its new management trainees already possessed career-related work experience (Rigdon, 1993). It is anticipated that companies will continue to raise requisite qualifications and demand ever richer skill portfolios unless the labor market changes significantly in the years ahead. Many employers have already targeted select schools for minority recruiting, and others hire only those who have interned or co-oped with them (Ward, 1992).

Reality #3. A "hidden" job market has developed, often bypassing formal college recruitment programs. Whether motivated by the fear of an avalanche of résumés, the threat of lawsuits from those rejected, or the off-cycle hiring demands of their businesses, employers are reluctant to give up their informal sources of select applicants. Professional association interns, minority scholarship winners, and college faculty recommendations can often provide ready sources of high-quality applicants to meet immediate hiring needs. Scheetz (1993) predicts "pockets of openings" despite an overall decrease in hiring. LaFevre (1993) recounts how several different events generated job opportunities for college graduates during a "hiring freeze" and a ban on campus recruiting. He stresses that opportunities abound for the new college graduate who knows how to job search.

Reality #4. Potential for abuse of applicants will increase in this tight job market. With competition for entry-level jobs increasing, some employers have begun using new and often abrasive tactics to recruit and select applicants. With so many college-educated white-collar professionals unemployed and thousands of others longing to change jobs, the potential for applicant abuse increases, according to Lopez (1993b). Ulrich and Lake (1990) describe the potentially intrusive psychological background screening questions posed to applicants at a U.S. Honda manufacturing facility. Job applicants may be reluctant to protest such non-job-related employer recruitment behaviors for fear of jeopardizing their hiring status.

Reality #5. Organizations will increasingly demand accountability and cost-effectiveness in all recruiting practices. Following the old business adage that "you can't manage what you can't measure," employers are now examining all avenues for human resource program cost savings, and recruiting is one of them. The already downsized recruiting staffs of most large employers will face growing accountability requirements. Results from the 1992 College Relations and Recruiting Survey show that college recruiters are facing increased workloads with reduced budgets and staffs. Defending the value and cost-effectiveness of recruiting programs will be increasingly necessary, according to Rhodeback (1991). She details a cost-benefit-based analysis of alternative recruiting strategies appropriate for the 1990s. As the rest of the organization has had to learn to "do more with less," so now must its recruiting professionals.

Reality #6. Demands for work force diversity will increasingly be met through college recruiting programs. Given that most current corporate work forces fail to reflect the racial and gender diversity of the U.S. population—especially at the upper management levels—college recruitment will provide a main remedial method to address this problem. New corporate recruiting efforts on minority college campuses have just started to meet objectives. Employers have reported that they were going greater distances to recruit minority candidates in an effort to maximize exposure to and involvement with campus minority and women's organizations (Major, 1993). The development of the Minority Graduate Database (12,000 graduates) and the HisPanData (5,000 minority résumés) computerized database provides ready sources of job candidates (Bargerstock, 1991).

What does this mean for white male college graduates seeking employment? Overall, not much is expected to change for them, given that their 47 percent representation in the current work force is expected to drop only to 45 percent by the year 2000 (Perry, 1991). Minority candidate shortages remain most acute in the engineering and technical fields (Scheetz, 1993).

Reality #7. Work force displacements will continue. According to Walker (1992), the work force in North America will continue to undergo major changes in structure and composition that will affect how companies recruit to meet their human resource needs. In a review article Cascio (1993) found that downsizing behavior begets more downsizing and that ongoing staff reductions have become etched into the corporate cultures of the 1990s. With the 1990s continuing to reflect a dynamic period of adjustment and change, job seekers will face intense competition for most available positions. An ability to adapt to change is an absolute necessity for new employees, according to the 504 employers surveyed in Scheetz's (1993) study. Understanding and acceptance of this volatile employment scenario will ready future job seekers for the task ahead.

It is important to note that all seven of these "realities" interact and have impact on multiple human resource activities and employment opportunities. Because recognition of any problem is the first step toward its solution, the combination of these factors will necessitate changes in recruiting strategies for job seekers and employers alike in the 1990s. The next portion of this article offers guidelines, based on available research and practitioner evidence, for both college graduate job seekers and employers.

Recruitment Guidelines

Successful management of the college recruitment function has significant payoffs for both employers and applicants, especially in today's volatile marketplace. Often time and energy are wasted on activities and processes that hold little promise for matching organizational needs with available talent. For organizations committed to gaining competitive advantage through human resources, recruitment activities present one of the first opportunities to make a difference. For the recent college graduate seeking employment, having a strategic plan for getting that job will focus efforts and help maximize career opportunities now and in the years to come. These guidelines, based on the previous analysis of marketplace "realities," are offered to help job applicants and employers better manage their respective recruitment efforts and agendas.

Applicant Guidelines

Management of the college recruitment function from the applicant's perspective is often overlooked until one recalls that joint decision making has to occur for a match to be successful. For most graduating seniors the quest for a job involves a quest for information. Information on *how* to search, *where* to search, and *what* information to search for all must be acquired. Although many of these informational needs have been addressed in popular best sellers, surprisingly little systematic research has been performed to validate these authors' recommendations to the novice job seeker. It is no wonder that most candidates have been found to base their job choices on very little information. Collecting useful information takes time, energy, and resources. Thus, getting a first job is a job in information gathering.

The primary goal of most college graduates is to obtain a job that is consistent with work environment preferences and, often, with career preparation efforts. Managing the applicant's role in the college recruitment process can be a full-time job, yet most students have to *add* this job to their current workloads. What guidelines can the individual follow to maximize the likelihood of a positive employment outcome upon graduation? What personal strategies have been found effective for managing the recruitment process? Here are five guidelines for the individual job seeker.

1. Job applicants should begin search efforts early. In the hypercompetitive marketplace of the nineties, students should try to build bridges to potential employers years ahead of their need for employment. A student should try to establish an informational network and a track record with potential employers before he or she needs to leverage a relationship into a full-time position upon graduation. Opportunities to explore the interfaces between school and work can include part-time jobs, internships, co-op arrangements, leadership posts in student chapters of professional associations, and academic semesters overseas.

These collective experiences fulfill three purposes. First, they let the student acquire critical career information in time to modify or add critical job prerequisites, such as second language or computer skills coursework. Second, they inform others of the student's skills and potential for future workplace contributions; by managing this interface experience effectively, the student can be positioned as an "inside candidate" for future job openings upon graduation. Finally, these experiences permit the student to assess his or her "fit" with company culture and career values. Early searching behaviors have also been positively linked with starting salary level and the number of offers received (Taylor & Giannantonio, 1993).

The element of effort is a significant issue here. Early search behavior clearly requires additional effort beyond the normal college workload, signaling to potential employers the student's overall motivation and commitment. A job search effort focused through a campus placement center just before graduation, by comparison, generates less information for the student and the potential employer. According to this logic, students who turn their job search responsibilities over to career placement center staff are at particular risk. Common sense reminds one that the person most interested in bringing the job search to a successful conclusion is the applicant.

2. Job applicants need to develop portfolios of demonstrable skills. In today's workplace, expectations are high that new hires will be able to contribute to firm productivity early in their careers without significant additional training. Recall that training and development activities have also been subjected to cutbacks in recent downsizing efforts. With employers expecting contributions from Day One, holding a skill portfolio that includes fluency in a second language, professional certification, or mastery of a particular computer software viewed as the industry standard enhances one's value. Although interpersonal skills are important, they are harder for employers to assess and verify than are demonstrable skills of the kinds just mentioned.

Many employers today seek only college graduates with prior real-world work experience and industry knowledge. Scheetz (1993) reports that some companies require job seekers to have direct sales experience just to apply for their sales representative positions. Internships, co-ops, and part-time jobs provide excellent opportunities to fatten one's skill portfolio.

3. Job applicants must master details of the recruitment process. Applicants must know the steps, protocols, and expectations of employers in the recruitment process to influence recruiters' decisions positively. In Scheetz's (1993) survey, employers reported an abundance of poorly prepared job seekers in today's competitive job market. These applicants exhibited poor job-hunting skills, neglected to research companies before interviewing, submitted poorly prepared résumés, and demonstrated marginal interviewing skills.

Simple gestures tell a potential employer a great deal about the job seeker's maturity, dedication, and professionalism. Employers expect applicants to send thank-you letters after on-campus interviews with recruiters or company site visits. Novice job seekers are also urged to recognize that delays and miscues on the employer's part are, unfortunately, part of the recruitment process in many organizations. LaFevre (1993) admonishes college graduates to learn the rules of a professional job search campaign and to refrain from the computer-generated résumé mailings that today's employers commonly view as job-search "junk mail." He states, "Companies always hire candidates who are well-qualified in job hunting, but only sometimes hire those who are well-qualified for available jobs."

4. Job applicants should maintain the widest possible sets of options. The job seeker is urged to use each recruiting contact to build a network that can sell his or her skills to others, even if the contact cannot result in a direct hire. In today's marketplace, all employment options should be investigated. Small employers, labor unions, "contract" recruiters, government agencies, and nonprofit organizations should be examined for potential employment opportunities.

Often attitude is just as important as action in the job search. Job seekers who remain open minded, enthusiastic, and adaptable send potential employers positive signals about their career maturity. Flexibility regarding geographical location, job travel requirements, starting salary, and entry level assignments can increase applicants' standing with employers. New job openings often arise after the campus recruiting period because of unanticipated events such as employee transfers, terminations, family leaves, and promotions. Applicants whom the employer recalls in a positive light have more chance of being contacted. The astute job seeker should treat each company contact as a collection of job opportunities rather than a fixed set of openings.

5. Job applicants should try to maximize "fit" over time, rather than in first jobs. Although college graduates should try to maximize the overall fit between their needs, skills, and preferences and the work environments capable of satisfying them, that process takes time. Graduates' first job expectations are often too high for today's job market conditions, reports Scheetz (1993). It may be more productive for job seekers to view em-

ployment as a continuous process of exploring and improving their fit within a workplace. The likelihood that a first job will ever meet one's optimal fit criteria is limited. Furthermore, dual careers (both spouses working) and uncontrollable workplace events (e.g., layoffs, bankruptcies) often make the fit process a dynamic one over time. Better to treat fit as a goal and a process rather than a destination, especially in a first job search situation.

Employer Guidelines

Human resource managers have several major tasks to accomplish through their college recruitment programs. First, they must develop recruitment strategies and programs to fill existing or anticipated job vacancies economically. Second, they are responsible for assessing applicants accurately, communicating job-related information honestly, and finally, extending job offers to those most likely to succeed in the firm.

Although "selling" and "sugarcoating" strategies have been used in the past, today's labor market conditions easily provide a large pool of job applicants. The expensive methods formerly used to attract qualified applicants are no longer as critical to successful recruitment. Therefore, the main focus of most recruiting programs today is on issues of selection, not attraction. The following guidelines are presented to help organizations manage their recruiting efforts in a timely, legal, effective, and efficient manner.

1. Employers should keep their recruiting programs strategic. Organizational staffing and recruiting activities should be directly tied to company business strategies and core mission statements. Business strategies can focus on cost reduction, global expansion, product innovation, or quality enhancement. These strategic choices should drive all recruiting efforts. Cost reduction recruiting strategies could include the identification of colleges with emerging reputations for excellence, where graduates' starting salary expectations might be lower than at top-tier institutions. More companies are pushing the strategic integration of all their functional activities. General Electric's global expansion plans have broadened applicant qualifications to now include foreign language ability and prior industry experience (Lopez, 1993b).

The integration of business strategies and human resource strategies should guide the development of recruitment programs to bring the right talent on board for the 1990s. Recruitment efforts not strategically anchored will waste time and resources, contributing little to the successful implementation of corporate strategies.

2. Employers should keep applicants informed throughout the recruitment process. The quality and quantity of information about the job and the organization are very important to applicants. Timely feedback throughout the recruitment process goes a long way toward establishing an employer as a smart choice for top graduates. Research results suggest that applicants tend to react negatively to delays in feedback and often make unwarranted attributions for the delays (e.g., the organization is poorly managed). Delays have also been found to cause the most marketable applicants to infer that something is "wrong" with the firm (Rynes et al., 1991). Perhaps most important is the option all applicants have, which is to accept other offers if delays become too extended.

Sound job-related information is important at all stages of the recruitment process. Recruiters should be trained to be rich sources of information about the organization and its job openings. Often job incumbents, when trained in effective interviewing skills, make the best organizational representatives for campus interviewing and during on-site visits. Job incumbents who spend more time gathering information about organizations and interacting with their representatives in the search process are expected to make better "fit" decisions, according to Taylor and Giannantonio (1993).

3. Employers should embrace work force diversity in recruiting. Competition between employers for top female and minority appli-

cants is currently fierce, especially in the short-supply disciplines such as engineering, information systems, and computer science (Scheetz, 1993). Affirmative action commitments make smart business sense when based on substance and not tokenism. The proactive multicultural recruiting efforts undertaken at Sun Microsystems, Inc., are one example. Through the use of strong employee focus groups, community outreach events, and well-coordinated fund-raising events, Sun has been able to build a good reputation that attracts good minority job applicants, especially in the technical disciplines (Major, 1993).

4. The employer needs to make every employee a recruiter. In today's marketplace, recruiting should be treated as a continuous process for identifying and hiring the best candidates for the organization. Many employers have successfully established a corporate "presence" on college campuses beyond the traditional fall and spring interviewing periods. For example, Microsoft has successfully established itself as a preferred employer by visiting over 137 campuses, some of them four times each year (Rebello, 1992).

Top employers have learned that furnishing classroom speakers, donating equipment for student projects, and funding faculty on-site visits to the employer can all help identify top candidates early in the recruitment process.

When employers are faced with unexpected vacancies, employees may be able to nominate promising candidates they have met on campus speaking visits, at local professional society meetings, or through family contacts. These employee recruiters usually are credible, understand the corporate culture, and are cost-effective.

5. Employers should reject applicants with tact. If employers recall that everyone is a potential customer, that students freely exchange recruiting experiences, and that every applicant can file an employment discrimination lawsuit, careful attention to policy details in the rejection of unacceptable applicants is a business necessity. With the abundance of applicants for each vacancy in today's marketplace, more individuals will be unhappy than pleased about an employer's final hiring decisions.

Limited research on the rejection process suggests that the employer can cushion the blow to rejected candidates by using rejection letters that are friendly and personal and that summarize the applicants' job qualifications so as to leave positive impressions. Overview information on the size and excellent quality of the applicant pool and the qualifications of the person hired also help soften disappointment and communicate fairness in the process. Managing rejected applicants' perceptions of fairness is very important, especially for employers who recruit annually on selected campuses.

Conclusion

College recruiting is still one of the most popular methods for infusing new talent and innovative ideas into corporate America. It remains an annual ritual that now has to cope with abundant applicant pools, minority candidate shortages in some disciplines, and an unforgivingly competitive marketplace. Employers and applicants who recognize and adapt to the pressing "realities" of today's marketplace are best positioned for recruitment success in the 1990s.

Ten guidelines were presented to help employers and applicants manage behaviors and outcomes throughout the recruitment process. It is hoped that presentation of both parties' agendas can foster more professionalism and career success in the recruitment process. However, the real test remains in the execution. Responsible participation in the process is needed if both parties are to meet their goals in the decade ahead.

References

Bargerstock, A. (1991). Computer databases: Windows to more effective recruitment. *Human Resource Professional, 4,* 9–14.

Beach, L. R. (1990). *Image theory: Decision making in personal and organizational contexts.* Chichester, England: Wiley.

Cascio, W. F. (1993). Downsizing: What do we know? What have we learned? *Academy of Management Executive, 7,* 95–104.

Chatman, J. A. (1991). Matching people and organizations: Selection and socialization in public accounting firms. *Administrative Science Quarterly, 36,* 459–484.

Chicci, D. L., & Knapp, C. L. (1980). College recruitment from start to finish. *Personnel Journal, 59,* 655–659.

Dawis, R. V., Lofquist, L. H., & Weiss, D. J. (1968). A theory of work adjustment: A revision. *Minnesota Studies in Vocational Rehabilitation, 23,* Minneapolis: University of Minnesota, Industrial Relations Center.

Greenhaus, J. H. (1987). *Career management.* New York: Dryden.

Johnston, W. B., & Packer, A. E. (1987). *Workforce 2000: Work and workers for the 21st century.* Indianapolis: Hudson Institute.

Judge, T. A., & Ferris, G. R. (1992). The elusive criterion of fit in human resource staffing decisions. *Human Resource Planning, 15,* 47–67.

LaFevre, J. (1993, Spring/Summer). My company is hiring. *National Business Employment Weekly: Managing your career,* pp. 24–25.

Lopez, J. A. (1993a, May 20). College class of '93 learns hard lesson: Career prospects are worst in decades. *Wall Street Journal,* p. B1.

Lopez, J. A. (1993b, October 6). Firms force job seekers to jump through hoops. *Wall Street Journal,* p. B1.

Major, M. J. (1993, June). Sun sets pace in work force diversity. *Public Relations Journal,* pp. 12–14.

Perry, N. J. (1991). The workers of the future. *Fortune, (123) 12,* 68–72.

Rebello, K. (1992, February 24). How Microsoft makes offers people can't refuse. *Business Week,* p. 65.

Rhodeback, M. J. (1991). Embrace the bottom line. *Personnel Journal,* 53–56.

Rigdon, J. E. (1993, May 20). Glut of graduates lets recruiters pick only the best. *Wall Street Journal,* pp. B1, B7.

Rynes, S. L. (1991). Recruitment, job choice, and post-hire consequences: A call for new research directions. In M. D. Dunnette & L. M. Hough (Eds.), *Handbook of industrial and organizational psychology* (pp. 399–444). Palo Alto, CA: Consulting Psychologists Press.

Rynes, S. L., & Barber, A. E. (1990). Applicant attraction strategies: An organizational perspective. *Academy of Management Review, 15,* 286–310.

Rynes, S. L., Bretz, R. D., & Gerhart, B. (1991). The importance of recruitment in job choice: A different way of looking. *Personnel Psychology, 44,* 487–521.

Scheetz, L. P. (1993). *Recruiting trends 1992–93: A study of business, industries, and government agencies employing new college graduates* (22nd ed.). East Lansing: Michigan State University.

Schwab, D. P., Rynes, S. L., & Aldag, R. J. (1987). Theories and research on job search and choice. In K. Rowland & G. Ferris (Eds.), *Research in personnel and human resource management* (Vol. 5, pp. 129–166). Greenwich, CT: JAI Press.

Sheridan, J. E. (1992). Organizational culture and employee retention. *Academy of Management Journal, 35,* 1036–1056.

Shingleton, J. D. (1993). The job market for '94 grads. In *Planning job choices: 1994* (pp. 19–26). Bethlehem, PA: College Placement Council.

Soelberg, P. O. (1967). Unprogrammed decision making. *Industrial Management Review, 8,* 19–29.

Stevens, C. K., & Beach, L. R. (1992). *Application of image theory to job choice processes: New directions for theory and research.* Paper presented at the meeting of the National Academy of Management, Las Vegas.

Taylor, M. S., & Bergmann, T. J. (1987). Organizational recruitment activities and applicants' reactions at different stages of the recruitment process. *Personnel Psychology, 40,* 261–285.

Taylor, M. S., & Giannantonio, C. M. (1993). Forming, adapting, and terminating the employment relationship: A review of the literature from individual, organizational, and interactionist perspectives. *Personnel Psychology, 19,* 461–515.

Ulrich, D., & Lake, D. (1990). *Organizational capability: Competing from the inside out.* New York: Wiley.

Walker, J. W. (1992). *Human resource strategy.* New York: McGraw-Hill.

Wanous, J. P. (1992). *Organizational entry: Recruitment, selection, orientation, and socialization of newcomers* (2nd ed). Reading, MA: Addison-Wesley.

Ward, J. (1992, September/October). How college recruiting has changed. *The Black Collegian,* pp. 137–139.

The Interview: Expecting
a Quick Decision?

M. Ronald Buckley and Robert W. Eder

In spite of the fact that research on the employment interview has yielded unimpressive reliability and validity coefficients relative to other selection techniques,[1] it remains the most extensively used tool in the selection program of most organizations. As Guion[2] has stated, "nor have repeatedly discouraging summaries of their reliabilities and validities deterred the use of interviews" (p. 367). In fact, a majority of executives view the employment interview as the most important component in the selection process.[3] Concurrently, "research on interviewing continues, whether in desperation or hope,"[4] and it appears as though management officials will continue to treat the employment interview as an especially important selection component.

It is really ironic that it appears as though managers believe that their decisions in selection interviews are made so quickly. In this paper, we examine the perception that a lot of executives have concerning interview decision time, the relevant literature which has yielded this assumption and recent research results which serve to contradict this management myth.[5] The paper concludes with a number of suggestions which, if implemented, will overcome some of the problems which inhibit the quantity and quality of the information which is collected in the interview.

At two separate executive development workshops we asked, "How important is the interview in your corporation's overall selection process?" We were not surprised by the rather uniform response that the interview is considered the most important component of the selection process. Academicians have found this to be somewhat of an enigma, given the consistent research finding that the interview is a less valid procedure for identifying job-related ability than most other selection techniques (e.g., review of biographical information, work samples, cognitive-aptitude tests). It is not uncommon for organizations to literally set aside all other pertinent information which has been collected and act as if, "O.K., it's down to these three, let's see who interviews the best."

We also asked the same group of 95 executives, "From what you have read and experienced, how long does it take interviewers to make a decision about the job suitability of the candidate?" Nine percent said it takes more than an hour, 17 percent said it takes between 6 and 60 minutes, and *74 percent said it takes 5 minutes or less.* The following are a sampling of the typical responses:

> It generally occurs within the first few minutes of the interview. First impressions must be good or the likelihood of obtaining the job will be minimal.

> It is easy to make a decision about an applicant soon after they respond to your first question. It is a feeling you get about whether the applicant hits you the right way or not.

> About 30 seconds, usually. First impressions last, and interviewers are usually looking for a type of person that will fit into the organization.

> Although we have instructed our people to weigh all of the information before they make a decision, I am sure that they make decisions about applicants quickly.

Given the singular importance attributed to the interview in the hiring process, it is interesting to note how short a period of time managers think it takes to make an interview decision. Are there any other strategic judgments which are approached in such a "snap decision" manner?—No? Then, why do executives believe that interview decisions are quick?

What Academicians Have Told Managers

We examined 68 post-1981 textbooks in the Personnel/Human Resources and the General Management area. Forty-five of the textbooks did not address the issue of anticipated quick decisions by interviewers. The remaining 23 did address this issue with the following results:

1. Seventeen of the textbooks cited Springbett,[6] or a recent literature review on the interview process that cited Springbett's 1954 research which led the textbook author to conclude that interview decisions were made in a relatively short time period, ranging from 2 to 6 minutes.

Some samples from these textbooks (citations are omitted but are available from the authors):

Decisions are made early in the interview process (often in the first 4 minutes) and are seldom reversed by later information.

Interviewers make up their minds about candidates during the first few minutes of the interview; prolonging the interview does little to change the decision.

There is a tendency for interviewers to make decisions about interviewees within the first 2 or 3 minutes of the interview.

Interviewers make decisions within an average of 4 minutes from the beginning of the interview.

Much research has shown that interviewers make a decision very early and conduct the rest of the interview searching for substantiating information.

2. Six of the textbooks were more equivocal, citing more current (replicated and generalizable) research that suggests interviewer decision time may be moderated under varying circumstances and by different contextual factors.

This widely disseminated "fact" that interviewers make quick decisions is grounded on a single study, the aforementioned dissertation work of Springbett. Ironically, Springbett's original finding that decisions were made in the first few minutes of interview has not been replicated.[7] Quite to the contrary, subsequent researchers found that interviewer decision time was delayed when the interviewer pre-assigned a longer interview time with the candidate, and when the qualifications of the candidate increased. In other words, if you schedule a 15-minute interview, like Springbett did, and simply ask for a reject/accept decision under well-defined qualifications, quick decisions will likely be the result. If more time is appropriated to the task, supposedly as a function of the need to go into greater depth into the candidate's qualifications and concerns, and the candidate is not of obvious low quality, decision times will substantially increase.

Interestingly, this is but a small sampling of the management myths which have crept into the mainstream of management knowledge.[8] This mythology points out the need for a continuing exchange between researchers and practitioners (in fact, the purpose of the *Academy of Management Executive*) for the purpose of integrating research findings into our thinking, teaching, and practice. Otherwise, researchers and practitioners work against each other and the research and practice in the management discipline suffers.

Implications for Practitioners, Educators and Researchers

There are a number of compelling reasons for the apparently widespread belief that selection decisions are made quickly. Experience (as indicated in the responses we received at the executive development workshop), textbooks and thus lectures may have fostered this notion. Systematic, controlled research, on the other hand, leads to the conclusion that decisions are made in a much more deliberative style. Who are practitioners to follow? It is difficult to follow the pronouncements of researchers when experience dictates otherwise. Why, then, do we believe that it is important for practitioners, educators, and other researchers to become more familiar with the research which has been done on this issue?

Practitioners: Because practitioners have come to believe that the quick decision in the interview is a reality, practitioners may adhere to the idea that the interview is typically over within the first few minutes. This may result in a self-fulfilling prophecy which deters the interviewer from investigating candidate qualifications in greater depth. This may result in the collection of insufficient information leading to suboptimal interview decision making. We often need to remind ourselves that, in an interview, an interviewer is attempting to obtain, process, and understand a lifetime of motivations, attitudes, and behaviors which surely will require more than a short amount of time to adequately assess.

Educators: As educators, we need to stop repeating this management myth of a quick decision in both our textbooks and in our lectures. When students hear about or read of this quick decision, what inspiration does it provide for them to be more effective and thorough when they are tasked with conducting interviews? Perpetrating this myth is a disservice to our students now and may be a stumbling block which hinders their later career achievement.

Researchers: There is a need for researchers to continue to advance research on the parameters that influence decision time in the interview. Researchers must include myriad variables in research in order to adequately capture the essence of the interview as it occurs in organizational situations. If researchers are able to gain an understanding of the conditions under which a brief or long decision time is necessary, researchers may be able to recommend an optimal length for the interview.

Guidelines for Avoiding the Needless Quick Interview Decision

First, if necessary qualifications are well defined and the candidate is clearly not qualified, a short interview and a quick decision is called for. However, how can today's manager avoid making too quick a decision and the deleterious consequences which accompany poor strategic decisions? Listed below are a number of guidelines that would be well worth considering.

1. Let the interview measure what it does best: oral communication skill, reasoning skills, and initial presentation skills. Give the interview a decision weight in your selection decision that reflects the extent to which job success is dependent upon effective oral communication skill, on-the-spot reasoning skills, and the ability to effectively present oneself to strangers. The interview should be more highly weighted when hiring a sales clerk than when hiring a computer programmer.

2. Adequately prepare for the interview. A more deliberate, reasoned decision is encouraged when the interviewer takes time to become familiarized with the job description, job specifications, historical performance difficulties, and considers the rating factors against which the decision is to be based. This suggests that the simple reject/accept decision (which often serves as the dependent variables in interview research) is less appropriate than the more complex attempt to assess relative candidate qualifications across multiple dimensions. The last step of adequate preparation is to formulate questions intended to tap these multiple rating factors. This is not the first step as is more commonly the practice.

3. Decide in advance upon an adequate amount of time to interview. This would be a function of job complexity and the criticality of the position to the unit's mission, and the overall quality level of the candidate pool. Try not to let the convenience of back-to-back rapid fire interviewing, under the guise that it only takes a few minutes to adequately size someone up, result in you scheduling short, terse interviews.

4. Use your intuition to signal the need to probe further. You will react to candidates on an intuitive level. Yet, do not let intuition alone rush you to a hasty decision. Instead, as you find yourself feeling pleased or displeased toward a candidate, probe further to uncover whether your intuition can be supported. Actively search for evidence which disconfirms your intuitions. Share your intuitions with others after everyone has interviewed. This, also, will provide a reliability check or confirmation that it was only you and not the candidate who was causing the reaction.

5. Decide to rate each candidate when the interview is over. This may create a recency effect where the last thing said will be remembered most vividly. However, postponing your decisions will effectively blunt your inclination to decide quickly, get it over with and move on to the next candidate. Require that ratings on each dimension be accompanied by confirming evidence. Summary ratings across dimensions should be postponed until all candidates are interviewed so that any contrast effects are avoided. Contrast effects would likely occur when the summary judgment on a candidate was influenced by the relative strength or weakness of the immediately preceding candidate interview.

We suggest that you not abide by what you have been told to regard as an absolute: Interviewers decide within the first few minutes. Due to the pivotal nature of interviews in organizations, optimal decision making is essential. Interviewees need to be given adequate opportunity to either change your mind or confirm your first impressions. Treat the interviewee with the rational, deliberative style which you would desire for yourself.

Combat the urge to make these important strategic interview decisions quickly. If you have waited until the end of this short subject to decide how you feel about this topic, we commend you for resisting the urge to be a quick decider.

Endnotes

1. See Hunter, J. E., and Hunter, R. E. (1984). Validity and utility of alternative predictors of job performance. *Psychological Bulletin, 96,* 72–98; and Reilly, R. R., and Chao, G. T. (1982). Validity and fairness of some alternative employee selection procedures. *Personnel Psychology, 35,* 1–62.

2. Guion, R. M., and Gibson, W. M. (1988). Personnel selection and placement. *Annual Review of Psychology, 39,* 349–374.

3. See Bureau of National Affairs (1976). *Personnel Policies Forum,* Survey No. 114, September.

4. Op. cit., Guion and Gibson, p. 367.

5. See Buckley, M. R., and Eder, R. W. (1988). B. M. Springbett and the notion of the snap decision in the interview. *Journal of Management, 14,* 59–68.

6. B. M. Springbett's 1954 doctoral dissertation, completed at McGill University, serves as the basis of the notion that quick decisions are made in the selection interview.

7. For example, D. H. Tucker and P. M. Rowe ("Consulting the application form prior to the interview: An essential step in the selection process," *Journal of Applied Psychology,* 1979, 669) used the same research methodology as Springbett and concluded the decision times in the interview averaged in excess of nine minutes. Similarly, J. M. Huegli and H. Tschirgi ("An investigation of the relationship of time to recruitment interview decision making," *Proceedings of the Academy of Management,* 1975, 234) reported that decisions in the majority of interviews were made in the second half of a 30-minute interview. Lastly, W. L. Tullar, T. W. Mullins and S. A. Caldwell ("Effects of interview length and applicant quality on interview decision time," *Journal of Applied Psychology,* 1979, 669) wrote that interview decision time depends upon the interviewer expectation of the duration of the interview and the quality of the applicant.

8. See A. C. Bluedorn, T. L. Keon and N. M. Carter ("Management history research: Is anyone out there listening?" *Proceedings of the Academy of Management,* 1985, 130) for a presentation of numerous management myths and their pervasiveness.

The Elusive Criterion of Fit in Human Resources Staffing Decisions

Timothy A. Judge and Gerald R. Ferris

Staffing positions in organizations may well represent one of the most important human resources (HR) management functions. Who is hired into the job from outside the organization as well as who is moved to another job internally (e.g., through a promotion decision), or who is moved out of organizations, ideally reflect job-relevant decisions and the maximizing of critical knowledge, skills, and abilities which contribute to an organization's overall effectiveness and its competitive advantage. That is the way we suggest it *should be* done. In practice, though, how are staffing decisions actually made? Can we apply the assumption of a rational model to staffing decisions, whereby decision makers are knowledgeable about the job in question (i.e., they know what characteristics, skills, and so forth it takes to succeed on the job), gather all relevant information about the candidate's job-relevant qualifications, compare these qualifications to job demands, and select the candidates with the best match? Or, is an alternative model more appropriate to capture the realities of everyday staffing decisions?

These questions have troubled us both for some time, which has led us to seek answers through systematic research as well as from managers, executives, and HR professionals who make these decisions frequently. For example, we have asked numerous recruiters who hire our students into HR management positions, "What is it you are looking for in a high-quality candidate?" Interestingly, after several requests for clarification from these decision makers, we have found an amazing degree of convergence on the responses provided. Inevitably, it comes down to a statement of "fit"—that is, they suggest they are looking for a candidate who fits. Sometimes they elaborate to specify someone who fits the culture, the value system, and so forth, but frequently it is merely stated as someone who fits. When pressed to define more precisely what it means to fit, many are initially hard pressed to provide a response. Again there tends to be amazing convergence across decision makers on a statement that goes something like this: "I can't articulate it, but I'll know it when I see it." Furthermore, we have had similar discussions with HR executives who also have articulated the importance of fit, but typically are hard pressed to define it.

One might find such a statement from a person responsible for making important screening/staffing decisions on behalf of the organization refreshing, enlightened, troublesome, or dangerous, depending on one's perspective. What is perhaps clearer is that such a statement challenges the rational model of staffing that has been so firmly entrenched for so long, and it suggests the importance of a criterion called fit, about which we know very little, as well as the introduction of a political perspective on staffing decisions. Furthermore, it appears that this process and the dynamics involving fit are most obvious through one particular HR staffing technique, the interview.

The purpose of this article is to model the HR staffing process more completely by highlighting the role of fit and blending the rational and political perspectives on staffing decisions. This model is intended to reflect the reality of how HR staffing decisions are

Reprinted with permission of The Human Resource Planning Society from *Human Resource Planning, 15:4* (1992): 47–67.

actually made. Furthermore, it is argued that the notion of fit, elusive and ill-defined as it typically has been, may be a constructive way to understand the use, and usefulness, of staffing decision tools such as the interview. Finally, the role of political influence behavior as a means of managing the impression of fit also is discussed. The article intends to provide a more comprehensive understanding of how fit actually affects the HR staffing process, and how our evaluation of the effectiveness of staffing decisions might be improved from a consideration of fit. Although a number of issues are raised in this article, such a broad and integrative approach is necessary in developing a more informed understanding of the notion of fit.

Human Resources Staffing in Organizations

When one considers HR staffing in organizations, it is common to assume that this entails considering external applicants for entry into the organization; however, Miller (1984), Sonnenfeld (1984), and others have argued that organizations should consider the staffing process more broadly than external selection. Human resources staffing entails internal staffing (i.e., promotion as well as demotion and termination decisions) in addition to external staffing. As pointed out by Beer, Spector, Lawrence, Mills, and Walton (1984), managing HR flows entails considering the flow of people into, through, and out of the organization. Effective staffing decisions are predicated on the ability of an organization to balance the HR inputs, outputs, and throughputs. In the present article, we adopt this broader view of HR staffing. Consistent with this perspective, a model of the HR staffing process is presented in Exhibit 1.

Exhibit 1 illustrates that the three HR staffing processes (in flows, through flows, and out flows) are not independent. For example,

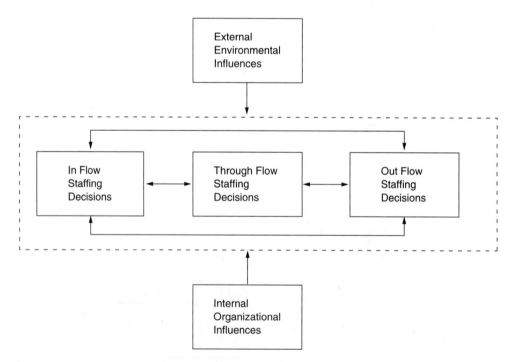

Exhibit 1.   Traditional Model of Human Resources Staffing

the quantity and quality of external hires (in flows) affects performance evaluations, promotions, and developmental mobility of employees (through flows), as well as the desirability and necessity of terminating existing employees (out flows). Similarly, the quantity and quality of existing employees may necessitate external hiring or termination of existing employees.

The exhibit also illustrates that all three staffing processes are influenced by internal and external environmental factors. External environmental factors such as laws and regulations place constraints on each of the three staffing activities. For example, equal employment opportunity laws and regulations limit the range of criteria upon which, and perhaps even the processes through which, staffing decisions are based. Internal organizational factors, such as organizational strategies and structures, also are influential. For example, the flattening of organizational hierarchies and expanding spans of controls may give HR managers more autonomy in the procedures used to carry out each of the three staffing processes. Furthermore, such structural changes may affect staffing decisions by influencing the types of people needed to perform their jobs effectively.

Exhibit 1 is a basic rational model of HR staffing which assumes that criteria for staffing decisions are explicit, clearly stated, and precisely specified. Furthermore, it is assumed that such criteria are only job relevant, with no extraneous factors entering in, that staffing decision makers have all the relevant information needed about candidates to make decisions, that they are knowledgeable about the job in question and have experience making such decisions, and that they are held accountable for their staffing decisions. Because a rational model includes these assumptions, these factors often are not included explicitly in staffing models. It may be quite reasonable to question such assumptions, though, given the staffing realities in organizations.

The foregoing model provides a framework within which to analyze staffing decisions. It is rational in its orientation by design, although, to more accurately reflect how staffing decisions are actually made in organizations, we might need to consider alternatives to the precision of the rational model. One such alternative is a political perspective (Ferris and Judge, 1991), and one of the realities we see increasingly in organizations is that HR staffing decisions are based on the criterion of fit.

The Notion of Fit

Observation, Anecdote, and Applied Literature

Whereas there appears to be little doubt that fit is used frequently in making HR staffing decisions, our current level of understanding of the fit construct is based more on anecdotal evidence than on systematic research. The business and popular press have provided some interesting accounts of the types of creatures that roam the corridors of corporate America, and the notion of fit is clearly in evidence. For example, Ferris, King, Judge, and Kacmar (1991) portrayed the importance of fit through a new corporate creature they call the "organizational chameleon." This creature embodies the philosophy of forced fit and adaptation, effectively becoming whatever you want it to be through feigning beliefs, values, attitudes, and so forth. Sofer (1970) appeared to characterize this creature when he stated, "It is said that the would-be successful executive learns when to simulate enthusiasm, compassion, interest, concern, modesty, confidence, and mastery, when to smile, with whom to laugh, and how intimate to be with others. If the operation succeeds, he will have fabricated a personality in harmony with his environment" (p. 61). Sofer's executive, then, is interested in fitting an image or stereotype of expected role behaviors.

Several accounts have been written of what really explains success, in terms of advancement and promotion, in some of the largest and most notable organizations in this country. Katz's (1987) analysis of top-level management succession at Sears, Roebuck, and Company involved fit as a key staffing criterion, whereby fit was operationalized in terms of height. Hence, the use of this criterion produced a succession of CEOs and executive committee members occasionally referred to as the Sears tall men, because an early CEO at Sears believed that height (i.e., at least six feet two inches) was an important staffing criterion leading to effectiveness in these top-level jobs.

Wright (1979) wrote a vivid account of management succession at General Motors (GM), which witnessed succession/promotion candidates trying to fit with not only the GM stereotype, but also the expectations of their superiors who controlled such decisions. Thus, success in the succession/promotion process was determined less by objective credentials and more by how skillful one was at flattering his superior and doing the things that made one appear to fit.

Von Werssowetz and Beer (1985) demonstrated how the notion of fit manifested itself throughout HR decisions at Hewlett-Packard (HP). In particular, rather than use statistical tests to predict narrow dimensions of job performance, HP relies on the interview to assess cultural fit. At HP, the overriding question in the selection process is not, "Does this person have the necessary specific skills?", but rather, "Will this person fit in our culture?" In the eyes of David Packard, focusing on this latter question in the staffing process better enables HP to meet its strategic imperatives such as technological innovation and leadership.

More recently, Bowen, Ledford, and Nathan (1991) provided an analysis of fit in the selection process. They suggested that in addition to basing selection decisions on job analysis data, an organizational analysis also is an important process underlying staffing decisions. The organizational analysis would identify the dominant values, social skills, and traits necessary to fit in the organization. This would then serve as the basis for selection decisions. Bowen et al. (1991) cited several organizations as examples of those that use fit as a central component of staffing decisions.

Kanter's (1977) in-depth, qualitative investigation of the employment practices of an organization sheds considerable light on how fit materializes as a principal criterion for internal staffing decisions. She coined the term "homosocial reproduction systems" to represent how internal staffing decisions are made. The criteria for advancement, she argued, were made up of a set of attitudes, beliefs, values, and characteristics that the key decision makers (i.e., the gatekeepers) deemed important, and this set of criteria, interestingly, often mirrored the characteristics possessed by these decision makers.

Indeed, one can readily see how this may not simply depict a passive process on the part of the candidates (i.e., whether they possess these characteristics or not), but could witness the candidate actually seeking to manage an image that fits with the decision criteria. Thus, we begin to see the transformation of our rational model of HR staffing into more of a political model, where instead of expending energy in the acquisition of important job-related knowledge, skills, and abilities, job candidates invest at least as much energy in honing their political skills, effectively working the system with smoke and mirrors to create an impression of fit which will prove instrumental to some desired outcome. Support for this recently was provided by Rynes, Bretz, and Gerhart (1991), who cited entry-level managerial applicants with quotes such as, *Especially after the offer, I started judging more.* In the beginning, it was just, 'Like me, please like me' " (p. 508), and, "Recruitment doesn't mean anything . . . it's a game and I think *a lot of people get screwed by it*" (p. 510).

The foregoing discussion of fit in HR staffing decisions implicitly raises the form versus substance problem articulated recently by Ferris and King (1991). The essence of this problem is the difficulties involved in distinguishing candidates who are truly qualified (i.e., substance) from those who merely construct images of qualifications and competence (i.e., form). Whereas it is easy to succinctly convey the essence of the form versus substance problem, it is quite another matter to sort out the process dynamics and adequately address it. The rational model of HR staffing decisions would suggest that candidates come to the selection context with knowledge, skills, abilities, and experience, and that decision makers come with an understanding of the job demands and specifications in addition to selection devices designed to best measure candidate characteristics. Both parties have known and acceptable motivations, and metaphorically, the decision maker attempts to hit a stationary target (i.e., make the best decision by identifying the most qualified candidate) using the best weapon at his/her disposal (i.e., the most accurate selection device).

In practice, however, we find that fit and the realities of the selection context suggest a somewhat different scenario. With candidates actively seeking to alter and manage images of competence, the decision maker is effectively attempting to hit, not a stationary, but a moving target. Selection research suggests we haven't traditionally performed well at hitting fixed targets (i.e., our hit rate, as reflected by validity coefficients, is not great), so one wonders how we could hope to hit moving targets. Let us further complicate the picture by suggesting that sometimes decision makers have other, personally beneficial, objectives they seek to achieve through the staffing process. That is, rather than seeking the candidate most qualified for the job (i.e., defined by a match between candidate skills and job demands), decision makers might seek to maximize their own self-interests by increasing their own power base through coalition building, thus seeking to select candidates who think like they do and fit their personal agenda. Extending our target metaphor, additional ambiguity is introduced here because the decision maker has altered the criteria, and effectively is aiming at a different target.

This section has addressed what we know about the construct of fit based on observation, anecdotal evidence, and some of the applied literature. Indeed, this construct has retained only anecdotal status until quite recently because of its lack of precision and definition. Some research has been conducted on fit in HR staffing, and the results of this work are reviewed in the next section.

Research Literature

Most investigations of fit have been plagued by imprecision, emphasizing nebulous terms such as "right types" (Klimoski and Strickland, 1977; Schneider, 1987). Rynes and Gerhart (1990) have argued that such notions add little to the understanding of fit. An explicit definition of fit is needed to clear the conceptual ambiguity in the construct. Fit was defined by Chatman (1989) as the degree to which the goals and values of the applicant or employee match those of employees considered successful in the organization. It is possible to add to Chatman's definition a more global construct—the degree to which the applicant is liked by the interviewer, co-worker, supervisor, or subordinate may be a direct manifestation of fit. Those who fit are liked by others; those who do not fit are not liked by organizational members. Because most selection decision makers probably consider themselves successful employees, as applied to the interview this may actually translate into how closely the applicant resembles and is liked by the decision maker(s). Similarity effects have been frequently mentioned in the performance evaluation process (Bernardin and Beatty, 1984). Perceived similarity between the interviewer and applicant appears to influence interviewer evaluations as well (Schmitt, 1976). Because managers may prefer individuals similar to themselves (Gilmore and Ferris, 1989b), similarity may be one way to construe fit; however, fit has not been explicitly included as a manifestation of this similarity.

Central to understanding the importance of fit to organizations lies in understanding what including fit in the criterion may accomplish for organizations. Four possibilities are suggested here: (1) *Fit as a control mechanism,* whereby selecting individuals with certain norms, beliefs, goals, and values, the organization imports control. Thus, rather than gaining control through socialization processes, control is achieved through the selection process; (2) *Fit as work force homogeneity*, where selecting similar people creates, or maintains, a homogeneous, not heterogeneous, work force. This leads to differing policy implications, because homogeneity can lead to groupthink (Schneider, 1983) and discrimination against members of the outgroup (Pfeffer, 1983); (3) *Fit as a job-related criterion*. With the growth in the service sector, hiring on the basis of fit to climate, values, or consumer orientation is indeed job-relevant, resulting in more effective employees being selected (Schneider and Bowen, 1992); (4) *Fit as an organizational image enhancer*. If employees are selected who accurately reflect the preferences of management, the predictability of employee public behavior is increased, and thus consistent with the image that the organization wishes to project. While we do not fully explore the organizational implications, these alternative definitions and uses of fit suggest some possible implications for organizations depending on how it is defined.

Using Fit to Reevaluate Staffing Decisions

Probably no HR decision tool has been as widely studied or as heavily criticized as the interview. Hundreds of studies have been published over the last eighty years investigating both the validity of the interview in staffing decisions and the psychological processes that influence the outcomes. Ten comprehensive research reviews on the subject have been published, the first in 1949 and the most recent in 1989, each integrating many studies in order to arrive at some generalizations about the interview. The ten reviews reached similar conclusions, the most significant probably being: (1) the reliability and validity of the interview is low; (2) there are many psychological biases that cause the interviewer to make inaccurate decisions; and (3) the interview is often an inhibiting factor in the selection process. Many have taken the unfavorable conclusions of these reviews and simply recommended against using the interview. For example, Howell and Dipboye (1982) stated, ". . . interviews as typically conducted are of limited practical value. They are subject to all sorts of biasing influences, and what information they do yield is irrelevant or could probably be obtained more efficiently in other ways" (p. 251). Heneman, Schwab, Fossum, and Dyer (1986) concluded, "In short, there is little reason to believe that the employment interview is efficiently accomplishing its selection purpose" (p. 320). While recent reviews (e.g., Harris, 1989) seem to have taken a more positive outlook than earlier ones, the general belief persists that the interview is not particularly valid (cf. Eder and Ferris, 1989). These conclusions are critical, because not only is the interview one of the most widely used external staffing methods, it often plays an important role in promotion decisions, as well as managing HR out flows (e.g., exit interviews).

It is probably safe to assume, though, that managers have at least some knowledge of the validity evidence on the interview (Dreher and Maurer, 1989). Thus, managers may continue to use the interview *despite* the past validity evidence. Rather than suggesting that staffing decision makers are erroneous in their continuing use of the interview, it may be that *researchers have been mistaken in condemning the interview*.

Researchers have implicitly assumed that the usefulness of the interview rests on the basis of how accurate the interview is in predicting job performance or productivity measures. This is not the only means of evaluating the interview, however. Inclusion of fit in the criterion is an important factor to consider in evaluating the interview, and may lead researchers to more positive conclusions about the usefulness of the interview. Specifically, the way performance has typically been measured in organizations may be deficient in that it does not fully capture the perceived value of employees to the organization (i.e., value that extends beyond employees' possession of key knowledge, skills, and abilities to perform the job). As indicated earlier, affect or liking apparently influences performance evaluation and interview decisions. Attempts to improve performance evaluations generally have been manifested by efforts to measure performance more objectively (Latham and Wexley, 1977; Smith and Kendall, 1963). In essence, this attempt is to move affective and other "biases" out of the evaluation, in order to obtain an accurate measure of employee's actual productivity. Efforts to remove affect from evaluations may only result in removing fit from performance evaluations under the assumption that this is simply error. The position we are taking here is that affect and fit reflect valid, job-relevant information with substantive implications for interview outcomes. This is crucial, because the conclusions researchers draw about the value of the interview may depend on the way the criterion is viewed.

If fit can reasonably be seen as representing the goals and values of an individual and directly manifested by the degree to which the individual is liked by others, the interview would seem to be situated better than other selection measures to assess the goals, values, and perceived likability of the applicant. In fact, past research has indirectly supported this proposition by showing that interviewer judgments seem to predict subjective performance better than objective measures of performance (Hunter and Hunter, 1984). Similarity effects have been demonstrated in both interviewer judgments (Keenan, 1977; Orpen, 1984) and performance evaluations (Ferris, Judge, Rowland, and Fitzgibbons, in press; Wayne and Ferris, 1990). If assessments of fit "contaminate" these judgments, this evidence would suggest that the interview will predict fit better than it predicts objective performance or productivity.

Thus, it is quite possible that we should not remove affect or liking from performance evaluations. Removing affect or liking (as an instrumental outcome of perceived fit) from performance evaluations may only ensure that the interview does not predict performance.

Yet, as has been argued here, affect is not irrelevant to judgments of employee value. Even if performance evaluations were totally free of affective processes, supervisor and co-worker affect or feelings toward the subordinate or fellow co-worker may be a legitimate criterion in itself.

Chatman (1989) has argued that organizations may continue to use the interview not to evaluate the technical qualifications of applicants, but rather to assess how well the applicants' values and norms will fit in the organization. Thus, while some selection methods are suitable for judging technical qualifications (e.g., ability tests, work samples, biographical information, and so on), the interview may be ideally suited to assess fit. If Chatman's arguments are true, it suggests reevaluating the interview based on its potential to contribute to the fit of the worker in the organization.

Interpersonal Influence and Fit

Practitioners have long recognized that there is a strong incentive on the part of candidates to actively manage the impressions that staffing decision makers form of them. It has been a relatively recent development, however, for researchers to examine systematically the effects of active influence attempts or impression management on HR decisions. In general, it is clear that impression management by candidates influences decision-maker judgments. In fact, in a recent study, impression-management techniques were found to have a more powerful effect on interviewer judgments than objective qualifications (Gilmore and Ferris, 1989a).

The significant relationship between perceived similarity and decision maker evaluations was reviewed earlier. Perhaps one of the more important goals of those using influence tactics in the selection process is to increase the evaluator's perception of the fit between the candidate and organization. In concept, this transcends similarity between the decision maker and the candidate to similarity between the candidate and the organization's culture. It may be that the specific influence tactics used depend on the situation, but the overall goal of enhancing the perception of congruence between the characteristics one has to offer and what the organization values remains the same. Therefore, the notion of fit may hold the promise of explaining how and why individuals seek to manage impressions in the selection process, and the extent to which they are effective in doing so.

Research has demonstrated that the extent to which a candidate is perceived to fit the job, culture, or organization substantially increases the candidate's likelihood of receiving a job offer (Rynes and Gerhart, 1990). Fit may be inherently vague, which allows it to take a number of forms and permits candidates to play upon this ambiguity and exercise a greater degree of influence over the selection process and outcomes. For example, fit has been viewed as attitude similarity between candidate and decision maker, and such perceived similarity in attitudes has been associated with more favorable evaluations (e.g., decisions to hire) of job candidates (e.g., Peters and Terborg, 1975; Schmitt, 1976). Fit also has been interpreted with respect to appearance, personality, and values, and the extent to which each of these is consistent with some expected or desired level. Molloy (1975) elevated appearance and dress to a higher level in the role it is believed to play in interpersonal evaluations including HR staffing decisions. Recent research has shown that appearance affects staffing judgments (Rynes and Gerhart, 1990).

The research on fit reviewed earlier suggested that assessments of fit typically have focused on the personality of the candidate. Organizations certainly differ in their strategic mission. Because differing strategic missions may require individuals possessing particular personality traits, it seems reasonable to expect that overall personality composition of employees significantly differs by organization. Several writers in the strategy literature have emphasized that the match between the characteristics of the individual and the strategic characteristics of the organization are of central importance in determining organizational success (Gupta, 1984; Hambrick and Mason, 1984; Szilagyi and Schweiger, 1984). For example, an organization that has typically pursued an aggressive business strategy may be more likely to have aggressive employees. If so, the organization may desire to hire and promote aggressive employees in the future. If the candidate perceived the personality desired, he or she might seek to manage the way in which his or her personality is perceived. For example, if the decision maker presents the impression that cohesiveness and cooperation is very important to the organization, the candidate may take particular care not to appear aggressive or stubborn.

It may be that the personality of the staffing decision maker alone is the dominant effect. The candidate may not be aware of the personality of the other organization members, only the decision maker's. If the staffing decision maker displays certain attributes, the candidate may seek to match the actions that manifest the traits. The decision maker displaying certain actions makes it more likely that the candidate will act in a reciprocal fashion. Thus, in such cases, the candidate has effectively managed the shared meaning of personality similarity, and the decision maker may well recommend hiring due to perceived fit to the job (when it is actually perceived similarity to himself or herself). Research on personality and fit has shown that job candidates who possess personality characteristics congruent with the job for which they are being evaluated tend to be judged as more suitable for that job (Paunonen, Jackson, and Oberman, 1987).

The Role of Fit in the Human Resources Staffing Process

In order to summarize our notions about fit, a model of fit in the staffing process is presented in Exhibit 2. First, it is hypothesized in Exhibit 2 that similarity, in terms of goals and values, will lead to higher assessments of candidate fit. This similarity is defined in terms of a match between goals and values of the candidate and those of the decision makers. It is then hypothesized that this match, defined as fit, will lead to the decision maker liking the candidate. Candidate interpersonal fit and decision maker liking of the candidate, in turn, are hypothesized to lead to higher evaluations of the candidate's suitability. The dimensions (as goals and values) used to categorize fit and affect, or liking, as the most immediate outcome of fit are by no means conclusive; however, they are dimensions of fit that have figured prominently in discussions of the construct. Judge and Bretz (1992) have discussed fit in terms of Ravlin and Meglino's (1987) four value classifications. Chatman (1989) also has discussed fit in terms of goals and values. Furthermore, drawing from the well-established similarity–attraction paradigm (Byrne, 1969), it has been suggested that fit probably operates on staffing decisions

through its influence on liking (Ferris and Judge, 1991; Ferris et al., 1991).

Exhibit 2 also shows that influence behavior, based on the previous discussion, is expected to affect both perceptions of fit and liking. This model does not assume that it is only the candidate who is using the selection process to his or her advantage. The decision maker also may have an agenda as well. For example, the decision maker may wish to select or promote (or fire) someone who happens to satisfy or further his or her self interest (e.g., hire or promote someone who shares their values and who will add to his or her own power base) (Beer et al., 1984; Ferris, Russ, and Fandt, 1989). Longenecker, Sims, and Gioia (1989) have illustrated how similar processes work with respect to performance evaluation decisions.

The model does not assume that fit exclusively leads to a select or reject decision. The match between the knowledge, skills, and abil-

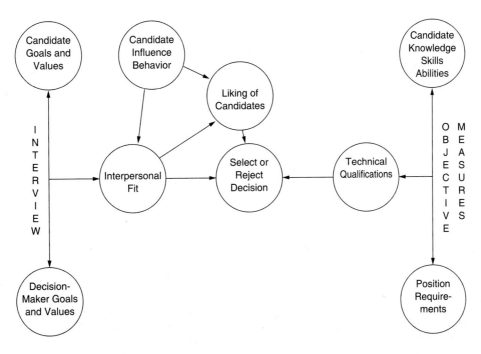

Exhibit 2. Role of Fit in Human Resources Staffing Decisions

ities of the candidate and the technical requirements of the position are also hypothesized to
influence the staffing decision. Further, the
model predicts that fit can best be assessed by
the interview. Conversely, the match between
the knowledge, skills, and abilities of the candidate and the technical requirements of the
position is hypothesized to best be predicted
by less subjective measures (e.g., ability tests
or work samples).

Understanding of the construct of fit also
depends on the benchmark or reference point
against which the individual is compared in
order to assess fit. That is, one could assess
the degree of fit to the group (Ferris, Youngblood, and Yates, 1985), the job (Rynes and
Gerhart, 1990), or the organization (Bowen et
al., 1991; Schneider and Bowen, 1992). One
would expect some degree of similarity between these sources (i.e., employees who fit
in the job are more likely to fit in the group
and the organization). For example, Rynes
and Gerhart (1990) found that interviewers
within the same organization gave more similar evaluations of job candidates' firm- or
job-specific employability than did interviewers from different organizations. It is
quite possible, though, that some differences
would be observed between these sources.
This conceptualization does not attempt to
make a distinction between these sources. We
assume that all may operate on selection decision maker's judgments of fit; however,
it would be useful for future research to investigate possible differences when considering fit at the job, group, and organizational
levels.

This careful analysis of the role of fit in HR
staffing decisions, as depicted in Exhibit 2,
has important implications for our overall
view of the HR staffing process. The model
presented in Exhibit 2 complicates the staffing
process by adopting a political perspective. We
believe this model is realistic because of the
centrality of fit to staffing decisions, and because of the potential complexities involved in
the process by which fit affects staffing decisions. We now need to bring this more com-

prehensive analysis to bear on our view of the
HR staffing decision process.

A Broader View of the Human Resources Staffing Process

The foregoing model and the ensuing discussion illustrate that the view of the staffing
process that was represented in Exhibit 1
was somewhat naive in its assumptions, and
simplistic in its depiction or characterization
of the process. The complexities of fit dynamics, as noted in the earlier sections of
this article, suggest the need for a broader
and more complete perspective on the HR
staffing decision-making process. Such a
view needs to address some of the challenges
introduced by the fit construct as well as deficiencies of the basic model of the HR
staffing process presented in Exhibit 1. This
new, broader and more expanded perspective
of HR staffing decisions and processes is
presented in Exhibit 3, and it strikes a balance in blending the rational and political
perspectives.

As Exhibit 3 illustrates, much of what is
contained in Exhibit 1 remains. Specifically,
staffing is still seen as consisting of three interrelated processes: in flows, through flows,
and out flows. Furthermore, external environmental influences and internal organizational
influences still affect the staffing processes in
the manner previously described; however,
the model adds several important elements
that more accurately depict the context in
which staffing decisions are embedded, and
provides a framework for understanding the
dynamics of fit in the staffing process. These
new elements are discussed next.

Organizational Staffing Philosophies and Practices

Organizational staffing philosophies and practices may affect each of the three staffing
processes. For example, until quite recently
IBM's full employment policy has meant
that few individuals are terminated due to layoffs. Similarly, some companies tout their

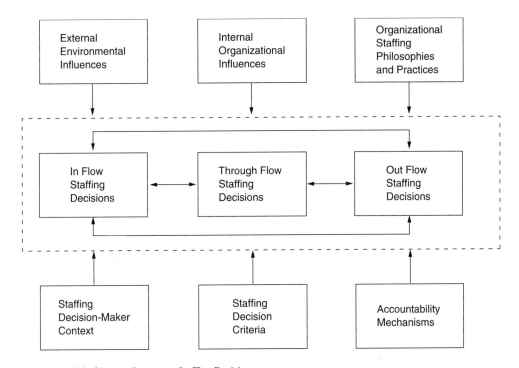

Exhibit 3.   Model of Human Resources Staffing Decisions

promotion-from-within philosophies which may translate into a greater number of positions being filled internally rather than externally. Another important philosophy is the velocity of flow (Beer et al., 1984). The velocity of flows concerns how rapidly individuals move and are expected to move in the organization. Thus, it is a reflection of whether the organization has a "fast track" philosophy, or a slower evaluation and promotion system. As discussed by Ferris and Judge (1991) and Ferris and King (1991), a fast track system involving quick movement potentially encourages at least as much symbolic behavior (perhaps political in nature) as actual effective performance. Because one is in a particular job or position a reasonably short period of time, and because standards of performance on many jobs are ambiguous at best, individuals are likely to be evaluated more on how much it appears that they are contributing than on the basis of their actual (objective) perfor-

mance level (Pfeffer, 1981). So, the velocity and direction of internal mobility, as well as the volume of in flow, will be influenced, in part, by the organization's particular staffing policies and practices.

Staffing Decision Criteria

Staffing decision criteria are concerned with whether or not there are clearly articulated standards for HR staffing decisions which are applied uniformly and consistently across all candidates so as to ensure procedural justice and job relevance. Because by its very nature fit is informal and subjective, the influence of fit on staffing decisions is probably greatest when there are fewer restrictions on the criteria that decision makers are able to use in reaching staffing decisions. Furthermore, even in organizations where fit is consciously weighted in selection decisions, there may be differences in the degree to which fit is precisely defined. Some organizations may constrain their decision makers to consider issues of fit only in terms of certain criteria such as values; other organizations may leave the definition up to the decision maker.

Staffing Decision-Maker Context

Gilmore and Ferris (1989b) suggested that some decision makers may be more easily influenced by candidate manipulation attempts than others because of a number of factors about their preparation for the decision task. For example, if the decision maker does not know the job requirements well, or what it takes to perform the job, it is difficult to know what to look for. Because organizations often do not provide systematic training for staffing decision makers, and there often are no requirements in terms of experience in making staffing decisions, the possibility that a particular selection decision maker is unsure or unknowledgeable about the criteria is often high. These individuals may serve as a "blank slate" upon which the candidate can create their own image. While this presents the candidate with an opportunity to manage the impression of fit, it also is somewhat of a dilemma since candidates may pick up few cues regarding the image against which they need to match themselves.

Accountability Mechanisms

Do we hold the decision maker accountable or answerable for his or her staffing decisions? In the case of staffing using college recruiting, the answer clearly seems to be "no" (Boudreau and Rynes, 1986). In the staffing context, reduced accountability allows the decision maker more latitude in terms of selection decisions. Thus, the decision maker has more opportunity to make decisions based on "illegitimate" criteria such as the ability of a candidate to augment the decision maker's power base, meet the decision maker's own needs or interests, and so on. It is likely, in this situation, that decision makers rely more on issues of fit, because they may more enjoy being around those who reflect their values and beliefs, and because similarity in terms of

outlook may be a fruitful basis upon which to build coalitions.

Implications for Human Resources Staffing Decisions and Processes

So, it seems that the construct of fit, indeed, plays a considerable role in HR staffing decisions. Given the foregoing discussion of fit in the staffing context, there appear to be some important implications for both research and practice.

Implications for Research

Clearly the construct of fit needs further investigation. Rynes and Gerhart (1990) and Bretz, Rynes, and Gerhart (1991) have offered data in support of the construct. The model proposed in Exhibit 2 is one attempt to capture the implications of the construct for staffing decisions, and needs to be empirically tested. Fundamental to supporting the model is that matches between goals and values of the decision maker and candidate lead to greater decision-maker affect or liking of the candidate, which subsequently leads to higher evaluations. This would support the existence of a fit construct influencing staffing decision-maker evaluations.

Perhaps more central to this article, research would need to demonstrate that subjective employment practices such as the interview predict fit better than do other HR staffing measures. This might be done by relating decision-maker evaluations of candidate acceptability to both decision-maker and candidate assessments of goals, values, and decision-maker liking of the candidate. Subsequently, acceptability ratings could be related to fit and job performance once the individual is on the job. If decision-maker evaluations did not predict these assessments of fit better than measures of objective performance, the framework presented in Exhibit 2 would be incorrect. However, caution needs to be exercised in how such research is conducted and thus the interpretations are made. For example, as noted by Ferris and Judge (1991) and Ferris et al. (1989), operating managers will frequently conduct interviews and make final decisions on those to be hired. If a manager hires a candidate, he or she is implicitly making a statement that the person hired is expected to succeed, which will likely influence the subsequent performance evaluations given to the worker. Such inherent bias may cloud the accurate interpretation of the true predictor–criterion relationship.

If these hypotheses were supported, it would suggest that many researchers have erred in condemning subjective selection measures such as the interview. By construing the criterion too narrowly, researchers may have ignored the principal contribution of these procedures in selection decisions. Further research on fit is also merited. Do those organizations that have a closer overall fit between their employees and management realize better overall performance and organizational effectiveness? If not, but if the construct influences evaluations nonetheless, managers may be sacrificing company profits/organizational effectiveness in order to meet their own personal desires.

Also needed is research mapping the construct of fit. To date, we only have a nebulous idea of its nature. We need to articulate more precisely the nature of the fit construct as well as the intermediate steps which characterize the dynamic process through which it operates. Work by Bretz et al. (1991) is helpful in this regard.

Implications for Practice

A major point made in this article suggests that use of the selection procedures such as the interview should depend on the staffing strategy of the organization. If this is so, what is the relative trade-off of technical qualifications versus interpersonal fit issues in making staffing decisions? Furthermore, staffing procedures should be matched to the criterion they are trying to predict. If one wants to predict productivity potential, why use the subjective procedures like the interview? We know ability tests and work samples do a better job of that than the interview probably ever

will; however, organizations that also want to examine fit should use the interview to assess it. A multimeasure procedure, using different methods to achieve different predictions, would seem to be the ideal strategy.

Research on the role of the interview in assessing fit holds the promise of increasing our knowledge regarding the utility of the interview in organizations and the usefulness of the concept of fit. If the major ideas presented in this article are supported, then it will demonstrate that HR practitioners have not been as errant in their use of the interview as we have been led to believe. Further, calls for structured interviews as a way to improve the validity of the interview (Latham, Saari, Purcell, and Campion, 1980; Schwab and Heneman, 1969; Carlson, Schwab, and Heneman, 1970) may be misplaced if the true goal, and utility, of the interview lies not in selecting the most technically qualified, but the individual most likely to fit into the organization. If this is the case, organizations might be well advised to use procedures other than the interview to assess overall qualifications, and use the interview to assess fit. Structured interviews may still play an important role. To the extent that we can situationally define fit, we will want to ensure that interviewers are accurately and reliably measuring candidate fit, and that might best be accomplished by structuring the interview in light of fit-related issues and dimensions.

The inclusion of fit as a criterion in the HR staffing process also may have strategic implications for organizations. By selecting individuals consistent with overall business strategies, organizational performance may be enhanced. Writers in the strategy area have argued this to be the case (Gupta, 1984; Hambrick and Mason, 1984; Szilagyi and Schweiger, 1984). A way to implement strategy is by designing an organization's culture to enhance strategic objectives (Butler, Ferris, and Napier, 1991). Firms may select employees who manifestly fit the existing culture. Schein (1990) contended that culture is perpetuated by the selection of new employees who already have the "right" set of beliefs and values. Similarly, others have contended that in order for a corporate culture to flourish, it is important that candidates fit into the existing value system of the organization (Fombrun, 1983). Thus, while using the interview to assess fit may not improve organizational performance through selection of employees with enhanced productive abilities, it may influence organizational effectiveness in the long run by matching the goals and values of the employee to those of the organization.

Although we have argued that fit can be considered in terms of goals and values, the notion of fit is undoubtedly even broader. For example, researchers and HR professionals have recently focused on the importance of HR competencies in obtaining a competitive advantage for organizations today and into the future (Jackson, 1989; Ulrich and Yeung, 1989). Ulrich, Brockbank, and Yeung (1989) have argued that HR competencies fall into three categories: knowledge of the business, delivery of HR practices, and management of change processes. Because these sets of competencies vary across organizations and industries (Ulrich et al., 1989), the fit of the individual to the organization is a very relevant concept. From a staffing standpoint, job applicants must be assessed according to the degree to which their current (or prospective) competencies match those required in the organization. Organizations that do a better job of matching the competencies of applicants to those required in the organization are likely to achieve a competitive advantage. Furthermore, because each of these categories of competencies may be difficult to assess from a formal testing standpoint, the interview is uniquely qualified to assess the degree to which applicants match the particular competency requirements extant in each organization.

Walker's analysis (1988) provides examples of how the notion of fit can be used to establish HR competencies. For example, Chase Manhattan Bank has established four areas of general competence (partner in the business, manages HR as a business, initiates/manages

change, and HR professionalism). In order to assess these capabilities, Chase evaluates applicants on personal attributes such as interpersonal skills, being a team player, communication skills, and judgment and decision making. Individuals who fit these requirements are those who possess the strategic capabilities that will enable Chase to perform into the future. Although the requisite competencies differ, similar competency-based assessment procedures are occurring at Union Carbide and Weyerhaeuser.

A final point is noteworthy regarding HR policy formulation and implementation. Indeed, it is important to formulate HR policies in a careful way, reflecting the organization's mission, goals, and strategy, as well as its philosophies and culture. We need to realize, however, that sound policy formulation by itself does not ensure effective implementation. The HR policy implementation process needs to be addressed directly with education/training of managers (i.e., decision makers) in the nature and specific features of the particular policy, and with accountability mechanisms to ensure compliance. This is no more apparent than in the case of HR staffing policy; these critical implementation aspects are noted in the model in Exhibit 3.

Conclusions

A central assertion made in this article is that fit is not a purely static concept. Although fit has traditionally been viewed in a passive sense, as a match between person and organizational characteristics, it is argued that fit also is a dynamic process, where impressions of fit are actively manipulated by the candidate and opportunistically employed by decision makers. It would be useful for future research to investigate this proposition as well. The challenges that these issues pose for theory, research, and practice on the interview are nontrivial ones. The interview needs to be selectively utilized where it is most appropriate, as noted above. Additionally, interviewers must be well prepared for their selection task by focusing on appropriate decision criteria in a way which will maximize decision outcomes.

Indeed, the fit construct has been an elusive one for both researchers and practitioners. We believe that fit can be a quite useful criterion, but not until it is more precisely defined and it is applied systematically and appropriately. In this article, we have proposed some potentially useful steps which should both increase our understanding of fit and improve the effectiveness of the interview. Finally, because of its pivotal role, conceptualizations of HR staffing decisions need to incorporate fit in efforts to gain a more informed understanding of how staffing processes actually operate in organizations, not simply how we believe they should operate.

References

Beer, M., Spector, B., Lawrence, P. R., Mills, D. Q., and Walton, R. E. *Managing Human Assets.* (New York: Free Press, 1984).

Bernardin, H. J. and Beatty, R. W. *Performance Appraisal: Assessing Human Behavior at Work.* (Boston: Kent, 1984).

Boudreau, J. and Rynes, S. "Giving It the Old College Try." *Personnel Administrator,* 1987, 32, pp. 78–85.

Bowen, D. E., Ledford, G. E. Jr., and Nathan, B. E. "Hiring for the Organization, Not the Job." *Academy of Management Executive,* 1991, 5, pp. 35–51.

Bretz, R. D., Rynes, S., and Gerhart, B. "Recruiter Perceptions of Applicant Fit: Mapping the Construct or Constructing the Map?" Working Paper, Center for Advanced Human Resource Studies, Cornell University, 1991.

Butler, J. E., Ferris, G. R., and Napier, N. K. *Strategy and Human Resources Management.* (Cincinnati, OH: South-Western, 1991).

Byrne, D. "Attitudes and Attraction." In L. Berkowitz (Ed.), *Advances in Experimental Social Psychology* (Vol. 4, pp. 35–90). (New York: Academic Press, 1969).

Carlson, R. E., Schwab, D. P., and Heneman, H. G. "Agreement among Selection Interview Styles." *Journal of Applied Psychology,* 1970, 54, pp. 8–17.

Chatman, J. A. "Improving Interactional Organizational Research: A Model of Person-Organization Fit." *Academy of Management Review,* 1989, 14, pp. 333–349.

Dreher, G. F. and Maurer, S. D. "Assessing the Employment Interview: Deficiencies Associated with the Existing Domain of Validity Coefficients." In R. W. Eder and G. R. Ferris (Eds.), *The Employment Interview: Theory, Research, and Practice* (pp. 249–268). (Newbury Park, CA: Sage Publications, 1989).

Eder, R. W. and Ferris, G. R. (Eds.). *The Employment Interview: Theory, Research, and Practice.* (Newbury Park, CA: Sage Publications, 1989).

Ferris, G. R. and Judge, T. A. "Personnel/Human Resources Management: A Political Influence Perspective." *Journal of Management,* 1991, 17, pp. 447–488.

Ferris, G. R. and King, T. R. "Politics in Human Resources Decisions: A Walk on the Dark Side." *Organizational Dynamics,* 1991, 20, pp. 59–71.

Ferris, G. R., Judge, T. A., Rowland, K.M., and Fitzgibbons, D.E. "Subordinate Influence and the Performance Evaluation Process: Test of a Model." *Organizational Behavior and Human Decision Processes,* in press.

Ferris, G. R., King, T. R., Judge, T. A., and Kacmar, K. M. "The Management of Shared Meaning in Organizations: Opportunism in the Reflection of Attitudes, Beliefs, and Values." In R. A. Giacalone and P. Rosenfeld (Eds.), *Applied Impression Management: How Image Making Affects Managerial Decisions* (pp. 41–64). (Newbury Park, CA: Sage Publications, 1991).

Ferris, G. R., Russ, G. S., and Fandt, P. M. "Politics in Organizations." In R. A. Giacalone and P. Rosenfeld (Eds.), *Impression Management in the Organization* (pp. 143–170). (Hillsdale, NJ: Lawrence Erlbaum, 1989).

Ferris, G. R., Youngblood, S. A., and Yates, V. L. "Personality, Training Performance, and Withdrawal: A Test of the Person-Group Fit Hypothesis for Organizational Newcomers." *Journal of Vocational Behavior,* 1985, 27, pp. 377–388.

Fombrun, C. J. "Corporate Culture, Environment, and Strategy." *Human Resource Management,* 1983, 22, pp. 139–152.

Gilmore, D. C. and Ferris, G. R. "The Effects of Applicant Impression Management Tactics on Interviewer Judgments." *Journal of Management,* 1989a, 15, pp. 557–564.

Gilmore, D. C. and Ferris, G. R. "The Politics of the Employment Interview." In R. W. Eder and G. R. Ferris (Eds.), *The Employment Interview: Theory, Research, and Practice* (pp. 195–203). (Newbury Park, CA: Sage Publications, 1989b).

Gupta, A. "Contingency Linkages between Strategy and General Manager Characteristics: A Conceptual Examination." *Academy of Management Review,* 1984, 9, pp. 399–412.

Hambrick, D. C. and Mason, P. D. "Upper Echelons: The Organization as a Reflection of its Top Managers." *Academy of Management Review,* 1984, 9, pp. 193–206.

Harris, M. M. "Reconsidering the Employment Interview: A Review of Recent Literature and Suggestions for Future Research." *Personnel Psychology,* 1989, 42, pp. 691–726.

Heneman, H. G. III, Schwab, D. P., Fossum, J. A., and Dyer, L. D. *Personnel/Human Resources Management.* (Homewood, IL: Irwin, 1986).

Howell, W. C. and Dipboye, R. L. *Essentials of Industrial and Organizational Psychology.* (Homewood, IL: Dorsey Press, 1982).

Hunter, J. E. and Hunter, R. F. "The Validity and Utility of Alternative Predictors of Job Performance." *Psychological Bulletin,* 1984, 96, pp. 72–98.

Jackson, L. "Turning Airport Managers into High Fliers." *Personnel Management,* 1989, pp. 80–85.

Judge, T. A. and Bretz, R. D. "Effects of Work Values on Job Choice Decisions." *Journal of Applied Psychology,* 1992, 77, pp. 261–271.

Kanter, R. M. *Men and Women of the Corporation.* (New York: Basic Books, 1977).

Katz, D. R. *The Big Store: Inside the Crisis and Revolution at Sears.* (New York: Penguin, 1987).

Keenan, A. "Some Relationships between Interviewers' Personal Feelings about Candidates and Their General Evaluation of Them." *Journal of Occupational Psychology,* 1977, 50, pp. 275–283.

Klimoski, R. J. and Strickland, W. J. "Assessment Centers: Valid or Merely Prescient?" *Personnel Psychology,* 1977, 30, pp. 353–361.

Latham, G. P. and Wexley, K. N. "Behavioral Observation Scales for Performance Appraisal Purposes." *Personnel Psychology,* 1977, 30, pp. 225–268.

Latham, G. P., Saari, L. M., Purcell, E. D., and Campion, M. A. "The Situational Interview." *Journal of Applied Psychology,* 1980, 65, pp. 422–427.

Miller, E. "Strategic Staffing." In C. J. Fombrun, N. M. Tichy, and M. A. DeVanna (Eds.), *Strategic Human Resource Management.* (New York: John Wiley, 1984).

Molloy, J. T. *Dress for Success.* (New York: Warner Books, 1975).

Orpen, C. "Attitude Similarity, Attraction, and Decision-Making in the Employment Interview." *Journal of Psychology,* 1984, 117, pp. 111–120.

Paunonen, S. V., Jackson, D. N., and Oberman, S. M. "Personnel Selection Decisions: Effect of Applicant Personality and the Letter of Reference." *Organizational Behavior and Human Decision Processes,* 1987, 40, pp. 96–114.

Pfeffer, J. "Organizational Demography." In L. L. Cummings and B. M. Staw (Eds.), *Research in Organizational Behavior* (Vol. 5, pp. 299–357). (Greenwich, CT: JAI Press, 1983).

Ravlin, E. C. and Meglino, B. M. "Effects of Values on Perception and Decision Making: A Study of Alternative Work Values Measures." *Journal of Applied Psychology,* 1987, 72, pp. 666–673.

Rynes, S. and Gerhart, B. "Interviewer Assessments of Applicant 'Fit': An Exploratory Investigation." *Personnel Psychology,* 1990, 43, pp. 13–22.

Rynes, S., Bretz, R. D., and Gerhart, B. "The Importance of Recruitment in Job Choice: A Different Way of Looking." *Personnel Psychology,* 1991, 44, pp. 487–521.

Schein, E. H. "Organizational Culture." *American Psychologist,* 1990, 45, pp. 109–119.

Schmitt, N. "Social and Situational Determinants of Interview Decisions: Implications for the Employment Interview." *Personnel Psychology,* 1976, 29, pp. 79–101.

Schneider, B. "An Interactionist Perspective on Organizational Effectiveness." In K. S. Cameron and D. A. Whetten (Eds.), *Organizational Effectiveness: A Comparison of Multiple Models.* (Orlando, FL: Academic Press, 1983).

Schneider, B. "The People Make the Place." *Personnel Psychology,* 1987, 40, pp. 437–453.

Schneider, B. and Bowen, D. E. "Personnel/Human Resources Management in the Service Sector." In G. R. Ferris and K. M. Rowland (Eds.), *Research in Personnel and Human Resources Management* (Vol. 10). (Greenwich, CT: JAI Press, 1992).

Schwab, D. P. and Heneman, H. G. "Relationship between Structure and Interviewer Reliability in the Employment Situation." *Journal of Applied Psychology,* 1969, 53, pp. 214–217.

Smith, P. C. and Kendall, L. M. "Retranslation of Expectations: An Approach to the Construction of Unambiguous Anchors for Rating Scales." *Journal of Applied Psychology,* 1963, 47, pp. 149–155.

Sofer, C. *Men in Mid-career: A Study of British Managers and Technical Specialities.* (Cambridge, England: Cambridge University Press, 1970).

Sonnenfeld, J. A. *Managing Career Systems.* (Homewood, IL: Irwin, 1984).

Szilagyi, A. D. and Schweiger, D. M. "Matching Managers to Strategies: A Review and Suggested Framework." *Academy of Management Review,* 1984, 9, pp. 626–637.

Ulrich, D. and Yeung, A. (1989). "A Shared Mindset." *Personnel Administrator,* March 1989, pp. 38–45.

Ulrich, D., Brockbank, W., and Yeung, A. "Beyond Belief: A Benchmark for Human Resources." *Human Resources Management,* 1989, 28, pp. 311–335.

von Werssowetz, R. O. and Beer, M. "Human Resources at Hewlett-Packard." In M. Beer, B. Spector, P. R. Lawrence, D. Q. Mills, and R. E. Walton, *Human Resource Management: A General Manager's Perspective.* (New York: Free Press, 1985).

Walker, J. W. "How Companies Develop Human Resource Staff." Working paper, The Walker Group, 1988.

Wayne, S. J. and Ferris, G. R. "Influence Tactics, Affect, and Exchange Quality in Supervisor-Subordinate Interactions: A Laboratory Experiment and a Field Study." *Journal of Applied Psychology,* 1990, 75, pp. 487–499.

Testing Is Not at Odds with Diversity Efforts

Charlene Marmer Solomon

It isn't easy to choose the right person for a job. We all know of high achievers who don't perform well on tests. We've had the experience of hiring brilliant people who have had dazzling recommendations, but who show up to work late or perform poorly on the job. Enter: employment tests (a commonly used tool for hiring, as well as training and placement decisions).

When the hiring of a diverse work force is of paramount importance, however, the appropriateness of pre-employment testing for a multicultural work force takes on a different cast. The major question, of course, is: Are these tests impartial?

Human resources executives are concerned that written and verbal aptitude, personality and achievement tests may not give them the accurate information they need when applied to applicants from diverse backgrounds. For example, can employers assume that a foreign-born bilingual applicant would select the same *right* answers as a person would who was born in the U.S. and whose native language is English? What about cultural factors that may persist, even when language isn't a problem?

Some companies use no paper-and-pencil tests. They rely strictly on interviews and recommendations. At the other end of the continuum are businesses that buy packs of tests, administer them, score them and key the results into a computer. The tests and assessment services run the gamut from inexpensive skill examinations that can be scored and interpreted in minutes to in-depth personality assessments that require extensive time and judgment on the part of both the test taker and the examiner.

Regardless of the scope of pre-employment tests, some are better predictors of success than others; some are *fairer* to all groups than others are. Most experts believe that tests should be only one component of the hiring process.

"In our opinion, it's best to take a battery approach. Look at all aspects of the person—as much as is feasible—and make decisions with everything in mind," says Scott G. Howard, president of Reid, Merrill, Brunson & Associates in Denver. The company provides tests for pre-employment, promotion and internal career-development purposes. The assessments include:

- Interest surveys
- Skill and aptitude tests
- Behavior and personality measures.

"We try to compare [potential employees] with people who are or have been successful in the position to be filled. We look at strengths and weaknesses, and make recommendations for improvement," says Howard.

Strengths and weaknesses, similarities and differences. These are key factors in a person's employment desirability. In this time of diversity awareness, many people believe that one of the advantages of conducting assessments is that tests point out differences between people.

"We're in an era of international competitiveness. We're looking for a variety of people to run our businesses, and to sell and make our products," says Charles F. Wonderlic Jr., vice president of Wonderlic Personnel Testing in Northfield, Illinois. "It means identifying the superb, not just the norm or average." This involves asking such questions as:

- How are you different from me?
- What do you like?
- What are you best at?
- What are you not best at?
- Where will you accelerate?
- Where are you not going to fit?

"These are questions that tests can begin to answer," says Wonderlic.

Although generalizations are risky, most experts agree that testing is far more sophisticated today—and more valid, in most respects—than ever. Still, human resources professionals who must use tests and nevertheless are interested in hiring a diverse work force need to know how to employ testing to their best advantage.

Job-specific tests are best. "Some employment tests lead to significantly different passing rates for minorities when compared with majorities," says John W. Jones, vice president of research and service for London House, a leading assessment publisher located in Rosemont, Illinois. "Companies seeking a culturally diverse work force prefer tests that don't discriminate unfairly." In addition, some employment tests clearly are job-specific, and others are more general, according to Jones. General tests originally were developed for clinical or educational settings, rather than for occupational settings. "Research shows that tests developed specifically for the workplace tend to be more accurate predictors of employees' on-the-job performance than the more general psychological tests are," says Jones.

Therefore, job-relevant tests that have no between-group differences are the ones to use. According to Jones, an example of this type of test is a multidimensional selection test that measures job applicants' attitudes toward a wide variety of workplace behaviors, including integrity, dependability, service, safety and productivity. Jones says that job attitude tests usually are fair to all protected subgroups. "They're ideal for the age of cultural diversity in the workplace," he says.

Jones says that general psychological tests that do yield differential scores for certain subgroups might include a clinical personality test that was designed to assess personal values, family adjustment or emotional health. There also are some intelligence tests that have been validated scientifically in the workplace, but which have an adverse impact on protected groups, and therefore are controversial. In addition, there are some tests that aren't accurate predictors of employees' behavior, although they don't impact any group adversely.

"I believe in valuing diversity and using the very differences that we were supposed to avoid," says Lewis Griggs, executive producer at Griggs Productions, a San Francisco–based company that produces diversity training films. "I feel that any test of anything is, of course, biased by its maker—it can't be otherwise. Still, any test is legitimate for what it tests. The individual using the results merely has to have the perspective to use that information responsibly and understand what he or she is testing for."

To Griggs, this means giving a woman the opportunity to prove that she can lift 100-pound hay bales or giving a man the chance to be a good cross-cultural Avon salesperson in predominantly minority areas of the city. "But isn't it a legitimate question to ask, 'Are you strong enough to lift the hay bales? Are you bicultural enough to be the appropriate salesperson for Avon or to sell insurance to Vietnamese immigrants?'" asks Griggs. "If we don't ask those obvious questions, we're putting our heads in the sand. We're denying the real differences. We're also denying the opportunity to discover differences that can be competitive advantages, all else being equal."

Identify skills needed for specific jobs. First, analyze the job. Find out which activities the person must accomplish. What does he or she have to do adequately or superbly? Focus on the things that the person has to do that require a high level of competence. Look at the necessary skills to achieve success on the job. In general, what qualities must that individual have if he or she is going to accomplish that success?

Then back off from there and remember that you aren't just assessing a person, you're assessing a specific person for a specific job. For instance, the job may require extensive contact with people. The employee has to perform customer-service-related activities and make customers happy. Find out the types of measures that would reveal whether an employee would be good at serving customers and whether he or she would be happy doing that type of work. In this case, you would need a personality test.

In other cases, testing is obvious and is used simply to weed people out. For example, if one skill required is the ability to type a minimum of 45 words per minute and the candidate only can type 20, it's clear that the person isn't adequate for the job. "At that point, regardless of your status or whatever the unique attributes are that the individual brings to the organization," says Wonderlic, "if he or she doesn't have the minimum skills required—and what we're really looking for is someone who has the maximum, who types 85 words per minute, who also can write, who has an understanding of the people in our community—then the test will help the human resources professional make the rejection."

Once the job needs have been identified, the next step is to look for a company that can be an information resource—a test vendor or publisher that will help determine your company's assessment needs and help put them into action.

Howard suggests that human resources professionals look at the testing company's research. What types of studies has it done? What groups did it use in these studies? What

control groups did it use? What was the level of detail?

"Ask the company to give you a description of the groups used in its studies, including the majority groups. Were they all males who have had two jobs each and who have been on the job 15 years, or is it a good representation of the entire population? Ask which protected groups were studied," says Howard. The answers should come back to you in easy-to-understand language that a businessperson can use, not psychobabble, he says.

Howard suggests that employers that routinely hire people who either don't have a lot of work experience or whose first language isn't English (in manufacturing, for example) ask the publisher of the test if it has analyzed that specific population. See if there's an adverse impact built into its test results.

Another crucial element is to be sure that test publishers track EEO and ADA data. If the company is good, it will update statistics, continuously track adverse impact and update norms.

"A good consulting provider can help people decide what they need," says Howard. Engage in a relationship with the provider. Some people call Reid, Merrill, Brunson & Associates (Scott's testing firm) saying that they need one thing when really they need something else, which becomes evident after they've described it.

Human resources professionals also should ask about alternative forms of specific tests. "A good test publisher will have as many alternative formats for each test," says Wonderlic. For example, Wonderlic's tests are translated into foreign languages. One test is available in 16 languages. He says that the company could make use of the test translated into even more languages.

Language isn't the only area in which differences can affect test taking. There are other subtle, but very important, language differences among people. For example, people who come from Puerto Rico use decimal points as Americans do, and those who come from Mexico use commas, although both groups are Hispanic and speak Spanish. A test should allow for these differences. "We want to make it as easy as possible for them to understand the questions," says Wonderlic.

London House has formed an alliance with Berlitz and other companies that do translations. Jones says that this is crucial because multilingual versions of tests are becoming important. Test designers are becoming more culturally sensitive as a result. "We aren't assuming that everyone should be forced into the English version," says Jones.

There's more to assessment than meets the eye, however. For instance, it isn't simply the translation. Let's say the human resources manager identifies a Vietnamese woman who doesn't speak English but has an IQ of 140 and is perfectly capable of handling any management learning objective. She could learn at a high level and solve problems on the level of any manager.

"You can assess her English-speaking ability or ability to learn English," says Wonderlic, "but you also have to assess her potential for integration into the workplace. You have to do the follow-up. How do you incorporate a person who scores well on a version of the test translated into her native tongue, but doesn't speak the language of the workplace?" He continues by saying, "We want to maintain and promote diversity. We also want to maintain and promote productivity. We want to find a way to do both."

The test format is another important criterion. This can mean large print, Braille or audio. This is especially important because of ADA requirements.

Finally, be sure that there's *scientific norming*. This is a process that assures that tests are equivalent across cultures. For example, all test questions should have the same meaning, regardless of a person's background.

Although there's a lot to consider when deciding whether to use pre-employment testing when hiring members of a diverse work force, many human resources executives deal with such considerations all the time. And these professionals don't always have the same opinion about pre-employment testing.

Kraft General Foods considers that testing is an investment. Charles Reid, director of diversity management at Kraft General Foods Inc. in Northfield, Illinois, always has been a proponent for pre-employment testing. The reason? "I think testing can provide information that's valuable to an individual or the tester but couldn't be obtained under other circumstances," he says.

When Reid came into the business arena from the world of education in 1972, he says that tests weren't being used correctly by business and industry. The courts ruled that some tests were discriminatory. When companies stopped using many of these instruments, interviewers were thrown into a quandary. They didn't know how to check for the sets of skills individuals had, what they were permitted to ask prospective employees, or what information they could look for to help them make valid decisions.

"A properly constructed test looks at the elements of the job and then measures the finite characteristics of the candidate that guarantee relative success. Those are the things that ought to be looked at in testing," says Reid. "For the past 20 years, when people have asked me about tests, I've encouraged them not to throw them out."

At Kraft General Foods, the company looks at testing from an entry-level perspective. It also uses tests to determine work-related abilities, such as mechanical skills. The organization's attitude is that it's better to test in the beginning for skills that will be used on the job, than to invest the time and energy in hiring people and then discover six weeks later that they can't do the job.

Reid describes himself as an African-American who has worked in industry for about 20 years and is trying to take an honest look at who the entrants are to the work force and what skills they're bringing. He supports the use of testing because he's finding that employees are lacking skills. "When you look at blue-collar workers, nonexempt clerical workers or professional managerial workers, you'll see that each situation is a little different. Because roughly 80% of the work force in most companies [in a manufacturing environment] is blue collar; however, this group has a greater impact. I think that the skill level of the blue-collar workers coming in today is less than it has been in the past," says Reid.

He says that you can't assume that just because a person has completed a four-year secondary program, he or she has adequate skills. Reid, who also serves on the National Board for the Literacy Volunteers of America, points out that at least one adult American in five is functionally illiterate. "If you don't use paper-and-pencil testing, you may miss the fact that the person is unable to read. I think a paper-and-pencil test gives you at least an indication of whether you have a problem."

Reid quickly adds that he isn't intimating that just because a person can't read doesn't mean he or she isn't skilled, because many illiterate people today are functioning adequately in their jobs. It's important, however, to have that information. A verbal interview generally wouldn't uncover this fact, Reid says, because many illiterate people have outstanding coping skills.

"When you think about what's happening in the educational system, people, especially people of color, are being undereducated. Therefore, we lack the skills that we need for a high-quality work force," says Reid. He goes on to explain that whenever there's competition for the highest-quality people, it means that companies are competing for the same people. When the applicant pool includes individuals who don't have adequate skills or who will need retraining if the company does employ them, testing is a way of establishing the level at which each person comes into the company. "It allows you to set up training programs to modify or develop skills that the individual brings to you, and to help him or her become a productive employee," says Reid.

Cahners tests only for some positions.   As a general rule, Newton, Massachusetts–based Cahners doesn't do pre-employment testing. The company does conduct some testing for sales positions and for certain management positions. "When we do test," says William Stevens, Cahners' director of human resources, "it's only to provide an additional tool to use in the employment process—in addition to such information as experience, things they may have published (for writers) and territories they covered for other companies (for sales)."

Cahners uses tests only with finalists in the selection process. If the company can narrow the field down only to 10 people, for example, it might use testing to narrow the candidate list further.

On the sales side, Cahners uses testing to find out if the individual is self-directed, motivated, needs guidance and, if so, what kind of guidance. Once the person is employed, the company uses the test results as a tool for the manager to help the person develop professionally on the job.

Cahners continues to use the test from time to time to focus on training needs and to help managers understand and pay attention to certain facets of the individual's personality. It's helpful to know, for example, if a worker doesn't like to work while someone looks over his or her shoulder.

Stevens, however, emphasizes that testing is merely one component. "You can talk to a recruiter and the recruiter will say, 'You can give me all of the test results you want, but there's something inside me that gives me a good feeling or a bad feeling about somebody. It's that gut feeling,' " says Stevens. "On tests, an individual can have a good day or a bad day, but in the interview process, if it's done properly, there's enough diversity that a person who doesn't do well with one manager might do better with another. In a test, you don't have that opportunity for variation."

Stevens believes that tests won't weed out particular cultures. In fact, he says that the problem for recruiters is having enough cultures to draw from in the beginning. "The problem is getting [diverse individuals] into the loop, and it's more difficult in different parts of the country," he says.

Cincinnati-based Procter & Gamble also believes that any testing procedure should be supplemented with other hiring tools. The company hires only at the entry level. "The use of testing at Procter & Gamble is of paramount importance," says Lynwood Battle, manager of corporate affirmative action. "Selection is critical because we grow all our management from inside the company."

Like the other companies mentioned, Procter & Gamble uses tests as part of a total assessment process of job candidates. "It has a lot of key indicators that offer a profile of the successful candidate," explains Battle, "and only a part of that process is a paper-and-pencil cognitive test."

For the previous four years, according to Battle, the company has recruited minorities at a rate of 20%, which is significantly higher than the percentage of available minorities who are receiving college degrees. The process must be working because, according to Battle, women and minorities at Procter & Gamble are moving up at a rate commensurate with their representation in the population.

He believes that skill tests generally are valid, although he says, "I can't emphasize enough that the test (a 45-minute cognitive test) is only one aspect of the total assessment process."

The assessment of a candidate will take several days, beginning at the college placement office on campus. It can proceed for a period of several weeks. The paper-and-pencil test is administered along with the other components of the company's job-hiring procedures. Only after all of the information is compiled and evaluated is the prospective employee reviewed. "The determination is based upon a total assessment process," says Battle.

It seems clear that within the proper framework, testing is a valuable tool for human resources professionals. Tests give reliable data about skills, and will point out deficits as well as strengths. When employers go outside the skill-testing arena, it becomes important to choose assessment professionals who can help meet their specific needs and focus on diversity.

CHAPTER 7

Performance Appraisal

Following the completion of organizational entry activities, the need soon arises to evaluate work performance to satisfy the organization's efforts to monitor and improve effectiveness and to give employees feedback about how well they are doing. Organizations' concerns about productivity have sparked interest in performance appraisal as an organizational control mechanism that, if used properly, can constructively influence future work performance. Furthermore, recent legislation has forced careful examination of performance appraisal and employee feedback as evidence to support internal administrative or termination decisions.

Historically, approaches to solving performance appraisal problems focused on issues of instrumentation or scale development and procedures. It was hoped that, through these means, better results would be achieved. More recently, the emphasis has shifted from the technical issues to the process issues or the dynamics of the supervisor-subordinate relationship in the work setting. The focus on process, as well as concerns with ensuring procedural justice, has highlighted the usefulness of incorporating self-appraisals along with supervisor appraisals of subordinates' performance. This additional source of input frequently enhances perceptions of fairness on the part of subordinates and increases the validity of the resulting evaluations. Such shared feedback on past performance also facilitates the establishment of jointly owned and often more challenging goals for the future.

In the first article in this chapter, Rice focuses on several problems that have plagued performance appraisal and then presents a number of ways in which these problems can be overcome. In the second article Longenecker,

Sims, and Gioia take a somewhat different and interesting perspective. They support the notion that managers often use performance appraisal as a political tool to maximize their own interests.

McGarvey and Smith, in the third article, suggest that performance appraisal is both a downward and an upward system of evaluation; theirs is a significantly different perspective. Fedor and Parsons take still another view: They explain that there is no simple formula for providing effective feedback because so many facets of the feedback process are open to inappropriate interpretations by both the sender and the receiver of feedback.

In the final article in the chapter, Austin, Villanova, and Hindman highlight the legal aspects of performance appraisal. They discuss how the courts' broadened interpretations of applicable legislation have brought performance appraisal under even closer scrutiny. These authors provide a useful interpretive review of the legislation and offer recommendations for ensuring that an organization's performance appraisal system is sound.

Suggestions for Further Reading

The benchmarking boom. (1993, April). *HR Focus,* pp. 1, 6+.

Day, D. (1993). Help for discipline dodgers. *Training & Development, 47,* 19–22.

Gupta, A., & Singhal, A. (1993). Managing human resources for innovation and creativity. *Research-Technology Management, 36,* 41–48.

Islam, N. (1993). Performance contract: Contractualization of the government–public enterprise interface. *Optimum, 23,* 53–59.

Joseph, J. (1993). Harnessing human resource technologies. *Business Quarterly, 58,* 71–75.

Korinek, J., & Thobe, D. (1989). Improving telecom pay and performance programs. *Business Communications Review, 19,* 33–36.

Murlis, H. (1993). New approaches. *Personnel Management, 25,* 7.

Reed, G. (1989). Employers' new burden of proof in discrimination cases. *Employment Relations Today, 16,* 111–113.

Smith, B. (1993). FedEx's key to success. *Management Review, 82,* 23–24.

Stewart, J. (1993). Performance management: Is it really working? *Benefits & Compensation International, 23,* 20–21.

Performance Review:
The Job Nobody Likes

Berkeley Rice

A common criticism is that it creates a kind of parent-child relationship between boss and employee. *Industry Week* calls it "a periodic agony thrust on both bosses and subordinates." A personnel administration expert laments, "Probably fewer than 10 percent of the nation's companies have systems that are reasonably good."

The focus of all this concern is the methods used to assess how well workers do their jobs. Personnel experts aren't the only ones dissatisfied with such procedures, known as performance review, evaluation, appraisal or rating. Supervisors and workers are unhappy too.

One reason for the general dissatisfaction with such systems is a lack of agreement on their purpose. Should they merely evaluate performance, or critique and improve it as well? Should they be used primarily to determine salaries and prospects for promotion, or as a means of training and career development? Should they focus on how an employee does the job or the results achieved? Just who are they supposed to help, the employee or the supervisor? No performance-review system can accomplish all these goals, but confusion about conflicting purposes often undermines attempts at effective evaluation.

Many employees complain that the forms and procedures used invite unfair evaluations. They are often based on personality traits or vague qualities such as reliability, initiative or leadership—factors difficult to measure objectively. Many standardized appraisal forms also use criteria that are not relevant to the job under review. Others provide a quick and superficial checklist that leaves no room for individual evaluation. Too often, one-sided performance reviews put employees on the defensive, particularly when they turn into lectures or harangues that end with the boss commenting on "how great it's been to have this open exchange of views."

It might surprise employees who feel threatened by performance reviews to learn that many bosses find them equally burdensome. They, too, grumble about the irrelevance of standardized review forms and the vague criteria. They complain that reviews require piles of paperwork, don't leave room for individual judgment and don't lead to improved performance.

Many managers feel they need more training in how to conduct reviews, but few companies offer any help. Robert Lefton, president of Psychological Associates, a firm that conducts such training sessions, describes performance review as a tough job, "the equivalent of walking up to a person and saying, 'Here's what I think of you, baby.' It requires knowing how to handle fear and anger and a gamut of other emotions which a lot of managers aren't comfortable with."

If you wonder why evaluating an employee's performance can be so difficult, consider a simpler appraisal: one made by the barroom fan who concludes that his team's quarterback is a bum because several of his passes have been intercepted. An objective appraisal would raise the following questions: Were the passes really that bad, or did the receivers run the wrong patterns? Did the offensive line give the quarterback adequate protection? Did he call those plays himself, or were they sent in by the coach? Was the quarterback recovering from an injury?

And what about the fan? Has he ever played football himself? How good is his vision? Did he have a good view of the TV set through the barroom's smoky haze? Was he talking to his friends at the bar during the game? How many beers did he down during the game?

Compared with barroom appraisals, evaluating performance at work is far more complex. Because evaluation is both difficult and important, it has grown into one of the busiest fields in industrial psychology. Since 1950, more than 300 studies have appeared in academic and management journals. Most of them, until quite recently, focused on the rating format used and on the biasing effect of various nonperformance factors such as race and sex. These latter concerns were spurred by the federal government's Equal Employment Opportunity guidelines, issued in 1969 and 1970.

No consistent pattern of sexual bias has emerged from the research. For example, Michigan State University psychologist Kenneth N. Wexley and a colleague studied nearly 300 manager-subordinate pairs in several companies and uncovered no evidence of sexual bias in the ratings. Research by psychologist Lawrence H. Peters of Southern Illinois University found a similar lack of sexual bias in supervisors' reviews of retail-store managers. When psychologist William H. Mobley studied more than 1,000 employees at another company, he found that women generally received higher ratings than did men, regardless of the supervisors' sex.

Occupational sex stereotypes are a different story. Laboratory studies of women working at traditionally masculine jobs show that they usually receive lower ratings than do men of comparable ability in the same jobs. (This effect may lessen as more women enter managerial and other "male" domains.) On the other hand, women in traditionally feminine occupations, such as clerical work, don't seem to benefit from a compensating bias in their favor.

Studies of racial bias have revealed a consistent pattern: White supervisors tend to give higher ratings to white subordinates, while black supervisors favor blacks. A study by psychologist W. C. Hamner and three colleagues found evidence of another, more subtle form of discrimination: White supervisors were more likely to differentiate between high and low levels of performance among individual whites than they did among individual blacks, whom they generally rated close to average on a performance scale.

Some critics of performance reviews suggest that ratings by supervisors may be less accurate than those by fellow workers or subordinates or even self-appraisals by the employees themselves. Several studies have shown that supervisors tend to give tougher evaluations than do fellow workers, while the fellow workers' ratings generally show greater consistency among several raters.

In a study of self-evaluation among job applicants, psychologist Cathy D. Anderson and others at the Colorado State Department of Personnel asked 350 men and women to rate their ability on a variety of job-related tasks. The list included several bogus skills, such as "matrixing solvency files," "planning basic entropy programs" and "resolving disputes by isometric analysis." Nearly half the applicants for what were mostly clerical jobs claimed they had experience with one or more of the nonexistent tasks. Among those who took a typing test, few achieved the speed they claimed, leading researchers to conclude that "inflation bias" in the self-appraisals was "prevalent and pervasive."

Several studies of actual and simulated work conditions have indicated that an employee's attitude and experience can affect the validity of a supervisor's ratings. In a field study, psychologists Ronald Grey and David Kipnis found that supervisors gave "compliant" workers higher ratings when the workers were surrounded by "noncompliant" peers and lower ratings when coworkers were more amenable. An early review by psychologists Rutledge Jay and James Copes of 47 studies showed that employees who had held their jobs longer, particularly in managerial jobs, usually got higher ratings than did peers of equal ability.

The appraisal method itself has received considerable attention from researchers. By far the most widely used format is still the traditional numerical or graphic rating scale. For each trait or skill being evaluated, the scale may be marked simply by numbers, say from 1 to 10, or by such vague adjectives as "unsatisfactory, below average, average, above average, outstanding."

In an attempt to improve the reliability of ratings, several researchers have experimented with varying the number of rating categories. The results indicate that consistency among raters drops significantly when there are less than 4 or more than 10 categories. Five to nine categories seem to produce the most consistent ratings.

Whether these ratings represent accurate measures of performance is another matter. According to industrial psychologist Robert Guion, editor of the *Journal of Applied Psychology,* "You get fairly valid ratings when you look mainly for the extremes of outstanding or very poor performance. But when you look closely at the middle or average range, distinctions among people are less accurate and valid."

That middle range, of course, is where most ratings fall, for several reasons. One is a manager's natural reluctance to cause pain by giving low ratings to poor performers. When supervisors know their subordinates will see the ratings, as they do in most systems, or that they will have to confront them with the ratings in a feedback session, they tend to be more lenient. This is perfectly human, but it doesn't lead to valid appraisals. Another factor may be what psychologists call "central tendency error," the fact that we tend to avoid the extremes when we rate almost anything. Then there's the problem of personal standards that lead tender-hearted managers to give consistently high ratings while "tough guys" rate consistently low. Both tendencies cause inequities when the reviews determine salary increases or promotions.

Some companies try to head off these errors with forced distribution systems that set minimums or maximums for the percentage of ratings in each category; for example, no more than 10 percent of one's subordinates can be rated outstanding, no more than 50 percent rated average. Many supervisors and psychologists object to such arbitrary limits, arguing that no one really knows what the distribution curve for such ratings should be.

Another common source of rating error is the "halo effect" whereby people who are generally well liked get favorable ratings on all categories. Bad chemistry between a subordinate and supervisor can have the opposite effect and produce unfairly low ratings. In both cases, ratings end up based on general impressions of the employee as a person rather than on specific aspects of performance.

Because of growing dissatisfaction with traditional ratings scales, and the search for more objective appraisal methods, many companies have adopted some form of "behaviorally anchored" rating scales (BARS). This development is based on the work of psychologists Patricia Cain Smith and Lorne Kendall, using John Flanagan's theory of critical incidents.

To create a BARS scale, companies first conduct a formal job analysis to determine what kinds of behavior constitute degrees of adequate performance for specific tasks in each job. They then use these behavioral descriptions to define or "anchor" the ratings on the scale. For example, for an item such as "perseverance," a BARS scale might offer choices ranging from "Keeps working on difficult tasks until job is completed" to "Likely to stop work on a hard job at the first sign of difficulty."

While the job analyses used to develop BARS scales are often conducted by outside consultants, many industrial psychologists feel that participation by the employees and their supervisors leads to more realistic performance expectations. Their involvement in the process should increase their awareness of what good work behavior is and thereby improve their performance.

While advocates of BARS, particularly the consultants who do a thriving business with it, claim it's a great leap forward, critics point to several drawbacks. The lengthy job analyses and complex scale construction require a major investment of a company's time and money. A scale designed for use in one department may not apply in another. In fact, separate scales may be necessary for each job category within the same department, since the requirements for good performance may differ markedly.

Comparative studies have found that the BARS method, because of its behavioral specificity, results in greater reliability than do traditional rating scales, and that it may reduce leniency, halo effects and central tendency error. But the improvements may be too slight to justify the time and money required. In addition, while BARS scales are suitable for jobs such as production or clerical work, they are harder to devise for managerial positions in which performance cannot easily be reduced to specific kinds of observable behavior. In such jobs, complex judgment, not easily reduced to a 6-point scale, may be more important than measurable behavior.

For managerial and supervisory jobs, many companies have adopted another form of evaluation, "management by objectives" (MBO), which focuses on results rather than behavior. MBO was proposed in the 1950s by psychologist Douglas McGregor. As customarily practiced today, supervisors and their subordinates sit down at the beginning of each year, or every six months, and agree (often in writing) on specific goals to be accomplished. At the end of the period, the supervisors evaluate their subordinates in terms of how well they have met those objectives.

MBO became popular because, in theory, it can be tailored to each individual job and because it lets subordinates know how their performance will be measured and gives them specific, mutually-agreed-on goals.

In practice, however, MBO appraisals are just as open to claims of unfairness as other systems of performance review are. One major weakness is the difficulty of setting reasonable goals well in advance, when they may be vulnerable to factors outside the employee's control, such as economic conditions, labor problems and price increases. Beyond that, the method's very individuality makes it difficult to compare one subordinate's performance with another's—one ostensible purpose of performance review. For these reasons, use of MBO has declined in recent years.

Frank J. Landy, a psychologist at Pennsylvania State University, reviews performance appraisal studies for the *Journal of Applied Psychology*. He has grown discouraged by the numerous attempts to build a better mousetrap by experimenting with rating scales or sources of bias. Even when those attempts reduce error, he says, the improvements are often so small that they're merely cosmetic.

"After more than 30 years of serious research," Landy wrote, "it seems that little progress has been made in developing an efficient and psychometrically sound alternative to the traditional graphic rating scale. . . . One major conclusion to be drawn from this research is that there is no 'easy way' to get accurate and informative performance data. Methods that aim toward easing the pain for managers who are busy will pay a price in terms of accuracy and value of the information obtained."

Faced with generally meager results from earlier studies, some researchers are turning to cognitive psychology in the hope of better understanding the processes of observation, information storage, retrieval, classification and communication that supervisors use, or should use, in performance evaluation. They suspect that perceptual and cognitive differences among raters may affect their ratings as much as or more than the nature of the rating scale itself and may be impervious to any changes in the evaluation system or the structure of the rating scale.

Many cognitive researchers point to the work of University of Washington psychologist Elizabeth Loftus and others who have demonstrated the fallibility of human observation and memory in studies of eyewitness testimony. Using videotapes of accidents and other incidents, those studies reveal the unconscious tendency of witnesses to "reconstruct" events based on cognitive biases, stereotypes and other unrelated information. If witnesses make all these mistakes on the comparatively simple task of recalling a few details about something that might have happened only a few hours or days before, imagine how difficult it is for a manager to evaluate the work of many subordinates over a period of six months or a year. Like witnesses at a busy intersection, managers often must base their judgments on only fragmentary evidence. It's understandable that unconscious mental habits play a vital part in their evaluations.

In his review of research on the cognitive processes involved in performance appraisal, Jack Feldman, a professor of management at the University of Texas at Arlington, showed that once a rater puts someone in a category, the category filters and colors the rater's observation and recall of that person's behavior. Supervisors thus attend chiefly to behavior that confirms the stereotype they have developed and ignore or forget behavior that conflicts with it. An admired employee whose performance declines may still receive excellent evaluations while another employee, who makes a serious effort to improve, may be condemned by a previous reputation.

When the time comes for evaluation, if the supervisor cannot recall any specific information relevant to a category on the rating form, he or she may unconsciously invent imaginary examples of "appropriate" behavior based on the stereotype. According to Feldman, these false memories are particularly likely when a supervisor has many subordinates to evaluate and little time or opportunity to observe them on the job.

This kind of categorical information processing is influenced not only by such obvious factors as age, sex, race and attractiveness but also by stereotypes about jobs. Thus some managers may evaluate the performance of all salespeople by how well they fit the traditional image of the fast-talking, aggressive go-getter and all bookkeepers by the image of the cautious, meticulous grind, whether or not these qualities apply to the particular job.

Personality or cultural conflicts can also create problems. Feldman cites the example of employees who act in what they feel is a friendly manner toward their boss, only to find that the boss considers it disrespectful. When review time rolls around, such employees may be shocked to find they have been labeled "insubordinate."

According to H. John Bernardin, professor of management at Florida Atlantic University, another type of error in performance reviews can be explained by attribution theory, which deals with the inferences people make as to why they and others act as they do. Bernardin has found that workers doing poorly on a job will attempt to justify their performance by attributing it to such situational factors as lack of supplies, unpredictable or excessive work load, difficult coworkers and ambiguous assignments. A worker's supervisor, however, is likely to blame personal factors such as lack of ability or motivation.

In one study of middle-level managers, Bernardin found that most of them cited low ability or motivation for their employees' unsatisfactory performance. But when asked to explain poor reviews of their own work, only 20 percent saw such personal factors as the cause. Most cited factors "beyond their control."

While many cognitive researchers are excited about the prospect of applying their findings to performance review, others remain dubious, particularly about using the work to improve rater training. In a recent research review, Bernardin points out that of the 34 rater-training studies he examined, only three involved data from real evaluations of real work. "It is a sad commentary on our discipline," he writes, "that an obvious applied area like rater training should be studied almost exclusively with student raters in an experimental context. . . . There appears to be an increasing emphasis on methodologically sound, internally valid laboratory research, the results of which have added little to our understanding of performance appraisal beyond what we already know."

According to a survey Bernardin did of personnel administrators and supervisors, inaccuracy in performance ratings stems more from intentional distortion than from rating error. Inflated ratings are one example. In tough times, managers may inflate ratings to make sure their subordinates qualify for raises, to keep their departments from being cut or to keep valuable employees from seeking transfers. Central tendency error is another example. It may make good administrative sense to lump most of one's subordinates in the middle range, thereby avoiding invidious comparisons and perhaps heading off arguments with or between employees.

Kevin Murphy, a psychologist at Colorado State University who has done considerable cognitive research on performance evaluation, also questions its relevance in training managers to be better raters. "The real problem is not how well managers can evaluate performance, but how willing they are," he says. "The problem is one of motivation, not ability."

In addition, he says, companies should stop trying vainly to improve rating forms and instead train managers in skills that would make them better observers: gathering and recording supporting evidence; discriminating between relevant and irrelevant information; doing selective work sampling when direct observation is infrequent; and deciding which aspects of performance are really measurable.

The discovery of how cognitive processes affect performance review, Landy says, has shaken the world of management psychology. "Eight years ago we would have given plenty of prescriptive advice about how to do an accurate review," he says, "but most of it would have been wrong. The bad news is that there's simply no easy way to do performance review. As appealing as the notion of a precise method of appraisal is, it's never going to be possible to measure such complex behavior in any absolute way.

"The good news," Landy adds, "is that we've discovered that a lot of that stuff about rating scales and evaluation formats is really trivial. The particular format doesn't make much difference. There is no one 'right' way to do it. There are dozens of ways. You just use whichever method feels right for your company. It may not be very accurate, but the degree of error won't make much difference."

"There's no one system that works," says management psychologist David DeVries, who conducts research and teaches courses on performance appraisal to corporate executives at the Center for Creative Leadership in Greensboro, North Carolina. "What we try to do here," he explains, "is show what the options are and how the companies' own managers can generally design a system most appropriate for them."

DeVries believes strongly that most managers "are much more sophisticated than the researchers realize. I think they understand the appraisal process pretty well because they are the ones who have to live with the results.

"Take traits like integrity, initiative, optimism, energy and intelligence. Researchers today feel such traits shouldn't be used in performance reviews because they're highly subjective, and therefore psychometrically suspect. But in business, those traits are very important, subjective or not. Executives make personnel decisions based on them all the time. If they do, then those traits should be evaluated, and we researchers can't afford to ignore them."

DeVries argues that companies can try to control the level of subjectivity in an appraisal system even though they can't make it go away. Despite the drawbacks of performance appraisal, he insists, "it's important to reward your top performers, and to make it clear to the others why they're being rewarded. . . . A good performance-appraisal system can help managers do this. It must be taken seriously by the managers, by the employees and by the company. It must be the basis for deciding who gets ahead and who doesn't."

Advice for Managers

However imperfect, performance reviews will continue to be required of most managers. Fortunately, along with all the criticism and research, there is also plenty of advice around on how to conduct them. The current edition of *Books in Print* lists more than 50 titles devoted to performance review or appraisal, and journals frequently publish articles on the subject. While not all of the advice is useful for every manager, much of it can be adapted to individual needs:

- Know precisely what you want to achieve (and what company policy says you should achieve) with your performance reviews, such as determining raises, evaluation, criticism, training or morale-building.
- Don't wait until the review itself to let your staff know what you expect. Let them know early on exactly what the job requires, what specific goals, standards and deadlines you expect them to meet and how you plan to evaluate and reward their performance.
- Keep a record of subordinates' performance so that you can cite specific examples to back up any criticisms or comments.
- Listen. Numerous surveys of employee attitudes reveal the feeling that "management doesn't care what we think." The review is your chance to get valuable feedback from your own subordinates about their jobs or company policy.
- Ask fact-finding questions to get employees to recall instances in which they performed well or poorly. See if they have a realistic estimate of their abilities.
- Go over your written evaluation with each employee. Find out if they feel your ratings are fair. They don't have to agree with you completely, but strong disagreements will lessen their motivation to improve.

- Focus steadily on each individual's performance. Show that you care about that person's career. Otherwise it looks like you're just going through the motions, and employees will get the message that the review, and perhaps their performance, doesn't really matter.
- When critiquing an employee's performance, do some stroking: Reinforce the good habits with praise.
- Be specific and constructive in your criticism. Don't just tell employees they're not "aggressive enough." Point out how they can improve, with specific examples.
- Critique the behavior, not the employee. Keep the discussion on a professional level.
- Be fair, but don't be afraid to give honest criticism when necessary. Most employees don't want a meaningless pat on the back. They want to know where they stand and how they can improve.
- Don't play the role of therapist. If personal problems are affecting an employee's performance, be supportive, but be careful about getting involved. Suggest outside professional help if necessary.
- Explain how the employee's performance in meeting goals contributes to department or corporate objectives. In this way, the review can help build morale and loyalty.
- Don't wait till the next performance review to follow up. Use informal progress reports or mini-reviews to help spot problems before they become serious.
- Use the occasion to get an informal review of your own performance. Encourage your staff to tell you about any of your habits that make their work difficult or to suggest changes you could make that would help them to do their jobs better.

Behind the Mask: The Politics of Employee Appraisal

Clinton O. Longenecker, Henry P. Sims, Jr., and Dennis A. Gioia

There is really no getting around the fact that whenever I evaluate one of my people, I stop and think about the impact—the ramifications of my decisions on my relationship with the guy and his future here. I'd be stupid not to. Call it being politically minded, or using managerial discretion, or fine tuning the guy's ratings, but in the end I've got to live with him, and I'm not going to rate a guy without thinking about the fallout. There are a lot of games played in the rating process and whether we [managers] admit it or not we are all guilty of playing them at our discretion.

According to management books and manuals, employee appraisal is an objective, rational and, we hope, accurate process. The idea that executives might deliberately distort and manipulate appraisals for political purposes seems unspeakable. Yet we found extensive evidence to indicate that, behind a mask of objectivity and rationality, executives engage in such manipulation in an intentional and systematic manner. In performance appraisal, it appears that some of the Machiavellian spirit still lives.

Our original goal was to conduct a scholarly investigation of the cognitive processes executives typically use in appraising subordinates. We held in-depth interviews with 60 upper-level executives who had extensive experience in formally evaluating their subordinates on a periodic basis. During these interviews, we heard many frank admissions of deliberate manipulation of formal appraisals for political purposes. In this article we'll discuss the "why and the how" of such politically motivated manipulation.

On the Appraisal Process

Almost every executive has dreaded performance appraisals at some time or other. They hate to give them and they hate to receive them. Yet, like them or not, every executive recognizes that appraisals are a fact of organizational life. In terms of time, a formal appraisal of a subordinate takes perhaps three or four hours out of the working year; in terms of impact on the lives of executives and their employees, appraisals have significance that reaches far beyond the few hours it takes to conduct them.

Because of the important role appraisals play in individual careers and corporate performance, a great deal of attention has been given to trying to understand the process. Special attention has been directed toward the issue of accuracy in appraisals.[1] Academicians in particular have expended (some might say wasted) substantial energy trying to design the perfect instrument that would yield an accurate appraisal. That effort now appears to be a hopeless, even impossible, task.

More recently, a flurry of activity has centered on the arcane mental processes of the manager who gives the appraisal. It is an intriguing approach because it involves a kind of vicarious attempt to climb inside an executive's head to see how he or she works. Predictably, however, this approach has confirmed the elusiveness of deciphering managerial thought

Reprinted with permission from *Academy of Management Executive, 1* (1987): 183–193.

Method

Our research approach involved in-depth semi-structured interviews with 60 executives. The participants in the study came from seven large organizations and represented 11 functional areas. As a group, they averaged more than 20 years of work experience and more than 13 years of managerial experience. Collectively, they had performance appraisal experience in 197 organizations. Conclusions reported here, then, are derived from a diversity of executives.

Each tape-recorded interview was designed to tap the executive's perception of his or her own performance appraisal processes. The interviews averaged more than one and one-half hours in length. Although the interview used some *a priori* "probes," the interviewing strategy mainly encouraged the subject to respond freely and subjectively.

The data collection yielded more than 100 hours of tape-recorded verbal data. All data from each interview were transcribed onto five-by-eight cards that mainly consisted of executives' directly quoted statements, with each card containing one statement, thought, or observation by an executive on a given topic. The transcription process yielded 1,400 cards, which were then classified according to various political issues that emerged during the interviews.

For a classification group to qualify as a potential "finding," a minimum of 72% of the respondents had to have brought up that issue. A research assistant then read each group of cards and assigned a label that captured the "essence" of the executives' views on a particular aspect of the appraisal process. The outcomes from this process were the designated findings of the study. To further enhance the reliability and validity of the research, two research assistants then independently developed frequency counts for each finding. They tallied the number of cards in each classification group that supported the finding that had been identified in the second step of the analysis. The frequencies tabulated by each judge ranged from a low of 43 responses (72%) to a high of 57 (95%). A correlation analysis of the frequencies revealed an $r = .94$ as a measure of interrater reliability in identifying the findings.

processes. Moreover, it has not yet resulted in appraisals that are any more accurate than existing appraisals.[2]

Even more recently, some effort has been directed toward demonstrating that appraisal is, in addition to everything else, a highly emotional process as well. When emotional variability gets dragged into the process, any hope of obtaining objectivity and accuracy in appraisal waltzes right out the office door.[3]

Taken together, all these approaches apparently lead to the depressing conclusion that accuracy in appraisals might be an unattainable objective.[4] More realistically, perhaps accuracy is simply a wrong goal to pursue. Even if we have a perfect understanding of instruments and mental and emotional processes, would that result in accurate appraisals? Our research indicates that it would not. All of

these avenues to understanding appraisal tend to ignore an important point: Appraisals take place in an organizational environment that is anything but completely rational, straightforward, or dispassionate. In this environment, accuracy does not seem to matter to managers quite so much as discretion, effectiveness or, more importantly, survival. Earlier research has either missed or glossed over the fact that executives giving appraisals have ulterior motives and purposes that supersede the mundane concern with rating accuracy.

On Politics in Performance Appraisal

Any realistic discussion of performance appraisal must recognize that organizations are political entities and that few, if any, important decisions are made without key parties acting to protect their own interests.[5] As such, executives are political actors in an organization, and they often attempt to control their destinies and gain influence through internal political actions.

Thus, it is likely that political considerations influence executives when they appraise subordinates.[6] *Politics* in this sense refers to deliberate attempts by individuals to enhance or protect their self-interests when conflicting courses of action are possible. Political action therefore represents a source of bias or inaccuracy in employee appraisal. To understand the appraisal process thoroughly, thus, we must recognize and account for the political aspects of the process.

Politics in Appraisal: Findings from the Study

The political perspective emerged as a surprisingly important and pervasive issue affecting the way executives appraise their employees. Conclusions derived from our interviews are summarized in Exhibits 1 through 4. Because a strong attempt was made to allow executives to speak for themselves in describing the politics of performance appraisals, direct quotations from the interviews have been included in our analysis, where appropriate. Our findings are discussed below.

Politics as a Reality of Organizational Life

The most fundamental survey finding was an open recognition and admission that politics were a reality in the appraisal process. In fact, executives admitted that political considerations *nearly always* were part of their evaluation process. One vice-president summarized the view these executives shared regarding the politics of appraisal:

> As a manager, I will use the review process to do what is best for my people and the division. . . . I've got a lot of leeway—call it discretion—to use this process in that manner. . . . I've used it to get my people better raises in lean years, to kick a guy in the pants if he re-

ally needed it, to pick up a guy when he was down or even to tell him that he was no longer welcome here. It is a tool that the manager should use to help him do what it takes to get the job done. I believe most of us here at _____ operate this way regarding appraisals. . . . Accurately describing an employee's performance is really not as important as generating ratings that keep things cooking.

Executives suggested several reasons why politics were so pervasive and why accuracy was not their primary concern. First, executives realized that they must live with subordinates in a day-to-day relationship. Second, they were also very cognizant of the permanence of the written document:

> The mere fact that you have to write out your assessment and create a permanent record will cause people not to be as honest or as accurate as they should be. . . . We soften the language because our ratings go in the guy's file downstairs [the Personnel Department] and it will follow him around his whole career.

Perhaps the most widespread reason why executives considered political action in the appraisal process was that the formal appraisal was linked to compensation, career, and advancement in the organization. The issue of money was continually cited as a major cause of intentional distortions in ratings.

> I know that it sounds funny, but the fact that the process is ultimately tied to money influences the ratings a person receives. . . . Whenever a decision involves money things can get very emotional and ticklish.

Although the logic of tying pay to the outcome of performance ratings is sound, pay linkages increase the likelihood that ratings will be manipulated. Both managers and the organization as a whole are guilty of using the rating process as an opportunity to reach salary objectives regarding employee compensation that have little, if any, relationship to pay for performance. A director of research and development very candidly described the predicament from the rater's perspective:

> Since the pay raise my people get is tied to the ratings I give them, there is a strong incentive to inflate ratings at times to maximize their pay increases to help keep them happy and motivated, especially in lean years when the merit ceiling is low. . . . Conversely, you can also send a very strong message to a nonperformer that low ratings will hit him in the wallet. . . . There is no doubt that a lot of us manipulate ratings at times to deal with the money issue.

At times, an organization uses the appraisal process as an instrument to control merit increase expenditures. The manipulative process can be summarized as follows:

> This thing [the appraisal process] can really turn into an interesting game when the HR [Human Resources] people come out with a blanket statement like, "Money for raises is tight this year and since superior performers get 7% to 10% raises there will be no superior performers this year." Talk about making things rough for us [raters]! . . . They try and force you to make the ratings fit the merit allowances instead of vice versa.

Influences on Political Culture

Executives made it clear that if an organization was political, the appraisal process would reflect these politics:

> Some organizations are more aggressive and political than others, so it just makes sense that those things carry over into the rating process as well. . . . The organization's climate will determine, to a great extent, how successful any rating system will be, and it follows that if any organization is very political, the rating system will be political. . . .

Several factors were identified by the executives as having a strong influence on the political culture in which the performance appraisal process operates. Perhaps the strongest was the extent to which the formal appraisal process was "taken seriously" by the

Exhibit 1
Politics as a Reality of Organizational Life

- Political considerations were nearly always part of executive evaluative processes.
- Politics played a role in the evaluation process because:
  —executives took into consideration the daily interpersonal dynamics between them and their subordinates;
  —the formal appraisal process results in a permanent written document;
  —the formal appraisal can have considerable impact on the subordinate's career and advancement.

organization. A plant manager in this study describes what it means for an organization to "take the process seriously":

> At some places the PA [performance appraisal] process is a joke—just a bureaucratic thing that the manager does to keep the IR [industrial relations] people off his back. At the last couple of places I've worked, the formal review process is taken really seriously; they train you how to conduct a good interview, how to handle problems, how to coach and counsel. . . . You see the things [appraisals] reviewed by your boss, and he's serious about reviewing your performance in a thorough manner. . . . I guess the biggest thing is that people are led to believe that it is a management tool that works; it's got to start at the top!

This quote suggests another important factor that turns the appraisal process into a political process: the extent to which higher level executives in the same company use political factors in rating subordinates. A "modeling" effect seems to take place, with managers telling themselves, "If it's okay for the guys upstairs to do it, then we can do it, too."

According to one executive we interviewed,

> I've learned how not to conduct the review from the bosses . . . but you do learn from your boss how much slack or what you can get away with in rating your people. . . . It seems that if the manager's boss takes it [the appraisal] seriously, the subordinate [manager] is more likely

to follow. If the boss plays games with the review, it seems like the subordinate [manager] is more likely to do so.

The economic health and growth potential of the organization appeared as important factors influencing the organization's culture and, consequently, the appraisal event. Similarly, the executive's own personal belief system—his or her perception of the value of the appraisal process—also seemed to have an impact. Generally, executives who honestly believed the process contributed to the motivation of their subordinates were less likely to allow political factors to affect the appraisal. Conversely, executives who saw the appraisal as a useless bureaucratic exercise were more likely to manipulate the appraisal.

Moreover, if executives believed the appraisals would be seriously scrutinized, reviewed, and evaluated by their superiors, then the influence of political factors was likely to be reduced.

> If somebody is carefully reviewing the marks you give your people, then the game playing is reduced . . . [but] as you rise in the organization, your boss has less direct knowledge of your people and is less likely to question your judgment, so the door is open for more discretion.

The degree of open communication and trust between executives and subordinates seemed to have some influence on the impact of political factors. The more open the communication, the less likely that politics would play a role:

> If the manager and employee have a trusting and open relationship and shoot straight with each other, then the manager is less likely to play games with ratings.

Last, but not least, the appraiser's level in the organization's hierarchy also seemed to have an influence. Executives generally believed the appraisal process became more political and subjective as one moved up the organizational ladder.

Exhibit 2
Factors Influencing the Political Culture of the Organization

---

- The economic health and growth potential of the organization
- The extent to which top management supported and, more importantly, did or did not practice political tactics when appraising their own subordinates
- The extent to which executives sincerely believed that appraisal was a necessary and worthwhile management practice or just a bureaucratic exercise
- The extent to which executives believed that their written assessment of their subordinates would be evaluated and scrutinized by their superiors
- The extent to which an organization was willing to train and coach its managers to use and maintain the performance appraisal system
- The degree to which the appraisal process was openly discussed among both executives and subordinates
- The extent to which executives believed the appraisal process became more political at higher levels of the organizational hierarchy

---

The higher you rise in this organization the more weird things get with regard to how they evaluate you. . . . The process becomes more political and less objective and it seems like the rating process focuses on who you are as opposed to what you've actually accomplished. . . . As the stakes get higher, things get more and more political.

Inflating the Appraisal

Although academicians have been preoccupied with the goal of accuracy in appraisal, executives reported that accuracy was not their primary concern. Rather, they were much more interested in whether their ratings would be effective in maintaining or increasing the subordinate's future level of performance. In fact, many reported they would deliberately misstate the reported performance level if they felt performance could be improved as a result:

> When I rate my people it doesn't take place in a vacuum . . . so you have to ask yourself what the purpose of the process is. . . . I use this thing to my advantage and I know my people

and what it takes to keep them going and that is what this is all about.

Overall, executives reported that deliberate distortions of the appraisal tended to be biased in the subordinate's favor:

Let's just say that there are a lot of factors that tug at you and play on your mind that cause you to tend to soften the ratings you give. It may not have a great impact all the time but when you know a "5" will piss a man off and "6" will make him happy. . . . You tell me which one you'd choose. . . . Plus, you don't want to be the bad guy, the bearer of gloom. It seems like ratings are almost always a little inflated at a minimum because of people aspects in the evaluation process.

Typically, executives tended to inflate the overall rating rather than the individual appraisal items. Interestingly, although the overall rating was generally the last item on the appraisal form, this overall rating was determined first; then the executive went back and completed the individual items.

Most of us try to be fairly accurate in assessing the individual's performance in different categories. . . . If you are going to pump up a person's ratings, for whatever reason, it's done on the subordinate's overall evaluation category. That's all they really care about, anyway. . . . The problem is these things have to match up, so if you know what the guy's overall rating is in the first place it will probably color the rest of the appraisal.

Of course, this backward procedure is usually contrary to the recommended procedure and is also inconsistent with the typical assumptions about how decisions are supposed to be made "objectively." Executives articulated several reasons as justification for consciously inflating subordinate ratings. The most frequently given reason was to maximize the merit increases that a subordinate would be eligible to receive. This reason was more likely to be given by executives in orga-

nizations that closely linked the numerical score on the formal appraisal and the subsequent merit raise.

Sometimes executives wanted to protect or encourage a subordinate whose performance was temporarily suffering because of personal problems. In a similar vein, executives would sometimes inflate a rating simply because they felt sorry for a subordinate. They wanted to avoid short-term "punishment" in the hope that the subordinate would recover and perform once again at an acceptable level.

It may sound kind of funny to say this, but sometimes there is a tendency to give subordinates ratings a little higher than they deserve because you feel sorry for them. . . . I just had a guy go through a divorce and I'm not going to kick him when he's down, even if his performance drops off. . . . If anything, you might use the review to help pick him up and get him back on his feet.

If the appraisal was reviewed by people outside the department, executives sometimes inflated ratings to avoid "hanging dirty laundry out in public." Clearly, many executives preferred to keep knowledge of problems contained within the department.

There are two reviews at times, the written one and the spoken one. The spoken review is the real one, especially if there are things of a sensitive nature. . . . I generally don't put those things down on paper in the review for the whole world to read because it is generally none of their damn business. . . . I could make all of us look bad or worse than we really are.

Executives also admitted to inflating a rating to avoid a confrontation with a subordinate with whom the executive had recently had difficulties. They took this action mainly to avert an unpleasant incident or sometimes to avoid a confrontation that they believed would not lead to an effective outcome.

On occasion, an executive might inflate the rating because the subordinate's performance had improved during the latter part of the performance period, even though the overall performance did not merit such a rating. Again, the motivation for this higher-than-deserved rating was a desire to encourage the subordinate toward better performance in the next period:

> Many of us have trouble rating for the entire year. If one of my people has a stellar three months prior to the review . . . you don't want to do anything that impedes that person's momentum and progress.

Executives also recognized effort, even though the effort might not pay off in actual performance.

> If a man broke his back trying to do the best job humanly possible, his ratings will generally reflect this if his boss understands people. Take two people with the same performance, but one tried much harder—their ratings will show it in my department. Low ratings might trample that person's desire to put forth effort in the future.

Last, although not frequently reported, a few executives admitted to giving a higher rating to a problem employee to get the employee promoted "up and out" of the department. Although executives only occasionally admitted to this, the "up and out" rating process was almost universally discussed as something *other* managers actually do. One plant manager candidly remarked:

> I've seen it happen, especially when you get a young guy in here who thinks he's only going to be here a short while before he gets promoted. People like that become a real pain in the ass. . . . If you want to get rid of them quick, a year and a half of good ratings should do it. . . . A lot of people inflate ratings of people they can't stand, or who think they are God's gift to the department, just to get rid of them. Amen.

Of course, this practice helps an executive avoid dealing with performance problems and passes the problem along to someone else. Mainly, this tactic was employed when an executive felt unable or unwilling to deal with a

Exhibit 3
Inflating the Appraisal

- Executives inflated the appraisal to provide ratings that would effectively maintain or increase the subordinate's level of performance (the primary concern was not the accuracy of the ratings).
- Inflated ratings occur primarily on the overall performance rating, as opposed to the individual appraisal items.
- Executive justification for inflating the appraisal:
  —to maximize the merit increases a subordinate would be eligible to receive, especially when the merit ceiling was considered low;
  —to protect or encourage a subordinate whose performance was suffering because of personal problems (feeling sorry for a subordinate also resulted in an inflated appraisal);
  —to avoid hanging dirty laundry out in public if the performance appraisal would be reviewed by people outside the organization;
  —to avoid creating a written record of poor performance that would become a permanent part of a subordinate's personnel file;
  —to avoid a confrontation with a subordinate with whom the manager had recently had difficulties;
  —to give a break to a subordinate who had improved during the latter part of the performance period;
  —to promote a subordinate "up and out" when the subordinate was performing poorly or did not fit in the department.

performance problem or, especially, when the source of the problem seemed to be based on "personality" or "style" conflicts.

Deflating the Appraisal

For the most part, executives indicated that they were very hesitant to deflate a subordinate's rating because such a tactic would lead to subsequent problems:

> I won't say I've never given a subordinate lower ratings than he or she deserves because there's a time and place for that type of thing, but let's just say I hesitate to do that sort of thing unless I'm very sure of what the outcome will be and that it won't backfire.

Nevertheless, negative distortions did occur. Executives gave several reasons for using this tactic. First, an overly negative rating was sometimes used to jolt a subordinate to rise to his or her expected performance level:

> I've used the appraisal to shock an employee. . . . If you've tried to coach a guy to get him back on track and it doesn't work, a low rating will more often than not slap him in the face and tell him you mean business. . . . I've dropped a few ratings way down to accomplish this because the alternative outcome could be termination down the road, which isn't pretty.

Also, a deliberately deflated rating was sometimes used to teach a rebellious subordinate a lesson:

> Occasionally an employee comes along who needs to be reminded who the boss is, and the appraisal is a real tangible and appropriate place for such a reminder. . . .

Deflated ratings were also used as part of a termination procedure. First, a strongly negative rating could be used to send an indirect message to a subordinate that he or she should consider quitting:

> If a person has had a questionable period of performance, a strong written appraisal can really send the message that they aren't welcome any longer and should think about leaving. . . . The written review sends a clear message if the person has any doubt.

Second, once the decision has been made that the situation was unsalvageable, negative ratings could then be used to build a strongly documented case against the marginal or poor performer:

> You'll find that once a manager has made up his or her mind that an employee isn't going to make it, the review [the written document] will take on an overly negative tone. . . . Managers

Exhibit 4
Deflating the Appraisal

- Executives indicated that they were very hesitant consciously to deflate a subordinate's ratings because of potential problems associated with such a tactic.
- Nevertheless, they sometimes deflated appraisals:
    —to shock a subordinate back on to a higher performance track;
    —to teach a rebellious subordinate a lesson about who is in charge;
    —to send a message to a subordinate that he or she should consider leaving the organization;
    —to build a strongly documented record of poor performance that could speed up the termination process.

are attempting to protect themselves. . . . The appraisal process becomes downwardly biased because they [the managers] fear that discussing and documenting any positives of the employee's performance might be used against them at a later point in time.

Of course, this tactic has recently become more common because of lawsuits challenging the traditional "employment at will" concept. The courts have clearly stated that terminations must not be frivolous; they must be justified by economic constraints or documentation of poor performance. In these cases managers will use the process to protect themselves from litigation associated with an unlawful termination lawsuit.[7]

Summary

Our research clearly showed that executives believed there was usually a justifiable reason for generating appraisal ratings that were less than accurate. Overall, they felt it was within their managerial discretion to do so. Thus our findings strongly suggest that the formal appraisal process is indeed a political process, and that few ratings are determined without some political consideration. Although research on rater "error" has traditionally suggested that raters can and do inflate ratings (leniency errors) and deflate ratings (stringency errors), researchers have typically not accounted for the realities of the appraisal context to explain why these errors occur.

In the minds of the managers we interviewed, these thoughts and behaviors are not errors but, rather, discretionary actions that help them manage people more effectively. Executives considered many factors beyond the subordinate's actual performance in their ratings. Thus, organizational politics was a major factor in the intentional manipulation of subordinate ratings.

Our findings provide support for the following political realities of organizational life: (1) Executives in large organizations are political actors who attempt to avoid unnecessary conflict; (2) they attempt to use the organization's bureaucratic processes to their own advantage; and (3) they try to minimize the extent to which administrative responsibilities create barriers between them and their subordinates.

We also conclude that the organizational culture in which the appraisal event occurs significantly influenced the extent to which political activity would both develop and operate. Of course, organizationwide patterns are also strongly influenced by the support and practice of top management. Indeed, we know that lower-level managers tend to emulate high-status executives, and the way they use the appraisal process is no exception. Thus, if top managers prepare ratings poorly or deliberately distort them, this behavior will tend to cascade down the organization.

Given these findings, what informative observations or constructive recommendations might we make to minimize, or at least manage, the detrimental effects of politics in employee appraisal? In fact, we have several for both the individual manager and the organization as a whole.

The Individual Manager

1. Quite frankly, our data suggest there are times in organizational life when political necessity supersedes the usually desirable goals of accuracy and honesty in appraisal. The ex-

ecutives interviewed suggested several compelling reasons for exercising managerial discretion contrary to traditional appraisal research recommendations. Clearly, there are times when individual employees and the organization as a whole can benefit as a consequence. The caveat, of course, is that the occasions when politics and discretion necessarily intrude on the appraisal process should be chosen judiciously. The overall effect on the organization should be given due consideration.

2. Performance appraisal is perhaps most usefully viewed as a high-potential vehicle for motivating and rewarding employees, rather than as a mandatory, bureaucratic exercise used only for judgmental or manipulative purposes. Ideally, it should be treated as an opportunity to communicate formally with employees about their performance, their strengths and weaknesses, and their developmental possibilities.

3. Executives should bear in mind that appraisal-related actions, like many other organizational activities, serve as guides for subordinates. Employees who must conduct appraisals often learn appraisal attitudes and behaviors from their bosses. Thus if appraisals are to be effective, high-ranking executives must treat the process as significant so that political manipulation is discouraged.

4. In addition, openness and trust between managers and subordinates seem to be associated with a lower level of detrimental political activity. Cultivating understanding seems to reduce the perceived need for resorting to interpersonal politics.

5. Finally, inflating or deflating appraisal ratings for political ends might serve temporarily to help executives avoid a problem with certain employees or to accomplish some specific purpose. However, such intentional manipulation may eventually come back to haunt the perpetrating executive and, ultimately, the organization as a whole. This is especially likely if the company comes to accept political manipulation of appraisals as part of the norm.

The Organization as a Whole

1. The appraisal process should operate in a supportive organizational culture. Effective appraisal systems are characterized by the support of top managers (who conduct appraisals themselves), training, open discussions of the appraisal process on an annual basis (perhaps a quality circle approach to appraisals), and rewarding the efforts of managers who do top-notch appraisals.

2. Systematic, regular, and formal appraisals should start at the top of the organization. We found that top executives want formal appraisals and rarely get them. If appraisals are not done at the top, the message sent to the rest of the organization is, "They aren't very important and thus shouldn't be taken seriously." As a result, the door to more political activity is opened wider.

3. Further, although training on *how* to do effective appraisals is important, managers also need to be trained on *why* they need to be done. Understanding the rationale for appraisals is important in building the perception that the appraisal process is an effective managerial tool and not merely a required bureaucratic procedure.

4. Open discussion of the political aspects of the appraisal process (and their legal ramifications) should be included in appraisal training programs. Although managers made it clear that political manipulation of ratings is commonplace, political issues were *never* openly discussed in either training programs or in management development efforts.

5. When money is tied to the rating process, politically oriented ratings tend to increase. This creates a dilemma: A "pay for performance" management philosophy depends on the "objective" measurement of performance. Yet the realities of politics in the measurement process often mean that measurement will not be objective. Should we therefore divorce appraisal ratings from salary decisions? We think not. Pay for performance is still a good concept in our view, even in light of our findings. Attention to the

recommendations we present in this section should minimize the impact of manipulative politics in appraisal ratings.

6. In addition, the number of people who have access to the written appraisal should be minimized. The more people who have access to the appraisal, the greater the temptation for the rater to "impression manage" it. Remember, the fact that the appraisal is written down often means that it is less than completely accurate, simply because it is publicly available.

7. The findings of this study have legal implications as well. Organizations are more susceptible to litigation involving charges of unlawful discharge or discrimination than ever before. Accurate, valid appraisals can help an organization defend itself; inaccurate, invalid appraisals can put the organization at risk. Of course, the relatively recent practice of extensive documentation of poor performance has been in part a response to the modern legal climate. Paradoxically, that climate has arguably *increased* the role of politics in formal appraisal, as organizations try to maintain legal grounds for termination decisions. Still, the often politically motivated practice of building a case for dismissal via documentation of poor performance has come under closer scrutiny as trends in employee appraisal are given closer examination. The best advice here is to stress honesty in appraisal as a "default option" policy. Credible and consistent appraisal practices are the best defense against litigation. Thus some counseling in the legal ramifications of appraisal should become part of executive training.

Conclusion

Perhaps the most interesting finding from our study (because it debunks a popular mythology) is that accuracy is *not* the primary concern of the practicing executive in appraising subordinates. The main concern is how best to use the appraisal process to motivate and reward subordinates. Hence, managerial discretion and effectiveness, not accuracy, are the real watchwords. Managers made it clear that they would not allow excessively accurate ratings to cause problems for themselves, and that they attempted to use the appraisal process to their own advantage.

The astute manager recognizes that politics in employee appraisal will never be entirely squelched. More candidly, most of us also recognize that there is some place for politics in the appraisal process to facilitate necessary executive discretion. The goal, then, is not to arbitrarily and ruthlessly try to eliminate politics but, instead, to effectively manage the role politics plays in employee appraisal.

Endnotes

1. For an extensive discussion of this point, see F. J. Landy and J. L. Farr's "Performance Rating," *Psychological Bulletin,* 1980, *87,* 72–107. This issue is further developed in Landy and Farr's book, *The Measurement of Work Performance,* New York: Academic Press, 1983. It is clear that the psychometric aspects of the appraisal process are only one part of understanding and improving appraisals.

2. DeNisi, Cafferty, and Meglino have recently discussed the key issues and complications associated with understanding the psychology of managerial decision making in the appraisal process in their recent article, "A Cognitive View of the Performance Appraisal Process: A Model and Research Prospective," *Organizational Behavior and Human Performance,* 1984, *33,* 360–396. For a discussion of further cognitive complications in the appraisal process as a result of unconscious information processing, refer to D. A. Gioia and P. P. Poole, "Scripts in Organizational Behavior," *Academy of Management Review,* 1984, *9,* 449–459.

3. For an exploration of some of the emotional and affective factors that might bear on appraisal processes, see O. S. Park, H. Sims, Jr., and S. J. Motowidlo's "Affect in Organizations: How Feelings and Emotions Influence Managerial Judgment," in H. P. Sims and D. A. Gioia and Associates (Eds.), *The Thinking Organization.*

4. Jack Feldman suggests in his article, "Beyond Attribution Theory: Cognitive Processes in Performance Evaluation," *Journal of Applied Psychology,* 1981, *66,* 127–148, that raters have certain cognitive flaws in information processing that make complete objectivity and validity in rating unobtainable. Also see W. C. Borman's "Exploring the Upper Limits of Reliability and Validity in Performance Ratings," *Journal of Applied Psychology,* 1978, *63,* 135–144.

5. Jeffrey Pfeffer, in his book *Power in Organizations,* Marshfield, MA: Pittman Publishing Co., 1981, makes a strong case that political gamesmanship and the use of power in organizations surround almost every important decision in organizational life. The implications of the appraisal process (e.g., pay raises, promotions, terminations) make the appraisal of performance an important decision-making enterprise.

6. Bernardin and Beatty, in their book *Performance Appraisal: Assessing Human Behavior at Work,* Boston, MA: Kent, 1984, suggest that extraneous variables that are not performance related have an effect on the rater's decision processes and that this influence is in fact a primary source of bias and inaccuracy in performance ratings.

7. For an in-depth treatment of the legal issues concerning performance appraisal, see P. S. Greenlaw and J. P. Kohl's *Personnel Management,* New York: Harper & Row, 1986, 171–173. See also W. F. Cascio and H. J. Bernardin's "Implications of Performance Litigation for Personnel Decisions," *Personnel Psychology,* Summer 1981, 217.

When Workers Rate the Boss

Robert McGarvey and Scott Smith

After six straight box-office flops, movie mogul Samuel Goldwyn knew he had a problem, but he didn't know where. So he decided to ask those who should know: his underlings. "I want you to tell me what's wrong with me and MGM," he ordered, "even if it means losing your job."

A half-century later, business leaders still find upward feedback discomfiting. But nowadays the trend is to encourage subordinates to speak up *and* to make the process safe for them. Upward feedback—essentially the appraisal of the boss by the employees—increasingly is recognized as information that can save companies from failures and boost bottom lines. That's why organizations as diverse as Federal Express and insurance giant John Hancock are taking pains to impress upon their managers that bad news needs to be heard.

"More and more organizations are recognizing that subordinates are in *the* best position to tell how their manager is doing," says Bob Abramms, a senior associate with ODT Inc., an Amherst, MA, consulting firm. "Why aren't employees getting the job done right? Often it's because the boss gets in their way. Upward evaluations [provide] the remedy."

"There is nothing as powerful as finding out what people think of you," adds Maxine Dalton, a manager in leadership resources at the Center for Creative Leadership (CCL) in Greensboro, NC. "Few of us really know how we are perceived unless we ask."

That's much easier to say than to do, particularly for high-ranking managers. "The higher up an organization's ladder, the more the incumbent usually is insulated from meaningful feedback," says Abramms.

The reason is simple. It's risky to spill the beans to any boss, a danger made vivid by Sam Goldwyn's quip. Accordingly, while most experts urge organizations to pursue the benefits of upward-feedback programs, they also raise a number of urgent caveats against casual stabs at gathering this kind of information. "The *wrong* way to go about this is for the boss to sit down with an employee and say, 'OK, now level with me about what you don't like about me,' " says Abramms. "The employee who answers honestly is out of his mind."

Another mistake is to confuse a solid upward-feedback program with "training managers to listen and sending them back for informal feedback," says Brian Davis, senior vice president at Personnel Decisions Inc. in Minneapolis. "That's a step, but it lacks the organized discipline necessary for getting the real benefits that can be had."

What's the right way to go about this delicate work? "It has to be an instrumented, facilitated process in order for managers and subordinates to get out of it what each wants, with the least amount of unnecessary pain," says Mike Glenn, training officer and branch head of employee development at NASA's Langley Research Center in Hampton, VA.

In practice, as Davis points out, that counsel translates into a prescription to buy an off-the-shelf upward-appraisal instrument or to develop an in-house version of one. Either way, however, the instrument itself must not be seen as an end-all. "The process must be carefully monitored to ensure it's implemented properly," says Davis. "Improperly administered, it can leave subordinates open to reprisals."

That is, of course, the chief worry employees will have about any upward-feedback scheme. Confidentiality is a staple ingredient in successful programs. But matters get tricky. For instance? "You need at least four people to make the feedback reasonably anonymous," says Dianne LaMountain, an ODT senior associate. "Managers with fewer than four reports generally ought to be excluded from the program—that's a basic safeguard."

Although the concern is common, actual reprisals against employees are rare, LaMountain says. "You hear human resources people worry about revenge for negative scores, but we haven't seen anything like that happen."

Even when confidentiality is built into the system, don't expect employees to take your word for it, at least not initially. Only longer-term experience with the program will provide people with the reassurance they need to be genuinely candid, says Davis. "As the process is repeated, people will become more comfortable and more honest," he says.

Fear of Frying

Employees aren't alone in fretting about upward-appraisal programs. Managerial worries are rampant. "About one-third of managers welcome upward appraisals and already encourage feedback from subordinates," estimates ODT's Abramms. "Another third will go along with whatever the organization dictates and, as they see results, many will become enthusiastic. The last third see this as intrusive and really want nothing to do with it."

Managerial fears aren't necessarily groundless. For instance, a recent national survey by St. Paul Fire & Marine Insurance Co. found one-third of U.S. workers unhappy or neutral about their supervisors. Then, too, employees may not understand or sympathize with the full range of pressures a manager operates under. If *his* marching orders from on high are to whip troops into shape, there's little chance his suffering subordinates will praise his performance to the skies. Or it may work the other way, cautions LaMountain. "Let's say your manager lets you express your ideas and helps get them implemented. You may forgive him or her a lot of other faults."

That's not the only hitch. Downward and upward evaluations alike are frequently marred by the same malady, "recency." LaMountain elaborates: "If you and the manager have been getting along well or badly for the last two months, the appraisal may tend to be biased by that rather than reflecting the whole prior year, as it's supposed to. It's not easy—it may be impossible—to fairly cover the entire reporting period without having done extensive preparatory work along the way."

Such as? Just as managers are encouraged to keep notes on employees' performance throughout the reporting period, says LaMountain, so should employees begin tucking away observations on their bosses' performance. "That's the only antidote for recency," she insists. Furthermore, she adds, employees need "meaningful training on objective behavioral criteria and to be taught the difference between offering their vague feeling about a manager and reporting concrete incidents." If Joe feels his boss doesn't respect him, that may be interesting, but it hardly carries the same weight as Joe's reporting a half-dozen concrete instances where the boss put him down. We don't expect managers to be able to do useful performance evaluations without some training, LaMountain points out, so why expect it of the rank and file?

Proponents of upward-appraisal programs insist that the expense of any such training effort is well warranted. "Employees see the manager on good days and bad, and their views are probably more valid than feedback from his or her boss," says H. John Bernardin, management professor at Florida Atlantic University in Boca Raton. Given at least some instruction, he says, employees should be able to deliver a fair evaluation, the biases of any one individual being balanced out by others in the group.

However, warns LaMountain, that does not necessarily mean that managers' pay or promotions should be linked to an upward-appraisal system right out of the box. Better to start by making the first few cycles of upward evaluations strictly developmental, to help managers see their weaknesses and work on them. "Experience and the comfort that comes with it are essential to making a program really work," LaMountain says.

Beyond that, the surest place to start the process is at the top. Hesitant managers will be won over to the process once *their* bosses have set the right example, says Henry Fontela, manager of human resources for a General Electric facility in Salem, VA. "Once they see how positive the results can be, they are likely to be willing to go ahead."

Henry Rosenbluth knows about that. As CEO of Rosenbluth Travel in Philadelphia, he once concluded a review of a vice president's performance by impulsively turning the tables and asking for a candid appraisal of his own leadership. After some prodding, the vice president opened up—and surprised Rosenbluth by saying he didn't feel the CEO listened well, a failing Rosenbluth promptly determined to remedy by attending a seminar on effective listening. In the aftermath, he emerged a committed convert to upward evaluations. These days, he insists on two written appraisals and one face-to-face interview from his direct reports each year. And he reads the appraisals aloud so his subordinates can hold him accountable for following through on any promises he makes.

"When your boss has the courage to do that, it's hard *not* to be open to the process," comments Rosenbluth's director of new ventures, Diane McFerrin-Peters. She adds that many companies jettison an open culture when coping with high-velocity growth like Rosenbluth's—from $20 million in revenues 14 years ago to $1.5 billion today. But the firm considers its openness to upward influence one of the keys to its success, according to McFerrin-Peters (coauthor with Rosenbluth of *The Customer Comes Second*). "The more involved employees become—and upward appraisals are a key involvement tool— the more customers can be served. We've seen it work."

Comparison Anxiety

A major source of concern for some about to be appraised is the prospect of comparison with others. Most people don't like being ranked against peers, and managers are no different. Off-the-shelf upward-appraisal instruments take this human tendency into account. For instance, ODT's instrument, called Prime Search, by design is "situational," not "normative." Its findings are meant to be compared only with that manager's own future appraisals, not with anyone else's, thus sidestepping the difficulties inherent in comparing a manager of 100 production-line workers with the manager of six nuclear physicists.

But Dalton of the Center for Creative Leadership, which uses norms in its upward-evaluation instruments, maintains that comparisons are helpful as long as precautions are taken. Such as? CCL describes for managers the group they are being compared with and also tries to make its database as diverse as possible, Dalton says. "Our [appraisal] results in a snapshot of where a manager stands with respect to the real world."

CCL's basic Skillscope and more intensive Benchmarks surveys are not just views from the bottom up, however. The person being rated also fills out the survey and is evaluated by peers and higher management, affording what CCL terms a 360-degree examination. The same approach is used by Personnel Decisions' Profiler, another normative instrument. Both firms try to erase the biggest managerial worry by insisting that the results of their instruments not be used for pay or promotion decisions; the information belongs only to the person being rated.

Shock Treatment

How do bosses react to their initial pass through an upward-appraisal program? "A lot of managers go into shock when they first read their results," notes Marty Fried, a Dallas-based program manager in executive education at GTE, the telecommunications company that has been a leader in the upward-feedback movement since the mid-1980s. "There is a lot of denial. One executive insisted the computer must have made a mistake. You have to proceed very delicately."

"We call it the SARAH reaction: Shock, Anger, Rejection, Acceptance, Help," says Bill Clover, director of the management learning center for Amoco in Downers Grove, IL. "Those are the stages people will move through, at first denying the feedback, then seeing it as useful."

According to Steve Jacobus, career development manager at Dun & Bradstreet in Murray Hill, NJ, executives, in particular, are prone to deny any findings they don't want to hear, often by dismissing the judgment of their subordinate evaluators: " 'They don't understand the real world,' or 'Those are just their perceptions,' " are common reactions to criticism, Jacobus says. "No matter how in tune with employees executives think they are, they are always surprised when they get their appraisals."

Managers *can* take the bad news, however. "Anyone can handle criticism as long as he or she has a core of basic competencies, strong points to build on," says ODT's Abramms. One key to a program's success, he adds, is providing managers with interpretations of results, not just raw feedback. "Constructive, frank, goal-specific conversations have to follow the survey, whether with the outside consultant or someone from in-house human resources."

Which to use? Outside consultants offer greater emotional distance, which may help employees open up and provide more honest answers. In addition, consultants presumably can draw on a wealth of knowledge and experience in presenting the feedback, along with suggestions on how to make changes. On the other hand, an outsider will not fully understand a client company's culture, and in fact may be limited to his own consulting firm's model of how the universe is supposed to work. "There is no one right answer," says LaMountain. "Much depends on the company, its internal resources and its hopes for the program."

The consultant or in-house trainer who administers the appraisals will also provide specific suggestions about how to apply the lessons of the feedback. "We stress that it is all about learnable skills, and our reports focus on what can be done to develop those," says CCL's Dalton. Adds Clover: "Some feedback reports are overwhelming, and you need to make them easier to take by giving the managers specific, concrete ideas for improvement."

Managers should not get fixated on their numbers, in any event, says GTE's Fried. "If they do, they will miss the point of the process, which is to open up communication."

NASA's Glenn agrees: "Upward appraisals are unfreezing instruments to get constructive discussions going between supervisors and employees. They are not meant to pronounce final judgments."

Picking Products

Months could be spent comparing the couple of dozen off-the-shelf instruments available for gathering upward feedback, says ODT's Abramms, though he claims that only about a third of them are really any good (that is, only one in three has sufficient validity, reliability and support to be an effective tool). Overlaps of questions are to be expected, and reading one after another can be mind-numbing. Typical themes:

- Does the supervisor distribute resources fairly?
- Are problems anticipated?
- Is input in decision making encouraged?
- Are instructions given clearly?
- Is the rater allowed the right amount of self-management?
- Is substandard work in the group confronted right away?
- Is the supervisor emotionally volatile?
- Is pressure handled well?
- Are mistakes readily admitted?

• Are sensible priorities set?

• Does the manager attract and hold talent?

While many upward-appraisal instruments ask the same sorts of questions, there are significant differences among them, beginning with their length. One off-the-shelf upward-appraisal tool from Pratt & Whitney contains 19 questions; another, William Steinberg Consultants' Managerial Self-Assessment Tool software, asks 500. ODT's Prime Search instrument has 50 questions. Personnel Decisions' Profiler has 135. CCL's Benchmarks and Skillscope surveys ask 156 and 98 questions, respectively. Stylus, an instrument from Human Synergistics of Plymouth, MI, asks 240.

"Superficially, the products may seem much alike, but when you get into a deeper examination, they are seen to be very different," says NASA's Glenn. Some have been researched more thoroughly than others. Some providers offer more extensive feedback and reports based on the survey findings. And not all instruments go after the same kinds of information about the boss.

Depending on order volume, the cost per individual rated can run from $100 to $300 (plus any fees to train company personnel to administer the surveys). These charges can be brought down through licensing where company size and frequency of surveying warrant.

Encore!

Like annual employee evaluations, upward appraisals aren't something to be endured once, then shelved. How often to do them?

NASA's Glenn thinks every two years is about right for putting an executive through the process. ODT's Abramms offers more situational counsel: "If your work group or task assignments change significantly, it's time for a reevaluation, but only after a few months with the new group or tasks. A manager needs time to settle into the job—and his reports need time to settle in with him—before the process can have validity."

But there are some cases in which an organization should do nothing at all. "Don't jump-start a process where you raise expectations if there is no intention of acting on them," cautions LaMountain of ODT. Better to have employees think their boss is indifferent than to have them feel betrayed. "Employees ought to know the process will result in at least some of their major itches getting scratched," adds Abramms. "If that's not in the cards, don't raise hopes by soliciting their feedback."

A broader warning from Personnel Decisions' Davis: "Organizations being downsized or any place with minimal communication up and down should not bother, because trying to do this will just feed paranoia."

Still, upward appraisals are expected to gain popularity as the '90s progress. Today, only about 10 percent of *Fortune* 1000 companies conduct full-blown upward-appraisal programs, by Bernardin's estimate, but he predicts the number will grow dramatically. "The trend is clear—and gaining strength."

"Upward appraisals can make the difference in getting to and staying at the cutting edge," adds NASA's Glenn. "That's why it's catching on at more and more organizations."

What Is Effective Performance Feedback?

Donald B. Fedor and Charles K. Parsons

Managers are more fully realizing that the way employees are managed is a critical component for achieving organizational effectiveness. One extremely important dimension of management is finding ways to influence employees' job-related attitudes, behaviors, and outcomes. Although managers have many methods at their disposal for directing and assisting employees, such as administering rewards and punishments or providing training and resources, one of the best tools can be the judicious application of performance-related feedback. This article explores the many facets of feedback and discusses the benefits and some of the possible pitfalls associated with its use.

Positive Attributes of Feedback

Feedback is usually discussed in favorable terms. Employees often use information about their performance to correct inappropriate behaviors. Besides having positive effects on performance, feedback can increase job satisfaction and alleviate stress arising from feelings of uncertainty. In the longer term, feedback helps employees establish a realistic idea of what is expected of them and how well they are meeting these expectations. Considering all its possible benefits, feedback is relatively inexpensive to administer, can be given immediately and frequently, and is not a scarce resource that must be rationed. With all of these positive qualities attributed to feedback, it is surprising that supervisors are often reluctant to give it, with the result that employees often feel "in the dark" about what and how they are doing.

The answer to this dilemma lies in the fact that feedback is a complex phenomenon and not simply a resource whose value can be measured objectively, like the value of raw materials or capital. Instead, the value of feedback is created in the context of interaction between the source of feedback (i.e., the supervisor) and the feedback recipient (i.e., the employee). An example will illustrate this statement: An employee is working in his office when the supervisor stops by for a short chat. The supervisor mentions that the employee did a very good job on a recent assignment. The two then talk about the project briefly, and the supervisor leaves to attend to other business. Although the employee has just received feedback about a particular aspect of his performance, it is not clear what the feedback really means and whether its effects will be positive or negative. As is often the case, the answer is—"It depends." Let us explore some of the factors that influence the effects of feedback.

Complexity of Feedback

Feedback is not simply a *resource* (i.e., some piece of objective information with some value) given by the supervisor to the employee. It is an *event* that occurs between the two parties in the context of their relationship, the employee's perception of his or her own performance, other recent feedback events, and the broader organizational environment. Feedback can be viewed by the recipient as information and/or reward or punishment.

Let us begin by assembling the easier parts of this puzzle. Research has indicated that certain aspects of feedback can greatly affect its impact. First, whether the feedback is positive or negative is a key issue. It may not come as a great surprise that employees tend to respond more favorably to positive feedback, perceive it to be a more accurate reflection of their performance, remember it better, and find it preferable to negative feedback. Second, the specificity of the feedback makes a real difference. For instance, telling someone that he or she is a poor worker is quite different from explaining that the person failed to complete two of the last three assignments or that the rejection rate for his or her product has been running 12 percent above the standard set for the department. Very general feedback does not supply much useful information. The more specific the feedback is in relation to goals, standards, or actual outcomes, the less recipients will tend to take the feedback as statements about them, and the more it will be received as useful performance-related input.

Third, the timing and frequency of feedback also have an impact on its effectiveness. For example, if a supervisor lets 2 weeks pass before evaluating an employee's performance on a particular project, some of the impact will be lost. The employee will then try to remember all the pertinent details. For jobs that continue to change, this memory exercise can be difficult. If the employee did not perform well, the time lag may unfairly obstruct efforts to improve as his or her attention has shifted to other tasks.

The appropriate frequency for feedback is a more difficult issue to address because feedback has something of a dual personality. On one hand, feedback contains useful information. On the other hand, feedback can represent a form of control. To see how this works, put yourself in the place of an employee who has just been given a new assignment. Your supervisor first shows you how to do the task and then stops by frequently to point out any mistakes you are making. Within a couple of days you begin to feel comfortable with what you are expected to do and how to do it. But how would you feel if your supervisor continued to come around and tell you how your performance could be improved? If you are like most people, the initial feedback would be welcomed, especially if the new assignment were relatively challenging. However, after a while the value of the information would decrease, while the perception of superfluous criticism and intrusion (i.e., exertion of unnecessary control) would increase. The proper frequency of feedback really depends on how much information the employee desires (this will be different for different individuals), how often a product is completed or a service provided, and the point at which evaluation or adjustment is appropriate or necessary.

To summarize, the positive or negative nature of feedback will have the greatest impact on the recipient's response to it: People respond much more favorably to positive feedback. In addition, feedback will be most useful if it is specific and provided relatively soon after the behavior or performance. Finally, feedback should be frequent enough to supply relevant information without exerting undue control over the recipient.

Sources of Feedback

Although our discussion has focused so far on the supervisor as the source of feedback, there are many alternative sources. These include the employee's co-workers; clients or customers; representatives of the organization (e.g., the personnel department); the job itself; and even the employee him- or herself.

Some feedback sources have direct contact with the recipient, and no one else is needed to pass along the performance information. This feedback is called *unmediated* feedback; it is not channeled through any source that could interpret or evaluate it. In other words, unmediated feedback is received directly—from the job, from oneself, or from a customer or client.

In contrast, feedback about job performance received from other sources, such as the supervisor or co-workers, is considered *mediated* feedback. For example, a customer complaining directly to an employee about a problem (i.e., unmediated feedback), and the supervisor passing along a complaint from a customer, can be two quite different situations. The supervisor may over- or understate the gravity of the problem. The employee must try to determine from the supervisor's feedback what will satisfy the customer and worry about how the customer's complaint will affect the supervisor's evaluation of the employee (i.e., feel apprehension about being blamed).

Before we look at the differences between unmediated and mediated feedback and consider why they might have different effects on an employee, we should note that these forms of feedback are not as independent as they might appear. For instance, a supervisor may decide to have the employee chart his or her own progress on a project or to allow direct contact between employee and customer. In this way the supervisor is influencing what information the employee uses from an unmediated source and thus may be able to affect the results without having direct involvement in the feedback process.

Now we need to address the question of how feedback sources differ. The key element that differentiates potential sources and determines their impact on the employee is the degree of credibility. The recipient's perception of the credibility of the source is influenced by a number of factors. The first is the source's perceived level of expertise—in other words, how much the source knows about the issue. The second factor relates more to historical judgment and concerns how reliable the feedback has been in the past. The third factor is the extent to which the recipient is attracted to the source. (This aspect of credibility is very important in advertising: To realize how it works, one need only turn on the television to see a famous sports figure selling a product.) The final factor is belief about the source's intentions toward the recipient. The recipient may ask, "Why is this person giving me this information? Is it to provide me with useful information and support my efforts or simply to put me in my place?" The recipient's estimate of the source's credi-

bility is based on these four factors; the judgment of credibility, in turn, conditions the recipient's acceptance of the feedback. This is especially true when the feedback is negative. If negative feedback comes from a highly credible source, people tend to accept it more easily.

As a general rule, the greater the distance between the recipient and the source of feedback, the less credible that source appears. In other words, one's co-workers would seem more credible than the personnel department as a source of feedback. Moreover, sources of unmediated feedback, such as the job or oneself, tend to be perceived as more credible than sources of mediated feedback. Therefore, falling behind on one's job is an indisputable signal that something is wrong because the job cannot have malicious intent and its expertise and reliability are not at issue.

In reading this you may have noticed a problem that organizations face in providing performance feedback. The agent usually responsible for this task is often viewed as having less credibility than the job, the employee him- or herself, and the employee's co-workers. As a result the organization relies on a source with only moderate credibility to influence behavior. For this reason a supervisor might be more effective by influencing the sources of unmediated feedback, such as specific, organizationally important aspects of the job, rather than by providing the feedback directly. An organization can use this method of providing feedback to improve the quality of employee work life and to give employees more involvement in decision making.

Recipient Responses

So far this discussion of feedback has focused mainly on the factors that influence recipients' responses. To complete the picture, we need to turn our attention again to the feedback source. Supervisors (as one specific source) are often reluctant to give employees feedback. If they do so, what kind of feedback will it be? For instance, a supervisor is considering telling a long-term, usually dependable employee that her current work is not up to the department standard. (This is not unlike the dilemma one faces when considering whether to give a friend feedback about a sensitive issue.) Ordinarily it would be the supervisor's duty to supply this information and, presumably, to attempt to improve the employee's productivity. Talking to this employee seems the perfectly logical thing to do until we examine the supervisor's perception of how the recipient will feel and respond. In other words, what does the source believe are the likely outcomes of the feedback event?

In the case of negative feedback from a supervisor, expected employee responses can range from constructive (i.e., taking steps to correct the problem) to nonconstructive. In the latter case an employee can be hurt emotionally, place some or all of the blame on the supervisor, withhold future cooperation, complain to others such as co-workers or personnel representatives, or perhaps even charge harassment and file a formal grievance. Unfortunately, criticism of employee performance in the form of negative feedback may render the supervisor vulnerable to counterattack or may negatively affect the supervisor's relationship with the employee or the entire work group.

Some feedback sources are equally concerned about potential harmful effects of positive feedback. In helping to install a performance appraisal system in a manufacturing facility, one of the authors of this article worked with supervisors who believed that praise would lessen the employees' motivation to perform well. Given this belief, they were reluctant to use positive feedback to influence employee performance. At the same time, they did not like dealing with the anger and other repercussions that could result from negative feedback. Essentially, their philosophy was to "let sleeping dogs lie" and use feedback only on occasions, such as the required annual performance appraisal, when it was absolutely necessary.

Another problem facing the giver of feedback is uncertainty concerning the recipient's possible response. Responses to feedback, as noted earlier, are based only partially on what the source does and says. Even good news can generate a negative reaction when it is not "good enough." Given the possibility of undesirable or unexpected reactions and responses, it is not difficult to understand why supervisors in particular might find it easier to withhold feedback than to offer it.

Using recipients' past responses and his or her own beliefs and expectations about the feedback's probable impact, a source may develop a certain feedback style, which will affect the recipient's interpretation of the feedback. For example, if a supervisor rarely provides feedback and then suddenly begins to lavish praise on the employees, initially they will wonder what the feedback really means because the supervisor's behavior appears out of character. Instead of focusing on the content, they may instead look for reasons behind the change in behavior. If there is an explanation for the supervisor's new style, such as a recent mandate for more feedback, then the employees may dismiss it as irrelevant to their own performance.

Feedback Seeking

A final, commonly overlooked aspect of the feedback process is the situation in which the recipient actively seeks feedback from the source. In such a case the employee may solicit the supervisor's impressions of a project or some other work activity. Where close supervision doesn't exist (e.g., work frequently performed in isolation) or where management has implicitly adopted the "let sleeping dogs lie" approach to feedback, an employee may only receive feedback that he or she actively seeks. While generally viewed as a positive employee attribute, feedback-seeking behavior (FSB, as it is called) raises another set of issues for the source.

Research has shown that FSB can occur for a number of reasons. The first and most obvious reason is that the employee is honestly looking for information in hopes of correcting or refining job performance. The value of this behavior is that the employee can select a credible source and perhaps catch small errors before they become large ones. For example, suppose that a bank employee is somewhat unsure about the bank's policy concerning account overdrafts from major business customers. After issuing such a customer a form letter about an overdraft, the employee may have second thoughts and ask the supervisor about the wisdom of the move. The supervisor, suspecting that the letter might insult the customer, may instruct the employee to telephone the customer immediately and handle the situation in a more personal manner.

Another reason that an employee might seek feedback is that he or she anticipates a positive reaction from the source and desires a "pat on the back" for motivational reasons. Suppose that an employee has put in extraordinary effort to finish a report. Upon completing it, the employee is drained but brings it to the supervisor, fully expecting the glowing remarks that are received. The positive feedback can be uplifting and perhaps provide a boost for future efforts.

Finally, an employee may seek feedback for impression management reasons. That is, the person may ask for either positive or negative feedback in hopes of earning credit for successful endeavors and avoiding blame for failures. Negative feedback may be solicited if the employee expects that the supervisor will eventually lose patience with lackluster performance and provide severe negative feedback. This short-circuiting of the negative feedback process may lead to a less severe reaction from the supervisor.

Whatever the reasons for seeking feedback, we notice that some employees are more likely than others to seek feedback actively. Though research in this area is still in the early stages, we believe that feedback sources should be aware both of the value of feedback seeking on the part of recipients and of its possible biasing effects on their evalua-

tions of these individuals (as a result of impression management).

Implications

The intent of this paper is not to discourage organizations or managers from using feedback, which is an extremely important management tool. Instead, the point is that they must use feedback wisely to reap the possible benefits. A supervisor can give feedback that has all the right qualities (i.e., it is constructive, specific, and immediate) and not realize the desired effects.

The feedback process is complex: The recipient interprets the feedback and combines it with other information. It may be discounted because of contextual factors (e.g., organizational rumors pertaining to the reason the feedback is given) or because it is discrepant with information from other sources. Therefore, simply giving feedback may not be enough. The source may have to explore with the recipient the latter's perceptions of the intentions behind the feedback and how it fits with other performance information. Some of the most effective feedback directs the recipient to other sources, such as important characteristics of the job. Performance feedback that one generates for oneself (i.e., unmediated feedback) will be more credible than feedback that is mediated through other sources. Moreover, we cannot forget that sources may hesitate to give feedback when they anticipate negative responses. Supervisors can be helped to understand that there are sources other than themselves for feedback on employee performance.

The implication for management training is that there is no simple formula for effective employee feedback. Merely instructing managers to give specific and timely feedback is not always adequate. Managers must learn to analyze feedback environments, determine the credibility of different feedback sources available to employees, and check employees' perceptions of the feedback. Only then can managers make good decisions about how to intervene in the feedback process.

Selected Bibliography

Ashford, S. J., & Cummings, L. L. (1983). Feedback as an individual resource: Personal strategies of creating information. *Organizational Behavior and Human Performance, 32,* 370–398.

Fedor, D. B. (1991). Recipient responses to performance feedback: A proposed model and its implications. In G. R. Ferris & K. M. Rowland (Eds.), *Research in personnel and human resources management* (pp. 73–120). Greenwich, CT: JAI Press.

Herold, D., & Greller, M. M. (1978). The definition of a construct. *Academy of Management Journal, 20,* 142–147.

Ilgen, D. R., Fisher, C. D., & Taylor, M. S. (1979). Consequences of individual feedback on behavior in organizations. *Journal of Applied Psychology, 64,* 349–371.

Jablin, F. M. (1979). Supervisor-subordinate communication: The state of the art. *Psychological Bulletin, 86,* 1201–1222.

Larson, J. R. (1984). The performance feedback process: A preliminary model. *Organizational Behavior and Human Performance, 33,* 42–76.

Larson, J. R. (1989). The dynamic interplay between employees' feedback-seeking strategies and supervisors' delivery of performance feedback. *Academy of Management Review, 14,* 408–422.

Taylor, M. S., Fisher, C. D., & Ilgen, D. R. (1984). Individuals' reactions to performance feedback in organizations: A control theory perspective. In K. M. Rowland & G. R. Ferris (Eds.), *Research in personnel and human resources management* (pp. 81–124). Greenwich, CT: JAI Press.

Legal Requirements and Technical Guidelines Involved in Implementing Performance Appraisal Systems

James T. Austin, Peter Villanova, and Hugh D. Hindman

Introduction

Performance appraisal (PA) involves evaluating how well individuals perform the activities and duties and otherwise fulfill the requirements of the positions they occupy. Unlike job analysis, which involves an impersonal description of the activities constituting a job, or job evaluation, which involves determining the relative worth of a job to arrive at appropriate compensation for the work done, PA focuses on an *individual's* record of accomplishment or success. Also, PA is an ongoing *process* that is repeated at least annually (Bernardin & Villanova, 1986; Bretz, Milkovich, & Read, 1992). When viewed from a systems perspective, PA is perhaps the most central HR (human resources) function in that PA data affect numerous decisions impacting on other HR system components. As shown in Figure 1, valid PA data are essential for (1) developing valid personnel selection procedures, (2) diagnosing training needs, (3) evaluating training effectiveness, (4) identifying candidates for promotion to other positions, (5) evaluating the effectiveness of a work design intervention, (6) distributing merit awards appropriately, and (7) making performance-driven reduction-in-force decisions.

Performance measurement systems in organizations vary on the extent to which judgment is required of appraisers. This variation forms a subjective-objective continuum along which different appraisal techniques fall, ranging from "products" to observer ratings. One option regarding extent of judgment is the use of relatively low-judgment performance criteria—for example, production records or managerial budget performance. Unfortunately, such criterion measures are often difficult to develop and, even when they can be developed, are problematic. Specifically, work output is not always attributable to one individual as distinct from others, nor is it always attributable to individual—as opposed to situational—factors. Also, objective criteria may suffer from the same deficiency and contamination problems that bias subjective ratings (Landy & Farr, 1983). A deficiency problem occurs when elements of an ultimate criterion are not included in the actual criterion; contamination occurs when irrelevant elements are included in the actual measure. Finally, judgment is involved in even the most objective criterion measures. For example, in the classification of absences or determination of what is "scrap," subjective evaluations are used extensively. Thus, illegal bias may still occur with low-judgment measures.

Although subjective performance appraisal instruments (e.g., rating scales) appear easier to develop and use than objective criteria, they can result in illegal bias against members of protected groups. Courts have long recognized that poorly designed and implemented appraisal systems "are a ready mechanism for discrimination against Blacks, much of which can be covertly concealed and, for that matter, not really known to management" (*Rowe v. General Motors,* 1972). Rating scales constitute the largest portion of operational performance appraisal systems (e.g., Guion, 1965; Landy & Rastegary, 1989; Locher & Teel, 1977), but because of their subjective nature

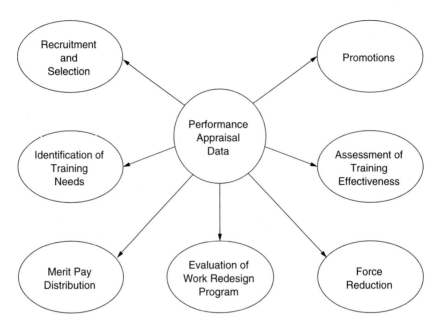

Figure 1.   Performance Appraisal in Relation to Other HR Functions

these scales may permit, conceal, and even fa-cilitate illegal discrimination. Raters may in-flate evaluations of in-group members, reduce the ratings of out-group members, or other-wise deliberately manipulate ratings to satisfy personal political agendas (Longenecker, Sims, & Gioia, 1987; Villanova & Bernardin, 1989, 1991). Unfortunately, PA ratings may be contaminated by effects related to rater and ratee age (Waldman & Avolio, 1986), race (Kraiger & Ford, 1985), and gender (Schmitt & Lappin, 1980).

Justifiably, PA is no trivial issue to employ-ers or employees. PA is essential to decision makers who need performance data to moni-tor organizational effectiveness adequately and to develop or implement policies in re-sponse to organizational performance. These data are particularly critical for the kinds of decisions that have become increasingly com-mon in contemporary organizations. For ex-ample, the catch phrase for the nineties ap-pears to be "organizational downsizing," or making an organization "lean and mean." Es-sentially, this involves reducing organiza-

tional redundancies, particularly with respect to personnel. Many firms use PA data in an effort to retain employees whose performance is superior and terminate more poorly per-forming employees. If the data used are not accurate, the effects of the downsizing on or-ganizational productivity may not be what management intended. Of course, seemingly arbitrary termination decisions have other repercussions, both for terminated employees and for those who remain. For example, em-ployees may perceive such decisions as capri-cious and unfair, lose faith in their employer, and become suspicious of any personnel deci-sion, thereby undermining the effectiveness of future HR programs. And, of specific rele-vance to this article, employees may formally challenge the *legality* of such decisions by fil-ing wrongful discharge or discrimination suits. In light of these potential employee re-sponses, it is not hard to understand why PA garners so much attention from management scholars and practitioners.

In this article we review legal requirements, processes, and technical standards to organize our discussion of PA systems. As the title implies, our discussion will focus on two classes of PA system determinants: (1) the legal environment—case law, executive orders, and legislation—that requires an organization's PA system to maintain specific procedures or content in order to satisfy legal dictum and (2) the professional and technical standards that serve as guides for effective PA system administration and offer some modicum of protection against allegations of illegal discrimination. A third section of the article illustrates the application of these concepts and the continually evolving nature of case law by describing three recent Supreme Court cases with significant implications for dispute resolution processes in Title VII cases. In the final section we provide a summary of prescriptive guidelines to assist in implementing more defensible PA systems based on both technical and legal developments.

The Legal Environment of Organizations

The legal environment within which contemporary organizations operate is a complex one that evolves as social pressure leads to the passage of legislation, decisions concerning the legislation are rendered by the courts, executive agencies interpret and implement those laws and decisions, and managerial responses are enacted (Ledvinka & Scarpello, 1991). Although the legislation itself may seem quite straightforward, its judicial interpretations and their subsequent application complicate matters (Arvey & Faley, 1988; Cascio, 1991; Corley, Reed, & Black, 1984; Miner & Miner, 1979). Both equal employment legislation and litigation have seen expansion over the past 25 years. Employment discrimination based on race, color, sex, religion, or national origin is prohibited by Title VII of the 1964 Civil Rights Act (1964 CRA). Through amendments to Title VII contained in the Civil Rights Act of 1991, Congress attempted to respond to a perceived erosion of the previous legislation brought about by recent Supreme Court decisions. The Age Dis-

crimination in Employment Act (ADEA; 1967, 1978) forbids discrimination against workers above age 40, and the Americans with Disabilities Act (ADA; 1990) protects people with mental and physical disabilities.

As legislation has broadened, the focus of litigation has also expanded because multiple selection decisions that are made affect people throughout their tenure with organizations. Thus, the focus of equal employment litigation has evolved beyond organizational entry decisions to encompass selection decisions made at later stages. Such expansion makes sense within a career and systems perspective on personnel and human resource management, a perspective in which a decision to hire is only the first in a series of personnel decisions (Byham & Spitzer, 1971; Cascio, 1991; Cascio & Awad, 1981).

Legal Requirements:
Legislation and Executive Orders

The five-member Equal Employment Opportunity Commission (EEOC) and its staff is the federal agency that oversees and enforces Title VII, ADEA, and ADA. Title VII and ADA (as of July 1994) apply to any organization that employs more than fifteen employees. ADEA applies to firms with twenty or more employees.

The EEOC has little statutory power to enforce legislation. Rather, it must turn to the courts for relief. When it receives complaints of discrimination, the EEOC uses a three-step procedure of investigation, conciliation, and litigation. Investigation involves gathering information about the complaint. Subsequently the EEOC attempts to resolve the complaint through conciliatory mediation between the complainant and the organization. If conciliation fails, the EEOC is vested with the authority to file suit in federal district court against a private sector employer on behalf of an individual (e.g., *Equal Employment Opportunity Commission v. Sandia,* 1980). Even where the EEOC declines to file suit, individuals can sue on their own after conciliation efforts have failed.

The EEOC also collects and disseminates information on equal employment opportunity through its annual EEO-1 form, which must be completed by most organizations. There are also state laws on fair employment practices, but these vary from state to state. Such laws are also subsumed by the Constitution, which establishes federal law as paramount. Table 1 summarizes the relevant laws regulating employment discrimination.

Presidential executive orders (EO) are a second broad means of combatting discrimination. Executive orders are rules, regulations, policies, or orders issued by the president that relate to the operation of the federal government. Within that sphere they carry the force of law. The most important order dealing with employment discrimination is EO:11246, first issued by President Johnson and reissued by every subsequent president. Although it applies principally to federal contractors and subcontractors, those categories account for a large number of organizations, including almost all large educational institutions, manufacturers of military equipment, and organizations that sell products and/or render services to the federal government. EO:11246 prohibits employment discrimination by federal contractors and, additionally, includes a requirement for affirmative action

(AA). AA goes beyond the notion of nondiscrimination or equal employment opportunity in that it requires employers to take active steps to ensure that underutilized populations—women and minorities—are identified and actively recruited; AA is a social force emphasizing the "righting of past wrongs" against minority groups (Ledvinka, 1982).

President Roosevelt issued the first nondiscrimination order in 1941; EO:8802 prohibited discrimination by defense contractors on the basis of race, creed, color, or national origin but not gender. In 1961 President Kennedy issued the first executive order (EO:10925) that incorporated the term *affirmative action* and thus formed the basis for subsequent orders by President Johnson. President Johnson's EO:11246 was largely similar to EO:10925, with the notable exception that it empowered individual federal agencies to impose sanctions and penalties prior to court action (Gutman, 1993). EO:11246 also established the Office of Federal Contract Compliance Programs (OFCCP) in the Department of Labor as the relevant enforcement agency, but it did not yet address gender-based discrimination. This oversight was remedied by EO:11375. Executive order 11478 (1969) changed the first part of EO:11246 to apply to federal government employment and established the Office of Per-

Table 1

Major Federal Legislation Regulating Employment Discrimination

Law	Date	Relevance
Equal Pay Act	1963	Prohibits sex discrimination in pay practices
Civil Rights Act	1964	Prohibits discriminatory employment practices
Age Discrimination in Employment Act	1967	Extends Title VII protection to workers aged 40 to 70
Equal Employment Opportunity Act	1972	Extends Title VII of 1964 CRA to public and private sector organizations
Rehabilitation Act	1973	Prohibits discrimination against mentally and physically handicapped persons
Americans with Disabilities Act	1990	Prohibits discrimination against people with disabilities and promotes affirmative efforts at "reasonable accomodation"
Civil Rights Act	1991	Restores evidentiary burdens established in *Griggs v. Duke Power Co.* (1971) but also requires plaintiffs to identify specific mechanisms responsible for discrimination

sonnel Management (OPM) as the supervisory agency. In addition, EO:11478 also prohibited discrimination on the basis of age and disability. Because the different federal agencies were inconsistent in their enforcement of EO:11246, President Carter in 1978 issued EO:12086, which recognized the OFCCP as the sole authority for enforcing EO:11246.

Decisions by the Reagan and Bush administrations tended to weaken EO:11246 by reducing staff and funds allocated to the OFCCP, filing amicus curiae (friend of the court) briefs in several reverse discrimination suits that challenged affirmative action programs, and appointing Supreme Court justices who maintain an opposition to affirmative action.

Dispute Resolution

Individuals who consider themselves wronged in a discriminatory manner may elect to use either state or EEOC channels to obtain relief. After exhausting the EEOC's conciliatory procedures, an individual may file suit in either the federal or the state court system. Two higher levels in both federal and state judicial systems are the courts of appeal and the Supreme Courts. The state court system is thus modeled on the federal system.

In an employment discrimination case, the employee is termed the plaintiff and the employer the defendant. Several important legal concepts involved in such cases include (1) *burden of proof* and its shifts between plaintiff and defendant during legal proceedings, (2) *disparate impact* and *disparate treatment* strategies, and (3) *business necessity* and *job relatedness.* We discuss these concepts next.

Burden of proof refers to the evidentiary tasks of plaintiffs (employees) and defendants (organizations). Disparate treatment and disparate (adverse) impact are the two theories the courts use when considering Title VII cases. *Disparate treatment* is the most frequently used theory, as it defines discrimination as the use of personal characteristics (e.g., sex, race), expressly prohibited by law, as a basis for treating people differently in any

personnel action. *McDonnell Douglas Corporation v. Green* (1973) and *Texas Department of Community Affairs v. Burdine* (1981) are the two leading Supreme Court cases that detail what a plaintiff must prove to win a disparate treatment case.

Cases develop in three stages. The first stage requires the plaintiff to establish a prima facie (i.e., possibly rebuttable) case of discrimination by proving four elements: (1) that the plaintiff is a member of a protected group, (2) that the plaintiff was qualified for and interested in the position, (3) that an unfavorable personnel action was taken (e.g., the plaintiff was not hired, was not promoted, or was terminated), and (4) that others with similar qualifications were not treated unfavorably. If these criteria are met, the case moves to the second stage. Here the defendant must produce evidence of a legitimate, nondiscriminatory reason for the personnel action. Note that the defendant's burden is merely to produce evidence and not to prove that the evidence is true; the burden of proof remains at all times with the plaintiff. If the defendant provides a legitimate, nondiscriminatory explanation for the action, then, in the third stage of the case, the plaintiff is given an opportunity to prove that the explanation is false and is merely a pretext or coverup for discriminatory motives.

The evidentiary burden for plaintiffs is more onerous in disparate treatment cases than in disparate impact cases. For example, in a disparate treatment case, the plaintiff must establish that the defendant *intended* to discriminate on the basis of a personal characteristic as proscribed by Title VII. Thus, disparate treatment refers to "motivated" or intentional discrimination, whereas disparate impact involves "unmotivated" or unintentional discrimination. Another major distinction between the two is that the disparate impact theory was conceived to be applicable to "facially neutral" or objective devices only. Furthermore, the plaintiff, in establishing a prima facie case of disparate impact, need not show that the discrimination was intentional.

By contrast, disparate treatment requires the presentation of evidence that intentional discrimination was present, certainly a much heavier burden for the plaintiff.

Disparate impact involves unlawful discriminatory employment practices that unequally impact groups of individuals as a function of sex, race, age, color, religion, or national origin. Such adverse impact on groups of individuals is illegal if the employment practice is not "job related." *Griggs v. Duke Power Co.* (1971) established the evidentiary burdens of plaintiffs and defendants in a disparate impact case. First, the plaintiff must demonstrate that a statistical disparity exists between protected class members (e.g., Blacks, females) and the majority class (white males) with respect to the number of individuals hired for a job versus the number who applied. This demonstration involves a comparison of selection ratios of the two classes. Prima facie evidence for adverse impact is said to exist when the selection ratio (i.e., the number of applicants hired divided by the total number of applicants) of the protected class members is less than 80 percent (four-fifths) of that of the majority class members. Once this evidence is established, the defense has the burden of demonstrating that the selection instrument used (e.g., cognitive ability test, interview) is job related or was adopted because of business necessity. If in fact the selection device is demonstrably job related, then the plaintiff has the burden of showing that less discriminatory, yet equally valid, alternatives for attainment of the employer's goals were available.

Business necessity and job relatedness are the two permissible defenses for the use of a selection device that has adverse impact. The two terms mean different things and are often confused (Hills, 1980). *Business necessity* refers to the right of business organizations to make personnel decisions based on business conditions. For example, *Coburn v. Pan American World Airways* (1982) involved a reduction in force mandated by economic conditions. In the eyes of the courts, such a business decision is best left to the organization because courts are not qualified to judge whether conditions warrant the reduction. However, having decided to make reductions, the organization is obligated to make fair and nondiscriminatory decisions (cf. *Nicholson v. Western Electric Co.,* 1982). *Job relatedness,* on the other hand, refers to whether a decision-making device is related to job performance. Standards for job relatedness in the case of selection tests were stated clearly by the Supreme Court in *Griggs v. Duke Power Co.* (1971) and have been elaborated since that decision.

Basically, establishing job relatedness requires evidence that a person's standing on a selection test has a manifest relationship with job performance. Although the statistical methods of formal validation are equally applicable to objective tests (e.g., intelligence tests) and subjective selection tests (interviews, performance appraisals), formal validation may not be required for a successful defense of informal standards (e.g., arrest records, credit information; Gutman, 1993).

Technical and Professional Standards

In addition to legislation, three sets of professional-technical standards cover all selection devices, in principle including both objective and subjective performance appraisals. Each takes a slightly different perspective. The *Principles for the Validation and Use of Personnel Selection Procedures* (hereafter *Principles;* Society for Industrial and Organizational Psychology, 1987) are guidelines for organizations that best incorporate recent research in personnel psychology. The *Standards for Educational and Psychological Testing* (hereafter *Standards;* American Educational Research Association, American Psychological Association, & National Council on Measurement in Education, 1985), on the other hand, are relevant to the overall development and evaluation of general assessment instruments for applied (educational, mental health, and organizational settings) and basic research purposes. A third set of standards is the *Uniform Guidelines on Employee Selection Procedures* (1978; hereafter *Guidelines*) from the Federal Equal Employment Opportunity Commission, Department of Labor, Department of Justice, and Civil Service Commission. The *Guidelines* and *Standards* were recognized by the courts as influential in several early Supreme Court decisions (e.g., *Griggs v. Duke Power Co.,* 1971; *Albemarle Paper Co. v. Moody,* 1975). Professionals and personnel workers depend heavily on these standards for guidance.

For performance appraisals, which constitute a primary source of data on employees after their entry into an organization, criterion validation would involve correlating appraisals across raters or with independent measures of job performance (e.g., work samples). If appraisal data are used to support promotion decisions, a stronger strategy would involve correlating employees' performance appraisal ratings with their subsequent performance at higher-level positions. Demonstrations of content-oriented scale development might entail showing linkages between behaviors rated in the appraisal device and behaviors judged important for task performance on the basis of job analyses. A construct validation strategy may be called for in specific instances (Austin, Villanova, Kane, & Bernardin, 1991; James, 1973). One way to implement this strategy is to develop and evaluate models of job performance; another is to combine criterion and content validation evidence in a series of studies. In certain situations courts have permitted the results of other studies, expert testimony, and the organization's prior successful experience with the challenged device to establish job relatedness. We do not mean to imply that organizations typically validate their performance appraisal systems; most do not. However, in the future it may be a sound practice to do so for legal defensibility. This practice would be especially valuable if the results of appraisals are used to make personnel decisions—for example, layoffs or terminations necessitated by downsizing.

Recent Supreme Court Decisions and the 1991 Civil Rights Act

As we mentioned earlier, the 1991 Civil Rights Act was passed largely in response to recent Supreme Court decisions that had upset established precedents regarding the evidentiary burdens of plaintiffs and defendants established in *Griggs. Wards Cove Packing Company v. Atonio* (1989) proved to be the watershed Court decision that fueled congressional action to pass legislation offering further protection for employees. Prior to *Atonio, Watson v. Forth Worth Bank & Trust* (1988) and *Price Waterhouse v. Hopkins* (1989) were two Supreme Court decisions directly relevant to performance appraisal that established new precedents for adjudicating cases involving subjective employment practices. In this section we briefly review details of these cases to illustrate the challenges the decisions posed to what had become accepted rules concerning plaintiff and defendant responsibilities in the course of litigation.

Watson v. Fort Worth Bank & Trust (1988)

Clara Watson filed suit in 1981 against her former employer, Fort Worth Bank & Trust Company, alleging that the bank had denied her promotion because of race. Watson joined the bank as a proof operator in 1973. She was promoted to teller trainee 2 years later and advanced to the position of commercial teller in 1980. She filed suit after applying unsuccessfully for four different promotions to supervisory positions between February 1980 and August 1981, when she resigned. Using the disparate impact model, Clara Watson's attorneys argued that blacks were less likely to be hired than whites, were paid less on the average, and progressed more slowly in comparison to whites (Sharf, 1988a).

The Supreme Court agreed to hear the Watson case because there had been conflicting decisions at the appellate court level about the appropriateness of the disparate impact strategy when the alleged discrimination involved subjective practices. Previously the adverse impact strategy, which involves demonstration of statistical disparity in hiring policies, had been applied only to instances where objective practices were at issue. In July of 1988 the Court ruled eight to zero (Justice Kennedy did not participate) that Title VII plaintiffs might use such a strategy to pursue claims of employment discrimination stemming from the use of subjective practices. The Supreme Court decision was influenced by an amicus curiae (friend of the court) brief filed by the American Psychological Association (1988; Bersoff, 1988). This brief contended that the subjective practices used by the bank (e.g., interviews and performance appraisals) could have been validated systematically, just as more objective devices can be validated. In short, the ruling is favorable for plaintiffs who wish to avoid the burden of proving intentional discrimination (Bernardin, 1988; Lee, 1990) that is required with the adverse treatment strategy.

A plurality of four justices, led by Justice O'Connor, utilized the *Watson* decision to lay a foundation for new evidentiary standards in disparate impact cases that are favorable to defendants. Their rationale was that because subjective practices were now open to challenge under the disparate impact strategy, the threat of increased litigation would prompt employers to shield themselves through the use of preferential treatment and quota systems. To avert such a scenario, the plurality sought to make it more difficult for plaintiffs to establish and prevail in disparate impact cases. The new disparate impact model (i.e., a disaggregation requirement to isolate the challenged practice and prove that it is specifically responsible for the differential impact) did not establish a precedent in *Watson,* although it foreshadowed the majority ruling in *Wards Cove* (described later in this section).

Price Waterhouse v. Hopkins (1989)

Ann Hopkins began working for Price Waterhouse in 1978 in the Office of Government Services. After amassing an impressive record of accomplishments, including playing a key role in the procurement of a multimillion-dollar contract with the State Department, she was nominated for partner status in 1982. She had earned more business for the firm than any of the other candidates (eighty-seven males) nominated that year. However, senior partners of the firm raised questions about her interpersonal skills and ability to work with others. In promoting to the partner level, Price Waterhouse uses a system whereby current partners evaluate candidates for partnership using a subjective rating format. Most of the negative comments Hopkins allegedly received came from short-form evaluations (completed by partners who knew her less well), although her supporters acknowledged questions about her abrasiveness with staff members. Nevertheless, many of the comments suggested that she had been evaluated differently than the other candidates on the basis of gender. Several partners suggested that Hopkins act in a more feminine manner by attending charm school, wearing jewelry, and styling her hair. Her candidacy was put on hold, and she was not renominated the following year. Hopkins filed suit in 1983 using a disparate treatment strategy.

In this case it was clear that Hopkins's interpersonal skills provided Price Waterhouse with a legitimate, nondiscriminatory reason for withholding partnership. At the same time it was equally clear that several partners had relied on impermissible factors in evaluating her candidacy. Hence, both legitimate and illegitimate motives were involved in the partnership decision. Attorneys for Price Waterhouse contended, in line with the traditional disparate treatment model, that once it provided evidence of a legitimate, nondiscriminatory basis for the decision that Hopkins could not disprove, the case should be dismissed. Hopkins's attorneys argued that once she proved that discriminatory motives had played a role in the decision, she should prevail. The Supreme Court agreed to hear this case to resolve the plaintiff's and defendant's respective burdens of proof in such "mixed motive" cases.

In May of 1989 the Court ruled six to three that after a plaintiff proves that an unlawful motive played a part in an adverse employment decision, illegal discrimination has been established. Thus, Price Waterhouse, the defendant, had violated Title VII. However, if the defendant can prove by a preponderance of the evidence that it would have reached the same decision in the absence of discriminatory motive, it may avoid liability (e.g., reinstatement, damages, or, in this case, granting of partnership to the plaintiff). In mixed motive cases, then, the respective burdens of proof differ somewhat from those in the traditional disparate treatment framework in the third stage of the case. Hopkins was able to prove that discrimination was one factor in the denial of her partnership. At this point, as Justice O'Connor noted, Hopkins had taken her proof as far as it could go. She was not able to prove that Price Waterhouse's legitimate, nondiscriminatory reasons were untrue and a mere pretext to mask illegal discrimination. So the court, in essence, separated the questions of determining illegal discrimination and establishing liability for that discrimination. Note that the employer bears the burden of proving that it should not be held liable for its illegal discrimination; this is the only aspect of a disparate treatment case in which the employer must carry the burden of proof.

Wards Cove Packing Company v. Atonio (1989)

This case involved the employment practices of two salmon canneries in Alaska. At the canneries there are two basic types of jobs: "noncannery" skilled positions (e.g., boat captains, machinists, engineers) and unskilled "cannery" positions. Virtually all of the higher-paying noncannery jobs are filled by white workers, whereas nonwhites, predominantly Filipinos and Native Alaskans, occupy a majority of the cannery positions. In 1974 Frank Atonio, along with other cannery workers, filed a class action suit charging that nonwhites were denied access to noncannery jobs on the basis of race. The plaintiffs charged that sixteen of their employer's practices were responsible for the work force's racial stratification. The practices at issue (e.g., nepotism, rehire preference, an English language requirement) involved a mixture of subjective and objective practices, and the plaintiffs invoked both disparate treatment and disparate impact models of discrimination. The district court rejected the plaintiffs' disparate treatment claims, whereas the appeals court (and subsequently, on remand, the district court) ruled that the plaintiffs had established a prima facie case of disparate impact. The Supreme Court agreed to hear the case "because some of the issues raised by the decision [vis-à-vis disparate impact] were matters on which the court was evenly divided in *Watson v. Fort Worth Bank & Trust Co*" (USLW, p. 4585).

In June of 1989 the Court rendered a five-to-four decision in the case, altering the disparate impact evidentiary burdens established by *Griggs* that we described earlier in this article. Throughout its decision the majority appeared to be heavily influenced by Justice O'Connor's plurality opinion in *Watson*. First, the Court ruled that to establish a prima facie case of disparate impact, the plaintiff must disaggregate the data, that is, identify the specific employment practice(s) at issue and demonstrate a causal link between it and the statistical imbalance. The majority noted that this requirement would not be unduly burdensome, given the *Guidelines'* requirements for maintaining records concerning individual components of selection processes where adverse impact exists. Liberal rules of discovery allow plaintiffs' attorneys access to these records. Second, once a prima facie case has been established, the defendant must articulate a business justification for the practice, although "there is no requirement that the challenged practice be 'essential' or 'indispensable' " (USLW, p. 4588). Third and most significant, the Court specified that the defendant's rebuttal burden vis-à-vis business justification is not one of *persuasion*—convincing the court—but merely one of *produc-*

tion—presenting evidence. According to the dissent, this standard inappropriately lessens the defendant's burden in disparate impact cases and blurs the distinction between the disparate impact and disparate treatment models. Relatedly, the majority also ruled that the ultimate burden of proof in disparate impact cases remains with the plaintiff at all times, again weakening the distinction between disparate impact and disparate treatment. And finally, in the last stage of a disparate impact case, the plaintiff may prevail by persuading the court of the existence of other devices that have less adverse impact and yet are equally effective in serving the employer's legitimate business goals. Cost factors and additional burdens are relevant considerations in the determination of effectiveness. The majority, reaffirming its decision in *Hazelwood School District v. U.S.* (1977), also ruled that the plaintiffs had made an inappropriate statistical comparison between the unskilled and skilled job groupings. This finding occurred because the cannery work force did not represent a pool of qualified applicants for noncannery positions.

The dissenting justices in *Wards Cove* contended that the additional proof required of plaintiffs, coupled with the lighter burden placed on defendants, tipped the scales in favor of employers and undermined the principles of fairness embodied in Title VII. They stated that the decision "takes three major strides backwards in the battle against race discrimination" (USLW, p. 4593) by (1) upsetting the burdens of proof in disparate impact cases, (2) barring the use of internal statistical comparisons, and (3) requiring of plaintiffs a practice-by-practice statistical disaggregation and proof of causation.

The 1991 Civil Rights Act

In response to the Court's decision in *Atonio* and a half-dozen other cases that seemed to undermine the evidentiary burdens established for plaintiffs and defendants, the U.S. Congress, after often caustic deliberation, passed the compromise 1991 Civil Rights Act. Following are some important elements of the 1991 CRA (*Congressional Quarterly,* 1991):

1. It reinstated the evidentiary burdens first established in the *Griggs v. Duke Power* decision (viz., the plaintiff must first establish a prima facie case and then the defendant must *persuade* the court of the test's job relatedness or business necessity).

2. The prima facie burden on plaintiffs was made more specific. That is, as in *Atonio,* the plaintiff must disaggregate the data to identify the specific employment practice responsible for the disparate impact. In the event that the elements of the organization's decision-making process are not separable, the entire decision-making process may be treated as a single employment practice. However, determination of whether a decision-making process can be disaggregated is left to the discretion of the court.

3. It let stand the Court's decision to allow the use of a disparate impact strategy in instances where subjective practices are at issue. Thus, promotion decisions, often based on performance appraisal data, are also amenable to statistical comparisons using the four-fifths rule in order to establish a prima facie case.

4. The 1991 CRA codified the decision in *Hopkins* regarding the deliberation of mixed motive cases. That is, contrary to *Burdine,* an unlawful employment practice is established when a worker demonstrates that race, color, religion, sex, or national origin was a motivating factor for any employment practice, even when other (job-related) factors also motivated the decision.

5. It provides plaintiffs in disparate treatment cases access to jury trials and offers winning plaintiffs the possibility of compensatory and punitive damage awards. Thus, the liability risks to employers associated with disparate treatment have been enhanced substantially.

Also of potential significance was the tone of the Court regarding the *Guidelines*. In a footnote, the *Watson* plurality noted that the four-fifths rule, endorsed by the *Guidelines,* had been criticized on technical grounds and had proved to be only a rule of thumb for the courts. It is unclear as yet whether this commentary will ultimately be translated into benefits for plaintiffs or defendants. The plurality in *Watson* further stated that formal validation studies might not be required of defendants, particularly in the case of subjective practices; the *Watson* minority concurred on this point. According to Landy (1989), because defendants need only present business justification as their defense, there is likely to be a decrease in the importance of the *Guidelines,* whereas the importance of the *Principles,* the *Standards,* and case law will likely increase. Regardless, the fact that plaintiffs are provided an opportunity to attack the employer's business justification defense with their own validation studies will likely motivate employers' continued adherence to one of the primary sets of professional-technical standards.

A third reference to the *Guidelines,* specifically its requirement that employers maintain adequate records documenting the individual components of their selection systems, was made by the *Wards Cove* majority and codified by the 1991 CRA. It is this reference that may create a substantial burden on employers (Kandel, 1989; Mitchell, 1990; Potter, 1989; Sharf, 1989). According to the *Watson* plurality, plaintiffs must disaggregate the data, "especially" when subjective and objective criteria are combined. Employers must therefore maintain disaggregated data on their subjective practices; this requirement may prove difficult (e.g., in the case of performance appraisal; Landy, 1989; Mitchell, 1990). However, employers failing to provide plaintiffs with such data under rules of discovery might be left with *no defense,* thus "forfeit[ing] any legal advantage gained through the Wards Cove decision" (Mitchell, 1990). Also, when disaggregation is not feasible, the courts may rule that the entire deci-sion-making process is prone to defense (1991 CRA).

Recommendations for Performance Appraisal Systems

The complexity of legal factors and their interaction with professional-technical standards has been noted by others (e.g., Bersoff, 1981, 1983; Nathan & Cascio, 1986; Novick, 1981, 1982). Professional practice concerning the design and operation of performance appraisal systems evolves from several sources, including societal pressures, personnel research, and consensus among researchers and practitioners on applications of performance appraisal. Personnel researchers investigate such topics as job analysis, predictor criterion development, and validity-utility analysis. Practitioners use this research within specific organizational contexts to implement and manage human resource management systems. However, the complexity of the legal environment means that practitioners in organizations cannot neglect the evaluation of appraisal systems until a complaint is filed and then expect their decisions to be defensible under challenge. Thus several sets of prescriptive recommendations have been proposed by various authors.

Specific prescriptive guidelines for performance appraisal systems have been provided by Burchett and De Meuse (1985), Ashe and McRae (1985), Bernardin and Beatty (1984), and Barrett and Kernan (1987). Based on previous court decisions and professional guidelines, these recommendations suggest that successful defense of performance appraisal systems is most likely when the following features are incorporated as the content and procedural basis of performance appraisal systems.

Criteria are developed from documented job analyses. In *Wade v. Mississippi Cooperative Extension Service* (1974), the court ruled that the performance appraisals used for promotion decisions were not based on the results of a job analysis and that appraisal of performance using a trait-based rating scale without reference to job analysis data was a suspect practice. On this point there is clear consensus among members of the professional community: A formal job analysis must be conducted as a prerequisite for the development of valid performance appraisal criteria. As a result of the court's decision, the organization was obligated to employ qualified minorities in large numbers within a prescribed period of time. Furthermore, the organization was warned that failure to comply with this order would result in more rigorous future minority staffing requirements.

In several other instances, practices inconsistent with professional standards were cited in the court decisions as reasons for defendant culpability. Several cases have underscored the importance of job analysis information in the choice and development of performance criteria (*Wade v. Mississippi Cooperative Extension Service,* 1974; *Albemarle Paper Co. v. Moody,* 1975; *Patterson v. American Tobacco Co.,* 1978). Also, in the case of *Carpenter v. Stephen F. Austin State University* (1983), the court held that updated job analyses were required in order to ascertain whether significant changes might have occurred in the job (changes had occurred). At present the best strategy is to follow the guidelines derived from previous court cases by Thompson and Thompson (1982).

Performance standards are communicated to employees in writing. This seems so obvious that one would wonder whether an organization that failed to communicate performance expectations to an employee could even remain in business. In fact, one of the world's largest organizations, General Motors, lost a case because it was found to base promotion decisions on standards not clearly communicated to employees (*Rowe v. General Motors Corporation,* 1972).

Employee performance is recognized as variable across job dimensions, and thus each dimension is rated separately (although overall ratings are not forbidden). Use of a single overall rating of effectiveness (e.g., *Bigby v. City of Chicago,* 1984) or ranking of employees on a similar global standard is not acceptable to the courts. Generally, court decisions have characterized such rating systems as "vague and inadequate" and "subject to racial bias" (*Albemarle Paper Company v. Moody,* 1975; *Watkins v. Scott Paper Company,* 1976). In *Bigby,* raters first provided a global rating of subordinates' performance and then completed subscale ratings that were required to average to the global ratings. The courts require that separate dimension ratings be combined through some formal weighting system to yield a summary score (e.g., *Allen v. City of Mobile,* 1978).

Subjective ratings reflect judgments of job-related behavior and are supported by objective criteria. The courts prefer performance appraisals that focus on job-related behavior rather than on global trait descriptions, as was the case in *Brito v. Zia Co.* (1973) and *Wade.* In *Brito v. Zia,* the Tenth Circuit Court of Appeals ruled that subjective performance appraisals were used as tests and should be evaluated against similar standards. Banks and Roberson (1985) have advocated that individuals involved in the development, supervision, and administration of performance appraisals regard themselves as test developers. This explicit realization that performance appraisal systems must be valid measures of relevant performance factors with controls against random error and irrelevant or biasing performance factors is of major importance in the development of an appraisal system that meets professional and technical standards. A good test should be content valid, have a standardized scoring procedure, and minimize susceptibility to contaminating effects. This concept is directly generalizable to the evaluation of performance appraisal effectiveness.

However, use of an advanced and carefully developed appraisal instrument does not ensure a decision favorable to the defendant. As noted by Nathan and Cascio (1986), "It is possible that in the presence of severe adverse impact a judge would rule against an employer regardless of what type of rating scale used" (p. 17).

A mechanism for employee appeal is available. In *Equal Employment Opportunity Commission v. E.I. du Pont de Nemours & Co.* (1978), the court was favorably impressed with the appeals mechanism that allowed employees to seek redress at multiple levels of the organization. Including a formal appeals process also might convey to raters that performance appraisal is considered an important component of their supervisory role. Also, it might make raters more reluctant to manipulate ratings deliberately to satisfy their own political agendas.

In a related vein, employees should have the opportunity to review and make comments, written or verbal, about their appraisals before they become final. This step can also be considered the first step in any formal appeals process, though it should be provided whether or not a formal appeals mechanism is available.

One appraiser never has absolute authority in determining a personnel action. This prescription involves two aspects: (1) provision for higher management review and (2) use of multiple raters. Some higher-level manager, perhaps the rater's own manager, should review all performance appraisals before they become final. Not only does this practice enable management to detect particular cases or patterns of rating that indicate illegal bias, but it also helps to ensure consistency among raters in use of formats, performance dimensions, and criteria.

The use of multiple raters is becoming more popular as many firms move toward team-based management systems. Use of multiple raters reduces the influence of idiosyncratic rating policies on personnel decisions. However, to implement this prescription faithfully, the organization must fulfill an additional requirement—namely, that the raters complete their evaluation independently of one another. That is, sharing ratings to arrive at a consensus is not an acceptable way of offsetting the bias of a single rater (*Loiseau v. Department of Human Resources,* 1983). An important caution in the use of multiple raters, illustrated by the *Hopkins*

case, is that illegal bias on the part of one or two raters can taint the entire process with illegal discrimination.

All information bearing on a personnel decision is documented in writing. The need to provide thorough documentation to support personnel decisions is of central importance to the defense of a performance appraisal system. For example, in *Marquez v. Omaha District Sales Office, Ford Division of the Ford Motor Company* (1971), the court ruled that the organization had not provided sufficient documentation of its reasons for removing an employee from a promotion list. Mr. Marquez maintained an excellent and promotable performance record during fifteen years with the company; he was never promoted, and for no apparent reason his name was removed from the company promotion list. In *Turner v. State Highway Commission of Missouri* (1982), the court ruled in favor of a defendant who was able to produce documented instances of inadequate performance. Documentation appears especially important in instances where performance appraisals are used for termination and promotion decisions (cf. Martin, Bartol, & Levine, 1986).

Without exception, courts condemn informal performance evaluation practices that eschew documentation (Ashe & McRae, 1985). In *Martinez v. El Paso County* (1983), the defendant organization asserted that a male clerical worker had been fired for lack of adequate typing skills. The plaintiff alleged that the company had discriminated against him on the basis of gender because a clearly inferior female typist had been retained (Ashe & McRae, 1985). The organization could offer scant empirical support for the decision to terminate on the basis of poor performance. And, somewhat unbelievably, the defendant argued that the absence of documented performance appraisals could not be used as evidence suggesting discriminatory practices because all employees were evaluated in the same way.

A major change in the employment discrimination arena is the 1991 CRA requirement that the plaintiff disaggregate the defendant's overall system to show specific discriminatory impact. So that organizations may defend against lawsuits, it will be necessary to maintain records that permit fine-grained analyses of components of the selection process. As an example, suppose that an organization uses ratings of past performance and two other predictors for promotion to first-line supervisor status. If there is evidence of disparate impact, the 1991 CRA requires the plaintiff to demonstrate to a court which of the components is responsible for the disparate impact.

Documentation should also serve the dual purposes of (1) establishing a systematic formal appraisal system that is applied equally to all incumbents performing the same job and (2) providing data on the operation of the system. With respect to the second purpose, the documentation can be used as input for conducting performance appraisal system diagnostics. For example, the information may facilitate identification of rater bias due to gender or to race differences between raters and ratees.

Supervisors are instructed and/or given training in the use of the appraisal instrument. Formal training of raters in the observation and rating of performance is acknowledged by both professionals and the courts to be a desirable characteristic of PA systems (Bernardin & Buckley, 1981; Burchett & DeMeuse, 1985). In the absence of a formal rater training program, an organization must at the least provide raters with written instructions for using the rating scale for evaluation of personnel. Such instructions are considered a necessary prerequisite to, not a guarantee of, systematic, unbiased appraisals.

Summary

Valid and accurate performance appraisal data may have a positive impact on the organizational "bottom line" (Banner & Cooke, 1984; Cascio, 1987; Landy, Farr, & Jacobs, 1982). It would also be inappropriate from an ethical standpoint, particularly given the high value placed on merit in our society, to devise a system on the basis of expediency at the cost of accuracy. One general caveat is in order. Although following professional standards for scientific and legal reasons is recommended, simple adherence to standards does not in and of itself guarantee a favorable court decision. The key may be a distinction between the design and the operation of performance appraisal systems. Recall that the courts' task is to decide whether unlawful discrimination in employment practices has occurred in a specific instance, not whether the appraisal system has been designed according to technical standards. It takes only one supervisor who violates the civil rights of an employee under Title VII to cast doubt on the entire system.

Related to our discussion of codified legal requirements for PA systems is a complementary literature that discusses individual perceptions of organizational justice. Two dimensions of perception within this framework relate to distributive and procedural justice (Greenberg, 1987). A question of distributive justice is said to be relevant when the issue concerns the fairness of the ends achieved. In the context of performance appraisal, distributive justice involves the levels of ratings assigned and the distribution of any outcomes that are linked to the ratings. Procedural justice issues revolve around questions pertaining to the fairness of the procedures (i.e., the means) employed to attain distributive outcomes. In performance appraisal this can include, for example, the extent to which members are allowed to participate in the development of performance criteria, have the opportunity to submit self-appraisals as part of the overall evaluation, and are entitled to submit appeals in cases where they disagree with supervisory ratings (cf. Greenberg, 1990). The importance of these procedural components should be apparent to the reader, as they mirror several of the prescriptions we outlined earlier. In addition, including the recommended procedural characteristics is consistent with the contemporary ethos, which places a premium on employee empowerment.

Adherence to professional and technical guidelines is neither necessary nor sufficient for successful defense of a performance appraisal system. Adherence alone cannot prevent lawsuits because a lawsuit alleges discriminatory behavior on the part of individual supervisors or the organization. However, we hope that it is obvious that performance appraisal systems that stress objectivity and accountability will tend to address these concerns better than systems that are undocumented and subjective. The tendency for individual raters to behave in a discriminatory manner is reduced when an organization adopts strong normative standards in favor of fair employment and backs up these norms with procedures that regulate appraiser behaviors throughout the performance appraisal process.

Such performance appraisal decisions and their associated debate can be viewed at general and specific levels. At a general level, the increasing cultural and ethnic diversity of the American population is forcing organizations to prepare for the future (Briggs, 1987; Johnson & Packer, 1987). Demographic shifts and patterns of increased immigration foreshadow today's minorities' becoming a large share of the work force sometime after the year 2000. Ethnic group members, women, and older adults will continue to constitute growing segments of the labor force. Early recognition of the demographic challenge and proactive planning will allow organizational scientists and human resource practitioners to have an impact on the bottom line through human resource management techniques that span employees' organizational careers. At the specific level, each organization must make multiple personnel decisions about individuals in the here and now (Novick & Ellis, 1977; Schmitt & Noe, 1986). For reasons of productivity, utility, and fairness, well-developed, well-implemented, and well-monitored subjective appraisal systems appear better than any more expedient alternatives.

References

Albemarle Paper Co. v. Moody, 422 U.S. 405 (1975).

Allen v. City of Mobile, 464 F. Supp. 433 (1978).

American Educational Research Association, American Psychological Association, & National Council on Measurement in Education. (1985). *Standards for educational and psychological testing.* Washington, DC: American Psychological Association.

American Psychological Association. (1988). In the Supreme Court of the United States: *Clara Watson v. Fort Worth Bank & Trust. American Psychologist, 43,* 1019–1028.

Arvey, R. D., & Faley, R. H. (1988). *Fairness in selecting employees* (2nd ed). Reading, MA: Addison-Wesley.

Ashe, R. L., & McRae, G. S. (1985). Performance evaluations go to court in the 1980's. *Mercer Law Review, 36,* 887–905.

Austin, J. T., Villanova, P., Kane, J. S., & Bernardin, H. J. (1991). Construct validation of performance measures: Definitional issues, development, and evaluation of indicators. In G. R. Ferris & K. M. Rowland (Eds.), *Research in personnel and human resources management* (Vol. 9, pp. 159–233). Greenwich, CT: JAI Press.

Banks, C. G., & Roberson, L. (1985). Performance appraisers as test developers. *Academy of Management Review, 10,* 128–142.

Banner, D. K., & Cooke, R. A. (1984). Ethical dilemmas in performance appraisal. *Journal of Business Ethics, 3,* 327–333.

Barrett, G. V., & Kernan, M. C. (1987). Performance appraisal and terminations: A review of court decisions since *Brito v. Zia* with implications for personnel practices. *Personnel Psychology, 40,* 489–503.

Bernardin, H. J. (1988). *EEOC v. Sears: A paradox in EEO litigation?* Unpublished manuscript, Florida Atlantic University, Boca Raton.

Bernardin, H. J., & Beatty, R. W. (1984). *Performance appraisal: Assessing human behavior at work.* Boston: Kent.

Bernardin, H. J., & Buckley, M. R. (1981). A consideration of strategies in rater training. *Academy of Management Review, 6,* 205–212.

Bernardin, H. J., & Villanova, P. (1986). Performance appraisal. In E. Locke (Ed.), *Generalizing from laboratory to field settings* (pp. 43–62). Lexington, MA: Lexington Press.

Bersoff, D. N. (1981). Testing and the law. *American Psychologist, 36,* 1047–1056.

Bersoff, D. N. (1983). Regarding psychologists testily: The legal regulation of psychological assessment. In C. J. Scheirer & B. L. Hammonds (Eds.), *Psychology and the law* (Master Lecture Series, Vol. 2, pp. 37–88). Washington, DC: American Psychological Association.

Bersoff, D. N. (1988). Should subjective employment devices be scrutinized?: It's elementary, my dear Ms. Watson. *American Psychologist, 43,* 1016–1018.

Bigby v. City of Chicago, 38 FEP 844 (1984).

Bretz, R. D., Milkovich, G. T., & Read, W. (1992). The current state of performance appraisal research and practice: Concerns, directions, and implications. *Journal of Management, 18,* 321–352.

Briggs, V. M., Jr. (1987). The growth and composition of the U.S. labor force. *Science, 238,* 176–180.

Brito v. Zia Co., 478 F.2d 1200 (1973).

Burchett, S. R., & DeMeuse, K. P. (1985). Performance appraisal and the law. *Personnel, 62,* 29–37.

Byham, W. C., & Spitzer, M. E. (1971). *The law and personnel testing.* New York: AMACOM.

Carpenter v. Stephen F. Austin State University, 706 F.2d 6708 (1983).

Cascio, W. F. (1987). *Costing human resources: The financial impact of behavior in organizations* (2nd ed). Boston: PWS-Kent.

Cascio, W. F. (1991). *Applied psychology in personnel management* (4th ed). Englewood Cliffs, NJ: Prentice Hall.

Cascio, W. F., & Awad, E. M. (1981). *Human resources management: An information systems approach.* Reston, VA: Reston.

Coburn v. Pan American World Airways, 32 FEP 722 (1982).

Congressional Quarterly (Volume 47, 1991). *Compromise civil rights bill passed,* pp. 251–261.

Corley, R. N., Reed, O. L., & Black, R. L. (1984). *The legal environment of business* (6th ed.). New York: McGraw-Hill.

Equal Employment Opportunity Commission v. E.I. du Pont de Nemours & Co., 445 F. Supp. 223 (1978).

Equal Employment Opportunity Commission v. Sandia Corporation, 23 FEP 810 (1980).

Greenberg, J. (1987). Using diaries to promote procedural justice in performance appraisals. *Social Justice Research, 1,* 219–234.

Greenberg, J. (1990). Organizational justice: Yesterday, today, and tomorrow. *Journal of Management, 16,* 399–432.

Griggs v. Duke Power Co., 401 U.S. 424 (1971).

Guion, R. M. (1965). *Personnel testing.* New York: McGraw-Hill.

Gutman, A. (1993). *EEO law and personnel practices.* Newbury Park, CA: Sage.

Hazelwood School District v. U.S., 433 U.S. 299 (1977).

Hills, F. S. (1980, March). Job relatedness vs. adverse impact in personnel decision making. *Personnel Journal,* 211–215, 229.

James, L. R. (1973). Criterion models and construct validity for criteria. *Psychological Bulletin, 80,* 75–83.

Johnson, W. B., & Packer, A. H. (1987). *Workforce 2000: Work and workers for the 21st century.* Indianapolis: Hudson Institute.

Kandel, W. L. (1989). Current developments in employment litigation: *Atonio* and *Betts. Employee Relations Law Journal, 15,* 267–272.

Kraiger, K., & Ford, J. K. (1985). A meta-analysis of ratee race effects in performance ratings. *Journal of Applied Psychology, 70,* 56–65.

Landy, F. J. (1989, September). *Implications of recent Supreme Court rulings on employment practices.* Presentation to the Metropolitan New York Association for Applied Psychology, New York.

Landy, F. J., & Farr, J. (1983). *Performance measurement.* New York: Academic Press.

Landy, F. L., Farr, J., & Jacobs, R. R. (1982). Utility concepts in performance measurement. *Organizational Behavior and Human Performance, 30,* 15–40.

Landy, F. J., & Rastegary, H. (1989). Criteria for selection. In M. Smith & I. Robertson (Eds.), *Advances in selection and assessment* (pp. 47–65). Chichester, England: Wiley.

Ledvinka, J. (1982). *Federal regulation of personnel and human resource management.* Boston: Kent.

Ledvinka, J., & Scarpello, V. G. (1991). *Federal regulation of personnel and human resource management* (2nd ed). Boston: PWS-Kent.

Lee, B. A. (1990). Subjective employment practices and disparate impact: Unresolved issues. *Employee Relations Law Journal, 15,* 403–417.

Locher, A. H., & Teel, K. S. (1977). Performance appraisal: A survey of current practices. *Personnel Journal, 56,* 245–247.

Loiseau v. Department of Human Resources, 567 F. Supp. 1211 (1983).

Longenecker, C. O., Sims, H. P., & Gioia, D. A. (1987). Behind the mask: The politics of employee appraisal. *Academy of Management Executive, 1,* 183–193.

Marquez v. Omaha District Office of Ford Motor Company, 440 F.2d 1157 (1971).

Martin, D. C., Bartol, K. M., & Levine, M. J. (1986). The legal ramifications of performance appraisal. *Employee Relations Law Journal, 12,* 370–396.

Martinez v. El Paso County, 710 F.2d 1102 (1983).

McDonnell Douglas Corporation v. Green, 411 U.S. 792 (1973).

Miner, M. G., & Miner, J. B. (1979). *Employee selection within the law.* Washington, DC: Bureau of National Affairs.

Mitchell, T. W. (1990). In the wake of Wards Cove. *MetroNews, 2,* 2–4.

Nathan, B. R., & Cascio, W. F. (1986). Introduction: Technical & legal standards. In R. A. Berk (Ed.), *Performance assessment: Methods & applications* (pp. 1–50). Baltimore: Johns Hopkins Press.

Nicholson v. Western Electric Co., 555 F. Supp. 3 (1982).

Novick, M. R. (1981). Federal guidelines and professional standards. *American Psychologist, 36,* 1035–1046.

Novick, M. R. (1982). Ability testing: Federal guidelines and professional standards. In A. Wigdor & W. R. Garner (Eds.), *Ability testing: Uses, consequences, and controversies* (pp. 70–98). Washington, DC: National Academy Press.

Novick, M. R., & Ellis, D. D., Jr. (1977). Equal opportunity in educational and employment selection. *American Psychologist, 32,* 306–320.

Patterson v. American Tobacco Company, 586 F.2d 300 (1978).

Potter, E. E. (1989). Supreme Court's *Wards Cove Packing* decision redefines the adverse impact theory under Title VII. *The Industrial-Organizational Psychologist, 27,* 25–31.

Price Waterhouse v. Hopkins, 109 S.Ct. 1775 (1989).

Rowe v. General Motors Corporation, 457 F.2d 348 (1972).

Schmitt, N., & Lappin, M. (1980). Race and sex as determinants of the mean and variance of performance ratings. *Journal of Applied Psychology, 65,* 428–435.

Schmitt, N., & Noe, R. A. (1986). Personnel selection and equal employment opportunity. In C. L. Cooper & I. Robertson (Eds.), *International review of industrial and organizational psychology* (Vol. 2, pp. 71–115). Chichester: Wiley.

Sharf, J. C. (1988a). APA & Civil Rights Bar opposed by Justice, EEOC, ASPA, IPMA, & EEAC before Supreme Court in *CLARA WATSON V. FORT WORTH BANK & TRUST. The Industrial-Organizational Psychologist, 25,* 27–34.

Sharf, J. C. (1989, October). *Practical solutions to real problems in the use of assessment.* Paper presented at the National Assessment Conference, Minneapolis, MN.

Society for Industrial and Organizational Psychology. (1987). *Principles for the validation and use of personnel selection procedures* (3rd ed.). College Park, MD: Author.

Texas Department of Community Affairs v. Burdine, 450 U.S. 248 (1981).

Thompson, D. E., & Thompson, T. A. (1982). Court standards for job analysis in test validation. *Personnel Psychology, 35,* 865–874.

Turner v. State Highway Commission of Missouri, 31 EPD 33, 352 (1982).

Uniform Guidelines on Employee Selection Procedures. (1978). *Federal Register, 43,* 38290–38315.

Villanova, P., & Bernardin, H. J. (1989). Impression management in the context of performance appraisal. In R. A. Giacalone & P. Rosenfeld (Eds.), *Impression management in the organization* (pp. 299–313). Hillsdale, NJ: Lawrence Erlbaum Associates.

Villanova, P., & Bernardin, H. J. (1991). Performance appraisal: The means, motive, and opportunity to manage impressions. In R. Giacalone & P. Rosenfeld (Eds.), *Applying impression management: How image-making affects organizations* (pp. 81–96). Beverly Hills, CA: Sage.

Wade v. Mississippi Cooperative Extension Service, 372 F. Supp. 126 (1974).

Waldman, D. A., & Avolio, B. J. (1986). A meta-analysis of age differences in job performance. *Journal of Applied Psychology, 71,* 33–38.

Wards Cove Packing Company v. Atonio, 109 S.Ct. 2115 (1989).

Watkins v. Scott Paper Company, 503 F.2d 159 (1976).

Watson v. Fort Worth Bank & Trust, 108 S.Ct. 2777 (1988).

CHAPTER 8

Compensation and Reward Systems

Pay, in the form of wages and salaries and a wide range of legally required and agreed-upon benefits, collectively represents the means by which employees are financially compensated for joining organizations, staying in them, and accomplishing certain levels of work performance. The compensation activity in personnel management, therefore, is a key people-processing activity, which begins with the planning that occurs before people enter organizations and continues until their exit and beyond. For a good many organizations, the compensation provided employees can account for as much as 50 percent of total cash flow. For others it can account for an even higher percentage, especially if the organization's product or service system is very labor intensive.

In addition to the equal employment opportunity laws—especially Title VII of the Civil Rights Act of 1964 and its amendment, the Pregnancy Discrimination Act of 1978, and the Age Discrimination in Employment Act of 1967—the legal environment in which the compensation activity is conducted is bounded by several other major pieces of federal legislation. The most basic of these is the Fair Labor Standards Act (FLSA) of 1938 and its amendments, including the Equal Pay Act of 1963, which contains provisions for minimum wage, overtime, and equal pay. Federal legislation also supports the Old Age, Survivors, Disability, and Health Insurance Program (OASDHI) and a number of legally required benefits associated with that program, such as Social Security and unemployment insurance. Another major piece of federal legislation is the Employment Retirement Income Security Act (ERISA) of 1974, which regulates the pension programs of employers and includes requirements regarding vesting, accrued benefits, funding, and so forth. Finally, the Revenue Act of 1978, the Economic Recovery Tax Act (ERTA) of 1981, and other tax laws define, as part of the Internal Revenue Code, the taxable or nontaxable status of benefits.

Organizations, in this context, must make their compensation systems both attractive and equitable to current and prospective employees. Information regarding the external labor market, often supplied through industry or area wage surveys, is necessary for determining an appropriate pay structure in making individual wage and salary decisions within that structure. Also necessary is information regarding the internal labor market. Again, is the compensation system attractive? Is it equitable? A variety of job evaluation methods are available for establishing pay grades and ranges for jobs on the basis of their relative worth to the organization. Attempting to match and then maintain a balance between the compensation demands of the marketplace and the compensation demands of employees is not an easy task. The task is further compounded by the rather subjective nature of the performance appraisal process (discussed in Chapter 7), which should be a primary source of information for making compensation decisions.

The first article in this chapter, written by Gomez-Mejia and Welbourne, deals with the strategic implications of compensation. The authors identify and delineate the compensation strategies associated with different organizational strategies, and they outline their opinions on important future issues.

The next two articles are concerned with the notion of pay for performance. Thornburg spells out the potential perils and advantages associated with a pay-for-performance system. McNally follows up with ideas about the most effective way to use pay for performance as a vehicle to facilitate the strategic direction of the organization.

Equal pay for work of comparable worth to an organization has been one of the most controversial issues in the compensation area; it is addressed by Benson and Hornsby in the final article in this chapter. The authors examine the legal background of sex-based wage discrimination and give primary attention to the pattern of court ruling concerning the issue of comparable worth.

Suggestions for Further Reading

Beatty, L. (1993, September). Pay increases with changing HR landscape. *HR Magazine,* pp. 78–80.

Brady, T. (1993). Employee handbooks: Contracts or empty promises? *Management Review, 82,* 33–35.

Brown, D. (1993). Centralized control or decentralized diversity: A guide for matching compensation with company strategy and structure. *Compensation & Benefits Review, 25,* 47–52.

Freedman, E. (1993). Workers compensation: A process management approach. *Benefits & Compensation International, 23,* 33–38.

Overman, S. (1993, September). You don't have to be a big fish to swim in international waters. *HR Magazine,* pp. 46–49+.

Schay, B. (1993). Broad-banding in the federal government. *Public Manager, 22,* 28–31.

Shilling, M. (1993, July). Avoid expatriate culture shock. *HR Magazine,* pp. 58–63.

Turk, H. (1993). Questions—and answers. *Employment Relations Today, 20,* 243–247.

Willey, T. (1993). Employee leasing comes of age. *Human Resources Professional, 5,* 18–20.

Yates, M. (1993). The bright side of a merger: A refined compensation plan and new spirit. *Human Resources Professional, 5,* 47–51.

Compensation Strategy: An Overview and Future Steps

Luis R. Gomez-Mejia and Theresa M. Welbourne

A number of writers are now arguing that compensation as a field of study is undergoing a transformation from being a micro-oriented, bureaucratically based, applied discipline that emphasizes tools and techniques to a broader field focusing on such concepts as "congruency," "fit," and "linkages" that involve close articulation between the pay system and other organizational functions, business unit strategies, and overall corporate strategy (e.g. Lawler, 1981; Henderson and Risher, 1987; Kerr, 1985; Wallace, 1987; Fay, 1987). The underlying assumption in most of this work is that the pay system is an essential integrating mechanism through which the efforts of individuals are directed toward an organization's strategic objectives, and that, when properly designed, it can be a key contributor to the effectiveness of the organization. For this to occur, careful analysis needs to be made of the role that compensation can and should play in the strategic plan of the organization.

Issues of variation, interrelation, and fit are well developed in the business policy literature. It contains many analyses of fit between strategy and other organizational variables, including formal organizational structure, technology, market competencies, and environment (e.g. Miller, 1986; Tichy, 1983; Prescott, 1986). Business policy research also suggests that coherent or matching strategy types are predictive of future firm performance (e.g. Woo and Cooper, 1981; Hambrick, 1983). The concept of match or fit is based on the notion that strategies are decomposable (Simon, 1981), consisting of components (e.g. technology) that are interesting for their individual importance as well as their role in overall strategic objectives. Because strategy "components" can be determined by a firm, an important normative test for a firm's strategy is internal consistency or equifinality (e.g. Porter, 1980; Galbraith and Schendel, 1983).

The question of strategic coherence has been operationalized in the business policy literature by examining sets of variables that typically fall within the realm of management responsibility; that is, controllable variables such as pricing, promotion, and research and development. Because they are controllable, it is possible to consider these in terms of functional area strategy, such as marketing strategy, financial strategy, human resource strategy, etc.

This paper reviews the emerging *compensation* strategy literature and offers some tentative answers to the following questions: (a) What is compensation strategy? The first part of this article focuses on the meaning of compensation strategy and the various dimensions that may be used to study this construct. (b) Are there any observable strategic compensation patterns? The second part of this article identifies those strategic pay dimensions that appear to cluster together and form discernible groupings. (c) What is the relationship between compensation and organizational strategy? This section identifies compensation patterns that are purported to be most appropriate for various corporate and business unit strategies. (d) What do we need to do to advance the state of the art in this area? The article concludes with a critical assessment of compensation strategy

Reprinted with permission of The Human Resource Planning Society from *Human Resource Planning, 11:3* (1988): 173–190.

notions and provides suggestions for future research.

What Is Compensation Strategy?

Compensation strategy is the repertoire of pay choices available to management that may, under some conditions, have an impact on the organization's performance and the effective use of its human resources. From this perspective, the degree of success associated with various pay choices depends on those contingencies facing the organization at any given time (Balkin & Gomez-Mejia, 1987b).

Eighteen different studies have explicitly examined strategic compensation choices. This literature spans such areas as executive compensation, diversification strategy, product life cycle, incentive pay, and research and development compensation. These articles are categorized in Exhibit 1 as either empirical, case studies, or conceptual. Conceptual articles include book chapters and theoretical or review articles. The dimensions shown in Exhibit 1 are broken down into those related to (a) the criteria or basis for determining pay levels, (b) the design of the compensation system, and (c) the administrative framework. Each of these dimensions is discussed below.

Job vs. Skills

Job-based pay is generally used in traditional pay systems where the company assumes that job value can be determined and that worth is primarily comprised of the contributions of the job (rather than individual incumbents) to the organization. Skill-based pay, on the other hand, tends to be used in nontraditional settings where jobs are fluid, employee exchanges are frequent, and the entire human resources philosophy fosters employee participation and trust (Tosi & Tosi, 1986). Few companies pay exclusively for individual skills rather than the job itself. These organizations tend to hire professionals such as academics, lawyers, and physicians (Lawler, 1981).

Performance vs. Seniority

Most authors agree that this decision should be evaluated in terms of organizational goals as well as the firm's ability to measure performance. If a company can accurately measure performance and align rewards accordingly, the system should be perceived as fair by the employees and serve as a powerful reinforcer of desired behaviors (Kerr, 1988). If not, the system will be perceived as unfair and become highly disruptive. Unfortunately, failures in pay-for-performance systems are not uncommon (Pearce, 1987).

Many firms want to pay for performance, but due to their inability to measure performance, they ultimately pay for seniority (Fombrun, 1984). Therefore, when recording perceptions of managers through either questionnaires or interviews, these individuals might claim that their company pays for performance when in reality their system primarily rewards seniority (Gomez-Mejia, Page & Tornow, 1985).

Individual vs. Group Performance

This issue is related to the problem of assessing performance discussed above. It has been argued that individual performance should be used as a basis for pay because it can be a powerful motivator (Carroll, 1987). However, management's inability to accurately measure individual contributions often results in rewards being incongruent with actual performance (Lawler, 1987). If the employees do not perceive a link between rewards and performance, the motivational effect disappears (Mount, 1987).

Using group performance as a basis for pay is recommended when corporate goals or the nature of work demands close cooperation in the work force (Carroll, 1987; Gomez-Mejia & Balkin, 1987). It has been suggested that combining group and individual performance criteria can enhance the reinforcement value of a pay for performance system (Tichy, Fombrun & Devanna, 1982). Lawler (1983) suggests using base salary contingent upon individual performance and bonuses dependent on

Exhibit 1. Strategic Compensation Dimensions Used by Various Authors

Author	Balkin & Gomez-Mejia	Balkin & Gomez-Mejia	Broderick	Carroll	Gomez-Mejia Tosi & Hinkin	Hambrick & Snow	Kerr	Kerr	Lawler	Miles & Snow
Year	1987a	1987b	1986	1987	1987	1987	1985	1982	1983	1984
Type of Paper	Empirical	Empirical	Empirical	Conceptual	Empirical	Conceptual	Empirical	Conceptual	Conceptual & Case Studies	Case Studies
STRATEGIC COMPENSATION DIMENSIONS										
Basis for Pay										
Job vs. Skills	X		X				X		X	
Performance vs. Seniority	X		X			X	X		X	
Individual vs. Group Performance	X			X			X	X	X	
Short vs. Long-Term Orientation	X			X	X	X	X	X	X	
Risk Aversion vs. Risk Taking	X								X	
Corporate vs. Division Performance			X			X	X	X	X	X
Internal vs. External Equity	X			X		X	X		X	X
Hierarchical vs. Egalitarian	X					X	X		X	X
Qualitative vs. Quantitative Performance Measures			X	X	X	X	X	X	X	
Design Issues										
Pay Level vs. Market	X	X	X	X					X	
Fixed Pay vs. Incentives	X	X	X	X	X	X	X	X	X	X
Frequency of Raises or Bonuses		X		X		X		X		
Intrinsic vs. Extrinsic Rewards						X			X	
Administrative Framework										
Centralization vs. Decentralization of Pay Policies	X		X			X			X	X
Open vs. Secret Pay	X		X						X	
Participation vs. Nonparticipation	X		X						X	
Bureaucratic vs. Flexible Policies	X		X			X				

Author	Murthy	Putts	Rappaport	Salschneider	Salter	Steers & Ungson	Stonich	Tachy Fombrun & Devanna	Total Frequency
Year	1977	1974	1978	1981	1973	1984	1981	1982	
Type of Paper	Empirical	Empirical	Conceptual	Case Studies	Case Studies	Conceptual	Conceptual	Case Studies	
STRATEGIC COMPENSATION DIMENSIONS									
Basis for Pay									
Job vs. Skills									4
Performance vs. Seniority									5
Individual vs. Group Performance								X	6
Short vs. Long-Term Orientation			X	X	X	X	X		12
Risk Aversion vs. Risk Taking					X				3
Corporate vs. Division Performance		X			X				8
Internal vs. External Equity	X					X			7
Hierarchical vs. Egalitarian									5
Qualitative vs. Quantitative Performance Measures	X	X	X		X	X	X	X	14
Design Issues									
Pay Level vs. Market				X					6
Fixed Pay vs. Incentives	X	X		X	X	X		X	16
Frequency of Raises or Bonuses			X		X	X	X		8
Intrinsic vs. Extrinsic Rewards						X			3
Administrative Framework									
Centralization vs. Decentralization of Pay Policies					X				6
Open vs. Secret Pay									3
Participation vs. Nonparticipation									3
Bureaucratic vs. Flexible Policies									3

group performance. Or a bonus pool could be established based on group performance and allocated based on individual performance. Lawler's suggestions are based on the presumed advantages of using both group and individual performance measures.

Carroll (1987) notes that firms with a strong concern for product and market innovation find it difficult to use individual-based performance measures due to their lack of stable individual output indicators necessary to conduct these evaluations. These firms are better off if they rely on narrowly defined group performance measures to make pay decisions. Carroll claims that this approach is more likely to foster creativity and cooperation in these types of companies. However, an empirical study by Balkin and Gomez-Mejia (1987a) found that within firms similar to those described by Carroll the compensation managers report that it is important to use both individual and group performance measures as a basis for pay in order to maximize the motivational impact.

Short- vs. Long-Term Orientation

Most of the work in this area focuses on top executive compensation, and there are many conflicting views on the subject. Some authors contend that executives are often provided incentives that cause them to consider only the short-term performance of the organization, and this often results in decisions that are inconsistent with long-term objectives (Lawler, 1983; Hambrick & Snow, 1987; Stonich, 1981; Rappaport, 1978). Moving to the opposite extreme, focusing entirely on the long-term picture can mean foregoing the reinforcement value provided by frequent rewards closely tied to desired behaviors (Andrews, 1987).

An extensive battery of measures can be used to provide managerial incentives. Included are return on assets, stock price, earnings per share, and net profit. New approaches are constantly being introduced to measure and reward long-term performance. Stonich (1981), for example, suggests three

methods: the weighted factor approach, the long-term evaluation method, and the strategic funds deferral method. However, no single method has been found that is entirely satisfactory (Crystal, 1988). One major problem is that a firm's long-term performance is a function of many factors beyond management's control (Deckop, 1987). A few case studies discuss alternatives for balancing short-term and long-term goals (e.g. Stata and Maidique, 1980), but there is little empirical research.

Gomez-Mejia, Tosi and Hinkin (1987) found that type of ownership significantly affects CEO pay. When there are dominant stockholders, CEO compensation reflects the firm's performance level. In such firms, CEOs are paid more for performance and less for the scale of operation, compared to CEOs in firms without dominant stockholders. This holds true for both pay level and its rate of change over time. However, long-term income, as a proportion of total compensation, appears to be closely associated with performance in both owner- and management-controlled firms. According to these authors, the U.S. tax system may promote this similarity.

The time horizon for pay may also be culture bound. According to Fombrun (1984), three levels of culture affect each employee's overall orientation toward short- or long-term performance: societal, industry, and corporate cultures. In the United States, all three of these tend to be much more concerned with short-term performance (Terpstra, 1978), so it will be difficult to reorient managers towards rewards contingent on long-term performance. One of the major challenges when making strategic compensation choices is to develop effective means of leading the change toward a long-term perspective. Unfortunately, boards of directors do not generally consider the performance of a firm's stock (a long-term measure of stockholder welfare) when rewarding top management (Kerr & Bettis, 1987).

There are numerous logistical problems encountered when dealing with long-term performance. Short-term performance is easily quantifiable, and the information needed for measurement is easily obtained. This is not true for measures of long-term performance. Executives are often reluctant to commit to long-term goals because they appear risky and rather nebulous.

Carroll (1987) and others argue that firms with business strategies emphasizing maintenance of current market share have objective data readily available and can use that data to reward short-term performance at various levels in the corporate hierarchy. Firms that are currently growing, taking financial risks, and acquiring new businesses do not have objective performance data available and tend to rely on subjective information, which results in an emphasis on long-term performance.

Risk Aversion vs. Risk Taking

According to Stonich (1981), the Japanese believe increased job security reduces individual risk and variability of income and so allows employees to make corporate decisions that involve taking risks, when needed. Job security permits managers to identify with corporate goals without worrying about the consequences of their business decisions for their personal life and standard of living.

There seems to be overall agreement that risk taking is rewarded in high growth companies while risk aversion tends to be reinforced in mature firms that concentrate their efforts on maintaining market share. The potential to earn large incentive payments in high growth companies is attractive to younger, risk-taking managers and technical personnel, and these individuals are necessary to support the entrepreneurial climate demanded by these firms. Mature companies seem to be disinterested in risking changes in their current technology or products and emphasize job security rather than monetary rewards.

Corporate vs. Division Performance

When utilizing only division performance as a measuring stick to distribute rewards, the corporation loses synergy and may find itself with less control over its business units than might be desired. Using only corporate performance

allows some divisional managers to receive undeserved rewards (Hambrick & Snow, 1987).

Rewarding based on corporate performance is more common in firms that have narrow and relatively stable product market domains and that are vertically integrated. The reasoning behind this association is that the headquarters' staff acts as an integrative force and is involved in decisions affecting division performance; therefore, performance should be assessed based on the amount of cooperation and synergy obtained across the various units in addition to financial measures of division performance. In these situations, the financial measures are not necessarily representative of only division performance but reflect the contributions of corporate involvement. Therefore, divisional managers should not be exclusively evaluated on division performance because it is not totally within their control.

Division performance has been recommended by Kerr (1985) and others as a reward criterion for firms at the start-up phase or those growing through acquisitions. Because firms that grow by acquisition tend to be autonomous and free from corporate controls and influence, measures of division performance are more accurate indicators of the contributions made by managerial and technical staffs. In order to spur growth, an entrepreneurial climate is desired in start-up and growth firms. This can best be accomplished by using division performance as a measure. Another justification for using division performance for these firms is that the corporation is not concerned with transferring employees between headquarters and the division because the product knowledge of employees is unique at each location. Therefore, these types of firms would not acquire the advantages associated with using corporate performance as a measure; they would only incur the disadvantages.

Compensation Level vs. Market

Milkovich (1988) refers to this dimension of compensation strategy as "competitiveness" which represents the total pay package in relation to the competition. This makes sense because the entire pay package is what will attract and retain employees. Unfortunately, researchers seem limited to measuring only base pay in relation to the market. Considering the problems associated with obtaining accurate survey data on base wage rates alone (Rynes and Milkovich, 1986), it is understandable that it might be virtually impossible to measure a more broadly defined competitive position.

Setting pay rates higher than market will usually enhance a firm's ability to attract and retain employees. Paying greater than market can also create a climate where employees feel part of an elite group. Paying lower than market can be an effective strategy for low skilled jobs or positions where qualified applicants are readily available.

High base pay should be associated with firms that continually search for new product and market opportunities because their employees take more risks, and their tasks are more complex (Carroll, 1987). However, Balkin & Gomez-Mejia (1987b) found that growing firms are associated with a lower base salary relative to the market. Their reasoning was that these firms had greater incentives in the pay mix in order to minimize fixed costs incurred at this stage of growth.

A pitfall associated with all the statements made regarding market positioning is that future income stream is seldom considered. For instance, start-up high technology companies might offer the lowest wages in the industry; however, they may be the only businesses that offer employees an opportunity to become millionaires within a few years.

Internal vs. External Equity

The emphasis placed on internal vs. external equity in the compensation system depends on whether divisions are autonomous or dependent. If autonomous, they are free to develop their own policies; therefore, internal equity in relation to the entire corporation is not critical, and external equity becomes the main concern. The opposite would be true for dependent divisions.

The findings of Balkin & Gomez-Mejia (1987a) indicate that "related products" strategy firms, which were the most highly diversified companies studied, emphasized internal equity over external equity. These authors suggest that more "freewheeling" pay practices that are responsive to varying conditions, contingencies, and individual situations seem to be most effective for single product firms and strategic business units at the growth stage. Formalized rules and procedures that tend to "routinize" pay decisions appear to work best for related product firms and strategic business units at the mature stage. A single product firm was defined as deriving 95 percent or more of its revenues from a single product line. A related products firm, on the other hand, derives 70 percent or less of its revenues from any single product but the remainder is derived from product lines that are related in some way.

Hierarchical vs. Egalitarian

Whether the reward system leads to a hierarchical or egalitarian atmosphere tends to be an indirect result of other strategic pay decisions rather than a goal in and of itself. If a company provides money and various perquisites for moving up the corporate ladder, the traditional hierarchy tends to result. If instead the firm de-emphasizes the traditional differentials between job grades, allows individuals to increase earnings without moving into management, and minimizes status-related perquisites, an egalitarian atmosphere becomes the norm.

Firms that concentrate on harvesting current market share and maintaining existing profit levels tend to reinforce a hierarchical structure. On the other hand, those firms making high investments and undertaking significant financial risks in order to expand market share attempt to foster a more egalitarian style. Milkovich (1988) suggests that the egalitarian atmosphere allows companies flexibility to deploy the work force into new areas, projects, or positions without pay changes. This could explain why growth firms prefer this style of management.

Fixed Pay vs. Incentives

Higher risks tend to be associated with opportunities for larger income. Mature firms or companies trying to maintain their present market share generally offer more job security, and that translates into higher base wages and benefits but less incentives (Salscheider, 1981; Balkin & Gomez-Mejia, 1984; 1987b). Those firms that are aggressively trying to expand their market share (causing employees to incur more personal risks) make use of higher incentives and lower base wages. This enables these firms to minimize fixed pay components and channel resources into additional growth areas. Tenure-related "long-term" incentives are also heavily utilized in the high technology industry to tie valuable scientists and engineers to the firm (Balkin & Gomez-Mejia, 1987b).

Quantitative vs. Qualitative Measures of Performance

It has been suggested that firms growing through mergers and acquisitions should use objective evaluation measures because they are more accurate indicators of performance for each quasi-autonomous unit, while companies expanding internally through vertical integration should use subjective measures for each unit due to their dependence on corporate headquarters (Kerr, 1985; Pitts, 1974).

It is also argued that firms that are trying to be "first movers" in new product and market areas should utilize subjective performance measures to better assess entrepreneurial activities because objective, quantifiable data are not easily found (Kerr, 1982; Carroll, 1987). Firms trying to maintain secure positions in relatively stable product or service areas are said to rely on objective performance measures because the quantifiable data is readily available. Objective measures ultimately result in an emphasis on short-term goals. Because of this drawback, Salter (1973)

recommended utilizing both types of measures to best serve the corporation's needs.

Bonuses vs. Deferred Compensation

Frequent bonuses and merit pay raises are associated with an emphasis on short-term performance while deferred compensation is associated with a long-term perspective (Salter, 1973; Rappaport, 1978; Carroll, 1987; Kerr, 1982). There is disagreement as to whether frequent rewards should be utilized by firms with a high need for cost efficiency and stable tasks or by companies with a high need for innovation and unstable tasks. This controversy reflects different views about whether short- or long-term goals are most important in each type of firm.

Intrinsic vs. Extrinsic Rewards

Lawler (1983) suggests that a firm can obtain a competitive edge if it combines a good pay package with intrinsic rewards (e.g. achievement, recognition) that meet the psychological needs of the employees the firm hopes to attract and retain. Hambrick & Snow (1987) argue that intrinsic rewards are important in organizations that seldom make major adjustments in their technology, structure, or methods of operation. This is because there is little glamour associated with this type of business so recognition and responsibility serve as important nonmonetary rewards to retain achievement-oriented employees.

Centralized vs. Decentralized Pay Administration

Pay decisions and administration can be tightly controlled by corporate headquarters or can be delegated to various plants, divisions, and other subunits within the firm. Lawler (1983) asserts that centralized pay works best when the expertise from headquarters is necessary and when internal equity is emphasized. Decentralized pay works best when local innovation is beneficial to the organization or when the strategic business units are either in different markets or at different stages in the product life cycle. Miles &

Snow (1984) suggest implementing centralized pay when economies of scale can be realized or when legislative requirements dictate centralization for ease of administration.

Centralized pay is associated with diversified "related products" firms trying to protect their present market share and business units interested in minimizing costs while retaining their position in the market (Carroll, 1987; Balkin & Gomez-Mejia, 1987a). Greater control over pay decisions is consistent with the higher bureaucracy associated with these corporate and business unit types. Single product firms carving out new market niches and undertaking projects with significant financial risks tend to exercise less direct control over pay decisions. These single product firms have a more organic management style, with less formal policies and the ability to decentralize decision making.

Open vs. Secret Pay

Lawler (1983) suggests that keeping pay issues secret breeds dependent employees. It also leads to low trust. Open pay, on the other hand, can encourage communication and involvement, in addition to pressuring management to effectively administer the system.

The empirical research conducted by Balkin & Gomez-Mejia (1987a) found open pay systems to be most effective (as reported by compensation managers) in organizations with pay policies that emphasize risk sharing, flexibility, strong "pay for performance" norms, decentralized decisions, employee participation in establishing agreed-upon objectives, and a long-term pay orientation.

Participation vs. Nonparticipation of Employees

Low participation appears to fit the traditional, bureaucratic compensation approach. Participation is associated with nontraditional compensation systems and highly knowledgeable workers who are actively involved in other aspects of organizational decision making (Lawler, 1983; Balkin & Gomez-Mejia, 1987a).

Bureaucratic vs. Flexible Pay Policies

Hambrick & Snow (1987) warn that frequent changes to the pay system can result in a lack of coherent policies leading to a compensation system misaligned with organizational strategy. They suggest that the system should be formalized yet flexible enough to allow for modifications when necessary.

What Patterns Emerge?

In order to determine which strategic compensation dimensions tended to be associated with each other, the work of the same 18 authors listed in Exhibit 1 was reviewed. This is an important task because, as noted by Milkovich (1988), a major challenge is "to extract any basic combinations or patterns of pay decisions that may be related to a variety of organizations and environmental conditions" (p. 3). The optimal method for uncovering strategic patterns of compensation dimensions would be to statistically analyze existing studies. However, the limited amount of empirical research precludes our conducting such an analysis. Instead, we used a heuristic approach to create a typology of compensation dimensions. To this end, the relationships among compensation dimensions postulated by various writers were manually recorded and sorted in order to discern underlying patterns (Note: For more information on this methodology, please contact the authors). Exhibit 2 summarizes the two patterns that were identified.

A proposed label for the first pattern is *mechanistic* because it reflects formalized rules and procedures that "routinize" pay decisions and are applied uniformly across the entire organization. These firms pay for the job performed, not the skills an employee brings to the organization; they emphasize base salary and evaluate individual performance; seniority is important, and long-term tenure with the firm is desired. Because these firms pay more than the market and reward for seniority, employees are often "locked into" these organizations and find it difficult to find comparable

Exhibit 2
Strategic Compensation Patterns

PATTERN A: Mechanistic Compensation Strategies	PATTERN B: Organic Compensation Strategies
Basis for Pay	**Basis for Pay**
Job	Skills
Seniority Emphasis	Performance Emphasis
Individual Appraisals	Group and Individual Appraisals
Short-Term Orientation	Long-Term Orientation
Risk Aversion	Risk Taking
Corporate & Division Performance	Division Performance
Internal > External Equity	External > Internal Equity
Hierarchical Emphasis	Egalitarian Emphasis
Quantitative Performance Measures	Qualitative Performance Measures
Design Issues	**Design Issues**
Pay Level > Market	Pay Level < Market
Fixed Pay > Incentives	Incentives > Fixed Pay
Frequent Bonuses	Deferred Income
Reliance on Intrinsic Rewards	Reliance on Extrinsic Rewards
Administrative Framework	**Administrative Framework**
Centralized	Decentralized
Secrecy Policies	Open Communication
No Participation	Participation
Bureaucratic Policies	Flexible Policies

compensation packages elsewhere. Internal equity procedures are carefully enforced in order to encourage transfers within the "internal labor market," resulting in longer tenure. Moving up the corporate ladder and hierarchical position are important values fostered by the organization's culture. Risk taking is minimal, quantitative performance measures are common, and the pay system has a short-term orientation. The administrative framework is characterized by centralization, secrecy, lack of participation, and bureaucratic policies.

The second pattern may be designated as *organic* because these pay practices tend to be more responsive to varying conditions, contingencies, and individual situations. The mechanistic and organic patterns have opposite orientations, with the latter emphasizing skills, performance, group and individual appraisals, long-term results, risk taking, division performance, external equity, and egalitarian approaches as bases for pay. In terms of

design and administrative issues for the compensation system, the organic pattern is associated with below-market salaries, high incentives in the pay mix, use of bonuses and deferred income, extrinsic rewards, decentralized and open pay policies, employee participation, and flexible compensation programs.

The reader should note that most of the studies used to develop the typology shown in Exhibit 2 are primarily descriptive and suggestive. The heuristic classification system is a first step at synthesizing the many diverse views expressed on this topic. We still have much to learn about the structure of strategic pay dimensions and contingency factors mediating their effectiveness.

What Are the Strategic Compensation Patterns Related To?

In this section we will discuss the overall organizational strategies that are presumed to be affiliated with the mechanistic or organic compensation systems. Exhibit 3 summarizes these relationships.

Mechanistic Compensation Strategies

The mechanistic pattern is associated with the corporate strategies of (a) internal growth, (b) related products, and (c) dominant business. The "internal growth" strategy is followed by firms that are vertically integrated, have a high commitment to their existing product(s), and cautiously expand in the current product areas. The related product strategy refers to a company that grows by diversifying into businesses or products that have a significant relationship to the core business and industry. The "dominant" business strategy describes those firms that diversify to some extent but that obtain a high percentage of their revenues from a single business.

In other words, it appears that the mechanistic compensation pattern is most often used by firms that are fairly secure with their present business and that, when expanding, use their expertise in that current business to grow into similar areas. The reward system complements this corporate strategy by providing pay packages and policies to maintain the ingrown talent needed to enhance the existing business. Work experience with the firm or seniority is rewarded because long-term tenure provides expertise needed to preserve the company's current strategy.

Business unit strategies found associated with the mechanistic pay pattern are the "defender" and "maintenance" strategies. Defenders are concerned with maintaining market share, and those following a maintenance strategy, as the name implies, are also concerned with retaining current position in the market. These business unit strategies have the same characteristics as the corporate strategies associated with the mechanistic pay pattern. The business units' primary concerns are with their existing product and existing market.

Organic Compensation Strategies

The organic pay pattern is related to the corporate strategies of (a) "single product," (b) "acquisition growth," and (c) "unrelated business." The "single product" strategy is characterized by firms at the initial stages of growth where they are preparing for rapid expansion along a narrow product line. The "acquisition growth" strategy is characterized by more mature companies utilizing acquisitions, mergers, and other forms of external activity as avenues for expansion. These firms grow by acquiring businesses unrelated to the current project or industry. Firms using the unrelated business strategy are not vertically integrated and diversify by entering new markets.

Exhibit 3

Compensation Strategies Associated with Various Organizational Structures

Mechanistic Compensation Strategies	Mixed Compensation Strategies	Organic Compensation Strategies
• Internal Growth • Related Products • Dominant Business • Maintenance • Defender	• Analyzer • Dominant Product	• Single Product • Acquisition Growth • Unrelated Business • Prospector • Dynamic Growth
SUMMARY Maintain current market share —mature companies—expand in their area of expertise.	SUMMARY Combines strategy—need flexibility due to culture—firms that are in transition.	SUMMARY Growing firms—expand through acquisition of unrelated businesses.

These corporate strategies are the opposite of those associated with the mechanistic compensation system. When at a mature growth stage, rather than expanding through the cautious acquisition of businesses related to the current product, these firms more aggressively acquire businesses inside and outside of their areas of expertise. While the main concern of companies utilizing mechanistic pay policies was internal equity, the primary concern of firms following the organic compensation strategies is external equity. These firms are interested in taking greater risks and need to attract a different caliber of employee who is challenged by a riskier environment. Kerr (1985) suggests that the reward pattern associated with these strategies should control outcomes versus behavior. The reason given is that when acquiring businesses outside the firm's area of expertise corporate headquarters does not have sufficient knowledge to control the managers in the acquired business. In order to spur successful operations, these firms attempt to set realistic operational goals and measure performance against goal achievement rather than evaluate the behavior used to attain goals. In addition, these growth firms are often more concerned with minimizing fixed costs due to the risky nature of their business and their fast growth; therefore, pay systems which help reduce these fixed costs are more beneficial to these companies.

The business unit strategies associated with the organic pay policies are "prospector" and "dynamic growth." The prospector strategy involves actively searching for new products and markets and pursuing opportunities both within and outside existing areas of expertise. The dynamic growth business strategy describes units that take significant financial risks frequently. Both of these business unit strategies have exactly opposite orientations to those associated with the mechanistic compensation system. Whereas the business unit strategies related to mechanistic pay policies emphasize maintaining current market share, the business unit strategies associated with the organic compensation pattern stress rapid expansion into new, often unrelated, markets.

Mixed Compensation Strategies

So far we have presented two extreme patterns of compensation decisions as summarized in Exhibit 3. We should actually think of these patterns as poles on a continuum. In addition to these two extreme positions on the continuum we have included a midpoint in Exhibit 3. The analyzer strategy, which is used by firms operating in both stable and growing markets, is associated with compensation policies between the mechanistic and organic pattern. This mid-position on our continuum is also associated with the "dominant product" strategy. This strategy is characteristic of firms whose diversification is limited and who obtain most of their revenue from a single product. These firms at the midpoint might be in a transitory state; their immediate needs dictate a compensation strategy that can provide both control and autonomy.

A Critical Assessment and Future Steps

While "think strategically" in terms of reward system almost has become a dogma during the past five years, our understanding of compensation strategy is incomplete, at best. The connection between organizational strategy and appropriate pay policies has not been sufficiently established. Work in this area tends to be prescriptive rather than theory driven, and empirical evidence (particularly in regard to performance results) is sparse or nonexistent. Future advancement in state-of-the-art application of strategic concepts to compensation requires more attention to the following substantive issues.

Strategic Focus

With few exceptions, most writers discuss compensation strategy in overarching terms. This frequently results in a nebulous and "mushy" treatment of the subject. It may be more fruitful to focus on strategic employee groups rather than organizational units, and on how strategic significance of different groups varies according to industry and firm characteristics. For example, Balkin and Gomez-Mejia (1987b) found that while scientists and engineers are crucial in the development of compensation strategies in small high technology firms, they may be less important when designing pay systems for mature manufacturing firms.

Milkovich (1988) suggests that strategic compensation issues be analyzed in terms of functional areas such as Research and Development, Marketing, and Finance. Other possible groups are exempt vs. nonexempt, plant vs. corporate, and professional, semiskilled, and unskilled. Appropriate pay policies for each of these employee groups can be quite different. Measures of success also vary. This suggests that major employee groups should be analyzed to determine their strategic importance and specific needs; compensation strategies appropriate for each employee group should be devised. Compensation strategy might best be divided into those pay policies affecting the entire corporation and pay policies which can be targeted for special employee groups. Additional research is needed to determine which strategic compensation policies should be made at each level.

Level of Analysis

When first reading textbook definitions of corporate and business unit level strategies, the distinctions between them appear clear. However, after carefully examining the typologies used in the compensation strategy literature, the distinctions between these two dimensions become blurred. For instance, the distinction between "dynamic growth" corporate strategy and "prospector" business unit strategy is not sharp. Both of these strategies are characterized as actively expanding into either related or unrelated product areas. Corporate and business unit strategies seem to deal more with the level of analysis than the actual strategies being used. Dynamic growth refers to the entire corporation's strategy while prospector refers to a strategy of one strategic business unit. If a business is not affiliated with a larger corporation, is at the introduction stage of the product life cycle, and is growing rapidly, it could use either definition of its strategy because the entire corporation's strategy is synonymous with business strategy. This issue is brought up to demonstrate two problems.

First, the typologies and designations used for describing corporate and business unit strategies are often unclear or loosely worded. The large number of labels used to describe various strategy types makes distinguishing between them difficult. Unfortunately, it is not uncommon for compensation investigators to borrow concepts from the business policy literature without providing careful justification of their application to pay-related issues.

Increased understanding of compensation strategy requires that more attention be devoted to this definition problem. This is needed to spur research and generate data that can be accumulated and analyzed for patterns and trends so that theories can be developed and tested. As noted by Milkovich (1988), very little is known about the linkages between compensation strategy and firm performance. Meaningful empirical research on this important issue demands better conceptualization of the overlap between compensation and organizational strategy. It is not clear, for example, why strategic compensation patterns should behave differently at the corporate versus the business unit level. Perhaps this distinction is not essential for a better understanding of the compensation policies that are most appropriate for the needs of these firms.

The second problem is that the studies conducted to date tend to focus on large manufacturing firms. These companies do have distinct corporate and business unit strategies and are able to articulate strategy. There is a need to study small and medium size firms in addition to nonmanufacturing companies. There is also a need for clearer descriptions of the firms studied. Any characteristics of the firms that might provide clues as to why their compensation strategies have failed or succeeded should be provided.

"Ideal" Types

The most common approach in compensation strategy theorizing and research to date is to adopt one of the many typologies from the business policy literature (there are at least 15 of these!), sort organizations into various categories of the chosen taxonomy, and then attempt to delineate the compensation features which are most appropriate for those firms in each cohort. The end result is an "ideal" type in terms of pay strategies for each strategic grouping (e.g. prospectors, defenders, etc.).

While taxonomies are often used in the early stages of science as a first step in understanding complex phenomena, it is important to recognize their drawbacks. A danger inherent with the use of typological thinking in compensation strategy is that only a handful of organizations or business units can be neatly classified into a predetermined classification scheme. Most existing business policy taxonomies are much too simplistic to capture the richness and nuances of organizational life that mold the reward system over time. Each firm has its own unique history and tradition, cultural norms, and sociotechnical and environmental forces that shape the framework within which the compensation system must operate. Most companies fall on a continuum along the multiple variables that could potentially influence pay level, pay mix, and compensation policies. Prescribing compensation strategies using an a priori taxonomy provides a general direction, but can be counterproductive if operational programs are faithfully built on such naive models.

Future work in this area would benefit from comprehensive case studies that provide in-depth description of successful compensation strategies employed by a diverse sample of firms. The typical questionnaire-based procedures used in previous studies fall short of providing these types of qualitative detail and insights. In addition, there is a need for nonclassificatory multivariate research using interactive models that can show the unique and combined effects of organizational and environmental variables on the pay system (e.g. pay level, pay mix, and pay policies). Ideally, longitudinal designs should be employed to ascertain how changes in compensation strategy (while controlling for such factors as firm size, extent of diversification, industry, etc.) predict subsequent pay effectiveness criteria (e.g. turnover, pay satisfaction, performance).

Concept of Fit

As discussed in the introduction, many authors have stated that the optimal conditions for corporate success include "fit" between corporate, business unit, human resources, and compensation strategy. But to date the concept of fit has only been tested on a very limited basis. We cannot be certain that fit is actually optimal for corporate success. In fact, Evans (1986) and Greene (1987) suggest that pursuing fit may lead to a rigid and inflexible system. If this is the case, naive concepts of "fit" need to be carefully reexamined and new, more complex paradigms may have to be developed. Is a company interested in adopting a system that will be reliable but possibly inflexible? Milkovich (1988) offers an alternate way of thinking about fit. Rather than alluding to fit as something static, he suggests that obtaining a state of fit is much like "shooting at a moving target." This implies that although fit is desired, the strategies that are appropriate today might easily become incongruent just around the corner. A major problem is that once a reward system is in place, employees develop a set of expectations that makes change difficult and potentially disruptive. Management should be reluctant to make strategic pay decisions that could be ideal under present conditions but may become obsolete in the near future.

References

Andrews, K. R. *The Concept of Corporate Strategy.* (Homewood, IL: Irwin, 1987).

Balkin, D. B. and L. R. Gomez-Mejia. "Determinants of R&D Compensation Strategy in High Tech Industry." *Personnel Psychology, 37(4), 1984,* pp. 635–650.

Balkin, D. B. and L. R. Gomez-Mejia. "Relationship between Organization Strategy, Pay Strategy, and Compensation Effectiveness: An Exploratory Study." (Paper presented at the 47th Academy of Management Meeting, New Orleans, 1987a.)

Balkin, D. B. and L. R. Gomez-Mejia. "Toward a Contingency Theory of Compensation Strategy." *Strategic Management Journal, 8(1), 1987b,* pp. 169–182.

Broderick, R. F. *Pay Policy and Business Strategy— Toward a Measure of Fit.* (Unpublished doctoral dissertation, Cornell University, 1986).

Carroll, S. J. "Business Strategies and Compensation Systems." In: Balkin, D. B. and L. R. Gomez-Mejia, *New Perspectives on Compensation.* (Englewood Cliffs: Prentice-Hall, Inc., 1987).

Crystal, G. "Executive Compensation." In: Gomez-Mejia, L. R. (Ed.), *Compensation.* (Alexandria, VA: Bureau of National Affairs/American Society for Personnel Administration, 1988).

Deckop, J. R. "Top Executive Compensation and the Pay-for-Performance Issue." In: Balkin, D. B. and L. R. Gomez-Mejia, *New Perspectives on Compensation.* (Englewood Cliffs, NJ: Prentice-Hall, 1987).

Evans, P. A. "The Strategic Outcomes of Human Resource Management." *Human Resource Management, 25(1), 1986,* pp. 149–167.

Fay, C. H. "Using the Strategic Planning Process to Develop a Compensation Strategy." *Topics in Total Compensation,* Winter, 1987, pp. 117–129.

Fombrun, C. "Environmental Trends Create New Pressures on Human Resources." *The Journal of Business Strategy,* 1984, January, pp. 61–69.

Galbraith, C. and D. Schendel. "An Empirical Analysis of Strategy Types." *Strategic Management Journal, 4(4), 1983,* pp. 152–173.

Gomez-Mejia, L. R. and D. B. Balkin, "The Effectiveness of Individual and Aggregate Incentive Strategies in an R&D Setting." (Paper presented at the Southwestern Academy of Management Meeting, Houston, TX, 1987.)

Gomez-Mejia, L. R., R. Page, and W. Tornow. "Improving the Effectiveness of Performance Appraisal." *Personnel Administrator,* January, 1985, pp. 74–82.

Gomez-Mejia, L. R., H. Tosi, and T. Hinkin. "Managerial Control, Performance, and Executive Compensation." *Academy of Management Journal, 30(1), 1987,* pp. 51–70.

Greene, R. J. "Effectively Implementing Compensation Strategy." *Topics in Total Compensation,* Winter, 1987, pp. 129–139.

Hambrick, D. "High Profit Strategies in Mature Capital Goods Industries: A Contingency Approach." *Academy of Management Journal, 26(2), 1983,* pp. 687–707.

Hambrick, D. C. and C. C. Snow. "Strategic Reward Systems." In: Snow, C. C., *Strategy, Organization Design and Human Resource Management.* (Greenwich, CT: JAI Press, 1987).

Henderson, R. and H. W. Risher. "Influencing Organizational Strategy through Compensation Leadership." In: Balkin, D. B. and L. R. Gomez-Mejia, *New Perspectives on Compensation.* (Englewood Cliffs, NJ: Prentice-Hall, Inc., 1987).

Kerr, J. "Assigning Managers on the Basis of the Life Cycle." *The Journal of Business Strategy, 2(4), 1982,* pp. 58–65.

Kerr, J. L. "Diversification Strategies and Managerial Rewards: An Empirical Study." *Academy of Management Journal, 28(1), 1985,* pp. 155–179.

Kerr, J. "Strategic Control through Performance Appraisal and Rewards." *Human Resource Planning* (1988, current issue).

Kerr, J. and R. A. Bettis. "Board of Directors, Top Management Compensation, and Shareholder Returns." *Academy of Management Journal, 30,* 1987, pp. 645–665.

Lawler, E. E. III. *Pay and Organization Development.* (Reading, MA: Addison-Wesley, 1981).

Lawler, E. E. III. "Strategic Design of Reward Systems." In: Tichy, N., C. Fombrun, and M. Devanna, *Strategic Human Resource Management.* (New York: J. Wiley & Sons, 1983).

Lawler, E. E. III. "Paying for Performance: Future Directions." In: Balkin, D. B. and L. R. Gomez-

Mejia, *New Perspectives on Compensation*. (Englewood Cliffs, NJ: Prentice-Hall, 1987).

Miles, R. E. and C. C. Snow. "Designing Strategic Human Resource Systems." *Organization Dynamics,* January, 1984, pp. 36–52.

Milkovich, G. T. "A Strategic Perspective to Compensation Management." In Rowland, K. and G. Ferris (Eds.), *Research in Personnel and Human Resources Management.* (Greenwich, CT: JAI Press, 1988, vol. 6).

Miller, D. "Configurations of Strategy and Structure: Towards a Synthesis." *Strategic Management Journal, 7(3),* 1986, pp. 233–249.

Mount, M. K. "Coordinating Salary Action and Performance Appraisal." In: Balkin, D. B. and L. R. Gomez-Mejia, *New Perspectives on Compensation.* (Englewood Cliffs, NJ: Prentice-Hall, 1987).

Murthy, K. R. S. *Corporate Strategy and Top Executive Compensation.* (Boston, MA: Harvard Press, 1977).

Pearce, J. L. "Why Merit Pay Doesn't Work; Implications from Organization Theory." In: Balkin, D. B. and L. R. Gomez-Mejia, *New Perspectives on Compensation.* (Englewood Cliffs, NJ: Prentice-Hall, 1987).

Pitts, R. A. "Incentive Compensation and Organization Design." *Personnel Journal,* May, 1974, pp. 338–344.

Porter, M. E. *Competitive Strategy.* (New York: Free Press, 1980).

Prescott, J. "Environments as Moderators of the Relationship between Strategy and Performance." *Academy of Management Journal, 29(3),* 1986, pp. 329–346.

Rappaport, A. "Executive Incentives vs. Corporate Growth." *Harvard Business Review,* July/August, 1978, pp. 21–40.

Rynes, S. L. and G. T. Milkovich. "Salary Surveys: Dispelling Some Myths about the Market Wage." *Personnel Psychology, 39(2),* 1986, pp. 71–89.

Salscheider, J. "Devising Pay Strategies for Diversified Companies." *Compensation Review,* Second Quarter, 1981, pp. 15–24.

Salter, M. S. "Tailor Incentive Compensation to Strategy." *Harvard Business Review,* March/April, 1973, pp. 94–102.

Simon, H. *The Sciences of the Artificial.* (Cambridge, MA: MIT Press, 1981).

Stata, R. and M. Maidique. "Bonus System for Balanced Strategy." *Harvard Business Review,* November/December, 1980, pp. 156–163.

Steers, R. M. and G. R. Ungson. "Strategic Issues in Executive Compensation Decisions." In: Balkin, D. B. and L. R. Gomez-Mejia, *New Perspectives on Compensation.* (Englewood Cliffs: Prentice-Hall, Inc., 1987).

Stonich, P. J. 1981. "Using Rewards in Implementing Strategy." *Strategic Management Journal, 2(2),* 1981, pp. 345–352.

Terpstra, V. *Cultural Environment of International Business.* (Cincinnati, OH: South-Western Publishing Company, 1978).

Tichy, N. 1983. *Managing Strategic Change.* (New York: J. Wiley & Sons, 1983).

Tichy, N., C. Fombrun, and M. Devanna. "The Organizational Context of Strategic Human Resource Management." In: Tichy, N., C., Fombrun, and M. Devanna (Eds.), *Strategic Human Resources Management.* (New York: J. Wiley & Sons, 1984).

Tosi, H. and L. Tosi. "What Managers Need to Know about Skill-Based Pay." *Organization Dynamics,* May, 1986, pp. 52–64.

Wallace, M. J. "Strategic Uses of Compensation: Key Questions Managers Should Ask." *Topics in Total Compensation,* Winter, 1987, pp. 167–185.

Woo, C. and A. Cooper. "Strategies for Effective Law Share Businesses." *Strategic Management Journal, 2(3),* 1981, pp. 301–318.

Pay for Performance:
What You Should Know

Linda Thornburg

Towers Perrin's Jim Nickel, one of the country's top compensation consultants, was meeting with senior HR executives interested in how they could link compensation systems to total quality management (TQM). He told a story about a Wisconsin manufacturer who moved to the South many years ago to escape union problems. Nickel designed an incentive-pay program for the company, requiring line employees to produce a minimum quantity each day; then they could work more for extra money or leave the line.

"Everybody finished by about 12:30 in the afternoon and spent the rest of the day playing cards in the cafeteria," Nickel said. "Before the holidays they worked more hours because they wanted more money. But the time they spent playing cards was valuable to them. If somebody didn't show up for the card game, the others asked him where he had been."

Here, a ritual that helped cement cultural ties was a more powerful draw than the money. Nickel's point is that employees have more control over quantity, quality and cost than management often gives them credit for. In thinking about how to design reward systems, compensation specialists have to walk some thin lines. There is always the danger that the system will send the wrong message or promote the wrong values.

As TQM becomes the paradigm for business, HR professionals search for ways to integrate the performance-management systems that became vogue in the '70s and '80s into the new TQM framework. Eighty percent of the businesses in the United States have at least one formal quality initiative in place, and most programs are less than five years old.

HR professionals must find ways to reward people for the values inherent in the TQM movement—teamwork, world-class competitiveness, internal and external customer satisfaction, incremental improvement and flexibility. But a major change, scrapping compensation systems that have been used during the past two decades and installing some strange new animal that leaves no room for individual evaluation or manager input, should not be made all at once.

"HR is saying, don't take away performance management, the only tool I have for evaluation," says Tom Pollack of Towers Perrin. "Operational management is saying the total-quality model doesn't fit easily with the performance measurement and appraisal method of paying."

Fortunately for HR professionals, there are dozens of different ways to implement reward systems that will complement quality programs. Companies are experimenting with combinations of individual merit-pay systems and teamwork systems; variable and fixed pay; rating and nonrating systems; and gain-sharing and individual incentive awards.

Steve Gross, the Hay Group's national director of variable compensation, says what's most important in any pay program is what one measures and rewards. The best base-pay system will measure behavioral competency, not accomplishments. The pay-at-risk component of the reward system can be tied to accomplishment factors, he says.

Customer Service Focus

In the model Gross likes to use, individuals are evaluated for base pay on such variables as ability to communicate, customer focus, dealing with change, interpersonal skills, ability to work on a team, and professional and technical knowledge. Managers are rated on employee development, group productivity and leadership. Variable pay for both managers and employees is based on what actually is accomplished. Variable pay can make up anywhere from 5 to 15 percent of a total compensation package for those at the bottom of the ladder, more at higher levels of the organization.

Because customer focus is a critical part of any TQM effort, a three-category rating system is easy to implement. These categories are used: not meeting customer expectations, meeting them or far exceeding them. Those employees who anticipate customer needs and actually develop partnerships with their customers are the stars in the system. Those who are available, approachable and able to identify their customers correctly get the average, or "C" grade; and those who are nonresponsive and unwilling get an "F."

It is important to remember that in the TQM framework, anybody you interact with is a customer. So the model works for all parts of the organization, not just those divisions that actually deal with the people who buy products or services.

Gross says such a system has several advantages. The rules are known and communicated to all employees. There is very little question about what types of behavior will be rewarded. At the same time, the individual merit-based pay that this country has traditionally used is not completely discarded.

In the TQM framework, merit pay is thought to foster an internal competition within the company that is counterproductive to the teamwork goals. Individual merit-based pay also may be grossly unfair, because it depends on the rating of a supervisor who may or may not like you. Some TQM gurus say individuals don't really control more than 10 to 20 percent of how they do their jobs. The rest depends on systems and processes in the organization. If this is true, it's difficult to reward individuals for individual efforts.

Gross's model says you can continue those individual rewards, based on specific, well-thought-out criteria that reward competencies supporting TQM values. Reward the competencies you desire and use the variable-pay component to spur employees on to greater productivity as teams, he suggests.

In designing pay-for-performance programs, you must identify those factors that will lead to group success and then communicate and reward them. Such programs reinforce those values that benefit the company even if products or services change, employees have to work on different teams, or supervisors are promoted to new levels. Employees are not punished for factors that are not in their control—and the "turkeys," those 5 percent or so of employees whose work really is unsatisfactory, are dealt with.

Managing Star Performers

This model is weakest in rewarding star behavior. Gross says stars are not always desirable for the system and can be destructive if they achieve at the expense of other people.

Robert Greene, SPHR, CCP, managing principal of James and Associates in Lincolnshire, Ill., says the star performer can cut the knees off the company. "The lone-ranger mentality isn't the model for us. It's the wagon trains that the Indians found hard to deal with. But the lone-ranger mentality is inbred very deeply in employees 40 or older, who were taught in school to get the answer first, to win while others lost, and to think independently and individually," Greene says.

"Do you know what the Japanese do in their schools?" he asks. "They sit around in a U-shaped formation discussing the question the teacher asks until they have a consensus about the answer. Then they all raise their hands at once. It doesn't matter who gets called on because everybody had a part in formulating the solution."

Still, this isn't Japan. Changing reward systems to discourage star players is not always the easiest or wisest thing to do. A Japanese quality expert once said he thought it was the height of arrogance for Americans to assume they could adopt the principles of TQM as easily as management experts have led them to believe.

Japan is a small country with limited land and natural resources. Since World War II, the Japanese have relied on an ethic of cooperation to achieve economic power. But the United States is a vast continent where, until recently, it seemed there was always room for the star player.

HR managers are uneasy with the idea of discouraging the star through a less-structured reward system. Where are all those good ideas, which the old management-by-objective models encouraged, going to come from?

Robert Greene says you can reward stars with career-development promotional tracking and with distinguished-performance awards. In some cases, such awards should not be money. In all cases, you'd better think carefully about what message you convey with the reward.

Pay at Risk

Jim Nickel of Towers Perrin has a matrix he likes to use when he consults with companies designing a reward system to complement their TQM initiatives. The matrix has an x axis for profit and a y axis for performance. There are four quadrants: high profit, high performance; low profit, high performance; low performance, high profit; and low profit, low performance.

In the high-profit, high-performance quadrant, an employer gladly rewards employees for increased quality and lower cost. In the low-profit, low-performance quadrant there is no problem. No employer wants to pay for sloppy work that causes a company to lose money. But what do you do when factors external to the company cause a low-profit, high-performance scenario?

For example, product liability insurance increases by $900,000 for the year. What do you do when the profitability your company experiences comes from something other than the good work of your employees, such as a change in the international value of the dollar? Do you share your good fortune with your employees? Employers need to think carefully about such elements before jumping into a new pay system.

Nickel says companies are including both financial and operational measures in their pay-for-performance systems. Performance measures in a rewards program have to be linked to overall business strategy. In a battle of priorities between your business plan and your quality plan, the quality plan rarely wins, Nickel maintains. Most reward programs use multiple measures, which can include such variables as improved financial performance along with improved customer service, improved customer satisfaction and reduced defects.

A good model for thinking about financial and operational measures together is the Nolan Norton Institute Scorecard. The scorecard was developed by several senior executives from *Fortune* 500 companies and Nolan Norton, a research organization of KPMG Peat Marwick.

Factors that create value in an organization are classified into four different areas: shareholder value, customer perspective, business processes and organizational learning. Shareholder value is determined by measuring cash flow, adjusted for risk and timing. Customer satisfaction is determined by measuring cycle time, quality and service. Business processes are defined by measuring cycle time, quality and productivity. Organizational learning measures how quickly performance changes. Such measurements can be linked to a pay policy that rewards broad competencies and promotes interdependence and teamwork.

"No facet of management provides a greater impact on our directions than performance measurement," Nolan Norton says.

"What we measure conveys to the organization what we think is important. If we measure it, it will happen."

Integrating Pay with Initiatives

In struggling to integrate pay with TQM initiatives, HR professionals need to remind themselves of the TQM concept of incremental improvement. Towers Perrin consultants say few organizations really implement TQM by the book. They draw from multiple theorists and they pick and choose what fits their particular organizational mission and culture.

Likewise, HR professionals can adapt their company's performance-management system to the TQM initiative, altering their performance-appraisal programs to make them reflect quality initiatives. You do not need to "throw the baby out with the bath water" to begin to implement the TQM paradigm.

Towers Perrin suggests that there are several approaches to choose from. In the most radical approach to performance management aligned with TQM, all values and objectives are based on the organization's mission and on customer satisfaction. Those providing feedback into the system include the managers, employees, teams, peer managers, customers and suppliers.

Measurements of all types are ongoing and improvements are incremental. There are no employee ratings, because workers always know exactly how they are doing. Goals are clear and measurement of key variables is highly calibrated and constant. Everything ties back to organizational mission and customer satisfaction. Rewards are based on how well the company does.

In other models, such as the team-driven model, evaluations may be done quarterly or monthly. Teams rate their peers. Still further down the scale are performance-management systems that are employee- and manager-driven, such as the model Steve Gross likes. Individuals are rated on a three-point scale either quarterly or once every six months by a manager and possibly by teams as well. In the manager-driven/employee-input model, ratings take place annually and are related to a five-point scale. In the old exclusively manager-driven model, what's measured is the task or tasks, not competencies, and annual ratings may contain an unlimited number of rating options.

Reward systems can be designed to reflect company missions and change employee behavior. But a company should never decide on a new reward system and then superimpose it on a culture that simply isn't ready for it. Consultants caution that you need to look at where your company is in implementing a TQM program and design a reward plan that is appropriate.

"You make a transition to an incentive program where a good deal of your pay is at risk," says Janet Fuersich, Coopers and Lybrand's National Line of Business expert. "With variable-based pay, you have to earn the incentive over and over, and you have to educate people about how to do that. So you make people earn a part of it, first. If the historical trends and the motivation aren't there when you institute the program, if the pieces of the program aren't in place, then you'll have employees who think you are just jerking them around. These changes have to be carefully plugged into your individual culture, your demographics, your benefits plan, objectives and mission, and existing profit-sharing plans," Fuersich says.

In designing systems, HR professionals must keep the ultimate goal of the rewards clearly in sight. Towers Perrin consultants say companies use rewards to obtain greater commitment, more flexibility, better cooperation and teamwork, more loyalty, better skills, improved productivity and improved bottom-line results. But employees, who in the TQM framework are the customers of the rewards program, want greater security, more control, more fairness, greater choice, more input and power, more vision, clearer expectations, more frequent feedback, greater trust in management, the ability to make a difference and more money.

To get employees to work better, management will have to communicate a shared vision, share information with employees at all levels to empower them, build trust and security through "walking the talk," and share the gains. Along the way, employers can reinforce the formation of teams as the basic elements of accomplishment.

Defining Performance Excellence

"There is incredible confusion about what constitutes excellence in performance right now," says Robert Greene. "Some of the most interesting things are happening in teams designed to accomplish a special project. Here, the goals of the team are crystal clear, and performance all of a sudden becomes real and visible. It's not some vague balance of MBO—more, better and doing what you're told. It's doing what needs to be done to accomplish the objective or objectives."

Nickel says companies miss some of their greatest opportunities in not rewarding the informal networks and temporary alliances that further the goals and objectives of the organization. The smaller the company, the more difficult it is to define what Greene calls the performance units, those team practices that work together, informally or formally, to get the job done.

In a small organization, one person may be functioning in many different ways on different teams. Any reward system that purports to capture the essence of this individual's responsibilities would have to be fairly complicated, and ratings by team members might not be possible. Multiratings, which included many peer ratings, could however be used in conjunction with the manager's evaluation, however. Greene says employers should evaluate and reward employees by three perspectives:

- How they excel as individuals.
- How they function as part of a primary performance unit.
- Where they fit in as citizens of the company.

Consultants have designed a variety of reward systems to meet these needs.

Ultimately, pay for performance is only one part of a reward system designed to complement total quality management. Employers should think about a total reward strategy that includes such factors as comfort and security, understanding and recognition, influence and power, and finally pay and wealth.

Compensation as a Strategic Tool

Kathleen A. McNally

Today there is a lot of talk about compensation, its cost to the organization and the company's return on its compensation investment. As a result, a variety of new pay systems have been developed, each with its own objectives, benefits and risks. Some companies have already installed new pay plans, and many more are considering it.

Many companies that have implemented various new pay plans find that plan objectives become disconnected from the larger picture; they have been designed with a local rather than a global view. These companies are looking for a way to integrate their pay systems into a cohesive whole so the plans drive the company objectives.

Other companies are beginning to look at new plans, wondering how these plans will fit into the current pay system.

Often, there is little connection between the new pay systems and the overall business plan of the organization. New pay systems are designed to achieve specific, departmental objectives or, worse, they are designed because "everybody is doing it."

The traditional function of pay to attract, retain and motivate employees has not changed with the introduction of new pay systems; but the emphasis has shifted from the attraction and retention functions to the motivation function.

The Planning Process

Strategic compensation planning allows an organization to focus on its strategic objectives and develop a comprehensive plan, considering base pay, short- and long-term incentives, benefits and growth opportunities. This kind of planning helps ensure that the compensation system will support the organization's long- and short-term objectives without overlap, which would have more than one pay plan driving the same objectives.

The ultimate objective of this process is to ensure that the compensation system attracts and retains the desired employees and that it motivates them to do those things that support the business plan.

The steps involved are:

Step 1: Identify business objectives. We begin the process by focusing on the strategic objectives of the organization. What does the company plan to do in the short and long term to gain and to keep a competitive advantage? Will it increase its market share? Expand into new markets or new market niches? Develop new products? Flatten its structure?

Next, the focus is on the tactical level: How will the organization achieve these objectives? Will it work in teams? Will it reduce materials or overhead costs? Will it focus on customer service? Will it improve the quality of its goods or services?

Some specific objectives can be extracted from the strategic plan—quality productivity, service, teamwork, cost reduction and so forth. The potential list is long and different for each organization.

Step 2: Assess the current compensation system. Look at the current pay system to assess the level at which it supports the objectives and the personnel necessary for the business. By taking this step, we will discover gaps or holes in the current system and uncover areas that are "overfunded."

Step 3: Identify potential plan types which can close the gaps. Finally, we can look at the gaps in the current system and identify new or existing pay systems and their funding sources. This step can help close the gaps and make the pay system work effectively.

ABC Company

Let's look at each of these steps in more detail for ABC Company, which wants to implement a new pay system:

Step 1: Identify business objectives. ABC Company has a strategic plan that calls for increased profitability while maintaining market share. To do this, ABC has decided that for the coming year, it will focus on customer service, quality, productivity and cost reduction.

Step 2: Assess the current compensation system. ABC currently has base pay that is at the 50th percentile, a merit pay system, executive stock options and productivity-oriented management incentives. All of these are competitive in the industry's market. In addition, ABC offers medical and dental coverage, pension, life insurance, disability coverage and paid time off, which are competitive in its market. Two years ago, ABC decided to offer on-site day care and flexible work hours for its employees. Last year ABC began to implement self-managed work teams in its operations area.

Exhibit 1, a strategy planning chart, allows ABC to evaluate how well its current pay system helps to attract, retain and motivate its employees.

Exhibit 1.

ABC Company
Compensation Strategy
Planning Chart

	Attract	Retain	Motivate				
			Profitability	Customer Service	Quality	Productivity	Cost Reduction
Base pay	X	X					
Merit increase	X	X					–
Stock options	X	XX	X				
Management productivity incentive	X	XX		–	–	XX	X
Medical insurance	X	X					
Dental insurance	X	X					
Life insurance	X	X					
Disability	X	X					
Paid time off	X	X					
Retirement	X	X					
older ees	X	X					
Day care							
younger ees	XX	XX					
Flexible hours	XX	XX					
Self-managed teams	X	XX					X

X Current system by itself cannot produce the desired objective.
XX Current system produces the desired objective.
– Current system works against achieving the objective.

Down the side of the chart are elements of the compensation system: direct pay, indirect pay (benefits) and several nonpay elements of the employee "contract" that differentiate this company from competitors.

To identify these elements in your organization ask: "Why would someone come to work here instead of for the competition, if pay and benefits were the same?" The answer may be such factors as career opportunities, a participative culture, promises to reduce staff only through attrition, or flexible work hours.

Across the top of the chart are the functions of pay: attraction, retention and motivation. The motivation column is further divided into the specific objectives identified in Step 1.

In assessing its current pay system, ABC used a simple code in which XX means that the current system is sufficient to produce the desired objective; X means that the current system will support the achievement of an objective, but is not strong enough to produce it alone; and minus (−) means that the current system works against achieving the objective.

In assessing the ability of pay elements to attract or retain, ABC compared its systems to those of its competition. In assessing the ability of its pay system to motivate employees, ABC considered both the objectives and the results of the pay system. Where possible, operational data (such as turnover or productivity reports) were used.

Base pay. ABC found that its base pay did not help significantly in attracting and retaining nonmanagement employees, because ABC keeps its base pay at the 50th percentile. It does not offer significantly more or less pay than the competition.

Merit pay. The merit system also does not help ABC attract or retain employees because ABC manages its merit pay system to match the market. Neither the base pay levels nor the merit system have had any effect on the motivational objectives of profitability, customer service, quality or productivity. The merit pay system, because it adds to base pay, has had the effect of increasing costs.

Stock options. ABC's executive stock options, being similar to those of the competition, are only supportive of attracting executives. However, ABC has found that the stock options do help to retain executives, because the options are more generous than those of the competition and have longer vesting requirements. Since the stock options were established, the executive turnover has decreased.

Management incentives. The management incentives, which reward individual managers for achieving productivity goals, have helped ABC retain the managers who are proficient at making their departments more productive. This productivity was achieved largely through increased output. However, in achieving this productivity ABC found that quality and customer service suffered.

Medical and dental coverage, retirement, life insurance, disability coverage and paid time off. All of these plans are competitive in ABC's market, thus they neither help nor hinder attraction and retention of employees.

Day care. No one else in ABC's market offers day care, and ABC has found that this has been an invaluable tool in recruiting and retaining employees with young children. Turnover within this group has decreased significantly since day care was offered. However, it has had no effect on turnover of mid-career and older employees.

Flexible work hours. Since the introduction of flexible work hours, ABC has found that it can easily recruit all levels of employees and that turnover has decreased significantly in all employee groups.

Self-managed work teams. This work structure is not a strong attraction tool, since many incoming employees are not familiar with it. However, it is a strong element in ABC's ability to retain those employees who are involved in the teams. In addition, the teams contributed to cost reductions, because the first layer of supervision was absorbed into the teams.

From the step-by-step analysis, ABC executives realize that the current pay systems are doing a fine job of helping to attract and to retain the kinds of employees ABC needs to do business. The management-productivity incentive is also producing the kinds of productivity improvements that will be required to increase profitability. However, as a result of those individual incentives, quality has suffered, and the managers' push for production has harmed customer service.

ABC would like to devise a pay plan that will help it to reward profitability, customer service, quality and cost reduction. This plan will have to either be integrated with the current productivity incentive or replace it.

Step 3: Identify potential plan types which can close the gaps. Three factors to consider in choosing any new pay plan are the objectives of the plan, the type of work processes in the organization and other programs in place. The objectives for the plan have been identified in Step 2. They are profitability, customer service, quality, cost reduction and possibly productivity. By looking at general categories of new pay plans available, we can find the ones that might produce these objectives.

Exhibit 2 shows four general categories of new pay plans and some of the possible objectives that they can help to achieve. (Neither list is exhaustive.) ABC Company discovered that group incentives, individual incentives and gainsharing can all help to achieve its objectives.

Exhibit 3 shows how different types of new pay systems support different work characteristics. Since most of ABC's work is done by interdependent, self-managed teams of 8 to 10 employees, group incentives seem to be a good choice.

Exhibit 4 shows how some other programs can help to support different types of new pay systems. ABC has a good system of work measurement at the team level. Considering the other programs in place, group incentives still seem to be a good choice for ABC.

Based on this analysis, ABC Company decided to implement group incentives for their self-managed teams. The targets for these group incentives are profitability, quality, cus-

Exhibit 2.

Plan Objectives

	Group Incentives	Individual Incentives	Gainsharing	Skill-based pay
Productivity improvement	XX	XX	XX	
Cost reduction	XX	XX	XX	(X)
Employee involvement			XX	XX
Quality improvement	XX	XX	XX	XX
Customer service	XX	XX	XX	
Employee relations			XX	XX
Job enrichment				XX
Participative management	XX		XX	XX
Team culture	XX		XX	XX
Smaller workforce		XX		XX
Flexible workforce				XX
Flatter organization			XX	XX
Profitability	XX	XX	XX	
Individual performance		XX		
Group performance	XX			

(X) Per-employee costs increase, but total payroll often is reduced.
XX Current system can produce the desired objective.

Work Characteristics

	Group Incentives	Individual Incentives	Gainsharing	Skill-based pay
Group processes	XX		XX	XX
Group size	5 to 15		<500	
Independent work		XX		
Discretionary work		XX		
Interdependent work	XX		XX	
Bottlenecks			XX	XX
Fluctuating volume		XX		XX

XX Current system produces the desired objective.

Exhibit 3.

Supportive Programs

	Group Incentives	Individual Incentives	Gainsharing	Skill-based pay
TQM	XX		XX	XX
Participative management			XX	XX
Employee involvement			XX	XX
Work measurement	XX	Required		
Self-managed teams	XX		XX	XX
Performance management		XX		Required

XX Current system produces the desired objective.

Exhibit 4.

tomer service, productivity and cost reduction. While some of the plans may not target all of these objectives, all plans must target some of them.

In addition, ABC Company has decided to change its management-productivity incentive to ensure that the managers are working together as a team. Consistent with their organizational culture, ABC Company will have the teams themselves, in consultation with a representative from HR, design the plans. One potential funding source is productivity increases from the teams, but ABC is also inves-

tigating the possibility of diverting some of the merit pool into the team incentives.

Taking the time to work through this planning process helped ABC to clarify which portions of its compensation package were attracting and retaining their employees. This understanding allowed them to identify gaps in their system and then to design new pay plans that will fill those gaps.

ABC Company has used the strategic compensation planning process to help strengthen its total pay system and position itself for the future.

The Conceptual and Legal Basis of Comparable Worth

Philip G. Benson and Jeffrey S. Hornsby

In the 1980s, human resources management witnessed the emergence of a well-publicized issue in the administration of employee pay systems. While the underlying issues have indeed been around for far longer, the amount of attention paid the comparable worth controversy in recent years has been tremendous. In this article, we review the nature of the controversy and why its eventual outcome is still uncertain. First, it is important to define the issue and to trace the development of the controversy.

The Meaning of Comparable Worth

The issue of comparable worth is essentially a question of fairness, or more properly, equity in the administration of pay. While it is easy to get people to agree that compensation systems should be equitable, defining precisely what *equitable* means in practice is difficult. Indeed, several forms of pay equity have been defined, and it is not always possible to reconcile them into a single pay plan (Milkovich & Newman, 1987; Wallace and Fay, 1988).

One form of pay equity is known as *external equity.* When we are concerned about external equity, we pay our employees at a rate that is fair in comparison to the labor market wages as defined by competing employers. In this way what is fair is a wage or salary that is similar to what a person could earn if he or she were to take a similar job in some other firm.

A second way to approach equity is to consider *internal equity.* From this perspective, we consider the variety of jobs performed within a single organization and determine the relative standing of the jobs in comparison to each other. In other words, a job is fairly paid when its salary is appropriate in comparison to the salary of other, different jobs in the organization.

It is also possible to define pay equity by comparing the salaries paid to different individuals in the same job. We usually assume that different people, even though they are doing the same work, have different levels of merit. Thus, we often pay people for the quality or quantity of their job performance, and we assume that such differentials are fair when truly based on individual merit.

Finally, we can consider the inherent fairness of the procedures used in setting up and administering the salary plan. Although this issue has seen less formal interest in human resources management until recently, it is clear that a pay plan may be considered unfair simply because of the way in which it was established regardless of the actual decisions made.

In raising the issue of comparable worth, the primary focus is on internal equity and how internal equity relates to external equity. The central issue is whether jobs traditionally held by females are typically paid at a rate less than their true worth, in comparison to jobs that have been traditionally held by males. The essential thesis of a comparable worth argument is that we should somehow pay jobs what they are truly worth to an organization, and that a fair comparison of male- and female-dominated jobs in an organization would often reveal that women are largely underpaid for the work they do. Such a view primarily criticizes the internal equity of a pay plan, although as we'll see, it is also necessary to consider the role played by external equity in this argument.

Indeed, the key pay differential that is often raised as an indication of pay inequity is based in the *earnings gap,* the difference in average earnings of fully employed men and fully employed women. To understand the source of the controversy, it is worthwhile to consider a few statistics based on labor market data and their implications for the issue of sex-based equity in pay administration.

The Earnings Gap

Men and women tend to be concentrated in different kinds of work, and on average they do not earn the same salaries. Women, for example, are heavily concentrated in occupational groups like nursing and teaching, whereas relatively few women work in occupations such as mining and truck driving. This in and of itself is not especially alarming, until one considers that women on average tend to earn about two-thirds the salary earned by the average man. The question, then, is whether or not this represents unfair discrimination against women.

Reskin and Hartmann (1986) have reviewed the literature on sex segregation in the workplace and the effects such segregation has on the earnings of women. They find that women are active participants in the modern labor force, and the trend toward full-time work for women is increasing. However, even though women are far more likely to be employed today than they once were, their earnings still fall far short of the earnings of men. Women are also segregated into relatively few occupational categories, partly because of direct discrimination and partly because women prefer to be in certain occupations. This raises an important question: To what extent are women forced into job categories they would prefer to not be in, and to what extent is sex segregation on the job the result of voluntary choices by women?

As pointed out by Cascio (1989), women who work are found in relatively few job classifications. Specifically, 80% of all women who work are employed in 20 of the 427 job classifications used by the Department of Labor. In addition, although the earnings gap has narrowed somewhat in recent years, women still earn (on average) about 30% less than men. In addition, as the proportion of women in a job classification increases, the average salary earned by workers in that classification decreases. Cascio reports that the annual salary decreases by about $42 for each percentage point increase in women employed in a job classification.

It is data such as this which raise the issue of comparable worth. The essential argument is that women are typically pressured into taking certain kinds of jobs and that those jobs are then undervalued in the labor economy. In addition, in setting pay, it is typical to use labor market data to adjust the results of job evaluation data. We consider the internal equity of the pay for jobs within an organization by rating those jobs on a number of dimensions, but in the final analysis we can set salaries only by comparing the job ratings to some criterion of job worth. This criterion, in typical practice, is the labor market (Schwab, 1980).

However, if the labor market is itself discriminatory and reflects many years of discriminatory practices in setting salaries for women, then its use as a fair criterion of job worth is questionable. It is this issue that makes job evaluation a questionable means of correcting such discrimination. On the other hand, it is also impossible to set up a salary structure without some criterion of fairness, and opponents of comparable worth are quick to point out that anything other than the labor market is arbitrary (Milkovich, 1980). Indeed, the solution to the comparable worth issue is often seen as a reduction in occupational segregation based on sex; if women are free to enter whatever job classifications they prefer, any unfair discrimination will presumably vanish in a free labor economy.

Resolving the earnings gap controversy will not be done easily, as it is precisely this issue that is the core of the comparable worth debate. In addition, it is not possible to simply calculate the differences in pay of women and men and assume that the entire differential is the result of discrimination. There are numerous other explanations for at least part of the wage gap (Milkovich, 1980).

For example, if the average education of full-time employed women is somewhat less than the average years of education found among full-time employed men, we naturally expect that men should on average be paid a somewhat higher wage. In fact, many such partial explanations of the earnings gap can be found, including the typical years of experience held by men and women (women are more likely to have dropped out of the labor market during their childbearing years), the extent to which men and women work in unionized environments, and other such variables. Thus, it is not possible to determine precisely the amount of the earnings gap that is the result of discrimination against women, although it is certain that some of the gap is due to such factors other than sex. In short, it is clear that an earnings gap exists, and it is very likely that it is at least in part the result of discrimination. However, trying to untangle the various arguments to resolve the comparable worth issue is nearly an impossible task.

To clarify the meaning of comparable worth, we must make the distinction between comparable worth and the principle of equal pay for equal work. To do this, it is useful to review two major laws that have implications for gender-based discrimination in pay administration.

The Equal Pay Act of 1963

In the 1960s, the U.S. government passed several laws that were designed to address various long-standing practices that had implications for social goals. One of these laws, the Equal Pay Act (EPA), was intended to forbid certain practices in pay administration that were regarded as discriminatory against working women. In particular the EPA made it illegal to discriminate in setting pay in any way that was directly based on the sex of the job incumbent. However, the EPA does allow for many bases of pay differentials, such that pay differentials do exist in the workplace. Essentially, the EPA requires that employers not discriminate on the basis of sex when establishing pay plans, when male and female employees are working on jobs that require equal skill, equal effort, equal responsibility, and that are performed under similar working conditions. In other words, men and women must be paid equally when they perform jobs that are equal, as defined by these characteristics.

However, in passing the EPA, Congress added what have become known as the four affirmative defenses. While general pay differentials are illegal when based on employee gender, the law specifically allows for pay differentials that are based on (1) a seniority system; (2) a merit system; (3) a system that is based in measures of quantity or quality of production; or (4) any factor other than sex. The law also allows for such practices as bonus systems, night-shift pay differentials, and other such pay practices, as long as these policies are applied to men and women in an equal manner.

The legislative history of the EPA has been reviewed by Williams and McDowell (1980), who make it very clear that the law was never intended to address the issue of equal pay for work of comparable value. While the comparable worth issue was raised initially, Congress quickly rejected the notion in favor of an equal work standard.

Under a comparable worth standard, jobs would be paid at the same wage or salary if those jobs were determined to be of comparable worth to the employing organization. Thus, two jobs that have virtually no duties in common and require different kinds of skills (although often the skills would be at similar levels) and that are not matched in any other of the bases of comparison used, would still be paid the same if they were found to have similar value to the organization. In contrast, the equal work standard requires that two jobs be (in a practical sense) identical before the organization is required to pay the same wage or salary for them. Indeed, under an EPA lawsuit, the first step required is that the plaintiff (i.e., the person filing suit for alleged discrimination) show that the jobs are truly equal. If this standard cannot be met, there is no basis for an equal work lawsuit.

Given this distinction, it is clear that the EPA defines unfair discrimination primarily from the standpoint of within-job comparisons. It is seen as inequitable and thus discriminatory when men and women, working together in the same job classification, with similar seniority and similar proficiency, are paid on a differential basis. Indeed, it was just such a practice that was the primary reason for passage of the EPA; before 1963, many employers openly paid a different wage or salary to men and women in the same job. Such practices were usually justified by the belief that women were "only working for pin money" and were likely to quit as soon as they found a husband, or that men were the only true providers for a family and therefore must be paid a higher wage. The passage of the EPA was a clear statement that Congress did not agree with such a line of thought, and such practices have essentially been banned since that time.

The comparable worth controversy, then, goes beyond the limitations set by the EPA. In this argument, the primary discrimination against women is not a result of within-job inequity but between-job inequity. Instead of equal pay for equal work, the question raised is how to equitably pay men and women who are engaged in very different work. Furthermore such a legal argument requires that laws other than the EPA be used, as the courts have been consistently very clear in requiring that the test for equal work be a prerequisite to other considerations of discrimination under the EPA. What other legal interpretations allow for charges of discrimination on the basis of comparable worth, and what other evidence sug-

gests that the true nature of pay discrimination is based on between-job inequities?

Title VII of the Civil Rights Act

Another law, very different from the EPA, is the Civil Rights Act of 1964. This law, passed very shortly after the EPA, has the goal of broadly addressing discrimination in U.S. society. In particular, Title VII of the Civil Rights Act defines the nature of discrimination in employment settings and sets very wide-reaching limits on acceptable employer practices. Although the law is often considered as regulating the recruitment and staffing aspects of human resources management, the law is in fact applicable to all areas of personnel administration, including compensation practice.

Under Title VII, practices can be found to be discriminatory when they lead to *adverse impact.* In other words, personnel practices that have a greater impact on one protected class of employees than on some other class of employees can be regarded as evidence of discrimination. In particular, as applied to compensation, it is *not* necessary for an employee to show that the jobs in question are equal for a lawsuit under Title VII. The result of such an interpretation is that comparable worth lawsuits need not be immediately rejected, as they are under the EPA. Given that comparable worth lawsuits seem to have a better chance of success under Title VII, it is not surprising that lawsuits were filed questioning the relationship between these two laws, and determining which should take precedence for complaints of gender-based comparable worth lawsuits. However, the relationship between the EPA and Title VII proved to be a complex issue (Williams & McDowell, 1980).

When Title VII was debated, discrimination on the basis of gender was given far less attention than was other discrimination, especially racial discrimination. Indeed, as pointed out by Scarpello and Ledvinka (1988), the addition of sex as a basis of illegal discrimination was largely an attempt to undermine the passage of the Civil Rights Act. Howard Smith, an outspoken opponent of the Civil Rights Act, introduced the amendment that included sex as a form of discrimination, and it can only be concluded from testimony given that his true intent was to block the act. Unfortunately, because the amendment was added late, little discussion was paid to the implications for the interpretation of the EPA. While it was clear that the relationship between the two laws needed clarification, such guidance was limited.

Given the potential problem in interpretation, the Bennett Amendment was added to the bill for the Civil Rights Act (see Williams & McDowell, 1980). This amendment stated that

> it shall not be an unlawful employment practice under this title for any employer to differentiate upon the basis of sex in determining the amount of wages or compensation paid or to be paid to employees of such employer if such differentiation is authorized by the provisions of [the Equal Pay Act].

However, the amendment was added very late in the debate over the Civil Rights Act, with the result that very little attention was given to its interpretation. This has turned out to be a critical issue, because the Bennett Amendment is subject to more than one interpretation.

Essentially, two major interpretations were defined shortly after the Civil Rights Act was passed. Does the Civil Rights Act allow any practice that is *not* a violation of the EPA? This first interpretation would effectively eliminate all comparable worth claims, as the EPA clearly is limited to cases involving equal pay for equal work. A second interpretation, however, is that the Bennett Amendment merely incorporated the four affirmative defenses within Title VII; such as interpretation would allow pay differentials that are based on seniority, merit, quantity/quality of production, and other non-sex bases of pay differentials. This latter interpretation would not thus necessarily require that work be equal under Title VII cases and would leave other avenues than the EPA for comparable worth lawsuits.

This issue was of primary concern in the case of *County of Washington v. Gunther* (1981). In this case, it was determined that male and female guards in an Oregon county prison were paid at a different rate. The jobs in question, however, were found to be not equal, as women guards performed more clerical duties and supervised fewer prisoners than did male guards. Thus, the question was whether the differences in the job classifications were substantial enough to warrant the pay differences. In addition, while external salary data were used as part of the pay-setting process, the female guards were paid at a rate of approximately 70% of the market, while male guards were paid at the market rate.

While a number of questions were raised in this case, the critical issue is the precise meaning of the Bennett Amendment. In short, the U.S. Supreme Court determined that the Bennett Amendment did not preclude a comparable worth lawsuit under Title VII, but only incorporated the four affirmative defenses within Title VII. Thus, it is not necessary to prove that two jobs are equal when filing a pay discrimination lawsuit under Title VII.

This does not mean, however, that comparable worth was supported by the Supreme Court in this case. Indeed, the justices wrote in their opinion that the

> claim is not based on the controversial concept of "comparable worth," under which plaintiffs might claim increased compensation on the basis of a comparison of the intrinsic worth or difficulty of their job with that of other jobs in the same organization or community. Rather, respondents seek to prove, by direct evidence, that their wages were depressed because of intentional sex discrimination, consisting of setting the wage scale for female guards, but not for male guards, at a level lower than its own survey of outside markets and the worth of the jobs warranted. The narrow question in this case is whether such a claim is precluded by . . . the "Bennett Amendment."

Thus, the court was very clear in pointing out that the decision neither endorsed nor rejected the theory of comparable worth, but only asked whether nonidentical jobs could be the basis of a Title VII lawsuit.

The issue that is not clear, given the outcome of the *Washington v. Gunther* case, is whether there is any basis to rule in favor of a comparable worth argument. While court cases have been inconsistent, in general the legal status of comparable worth seems questionable.

Demonstrating Adverse Impact

Historically, plaintiffs in employment discrimination cases employ either a disparate impact or a disparate treatment argument in establishing an argument for illegal discrimination. While the courts usually prefer the class action aspect of disparate impact arguments, Ledvinka (1987) suggests that this approach may not be viable for comparable worth cases. Several cases support this point.

For example, the case of *County of Washington v. Gunther* was based on the notion of intentional discrimination. The use of intent as a basis of a Title VII lawsuit makes it more difficult to prove that discrimination has taken place, and several cases since the *Gunther* decision have suggested that intent must be shown (e.g., *Power v. Barry County* [1982]). Taking this further, showing of intent was seen as requiring that a specific employment practice must be identifiable to justify a disparate impact case in *Coe v. Yellow Freight System* (1981), and this has been further affirmed in several more recent cases (e.g., *Pouncy v. Prudential Insurance Co.,* [1982]; *Spaulding v. University of Washington,* [1985]). In addition, the cases of *AFSCME v. County of Nassau* (1985), *AFSCME v. State of Washington* (1985), and *Spaulding v. University of Washington* (1985) have all suggested that market forces can be a legitimate basis for pay differentials between jobs that are primarily held by women and jobs that are primarily held by men. All of these decisions make it difficult to establish disparate impact as a basis of a comparable worth lawsuit.

As a result of such decisions, a disparate impact strategy offers little hope in addressing the comparable worth issue. In the area of pay determination, the courts very clearly restrict this practice. The overall ramifications of a pay system (i.e., the wage gap) does not establish a disparate impact argument (*Spaulding v. University of Washington*). Essentially, a pay plan that structurally underpays female-dominated jobs does not imply intent on the company's part.

The tone of these court decisions indicates a need for a different direction. In fact the courts appear to more readily accept a disparate treatment strategy for showing adverse impact.

The first court case that legitimized a disparate treatment approach was *County of Washington v. Gunther* (1981). While essentially an equal pay case, the court established the notion that comparable worth is a viable option for addressing pay differentials between male and female jobs. In this case, jail matrons were able to successfully argue that the county intentionally discriminated against them because of their sex by setting wage levels that were lower than male jailers even though a job evaluation showed them to be equal in value to the county. The fact that they went against an adopted pay plan seemed to be the key issue in whether or not a favorable comparable worth decision was rendered (Katz, Lavan, & Malloy, 1986; Ledvinka, 1987). The failure to adhere to "adopted" job evaluation results led to the determination of intentional discrimination.

However, the failure to adhere to adopted job evaluation results seems to be the only evidence accepted for proving intentional discrimination. Several other cases support this contention. For example, in *AFSCME v. State of Washington* (1983) the courts held that unfair wage discrimination had taken place, as the state had conducted a job evaluation, found that women were largely underpaid, agreed to remedy the situation, and then failed to follow through with the needed corrections. (Note that this case was later overturned in 1985.) In addition, in other cases the failure to properly implement the outcomes of a job evaluation study, in a manner consistent with the study, has been seen as the basis for intentional discrimination in *AFSCME v. County of Nassau* (1985). In contrast, the fact that the case of *AFSCME v. State of Washington* was overturned suggests that even these practices are not always illegal. Further support that employers have wide latitude in setting pay can be found in *American Nurses Association v. State of Illinois* (1985, 1986); although the defendant ignored the results of a job evaluation study that had been commissioned, it was successfully argued that the results had never been formally adopted and therefore do not need be followed. This tends to further limit the cases in which job evaluation data can be used to justify an argument for intentional discrimination under Title VII, thus limiting the applicability of the comparable worth argument.

In summary, the strategies allowed by the courts to argue comparable worth are extremely limited. Disparate treatment appears to be the only option and even then the burden on the part of the plaintiff to prove intent is great.

Characteristics of Comparable Worth Cases

Katz, Lavan, and Malloy (1986) analyzed a total of 68 litigated comparable worth cases. In their study they considered several specific hypotheses regarding the likely outcome of such cases. Specifically, they suggested each of the following four hypotheses:

1. Companies that conduct job evaluation studies and market surveys and accurately implement them are more likely to win the case and be subject to less back pay awards.

2. Professional and technical employees are more likely to win a comparable worth case and receive higher back pay awards than are lower-level employees.

3. Employers appealing to the Bennett Amendment are more likely to win the case and be less susceptible to back pay awards.

4. Multiple plaintiff cases are more likely to result in a favorable ruling for comparable worth and back pay awards.

The important characteristics of the 68 cases studied were summarized by Katz et al. (1986) and include a number of findings. First, the cases came from the private sector (62%) more than the public sector (38%), and dealt most typically with blue-collar employees (41%). More of the cases came from service industries (66%) than manufacturing firms (34%) and were fairly evenly split as to whether or not they were filed as a class action lawsuit (53% of cases).

The major issues raised tended to focus more on job evaluation (62% of cases) than on wage surveys (9% of cases), and defenses tended to rely on Bennett Amendment appeals (12% seniority, 8% merit, 4% productivity, and 44% on other bases than gender). Unions were involved in only 16% of cases, and the EEOC was involved in only 19% of cases.

Decisions rendered were consistent with the arguments against a comparable worth theory, although this was far from universal. The defendant won 49% of the cases, the plaintiff won 32% of the cases, and the remainder were split. Back pay was awarded in 25% of cases, and the average settlement was $67,400 (with a range of $2,885 to $190,000).

In considering the four hypotheses given by Katz et al. (1986), a significant difference was found for only one. A company was likely to succeed in its defense against comparable worth if its defense was based on merit, seniority, productivity, or any factor besides sex. The company's use of a systematic job evaluation, the type of employee, union involvement, and number of plaintiffs had no significant impact on the outcome of the cases.

Major Court Cases for and against Comparable Worth

While Katz et al. found 68 cases that litigated the issue of comparable worth, 11 cases are often cited for their relevance to the critical issues pertinent to how the case was decided. All these cases date from 1982 to 1985 and, due to the lack of any law making comparable worth mandatory, provide guidance for more recent and future court decisions.

Pro–comparable worth cases. The following four cases, in chronological order, are cases in which the court's decision could be construed as pro–comparable worth.

1. *County of Washington v. Gunther* (1981). This case led the way for comparable worth cases to be filed under Title VII by endorsing the validity of a company-sponsored job evaluation. However, it did not endorse the issue of comparable worth. Specifically, the court's decision enabled plaintiffs to mount a disparate treatment argument by establishing a means of proving adverse impact. The theory is that if an organization ignores the results of its own job evaluation study and pays a lower-than-prescribed wage to female-dominated jobs, intent to discriminate is proven and the burden shifts to the defendant to show a bona fide occupational qualification.

2. *Lanegan-Grimm v. Library Association of Portland* (1983). In this case, the court ruled against the Library Association because they paid bookmobile drivers (who were mostly female) less than delivery truck drivers (who were mostly male). The court ruled for the females because the jobs were shown to be similar though not equal.

3. *AFSCME v. State of Washington* (1983). In this case, the State had conducted a job evaluation study but had failed to adjust the wages of female-dominated jobs based on the results of the job evaluation.

4. *AFSCME v. County of Nassau* (1985). The court allowed the use of a job evaluation study to establish intentional discrimination based on a previous percent set by the *County of Washington v. Gunther* case.

Cases decided against comparable worth. A considerable amount of case law has struck down the notion of comparable worth. The courts have forced the usage of a disparate treatment argument and seem to be shying away from the use of a job evaluation study for proof of intentional discrimination. The following is a description of six fundamental cases that have been decided against comparable worth.

1. *Briggs v. City of Madison* (1982). In this case, public health nurses claimed that they were paid less than public health sanitarians. While the court ruled that the burden of proving intent was satisfied, the City of Madison successfully argued that the salary differential was based on market demand.

2. *Pouncy v. Prudential Insurance Co.* (1982). The court ruled that a disparate impact argument is not allowed when the case involves a company's general employment practices.

3. *Power v. Barry County* (1982). The court ruled that Title VII pay discrimination claims are limited to situations in which intentional discrimination can be proven.

4. *Spaulding v. University of Washington* (1984). In this case, the court ruled that companies are "price takers" in that they must deal with the market as a given. This decision validated a market pricing strategy over job evaluation, thereby diluting the impact of job evaluation results in comparable worth cases.

5. *AFSCME v. State of Washington* (1985). This appeals court decision overturned the earlier 1983 decision. The court stated that job evaluation results were insufficient evidence of intentional discrimination. Furthermore, the court held that a company is not bound by a job evaluation that it commissioned since it is only "one factor influencing the rate of compensation."

6. *American Nurses v. State of Illinois* (1985). This court decision supported the findings in *AFSCME v. Washington* (1985) and *Spaulding v. University of Washington* (1985) by stating that an employer is not bound by job evaluation results even if they indicate a more equitable job structure.

Recent Court Decisions

While the cases described have often been cited in the literature on comparable worth, relatively little has been said about more recent developments. Indeed, in very few cases since 1985 has litigation centered on the comparable worth debate. This lack of cases is probably due to the impact of the Spaulding and AFSCME court decisions. However, four cases have been decided to support the notion that, at least in the near future, comparable worth is a moot issue. The following is a brief discussion of the cases.

1. *American Nurses Association v. State of Illinois* (1986). This appeal to the 1985 district court decision by the plaintiffs reaffirmed the notion that a salary structure is market driven (at least in the eyes of the courts). The court decision discussed the fact that "upsetting the market equilibrium by imposing such a conception would have costly consequences, some of which might undercut the ultimate goals of the comparable worth movement."

2. *Colby v. J.C. Penney Company Inc.* (1987). The appeals court decision ruled that, just as in the American Association of Nurses case, the relative market value of the jobs, not the predominant sex of the incumbents, was the basis for pay differences. The court also ruled that since females were not barred from the higher-paying jobs, no intent to discriminate existed.

3. *Equal Employment Opportunity Commission, Cole, and Long v. Madison Community Unit School District No. 12* (1987). In this case, Long, a female girls' track and tennis coach, was paid less than the boys' track and tennis coaches, even though equivalent numbers of students were coached and an equivalent amount of time was spent on the job. Specifically, the appeal centered on whether the case was based on equal pay or comparable worth. The question raised was whether or not the coaching jobs were "very much alike" or just "comparable." The court ruled that paying coaches of girls' teams less than coaches of boys' teams violated the Equal Pay Act when the same sport was concerned. However, comparisons across different sports (i.e., a female tennis coach and a male track coach) were ruled erroneous because there were pay differentials across coaches of different men's sports.

4. *Forsberg v. Pacific Northwest Bell Telephone* (1988). The court ruled that the tele-phone company did not violate the Equal Pay Act by paying telephone maintenance administrators (a female-dominated job) less than their predecessors, test desk technicians (a male-dominated job). Since the male-dominated position was phased out because of advances in technology and the new female-dominated position required less skills (even though the work was comparable), the court ruled against Forsberg and the notion of comparable worth.

In summary, the recent court cases center around identifying whether or not the case is an Equal Pay Act case or a comparable worth case. Plaintiffs who successfully argue that the Equal Pay Act applies have a reasonable chance of winning the case. However, if the jobs are not proven to be reasonably equal, the case shifts to the now skeptical comparable worth arena. Barring a federal or state law that gives comparable worth the same legal status as equal pay, the instances of comparable worth cases in the 1990s will be virtually nonexistent. The trend is beginning as evidenced by the lack of cases in the past few years.

Conclusion

Comparable worth has been an issue to receive substantial attention, both in the popular press and in the professional literature. Indeed, the view toward comparable worth was argued as one of the differences in the 1988 U.S. presidential candidates. However, the legal status of the comparable worth theory is developing as without support, and for all of the attention paid to it, it seems that equal pay for equal work remains the applicable standard.

In practice, the greatest legal liability for human resources managers appears to be in the failure to fairly pay women and men in the same job classification. In addition, the practice of conducting a careful job evaluation, and then ignoring the results of such a study, seems to be a potential violation of law. In particular, the practice of deliberately paying women at less than market, while paying men in very similar jobs at the market, seems likely to lead to the same decision that emerged in the *Washington v. Gunther* case.

Even though the courts have been generally unsympathetic to comparable worth claims, the issue should not be ruled out as dead. Indeed, the political aspects of this issue could lead to efforts to change the applicable laws, with any variety of interpretations. In addition, while the courts have been reasonably consistent, it is always possible for a Supreme Court decision to alter the precedent interpretations. However, neither of these possibilities seems immediately likely, and at present comparable worth seems to have little legal basis.

References

AFSCME v. County of Nassau, F. Supp., 37 FEP Cases 1424 (E.D.N.Y. 1985).

AFSCME v. State of Washington, 578 F. Supp. 846 (W.D. Wash. 1983).

AFSCME v. State of Washington, 770 F 2d 1401, Nos. 84–3569, 3590, slip op. (9th Cir. 1985).

American Nurses Association v. State of Illinois, 606 F. Supp. 1313 (N.D. Ill. 1985).

American Nurses Association v. State of Illinois, 783 F. 2d 716 (7th Cir. 1986).

Becker, G. S. (1985). How the market acted affirmatively for women. *Business Week,* 10.

Briggs v. City of Madison, 536 F. Supp. 435 (W.D. Wis. 1982).

Cascio, W. F. (1989). *Managing human resources: Productivity, quality of work life, profits.* New York: McGraw Hill.

Civil Rights Act of 1964, Title VII, 42 U.S.C., 2000e, *et seq.*

Coe v. Yellow Freight System, 646 F 2d 407 (10th Cir. 1981).

Colby v. J. C. Penney Company Inc., 811 F 2d (CA-7. 1987).

County of Washington v. Gunther, 452 U.S. 161 (U.S. S. Ct. 1981).

Equal Employment Opportunity Commission, Cole, & Long v. Madison Community Unit School District No. 12, 43 EDP (CA-7, 1987).

Equal Pay Act of 1963, 29 U.S.C., 206(d)(1) (1976).

Forsberg v. Pacific Northwest Bell Telephone Co., 45 EPD 1988 (CA 9 affirming DC Oregon 1985).

Katz, M., Lavan, H., & Malloy, M. S. (1986). Comparable worth: Analysis of cases and implications for HR management. *Compensation and Benefits Review, 18,* 26–38.

Ledvinka, J. (1987). The legal status of comparable worth. In D. B. Balkin and L. R. Gomez-Mejia (Eds.), *New perspectives on compensation.* Englewood Cliffs, NJ: Prentice-Hall.

Milkovich, G. T. (1980). The emerging debate. In E. R. Livernash (Ed.), *Comparable worth: Issues and alternatives.* Washington, DC: Equal Employment Advisory Council.

Milkovich, G. T., & Newman, J. M. (1987). *Compensation.* Plano, TX: Business Publications, Inc.

Pouncy v. Prudential Insurance Co., 668 F 2d 795 (5th Cir. 1982).

Power v. Barry County, 539 F. Supp 721 (W.D. Mich. 1982).

Reskin, B. F., & Hartmann, H. I. (Eds.) (1986). *Women's work, men's work: Sex segregation on the job.* Washington, DC: National Academy Press.

Scarpello, V. G., & Ledvinka, J. (1988). *Personnel/ human resource management: Environments and functions.* Boston: PWS-Kent.

Schwab, D. P. (1980). Job evaluation and pay setting: Concepts and practices. In E. R. Livernash (Ed.), *Comparable worth: Issues and alternatives.* Washington, DC: Equal Employment Advisory Council.

Spaulding v. University of Washington, 740 F 2d 686 (9th Cir. 1985).

Wallace, M. J., Jr., & Fay, C. H. (1988). *Compensation theory and practice* (2nd ed.). Boston, MA: PWS-Kent.

Williams, R. E., & McDowell, D. S. (1980). The legal framework. In E. R. Livernash (Ed.), *Comparable worth: Issues and alternatives.* Washington, DC: Equal Employment Advisory Council.

CHAPTER 9

Training and Development

The training and development of human resources is an important activity in organizations. The outcomes of any of the previous activities (e.g., recruitment and selection, performance appraisal) may indicate need for improvements in work performance, updates in job knowledge, modifications of existing skills and abilities, or a new awareness of and response to changing environmental conditions. Training and development, in its many aspects, is used by organizations and employees to advance their individual and collective self-interests.

Estimates suggest that U.S. organizations spend more than $200 billion a year on the planning and implementation of all types of training and development programs, ranging from technical skill training to management development. With an investment of this magnitude, one would expect organizations to have a good deal of evidence concerning the benefits of those programs. However, the contrary is true: In most organizations the quality of the evaluation component of training and development has been seriously neglected. Organizations are fairly conscientious in their efforts to determine training and development needs and to design the content, structure, and techniques of programs to meet those needs, but few if any systematic efforts are exerted in program evaluation. Much program evaluation today is limited to collecting the subjective reactions of program participants rather than evaluating the longer-term, more objective measures of change in behavior. But, with an increasing focus on accountability and strategic human resources management, we will very likely see more careful attention paid to program evaluation in the future.

The first article in this chapter, by Chachere and Martocchio, points out the close link between training and organizational effectiveness and discusses the pivotal nature of this relationship for organizations of the future. Next, the Wilson and Elman article addresses the beneficial effect of mentoring, which leads to many positive organizational outcomes. McCall draws upon the extensive research base of the Center for Creative Leadership concerning management development to present a somewhat different view concerning the best way to develop managers. The conclusion from these latter two articles is that training within organizations does not stop—it is an ongoing organizational activity.

The last article, by Urban, Ferris, Crowe, and Miller, is concerned with the evaluation of training in relation to other organizational needs. These authors make the point that the primary criterion for assessing the effectiveness of training is the dollar criterion. Training must pay for itself and yield positive organizational outcomes, or it becomes an unaffordable luxury.

Suggestions for Further Reading

Carlisle, K., & Henrie, D. (1993). Are you doing high-impact HR? *Training & Development, 47,* 47–53.

Greengard, S. (1993). How technology is advancing HR. *Personnel Journal, 72,* 80–90.

Laabs, J. (1993). How Gillette grooms global talent. *Personnel Journal, 72,* 64–76.

May, B. (1993). Youthful problems—Adult solutions. *Supervision, 54,* 3–6+.

Mirvis, P. (1993, September). Is human resources out of it? *Across the Board,* pp. 50–51.

Optimism for workforce growth varies among regions. (1993, September). *HR Focus,* p. 2.

Overman, S. (1993, September). Under HR umbrella, career development pays dividends. *HR Magazine,* pp. 67–68.

Shull, G. (1993). Stretching the boundaries of sexual harassment. *Training, 30,* 74.

Smith, J. (1993, August). Train managers on HIV/AIDS issues. *HR Focus,* p. 10.

Soloman, C. (1993). HR is solving shift-work problems. *Personnel Journal, 72,* 36–48.

Linking Training with Productivity: Taking Training into the Twenty-First Century

Denise R. Chachere and Joseph J. Martocchio

Introduction

Since the late 1970s a literature has emerged that maintains that the use of human resource management (HR) practices (performance appraisal, training and development, and so on) represents a potent influence on the attainment of competitive strategy (Lengnick-Hall & Lengnick-Hall, 1988; Wright & McMahan, 1992). Competitive strategy refers to the goals that top management sets to position its business within the market for the purpose of achieving and sustaining a competitive advantage or the value an organization or firm is able to create for its customers that exceeds the cost of creating it (Porter, 1985). Competitive advantage is revealed in various organizational performance measures such as return on investment, sales revenue, and market share. One of the key determinants of competitive advantage is labor productivity.

Moreover, employee skills and abilities are essential for "moving" an organization toward operating consistently with its strategy (Lengnick-Hall & Lengnick-Hall, 1988). In no other HR function is employee skill and ability development addressed more than in training. Indeed, many case studies in the applied HR literature showcase firms that have "successfully" aligned specific HR practices such as training with competitive strategies for organizations (Carnevale, Gainer, & Villet, 1990). Noticeably absent from this literature are evaluative data on the role of training in meeting organizational goals (Tannenbaum & Woods, 1992). In other words, we have relatively little of the information necessary to *demonstrate* that training, in fact, contributes to the achievement of competitive advantage.

Taking training into the twenty-first century will require that HR professionals team up with top management to monitor regularly the degree to which training contributes to competitive advantage. A recent estimate indicates that U.S. companies spend over $200 billion annually on training and development (McKenna, 1990). This investment signals the importance of training activities in the workplace in this country. In addition, as the globalization of business intensifies, it is imperative to understand how a multinational enterprise operates in accord with its competitive strategy (Ghoshal, 1987). Meeting the imperative of competitive strategy mandates that the operation of a multinational enterprise be sensitive to global competition and local customs, which are not always compatible (Bartlett & Ghoshal, 1991). For example, an American-owned multinational enterprise would typically operate under a capitalist ethic. However, the firm's employees in a foreign country—say, China—might be totally unaccustomed to that profit maximization ethic inasmuch as the vast majority of business in China is owned by the government. This example underscores the importance of training in orienting foreign employees toward sufficient productivity.

Being well aware that productivity is essential to the attainment of competitive advantage, we have witnessed in our nation a continuing decline in its growth. The rate of growth is defined as the percent change from the previous year in the ratio of output to labor hour. As Table 1 shows, the rate of

Table 1
Percent Change in Output per Hour of Labor, Nonfarm
Business Sector, U.S., 1954–1991

Year	Percent Change	Year	Percent Change
1991	0.6	1974	−2.5
1990	−0.1	1972	3.7
1989	−0.9	1970	0.3
1988	0.9	1968	3.3
1987	0.8	1966	2.5
1986	1.6	1964	3.9
1984	3.1	1962	3.6
1982	0.2	1960	0.8
1980	−0.7	1958	2.4
1978	0.6	1956	0.3
1976	3.2	1954	1.4

Source: *Economic Report of the President,* 1985 and 1993.

growth in American labor productivity slowed considerably in the 1970s and 1980s, remaining virtually stagnant from 1977 on.

Beyond mere talk of productivity, there are widespread signs of serious and sustained efforts to create new opportunities for recovery: Organization-wide productivity improvement programs are increasing, firms are expanding efforts to improve employee job satisfaction, productivity is surfacing as a key issue in union negotiations, and, at the national level, various committees have been created with the aim of halting America's industrial decline. Indeed, neither the federal government nor business leaders are totally convinced that we have taken all possible steps to increase operational efficiency through engineering and other techniques.

When we consider the potential array of impediments to an organization's productivity, it is not the technology that will normally prove at fault. Rather, the real problem will most often have its roots in the attitudes and behaviors of people within the system. Thus, the source of improvement in the organization's productivity position is directly traceable to people; it follows that the achievement of a better bottom line of productivity becomes everyone's business.

Recognition of the centrality of people in the total productivity scheme of the organization requires managers who are capable of utilizing the organization's human resources in a superior manner, and it calls for a commitment to a systems approach to productivity enhancement in which all members of the organization are involved in a partnership toward its attainment.

What else could this point to but some link between productivity and effective training? Yet, for the volumes written on the separate subjects of training and productivity, the literature is virtually silent on the subject of training-productivity linkages.

The purpose of this article is to convince you that we must link training and productivity if American business is to prosper. Thus, we will provide a simple framework for linking training and productivity. But first, we will address the essential concepts of training, competitive strategy, and productivity.

Training

This part of the discussion is divided into concise sections that together will give you a good idea of what training is all about. First we propose a working definition of training. Then we offer a brief history of training, noting the key milestones in the evolution of training during this century. Recent history can provide useful input into plans for the future—in this case, plans for taking training into the twenty-first century. Finally, we consider criteria for evaluation of training.

Defining Training

According to Cascio (1991), training activities are planned programs of organizational improvement undertaken to bring about a relatively permanent change in employee knowledge (e.g., familiarity with all the items in a particular product line), skills (e.g., ability to deal diplomatically with irate customers), attitudes (e.g., satisfaction with training, which may lead the employee to seek out further training), or behavior (e.g., acceptable performance of the job for which training was provided). Organizations incur fiscal costs due to the development, implementation, and evaluation of these planned programs of improvement. For training to be deemed successful, it must be associated with improvements in knowledge, skills, attitudes, or behavior that outweigh the fiscal cost to develop, implement, and evaluate training. Does it sound simple? Before answering, let us consider some of the milestones in the evolution of training.

History of Training

Evidence of training can be traced as far back as several thousand years. Training must have been prerequisite to the construction of many ancient architectural wonders, such as the Egyptian pyramids. Certainly, the pyramids were not built by a few individuals. In fact, history books recount that thousands of people built the pyramids over a period of years. It is reasonable to infer that training occurred insofar as those who initiated the construction of the pyramids, perhaps experts in architectural design and stone masonry, transferred their knowledge to others. No doubt, training has come a long way since ancient Egypt. Let us focus on the evolution of training in the twentieth century as we prepare to take it into the twenty-first century.

The 1910s. Developments in training between 1910 and 1920 resulted from changes in the automobile industry and necessities created by World War I. Ford Motor Company initiated the assembly line approach to automobile manufacturing. By design the assembly line resulted in workers' performing specific tasks repeatedly. Training was instituted to teach workers to manufacture cars in this way. During World War I there was a tremendous need for warships, but not enough skilled workers were available to meet this demand. Consequently, unskilled workers were employed, and large-scale training programs were instituted to train these individuals quickly.

The 1920s. During the prosperous 1920s neither the surplus workers who had supported

the war effort nor their skills were needed because World War I had ended. With this slowdown, there were fewer opportunities in the workplace for training. As a result, correspondence schools became the prevalent means by which individuals learned technical skills related to their trades. In addition, sales training became popular as a result of the advent and growing popularity of consumer appliances.

The 1930s. The severe economic depression of the 1930s created a training paradox. On one hand, there was widespread termination of training throughout the business community stemming from the failure of businesses, which obviously eliminated training opportunities. Business failure also led to a surplus of skilled workers, who found themselves unemployed. On the other hand, the government stimulated training by providing funds for training in handicrafts, such as leather work, that provided individuals with practical skills they could use to make a living.

The 1940s. Like the 1910s, the 1940s were a time of expanding employment and attendant training efforts that were stimulated by the government as a result of World War II. Because the technology of war was becoming more advanced and involved many different kinds of implements (tanks, airplanes, and so on), diverse training methods were created. Also, during this decade, the formation of the American Society of Training and Development (ASTD) first signaled the professionalization of training practitioners.

The 1950s. During the 1950s videotape and television became the prominent media for delivering a variety of training opportunities. These media enabled companies to teach their employees a wide range of job-related skills efficiently and cost-effectively. This decade also saw increased interest among trainers in the evaluation of training, a matter that, for obvious reasons, could not be considered in its own right during the war era.

The 1960s. During the 1960s training became a topic of interest to academic researchers, and training practitioners and academicians formed partnerships to develop effective training. Evidence of this partnership can be seen in the reporting of training research in various scholarly journals and in the genesis of *Training and Development Journal,* an outlet that continues to showcase training innovations. The importance of training needs assessment and evaluation was also recognized during this time.

The 1970s. The 1970s reflected a quantum step in the evolution of training. Training became recognized as a *system* of practices, rather than separate practices, that could be designed to meet established organizational objectives. Training was deemed essential to effective personnel development, organizational structure, management methods, interpersonal relations, and group dynamics. This change can be considered the precursor of the use of training as a strategic tool for attaining and sustaining competitive advantage.

The 1980s. With the sharp economic recession in the early 1980s, training professionals received increasing pressure from top management to justify expenditures on training programs. As a result, a great deal of research went into developing methods to assess the utility, or future payoff, of training. This research yielded a plethora of prescriptive articles urging training practitioners to consider ways to evaluate the return on investment in training but offering little substantive information.

The 1990s. We are rapidly approaching the beginning of the twenty-first century. The developments of the 1990s suggest that we have not moved much closer to *actually* assessing the return on investment for training and development, in spite of the extraordinary sums of money American businesses spend each year on training (as mentioned earlier, an estimated $200 billion!). Given the lengths to which businesses go to protect their annual profit margins, virtually no expense on the balance sheet goes unnoticed. Moreover, almost no employee is sacred. Just consider IBM, which earned its

claim to fame partly through its practice of lifetime employment. To help ensure its survival in the marketplace, IBM laid off tens of thousands of employees in 1993. We believe that if training is to remain viable and flourish in the twenty-first century, it is more essential than ever to give serious thought to the link between training and productivity.

This brief history has shown that oftentimes training was implemented reactively, as during World Wars I and II. The implication is that little opportunity was afforded to consider training effectiveness. Another fact revealed by this history is that for most of this century, training has been conceptualized primarily at the level of the individual (the employee) rather than the organization. Thus, it is reasonable to infer that the expertise gained during this century about training evaluation centers on the individual rather than the organization, particularly given the prescriptive nature of the recent organization-level training literature. Recognizing the relative lack of attention to the evaluation of training, let us examine some of the ways in which evaluation is conducted.

Training Evaluation Criteria

Kirkpatrick (1987) advanced four levels of training evaluation criteria that have been generally accepted by training practitioners. Each criterion addresses different questions.

Level 1. The first criterion, *trainee reactions,* refers to trainees' judgments of the usefulness of the training program and the quality of its delivery. Trainee reactions, when assessed, are measured by survey at the completion of the training session. The survey questions can be specific or general (e.g., "How satisfied were you with the presentation of sales skill strategies?" versus "How satisfied were you with the overall training program?"). The survey information may help training designers pinpoint potential problems in the training as well as possible reasons for any shortcomings.

Level 2. The second criterion, *learning,* refers to the extent to which principles, facts, and techniques are understood and retained in memory by the trainee. Like trainee reactions, learning is often assessed at the completion of the training program—and, sometimes, throughout the program—via appropriate tests (e.g., assessment of typing speed or recall of concepts from memory). The first two criteria are important because both positive trainee reactions and learning are expected to lead to more job-related and concrete ways of assessing training.

Level 3. The third criterion, *behavior,* relates to changes in job-related behaviors or performance that can be attributed to training. Specifically, this criterion assesses the extent to which an employee (1) generalizes knowledge and skill acquired in training to the workplace and (2) maintains the level of skill proficiency or knowledge acquired in training. Generalization, for instance, might mean applying techniques for dealing effectively with "difficult" individuals, learned and practiced in a training setting, to dealing diplomatically with irate customers or managing a highly competitive co-worker in the workplace. A test of skill maintenance might be whether a typing speed of 90 words per minute demonstrated during training is sustained over time when the employee is back on the job.

Level 4. The fourth criterion, *results,* refers to the extent to which the organization realizes tangible outcomes that can be attributed to training. Results are such outcomes as enhanced productivity, lower costs, and higher product or service quality. Results in the context of training indicate whether (and how well) an organization has attained competitive advantage. Likewise, assessment of results over time can reveal whether (and how well) competitive advantage has been sustained over time. Whereas much research on trainee reactions, learning, and behavior has been amassed over the last several decades, relatively little has been documented concerning results. In the next section we discuss competitive strategy as the context for the re-

sults criteria that must be met if an organization is to attain and sustain competitive advantage.

Competitive Strategy and Training for Competitive Advantage

A plethora of strategy types—and an associated proliferation of terminology—are discernible in the literature. Overall, they fall into the categories of three widely accepted generic competitive strategies: (1) differentiation, (2) highest quality, and (3) lowest cost (Porter, 1985). Porter argues that these strategies represent the essence of competitive advantage, and we will invoke them for this discussion.

Differentiation

An organization uses the differentiation strategy to develop products or services different from those of competitors. Iams dog food company is a good example of a company that has successfully pursued this strategy. Within its primary focus on dog food, Iams offers two differentiated lines, one that is nutritionally well balanced for dogs and contains quality ingredients and an ultrapremium line, Eukanuba, with products that contain only top-grade sources of meat protein. In differentiating, Iams has created an image that appeals to the general population of dog owners with its standard line of products and an image that appeals to dog enthusiasts who want "the best you can do for your dog."

Highest Quality

The second strategy, the highest-quality strategy, emphasizes the enhancement of product or service quality. Motorola Corporation is one organization that pursues a quality enhancement strategy. Motorola initiated a program, *Sigma Six,* that sets a standard for virtually eliminating defects from its manufacturing and service delivery processes. Accordingly, there will be no more than three defective components per one million manufactured.

Lowest Cost

The third broad strategy, the lowest-cost strategy, focuses on gaining competitive advantage by being the lowest-cost producer. United Parcel Service (UPS) is an excellent example of an organization that pursues a cost reduction strategy. In a highly competitive market (including, for example, Federal Express and Emory), UPS has successfully gained and is sustaining competitive advantage through the elimination of wasteful steps in the parcel delivery process. For example, observers frequently accompany UPS drivers on their routes, literally counting the motions, steps, and time it takes to complete a parcel delivery.

Successful pursuit of these overall strategies depends upon a complex of factors. Our concern is with the use of training practices to support these strategies. Already, researchers have begun to conceptualize the optimal design of HR practices that are expected to elicit employee behaviors that are consistent with the chosen strategy (Schuler & Jackson, 1987). Left relatively unexplored is the determination of the best training evaluation criteria for each competitive strategy. We will speculate about some possible criteria for training that may be used to enhance productivity. But first, it is essential to consider the kinds of employee behaviors that should be elicited to support each of these strategy types.

According to Schuler and Jackson (1987), an organization in pursuit of a differentiation strategy might expect employees to be actively involved in making suggestions for improving their work methods, or it might grant employees a limited time to experiment as well as to exhibit cooperative and interdependent behaviors. Pursuit of a highest-quality strategy will likely mandate highly reliable behavior from employees who can identify with the organization and, when necessary, adapt to changing circumstances (Schuler & Jackson, 1987). An organization in pursuit of the lowest-cost strategy might expect employees to perform their jobs efficiently, perhaps

with monitoring from management (Schuler & Jackson, 1987).

Until this point we have considered individual employee behavior and competitive strategy. Ultimately, each employee is the fundamental component; however, establishing the link between training and productivity requires aggregation to the unit of analysis for which training is targeted. Likely units of analysis range from formal work teams through functional departments to organizational subunits. A formal work team may consist of a group of individuals who are responsible for the complete manufacture of a product or the conception and delivery of a service; such a team may receive technical training or self-management training. A functional department is responsible for a traditional functional operation within an organization—for instance, accounting, finance, or manufacturing. Training within a functional department may be targeted toward specific groups of employees such as clerical staff (word processing training) or professionals (time management skills and related professional development topics). Finally, an organizational subunit (alternatively, a division or strategic business unit) includes all employees across functional departments and work team configurations, as in General Electric's Appliance business. Training within such a division may include diversity training and intensive seminars designed to educate employees about the division's products and services. Recall that each employee is the fundamental component.

Productivity: What Is It?

To understand productivity, it is useful to know what it is and how it is measured. For the context of this article, it is also useful to know how it is related to strategy.

Productivity is often discussed in the national context, as it was in our introduction (see Table 1). However, analysis of productivity must be undertaken at various levels (Mitchell, 1989). The *individual employee* can be more or less productive than other employees. It is generally accepted that labor productivity is influenced by HR policies and practices. At the level of the *plant* or *firm,* productivity is influenced by the use of capital and the use of technology as well as the use of labor. A firm uses comparisons with other firms in its industry to evaluate its relative position. Finally, overall *national* productivity is the aggregate performance of all firms in the economy. You may have noticed that U.S. politicians and business leaders become quite concerned when Japan reports a higher value, or a more rapid change since the previous reporting period, than does the United States.

The formal definition of productivity is quite simple: *the ratio of outputs to inputs.* This definition applies whether we evaluate productivity at the individual level, at the plant level, or at the national level. However, two caveats accompany this simple definition. First, productivity is a *relative* concept. It would not be of much value, for example, for Iams to know that its productivity is 3.1 cases per labor hour. However, if Iams management compares that figure with last month's figure or with the productivity of Ralston-Purina, then management has useful information for decision making. Second, productivity is related to *competitiveness.* Whether the focus is on individual, plant, or national productivity, it is safe to assume that one examines the figures to identify one's competitive position: *the bottom line.*

To review, productivity—outputs divided by inputs—is used to identify competitive advantage relative to one's own previous position or relative to a competitor's current position. The next step is to specify the inputs and outputs used in the equation.

Inputs

Inputs are the factors of production—labor, capital, materials—used in making goods and delivering services. They are classified as either variable or fixed, depending on the planning horizon of the firm. In the short run, firms cannot easily change their technology in ways that allow them to substitute capital for labor; capital is a fixed input. In the long run, however, firms have time to adjust their production processes in ways that allow them to substitute capital for labor.

Labor. Labor is the most common input used for measuring productivity (Mitchell, 1989). The reason is that measurements of labor hours and/or labor costs are (1) simple to calculate with accuracy, (2) readily available and widely reported, and (3) easily interpreted. Labor inputs are also known as variable inputs because their quantity can be changed during the relevant period (Mansfield, 1989).

Capital. Capital is also used in productivity measurements, but it is used less frequently than labor inputs. Among the most important capital inputs are the firm's plant and equipment—the buildings, machinery, tooling, and transportation facilities. Capital inputs are called fixed inputs because their quantity cannot be changed during the period under consideration (Mansfield, 1989).

Raw materials. Because an input is anything the firm uses in its production process, raw materials such as electricity, trees, metal, oil, water, and even air can be used in calculations of its own unique productivity. As you can guess, these are also variable inputs because it is possible to alter the amount used at any given time (Mansfield, 1989).

Outputs

Outputs are the resulting products—goods and services—of the transformation process of production. Measuring output tends to be more complex than measuring input because firms can produce multiple products, product quality can be variable, and some products may not be easily standardized.

Quantity. Measuring quantity output can be simple or complex (Mitchell, 1989). For example, think of tons of steel, barrels of oil, and bushels of corn: All of these are easily quantified. Now think of health care, police protection, and entertainment. It is not so easy to determine output quantity in these latter examples.

Revenue. When firms produce multiple products, when the output is not quantifiable (as with most services), or when outputs are aggregated at the national level, quantities cannot be added directly. This poses problems for productivity measurement. In such cases the total dollar amount of sales (revenues) is used as the output.

Productivity: How Is It Measured?

Because our concern in this article is with the linkage between training and productivity, we will limit our discussion to labor productivity (labor inputs). We will not investigate measurement of productivity at the national level of analysis. Keep in mind, however, that the framework for doing so would be similar.

The two standard measures of labor productivity are (1) *dollar revenue (sales) / labor costs* and (2) *total quantity / labor hours.* Each can be evaluated at the individual and the firm level of analysis.

The Individual Level

In the field of human resource management, we often speak of increasing employee productivity. What is meant by employee productivity in this sense, and how can it be increased? In view of the previous discussion, can you imagine that employee productivity reflects environment, capital, and/or technology rather than individual effort? If so, how can individual effort and ability be distinguished from the external influences on productivity (Mitchell, 1989)?

The simple economic model. A production function is defined as the functional relationship (f) between the quantities of various inputs of labor (L) and capital (K) used per period of time and the maximum quantity (Q) of the commodity that can be produced per period of time. That is, $Q = f(L,K)$. As the amount of labor input increases, so does the output, but the amount of extra output varies depending on the current amount of labor input being used. This phenomenon is known as *diminish-*

ing marginal product, and it leads directly to a downward-sloping marginal product of labor curve. Under the assumptions of this simple economic model, every employee is paid the same wage as determined by the market.

A standard example is work in a fast-food restaurant. When there are usually two employees working behind the counter but the inputs are doubled for the expected lunch-hour rush, it is easy to imagine that the four employees will produce more output than the usual two. It is less easy, but not impossible, to imagine their diminishing returns. When there is a fixed amount of capital (one milk-shake machine, one soft-drink dispenser, and so on), all employees cannot use the equipment at the same time. As the amount of time spent waiting to use equipment increases with additional employees, the quantity of output declines. Even though total quantity is increasing with more labor, the rate at which it increases declines. Furthermore, all workers are paid the same wage even though the fourth worker's contribution to increased productivity is less than the contribution made by the second worker.

In the simple economic model, productivity is not related to employee motivation, ability, or rewards (Mitchell, 1989). However, HR managers realize that these components do matter, and it is easy to adjust the assumptions of the economic model to fit their perspective.

Diversity and imperfect information. When we remove the economic assumptions that all workers are equal and that everyone has perfect information, we are essentially creating a need for HR managers. They are the people who can devise systems to identify the more motivated and more able workers who will enhance the firm's productivity. Instead of offering the market wage to every employee, the HR specialist can offer lower wages to low performers and higher wages to high performers. Notice that this system pays each worker according to his or her productive value, and the wage is at the firm's discretion rather than being determined by the market.

Screening costs. Profit-maximizing firms want simultaneously to avoid hiring low-performance workers and to retain high-performance workers. There are costs associated with maintaining an HR department; however, under certain conditions a firm may find it more profitable to pay these administrative costs. If the HR representatives can screen for productivity before hiring and can implement policies and practices that keep productive workers satisfied and committed to the firm, then the HR department is also associated with benefits. A simple cost-benefit calculation will reveal the trade-offs. Then, following the simple rule of adopting a practice when the benefits exceed the costs, the firm can make an effective decision.

Modifying productivity. Finally, we drop the economic assumption that individual productivity is a given that remains constant for each employee. This creates a need for the HR department to find ways to increase productivity through education, training, and motivational techniques. Workers can be stimulated through reward and penalty programs such as merit pay systems, career ladders, and discipline policies.

The Firm Level

Knowledge of firm-level productivity helps us answer such questions as "Why are some firms finding it so difficult to compete?" and "At what point does the continued education or training of employees cease to add to their ability to provide output?"

Simple economic model. The notion of productivity at the firm level is actually an efficiency principle. Given that a firm desires to produce a given quantity of output, it considers the lowest-cost combination of inputs to do so. Similarly, a firm can choose to maximize the quantity it produces for a given amount of input. The firm bases these decisions on calculations of marginal product.

The basic idea is that the firm will minimize cost by combining inputs in such a way that the marginal product (MP) of every input used is proportional to the price of the input. Consider the fast-food restaurant again. The manager has decided to produce 100 hamburgers per day at the lowest cost. The inputs for this simplified production process are the food ingredients and the labor (of cooks and servers). In line with the economic efficiency rule, the input combination is chosen such that

$$\frac{MP \text{ Ingredients}}{\text{Ingredient Prices}} = \frac{MP \text{ Labor}}{\text{Labor Prices}}$$

When we multiply both sides of this equation by the ingredient prices and divide both sides by the marginal product of labor, we get

$$\frac{MP \text{ Ingredients}}{MP \text{ Labor}} = \frac{\text{Ingredient Prices}}{\text{Labor Prices}}$$

So, to minimize costs, a firm should set a previously calculated ratio of marginal product of inputs equal to the ratio of the input prices.

Numerous suggestions have been made for improving productivity growth (Mitchell, 1989). These include fostering an improved HR management climate and improving education and training.

Improved HRM climate. Levine and Tyson (1990) found that an improved HR management climate is fostered through voluntary cooperative and participative programs designed to afford employees input into the decision-making process. They ascertained that such programs worked best under the four additional conditions of (1) profit sharing or gainsharing, (2) guaranteed long-term employment, (3) relatively narrow wage differentials, and (4) guarantees of worker rights.

Improved education. One suggestion for improving productivity is to encourage schools to produce skilled and disciplined workers (Zemsky & Cappelli, 1992). According to Zemsky and Cappelli, this can be accomplished when schools (1) focus more on product and less on process; (2) teach the core competencies in mathematics, communication skills, and citizenship; and (3) recognize firms, as well as students, as customers.

Innovative training. When firms provide training that enables workers to assume greater responsibility, productivity rises. Ichniowski (1992) found that one training concept, multiskilling, had strong productivity-enhancing (PE) effects in paper mills. This training procedure was implemented to help ensure that (1) employees acquired the skills necessary to perform various jobs in a team rotation framework and (2) management had the flexibility to adjust worker assignments according to cyclical variations in the production process. Productivity was increased under multiskilling in the paper mills studied because with greater job security, workers were more willing to express their productivity-enhancing ideas.

Strategically Linking Training and Productivity

As shown in Table 2, the three strategies—differentiation, highest quality, and lowest cost—can all have positive impacts on our two productivity measures (output and revenues). Look, for example, at the first column under productivity for the differentiation strategy, the one used by Iams. If a firm adopts this strategy, we can predict that both dollar revenues and labor costs will increase. For the firm to achieve an increase in productivity under these conditions, training should result

in an increase of revenues that is greater than the increase of the cost of labor. That is, for a higher ratio to result, the numerator must increase more than the denominator increases.

Now look at the first productivity column for the highest-quality strategy, which Motorola used. If a firm desires to increase the quality of its products and to achieve a higher level of productivity, then the numerator must increase while the denominator remains unchanged. The idea is to produce the maximum quality for a given amount of input. It is the same principle as profit maximization, except that now the firm has as its objective to maximize quality.

Let us consider one more example. In the second column for the lowest-cost strategy, adopted by UPS, we see that for productivity to increase, the denominator must decrease while the numerator remains unchanged. Recall from the previous section the simple economic model and the rule for a cost minimization objective: For a specified quantity of output, what is the lowest-cost combination of inputs? Again, the principle is the same.

Now we are ready to make the linkages we hinted at in the introduction. Can you think of ways in which training might change the output and input values in the desired directions?

Strategic Linkages for Increased Productivity

Differentiation. We maintain that the differentiation strategies require training that promotes creativity. So, where does this begin?

Table 2
How to Increase Productivity under a Particular Strategy

Productivity Strategy	Dollar Revenues / Labor Costs	Quantity Output / Labor Hours
Differentiation	Increase revenues more than labor costs increase	Increase quantity more than labor hours increase
Highest quality	Increase revenues while labor costs remain unchanged	Increase quantity while labor hours remain unchanged
Lowest cost	Decrease labor costs while revenues remain unchanged	Decrease labor hours while quantity remains unchanged

The starting point is basic education, but not as we usually think of it. By basic education, we mean going beyond traditional classes and the mere satisfaction of administrative requirements to classes that stress core competencies in mathematics, communication skills, and citizenship. This last point, citizenship, relates to the nurturing of interpersonal relationships across occupational and personal aspects of life. Enhanced relationship skills may make team-based training and the formation of semiautonomous work groups more readily attainable and, when in place, more productive.

Highest quality. We assert that the highest-quality strategies require employer-sponsored training that is vocational in nature. That is, the employer should invest heavily in teaching employees to perform their specific job duties and related duties. For example, this kind of training might educate employees in ways to cut down on scrap or waste, minimize their mistakes, maximize customer satisfaction, and reduce product liability claims. In short, we believe that firms that adopt the highest-quality strategy should institute systematic programs of vocational training for all employees.

Lowest cost. We endorse training programs that are designed to help employees work more efficiently than their counterparts at competitor firms. This may be accomplished through either of two approaches. The first entails management's learning the employees' jobs. That may mean working closely with employees in mapping out the tasks and duties that constitute their jobs and jointly identifying the "best" ways of performing jobs. The second approach involves training employees for multiple skills that lend themselves well to job rotation; it requires employer flexibility in response to varying business conditions.

Situational Constraints

Situational constraints are one set of important variables that interfere with the translation of abilities and motivation into effective performance (Peters & O'Connor, 1980). Pe-

ters and his associates (Peters & O'Connor, 1980; Peters, O'Connor, & Eulberg, 1985) have identified eight situational resources that are relevant to productivity outcomes. As you read this listing of resource variables that adversely affect productivity, can you identify the three main dimensions to which poor performance is attributed?

Job-related information. The information needed to do the job assigned. Necessary information can come from supervisors; peers; subordinates; customers; company rules, policies, and procedures; and so on.

Tools and equipment. The specific tools, equipment, and machinery needed to do the job assigned.

Materials and supplies. The materials and supplies needed to do the job assigned.

Budgetary support. The financial resources and budgetary support needed to do the job assigned. These are the monetary resources necessary to accomplish aspects of the job, including such things as making long-distance calls, traveling, hosting job-related entertainment, hiring new employees and maintaining and/or training existing employees, hiring emergency or temporary help, and so on. This category does not relate to an incumbent's own salary but rather to the monetary support necessary to accomplish tasks that are part of the incumbent's job.

Required services and help from others. The services and help from others needed to do the job assigned.

Task preparation. The personal preparation, through previous education, formal company training, and relevant job experience, needed to do the job assigned.

Time availability. The availability of the time needed to do the job assigned, taking into consideration the time limits imposed as well as interruptions, unnecessary meetings, non-job-related distractions, and so on.

Work environment. The physical aspects of the immediate work environment needed to do the job assigned. That is, the characteristics that facilitate rather than interfere with doing the job assigned. A helpful work environment is one that is not too noisy, not too cold, or not too hot; that provides an appropriate work area; that is well lighted; that is safe; and so on.

So what are the three main dimensions to which Peters and his associates (Peters & O'Connor, 1980; Peters et al., 1985) attributed poor performance? They are (1) finding the needed resource unavailable, (2) not receiving enough of the needed resource, and (3) receiving a needed resource but finding its quality poor. In other words, the three main dimensions to which poor performance is attributed—in spite of training efforts aimed at increasing productivity—are unavailability, inadequate quantity, and inadequate quality.

One final comment. Bartel (1989) attempted to identify the actual impact of training programs on labor productivity from responses to a national survey on HR practices. Her results are quite interesting: (1) Employees who received training were likely to be young white males, (2) private sector training played a significant role in the wage determination and career patterns of young workers, (3) individuals with more training had significantly greater wage growth and longer job tenure, and (4) those who received training in their first 3 months of employment had significantly faster productivity growth during their first 2 years with the employer.

Summary

We have considered the linkages between training and productivity in support of competitive strategy, a much-neglected focus of training research and practice in the twentieth century. To move training forward into the twenty-first century, we want you to keep in mind our strategic linkages framework. At present this framework represents initial thoughts. We invite you to develop these ideas and refine them further as practitioners of the twenty-first century. For now, we leave you with these prescriptions.

Souza and Vining (1990) wrote about productivity for the hospital industry, which is currently undergoing major competitive changes. They identified four principles that lead to productivity enhancement (PE), principles that we believe can be applied to training and to organizations in any industry. The first is that productivity is a management philosophy, not a tool or a statistic. If a manager is having difficulty with the bottom line, then PE training should not be viewed as a one-time activity. The second principle is that productivity is multidimensional. To be most effective, PE training should mirror the organization's primary work flow or process. The third principle is that productivity is a dynamic, relative process, not a static condition. Unless PE training adds value by helping the organization fulfill its mission, its productivity is missing. In other words, keeping busy is different from being productive. The final principle is that productivity is the means to a strategic end. PE training should mean working smarter, not harder.

References

Bartel, A. P. (1989). *Formal employee training programs and their impact on labor productivity: Evidence from a human resources survey.* Washington, DC: National Bureau of Economic Research Working Paper No. 3026.

Bartlett, C., & Ghoshal, S. (1991). *Managing across borders: The transnational solution.* Cambridge, MA: Harvard Business School Press.

Carnevale, A. P., Gainer, L. J., & Villet, J. (1990). *Training in America: The organization and strategic role of training.* San Francisco: Jossey-Bass.

Cascio, W. F. (1991). *Applied psychology in personnel management* (4th ed.). Englewood Cliffs, NJ: Prentice Hall.

Ghoshal, S. (1987). Global strategy: An organizing framework. *Strategic Management Journal, 8,* 425–440.

Ichniowski, C. (1992). Human resource practices and productive labor-management relations. In D. Lewin, O. S. Mitchell, & P. D. Sherer (Eds.), *Research frontiers in industrial relations and human resources* (pp. 239–271). Madison, WI: Industrial Relations Research Association.

Kirkpatrick, D. L. (1987). Evaluation. In R. L. Craig (Ed.), *Training and development handbook: A guide to human resource development* (3rd ed., pp. 301–319). New York: McGraw-Hill.

Lengnick-Hall, C. A., & Lengnick-Hall, M. L. (1988). Strategic human resources management: A review of the literature and a proposed typology. *Academy of Management Review, 13,* 454–470.

Levine, D. I., & Tyson, L. D. (1990). Participation, productivity, and the firm's environment. In A. S. Blinder (Ed.), *Paying for productivity: A look at the evidence* (pp. 183–237). Washington, DC: The Brookings Institution.

Mansfield, E. (1989). *Economics: Principles, problems, decisions* (6th ed.). New York: W. W. Norton.

McKenna, J. F. (1990). Take the "A" training. *Industry Week, 239,* 22–29.

Mitchell, D. J. B. (1989). *Human resource management: An economic approach.* Boston: PWS-Kent.

Peters, H. L., & O'Connor, E. J. (1980). Situational constraints and work outcomes: The influences of a frequently overlooked construct. *Academy of Management Review, 5(3),* 391–397.

Peters, H. L., O'Connor, E. J., & Eulberg, J. R. (1985). Situational constraints: Sources, consequences, and future considerations. In K. M. Rowland & G. R. Ferris (Eds.), *Research in personnel and human resource management* (Vol. 3, pp. 79–114). Greenwich, CT: JAI Press.

Porter, M. E. (1985). *Competitive advantage: Creating and sustaining superior performance.* New York: Free Press.

Schuler, R. S., & Jackson, S. E. (1987). Linking competitive strategies with human resource management practices. *Academy of Management Executive, 1(3),* 207–219.

Souza, M. G., & Vining, G. W. (1990). Four principles that lead to greater productivity. *Healthcare Financial Management, 44(11),* 19–25.

Tannenbaum, S. I., & Woods, S. B. (1992). Determining a strategy for evaluating training: Operating within organizational constraints. *Human Resource Planning, 15(2),* 63–81.

Wright, P., & McMahan, G. (1992). Theoretical perspectives for human resource management. *Journal of Management, 18(2),* 295–320.

Zemsky, R., & Cappelli, P. (1992, July). The challenge: To revitalize the nation's economy by making long-term investments in a skilled workforce. *EQW Issues.*

Organizational Benefits of Mentoring

James A. Wilson and Nancy S. Elman[*]

When Odysseus went off to fight the Trojans, he left an old and trusted friend in charge of his household and his son's education. Three thousand years later, when we speak of the process by which an older, more experienced member of an organization counsels a younger colleague on the unwritten facts of life in that organization, the name of this trusted servant is often invoked. Odysseus' friend, Mentor, has been immortalized by the attachment of his name to this widespread form of intergenerational knowledge sharing.

The subject of "mentoring" has often been discussed, along with the benefits that accrue to the mentee and the mentor; however, the benefits that accrue to the organization that encourages mentoring within its ranks are referred to less often. To apply the Homeric analogy, most discussions of mentors have missed an explicit focus of the benefits received by Odysseus or, more generally, by the Kingdom of Ithaca, as a result of the first historically recorded (so to speak) mentoring relationship. This article addresses this subject directly, delineating what modern corporate Ithacas can hope to gain through the fostering of mentoring relationships.

It is probably a safe assumption that different types of organizations benefit in different ways and to various degrees from mentoring. It is also a safe assumption that the character of mentoring will change as the participants move up the corporate hierarchy. It is our opinion that mentoring is not and should not be a phenomenon restricted to lower or entry level personnel, but, rather, that it has a place at the very highest levels of organizations (as in the grooming of the next CEO). Within the context of these assump-

tions, we can examine the organizational benefits of mentoring.

Organizational Benefits of Mentoring

The most obvious and often discussed benefits are those related to the development of human resources. Mentoring can contribute to employee motivation, job performance, and retention rates. However, other important benefits are often overlooked. These are related to the long-term health of the organization as a social system. One such contribution is that mentoring provides a structured system for strengthening and assuring the continuity of organizational culture. The existence of a strong corporate culture that provides members with a common value base, and with implicit knowledge of what is expected of them and what they in turn can expect from the organization, can be vital to organizational success and effectiveness. The mentoring system is also useful when the organization requires modification or redefinition of culture, i.e., during times of leadership succession. The alternative in many cases is to rely solely on an expensive, intrusive, and highly formalized monitoring and control system. Mentoring can thus be used as an adjunct to the typical performance appraisal and salary-based sources of information about how well one is doing in the system.

In addition to being transfer agents of corporate culture, mentors also provide immediately practical services for their mentees. Such diverse "services" as informing their proteges of the best ways to navigate the subtleties of the organization's informal political system, acting as a sounding board for ideas with which a junior colleague might be hesitant to

Reprinted with permission from *Academy of Management Executive, 4* (1990): 88–94.

approach a supervisor, and even providing mundane advice about appropriate styles of dress all fall within the purview of mentoring.

It is clear that mentors serve as nodes in an information transmission network. Data on this network runs in both directions. While the messages that mentors pass down will shape the future, the messages they send up can be vitally important also. This suggests another contribution of mentoring, the placement of "deep sensors" within the organization.

Mentors in their occasional role as deep sensors of workforce mood, attitude, etc., can transfer early warning signals to upper management long before news of such trouble becomes common knowledge, is communicated through formal channels, or manifests itself through reduced levels of performance. In discussing this deep sensing role, we are not suggesting that mentors should pass on specific information provided to them in confidence. Rather, we are suggesting that mentors are in a position to detect increasing levels of "noise" emanating from various quarters within the organization before it becomes figural or specific information.

The deep sensing role is made possible by matching mentors and mentees who are two to three levels apart in the organizational hierarchy and who are not in the same immediate chain of command. Information which might ordinarily be suppressed by direct middle level supervisors now has an opportunity to make an "end run" around those who would prefer to see it squashed. The separateness of mentor and mentee across levels of the organization can help prevent interference or undercutting of the direct supervisor.

In their role as sensors, mentors are not restricted to looking out for negative signals. Mentors are in a good position to spot talent which might not otherwise be noticed and to aid in the development of this talent. Mentors can work to draw out the best in young proteges who may for some reason lack the confidence or the ability to communicate their ideas and might otherwise be overlooked. Of course, mentors can also aid in the develop-ment of those "fast trackers" who are already acknowledged to be gifted.

Choosing Mentors

The questions of who should be mentors and how they should be chosen are extremely important. It is not always obvious in modern corporate societies who should play the role of "tribal elder." From the previous discussions of the deep sensing role, it seems that immediate supervisors would generally be unsuitable mentors for their underlings. The inherent conflict of interest and tension involved, particularly in the valuative judging aspects of the supervisory role, could be likely to stifle meaningful communication. Sometimes the actions of a supervisor are topics which one might like to discuss with a mentor. Obviously, this opportunity would be compromised if the supervisor were the mentor.

Likewise, managers positioned directly above the mentee's supervisor would also be awkwardly placed to be mentors. The mentor could be in the position of having to choose between providing support for the younger protege and undermining the authority of the protege's supervisor. Still, the mentor should be relatively close to the mentee in the organization. There must be a common base of shared experience from which the relationship can draw.

From another angle, the selection of mentors depends as much on individual personality development as on their position in the organizational hierarchy. Some people are not psychologically or positionally secure enough to give of themselves to the younger generation. They may see younger members of the organization as threatening competitors or as unworthy "brats." Others may have been embittered through their own experience in the organization. It would be deleterious to the mentee for either type of person to attempt to provide the personal guidance required by the mentoring function. It would be a mistake for the organization to assign these people to mentoring duties.

The increasing diversity of the workforce in contemporary organizations adds another dimension to the mentor-mentee matching problem. People naturally move to mentor and can more easily communicate with those with whom they most closely identify. If the prospective mentee looks somewhat like the potential mentor in terms of gender, race, ethnicity, religion, etc., the identification process becomes more immediate. If mentor-mentee matching is left to occur naturally, the danger is that quality mentoring may only be available to white males from dominant ethnic or religious groups rather than to the full range of people represented in the contemporary organization. Organizations implementing mentoring programs will likely need to provide special training and coaching of potential mentors of special groups such as women and minorities, if only to increase confidence and motivation to enter mentoring programs. Any such training program should explicitly deal with the dangers and unacceptability of sexualizing any mentoring relationship in any direction by either party.

Mentoring is an activity that can and should be promoted by the organization, but should never be required. The mentoring relationship must be a voluntary one, so mentors and mentees cannot simply be paired off by some higher authority. This may be a difficulty in establishing company-sponsored mentoring programs, but it is necessary to deal with this structure. Some people who would make the most outstanding role models should be actively encouraged to become mentors (although those most suited may already be functioning as mentors informally). The other side of the coin is that some people may have to be quietly discouraged from mentoring. Outside consultants and senior human resource professionals might serve in the initiation and development of a working mentoring program.

Mentoring in the Upper Echelons

As stated previously, the value of mentoring is not restricted to the indoctrination or inspiration of entry level personnel. Its value is maintained through the highest levels in the organization. At each level in the organization there is a new and different "subculture." As employees assume positions of increasing authority, they require new and different advice, and access to more closely held organizational secrets and realities become important.

When persons penetrate the uppermost reaches of the organizational hierarchy, their need for good mentoring does not cease, although it does assume another character. Far from being organizational novices in need of "socialization," advancing executives are well acquainted with the broad and complex corporate culture. However, there is another culture to which they must become accustomed. This is the culture of institutional leadership. Mentoring of executive-bound upper level staff will thus be occurring even as these staff take on mentoring roles of their own with younger employees. This further multiplies the impact of mentoring across the organization.

Managers operating at the higher institutional levels of organizations must learn to think differently than those securely sheltered somewhere in the middle of the hierarchy. Ultimate responsibility now falls upon them. They must develop their own vision and learn how to share this vision with others. Elliot Jaques describes the increasing levels of psychological complexity required by managers as they rise through the organizational ranks.[1] As Jaques sees it, there are four levels of complexity, ranging from the lowest, manifested in the ability to deal with tangible phenomena, through capabilities with the symbolic and the intangible, and finally to the highest, a facility with universalistic concepts. Mentoring can help rising managers develop the integrative vision necessary to function at the universalistic level. The primary role of the mentor in the upper echelons is thus twofold. One part of this role is the sharing by the mentor of his or her own vision. This establishes a continuity of leadership. The other part of this role is to nurture within the mentee the confidence to develop his or her own vision. The latter is ultimately the more important and challenging function of mentoring which inspires creative growth and change for the organization.

Secondary roles of the institutional level mentor include assisting the newly arrived to adjust to life at this elite plane. This aspect of mentoring increases in importance when the class and social background of the mentee differs from peers at the institutional level of corporate leadership.

Mentoring the Mentors

It should not be forgotten that as mentees gain competence and move up the corporate ladder they may surpass their mentors. In a pyramidal-shaped organization, this must occur. Thus, the mentor-mentee relationship is not a lifetime one, nor is it exclusive. Over the years, mentoring relationships outlive their function and die out, and new ones form. An individual may have many mentors over the life of a career; a mentor may advise many proteges. It is also possible and, from the point of view of the authors, desirable that one person might function simultaneously as a mentor and mentee, as described previously.

How then is this complex web of interrelationships to be managed? Official and semiofficial but sanctioned mentoring programs have been established by a number of organizations with varying degrees of success. It is crucial to note that *how* the program is established has much to do with the success of the program itself. Junior managers especially must trust the benign intent of the organization's senior managers and be provided with the degree of autonomy that they need to open themselves to mentors. Without building trust, they will not make themselves sufficiently vulnerable to the mentor so that the mentor can assist with meaningful and nontrivial aspects of personal and managerial development.

A fairly typical design for instituting a mentoring program at the entry level or one or two levels higher in the organization frequently takes the form of a "sponsored but voluntary" effort. Sometimes potential mentors and mentees are identified through survey or "hotline" sign-up procedures, with matching and interviews proceeding until "matches" are made. More promising is a formal design in which interested persons are gathered together for snacks and coffee or wine and cheese accompanied by an "inspirational" introduction of the program and concept by the CEO or other high-ranking officer. Internal or external consultants handle the actual process of the meeting, which involves an explanation of the process of mentoring and its benefits, along with a period of informal "milling about" during which potential mentors and mentees can meet and assess each other. Multiple meetings may have to be held to include everyone interested and yet keep the number of participants down to a workable size. A second training session of two to four hours is appropriate in which the benefits, opportunities, and dangers of mentoring are fully aired. Details of how to initiate and, importantly, dissolve mentoring relationships should be discussed.

People who wish to become mentors should make public a listing of times when they will be available for fairly brief interviews. Mentees should be encouraged to call on and consider four to six potential mentors. They should interview their whole culled listing and not settle for the first agreeable person. If a mutual interest exists between a prospective mentor-mentee pair, a contract specifying the procedures and norms of the relationship should be agreed upon. This informal, but contractual, step is especially important for women and minorities and should include such seemingly mundane issues as whether doors will be open or closed during meetings, who can initiate meetings, and whether meetings can be held off-site, etc. It is a good idea to hold an additional general meeting after the first batch of matched pairs have begun to work together to check progress and address any problems which may have developed. Managers or consultants can serve as counselors for pairs who are experiencing difficulty. After several matching cycles, mentoring may become spontaneous as the organizational culture accepts it as a norm that mentoring is "good for us" and those both able and willing consider it part of their job.

Whatever the specific procedures employed to institute a mentoring program,[2] there must exist some mechanism for the establishment— as well as for the polite termination—of mentoring relationships. Termination is sometimes difficult, but both parties must realize that just as the child grows up and leaves the parents, so too must the mentee leave his or her mentor. Yet, the mentor remains a part of the former mentee, just as the parent remains a part of the adult child; the values of the current generation are carried on by the next. The former mentor can take some satisfaction from the role of shaping the organizational character of the younger person. The latter may feel a sense of gratitude toward the former mentor. Overall, these interrelationships only serve to strengthen the bonds with the organization.

Unintended Consequences

Any program as significant and powerful as an effectively designed mentoring program may well have some unintended negative consequences. One such problem is that the organizational values passed on through mentoring may already be obsolete or on the road to obsolescence in an age of rapid technological, economic, and social change. It might be argued that mentoring could actually stifle the fresh insights brought into the organization by new members. However, the problem of the adaptation of the organizational culture to an environment in flux is something that should be addressed within the larger context of organizational change. A mentoring program may not be of much help with this issue, except insofar as mentors, by virtue of their experience, can sense the change that is occurring and advise mentees accordingly, or conversely, mentees can open the eyes of their mentors to new environmental realities.

Concerning consequences more specific to the mentoring process, we are sure that there are many individual cases of mentoring gone awry in idiosyncratic or unusual ways. These unfortunate occurrences often have their beginnings in poor "matching" or improper or incompetent behavior on the part of either the mentor or mentee (e.g., a sexualizing of the relationship). Sometimes mentors pass on incorrect, incomplete, or politicized information based wholly on their own opinions or the viewpoints of the particular office "clique" to which they belong. It is the responsibility of the designers of the organizational policy concerning mentoring to establish selection, training, and reward mechanisms that foster fairness, competence, and discretion on the part of mentors.

Conclusion

Organizations should come to see mentoring as a strategy for the future and approach it as such. Odysseus knew his son needed to be prepared to assume the duties of leadership, and he recruited the original mentor to provide this preparation. Modern-day corporations must provide the guidance required by future generations of leaders so they too are prepared to take command. Obviously, effective mentors should be rewarded for making a central contribution to the organization. Mentoring is a way to speed the development of talent. It is also a way to spot talent that might otherwise be overlooked, sometimes by bosses who are hoarding human talent to bolster their own success. Further, it is simply the best method of passing along the norms, values, assumptions, and myths that are central to an organization's successful survival.

It is not only the small percentage of young managers who will someday reach the ranks of VPs and CEOs who benefit from the promotion of mentoring. The entire organization benefits not only because its leadership has been carefully groomed, but also because a strong culture has been developed and transmitted. This strong culture assures that past lessons and successful core values will not be forgotten and that excessively rigid, bureaucratic systems can be avoided. Furthermore, the organization with an extensive informal mentor-based information network can be more responsive to brewing internal controversies, discontent, and latent opportunities. These benefits can only serve to enhance an organization's prospects for future success.[3]

Endnotes

*We are indebted to Mr. William D. Oberman, Doctoral Candidate in the Katz Graduate School of Business, University of Pittsburgh, for valued contributions toward an earlier version of this article and to Professor James Craft, KGSB, for comments.

1. Elliot Jaques, *Requisite Organization: The CEO's Guide to Creative Structure and Leadership,* (Arlington, VA.: Cason Hall and Co., 1989).

2. There are other ways of promoting mentoring besides the formal matching procedures discussed. Reward systems, educational interventions, and job assignments can all facilitate mentoring relationships. Interested readers should consult the book by Kathy Kram cited below.

3. Readers seeking further information and insights on the subject of mentoring may be interested in a new journal, *Mentoring International,* published in Vancouver, British Columbia. The following books are also available:

Nancy W. Collins, *Professional Women and Their Mentors: A Practical Guide to Mentoring for the Woman Who Wants to Get Ahead,* (Englewood Cliffs, NJ: Prentice-Hall, 1983).

Kathy E. Kram, *Mentoring at Work: Developmental Relationships in Organizational Life,* (Glenview, IL: Scott Foresman, 1985).

A. Missirian, *The Corporate Connection,* (New York: Prentice-Hall, 1982).

Linda Phillips-Jones, *Mentors and Proteges,* (New York: Arbor House, 1982).

Developing Executives
through Work Experiences

Morgan W. McCall, Jr.

I learned to take risks on people and to keep my cool as a leader. I learned the importance of a leader's ceremonial role to subordinates . . . , how to manage a large team harmoniously, and the importance of a company "culture." (Lindsey, Homes, & McCall, 1987)

I had to learn to work with two customer systems and sales forces almost overnight. I learned how to balance the needs of the company with risk to the project and to myself, how to manage upward effectively, and how to build and maintain a motivated team. (Lindsey et al., 1987)

These two executives were not describing what they had learned from a job assignment, nor from a management seminar or from reading the latest management text. They were describing lessons learned from starting an operation from scratch. Even though commitment to developing managerial talent is often measured by the size of a training budget, the role the classroom plays in the development of executive skills is unclear. A recent article by Short (1987) reported that the "corporate classroom" is budgeted at over $40 billion for its more than 8 million "students." Bennis and Nanus (1985) put the figure between $30 and $40 billion. Kotter (in press), in a recent study of 15 corporations well known for the quality of their executive cadre, concluded that "as important as formal training can be, it never seems to be the central ingredient in development at these firms. It may be rather obvious that if people spend 98–99% of their work time on the job, and only 1–2% (at most) in formal training, that most learning must occur on the job."

The two executives quoted earlier and their corporations took substantial developmental risks in these assignments. Unlike the relatively tangible cost of educational programs, the expense of on-the-job development is difficult to calculate. That it can be astronomical is reflected by the following comment from a member of the executive committee of a major corporation:

> I assigned him to that job because I thought he would learn from it. He clearly wasn't the most qualified candidate. I figured if he couldn't cut it, it would cost us two million. In a two billion dollar business, we could afford it.

While it may be obvious that executives learn on the job, relatively little is known about such learning. A recent review "revealed no systematic body of research focused on what experiences or events may be important in managers' careers" (McCauley, 1986, p. 2). However, this review did identify several studies showing that early job challenge, early broad responsibility, early leadership opportunities, and task force and staff assignments can have developmental significance.

In Kotter's study (in press), the better firms made use of a broad array of developmental experiences, "including adding responsibilities to jobs, creating special jobs, using inside and outside training, transferring people between functions and divisions, mentoring and coaching employees, giving those people feedback on progress, and giving them instruction in how to manage their own development."

What evidence there is indicates that work experiences are critical for developing man-

Reprinted with permission of The Human Resource Planning Society from *Human Resource Planning, 11:1* (1988): 1–11.

agerial talent. But some stubborn questions remain, including three that I can address here. To make effective use of work experiences, we must first understand, "What makes an experience developmental?" Research to date suggests that job challenge is crucial to development, but it tells us little about the *kinds* of experiences that develop executives. Not all experiences are equally challenging: What makes the difference and what differences does it make?

Second, "What can experience teach?" It's one thing to talk about the importance of exposure, breadth, and visibility, but what specifically might someone learn from such developmental experiences?

Finally, even if we knew what makes an experience developmental and what a person might learn from it, "How can we design systems to take advantage of our knowledge?" Can we do a better job of strategically managing the careers of executives than simply providing periodic job rotations?

Job Challenge

Why is it that so many of the most successful corporations emphasize job challenge for developing managers (see, for example, Hall, 1976)? Kotter (in press) concludes that "challenging entry-level jobs help attract good people in the first place, and challenging promotion opportunities help firms hold onto those people. . . . The challenges, in turn, both stretch people, and allow them, often early in their careers, to exercise some leadership. And that, of course, is at the heart of development."

If good people want challenge, and if challenge is at the heart of development, then what is challenge? The answer is not as obvious as it seems. A longitudinal study at AT&T (cited in McCauley, 1986, p. 4) used four characteristics to examine the challenge of managerial jobs. A single index was created by combining measures of "job stimulation and challenge, supervisory responsibilities, degree of structure of assignments, and degree to which the boss was an achievement

model." They found a significant relationship between early job challenge (as reflected by these characteristics) and subsequent managerial success. By implication, then, challenging jobs are those that require people to supervise others, are relatively less structured, and involve working for a good boss. This leaves me with the unsettling feeling that there must be more to challenge.

Our studies (McCall, Lombardo, & Morrison, in preparation; Lindsey et al., 1987; McCall & Lombardo, 1983) looked a little deeper. We examined 616 descriptions of experiences that made a lasting developmental difference to 191 successful executives from six major corporations. We were able to identify 16 types of experiences or "key events," including (a) assignments, (b) other people, (c) hardships endured, and (d) other events (see Exhibit 1).

These key events can help us to understand what underlies the challenges that make work experiences developmental. Consider five kinds of assignments identified in Exhibit 1. These are *not* distinguished by title, Hay points, function, business unit, status, salary, hierarchical level, or product line. Rather, they reflect dramatically different managerial challenges. In three of them—starting from scratch, turnarounds, and large scope jobs— the manager is clearly in charge and has line responsibility. The other two, project/task force assignments and line-staff switches, put a premium on persuasion, that is, leading without formal authority or position power.

When "other people" were identified as the pivotal force in developmental experiences, their role was surprisingly narrow. Virtually all of the significant other people were bosses or hierarchical superiors (not subordinates, peers, friends, spouses, or gurus, as some might expect), with the primary variability coming in how long the manager was exposed to the particular boss (from a few minutes to several years), and whether the boss was exceptionally good (about 2/3) or exceptionally bad (about 1/3). Having a good boss seemed to matter most in a manager's first supervisory job and in big scope jobs. In

Exhibit 1
16 Developmental Experiences

Assignments
- **Starting from Scratch**—building something from nothing
- **Fix It/Turn It Around**—fixing/stabilizing a failing operation
- **Project/Task Force**—discrete projects and temporary assignments done alone or as part of a team
- **Scope**—increases in numbers of people, dollars, and functions to manage
- **Line to Staff Switch**—moving from line operations to corporate staff roles

Other People
- **Role Models**—superiors with exceptional (good or bad) attributes
- **Values Playing Out**—"snapshots" of chain-of-command behavior that demonstrated individual or corporate values

Hardships
- **Business Failures and Mistakes**—ideas that failed, deals that fell apart
- **Demotions/Missed Promotions/Lousy Jobs**—not getting a coveted job, or being exiled
- **Subordinate Performance Problem**—confronting a subordinate with serious performance problems
- **Breaking a Rut**—taking on a new career in response to discontent with the current job
- **Personal Traumas**—crises and traumas such as divorce, illness, and death

Other Events
- **Coursework**—formal courses
- **Early Work Experiences**—early nonmanagerial jobs
- **First Supervision**—first time managing people
- **Purely Personal**—experiences outside of work

See Lindsey et al., in press, for complete definitions.

other situations, for example in start-ups, it was often the absence of supervision, not the qualities of the boss, that allowed development to occur.

In addition to developmental work experiences based on assignments and other people, executives discussed five kinds of experience we categorized as hardships (see Exhibit 1): Being set back by mistakes or distasteful jobs, being forced into all-or-nothing career decisions, being confronted with difficult personnel problems, or dealing with traumatic personal events. These were experiences that forced their victims to dig deep and confront a level of self not usually dealt with in other kinds of situations.

The Elements of Job Challenge

The "elements" that make up these developmental events write the encyclopedia of job challenge. Content analysis of the hundreds of experiences described by executives surfaced eight fundamental challenges: bosses, incompetent or resistant subordinates, dealing with new kinds of people, high status, business ad-

versity, scope and scale, missing trumps, and degree of change.

Bosses were a particular challenge when managers had to adapt to their bosses' ogre-like qualities or stylistic differences. Bosses were also developmental if they modeled an exceptional skill or attribute, and in certain jobs where the manager needed and got the boss's advice and support. It was by learning to adapt to a variety of bosses that executives developed the ability to deal effectively with a diverse array of people in authority.

While both good and bad bosses could create a developmental work context, managing competent subordinates was seldom mentioned as a developmental experience. The challenge came in overcoming *incompetence and resistance from subordinates,* or in having to build an effective team from scratch. There were also developmental challenges in learning to manage former peers or bosses, or older or more experienced employees. These kinds of situations led to the realization that no "one way" of leading would work all the time. These experiences forced the development of alternative approaches to fit various situations. As one executive learned, "You can't fire everybody."

One's boss and subordinates are obviously important to executive development, but learning potential was increased every time managers worked with *types of people they had not dealt with before.* Higher-level executives, clients, suppliers, unions, vendors, governments, people from other cultures, and joint venture partners were among the new relationships executives frequently confronted and learned from.

Simply dealing with these people could be challenging, but the developmental ante was further raised when managers had to do the dealing without any formal authority over them, and when there was no requirement to cooperate. As was true with bosses and subordinates, encounters with these different kinds of relationships led managers to develop new skills to deal with various situations. Negotiating with a union and working with a joint venture partner are not the same thing.

Yet another developmental aspect of experience was *playing for high stakes,* for example: being out on a limb with a project highly visible to top management, working against a tight deadline, taking a huge financial risk, and maybe having to go against one's bosses' preferences or advice. Managers had to learn to cope with the pressures, handle the risks, and take effective actions in the face of enormous consequences.

Managers are responsible for the performance of the business; consequently job challenge increases along with *business adversity.* The developmental demands described by executives increased as markets went sour, suppliers or customers went out of business, competitors seized the moment, unions went on strike, the economy changed unpredictably, natural resources ran short, technology changed, or equipment failed. Responding to these kinds of situations taught critical lessons: how to take action quickly, how to cope with ambiguous problems, how to make choices without sufficient information, and how to play for big stakes.

As one takes on responsibility for more people, dollars, functions, products, markets, or sites, *scope and scale* emerge as a major challenge. Particularly for managers who have developed personal leadership skills, changes in scope present countless demands to learn to "lead by remote control," to find ways to run things when it's impossible to keep one's arms around them.

In many of their significant learning experiences, managers came into the situation with *at least one missing trump.* They routinely faced unfamiliar functions, businesses, products, or technologies. Sometimes they were too young, had the "wrong" background, or had to master computerese or financialese or legalese. Some found themselves in foreign countries, unable to speak the language or communicate with the people they managed. In all these cases, the challenge was not to let the missing trumps do them in; the development was in learning how to work around a significant disadvantage.

Not surprisingly, challenge also seemed proportional to the *degree of change* a new situation presented to the individual. People were promoted two or more levels at once, moved into new businesses, or plucked from years on the line into some technical staff assignment with no subordinates and no clear bottom line. Hot shots found themselves exiled to less significant jobs, free-wheelers got bridled by a hands-on boss, fix-it managers were sent to start something up. In these situations, managers had to find ways to deal with huge and usually unexpected change. From the feeling of being overwhelmed, they developed the ability to adapt.

Making Use of Job Challenge

The message of this study is simple. There were identifiable and categorizable things that executives said challenged them. Meeting these challenges left little choice but to learn and develop new abilities. In this respect, development came from inside, from individual desire to succeed. This leads us to our first rule: Development is not something you can do to or for someone. Development is something people do for themselves. On the other hand, a lot can be done to provide talented people with the kinds of challenges that will give them opportunities to develop new skills. This leads to our second rule: The developmental potential of a work experience is driven by the challenges it presents; exposure to a different function, product, division, or the like is not enough. While the exposure can be useful, even enriching, what matters is what one is doing while being exposed.

What Work Experiences Can Teach

> There is no simple formula, no cookbook that leads inexorably to successful leadership. . . . Learning to be a leader is somewhat like learning to be a parent or lover; your childhood and adolescence provide you with basic values and role models. Books can help you understand what's going on, but for those who are ready, most of the learning takes place during the experience itself. (Bennis & Nanus, 1985, p. 223)

To say an experience is developmental begs the question, "Developmental of what?" As we studied what executives learned from their most developmental experiences, we found many examples of "exposure" learning—gains in cognitive knowledge of technical or business issues. But such lessons are just the beginning, representing only two of what turned out in our content analysis to be thirty-four categories. Just as experience is highly differentiated, its lessons pertain to a broad spectrum of skills, abilities, attitudes, philosophies, perspectives, knowledge, and values. This overwhelming array of bits and pieces, the puzzle-pieces of managing, can be arrayed into the five clusters shown in Exhibit 2: (1) Setting and Implementing Agendas; (2) Handling Relationships; (3) Basic Values; (4) Executive Temperament; and (5) Personal Awareness.

The lessons in the first cluster relate to obtaining the knowledge and skills needed to set and pursue agendas. John Kotter (1982) observed that effective general managers were able to set agendas for themselves and their businesses that consisted of "loosely connected goals and plans." Their agendas included issues covering a variety of time frames, a broad range of business issues, and both "vague and specific goals." These agendas were not usually written and were only loosely related to formal plans (Kotter, 1982). Lessons that enable managers to form agendas are those that teach business and technical knowledge, organizational design skills, how to think broadly and accept responsibility for direction, and finding alternative ways to accomplish one's ends.

The second cluster of lessons shown in Exhibit 2 are related to handling relationships. The kinds of relationships an executive must deal with are quite diverse. While all the lessons in this cluster require the ability to understand the other person's point of view, there is no such thing as "a man for all interpersonal seasons." The ability to work effectively with one group does not guarantee that a manager is equally adept with other constituencies.

Basic values, the third cluster of lessons, refers to the development of moral and philosophical perspectives on how people should be treated and the standards of conduct appropriate in a leadership role. Here executives hone and shape their fundamental values based upon their work-related experiences.

Executive temperament, or "what executives are made of," describes the fourth constellation of lessons. Coping with ambiguity, persevering through adversity, rolling with the punches, and making tough decisions are part of the daily menu of executive life. These abilities may spring from the common root of self-confidence.

Finally, five lessons form a personal awareness theme. At various points in their careers, many of the executives we studied came to grips with what they really liked to do, what they were going to do with their careers, and the sacrifices they were willing to make in their personal lives to achieve their ambitions. Many aspects of development require self-awareness:

Learning Experiences: Developmental Events

Learning Content: Leadership Qualities

Column groups and headings (left to right):

- **Assignments:** Scratch · Fix It · Projects/Task Forces · Scope · Line to Staff
- **Hardships:** Business Failures · Lousy Jobs · Subordinate Performance Problem · Breaking a Rut · Personal Trauma
- **Other People:** Role Models · Values Playing Out
- **Other Events:** Course Work · Early Work · First Supervision · Personal

Row groups and leadership qualities:

Setting and Implementing Agendas
1. Specific technical knowledge
2. How the business works
3. Standing alone, being decisive
4. Seeing organizations as systems
5. Solving and framing problems
6. Building/using structure and control systems
7. Doing, not talking about it

Handling Relationships
8. Directing and motivating others
9. Dealing with people's perspectives
10. Politics is part of organizational life
11. Getting cooperation: non-authority relationships
12. Working with executives
13. Strategies for negotiating
14. Confront subordinate work performance problems
15. What executives (and managers) are like
16. Management vs. technical work
17. Developing your people
18. Managing people with more experience than you (former bosses, etc.)
19. Dealing with conflict
20. Management models and theories

Basic Values
21. Basic values: trust, integrity, credibility
22. Human values: sensitivity to needs

Executive Temperament
23. Can't manage it all by yourself
24. Self-confidence in skills and judgment
25. Comfort with ambiguity, stress, uncertainty
26. Persevering under adverse conditions
27. Learning to be tough

Personal Awareness
28. Coping with situations beyond your control
29. Using, and not abusing, power
30. Recognizing personal limits and weaknesses
31. Learning which jobs are and aren't enjoyable
32. Taking control of own actions: career
33. Perspective on life and work
34. Being prepared for opportunities

Note: From *Key Events in Executives' Lives* by Lindsey et al., in press. Reprinted by permission.

Exhibit 2. Executive Leadership Qualities and the Experiences Associated with Them

By recognizing and accepting their blind spots and weaknesses, these managers learned to direct their own development and realistically assess their aspirations.

There is not space here to fully define each of the thirty-four lessons shown in Exhibit 2, or to explore the subtleties within and among them (for that, the reader is referred to Lindsey et al., 1987). There are a number of conclusions, however, that have implications for using experience as a way of strategically developing executive talent. Among them are the following:

1. Different kinds of experience can provide opportunities to learn quite different things (these are summarized in Exhibit 2). There is a technical or business lesson to be learned from almost any assignment, but such lessons are seldom the primary lessons learned from a truly developmental experience. It is crucial, therefore, to think seriously about what a person might learn from a particular experience and not to stop at the "exposure" level.

2. A job that is incredibly developmental for one person can be largely redundant in the growth of another. However obvious that is, it is still tempting to think of development in absolutes—that through this experience a person learns "x," regardless of the person who goes through it. Our data show two things bearing on this issue. First, executives with repeat experiences (e.g., two turnarounds) learned fewer, and usually similar, lessons the second time. Second, executives who became "specialists" by virtue of successful repetition (e.g., "start-up" managers) sometimes derailed later in their careers because they failed to develop the broader array of skills required to handle other kinds of situations.

3. There can be no guarantee that an individual will learn the lessons that an experience offers. Even companies that make extensive use of developmental assignments often fail to consider what they might do to help individuals learn. It's as if the sink-or-swim approach we associate with selection has been applied to development, too: Throw them in and leave the learning outcome up for grabs.

Even if development is ultimately up to the individual, we think a great deal could be done to help people make more of the job experiences they have. At the simplest level it might mean giving managers time between assignments to reflect on what they've just been through (as opposed to showing up on Monday to take over New Guinea operations). It could also mean providing a structured experience after a significant assignment to help a person make systematic sense of it. A great deal of thought and effort goes into designing classroom experiences, and it will probably require at least as much effort to take advantage of key work experiences. Sometimes executives do not stay in important assignments long enough to learn much from them at all (Gabarro, 1987)!

Implications for Career Management

It is clear that effective use of work experience for development will be difficult unless the culture of the corporation supports the practice. A supportive culture is more than a statement of mission and values endorsing development. It is an environment in which *at least* the following four concrete things happen:

1. Executives risk a portion of the bottom line to put talented people in jobs for which they may not be fully qualified. Such decisions are common, and the developmental choice is made on purpose. Placement decisions are a behavioral reflection of management's recognition that a person fully qualified for a job is the least likely to develop in it.

2. Managers are allowed—encouraged—to take risks and make mistakes. Mistakes aren't fatal as long as they aren't repeated, they result from real effort to do something new and beneficial, and they teach the manager something useful. Because managers need to take responsibility for their mistakes, the organization may need to use temporary punishments ("penalty boxes"). There are many examples of people taking reasonable risks, both in business decisions and in career moves. In-

terestingly, this propensity toward taking reasonable risks and tolerating failure is a characteristic of the "excellent" firms described by Peters and Waterman (1982).

3. Movement across organizational boundaries occurs regularly and easily. There are formal or informal mechanisms for identifying talented managers in other parts of the organization and for keeping them challenged even when that means crossing barriers. Because they identify with the larger corporate entity, managers do not have to protect their turf, and they do not tolerate games of "pass the turkey."

4. Developing executive talent is accepted as a line responsibility—commitment is demonstrated by the amount of time executives devote to it. Sometimes very serious incentives (such as a percentage of the bonus) are attached to achieving developmental goals.

One could list other characteristics of a culture that supports development, but the main point is that the behavior of executives is a clear demonstration of their commitment. People do not have to search to find examples of significant developmental moves. Action signifies their commitment—rewards and reprimands are consistent with developmental moves. In organizations where contrary patterns exist—where the folklore, for example, is replete with examples of fatal mistakes—the more practical human resource approach might be to emphasize selection and leave development to the occasional unsung hero. In these organizations, nothing short of a significant cultural shift, usually requiring several years of intense senior management effort, will work well.

If the organizational culture is at least partially supportive of development, the next step is doing something. While there is no "right" answer, effective development begins with the basic business strategy of the company. Take, as an example, whether or not to have a high-potential talent pool. In a conglomerate that has opted to be a holding company driven by financial criteria, the idea of developing executive talent for the corporate staff is moot. Any decisions on talent pools would best be left to the business units. However, a company that wants or has a strong corporate identity, but has numerous business units, needs some way to identify corporate resources across its many parts.

The salience of business strategy for executive development is even more pronounced in the case of cross-boundary movement. Our findings strongly suggest that variety in assignments over time is very important to development. Such variety is often attainable only through moves that cross functional, product, or business boundaries—leaps that sometimes defy past practice, and that almost always entail great risk to those who leap. Such moves should not be made lightly or because "it seems like a good idea." Rather we suggest that the business strategy dictates the need for such moves and the degree of acceptable risk associated with them. One company we work with has a strategic plan that calls for a new product line that will require the particular expertise held by two traditionally separate parts of the business. Success will depend upon finding managers for the new enterprise who are hybrids of these two parts, and this seems to justify the risk of developmental boundary spanning. Another company anticipates strategic realignment that will place a premium on skills most readily developed in a small part of the business historically considered a dead end. Once again, the strategy dictates breaking boundaries for the sake of developing people for the future.

Business strategy affects development in more subtle ways as well. Research suggests that "growing" a general manager takes 10 to 20 years (Kotter, 1982), and there are no shortcuts. Confidence in business plans that go beyond five-year projections is low, at best, and obviously one cannot expect better accuracy with human resource strategy than with the business plan itself. Given the uncertainty of the future, it makes sense to insure that a variety of managerial styles and abilities are in the corporate pool. Business strategies can work against this if they result in the reduction of opportunities for people to:

- have responsibility for multiple functions and a bottom line at a relatively early age (e.g., to run small business units);
- roll out or start up operations (e.g., Bechtel reportedly takes on small, uneconomic projects just to give high-potential managers a whole job early);
- take responsibility for solving significant organizational problems and requiring people to reach their particular technical or functional specialties.

In our vernacular, we are suggesting that a developmentally oriented company will find ways to keep start-ups, turnarounds, big-scope assignments, and meaningful projects and staff jobs available for its high-potential people, even if short-term business objectives suggest that it is inefficient to do so. And that is the crux of the argument—*having* managerial talent to run the business is just as significant as making optimal business and financial choices. Whether a corporation chooses to develop its own talent, or to refine its selection procedures to choose talent as needed, is itself a crucial strategic business decision.

The procedures used to develop executive talent through on-the-job experience must make sense in the context of a particular organization's culture and business strategy, so offering general advice is tricky. Nevertheless, we can identify several elements that are likely to be present in a career management system. The conclusions we have drawn from our research and from working with corporations on executive development issues suggest that a solid system will have many of the components described below.

A. A means for identifying and tracking high-potential people across the corporation and all levels of the hierarchy. Whatever system is used, it will be characterized by frequent updating and fluid membership;

B. A mechanism for assessing and facilitating self-assessment of accomplishments, career experiences, and demonstrated learning over time;

C. A means of identifying developmental jobs throughout the company, a means for keeping track of them and what they might teach, and procedures for unblocking key assignments without losing solid performers in the process;

D. A way to ensure that placement decisions are made in light of developmental as well as business interests, and that line managers take reasonable risks for developmental purposes;

E. A way of keeping the managers who make placement decisions informed of available candidates from other parts of the business, and provisions for keeping track of the high potentials as they move to new assignments, particularly when they go overseas;

F. A tangible reward system for executives who identify and develop their people and who allow good people to move across boundaries in the interest of the corporation;

G. A program geared to helping talented managers get the most out of the work experiences they have, possibly including such things as coaching or training interventions at crucial times, or readily available training and educational opportunities that support and help to synthesize what is learned on the job;

H. A human resources staff intimately knowledgeable about the business of the corporation, the demands of executive jobs, the pool of managerial and executive talent needed, and ways to work effectively as resources to line management.

Elegant formal systems do not guarantee effective executive development practice. Rigid career paths, forced mentoring and coaching programs, lock-step rotation plans, catalogs of training programs, and elaborate succession planning tables may actually be counterproductive. Our studies suggest that the development of executive talent is highly individualized. While no one would suggest that the processes should be random or devil-may-care, rigidity is not the answer either. Much as the successful executive is pragmatic, flexible, and action oriented, we believe a system to develop such people should have those same characteristics.

References

Bennis, W., and B. Nanus. *Leaders: The Strategies for Taking Charge.* (New York: Harper and Row, 1985.)

Gabarro, J. J. *The Dynamics of Taking Charge.* (Boston, MA: Harvard University Press, 1987.)

Hall, D. T. *Careers in Organizations.* (Pacific Palisades, CA: Goodyear Publishing Company, 1976.)

Kotter, J. P. *The Leadership Factor.* (New York: The Free Press, in press.)

Kotter, J. P. *The General Managers.* (New York: The Free Press, 1982.)

Lindsey, E. H., V. Homes, and M. W. McCall, Jr. *Key Events in Executives' Lives.* (Greensboro, NC: Center for Creative Leadership, 1987.)

McCall, M. W., Jr., M. M. Lombardo, and A. M. Morrison. *The Lessons of Experience.* In preparation.

McCall, M. W., Jr., and M. M. Lombardo. *Off the Track: Why and How Successful Executives Get Derailed.* Technical Report No. 21. (Greensboro, NC: Center for Creative Leadership, 1983.)

McCall, M. W., and C. D. McCauley. "Analyzing the Developmental Potential of Jobs." Presentation at the Annual Meetings of the American Psychological Association. Washington, DC, August, 1986.

McCauley, C. D. *Developmental Experiences in Managerial Work: A Literature Review.* Technical Report No. 26. (Greensboro, NC: Center for Creative Leadership, 1986.)

Peters, T. J., and R. H. Waterman, Jr. *In Search of Excellence.* (New York: Harper and Row, 1982.)

Short, A. "Are We Getting Our Money's Worth?" *New Management,* 4, Winter, 1987, pp. 23–26.

Management Training:
Justify Costs or Say Goodbye

Thomas F. Urban, Gerald R. Ferris,
Daniel F. Crowe, and Robert L. Miller

During the 1970s, management training delivered developmental skills to a rapidly growing managerial cadre. The attitude was that if training is good, more is better. During the 1980s, however, the survival of the training and development function depends on the answer to the question, "How do we *know* training is good?"

Rigorous, systematic efforts to demonstrate effectiveness generally have been neglected. A recent study of 20 corporations regarded as leaders in corporate training concluded that, "To the degree that evaluation efforts have been undertaken, they seem to have focused on technical training. . . ."[1] Even when evaluation took place, there was no consensus on the best type of evaluation criteria. More top management is agreeing with Odiorne's contention that if management development programs do not show quantifiable economic gains the programs should be discontinued.

Recent discussions of management development recommend a multi-method approach to assessing its effectiveness. Campbell recommends that subjective evaluations by participants (internal criteria) be combined with measures assessing behavioral change on the job (external criteria) in order to evaluate fully the effectiveness of management development programs.[2]

Our research outlines a multi-criterion approach to evaluating a large-scale supervisory training program in a major U.S. oil company. In addition to the internal criteria of participants' reactions to the program, longitudinal measures were taken in regard to subsequent attrition and career progressions of participants or external criteria. We also developed measures of participants' organizational investment and conducted a cost/benefit analysis. While some evaluation approaches build on existing notions, comprehensive multi-evaluation criteria go beyond these in scope, permitting the convergence of both internal and external criteria to be examined.

The Supervisory Training Program

The supervisory training program (STP) was designed for employees newly promoted into first-level supervisory positions and supervisors who had not attended a supervisory training program in the last five years. Program participants were nominated by their managers for a specific program based on the manager's assessment and discussions of the supervisor's training needs.

The content of the programs included communication, group dynamics, problem solving, decision making and other supervisory skills. Conducted six to ten times per year, each program contained the same generic content and was conducted by three in-house members of the training staff at an off-site location. Participants were selected from diverse functional areas and geographic locations.

This training evaluation effort focuses on STP programs offered between September 1979 and July 1981. The average age of the 533 participants was 36 years, approximately

Reprinted with the permission of *HRMagazine*, published by the Society for Human Resource Management, Alexandria, VA.

90 percent earned between $25,000 and $63,000, and approximately 22 percent were female and minority group members. The majority of participants came from Texas, Alaska and Louisiana.

Conceptual Model

An understanding and cost justification of the STP effectiveness was developed through use of multiple methods and criteria. Evaluation criteria were developed from a conceptual model outlining the multi-criterion approach to evaluation. The STP project was evaluated relative to participant reactions concerning content and context as well as promotions, grade increases and attrition (performance effects). At the end of each program, participants evaluated their interest in the program, perceived relevance of the program content, the trainers and the overall course.

Participant interest in the course material was determined to be a necessary, but not sufficient condition for implementation on the job. For the 15 programs, overall interest received an average of 5.04 on a 6-point Likert scale, and perceived applicability of the course material an average of 5.02 on a similar scale. The overall course rating average was 3.46 on a 4-point scale, with the trainers' ratings averaging 3.63. Participant reactions suggested that the STP rated high in terms of interest, perceived applicability, course and trainers. Participants' narrative comments, which were content analyzed, were also favorable.

While participant reactions are useful, additional criteria were used to determine program effectiveness and to provide a basis for comparison across methods.

Attrition

Training programs may not change observable behavior on the job, but they may have value in reducing attrition. Perhaps the most important effect of a development activity is the positive feelings resulting from participants' perceptions of corporate interest in their personal and career development. Participants selected for organizational rewards, such as developmental experiences, may reciprocate through increased loyalty and commitment, and longer tenure with an organization. Not only is training costly, but so is turnover. Yeager notes that replacement costs for managers is equal approximately to their annual salary.[3] Therefore, a central question in measuring training effectiveness is whether the participants remain with the organization providing the training.

During 1980–1981, the attrition of experienced personnel was of vital importance to the energy industry. Smaller independent oil firms were raiding the major firms to secure experienced engineers, geologists, geophysicists, landmen and managers. Retaining these professionals was of paramount importance for the exploration and production of energy resources by the major oil companies. Of the 533 supervisors participating in the 15 STP programs between 1979 and 1981, 20 subsequently left the organization. This is an annualized average attrition rate of 2.2 percent compared to an overall 6.4 percent for all employees in this category.

Table 1 provides a more specific analysis of the turnover rate among program

Table 1

Comparison of Annualized Average Attrition Rate for Critical-Skills Personnel

Skill Category	STP Participants	Overall	Z
Reservoir engineers	2.6%	8.1%	3.44**
Drilling engineers	3.2%	8.5%	1.71[a]
Production engineers	0.0%	5.1%	2.55*
Geologists	12.8%	11.8%	.38
Geophysicists	2.9%	6.5%	2.02*
Landmen	0.0%	13.9%	4.63***

[a]While this value did not reach statistical significance at conventional levels, it was marginally significant (p < .08).

*p < .05

**p < .01

***p < .001

participants, showing the annual average attrition rates for critical-skills employees in the STP program compared with the overall turnover rates for specific categories of professionals.

The attrition rate for all critical-skill categories, except geologists, was significantly lower for STP participants. The low or nonexistent availability of experienced critical-skills employees magnified the significance of the low attrition rate.

Career Progression

Enhancing performance on the job is a central focus of any developmental activity. Since observing performance changes was not possible, the outcomes of the organization's reward process served as a surrogate measure. Participants' grade increases and title changes gauged organizational rewards. A longitudinal analysis determined organizational reward and career progression of participants in the three programs offered in 1979. Table 2 shows the comparison of pre- and post-positional and grade data for the 1979 participants and for employees who did not participate in STP.

Table 2

Comparison of Pay Increases and Title Changes for STP Participants and Nonparticipants

	Participants (N = 105)	Nonparticipants (N = 105)	z^a
Percentage receiving at least one pay grade increase	70.1%	49.5%	4.39**
Percentage receiving position title changes	66.0%	37.1%	6.16**
Total pay grade increases	104 (ratio = .99)	50 (ratio = .48)	14.57**

[a]This z-test examines the significance of the difference between two proportions.[4]

**p < .001

The analysis in Table 2 indicates that STP participants received more grade increases and title changes than those in the nonparticipant sample. The 105 participants received a total of 104 grade increases—more than twice as many as the nonparticipants. Statistically significant differences existed between participants and nonparticipants on all measures.

Cost/Benefit Analysis

A systematic and informed evaluation effort should provide an indication of program investment or costs to use a benchmark against which to evaluate benefits. In this study, the costs of a single program appear in Table 3. A single STP program costs approximately $65,000, or nearly 4.0 percent of the participants' annual average salary. If training and development efforts are viewed as investments in human resources, then a long-range investment perspective seems desirable. Comparing the $65,000 program cost with the total tenure of the STP program participants, the investment per year was $218.86. If the cost of the program was amortized over the projected organizational tenure of the participants, the amortization per year would be $77.20. This expense is minimal relative to projected returns from a supervisor's career.

Another analysis, conducted on October 1981 participants, is analogous to a break-even calculation for cost-benefit justification.

Table 3

STP Program Cost Calculation (July 1981 Session)

Participant salaries (1 week at average salary):	$21,500
Trainers' salaries (3 trainers for 1 week at average salary):	2,200
Transportation, lodging and meals (participants and trainers):	36,000
Program expenses (materials, conference rooms, etc.):	5,000
Approximate total cost:	$64,700

Table 4

Comparison of Total Resources under Participants'
Control with Total STP Expenses

Resource	Amount
Direct labor	$ 47,737,800
Overhead expenses	254,123,400
Company equipment	806,902,000
Contract allocations	80,849,000
Total resources	$1,189,612,200
Total cost of STP (9/79–10/81)	$1,200,000

Information on the resources that they had under their control was collected from participants. Table 4 shows a comparison between these resources and the total amount expended for the 15 programs conducted between September 1979 and October 1981. The total expenses for STP programs would be covered if participants in one program subsequently increased their resource utilization (e.g., through better management skills) by only 0.1 percent.

In addition, if the supervisors could get their 253 direct reports to increase resources an average of $256.92 per direct report, the program expense would be covered.

Summary and Conclusions

This study reports a program evaluation effort of a large-scale management training and development program in a major oil company. The evaluation approach employs multiple criteria, rather than relying on a single dimension which typically is of questionable validity. Using several different methods allows the examination of convergence in the results from the different criteria, thus permitting more confident conclusions concerning the program's effectiveness. In our study, positive participant reactions, post-program promotion and pay grade increases, reduced turnover rates and effective cost measures converged in supporting the effectiveness of the STP program.

In the current uncertain economic climate, fewer resources will be allocated to support training programs without evaluation. Human resource professionals contend that development is an important organizational activity, and managers and other professional employees view development as important to their careers. However, the training and development function must be able to justify, with sound evidence, that programs are actually effective. Multi-evaluation methods that provide accurate measures of program effectiveness assist in the cost justification of training efforts. As training professionals, we are challenged to evaluate corporate development activities before evaluation is forced upon us.

References

1. Lupton, A. H. (1983). An overview of the NIE study of corporate education training. *Academy for Educational Development.* Washington, D.C.

2. Campbell, J. P., Dunnette, M. D., Lawler, E. E. & Weick, K. E. (1970). *Managerial behavior, performance, and effectiveness.* New York: McGraw-Hill.

3. Yeager, J. (1982). Coaching the executive: Can you teach an old dog new tricks? *Personnel Administrator, 27,* 37–42.

4. McNemar, Q. (1969). *Psychological statistics.* New York: Wiley.

PART 4

Management of the Employment Relationship

An important issue that is currently the subject of much discussion is work force governance. Should organization leaders permit and encourage participation in discussions concerning the direction of the organization? To what extent should authority be shared with the organization's employees? Who should have input into organization decisions? These questions are addressed by the articles in Chapters 10 and 11.

The articles in Chapter 10, though in some respects concerned with traditional themes related to unions, are progressive in flavor, concentrating on the development of new and different ways in which unions and management can interact in a less adversarial manner. Cooperation between union and management will do more to facilitate organizational success than will its opposite—poor union-management relations.

Involvement of workers in organizational decision making can do much to engender positive organizational outcomes (e.g., commitment, satisfaction). Chapter 11 includes articles that offer some caveats and outline some benefits associated with employee empowerment. Empowerment can be an effective tool, but it must be part of an overall strategy of employee involvement in organizational processes.

CHAPTER 10

Union-Management Relations

A consensus prevails that labor-management relations in the United States are changing—rather dramatically, some believe. For example, the percentage of unionized employees in the nonfarm work force dropped from a high of nearly 33 percent in 1950 to 19 percent in 1985 and is predicted to decline further. But this still means that approximately one out of every five employees today is a union member, with the ratio of unionized to nonunionized employees much higher in such industries as auto manufacturing, mining, steel, construction, food retailing, air transport, and trucking. Those responsible for the personnel function in unionized organizations, therefore, whether they are directly or indirectly involved with labor-management relations, should become familiar with current trends in the labor movement, the reasons employees want unions, the ways union campaigns are conducted, the implications of concession bargaining for the employee-employer relationship, and the strategies that organizations might follow in the labor relations area.

Although the labor movement is now in a period of declining size and strength, unions and the underlying philosophies of unionization will probably continue to affect the field of personnel and human resources management. Unions and threats of unionization have played a significant role in the development and elaboration of several human resources activities, especially compensation and safety and health. Non-unionized organizations have in many instances modified their personnel policies and practices to discourage unionization.

Labor-management relations are affected by numerous federal laws and court decisions. The most important federal laws are the National Labor Relations (Wagner) Act of 1935 and its two amendments, the Labor-Management Relations (Taft-Hartley) Act of 1947 and the Labor-Management Reporting and Disclosure (Landrum-Griffin) Act of 1959. Each piece of legislation has a somewhat different focus. The Wagner Act encourages unionization, specifies a number of unfair employer labor practices, and establishes the National Labor Relations Board to enforce its provisions. The Taft-Hartley Act, enacted in response to union growth and a series of major strikes and boycotts during the years following the passage of the Wagner Act, seeks to achieve a balance of power more favorable to employers by specifying a number of unfair union practices in such areas as union membership, bargaining requirements, strikes, and boycotts. The primary purpose of the Landrum-Griffin Act is to prevent corruption and abuses of power by union leaders.

Atchison, in the first article, examines the relationship between the individual and the organization. Has enough been done—or does more need to be done—to develop a cooperative relationship between labor and management? In the second article, Lawler and Mohrman address the notion of a new style of management that has implications for union-management relationships.

Reed, in the final article, provides a practical guide for managing employees in a unionized environment. In addition to important background information about unions and labor law, he offers specific advice to current and prospective managers.

Suggestions for Further Reading

Carnevale, D. (1993). Root dynamics of alternative dispute resolution: An illustrative case in the U.S. Postal Service. *Public Administration Review, 53,* 455–461.

Ettorre, B. (1993). Will unions survive? *Management Review, 82,* 9–15.

Frey, R. (1993). Empowerment or else. *Harvard Business Review, 71,* 80–94.

Green, D., & Valdez, C., III. (1993). Mutual-gains bargaining assists contract negotiations. *Personnel Journal, 72,* 60.

Kochan, T., & McKersie, R. (1989). Future directions for American labor and human resources policy. *Industrial Relations, 44,* 224–244.

Lynn, M., & Brister, J. (1989). Trends in union organizing issues and tactics. *Industrial Relations, 28,* 104–113.

Murphy, B., Barlow, W., & Hatch, D. (1993). DuPont's employee committees ordered disbanded. *Personnel Journal, 72,* 24.

Reynolds, L. (1993). Ronald Carey: No more business-as-usual in the teamsters. *Management Review, 82,* 16–19.

Stuart, P. (1993). Labor unions become business partners. *Personnel Journal, 72,* 54–63.

Zellner, W. (1989, November 6). Suddenly, the UAW is raising its voice at GM. *Business Week,* pp. 96, 100.

The Employment Relationship: Un-Tied or Re-Tied?

Thomas J. Atchison

Employees are running so scared that there is a whole culture that says don't make waves, don't take risks—just at the time we need innovation.[1]

This executive's statement reflects employees' fear and anxiety about their jobs today. It also highlights three concerns about changes occurring in the employment relationship.

The first concern is that the nature of the employment relationship has changed considerably. "Companies want fewer obligations to their employees, not more," said one economist in a recent *Time* article.[2] The way that employees are responding to these changes is the second concern. The title of the *Time* article, "Where Has the Gung-Ho Gone?" effectively sums up the motivational problem which is being created. It shows how this motivational problem is negatively affecting productivity. The timing for employee malaise is terrible. This is the third concern. Competitiveness, which has spawned the movement for lean and mean organizations, will only occur if employees are more productive, not less.

This is not the first time that the employment relationship has undergone radical change. Entrepreneurs, at the beginning of the Industrial Revolution, sought to free themselves from the responsibilities of being the master in the master-serf relationship established in the Middle Ages.[3] After decades of labor strife, a labor-capital accord was finally reached in the 1930s. Labor relinquished claims over the control of production, thereby granting management broad powers to operate organizations without interference. This included the ability to adjust the size of the

work force to meet economic conditions. In return, wage increases were to keep up with the increasing growth of the economy. In addition, rules governing procedural justice, such as job classification, movement of employees between jobs, and how wages were to be set were established.[4] Both labor and management agreed to this arrangement because they wished to prevent further government intrusion into the employment relationship.

In 1980, this accord came apart. External pressures, such as foreign competition and deregulation, led management to believe that employment conditions must change if American industry was to be competitive.[5]

What is emerging out of the current situation? One view is that a new employment relationship emphasizing cooperative rather than adversarial relations between management and employees is coming about and will be the answer to America's productivity crisis.[6] This new cooperative relationship is patterned after the Japanese style.[7] While seemingly new, philosophically it is like Frederick W. Taylor's idea that management and labor should "take their eyes off the division of the surplus as the all important matter, and together turn their attention towards increasing the size of the surplus. . . ."[8] Such cooperation did not occur in the 1920's; will it happen today?

Cooperation at What Cost?

Cooperation assumes two parties working together to achieve a desired end. Much of what has occurred in the past ten years does not fit this model. Massive layoffs at all organiza-

Reprinted with permission from *Academy of Management Executive*, 5 (1991): 52–62.

tional levels, wage reductions in most union contracts, takeovers and mergers destroying jobs as well as pensions systems have been all too common. Job classifications have been changed and white-collar employee layoffs have reduced their job security. These actions, more typical of an adversarial relationship than a cooperative one, make management look like it's taking unilateral action to the detriment of its employees.

The following allegory illustrates employee confusion about talk of cooperation in the employment relationship. In this example, the employment relationship is replaced with the marriage relationship:

Suppose as the two of you come in the door from work your spouse says to you:

"Sit down. I want to talk to you. Our relationship has got to change. The reasons for this are partly you and partly outside pressures. You have been asking for too much and giving too little. At the same time we are facing a deteriorating financial condition so there is not as much for us to share. I have given this a great deal of thought and here are the changes that must take place.

"I need more from you. I want you to be more cooperative and involved with our relationship. You need to look around the house and see what needs to be done and do it. Then we should sit down more often and decide on what things need to be done and how. We are not going to be able to afford help so you need to devote more time and do more around here. All this means you must be more flexible and take on a wider variety of responsibilities around the house.

"You are going to have to cut back on the amount of money you use each week. I have had to borrow a large amount of money to keep this house going and at the same time have needed money for maintaining other activities so there is less for you. There is an up side to this, however. First, you will be on an incentive system that will give you a share of any savings in expenses that we can make by sitting

down together and working through ideas to save costs. Second, since you are doing a wider variety of tasks around the house and experiencing more responsibility, you should find this to be intrinsically satisfying.

"This is not all. We cannot afford to put any more money into the savings account we established for retirement. But I did find that, with the increase in the value of our investments, the account has gained more value than we planned so I didn't think you would mind if I used that money for other purposes.

"Oh! By the way, I have been working on a deal with some other people. It is possible that in the near future I will be offered an opportunity that involves me moving on and leaving you with a new partner. I realize that this might seem tough on you but it is the best thing for me and I know you can survive the change.

"Last, I am concerned that our relationship is not productive enough to survive. If I find that it is not in the next six months, you will find your bags packed and outside the front door when you come home some evening."

This is not a new cooperative relationship at all but a coerced one which one party has imposed upon the other. True cooperation will require management to change its attitudes toward the capabilities of employees to make decisions and be involved with the operation of the company. The tone in this allegory is autocratic, where one person makes all the family decisions. It is to this view of the organization as family that I now turn.

One Big Happy Family?

In the recent movie *Roger and Me* the narrator is talking to a public relations official who is leaning out of a plant window. He questions her about a pending layoff and she replies that this is "family business." The image of company as family is popular and, given the ideas of cooperation discussed above, it seems to be becoming more popular. The smaller size of organizations today also fosters this view of the organization.

But such metaphors, intentionally or not, convey the characteristics of the image onto the object.[9] While the image of business as a family may be comforting to many business executives, like all metaphors, it focuses on some aspects of reality while ignoring others. In this case, when the metaphor is more closely examined it suggests some unattractive comparisons for both management and the employee.

In the "organization as family" metaphor the manager is the parent and the employee is the child. Decision making is placed on management and employees are dependent on their managers. While management may find this a comfortable arrangement, it is not what is needed to create a climate of cooperation. A more enlightened view may be that of an older family, where the children are grown and independent or in the extreme where the children are grown and caring for the elder parent. But this image would be discomforting to managers. It suggests that employees would strive for independence from the employer or even seek to make the employer dependent upon them.

An image of organizations as family may make more sense in the Japanese culture.[10] The concept of family is collective. It encourages loyalty from the employee and protection by and from the employer. The push towards ridding the organization of low performers and downsizing in general are antithetical to the idea of family. Families turning out or leaving behind children are illustrations of the most extreme negative circumstances in literature and history.

The parental role in this "organization as family" metaphor focuses on the child's achievement and performance. But what of the parents' nurturing role? It is absent. Including the nurturing role refocuses the metaphor on a different and more affective employment relationship. For instance, focus may shift to caring, listening, and developing employee self-esteem.[11]

Is there a place in organizations where this more nurturing, caring, and protective role is fostered? Is this a major function of the human resource department?

The Human Resource Department: Ombudsman or Strategist?

Fairness is a major concern in any relationship. The management literature calls this organizational justice and it has three aspects: distributive, procedural, and corrective. All three have been damaged by changes to the employment relationship in the past ten years.

Distributive justice, which is the allocation of revenues, has experienced a shift. Employees are receiving a smaller share of the organizational income pie, even as that pie has grown. Leveraging, with its consequent burden of huge interest payments, has taken a larger proportion. Large increases in executive salaries, while not a major portion of the total pie, have increased pay differences between the top and bottom of the organization. This has created a negative impression with employees.[12] Finally, the upsurge in the stock market during the 1980s significantly increased stockholders' wealth. Wages have not risen proportionately, thereby violating employees' feelings of distributive justice.

Procedural justice involves establishing rules for how to divide the pie and corrective justice has to do with correcting mistakes. These two have also been changed to the detriment of the employee recently. With unions, procedural and corrective justice were accomplished by collective bargaining and contract administration. Today, as fewer employees are union members, fewer have their rights protected.

In *The Transformation of American Industrial Relationships,* the authors (Kochan, Katz, and McKersie) see the rise of a strong and enlightened human resource department within the organization as the replacement for unions.[13] The strength of this modern human resource department emanates from a strategic focus which contributes to the organization's overall strategy. This focus is necessary if human resources are to be considered truly important.[14] The way this often gets interpreted, however, is disturbing. The human resource administrator is to "contribute to the bottom line" and show the result of human resource activities in financial terms. While there are places where this is appropriate, such as with cost containment of benefits, in general good human resource management is better stated in terms of productivity than profits. Human resource management best fits with organizational strategy when the strategist's role is perceived to represent the organization's stakeholders rather than the stockholders.[15]

These events have long-term consequences to organizational strategies. Changes in employee attitudes are one documented consequence. Employees become more cynical.[16] Employees who once gave their commitment and energy to the organization vow that they will never be fooled again. Such employees are hard to gain cooperation from or to motivate for higher productivity.

If the human resource department is to effectively replace unions, the strategic model may not be the best approach. Viewing the human resource executive as an ombudsman may be a more apt model. An ombudsman is a person who knows the system and can protect the individual from the excesses of that system.[17] This, however, places the human resource executive back in a role perceived as not central to accomplishing organizational goals.

In pursuing a more competitive strategy, management has taken many unilateral actions during the past decade which have proved to be detrimental to employees. Neither unions nor an enlightened human resource department have been able to soften the negative impact on employees. Is management to be allowed the latitude to continue to make these decisions unfettered, or will its power be curtailed?

Where Is the Countervailing Power?

The concept of countervailing power is central in American political science and extends to most other aspects of our society as well. No single decision maker or decision-making body is to have total power. Galbraith in *American Capitalism* extended this idea into the economic sphere with a tripartite relationship among management, labor unions, and the government where a rise in the power of one leads to a rise in the power of at least one of the other two.[18] But with the weakened power of unions, the relationship is out of balance. A redress of the power balance could come from three sources: employees, government, or resurgent unions.

Employees

Employees must be able to influence the terms of a new relationship. It is the only long-term solution that will be acceptable to employees and society. In fact, employees are soon likely to possess more power in determining their work relationships. The labor market, which for the last twenty years has experienced a surplus of employees due to the baby boom, is drying up as the baby bust generation moves into the work force. Predictions indicate that there will be a shortage of employees in most skilled and professional areas.[19] A surplus of employees will occur only in unskilled areas where demand is falling and the labor pool is poorly educated. Thus, there will be a valued group of employees with more power and another group that is less valued with reduced power. This split in the work force is being reflected in society and creates a "have-not" class which could threaten the stability of our social and political structures.[20]

Women will represent the majority of new entrants into the work force during the next ten years. Obtaining their commitment and involvement will require substantial changes in human resource policies. One major area that must be addressed is the work-family conflict. Organizations need to revise policies to provide more flexibility in employment: time and place of work, career paths, and benefit options, for example.

New forms of communication and the computer enable organizations to adapt and be more flexible on hours and work locations. But even more important is the attitudinal change that balances the organization's needs with the employee's home life. The separation of work and family which began with the industrial revolution may be reversing.[21]

The highly educated, including women, will definitely impact organizations, not because they are organizing to do so, but rather as a result of organizations attempting to recruit them and adopting policies to maintain an adequate labor force. It is here that the enlightened human resource department can have a significant impact by introducing sophisticated personnel planning systems to complement the organization's other planning systems.

Government

Recently, government has been steadily increasing its role in defining conditions of the employment relationship, both through legislation and the courts. Legislation regarding the employment relationship has moved from a reliance on collective labor law which encouraged collective bargaining to individual labor law which provides specific protection to all employees.[22]

The most dramatic change in individual labor law has come from the redefinition of the at-will principle of employment. This doctrine has allowed employers to dismiss any employee for any reason whatsoever. The United States is the last of the industrialized countries not to have replaced this doctrine with an unjustified discharge law, one that restricts employers to firing employees only for cause. Even so, the impact of the at-will principle has been steadily eroding as select employee groups have been protected from arbitrary discharge. The Civil Rights Act is a case in point. In addition, courts have begun to de-

velop exceptions to the at-will principle for violations of public policy, implied contract, and bad faith. Clearly we are close to replacing the at-will principle in the United States with a doctrine of justifiable discharge.

As the move for a new civil rights bill and family leave benefits indicate, there is a continuing push for new labor legislation. The long-term results of this intrusion by law are clear and should be disturbing to the business executive; the demands of employees through elected union representatives are being replaced by legislation and court decisions. These constraints are more unilateral, leaving the manager less room for negotiating reasonable change.

Unlike collective labor law, which established the system for determining the details of the employment relationship, these individual labor laws focus on specific perceived problems without defining any overall employment policy. The result is a mass of overlapping laws and regulations that requires an expert to understand.

Dealing with these pressures is another major challenge for the human resource department. It becomes the organizational watchdog responsible for "keeping the organization legal." It is a necessary but not necessarily desirable role.

Resurgent Unions?

Collective bargaining is the alternative to individual bargaining or government control. But the prospect of unions being a powerful force in redefining the employment relationship is not good. Union membership and power has been steadily declining for the past twenty years. The movement from a manufacturing to a service economy which led to this decline is not likely to change.

Unions would have to attract large numbers of white-collar employees in the service industries in order to grow. A high level of dissatisfaction and powerlessness would have to exist in these employees for this to happen.[23] Preventing these conditions is exactly what Kochan, Katz, and McKersie see as the human resource department's contribution.

Why have unions stood by passively as management has made drastic changes in the employment relationship during the last ten years? Increased global competition and an emerging world economy may be part of the answer. The United States must become more competitive and changes and hardships are perceived as the cost that union members must pay for their role in the problem. However, as a 1987 *Los Angeles Times* Labor Day editorial stated, management must beware that it does not use this feeling on the public's part as a way to exploit its employees.[24]

Further, Kochan, Katz, and McKersie explain that with the rising power of management, a latent dislike for unions has emerged, resulting in a resurgence of anti-unionism.[25] Is this attitudinal change only restricted to the union? Or is it the organization's attempt to create a stable situation by turning employees into a compliant resource? This kind of thinking, however, is not conducive to cooperation. Compliance and cooperation are not the same thing. Trust, built on mutual respect, is the major building block for cooperation between management and the employee. In the labor accord forged in the 1930s both sides gained and paid for some advantage. A new accommodation is needed if American industry is to survive. Employees must be empowered to control their work and influence the operation of the organization.

The New Employment Relationships

Despite the concerns expressed here, the outlines of some new employment relationships are already clear. Changes in American industry and the work force are creating not one but a number of new employment relationships. C. Handy in *The Age of Unreason* expresses this best by observing that organizations today can be pictured as a shamrock with three leaves, each representing a different group of employees with a different employ-ment relationship. These groups he calls the core, contractor, and flexible.[26]

The Core Group

The labor accord of the 1930s began to unravel because of changes in U.S. work patterns. A redefined employment relationship for the organization's core group of employees is being built upon these changes. A discussion follows of the major characteristics needed to establish a new employment relationship with the employees that perform the organization's base operations—the core group.

1. The nature of the new work. The employment relationship of the 1930s encouraged job simplification. The life cycle of products today, competition, and new technology all combine to require greater employee skills. Technology has made the work environment more complex and requires employees to change the way they perform their jobs. Flexibility is now a major requirement. Employees must be able and willing to do different tasks every day.

How do we obtain this flexibility and willingness to change? One way is to provide jobs that allow the employee to exercise more discretion on the job—to be empowered. In a way, empowerment is an updated version of an old idea—participative management.[27] How is it different? First is a focus on work. The new work requires decision making, flexibility, and higher skill levels. Second, the work group as opposed to the individual is key. Self-managing work teams are held accountable for producing a product and making all the necessary production decisions.[28]

The idea of empowerment reverses a trend that began with the Industrial Revolution. It was strongly influenced by scientific management, which put managers in charge of determining what was to be produced and how production was to be accomplished. F.W. Taylor, in *Principles of Scientific Management,* suggests that planning the work should be completely separate from doing the work which characterizes this trend.[29] Reversing this way of thinking will not be easy because doing so jeopardizes traditional power relationships.

Suggesting the use of company work groups changes the metaphor from family to team. Employees cooperate within their team to accomplish a goal. Teamwork also suggests a new role for the supervisor—that of coach. The supervisor focuses on teaching and learning instead of authority and command.

2. Employee training. Empowerment requires that employees possess skills at three levels: reading and computation, job knowledge, and interpersonal skills. Finding employees who have all these qualities is becoming difficult. Part of the problem is that there is a shortage of young employees entering the work force. School systems are struggling to educate today's diverse student population. The result is a work force which is deficient in language and computational skills.

The most positive change American business could make is to increase employee training. To build on the strength of our diverse work culture, companies must provide educational opportunities for language competence, work skills, and company work ethic standards. The evidence suggests that such training pays off. For example, Motorola and Corning have extensive training programs which complement work reorganization. These programs have been successful in making the companies more competitive.[30]

Linking jobs to specific educational requirements is another step companies can take. Unlike countries like Germany, that have a strong apprenticeship tradition, organizations in the United States have not required either particular levels or types of education to obtain specific jobs. Given the changing job requirements, organizations would do well to establish a clear "line of sight" between the completion of courses and degrees and employability. Countries that have made this connection have a lower unemployment rate and higher productivity among young employees.[31]

3. Work continuity. Job security is the number one concern of employees today. The down-

sizing of American industry has affected all types of employees, including executives and professionals. Finding new jobs has been difficult and finding jobs at the same level of work has been even harder.

If American industry is going to engage in empowerment and training, then job security is a necessity. Organizations lose an enormous investment in human resources when downsizing. The more training invested in the employee, the greater the loss of human capital. Costs associated with downsizing are large and planned cost savings almost never achieved. Remaining employees feel guilty and fear that they will be next.[32] The atmosphere that job insecurity produces is detrimental to employees' mental health and decreases productivity in the organization.[33]

4. Flexibility in work arrangements. Organizations are slowly changing policies to increase workplace flexibility—when, how much and where people work. Workplace flexibility is often suggested as a female issue. It should be viewed, however, as a changing society issue. Women need to work for economic reasons and organizations need the skills represented by the best-educated segment of our society. Since the U.S. family structure is being altered, the issue shifts to families, in which case all of us are affected.[34]

Flexibility and responsiveness to family life is congruent with empowerment. Organizations need to offer employees choices so that they can balance their professional and personal life. Management must trust employees to use good judgment in arriving at mutually acceptable work patterns.

5. Work rewards. Compensation practices changed little in the United States for more than fifty years. Emphasis was placed on internal equity and external competitiveness. The past ten years has seen a trend toward relating pay to performance and making it variable with the fortunes of the company. Some portion of the employee's pay is "put at risk" to give the organization flexibility and to focus employee attention on the organization's success. This trend has encouraged interest in incentive plans, particularly those that are oriented to organizational success, such as gainsharing.

Contractors and Flexible Employers

The five conditions just discussed define the employment relationship for a core group of employees. In the past decade, the downsizing of American industry and technology changes has considerably reduced the size of the core group.

Two other groups fill out the shamrock organization and create very different employment relationships.

Contractors are the first of the two. These people may be former core employees brought back as consultants, independent professionals who perform work for a group of organizations, or employees of organizations who provide specific services. The employment relationship for this group is defined in a contract and usually in terms of specified outcomes for a set price. The positive side of this relationship is that work can be expanded and contracted by the organization easily. A negative aspect is that in expansionary times a low supply of these people may leave the organization without sufficient human resources.

The flexible work force, or temporary and part-time employees, is the third leaf of the shamrock. This group is often viewed as being disposable. Organizations often fail to treat these employees as important assets. Handy pointed out that "treated as casual labor, such people respond casually."[35] Most organizations, however, depend on this group when the production level is anything more than the minimum.

Many people prefer to be in this flexible group. They do not wish to work the long hours or make the commitment required of the core group. This, however, does not mean that they should not be treated equitably. The cornerstone of this employment relationship from the organization's standpoint is the ability to adjust the work force at will. The employee's focus is on time, the job, and being rewarded fairly. This group should not be expected to express commitment to the organization. Rewards systems should focus on competitive pay and short-term bonuses for good work.

Conclusion

That these new employment relationships require new employee behavior and attitudes is clear but the change also affects managers. The new employment relationship requires that employees be self-reliant and active in defining their future. Gone is the paternalism of yesterday. Each party in the employment relationship must focus on defining their needs and taking responsibility for meeting them.[36]

Treating employees as adults, empowering them, and creating true cooperative relationships are all part of a new dynamic employment relationship. Achieving this new relationship is difficult for managers. Two recent articles in the *Harvard Business Review* identified some principles that worked for two executives. Ricardo Semler, who heads a manufacturing company in Brazil, was guided by three principles when turning the company around to a profitable position. Work force democracy, profit sharing, and free access to information are three interrelated principles to Semler. Work force democracy, or treating people like adults, led to employees making corporate decisions, determining their own flexible work arrangements, and browsing through the company's books.

Ralph Stayer heads up a family business called Jacksonville Sausage. He also found that the company needed to be turned around if it was to survive. Stayer was concerned that people did not seem to care about the company or their own job performance. What he began to realize after a few false starts was that he had to give up his hold over the decisions made in the company and thereby his authority. The line workers have now taken over quality control, personnel functions, scheduling, budgeting, and capital improvement. Stayer believes that he has now worked himself out of a job and the organization is doing just fine.[37]

Growth and productivity will come when the employees share in the rewards and take responsibility for increasing productivity. Employee empowerment must not be limited to work methods but must also include the broader set of rules that defines the procedural justice pattern within the organization, as well as strategic policy decisions. Without this, the employees' perception of cooperation will be too narrow. The purpose of empowerment must go beyond "giving employees the feeling of participation" to a true sharing of power in the organization. As also seen in the previous examples, empowerment threatens traditional management power. Empowerment is not just listening to employees but allowing them to make decisions about their work and the organization's operations.

If the appropriate metaphor for the organization is the team, then the appropriate metaphor for the manager is the coach. This focuses the manager on motivating employees through training and getting the best out of them, not by commanding them. Such an approach requires managers to respect their employees and perceive that they are competent adults who can be depended on to do their work.

Endnotes

1. J. Castro, "Where Did the Gung-Ho Go?" *Time,* September 11, 1989, 52–56.

2. "The Password is 'Flexible'," *Business Week,* September 25, 1989, 154.

3. R. Bendix, *Work and Authority in Industry,* (New York: Harper and Row, 1956).

4. See for instance: S. Bowles, and H. Gintis, "The Labor-Capital Accord" in F. Hearn, *The Transformation of Industrial Organization,* (Belmont, CA: Wadsworth Publishing, 1988), 75–84 and P. Osterman, *Employment Futures,* (New York: Oxford University Press, 1988).

5. Osterman, Ibid.

6. See for example: E. E. Lawler, *High Involvement Management,* (San Francisco: Jossey-Bass, 1988) and T.J. Peters, and R. H. Waterman, *In Search of Excellence,* (New York: Harper and Row, 1982).

7. C. J. Grayson, and C. O'Dell, *The Two Minute Warning,* (New York: The Free Press, 1988).

8. F. W. Taylor, *Principles of Scientific Management,* (New York: Harper and Row, 1912), 29–30.

9. G. Morgan, *Images of Organization,* (Beverly Hills, CA: Sage Publications, 1986).

10. G. Hofstede, "Cultural Dimensions in Management and Planning," *Asia Pacific Journal of Management,* Jan. 1984, 81–99.

11. P. C. Lunneborg, *Women Changing Work,* (New York: Bergin and Garvey, 1990).

12. "Is the Boss Getting Paid Too Much?" *Business Week,* May 1, 1989, 46–52.

13. T. A. Kochan, H. C. Katz, and R. B. McKersie, *The Transformation of American Industrial Relations,* (New York: Basic Books, 1986).

14. R. S. Schuler, "Repositioning the Human Resource Function: Transformation or Demise?" *Academy of Management Executive,* August, 1990, 49–60.

15. I. Mitroff, *Stakeholders of the Organizational Mind,* (San Francisco: Jossey-Bass Publishers, 1983).

16. D. L. Kanter, and P. H. Mirvis, *The Cynical Americans,* (San Francisco: Jossey-Bass, 1989).

17. M. Waxman, "Reactive and Proactive Resolution of Employee Responsibilities and Rights Staff Issues via the Ombudsman Concept," in C. A. B. Osigweh, Ed., *Managing Employee Rights and Responsibilities,* (New York: Quorum Books, 1989), 161–174.

18. J. K. Galbraith, *American Capitalism,* (Boston: Houghton Mifflin Co., 1962).

19. M. M. Greller, and D. M. Nee, *From Baby Boom to Baby Bust,* (Reading, Mass: Addison-Wesley Publishing, 1989).

20. "Where the Jobs Are Is Where the Skills Aren't," *Business Week,* Sept. 19, 1988, 104–108.

21. F. S. Rogers, and C. Rogers, "Business and the Facts of Family Life," *Harvard Business Review,* November-December 1989, 121–131.

22. K. L. Sovereign, *Personnel Law, 2nd. Ed.,* (Englewood Cliffs, New Jersey: Prentice-Hall, 1989).

23. J. M. Brett, "Why Employees Want Unions," *Organizational Dynamics,* Spring 1980, 47–59.

24. "Looking at Labor and Business," *Los Angeles Times,* September 7, 1987, II, 6.

25. Kochan et al., Op Cit.

26. C. Handy, *The Age of Unreason,* (Boston: Harvard Business School Press, 1989).

27. Lawler, *High Involvement Management,* Op Cit.

28. See for example: M. A. Frohman, "Human Resource Management and the Bottom Line: Evidence of the Connection," *Human Resource Management,* 1984, 315–34.

29. F. W. Taylor, *Scientific Management,* Op Cit.

30. W. Wiggenhorn, "Motorola U.: When Training Becomes an Education," *Harvard Business Review,* July-August 1990, 71–83 and J. Hoerr, "Sharpening Minds for a Competitive Edge," *Business Week,* Dec. 17, 1990, 72–8.

31. Hoerr, Ibid.

32. J. F. Bolt, "Job Security: Its Time Has Come," *Harvard Business Review,* November-December 1983.

33. J. Hartley, D. Jacobsen, B. Klandermans, and T. Van Vuuren, *Job Insecurity,* (Newbury Park, CA: Sage Publications, 1991).

34. Rodgers, Op Cit.

35. Handy, Op Cit. 100.

36. K. P. DeMeuse, and W. W. Tornow, "The Tie That Binds—Has Become Very, Very Frayed," *Human Resource Planning,* 1990, no. 3, 203–213.

37. R. Stayer, "How I Learned to Let My Workers Lead," *Harvard Business Review,* November-December 1990, 66–83 and R. Semler, "Managing without Managers," *Harvard Business Review,* September-October 1989, 76–84.

Unions and the New Management

Edward E. Lawler III and Susan A. Mohrman

The union movement in the United States is in trouble. Indicators of its health show it is very ill. The only debatable point is whether the illness is terminal or simply represents another one of the down cycles from which the union movement has suffered during its lifetime. The severity of the illness is best illustrated by declining membership: Data from the Bureau of Labor Statistics show that union membership has fallen from 23% of the workforce in 1980 to 18.8% in 1984, the lowest in recent history and the lowest of any other free industrial nation, with the possible exception of Spain. This decline represents a loss of 2.7 million union members. As recently as the 1950s, over 30% of the workforce belonged to unions. Data from decertification and certification elections point to a significant decline as unions lose an increasing number of elections.

The reasons commonly cited for the decline in union membership are many and varied. Some reflect trends in the economy: globalization resulting in the decline of traditionally unionized industries such as automobiles, garments, food processing, and steel; a sharp growth in the service sector, which is harder to organize; the emergence of nonunion competition in newly deregulated industries such as airlines and trucking; and a decrease in demand and/or overproduction in industries, e.g., meat packing. Other threats to unions include automation, the changing legal situation with respect to union organizing and employee rights, and, finally, the changing expectations of the new workforce.

Unions are not the only institutions threatened. The changing environment has made its impact on the viability of many businesses themselves and on the way in which they are managed. In fact, management's actions in adjusting to an altered environment have constituted further threats to the health of unions. Believing unions to be an encumbrance to competing effectively in a rapidly changing global economy, some managements resort to antiunion tactics with increased intensity, sophistication, and success. More important, from our perspective, management is trying to create a new way of managing, one more suitable to a rapidly changing economy, increasingly advanced technologies, and a better educated, more sophisticated workforce. This new approach to managing includes greater responsiveness to employee needs for involvement, responsibility, and meaningful work. As part of the new way of managing, these organizations accept responsibility for creating a positive and motivating work environment for their employees. In doing so, they discover that the result is a stronger, more competitive enterprise.

The increased adoption of involvement-oriented management approaches raises the question of what role there is for unions. The role unions once filled is not viable in the new management environment: They must change or continue to decline.

Should we worry about their decline and possible extinction? We take the position that society should be very concerned about the rapid weakening of organized labor. It potentially eliminates effective input by a major stakeholder, labor, into the decisions shaping businesses of the future. In the past, unions have been the primary voice for workers. Now their survival depends on finding a new role, given the changes that have taken place. Before we can discuss some of the changes that

Reprinted with permission from *Academy of Management Executive, 1* (1987): 293–300.

unions will have to make, we first need to consider the success in fulfilling their traditional role. We will then look at the "new management" to which unions must adjust.

Traditional Role of Unions

Union-management relationships in the United States have traditionally been adversarial, with unions consistently taking the position that this is the best way to accomplish their objectives. In many ways this attitude follows directly from union objectives and the type of promises union officials make to their membership. Essentially, unions have presented themselves as the sole recourse for employees seeking certain tangible benefits from their company. These benefits are primarily in the area of wages, working conditions, job security, and due process appeals. The famous statement by Samuel Gompers that what unions want is "more" is a clear indication of this bread-and-butter approach. Jimmy Hoffa, the late president of the Teamsters, said the success of unions depended on their ability to deliver "the highest buck."

Few question that unions have been effective in accomplishing many of their objectives. The wages of unionized employees have been estimated to be as much as 33% higher than those of nonunion employees, and unions are often credited with dramatically improving working conditions and safety in the United States.[1] The protection that unions offer against arbitrary management actions are also well documented. Grievance procedures and contractual terms protect employees from unfair salary practices, layoffs, and discipline. Overall, the evidence supports the view that unions have been highly successful in accomplishing what they set out to do for their members.

Indeed, there is evidence to suggest that not only have unions have won improved working conditions for their membership, but that many of these improvements have spread to the workforce in general. This is a result of legislation that unions have supported, as well as companies' giving their nonunion employ-ees comparable working conditions to avoid unionization. Indeed, unions have served as a "countervailing power" within our democratic system. It is the union movement that has established many of the employment standards that are generally accepted in today's society.

If unions have been highly successful, why then are they in a state of serious decline? Essentially, unions have been so successful in accomplishing their objectives that many people now believe they are no longer needed and should go out of business. However, we believe that there are serious problems with this suggestion. First, there is considerable work still to be done with respect to the traditional issues that unions have addressed. Far too many people in the United States continue to be injured and even killed in workplace accidents, too many rogue managements still engage in unfair and unreasonable practices, and there certainly is room to improve the economic plight of many employees. Furthermore, the existence of unions probably motivates many managers, even those in nonunion settings, to deal fairly with their subordinates. Second, we are at a point in history when fundamental changes are occurring in the organization of work and the structure of the economy. Organized labor can be an important institutional voice for the workforce during this time of change. Thus, from a societal point of view, it is clearly desirable to have a vibrant, viable union movement in the United States. However, there is no denying the declining market for traditional adversarial unionism. The challenges our organizations face are so major that effective representation of labor requires an expanded agenda and new approaches. Failure to adopt these new approaches could lead to the demise of unions even though it is in the best interest of society for them to continue.

The declining market for traditional unionism is being recognized by the leadership of some major U.S. unions, and there is evidence that changes are taking place. The Communications Workers of America (CWA) began a study in 1981 that developed a new framework for its future. The results of a 1985 study by the AFL-CIO that addresses the issue of the future of unionism in the United States represents a revolution in thinking within the top echelons of the union movement. The study points out that unions often find themselves behind the pace of change, and states that "It is not enough merely to search for more effective ways of doing what we've always done: We must expand our notions of what it is workers can do through unions."[2]

What can employees do through unions that is new and different? What are the new services or products that unions can offer people that will prevent unions from becoming obsolete? How can unions be an effective voice for the people they represent as our businesses and society adjust to the new global economic order? In answering these questions, unions must deal with the changes management is making, for management is developing strategies to cope with the same changes that are causing such severe problems for unions.

The New Management

A minirevolution, or at least a significant change in the way a number of American corporations are being managed, started in the 1970s and has gained major momentum in the 1980s. These new management approaches were developed in response to such challenges as increasing foreign competition, the complexities of a global economy, and a decline in the growth rate, and aim toward greater power sharing and participative decision making. Information, knowledge, and power have increasingly been disseminated and moved to lower levels. Motorola, General Motors, Ford, Honeywell, Mead, Xerox, and GTE are among the major U.S. corporations that have publicly committed to corporate-wide changes in the way they manage their people. They are adopting management practices that consciously blur the line between workers and managers and create an organizational culture characterized by employees caring more, knowing more, and doing more. This represents a substantial departure from the traditional management approach of emphasizing control and compliance to get effective behavior from lower-level employees. In short, it emphasizes getting effective behavior through commitment to the goals of the organization.[3]

Some of the design components of this new approach to managing are listed in Exhibit 1. Briefly, organizations attempting to change in this direction recognize the need for conscious and public articulation of a new philosophy emphasizing shared values at all organizational levels and trust in the willingness of all employees to work in the company's best interest. This philosophy is then backed up by lean, flat structures that push responsibility and authority down to those who do the work, typically in self-contained teams and organizational units that have responsibility for a product, service, or market segment. Reward systems formally link the interests of individuals with those of the company, and acknowledge the increased skills, flexibility, and teamwork required of employees in this kind of organization. Employees are fully informed about the business, and their expanded job responsibilities are complimented by greater participation in decisions about how work is done and the policies and practices that affect the workplace. The climate is designed to encourage higher standards of organizational performance.

In examining Exhibit 1, it is apparent that some of the attributes of the new management, such as flexible job duties, emphasis on "stretch" goals, and participatively developed personnel policies, appear antithetical to such traditional union issues as clearly defined job classifications, avoidance of arbitrary increases in standards of performance (sometimes called "speed-ups"), and collective bargaining to resolve conditions of employment. Indeed, to a great extent the new management philosophy is a clear alternative to the world of work advocated by many traditional unionists.

Exhibit 1
Characteristics of the New Management

Philosophy	• Shared values, trust
Organizational structure	• Flat
	• Light on staff
	• Self-contained organizational units responsible for product or customer
	• Decentralized decision making
Job design	• Individually enriched jobs or teams
	• Flexible job duties
	• Cross-training
	• Responsible for "doing" and "improving"
Employee voice	• Participate work teams
	• Task forces
Information systems	• Business data widely shared
Performance standards	• Goals and standards participatively set
	• "Stretch" goals emphasized
Reward systems	• Variable rewards share in business gains
	• Linked to skills and mastery
	• Team rewards
Personnel practices	• Developed participatively

This new management approach is probably best represented by the more than 200 "high-involvement" plants that have been started by U.S. manufacturing organizations in the last decade.[4] Many of these began as nonunion plants, often in traditionally organized industries, and have successfully resisted union organizing drives. In essence, these organizations have made unions unnecessary in the eyes of their employees, not so much because they offer the same benefits as do unions but because they have created a work environment that has more appeal to today's workforce than the one offered by unions. In high-involvement plants distinctions between managers and workers are blurred and team-based job structures with enhanced variety and responsibility are present. Employees often control the organization to such an extent that they determine their own

wages, the distribution of overtime, the structure of their work, and who will be laid off. This creates an environment in which workers already make decisions about issues covered by union contracts and historically subject to grievances. In this environment, it is difficult to see the role for traditional unionism. When interviewed about the desirability of a union, over half the employees in a plant we studied said they would lose power with a union because the contract would take away decision-making responsibilities they currently had.

It is possible to conclude here that as organizations move toward more employee involvement there is no role for unions because management is meeting the needs of employees. In fact, some observers of this trend see it as a sophisticated union avoidance strategy.[5] There is little doubt that management has been more responsive to research evidence that for decades has shown that employees want to participate in workplace decisions and to have interesting, challenging jobs. As a result of management leadership, many unions now find themselves playing catch-up and trying to develop a role for themselves in participatively managed organizations.

Before concluding that unions are unnecessary, we should note that some new high-involvement organizations are, in fact, organized. The United Auto Workers union (UAW) has initiated a joint venture with General Motors in a number of high-involvement plants, is a partner with Toyota in a plant in Fremont, California, managed along high-commitment principles, and is currently involved in the start-up of General Motors' Saturn operation. The Shell polypropelene plant in Sarnia, Ontario, has a high-involvement design that was jointly implemented with the Oil, Chemical, and Atomic Workers union (OCAW). In these efforts, the union has fully participated in planning the organization, developing its philosophy, and monitoring adherence to the new way of operating. Although the research evidence from these settings is still slim, it does suggest there can be a viable and important role for unions in the design and ongoing maintenance of high-involvement, high-performing organizations. Indeed, this is our view as well.

Now, let us consider what this new role for unions entails.

A New Role for Unions

The role of unions in high-involvement organizations is primarily one of assuring participation rather than fomenting adversity. Participation needs to occur at two levels. First, unions must actively work with management to create an organizational climate and a way of operating that allow employees to participate directly in decisions made in their work areas and in task teams and problem-solving groups. In short, unions must emphasize direct participation and high involvement as important organization design features. This differs from the traditional practice of emphasizing participation by union officials through formal collective bargaining and grievance channels. The difference is not subtle, as it implies a willingness on the part of union leaders to make their own decisions.

Second, unions must become representative of members in decision making and assure that their inputs and views are effectively represented in the decision-making process, not just in collective bargaining. This implies both an expanded agenda and a shift in the format and quality of the relationship between union and management. The agenda needs to expand to include multiple goals. Beyond issues of working conditions and labor's share of the pie, unions must become concerned with the health of the business in a changing economic environment and with issues, such as the adoption of new technology, that relate to competitiveness and business survival. This expanded agenda requires that unions come to the business process not just periodically, as an adversary trying to grab an even larger share of the pie, but as a stakeholder in an ongoing, complex, multi-stakeholder organization designed with the shared objectives of ensuring survival of the business and an equi-

table return for all. This is not to say that the union should abandon the collective bargaining process. Collective bargaining will continue to have an important role but it, too, must change.

Exhibit 2 lists the important differences between the traditional union contract and one that might be negotiated using this new approach. The latter suggests that the entire contract might be only a few pages long, containing a general statement of corporate philosophy and culture. It needs to focus on establishing decision processes that allow the details of work methods, procedures, and pay to be handled on an ongoing basis through an organization structure based on participation. With respect to the reward systems, rather than detailing the actual reward levels for individuals, the contract should talk about the type of reward system that will be put in place and leave it to the participative process to decide how specific individuals will be affected. Rather than establishing a time-bound legal template and a "judicial" appeals process to handle violations, the new contract should bind the parties to general participative processes for determining the particulars, introducing change, and addressing problems that arise.

Perhaps the best example of a new contract is the one at the Shell plant in Sarnia, Ontario. It is only three pages long and largely deals with goals and philosophy. It calls for cross-training, employee involvement, and joint decision making. A somewhat similar contract has been developed to cover the new GM Sat-

Exhibit 2
The Role of Contract Bargaining

Traditional Approach	New Approach
• Detailed; covers all contingencies	• Set culture, philosophy
• Fixed/regular negotiations	• Open, participatively altered on-line
• Reward level determined	• Reward system determined

urn plant. In its preamble, it calls for cooperation, gainsharing, and teams.

Exhibit 3 carries the idea of a new union role further. In several areas it calls for unions to take on a much more important role than they have in the past, and in others it suggests a dramatic change in their activities. For example, with respect to corporate policy and organizational effectiveness, this new role calls for unions to become active because they are the employees' elected representative. One way to do this is for the union to have a seat on the board of directors. The boards of Eastern Airlines, Wheeling-Pittsburgh, and Chrysler and such employee-owned companies as Wierton Steel and Hyatt Clark already have union representation.

A second way union leaders can represent their membership is through task forces and operating committees that set policy and make business decisions. For example, a joint union-management task force at the Saturn plant participated in virtually all the important decisions concerning the operation. The task force dealt with site selection through job design. Amalgamated Clothing and Textile Worker members have participated in Horizon Study Teams with Xerox, investigating and making recommendations on a wide range of strategic business decisions. At AT&T, the CWA has participated in Common Interest Forums for the same purpose.

With respect to organizational effectiveness, the union represents an organized vehicle for building employee commitment to an effective organization as well as assuring that employee knowledge and expertise are well utilized by the organization. Unions such as the Southern California Professional Engineering Association have initiated company/union efforts to examine issues of obsolescence and utilization of the professional expertise of members by employers. They have also sponsored sessions to educate their membership on the importance of these issues.

Unions can also play a key role by helping assure that management acts in ways that increase organizational effectiveness by challenging management actions that are poorly thought out, unwise, and self-serving and hence unlikely to increase effectiveness. Theoretically, the investors should play this role, but for many reasons they are not in a position to do so. Unions, on the other hand, often are because they participate in the day-to-day activities of organizations. For this to happen, however, unions must accept part of the responsibility for organizational effectiveness. Although this does not fit the traditional role of unions, it fits well with the idea that unions exist to help their members, and effective organizations are in the position to create a high quality of work life for workers.

Exhibit 3
Union Role

	Traditional Approach	New Approach
• Corporate policy	No role	Represents workforce at top level
• Due process	Grievances	Grievances as a last resort
• Rewards	Bargaining for specific levels	Bargains for and helps administer general guidelines, may include gainsharing, skill-based pay, profit sharing, all salary workforce
• Organizational effectiveness	No direct role	Facilitates input, improves decision making
• Work methods, job designs	Bargaining	Participates in design process
• Quality of work life	Bargaining grievances	Facilitates decision input, improves job design, assures employee input
• Job security	Bargaining	Skills, organizational effectiveness

In the important area of rewards, the union's role should be that of an active participant in designing and structuring the reward system that will be used. This can include such new practices as skill-based pay and profit sharing, which align the interest of company and employees in well-trained workers and high-performing business units.[6] For example, we recently studied a joint project between a steel company and the International Brotherhood of Boilermakers, in which the two parties jointly developed a gainsharing plan, worked on bid prices, and adjusted base wages to fit the economics of the global competitive bidding situation. The reduction in wages was accepted by the membership at least in part because the union was a partner in the decision process.

In gainsharing systems the union also needs to take on the role of monitoring the operation and assuring the effectiveness of the gainsharing plan. Here, too, the union can offer something that is less available in the absence of a union: credibility and trust. Serving as representatives of the rank and file, a small group of union officers or members can learn to understand the financial system, examine the books, and monitor payouts. When a *joint* union-management group says a program is fair, it is much more likely to be accepted.

Unions also should be quite active in the design of work methods and job structures, as they were at the Saturn plant. This means that they will inevitably be involved in selecting and implementing new pieces of technology and that they will become partners in the design process. Union involvement in work design, pay, and other decisions can have a dramatic and positive impact on the quality of work life that employees experience.

Unions can do a great deal to ensure that the participative process and attention to quality of work life, which are characteristic of the new management, become integral parts of the management process. Indeed, the single most important role that unions can fulfill may be as a check and balance on the management group. As numerous studies of participative

practices have shown, it is all too easy for management to slip in and out of participative management practices as the environment and the management personnel change.[7] Likewise, in the absence of a union, management can pick and choose the issues on which participation is permitted, soliciting no input in issues in which the workforce is centrally concerned, such as the introduction of new technology. A union that is firmly committed to involvement can be an important safeguard that ensures worker input in these key decisions.

Finally, with regard to job security, the new role represents an interesting change for unions. It suggests that union members get their security through their own skills and through the effectiveness of the organization. As we have already mentioned, members can help ensure that the organization remains effective in its actions, and that they are trained and developed in ways that will give them the personal security that comes from having transferable skills and the ability to cope with a turbulent economic environment. This, of course, is a quite different kind of job security from the one that typically comes with seniority-based union contracts. In recent contract negotiations, the UAW and CWA have achieved commitment to job-retraining programs jointly administered by management and union. General Motors and the UAW have even worked out an approach to jointly planned ventures to create new businesses and new job opportunities.

The details of the new role that unions may have in participative organizations clearly need to be established. At the moment there are no union-management relationships that incorporate all the elements suggested in Exhibit 3. Perhaps the closest example is the work that GM and the UAW have been doing on the Saturn Project. There, union and management have jointly made policy decisions and participated in structuring the work environment. It could become a prototype of the new union-management relationship in the United States.

Right now GM, Ford, Xerox, and a number of steel companies have highly publicized quality of work life programs in operation. These programs clearly represent a step toward establishing a strong role for unions in more participatively managed organizations. In most cases they have stimulated employee involvement through problem-solving groups and reduced the grievance levels by using cooperative problem solving for day-to-day disputes—further evidence that it is possible to have viable, cooperative union-management relationships in the United States.[8] However, so far most efforts fall far short of the role relationship that can be developed if unions commit themselves to a participative management model and a cooperative working relationship with management, as the UAW did with Saturn and the OCAW did with Shell Sarnia. In essence, most quality of work life projects create a parallel organization structure that leaves the contractual adversarial relationship intact. Cooperation typically focuses on noncontractual issues and, thus, is encapsulated and limited. This approach has some advantages over the traditional one, but falls far short of a high-involvement model. It may, however, represent a first step in the transition toward high involvement; for example, it seems unlikely that GM and the UAW would have gone ahead with Saturn if they had not successfully experimented with problem-solving groups in other plants.

How Unions Must Change

Adopting a high-involvement approach represents a fundamental change in orientation for the union movement and thus creates a need for a change in behavior on the part of union leaders. Different skills are needed when union leaders assume a role in business decision making. They must understand the business and problem solve around its issues. Under Lynn Williams, for example, the United Steelworkers union has sought counsel from Wall Street investment bankers in formulating union reactions to the problems in the steel industry. Of course, unions also need to remain in touch with the needs, desires, and

views of their membership. In some cases the need may actually be to *regain* touch with the job attitudes and preferences of a changing workforce doing new kinds of work.

Because of the personal changes required, it is not surprising that some union leaders are opposed to cooperative union-management employee involvement programs. The Saturn Project, for example, is highly controversial within the UAW. One UAW official has stated that "inherent in this agreement is the demise of the UAW and the trade union movement as we now know it." Another noted at the UAW's 1986 annual convention that "Saturn is a sellout of everything this union has ever fought for." We take issue with both these statements. Quite to the contrary, the Saturn Project may signal a new beginning for organized labor. Clearly, there is support for Saturn-type agreements: A movement at the 1986 UAW convention to prevent future Saturn-type agreements was defeated by an overwhelming vote, and the National Labor Relations Board has rejected a legal challenge to this agreement. As one union representative noted, "We have to find a new approach. It's not just management we are fighting now; the foreign automakers are taking our jobs."

There are indications that rank-and-file sentiment may also be changing. In 1986 workers at a GM plant in Van Nuys, California voted to try a team-style approach similar to the NUMMI joint GM/Toyota/UAW venture in Fremont, California. This vote occurred despite vocal objections from some of the key officers in the union.

Some union leaders recognize the opportunities that are present in employee involvement. Glen Watts of the CWA and Irv Bluestone and Don Ephlin of the UAW are among those union leaders who see the opportunity for a new role for unions and are trying to move their unions in this direction. Presently, however, they probably represent a minority of all union leaders. For example, although UAW President Owen Bieber backs the Saturn and NUMMI approaches, he has not made a strong commitment to the high-involvement approach. Many others seem to prefer the traditional adversarial model, perhaps because they view leaders like Ephlin as "getting in bed with management."[9] They remain convinced that the pendulum will swing back toward them and that unions will once again be strong and adversarial. Perhaps they are right, but if they are not the union movement is in for a long period of decline and possibly even eventual demise.

The macroeconomic trends affecting the United States suggest to us that the adversarial model is doomed because of the restructuring of work and organizations. The current economic challenges facing American organizations are far too complex to be easily addressed by single-stakeholder advocacy and wasteful adversarial struggles. In many respects, the economic realities of a global economy mean that to survive, organizations and their unions need to focus more on how they can jointly create wealth and less on antagonistic approaches to dividing wealth. By including gainsharing and stock ownership, high-involvement approaches can direct the energies of both labor and management toward creating organization effectiveness and wealth. Companies that fail to do this could well face extinction because their adversarial practices make them noncompetitive in a global economy.

Implications for Management

The behavior of managers may be an important factor in what ultimately happens within the union movement. In many industries the fates of unions and management are closely intertwined and positive outcomes depend on both finding innovative responses to the changing environment. Clearly, there are some things that managers can do that will help their unions change. It is an old truism that management gets the kind of union it deserves. If management decides it wants a high-involvement relationship, we believe they can do a great deal to make this happen, although it may be a slow process, particu-

larly in situations where there is no immediate threat to survival. Neither management nor unions can afford to wait until survival is at stake to make the changes necessary to revitalize their industries. The steel industry is one unfortunate example.

In our experience, reorientation toward cooperation with the union is no easier for managers than for union officials. Management is used to seeing the union and the collective contract as a constraint, with all the negatives implied by that word. Although the contract may constrain, it is also a given around which it is possible to plan and manage. Furthermore, the contract is limited in scope, leaving a whole host of areas in the category of "management's prerogatives." The notion of voluntarily conferring with the union about an expanded set of issues appears nonsensical within the traditional management mind-set. However, it is a good way to start a change process that is intended to create a more cooperative union-management relationship. The mind-set change is most easily made by managements whose backs are to the wall. More enlightened top managers are anticipating the need to have a fundamentally changed relationship with the union and, thus, have the flexibility to adjust to changing business conditions.

Perhaps the most basic step management can take is to provide the union and its leadership with a secure position as the legitimate, permanent representative of the bargaining unit. A union is unlikely to cooperate with a management working toward its destruction. This means abandoning efforts to decertify the union and may mean recognizing the union in new facilities, as GM has done with Saturn and a number of other plants. It may also mean taking many first and even second steps toward starting a cooperative relationship. Unions are political organizations and, as such, they may not respond to overtures in the way managers expect or like when it comes to cooperation and involvement. For example, the time may not be right because of an upcoming election, or it may take many different types of offers for the unions to believe the efforts are genuine. It is imperative that top management personally become more aware of the political realities of the union, and not rely exclusively on a small group of labor relations specialists. Cooperation in developing innovative approaches to solving business problems is possible only if union leaders feel secure in their ability to manage the internal union politics of an inevitably divisive strategy. To do this, management must be trusted not to deliver "surprises" that will undermine the trust of the workforce. Union officials can help management avoid these land mines.

Conclusion

In our opinion, the window of opportunity is now open. Throughout the country, managements are beginning serious efforts to alter their management style and introduce new participative systems, structures, and practices. New technologies are being introduced that require more highly skilled, responsible workforces. If these changes are developed and put into place without the involvement of unions, it may be nearly impossible for unions to find a role. Unless their leaders endorse and take an active participative role, unions are headed for continuing decline. If this occurs, the new management that will arise will lack workforce representation; employees will have only spotty input into the organizational changes that will determine the form and vigor of American business. In our opinion, this is not a desirable set of events. There is a need for unions to assure the permanency of participation and represent the workforce in major organizational decisions. They are uniquely capable of performing these functions. Thus, it is important that unions revitalize themselves. There is an important role for the union to play in participatively managed organizations and in contributing to the emerging innovative organizational practices.

Endnotes

1. See R. B. Freeman and J. L. Medoff's *What Do Unions Do?* New York: Basic Books, 1984.

2. *The Changing Situation of Workers and Their Unions,* AFL-CIO Committee on Evolution of Work, 1985. For more, see *New Management,* 1986, *3*(3).

3. More in-depth discussion of these changes can be found in E. E. Lawler's *High Involvement Management,* San Francisco: Jossey-Bass, 1986; J. O'Toole's *Vanguard Management,* New York: Doubleday, 1985; and R. E. Walton's "From Control to Commitment in the Workplace," *Harvard Business Review,* 1985, *63*(2), 76–84.

4. The format of these plants is fully described in E. E. Lawler's "The New Plant Revolution," *Organizational Dynamics,* 1978, *6*(3), 2–12.

5. For insight into a cautious interpretation of new management and its impact on unions, see J. Barbash's "Thinking Ahead: Do We Really Want Labor on the Ropes?" *Harvard Business Review,* July-August 1985, 10–20.

6. More about innovative approaches to pay can be found in E. E. Lawler's *Pay and Organization Development,* Reading, MA: Addison-Wesley, 1981.

7. For an in-depth case analysis that demonstrates the difficulties of maintaining a consistent philosophy, see D. Perkins, R. Nieva, and E. E. Lawler's *Managing Creation: The Challenge of Building a New Organization,* New York: Wiley, 1983.

8. Studies that demonstrate this impact on grievances include J. Simmons and W. Mares, *Working Together,* New York: Knopf, 1983; S. E. Seashore, "Quality of Working Life Perspective," in A. Van de Ven and W. F. Joyce (Eds.), *Perspectives on Organization Design and Behavior,* New York: Wiley-Interscience, 1981; E. E. Lawler and G. E. Ledford, "Productivity and the Quality of Work Life," *National Productivity Review,* 1982, *1,* 23–26; and E. E. Lawler and L. Ozley, "Winning Union-Management Cooperation on Quality of Work Life Projects," *Management Review,* 1979, *68*(3), 1924.

9. For the views of some key union leaders and government officials on employee involvement, see the Winter 1986 issue of *New Management.*

Advice to a New Manager in a Unionized or Double-Breasted Company

Thomas F. Reed

Working as a supervisor or manager in a unionized or double-breasted company[1] presents many exciting opportunities to a new college graduate. You are assigned duties to be carried out, timetables to meet, and employees to supervise. Perhaps you are even responsible for a budget. Working in a unionized organization presents additional challenges that should not be underestimated. In fact, unassuming new managers in a unionized environment may find themselves operating in a mine field, with traps and pitfalls all around them. The purpose of this article is to alert the new or aspiring manager to some of these dangers.

This article is divided into two parts. First, some general information about unions is presented. This section summarizes some recent findings by labor economists and industrial relations researchers that highlight both the positive and the negative effects of unions on workers, firms, and society. The second part of the article offers specific advice about managing workers in a unionized organization. This advice falls into three categories: (1) learning the turf; (2) managerial prerogatives; and (3) managing your relationships with union members, representatives, and officials.

The Pros and Cons of Unions

Unless your parents are committed union members or you had a college professor who taught the positive aspects of unions in a labor history or industrial relations course, your view of unions may well be negative. When the media in the United States present a story on unions, they usually tend to focus on nega-

tive issues such as alleged corruption or labor-management conflict. Rarely are the positive actions or effects of unions highlighted. The purpose of this section is to review some of the recent research on the impact of unions to provide you with a more balanced view of the positive and negative effects of unions.

Research by Freeman and Medoff (1984) suggests that it is useful to look at the two faces of unions: the monopoly face, which is concerned with the economic power of unions in labor markets, and the collective voice/ institutional response face, which is associated with union representation of workers in a collective bargaining relationship with management. We shall focus on the effects of unions on three important dimensions: (1) economic efficiency; (2) income distribution; and (3) social aspects.[2] Table 1 presents some arguments and evidence about the effects of unions on these three dimensions.

Economic Efficiency

Much of what you have learned about unions probably emphasizes the monopoly face of unions. This view holds that unions act as monopolies in the labor market and cause harm to workers, firms, and society. In terms of economic efficiency, unions are alleged to harm economic efficiency by disturbing the optimal ratio of capital to labor. Microeconomic theory[3] shows that the optimal ratio of capital to labor in a firm is achieved when the marginal product of labor (MP_L) divided by the price of labor (P_L) equals the marginal

Table 1
The Two Faces of Trade Unionism

	Union Effects on Economic Efficiency	Union Effects on Distribution of Income	Social Nature of Union Organization
Monopoly Face	Unions raise wages above competitive levels, leading to too little labor relative to capital in unionized firms. Union work rules decrease productivity.	Unions increase income inequality by raising the wages of highly skilled workers. Unions create horizontal inequities by creating differentials among comparable workers.	Unions discriminate in rationing positions. Unions (individually or collectively) fight for their own interests in the political arena. Union monopoly power breeds corrupt and nonde-mocratic elements.
Collective Voice/Institutional Response Face	Unions have some positive effects on productivity—reducing quit rates, inducing management to alter methods of production and adopt more efficient policies, and improving morale and cooperation among workers. Unions collect information about the preferences of workers, leading the firm all to choose a better mix of employee compensation and a better set of personnel policies.	Unions' standard-rate policies reduce inequality among organized workers in a given company or a given industry. Union rules limit the scope for arbitrary actions in the promotion, layoff, and recall of individuals. Unionism fundamentally alters the distribution of power between marginal (generally junior) and more permanent (generally senior) employees, causing union firms to select different compensation packages and personnel practices from those of nonunion firms.	Unions are political institutions that represent the will of their members. Unions represent the political interests of lower-income and disadvantaged persons.

Source: Table from page 13: "Two Faces of Trade Unionism" from *What Do Unions Do?* by Richard B. Freeman and James L. Medoff. Copyright © 1984 by Basic Books, Inc. Reprinted by permission of BasicBooks, a division of Harper-Collins Publishers, Inc.

product of capital (MP_K) divided by the price of capital (P_K):

$$MP_L/P_L = MP_K/P_K$$

In other words, the optimal ratio of labor to capital is achieved when the last dollar spent on labor yields the same output as the last dollar spent on capital. By raising the price of labor above competitive market levels, holding all else constant, unions cause the equilibrium condition presented in the equation to change: P_L increases, so the value MP_L/P_L declines. To restore equilibrium, the firm must employ more capital and less labor. Therefore, by raising wages above competitive levels, unions lead firms to employ fewer workers and more capital than is optimal; this leads to economic inefficiency (Kleiner, McLean, and Dreher, 1988).

Critics of unions also charge that unions create economic inefficiency through work rules and featherbedding.[4] These rules, which define how much and what type of work may be done by various groups of workers, lead to reduced productivity. Strikes also reduce overall economic efficiency by reducing the gross national product, the sum value of goods and services produced by the economy.

Other industrial relations researchers and labor economists argue that unions may have positive effects on economic efficiency; these views are summarized under "Collective Voice/Institutional Response Face" in Table 1. We know from many empirical studies that unionized workers are less likely to quit their jobs,[5] and lower quit rates in a firm lead to lower recruiting, selecting, and training costs. Unionized workers tend to have longer tenure in the organization and consequently accrue job experience. This experience should make the workers more productive than less experienced workers. Finally, the longer tenure with the firm provides greater incentives for both firms and workers to make human capital investments that lead to greater productivity.

Unions can increase productivity in a variety of other ways. Since unions reduce firm profitability, managers have the incentive to find ways to make their operations more productive and efficient in an attempt to raise profits. Unions can help firms to be more efficient by providing managers information about workers' desires for compensation plans (i.e., the mix of wages to benefits, and the types of benefits desired) and personnel policies. The use of seniority to determine promotions and opportunities for lateral transfers within the firm can reduce rivalry and competition among workers and may lead more senior workers to help train younger workers without fear of being replaced by the younger workers.

Distribution of Income

Advocates of the monopoly face of unions allege that unions increase income equality. They do so in a number of ways. As we have seen from the preceding discussion, raising the wages of unionized workers in an industry leads the firm to employ fewer workers and more capital. What happens to workers who would have been employed in the industry but are now replaced by capital? These workers shift to other industries or occupations, causing the supply of workers in those labor markets to increase and wages to decline. Therefore, the argument goes, high union wages in one industry or occupation cause lower wages in other, nonunionized industries or occupations. This leads to increased wage inequality among workers.

A second type of wage inequality is introduced when one considers that unions tend to organize workers who are already highly skilled. These highly skilled workers receive better wages than low-skilled workers to begin with, and the effects of the collective bargaining agreement are to increase the disparity in total compensation between these two classes of workers.

Finally, critics charge that unions create further inequality by establishing wage differentials among workers who perform the same jobs in the same industries. Microeconomic theory suggests that workers' wages should be set equal to the marginal product of labor. Therefore, if workers are equally productive, they should earn the same wage (if all else is held constant). If we observe that unionized workers earn more than nonunionized workers *and that they are equally productive,* then wage inequality is introduced.

The collective voice/institutional response face proponents argue that unions help to reduce income inequality in several ways. By attempting to establish standard compensation levels, unions reduce inequality among organized workers both within firms and across the industry. Within a firm, unions also attempt to limit managerial discretion in the awarding of pay increases, so unionized workers in the same job tend to receive the same pay increases, thus reducing inequality. Finally, by organizing workers with lower skills and by securing collective bargaining agreements that provide substantial compensation increases, unions have helped to alleviate some of the wage inequality in the national economy.

Social Aspects

The monopoly face advocates argue that unions are corrupt institutions that use violence or threats of violence to extort from firms greater compensation for unionized workers and kickbacks for union leaders. They argue that unions are undemocratic, meaning that power is held by a small group of insiders. Finally, this view holds that, in the political arena, unions pursue public policies that benefit their own narrow interests at the expense of nonunionized workers and the community at large.

Advocates of the collective voice/institutional response face of unions argue that, by and large, unions are democratic organizations that pursue their members' interests in a pluralistic political system. These advocates also point out that unions have actively supported many legislative proposals—such as the Public Accommodation Act of 1964, the Voting Rights Act of 1965, and antipoverty programs—that would provide little if any direct benefit to the majority of their members.

Freeman and Medoff's (1984) studies on the effects of unions on economic efficiency, income distribution, and social factors present some challenging results for those who think that unions are predominantly a negative force in society. Although space limitations prevent a complete discussion of their results, a few can be highlighted. First, unions do have a substantial wage impact, but the effect is greater for younger and less educated workers than for older and better educated workers. They estimate the social costs of this monopoly wage impact to be a modest 3/10 of 1% of the gross national product.

Second, unions affect the compensation packages of workers and tend to increase the proportion of compensation taken in the form of fringe benefits. Much of these fringe benefits are in the form of deferred benefits such as pension plans and various forms of insurance.

Third, Freeman and Medoff's research suggests that unions reduce wage inequality: "The inequality-reducing effects of unionism outweigh the inequality-increasing effects, so that on balance unions are a force for equality in the distribution of wages among individual workers" (1984, p. 20).

Fourth, unions provide workers with procedural justice and opportunities to voice grievances and suggestions with little fear of reprisal. This, in turn, helps to reduce turnover and may lead to productivity improvements.

Fifth, considerable evidence suggests that unionized firms are more productive than nonunionized firms. Although unionized firms are less profitable than nonunionized firms, this greater productivity may explain why unionized firms can pay the union wage premium and still successfully compete with other firms.

Sixth, unions are not as successful in the political arena as their critics allege, and aside from a few unions that have well-deserved reputations for corruption and undemocratic practices, most unions are highly democratic, particularly at the level of local unions.

The preceding discussion of the effects of unions on workers, firms, and society raises several important issues to consider when evaluating the role of unions in our society. However, this discussion ignores the extremely conservative role that unions play in our society as preservers of the status quo. It was no accident that the National Labor Relations Act (NLRA, also called the Wagner Act) was passed in the depths of the Great Depression. There was much unrest in the nation among workers, and "radical" labor unions and political parties were finding receptive audiences for their socialist and anarchistic programs.

In the midst of the collapse of the capitalist economy and growing dissent among workers, the NLRA was passed by the Congress, signed by President Franklin D. Roosevelt, and subsequently deemed constitutional by the United States Supreme Court. The stated primary purpose of the NLRA is to promote full and free commerce, *not* to grant workers the right to join together in unions and collectively bargain over wages, hours, and conditions of employment. Collective bargaining was viewed as the *means* to achieve the desired end: a rehabilitated capitalist economy.

Although many managers, government officials, and workers decry conflict, the astute student of labor-management relations will recognize that industrial conflict is endemic in a capitalist economy (and, as we have seen from labor unrest in countries like Poland, industrial conflict is probably endemic in socialist economies as well). Conflict between workers and owners (and owners' representatives and managers) is a natural outcome of the separation of ownership of capital from those wage earners who use the capital to produce goods and services. (In fact, recent experiments with employee ownership of firms have revealed that labor-management conflicts occur even when the workers themselves own the company!) The interests of workers and owners/managers are not identical, and disagreements occur. What collective bargaining does is not to eliminate conflict but to channel the conflict into *socially acceptable* expressions of conflict and avenues of resolving the conflicts. In other words, the institutions of unionism and collective bargaining do not create industrial conflict; conflict will exist with or without unions. The institutions of unionism and collective bargaining help to manage conflict and to channel the conflict into socially acceptable behaviors such as grievances, contract negotiations, and even strikes. Through collective bargaining, limits are put on the type of conflicts that are played out in the workplace and the tactics that may be used by both labor and management to resolve the conflicts. Gone are the days of the Old West, when labor conflicts were resolved at the end of a gun barrel. Although strikes are disruptive to the economy, to firms, and to workers, society has recognized through its laws that labor problems naturally occur in society, and the goal of labor law should be to reduce and manage conflict through the establishment of laws and societal norms. Therefore, managers with a sense of history will recognize the importance of unions and the institution of collective bargaining as a conservative force in our society.

Advice to the New Manager

This section offers advice to the new or aspiring manager in a unionized or double-breasted organization. The advice is intended to suggest the types of issues to which you should be sensitive when you manage in a unionized environment. Three categories of advice are offered: learning the turf; managerial prerogatives; and managing relationships with union members, representatives, and officials.

Learning the Turf

Learn labor laws. It is imperative that you have a clear understanding of labor law if you are to successfully manage in a unionized environment. For most, that means learning the provisions of the National Labor Relations Act. The NLRA covers most private-sector firms with substantial interstate commerce. Those who manage in the public sector need to become familiar with the particular state's labor law. If you work in the transportation industry for an airline or rail company, you need to become familiar with the Railway Labor Act.

It is important for the new or aspiring manager to know the appropriate labor law, because the law specifies the boundaries of legal employer, employee, and union behavior and the rights and responsibilities of both parties. For example, a new manager without the requisite knowledge of appropriate managerial behavior during a union organizing campaign may inadvertently commit unfair labor practices during the campaign. A helpful book for those interested in learning more about the NLRA is Gould's (1982) labor law primer.

Learn the contract. The collective bargaining contract that covers the workers in your company is the written law governing labor-management relations in your specific organization. The contract identifies which workers are covered under the agreement, specifies wage levels, fringe benefits, and the seniority system, and in all likelihood establishes a grievance system to redress problems and complaints at the workplace.

You can be assured that the union shop stewards and activists, not to mention the typical rank-and-file member, will know the contract inside and out. It is in your own best interest, as well as the organization's, for you to know the contract as well as the union representatives and workers do. This reduces the chances of your making avoidable mistakes concerning things like work assignments and selection of workers for overtime. If you have questions about the contract or its interpretation, you should consult your superior or the personnel/labor relations office in your organization.

Learn the common law. Not all of the law governing labor-management relations can be found in relevant statutes or the collective bargaining agreement. You need to learn the common law in your organization. The common law in your company is comprised of practices concerning union-management relations, work rules, or other topics that are widely accepted in your organization by both union and management but cannot be found written in any document.

An example may clarify the point. Suppose it has been common practice in your organization for unionized workers to skip their morning coffee break on payday so that they can add an extra 15 minutes to their lunch break. The workers use the longer lunch break to cash their checks at a local bank. This arrangement is informal: The collective bargaining agreement says nothing about this arrangement, and labor law certainly does not address the point. The arrangement has become common law, however, by virtue of its having been practiced for a number of years without being contested by management.

Let's assume that a new manager is not told about this arrangement. On the first payday after she is hired as a manager in the organization, she gives worker warnings to several workers who are 15 minutes late returning to work after lunch. The workers protest that this arrangement has been in effect for years, and they have every right to return from lunch 15 minutes later than usual because they worked through their coffee break. Since the new manager and the workers are unable to resolve the dispute, the workers file a grievance against her actions and the arbitrator rules in their favor: A common law was established that permitted workers to forsake their coffee break on paydays so they would have time to cash their paychecks.

This situation could have been avoided if the new manager had learned the common law at the company. Learning the common law can be difficult, however, since by definition it is not written down. The best advice that can be offered to a new manager is to check with more experienced colleagues as questions arise. Also discuss the situation with the workers and the shop steward; you need not pretend that you know everything.

Learn about your firm's union-management relations. The new manager should learn about the history of labor-management relations in the organization. Perhaps the union is new to your company and the union was able to secure a contract only after a long and bitterly fought representation campaign. On the other hand, perhaps the union has represented workers in your organization for decades, and a mature bargaining relationship has been developed over time. The new manager must learn about these things to better understand current dynamics between union leaders and company officials.

The new manager should also try to assess what the recent history has been with respect to collective bargaining at the particular work site. Did the last round of negotiations include a bitter strike, or were the negotiations relatively trouble free? A knowledge of history may help the new manager understand seemingly inexplicable behavior by both union and management officials. Remember the adage that those who do not know history are destined to repeat it.

Read the union newspaper and newsletter. The union newspaper and newsletter are excellent sources of information about the union's goals and concerns. While the union's paper (national or international) focuses on issues of concern to the majority of members throughout the nation, the local union's newsletter or other publication highlights issues of concern to workers in your organization. The new manager—and more senior managers—can learn a lot about what is on members' minds. Perhaps workers are concerned about the upcoming contract negotiations, the backlog of grievances, or health and safety problems in your organization. Issues raised in the union's periodicals may be raised in workers' discussions with you, and the well-prepared manager is aware of these concerns and has a well-thought-out response to offer the workers.

Managerial Prerogatives

Learn the difference between managerial power, authority, and influence. The new manager needs to clearly understand the differences between power, authority, and influence. *Power* involves the ability to achieve or effect some outcome through the imposition of will accompanied by the threat of a negative sanction. *Authority* involves the ability to achieve or effect some outcome by virtue of the legitimacy attached to one's organizational position. *Influence* is the ability to achieve or effect some outcome by virtue of the deference that others pay you because of your personality, experience, or knowledge.

It is important for the new manager to understand that managerial power is constrained by the contract, but that influence and authority are not necessarily constrained. One major purpose of the collective bargaining agreement is to reduce managerial discretion with respect to treatment of workers, the distribution of rewards, and the levying of penalties. The contract grants certain property rights to unionized workers and constrains the types of behaviors managers may engage in when problems arise in the organization. Without a union contract, the employment relationship is dictated by the legal concept of employment at will. The two parties—worker and manager—freely enter into an employment relationship that may be severed at any time by one or the other party for almost any reason (except those specifically excluded by law, such as race, age, or sex discrimination). Under the union contract, however, manager-

ial discretion is reduced and procedural justice is formalized in the organization through the grievance system. While reduced discretion is often lamented by managers, procedural justice is highly valued by workers.

Authority comes from your position in the organization, not from your personality. By virtue of your position as a manager at a particular level and position in the organizational hierarchy, you have the ability to expect and indeed demand certain outcomes from people in your charge. It is important to remember, however, that workers do not like to be ordered to perform. Your expectation of performance by the individuals under your supervision is rooted in your position in the organization. New managers must be careful not to overstep their authority by assuming that their authority emanates from themselves as individuals.

Finally, your influence comes from your personality, experience, or knowledge, not from your position in the organization. Effective managers are those who can combine their organization-derived authority with an influential personality that motivates workers to perform.

Use the grievance system with extreme care. The new manager must learn to use the grievance system carefully. Grievances are time-consuming and very expensive for the organization: There are direct costs such as lawyer fees, and indirect costs associated with lost productivity for the manager or supervisor and the worker involved in the grievance. Although grievances are inevitable because of differences of opinion and interests among workers and managers, the astute manager attempts to resolve petty differences well before they reach the top level of the grievance system and leaves the grievance system for the resolution of disputes of great importance to the organization, worker, or union.

Managing Relationships with Union Members, Representatives, and Officials

Don't disparage the union or its leaders. This is simply common-sense advice. But, amazingly, managers quite often make disparaging remarks about unions and union officials in the presence of workers. Whether a particular worker likes or dislikes the incumbent union leadership, the manager achieves nothing but ill will by criticizing union leaders and officials in the presence of the rank-and-file worker. Because good labor-management relations are built not only on economic power but also on trust, a respectful attitude toward the union and its officials pays off in the long run.

Use union representatives to solve problems. The intelligent manager knows how to use shop stewards and other union representatives to help solve problems at the workplace. This intelligent use includes soliciting the involvement of a responsible and reasonable shop steward when certain problems arise. An example from my own experience may help to illustrate this point.

On a couple of occasions, when I was a manager in a private hospital, a nonprofessional staff member appeared at work under the influence. The supervisor called me in to help deal with this problem. On both occasions, the shop stewards were responsible, reasonable individuals with whom I had developed good rapport. In each case, I notified them of the problem and asked them to meet me at the affected worker's location. I spoke to the worker and explained that I wanted him to take a test in the hospital's emergency room because his supervisor and I were concerned that he would be unable to perform his job because we suspected he might be under the influence of some substance. The shop steward stayed with the worker, spoke with him, represented his interests, and helped to remove the worker from the job site while protecting his rights. By including the shop stewards in the process, there was a greater assurance that the worker's rights would be protected and that the union could not later allege that the worker had been treated unfairly. The presence of the shop steward—an advocate for the worker—also helped to defuse any potential problems that may have arisen.

Conclusion

The purpose of this article is twofold: to present a balanced view of the pros and cons of unions in modern organizations; and second, to offer some specific points of advice for the new or aspiring manager. Most of the advice is based on common sense, but failure to abide by it may prove costly to you and your organization. Managing in a unionized environment can be frustrating at times for managers, but also exciting when contract negotiations are in process or when new forms of labor-management cooperation are being experimented with in the organization.

References

Freeman, R. B., and Medoff, J. L. (1984). *What do unions do?* New York: Basic Books.

Gould, W. B. (1982). *A primer on American labor law.* Cambridge, MA: MIT Press.

Kleiner, M. M., McLean, R. A., and Dreher, G. F. (1988). *Labor markets and human resource management.* Glenview, IL: Scott, Foresman.

Endnotes

1. A double-breasted company is one that operates production processes in both unionized and union-free modes.

2. Much of this discussion is based upon what is arguably the most important book on unions written in the last decade, *What do unions do?* by Richard Freeman and James Medoff. You are encouraged to read this book to gain a better understanding of the effects of unions on workers, firms, and society.

3. See Kleiner, McLean, and Dreher's *Labor markets and human resource management* for a full exposition of this point.

4. This charge ignores two facts—first, that work rules are a negotiated outcome of the collective bargaining agreement, so both labor and management bear responsibility for them; and second, that work rules which reduce employee effort may be viewed as a component of the employee's total compensation package. The restrictive work rules are a form of compensation, just as higher wage increase or additional fringe benefits are components of the compensation package.

5. Reasons for this include the higher-than-average compensation that unionized workers make, their job security, pension plans, and the representation given to workers in disputes with management (i.e., the "voice" dimension of unions).

CHAPTER 11

Employee Participation and Empowerment

Allowing employees to participate in organizational decision making has a number of positive ancilliary benefits. Participation can help subordinates understand the circumstances surrounding and required by a decision. This is normal adult behavior that satisfies individual needs for autonomy and achievement. Cooperative social and work interactions, a goal of human resources programs, are facilitated when participation is allowed. In fact, many behavioral scientists believe that participation will result in better decisions to the extent that the talents and skills of the entire group are tapped. This belief has been operationalized as a move toward "empowering" people in organizations—sharing power with organization members.

Is empowerment an effective strategy? Is it right for all organizations? From a human resources perspective, the correct answer is that it all depends upon a number of related issues. The articles in this chapter are aimed at elucidating the important issues surrounding the question of whether empowerment is right for a particular organization.

The first two articles in this chapter deal with employee involvement. First, Coye and Belohlav examine the degree to which participation occurs in U.S. organizations. They discuss key issues in employee involvement programs and the benefits associated with those programs. In the following article Lawler focuses on guidelines for selecting an employee involvement program and issues that need to be addressed before an organization moves in the direction of systematic employee involvement.

In the final article Dobbs describes the empowerment environment, providing insight into factors that need to be present if empowerment is to facilitate the attainment of organizational objectives. Not surprisingly, the personality characteristics of the leader are closely related to the success or failure of empowerment. This article is an excellent starting point for the development of a program to empower individuals and tap their resourcefulness.

Suggestions for Further Reading

Bernstein, A. (1992, July). Why empowerment programs often fail. *Executive Excellence,* p. 5.

Covey, S. (1993). Transforming a swamp. *Training & Development, 47,* 42–46.

DeLong, T., & DeLong, C. (1992). Managers as fathers: Hope on the homefront. *Human Resource Management, 31,* 171–181.

Dubnicki, C., & Williams, J. (1992). The people side of TQM. *Healthcare Forum, 35,* 54–61.

Galagan, P. (1992). The truth about empowerment, according to D. Quinn Mills. *Training & Development, 46,* 31–32.

Leifeld, N. (1992). Inside the Baldrige Award guidelines—Category 4: Human resource development and management. *Quality Progress, 25,* 51–55.

Ripley, R., & Ripley, M. (1993). Empowerment: What to do with troubling employees? *Journal of Managerial Psychology, 8,* 3–9.

Whittle, D. (1992, July). Conferencing communications. *Executive Excellence,* p. 7.

Wickens, P. (1993). Steering the middle road to car production. *Personnel Management, 25,* 34–38.

Wynne, J. (1993). Power relationships and empowerment in hotels. *Employee Relations, 15,* 42–50.

Employee Involvement
in American Corporations

Ray Coye and James Belohlav

Introduction

The escalating competitive gap among American companies and their international counterparts has been commented upon by many people from casual observers to the leaders of corporate America. The magnitude of the competitive gap is becoming increasingly difficult to dismiss as the yardstick of performance, based upon the achievements of global competition, and is being used to measure the success of American firms. The failure of many American companies to meet the strategic challenge has led to second guessing, thoughtful analyses, and in a few instances even some serious soul-searching.

Why is this competitive gap occurring? Are the strategies that American companies pursue ill-conceived and poorly thought out? Invariably, discussions about the lack of competitiveness consider the impact of poor worker performance on overall productivity. Some basic insight into the issue of competitiveness is provided by the Public Agenda Foundation in the study *Putting the Work Ethic to Work* (Yankelovich & Immerwahr, 1983). It is pointed out that there is a growing disparity between the performance of which American workers are capable and the performance they are delivering. For example,

- Nearly one-half of the work force (44%) say they do not put a great deal of effort into their jobs over and above what is required.
- Fewer than one out of four [workers] (23%) say that they are performing up to their full capacity and are being as effective as they

are capable of being. The majority say they could increase their effectiveness significantly.

However, equally revealing were statements from the same individuals that

- Management doesn't know how to motivate the workers (75% agree).
- All workers get the same raise regardless of how hard they work (73% agree).
- Today, people want more of a challenge on the job (67% agree).
- People don't see the end result of their work (68% agree).

These and other findings lead the authors Daniel Yankelovich and John Immerwahr to conclude, contrary to some prevailing opinions, that there is no lack of work ethic in America. The human dimension of declining productivity is not a structural problem and, in fact, need not exist.

The blame for the lagging growth of productivity should not rest solely with management techniques either. A recent study (Belohlav, in press, p. 19) recognizes that American firms continue to utilize new and evolving managerial techniques. However, in comparing the operations of American and Japanese manufacturing companies the study also points out that "Americans understand JIT (just in time inventory method) as techniques, 'things to adapt and adopt.' Japanese understand JIT as techniques, but integrated as a way to strengthen people." It appears that the firms from both countries understand the

Reprinted with permission of Plenum Publishing Corporation, Ray Coye and James Belohlav from *Employee Responsibilities and Rights Journal, 4:3* (1991): 231–241.

content of the techniques, but it is the actual application that differentiates the two approaches. Hall and Nakane (1988) remark that the success of the Japanese seems to occur because they "see JIT as a neverending *reform and improvement of themselves.* Improvement is first of the people then *through* the people" (p. 21).

From the preceding discussion, what seems to be the strategic issue of concern for American companies is how people are involved in the operations of the organization. As Ron Brooks, manager at Digital Electronics Corp., characterizes it, "The employee involvement process is the glue that holds all of the techniques together" (4, p. 108). The competitive gap referred to in the initial discussion may in fact arise from this deficiency—the organization-individual disparity present within many American companies. Poor strategies may be, in reality, only poorly executed strategies.

Indeed, one might even conclude that such varied problems as the lack of innovation, inferior quality, the generally slow growth of productivity, and inadequate concern for the customer all really stem from a perspective that places people apart from the organization and its processes. Steve Palm, division manager for Midland Brake, Inc., remarks, "The real reason American industry is losing its preeminence is the lack of total human involvement and participation." What are the attendant consequences of this lack of involvement? He goes on to further comment, "We no longer know how to work as a unified team. We have become different teams, working on different problems, indifferent towards one another" ("Making Manufacturing Human," 1988, p. 1).

The preceding discussion of employee involvement comes from research as well as anecdotal evidence. But what is employee involvement? Some individuals see it as relatively simple activities influencing limited areas of an organization. Other people see it as a grand philosophy influencing virtually every aspect of organizational life. A recent article by Edward Lawler (1988) provides a framework to help in conceptualizing employee involvement. According to Lawler, employee involvement relates to the degree to which four key elements are moved down to the lowest level in the organization. These features are "(1) information about the performance of the organization, (2) rewards that are based on the performance of the organization, (3) knowledge that enables employees to understand and contribute to organizational performance, and (4) power to make decisions that influence organizational direction and performance" (p. 197).

Involvement strategies differ in the extent to which these elements are moved downward in the organizational hierarchy. Lawler uses the terms "suggestion involvement," "job involvement," and "high involvement" to describe three levels of progressively increasing downward movement of power, knowledge, information, and rewards. Commonly recognized activities which fit these categories include the following:

1. Suggestion involvement: written suggestion programs, quality circles;
2. Job involvement: job enrichment, work teams, gainsharing;
3. High involvement: employee participation in organizationwide decision making.

As efforts are made to move these elements downward in the hierarchy, certain issues become keys to success. Appropriate training, equality of treatment, and trust are a few of the factors that can be vital to effective employee involvement.

Information recently gathered in a federal study provides some insights into the nature and extent of employee involvement efforts in American companies. The purpose of this article is to investigate the following questions: (1) What are the existing practices with respect to employee involvement within the current corporate operating environments? (2) What has been the impetus for undertaking employee involvement programs? (3) What have been the most significant barriers encountered in implementing employee involvement programs? and (4) What have been the consequences of the employee involvement approaches on the operations of the organization?

Characteristics of Responding Organizations

A survey of private sector organization employee involvement efforts was undertaken by the U.S. General Accounting Office (1988) and reported to the U.S. Senate Subcommittee on Governmental Affairs. The purpose of the survey was to obtain information on the factors used in the design, implementation, and operation of employee involvement systems within major American corporations. For the purpose of the survey, employee involvement was defined as the "process that provides employees with the opportunity to make decisions affecting their work and work environment."

The survey questionnaire was mailed to the top management of the 500 largest manufacturing and 500 largest service companies as defined by *Fortune* magazine. A total of 476 corporations responded, with the responding individual being identified as the chief executive officer in 4.2% of the cases, as a vice president in 50% of the cases, and all other titles combined (corporate manager of operations, director of employee involvement, etc.) in 45.8% of the cases. The median number of full-time American employees within the responding companies is 9,000 people, who are divided occupationally into four categories: hourly/clerical 59%, technical/professional 20%, supervisors/managers 14%, and all others 9%.

Survey Results

This study views corporate responses on existing business practices, employee involvement activities, the rationale for implementing employee involvement, perceived barriers to implementing employee involvement programs, and the perceived results of the programs. The preliminary results of the survey provides informative and revealing results.

General Business Practices

Before the actual employee involvement activities are viewed, it would be useful to examine the general characteristics of the operating environment. The major elements included in this section are: specific personnel practices, the extent of information sharing with employees, and the types of training provided. In general, it seems reasonable to infer that the existing practices present in the operating environment provide an indication of the predisposition of companies toward employee involvement.

First, several personnel practices were investigated relating to the quality of the employer-employee relationship. Of the personnel practices queried, career counseling appears to be the most broadly applied among the responding companies. Employment security, which was defined as company policies designed to prevent layoffs, varied widely among the responding companies. Although the data seem to show that most of the responding firms cover relatively few employees with employee security, it should also be noted that a significant minority of firms (about one-third) covered a large portion of their employees. The final personnel practice viewed, multiple career tracks, tended to show a limited range of coverage within the responding companies. Overall, it can probably be said that the preceding personnel practices tend to relate to the degree of value placed upon individuals as organizational members.

Traditional practices appear to prevail in the dissemination of information to employees. For example, few employees are told what fellow workers are paid, while most have knowledge of overall company performance. In general, the majority of the companies seem to provide a large segment of their employees with internally based types of information (overall and unit operating results, and business plans and goals); however, it appears that far fewer individuals receive information as it develops a more external focus. In general, the degree of information sharing relates to the degree of mutuality between the organization and its members.

Finally, the primary types of training examined within the survey involved skills related to the understanding of the operation of the overall business and the management of people and groups in the company. Training in its broadest sense implies a sharing of power. While the single training activity provided to the greatest number of people is cross training, it can quite accurately be stated that few organizations provide training for large numbers of employees regardless of the type of training involved (Table I). One-third to one-half of the companies provide training to, at most, only one of five employees.

From the preceding data, it appears that the potential for employee input into organizational decision making and practices is quite confined. In terms of general business practices, most of the responding companies can be characterized as providing only limited opportunities for training, insulating their employees from external information that has di-

rect bearing on their well-being, and in general do not promote a widespread sense of value among individuals. Thus, it becomes evident that many companies are not creating environments conducive to active employee involvement.

Organizational Employee Involvement Activities

Corporations were asked to provide details about specific employee involvement activities—that is, which types of programs were being undertaken and the extent of application of each program within the organization. In general, it appears that very few of the responding organizations are utilizing employee involvement programs that encourage input from large numbers of their employees (see Table II). Furthermore, approximately 12% of the responding companies failed to utilize any employee involvement programs at all.

Although suggestion systems seem to be the most popular of the employee involvement mechanisms, less than half of the responding companies use it on a scale that encompasses a

Table I.
Business Practices

Practice	Number of employees covered		
	Less than 20%	20% to 60%	More than 60%
Personnel			
Career counseling	40%	26%	34%
Employment security	61%	9%	30%
Multiple career tracks	55%	27%	17%
Information sharing			
Company's overall operating results	7%	15%	78%
Unit's operating results	9%	33%	59%
Business plans and goals	12%	43%	45%
Advance information on new technology	18%	54%	28%
Competitor's relative performance	33%	50%	17%
Training			
Cross training	35%	51%	14%
Team building	48%	47%	5%
Group decision-making/problem-solving skills	43%	52%	5%
Understanding the business (finance, accounting, etc.)	50%	46%	4%

Table II.

Employee Involvement Programs

Type of program	Number of employees covered		
	Less than 20%	20% to 60%	More than 60%
Suggestion system	33%	24%	42%
Survey feedback	54%	23%	23%
Employee participation groups other than quality circles	63%	30%	6%
Job enrichment	78%	18%	5%
Quality circles	71%	25%	3%
Union-management quality of work life committees	90%	9%	2%
Gainsharing	93%	5%	2%
Minienterprises	93%	5%	1%
Self-managing work teams	92%	7%	0%

significant part of the organization. The survey feedback method was a distant second overall, with less than one-quarter of the responding companies using it with substantial numbers of employees. All of the other forms of employee involvement received relatively limited usage. Even some of the more widely recognized and discussed activities such as job enrichment and quality circles were applied to less than one-quarter of the employees within that vast majority of companies employing those techniques.

Why Companies Use Employee Involvement

Those firms who have implemented employee involvement programs report a variety of reasons for doing so. The reasons for implementation (Table III) can be classified into four broad categories: output reasons, employee satisfaction reasons, operating reasons, and ethical reasons.

The reasons most frequently cited as having a large degree of influence on creating em-

Table III.

Reasons for Implementation of Employee Involvement Programs

Reason for implementation	Degree of influence in initiating employee involvement programs		
	Small	Moderate	Large
Improve quality	10%	19%	72%
Improve productivity	10%	20%	70%
Improve employee motivation	13%	28%	58%
Improve employee morale	16%	30%	54%
Reduce costs	26%	30%	44%
Adapt to future changes in the environment	32%	24%	44%
Strengthen the management of the company	33%	29%	38%
Improve employee skills	33%	34%	34%
Easier to introduce changes	41%	27%	32%
Ethical/value reasons	54%	26%	19%

ployee involvement programs are principally output related—improving productivity and quality. A smaller yet still significant group reported an employee focus—improving employee motivation and morale of people within the organization. Less than half of the respondents focused on reasons in the third cluster, which related to various operating practices—reducing costs, adapting to future changes, and so forth. The least-cited rationale for implementing employee involvement programs was for ethical or value reasons, where fewer than one of five respondents report this as a significant factor in implementation decisions.

Barriers to Employee Involvement

As we might have expected from the popular business literature, short-term performance pressures seem to provide the most significant barrier in implementing employee involvement programs (Table IV). Over two-thirds of the respondents felt that short-term pressures presented a moderate to large barrier in pursuing employee involvement programs.

While there are varying percentages of companies reporting on the balance of the barriers, practically speaking the remaining reasons have similarly perceived impacts on program initiation. Turnover of top management, an intuitively reasonable and perhaps expected barrier in light of current business conditions, was surprisingly the least-reported hindrance to employee involvement.

Results of Using Employee Involvement

What impact did these involvement programs have on the operations of the firms surveyed? Respondents were asked about the impact on various performance indicators, and the degree of change in the internal business environment. Overall, the companies with employee involvement programs seemed to indicate that they were worthwhile (Table V). For the majority of the performance indicators, primarily positive effects far outweighed "no change." Virtually none of the organizations reported any negative impacts. Only absenteeism and turnover were reported to have

Table IV.
Perceived Barriers to Implementation[a]

Barriers	Degree of influence in initiating employee involvement programs		
	Small	Moderate	Large
Short-term performance pressures	27%	26%	43%
Lack of an employee involvement "champion"	54%	15%	26%
Lack of a long-term strategy	45%	23%	25%
Lack of training	50%	23%	23%
Unclear objectives	46%	25%	21%
Lack of tangible improvements	55%	20%	20%
Lack of a feedback system	56%	20%	18%
Centralized decision making	53%	23%	17%
Culture opposed to involvement	63%	17%	15%
Worsened business conditions	67%	12%	14%
Lack of coordination	50%	28%	12%
Turnover of top management	79%	11%	6%

[a]The difference the overall percentages reported and 100% arises from the number of individuals responding that they had "no basis to judge" a particular barrier or that the barrier was "not applicable."

Table V.
Perceived Effects on Performance Indicators[a]

Performance indicators	Effect on the performance of the organization		
	Primarily negative	No change	Primarily positive
Worker satisfaction	1%	9%	78%
Quality of product/service	0%	13%	72%
Product	0%	14%	69%
Customer service	1%	14%	68%
Employee quality of work life	0%	15%	68%
Profitability	0%	25%	47%
Competitiveness	0%	28%	43%
Absenteeism	0%	44%	24%
Turnover	1%	48%	23%

[a]The difference between the overall percentages reported and 100% arises from the number of individuals responding that they had "no basis to judge" that particular performance indicator.

a greater frequency of "no change" than positive effects. Also, the reporting organizations found it more difficult to assess the impact on profitability and competitiveness, with approximately 30% reporting that they had no basis for judgment.

In terms of change to the internal business environment, there was no single change attributable to employee involvement that stands out above all of the others (Table VI). There appears to be a greater flow of information through the organization. However, there is no real consensus that layers of management have been eliminated, that decision making has moved down in the organization, or even that management-union relationships have improved. At best, it can probably be said that the companies have experienced mixed results in their operating environments because of their employee involvement programs.

Discussion

Although the arguments for employee involvement are widespread and presumably

Table VI.
Degree of Change in Internal Business Environment[a] as a Result of Employee Involvement

Domain of change	Extent of change		
	Limited	Moderate	Substantial
Increased flow of information	37%	31%	24%
Change of management style	43%	29%	20%
Increase of employee trust	40%	32%	16%
Improved technical implementation	42%	28%	14%
Skill development at lower levels	46%	31%	14%
Improved management decision making	45%	28%	14%
Improved organizational process and procedures	46%	29%	14%
Eliminate management layers	67%	12%	11%
Moved decision making to lower levels	56%	26%	11%
Moved performance-based rewards to lower levels	68%	14%	11%
Improved management-union relations	55%	11%	10%
Improved employee safety	50%	21%	10%

[a]The difference between the overall percentages reported and 100% arises from the number of individuals responding that they "don't know" about that particular internal business condition.

compelling, the actual practice of such efforts, as reported by this study, appears to be relatively limited. From the results of this study, two observations appear to stand out. First, among companies that are undertaking involvement programs, few seem to be involving large percentages of employees. Second, internal operating environments do not appear to encourage and support involvement.

For example, firms report that an incentive for undertaking involvement efforts is anticipated productivity improvements, yet few provide their employees with employment security. What should be obvious (but apparently is not) is that employees are unlikely to take seriously their role in such corporate efforts if they end up "participating" themselves out of a job.

How do we interpret the findings present in this study? The results of the survey allow for several interpretations. One interpretation might be that because this sample was limited to very large firms it does not account for a significant number of involvement efforts in smaller corporations. Given the particular demands placed on the organization when implementing such efforts, the smaller firm may be more receptive to employee participation.

A second interpretation comes from the observation of the authors that at least in some instances companies are "piloting" employee involvement initiatives in only small segments of their organization. In other instances, there is a type of covert "piloting" by lower-level managers who believe in the employee involvement concept without the blessing or possibly even the knowledge of people higher up in the organization. These personal observations are validated somewhat by the fact that some of the more tangible performance indicators had the highest percentage of "no basis to judge" responses. That is, one would expect items such as absenteeism, turnover, profitability, and competitiveness to be the easiest to assess and report, yet we observe just the opposite of what we might expect in terms of response.

There is one last interpretation of these results. From the study cited at the beginning of the article, there is a tendency in some American companies to take the less uncomplicated but naive "adapt and adopt" route to achieved prosperity. Thus, it may be that some U.S. firms are attempting, without great success, to apply a "managerial technique" in the wrong way, for the wrong reasons. Daniel Bills, chairman and president of Granville-Phillips Co., probably best articulates this problem with the experience of his organization. When Granville-Phillips initiated its productivity improvement programs, the company took whole programs "as is" from the Japanese companies Granville-Phillips studied. As it turned out, the actions by Granville-Phillips worked. Daniel Bills observes, though, "Some actions were taken out of sequence by not realizing why they worked for the Japanese. We no longer make this type of mistake because now we have a very effective process for identifying root causes in a business environment" ("Managing Cause and Effect," p. 3).

All of the preceding interpretations are probably correct to some degree. Companies that may eventually be part of *Fortune*'s 500, but are not today, are undertaking some very innovative activities in employee involvement. Some of the *Fortune* 500 companies are, indeed, undertaking employee involvement, but since we are dealing with America's largest corporations, the process is undeniably one of gradual change and rejuvenation. In addition, we are undoubtedly observing companies that are trying things because everyone else is, and consequently there is no real commitment to employee involvement.

The overall picture provided by the results of this survey taken in light of Edward Lawler's earlier comments is not very encouraging. Although firms appear to believe that involvement efforts are worthwhile, it appears that only a relatively limited number are, in fact, making the commitment necessary to ensure their success. Some firms use "suggestion involvement," few firms are using "job involvement," and there was little evidence of "high involvement" among the respondents.

Although there are a variety of motives and actions, it can probably be fairly stated that, regardless of the desires of management, any corporate efforts can only succeed if employees want them to succeed. Companies employing successful strategies invariably realize that such efforts must be applied "through" people, not "to" people, as not only Japanese companies, but American companies as well, have demonstrated in the past and are showing today.

While the findings of the survey are not encouraging, the prognosis is certainly not terminal. Not every American company is a victim of the competitive gap. In fact, there are companies such as ServiceMaster and Lincoln Electric that are not only doing well but in many respects dominate their competition. The factor common to these and other successful organizations is the manner in which they utilize the people within their organization: That is, the amount of employee involvement present at all levels in the organization.

The success of an employee involvement strategy ultimately rests in focusing on the "how" rather than simply looking at the "what."

References

Belohlav, J. A. (1991). *Championship Management.* Cambridge, MA: Productivity Press.

Hall, R. W., & Nakane, J. (1988). Developing flexibility for excellence in manufacturing: Summary results of a Japanese-American study. *Target, 4*(2).

Lawler, E. E., III (1988). Choosing an involvement strategy. *Academy of Management Executive, 2*(3).

Making manufacturing human (1988). *Productivity Newsletter, 9.*

Managing cause and effect (1987). *Productivity Newsletter, 8.*

US GAO (1988, May). *Survey of Corporate Employee Involvement Efforts.* Washington, DC: U.S. General Accounting Office.

Yankelovich, D., & Immerwahr, J. (1983). *Putting the Work Ethic to Work.* New York: The Public Agenda Foundation.

Choosing an Involvement Strategy

Edward E. Lawler III

The most prevalent approach to designing work organizations calls for such features as hierarchical decision making, simple repetitive jobs at the lowest level, and rewards based on carefully measured individual job performance. But this "control" approach appears to be losing favor. Numerous articles and books have recently argued that work organizations need to move toward an "involvement" or "commitment" approach to the design and management of work organizations.[1] The advantages of the involvement approach are said to include higher quality products and services, less absenteeism, less turnover, better decision making, and better problem solving—in short, greater organizational effectiveness.[2]

Careful examination of the suggested ways to increase involvement reveals not one but at least three approaches to managing organizations. All three encourage employee participation in decision making. These three approaches, however, have different histories, advocates, advantages, and disadvantages. An organization interested in adopting an involvement-oriented approach needs to be aware of the differences among these approaches and strategically choose the approach that is best for it.

The three approaches to involvement are (1) parallel suggestion involvement, (2) job involvement, and (3) high involvement. They differ in the degree to which they direct that four key features should be moved to the lowest level of an organization. Briefly, the features are: (1) information about the performance of the organization, (2) rewards that are based on the performance of the organization, (3) knowledge that enables employees to understand and contribute to organizational performance, and (4) power to make decisions that influence organizational direction and performance.

Information, rewards, knowledge, and power are the central issues for all organizations. How they are positioned in an organization determines the core management style of the organization. When they are concentrated at the top, traditional control-oriented management exists; when they are moved downward, some form of participative management is being practiced.

The parallel suggestion approach does the least to move power, knowledge, information, and rewards downward, while the high involvement approach does the most. Because they position power, information, knowledge, and rewards differently, these approaches tend to fit different situations and to produce different results. It is not that one is always better than another, but that they are different and, to some degree, competing. Let us consider how these three approaches operate, and the results they produce. Once we have reviewed them, we can discuss when and how they are best used.

Parallel Suggestion Involvement

Probably the oldest approach to employee involvement is suggestion involvement. Formal suggestion programs are perhaps the original way of establishing a problem-solving relationship between lower-level employees and their work. In suggestion involvement, the employees are asked—probably for the first time—to problem solve and produce ideas that will influence how the organization operates.

Reprinted with permission from *Academy of Management Executive, 2* (1988): 197–204.

Traditional suggestion programs often include the implementation of a supportive reward system as well. For example, an individual who is not in a management position may be given a reward based on one year's estimated savings from the suggestions he or she produces. Interestingly, managers typically are not rewarded for suggestions because developing workplace improvements is considered "part of their job."

A much more extensive reward system is involved in gainsharing plans.[3] The oldest and best-known gainsharing plan is the Scanlon Plan. Other gainsharing plans include the Improshare Plan and the Rucker Plan. Unlike traditional suggestion programs, gainsharing plans offer employees a share in gains for as long as the gains are realized by the organization. In the typical gainsharing plan, employees are asked to suggest improvements, and they share in any performance improvement the organization makes. Some gainsharing plans also move new information downward because they focus on organizational performance. In some cases, gainsharing plans go beyond suggestion involvement by creating a joint union/management committee structure that decides on the implementation of suggestions, designs and alters the plan, and makes other policy decisions.

Recently quality circles have become an extremely popular approach to suggestion involvement. At this point, quite a bit is known about the effectiveness of quality circles and how they operate.[4] Like written suggestion programs and Scanlon Plan suggestion programs, they encourage employees to recommend ways that the operations of the organization can be improved. The traditional quality circle approach uses groups, or quality circles, rather than individual written suggestions. According to quality circle advocates, the group process typically leads to better suggestions— and better-developed suggestions—than the written suggestion process does. In addition, in quality circles, considerable training is done to enable the group to function effectively and to help individuals become efficient problem

solvers. In the more advanced programs, employees are trained in problem analysis and statistical quality control.

As is true with written suggestion programs, quality circle programs provide participants only with recommendation power; they do not have the power to implement and decide on the installation of their suggestions. In this sense, they are a parallel structure to the ongoing organization. They are also a parallel structure because they take people out of their regular organizations and put them in a separate new structure that operates differently than the traditional organization does. Quality circles and other parallel structures are often easy to install, and they start quickly. The problem-solving groups can be small and need not be disruptive to the organization. They can easily be installed in a single plant or in a department of a larger organization. However, they do not change the existing organization structure, and they usually affect only a small percentage of the workforce.

Exhibit 1 summarizes the general characteristics of suggestion involvement plans. As the exhibit shows, these types of plans do not represent a major shift in the way control-oriented organizations deal with most issues. Instead, they rely on a special parallel structure to change the relationship between individuals and their work. This structure gives people the chance to influence decisions that they would not normally influence and, in some cases, to share in the financial results of their new role. It also usually leads to the communication of some additional information and to greater knowledge on the part of employees. However, this change in knowledge, information, and rewards often is limited to a small percentage of the workforce. In addition, the change is contained because individuals are asked to use this new knowledge and information only when they are operating in special suggestion-type activities. During their regular work activities, it is very much work as usual.

Research on the parallel structure or suggestion involvement approach suggests that it

Exhibit 1
Suggestion Involvement

Job Design:	Traditional, simple, specialized, focused on the individual
Organizational Structure:	Functional organization
Parallel Structures:	Quality circles; written suggestions; screening or review committees
Performance Information:	Focused on the value of savings from suggestions
Knowledge:	Group skills and problem solving
Decision Power:	Traditional top-down; suggestions decided upon by hierarchy
Rewards:	Traditional job-based with merit pay; possible awards for value of suggestion
Personnel Policies:	Traditional

position of having to do extra work. Conflict can develop between those who are in parallel structures and those who are not. Nonparticipants can come to resent being left out. Sometimes parallel structures can lead to a call for a systematic restructuring of the organization for greater involvement. In essence, employees like the taste of involvement they have gotten and want more.

Finally, over time suggestion involvement approaches that are not supported by reward system changes may lose their momentum and disappear. This comes about because they do not systematically change an organization's way of operating or the way the total workforce relates to the organization and its performance. Gainsharing plans, because they affect the way everyone is rewarded, typically do not suffer from this limitation. Gainsharing companies like Herman Miller and Donnelley Mirrors have maintained gainsharing plans for decades.

Job Involvement Approaches

Job involvement approaches focus on enriching work to motivate employees to achieve better job performance. One strategy, job enrichment, focuses on creating individual jobs that give people feedback, increases their influence over how the work is done, requires them to use a variety of skills, and gives them a whole piece of work.[6] This approach has an extensive research history going back to the 1950s, when behavioral scientists tried to design alternatives to traditional, standardized, simplified work. Perhaps the most visible champion of this approach has been Herzberg.

A second strategy for job involvement creates work groups or teams. This approach, too, has an extensive research history going back to the 1940s and the pioneering work of Trist, Emery, and Thorsrud.[7] It differs from individual enrichment in that it considers the work group as the primary unit of involvement. It creates group goals, tasks, and control with the objective of making all group members feel responsible for the group's performance.

can lead to an improvement in organizational performance. Case after case shows that individuals and groups often come up with suggestions that save the company a considerable amount of money.[5] There also seems to be no question that employees enjoy the opportunity to participate in problem solving. As a result, they are often more satisfied with their work situation, are absent less, and are less likely to leave the company.

The parallel suggestion involvement approach, however, has a number of well-documented limitations. First, it tends to have a "program character" about it, which often makes it a temporary system in an organization. In addition, parallel structures are expensive and difficult to maintain. In some situations, they run out of suggestions because individuals do not have enough expertise to solve the more complex problems in an organization. They also often are resisted by middle-level managers because parallel structures threaten their power and put them in the

Groups designed according to this approach are often called autonomous work groups, self-managing groups, semi-autonomous work groups, or work teams.

As Exhibit 2 shows, the job involvement approach does have significant implications for how an organization is structured and managed. In essence, individuals are given new skills and knowledge, new feedback, an additional set of decisions to make, and they may be rewarded differently. Both the individual and the team approach have these effects, although the team approach carried to its fullest extent has them to a greater degree.

With the team approach, interpersonal skills and group decision-making skills are needed in addition to those that are needed for individual enrichment. The reward system also is changed more with groups or teams than with individual job enrichment, since skill-based pay is often used. Finally, teams can make certain decisions that individuals usually cannot. Both individuals and teams can control the way the work is done, per-

forming quality-management, inventory, and other task-related activities, but teams can also decide personnel-management issues. Teams, for example, can make decisions about hiring and firing, and may select their own supervisors. Perhaps the most successful examples of teams are found in the new plants built by Procter and Gamble, Mead, and a host of other manufacturing companies during the last 20 years.[8]

Overall, job involvement represents a significant change in the fundamental operations of an organization. Individuals at the lowest levels get new information, power, and skills, and they may be rewarded differently. The new information, power, knowledge, and rewards correspond to their particular work tasks, and typically do not have to do with the structuring and operating of the whole organization or the development of its strategic direction. Unlike parallel suggestion approaches, job involvement affects the day-to-day work activities of all individuals. Involvement is not an occasional thing, it is the standard way in which business is done.

Theoretically, the decision to use either teams or individual job enrichment should be based on the technology of the workplace. Teams are more complicated to build and maintain, but may be necessary if the work is such that no one individual could do a whole part of it and get feedback about it. Teams are often appropriate, for example, in process production facilities such as chemical plants and oil refineries, and in complex service organizations such as banks and airlines. Where the technology allows an individual to do a whole task or offer a whole service, individual designs are preferred because they are simpler to install and give the individual more direct feedback.

Studies of job involvement approaches show improvements in productivity, quality, absenteeism, and turnover among individuals working in enriched jobs and in teams.[9] The net result for the organization is usually significant performance improvement over that found with traditional job structures. Unlike

Exhibit 2
Job Involvement

Job Design:	Job enrichment or teams
Organizational Structure:	Traditional, functional
Parallel Structures:	None
Performance Information:	Focused on job and/or team performance
Knowledge:	Job specific, team skills
Decision Power:	Performers control how work is done
Rewards:	Traditional for job enrichment; skill-based pay possible for teams
Personnel Policies:	Traditional; some team-based decision making

suggestion programs, job involvement structures seem to be reasonably stable. This is particularly true of teams, since they represent cohesive organizational units that are difficult to dissolve.

The limitations of the job involvement approach are primarily those of lost opportunities. Because they limit employee involvement to immediate work decisions, they often fail to capture the contributions that individuals can make to strategic decisions and to higher-level management work. As a result, individuals in work teams may tend to optimize their own performance without paying a great deal of attention to overall organization performance.

Work involvement efforts do entail some significant start-up costs because they require considerable training. Often overlooked is the need to train the supervisor and dramatically change the supervisor's job. Some evidence exists that many supervisors have difficulty moving from a traditional management environment to one characterized by job involvement.[10] In some cases, job involvement efforts call for an extensive and expensive physical reconfiguration of the workplace to allow for team interaction and control of a whole piece of work by individuals. Also, these efforts are often resisted by middle managers because they feel threatened by the new power that others have.

Finally, job involvement approaches may be subject to cancellation if they do not influence higher-level strategic decisions concerning organization structure, power, and the allocation of rewards. This is particularly true with individual job enrichment. Unless major restructuring is done to support the program, supervisors are often able unilaterally to change jobs in ways that take away the decision-making power that is critical to enrichment. Job involvement efforts are particularly likely to be cancelled when they affect small parts of an organization. Like parallel structures, they can be installed only on a limited basis and, as a result, create friction between participants and nonparticipants. This friction

can, in turn, lead to pressures to eliminate the job involvement program.[11]

High Involvement Approach

The high involvement approach has also been called the commitment approach or, perhaps more descriptively, the business involvement approach. It is relatively new although it has roots in the early work of Likert on System 4 management, McGregor on Theory Y, and Trist and others on sociotechnical systems.[12] In many respects, it also builds on what has been learned from the suggestion involvement and job involvement approaches. It tends to structure an organization so that people at the lowest level will have a sense of involvement not just in how they do their jobs or how effectively their group performs, but in the performance of the total organization. It goes considerably farther than either of the other two approaches toward moving power, information, knowledge, and rewards to the lowest organizational level. It is based on the argument that if individuals are going to care about the performance of the organization, they need to know about it, be able to influence it, be rewarded for it, and have the knowledge and skills to contribute to it.

As Exhibit 3 shows, in order to have high involvement management, virtually every major feature of the organization needs to be designed differently than it is with the control approach. The high involvement approach builds upon what is done in the job involvement and the suggestion involvement approaches: Parallel structures are used for certain kinds of problem solving and policy setting, and work is designed according to the principles of individual enrichment and work teams. High involvement is different, however, in the kind of information that is shared, and in the decision power and reward systems areas. In the case of decision power, employees are not only asked to make decisions about their work activities, they are also asked to play a role in organizational decisions having to do with strategy, investment, and other

Exhibit 3
High Involvement

Job Design:	Work teams and job enrichment
Organizational Structure:	Business or customer focused
Parallel Structures:	Task forces for major business issues
Performance Information:	Focused on business performance
Knowledge:	Team skills; business economics; problem solving
Decision Power:	Performers make work-method and work-unit management decisions, have input to strategic decisions
Rewards:	Egalitarian; skill-based pay; gainsharing and/or profit sharing; employee ownership
Personnel Policies:	Employment stability; equality of treatment; participatively developed and administered policies

major areas. Rewards are based on the performance of the organization; hence, profit sharing, gainsharing, and some type of employee ownership are appropriate.

Creating a high involvement organization is clearly a much different and more complex task than implementing job involvement or parallel suggestion involvement is. Virtually every feature of a control-oriented organization has to be redesigned and, in some cases, innovation in design is necessary. Many of the methodologies and approaches for such policies as pay, selection, and training are readily available and well developed for control-oriented management; installing them is simply a matter of taking established systems "off the shelf" and making them operational. On the other hand, there is a relative paucity of technology to support the development of high

involvement organizations. This is largely due to the fact that this approach to management is new and the technology has not yet been fully developed. Therefore, those organizations that adopt it are forced into somewhat of a research and development mode with respect to the technology of management.

This point is well illustrated by the now defunct airline, People Express. It had to invent new work scheduling approaches, pay structures, training programs, and a new organization design in order to operate in a high involvement mode. Because no airline had ever operated as a high involvement organization, there simply were no examples around. Not surprisingly, the need for so much invention and system debugging contributed to some operating problems.

There are relatively little data on the effectiveness of high involvement organizations. Indeed, there are few examples to study. The closest examples of organizations using this approach would appear to be the many new team-based plants that have been started around the world. The data on the plants are largely favorable, but limited. In addition, there are some new organizations that have started with this approach and some employee-owned companies that are moving toward operating in a high involvement mode.[13]

It is hardly surprising that the best examples of high involvement organizations are new start-ups. The high involvement approach represents such an extensive change from the control approach to management that the difficulties in making a conversion are enormous. It is much easier to start with a clean sheet of paper and design the organization from the ground up.[14] This is in notable contrast to job involvement and suggestion involvement approaches, which are often put in place in existing organizations.

The admittedly sketchy, testimonial-type evidence that does exist on high involvement organizations generally shows superior operating results.[15] They tend to be low-cost, relatively flexible, adaptive organizations that are very quality and customer oriented. However, this approach is not cheap to use, since it requires a large initial investment in selection, training, and system development. In addition, as we will discuss, it does not fit every person, situation, and business.

The Strategic Choice

Decisions about which approach an organization should adopt ought to be guided by a number of factors. The different approaches to involvement fit different types of businesses, situations, and individuals. The key to effective utilization of any of them is installing them in conditions to which they are suited. Three major factors need to be examined in deciding which approach to pick: (1) the nature of the work and technology, (2) values of the key participants, and (3) the organization's current management approach.

Work and Technology

Perhaps the overriding determinant of how an organization should approach involvement is the kind of work it does and the technology it uses. Managers' values and attitudes can be changed over time, and the traditional practices of older, control-oriented organizations can evolve into high involvement policies, but organizations cannot necessarily change the kind of technology they use or the kind of jobs that the technology dictates.[16]

Admittedly, technology is only partly driven by the products and services an organization offers. As many advocates of the work redesign approach have pointed out, there is some flexibility in the technology an organization chooses to use. In addition, the technology does not completely dictate the nature of the jobs an organization has. Some technologies can be modified to produce the types of jobs that are congruent with the desired form of involvement. An example of this is Volvo's heroic effort to alter its auto assembly technology to make it congruent with work teams. But in many cases the control of a single organization is limited. There is, for example, little flexibility when it comes to refin-

ing oil and generating electricity. It is very difficult to change the telephone operator's job, given the way telephone equipment has been designed. As a result, there are some situations in which the technology is not amenable to any of the involvement approaches, with the possible exception of suggestion involvement.

Two aspects of technology are particularly critical influences on the appropriateness of different involvement approaches: (1) the degree of interdependence and (2) the degree of complexity. Interdependence refers to the extent to which individuals need to coordinate, cooperate, and relate to others to produce the product or services the organization offers. Organizations vary on this dimension from very high interdependence to low interdependence. For example, university professors and insurance salespeople are typically in a low interdependence situation, while chemical plant operators and computer design engineers are in high interdependence situations.

High interdependence argues for teams and against individual approaches to work design. Low interdependence favors maximizing individual performance through job enrichment or well-structured individual tasks that offer large amounts of incentive pay.

A crucial issue in determining which way to go with low interdependence jobs is the complexity of the work involved: High complexity calls for job enrichment, while low complexity calls for simple jobs and incentive pay.

Technology, to a substantial degree, tends to influence the complexity of the work. Complexity can vary from the repetitive jobs associated with assembly lines to the highly complex knowledge-based work required by professional jobs and jobs in state-of-the-art manufacturing facilities. Where the work is simple and repetitive by necessity, it is hard to put in place a high involvement or even a job involvement approach (unless the technology can be changed). These situations are often limited to parallel suggestion involvement approaches, as they can operate with most approaches to work design and most types of technology.

With complex knowledge work, the clear choice is one of the involvement approaches. At the very least, job involvement is called for—job enrichment in the case of independent work and teams in the case of interdependent work. If other conditions are right, high involvement would seem to be the best choice. High involvement flourishes where complex knowledge work exists because individuals who do this kind of work possess the ability to participate in a wide range of decisions, and they often expect and want this approach to management.

Values and Beliefs

The values and beliefs that key participants in an organization need to have vary widely among the involvement approaches. If the values do not match the chosen approach, the approach is unlikely to be fully implemented and effectively operated.

In the case of the suggestion approach, key managers do not need to have a profound belief that employees can and will exercise self-control, manage themselves, and be able to contribute to major organizational decisions; they simply need to believe that employees have useful ideas about how things can be improved.

The high involvement approach, on the other hand, requires that managers believe in the capabilities, sense of responsibility, and commitment of people throughout the organization. In short, they need to believe that people not only are a key organization resource, but that people can and will behave responsibly if given the opportunity.

The beliefs of management are often captured in the philosophical statements they endorse and write. High involvement organizations typically have clearly stated, widely circulated management philosophy statements that highlight their commitment to employee involvement and their desire to push decision making and information to the lowest levels of the organization. On the other

hand, managers who feel most comfortable with suggestion involvement usually make no such statements. If they say anything, it is that employees are an important asset of the organization and know how to do their jobs best.

The values of the employees are also important to consider. For any form of involvement to work, most employees have to want to learn, grow, develop, contribute, and take on new responsibilities. Most researchers have argued that the vast majority of American workers do want to be involved in their work, but few argue it is universally true. Particularly where there has been a long history of autocratic management, the majority of the workforce may not want to be more involved. They may have become conditioned to the control-oriented approach and appreciate the fact that they can just put in their eight hours and not have to take the job home with them. In addition, self-selection may have taken place so that those who most value involvement quit long ago, leaving behind those who are less attracted to it.

Societal values can also come into play in determining the appropriate approach to involvement. Democratic societies provide much more supportive environments for the high involvement approach than do traditional autocratic societies. The United States, with its long democratic tradition and commitment to individual rights, appears to provide the ideal setting for involvement-oriented management. Historically, our society has exempted the workplace from our commitment to democracy and individual rights, but there are many signs that this is breaking down in the area of individual rights and it seems inevitable that the exemption will also disappear as far as participation and involvement are concerned.[17]

Organizational Starting Point

In considering employee involvement strategies, organizations need to assess their current operating approach. As noted earlier, it is hardly surprising that many job involvement and high involvement organizations start as "green field" operations. Without question, it is easier to install involvement-oriented management where no management system currently exists. Not only is it possible to select managers who have values that are supportive of involvement, but it is not necessary to overcome all the traditions, practices, and policies that are inconsistent with it. This is not to say that it is impossible for an organization to evolve toward high involvement; if it seems to be called for because of the kind of work and technology the organization has, and if the values of managers support it, it certainly is possible. However, it may not be feasible to change immediately to a high involvement approach.

In starting a change process toward high involvement, it is critical to see where the organization is and then map out a long-term strategy. If the organization is currently operating in an extremely traditional way, the best first step may be to move to quality circles or another suggestion involvement approach. This approach should be structured in ways that make movement to job involvement relatively easy. Quality circles, for example, can be converted into work teams if they are led by a supervisor and organized around natural work units. As noted earlier, work teams are an important part of the high involvement approach, and getting them in place is an important step toward high involvement management. Thus, there can be a natural transition from the parallel structure approach to job involvement and finally to high involvement.

If an organization is already relatively participative in a number of its personnel policies, its work structure, and managerial behaviors, it may not be necessary to start with a suggestion involvement program. The organization can immediately start with the job involvement approach. On the other hand, if an organization is very traditional in the way it operates, and managers are very hesitant to give up decision-making power, then the only way to start involvement is often with a parallel suggestion approach. Quality circles or Scanlon written suggestion programs are particularly appropriate, since they present a minimal threat to existing management prerogatives and power. Sometimes their success can convince management to move ahead to other forms of involvement. As noted earlier, however, suggestion programs are limited in what they can accomplish because they do little to share power, knowledge, rewards, and information among all levels of the organization.

The presence of a union organization can make a significant difference in which approach to involvement is most appropriate. Many unions have been willing to create jointly sponsored parallel structure approaches to involvement. Scanlon plans, for example, have been widely used in unionized workplaces, as have quality-of-work-life programs. The latter usually create a hierarchical structure of joint union/management committees.[18] These committees are involvement devices in their own right, and they typically sponsor problem-solving groups and other participative activities for rank-and-file union members. A common problem with quality-of-work-life programs is that they end up dealing with a very limited set of issues, including primarily those related to workplace hygiene. In a few instances, this type of parallel structure involvement has led to the creation of high involvement efforts. A good example of this is the General Motors Saturn project. General Motors had quality-of-work-life projects for years before it decided to ask the United Auto Workers to create jointly a new company called Saturn, which was to be developed and run in a high involvement manner.

Conclusion: Analyzing Situational Factors

Our argument so far suggests that there is no one right approach to involvement. The approach needs to be dictated by a number of situational factors. At the extreme, an organization may be able only to progress from control to suggestion involvement. At one extreme if all of an organization's systems are traditional, well developed, and firmly in place, and its technology leads to relatively independent, simple, repetitive tasks, then suggestion involvement is appropriate. However, if the organization is new, has complex knowledge work, interdependent tasks, and managers who value employee involvement, it is possible to move to high involvement management and reap the rewards it has to offer.

Because involvement is not universally good for all organizations, it is important to take a differentiated view toward it. If organizations carefully analyze where they are and where they want to be, they can lay out a series of steps that will lead to the type of involvement that fits their situation. In the absence of this kind of process, they run the risk of managing in a way that compromises the potential effectiveness of the organization.

Endnotes

1. See, for example, E. E. Lawler, "High Involvement Management," San Francisco: Jossey-Bass, 1986; E. E. Lawler, "Transformation from Control to Involvement," chapter in R. Kilmann, J. Covin and Associates' (Eds.) *Corporate Transformation,* San Francisco: Jossey-Bass, 1987, pp. 46–65; R. E. Walton, "From Control to Commitment in the Workplace," *Harvard Business Review,* 1985, 63(2), 76–84.

2. Some interesting but limited data are provided by D. Dennison in "Bringing Corporate Culture to the Bottom Line," *Organizational Dynamics,* 1984, 13(2), 4–22.

3. A good overview is provided by B. Graham-Moore and T. Ross, *Productivity Gainsharing,* Englewood Cliffs, NJ: Prentice-Hall, 1983.

4. E. E. Lawler and S. A. Mohrman, "Quality Circles After the Fad," *Harvard Business Review,* 1985, 85(1), 64–71; E. E. Lawler and S. A. Mohrman, "Quality Circles: After the Honeymoon," *Organizational Dynamics,* 1987, 15(4), 42–54.

5. See the following for examples: Carl F. Frost, John H. Wakeley, and Robert A. Ruh, *The Scanlon Plan for Organization Development: Identity, Participation, and Equity,* East Lansing: Michigan State University Press, 1974; Tom Peters, *Thriving on Chaos,* New York: Knopf, 1987; M. H. Schuster, *Union-Management Cooperation,* Kalamazoo, Mich.: W. E. Upjohn Institute, 1984.

6. Three seminal writings in this area are J. R. Hackman and E. E. Lawler's "Employee Reactions to Job Characteristics," *Journal of Applied Psychology,* 1971, 55, 259–286; J. R. Hackman and G. R. Oldham's *Work Redesign,* Reading, Mass.: Addison-Wesley, 1980; F. Herzberg's *Work and the Nature of Man,* New York: World, 1969.

7. T. G. Cummings's "Self-Regulating Work Groups: A Socio-Technical Synthesis," *Academy of Management Review,* 1978, 3, 625–633; F. Emery and E. Thorsrud's *Industrial Democracy,* London: Tavistock, 1969.

8. An overview of how these plants operate is provided in E. E. Lawler's "The New Plant Revolution," *Organizational Dynamics,* 1978, 6(3), 2–12.

9. See Endnote 6.

10. R. E. Walton and L. A. Schlesinger, "Do Supervisors Thrive in Participative Work Systems?" *Organizational Dynamics,* 1979, 8(3), 25–38.

11. E. Trist and C. Dwyer, *The Limits of Laissez-Faire as a Sociotechnical Change Strategy,* in R. Zager and M. Rosow (Eds.), *The Innovative Organization,* New York: Pergamon, 1982, pp. 149–183.

12. See, for example, R. Likert's *The Human Organization,* New York: McGraw-Hill, 1967, and D. McGregor's *The Human Side of Enterprise,* New York: McGraw-Hill, 1960.

13. C. Rosen, K. Klein, and K. Young's *Employee Ownership in America,* Lexington, Mass: Lexington, 1986.

14. See D. Perkins, V. Nieva, and E. E. Lawler, *Managing Creation: The Challenge of Building a New Organization,* New York: Wiley, 1983.

15. See, for example, Endnotes 1 and 5, as well as *Fortune* (Eds.) *Working Smarter,* New York: Viking, 1982.

16. The following stress the importance of technology: J. Thompson's *Organizations in Action,* New York: McGraw-Hill, 1967, and J. Woodward's *Management and Technology,* London: Her Majesty's Stationery Office, 1958.

17. D. W. Ewing, *Freedom Inside the Organization,* New York: Dutton, 1977, and M. Sashkin, "Participative Management Is an Ethical Imperative," *Organizational Dynamics,* Spring 1984, 5–22.

18. E. E. Lawler and L. Ozley's "Winning Union-Management Cooperation on Quality of Work Life Projects," *Management Review,* 1979, 68(3), 19–24.

The Empowerment Environment

John H. Dobbs

I recently met a young, capable engineer during a visit to Coors Electronic Packaging in Chattanooga, Tennessee. The engineer's job was designing ceramic carriers for semiconductor chips, a complex operation. The engineer said one of the problems he faced was getting timely approvals on design changes from customers. To get approval, he had to mail overnight shipments of large, expensive drawings almost daily.

The engineer wanted to save time and cut costs by installing a linked computer terminal—at no expense to the customer—at a key customer's worksite. That way, the designer could simultaneously transmit and discuss design changes with the customer.

Did I mention that the engineer was also highly empowered? The engineer's employer, Coors Brewing Company, is committed to innovation, an essential condition for empowerment. One of Coors's strategic initiatives is a monitoring process that measures the rate at which innovation occurs in various parts of the company. Not surprisingly, Coors adopted the engineer's idea, greatly reducing the design-to-prototype cycle time.

The lesson is that an action by a single empowered employee can result in dramatic benefits for an organization. In Coors's case, the engineer's innovation enhanced the efficiency of new-product development and improved customer service.

In many organizations, empowerment has become a buzzword. Although the term is used often, it's not always understood. Empowerment is usually vaguely characterized as "something managers do to their employees." Despite the lack of a definitive definition, many organizations have recognized that empowerment is critical to the achievement of total quality, customer satisfaction, and continuous improvement.

Organizations—and managers—who are trying to empower people may be fighting an uphill battle. That's due, in part, to the economy. Every day, about 2,500 people are laid off in the United States. Managers may be more worried about keeping their jobs than about empowering employees. They may even worry that empowering subordinates might jeopardize their own jobs. Some managers may be asking, "If I empower my employees, who will empower me?"

Where does empowerment begin? What must organizations be like in order for empowerment to occur? People seem to agree about the way an empowered employee should behave. But they don't always agree about which conditions are necessary for fostering enough empowerment to change a traditionally hierarchical organization into a more participative one.

To complicate matters, people seem to desire and fear empowerment at the same time. In some organizations, it's as sought after as the Holy Grail; in others, it's avoided like the plague.

Conditions for Empowerment

Understanding empowerment may be the first step to achieving it. In order for empowerment to take root and thrive, organizations must encourage these conditions:

• participation
• innovation

• access to information

• accountability.

Those factors produce an organizational feeling and tone that can have a dramatic, positive effect on employees.

Participation. People must be actively and willingly engaged in their jobs. They must care about improving their daily work processes and work relationships.

Such involvement doesn't happen just because managers ask for it. Willingness to participate can't be mandated. It has to come from each individual's desire to contribute and to make a difference.

The good news is that a 1991 survey, conducted by Brooks International, shows that 93 percent of U.S. workers do feel personally responsible for organizational quality and performance. But bureaucratic, highly controlled work environments can thwart employees' willingness to participate. Organizations that are less hierarchical are encouraging their employees to become more involved. Some even provide empowerment training.

For example, at the chemical division of Georgia-Pacific Corporation, a quality-and-environmental-assurance supervisor and a plant operator thought of a more effective way to prepare test samples of a certain chemical. They had been trained in collaboration skills, so they felt comfortable sharing their idea. Instead of simply writing down the new procedure, they produced a demonstration video.

After seeing the video, managers asked the two employees to share the tape with quality-assurance supervisors at other Georgia-Pacific plants. In turn, the supervisor and operator encouraged employees at other sites to provide feedback and to share their own ideas. Such collaboration and sharing exemplify a shift toward empowerment.

Georgia-Pacific also uses a concept called "100 percent responsibility," which encourages managers and other employees to examine their job responsibilities differently than they have in the past. The goals are to get em-ployees to take more initiative and to be more accountable for results.

Other organizations are training their workforces on total quality tools and concepts in the hope that such training will make employees want to apply new techniques and improve performance.

Whether the topic is collaboration or total quality, training can encourage people to participate more actively by helping raise their levels of confidence. Sometimes people simply lack enough self-assurance to address problems and try to solve them.

Innovation. It's almost impossible for empowerment to exist in environments in which innovation is ignored, stifled, or discouraged. Empowerment can't exist in an organization that expects employees to do their jobs the way they've always done them.

Organizations need to give employees at all levels permission to innovate. The most valuable innovations often come from employees in "the trenches"—the workers who have direct contact with an organization's manufacturing processes or who deliver service to customers.

Unfortunately, many organizations pay only lip service to innovation and do little to foster it. Michael Schrage, in the November/December 1989 *Harvard Business Review,* describes organizational environments that encourage innovation:

> The most successful corporate innovation systems aren't systems at all. They are environments that are hospitable to interesting people with innovative ideas—environments that encourage people to explore new paths and to take meaningful risks at reasonable costs, environments in which curiosity is as highly regarded as is technical expertise. Organizations that succeed at innovation are those that make an unwavering commitment to it. Innovation is as much a core value as is an acceptable return on investment.

Access to information. In traditional organizations, the senior managers decide who receives what kind of information and how much. In organizations in which employees are empowered, people at every level make decisions about what kind of information they need for performing their jobs.

In many organizations, information can be a source of power. In some instances, a manager may restrict subordinates' access to information as a means of controlling employees. In organizations in which such restriction occurs, employee participation is bound to be low.

At a General Mills plant in Covington, Georgia, small, self-managed teams of about 28 employees each successfully operate a 400,000-square-foot manufacturing operation. Employees, whose access to information is virtually unlimited, receive training on such diverse topics as profit and loss statements and manufacturing processes.

Accountability. Empowerment has its benefits, but what about the risks?

K. Grahame Walker, as quoted in *Industry Week* (November 18, 1991), says he advocates doing away with the term *empowerment* in favor of another word—participation, contribution, involvement, or responsibility. Why? Because, Walker says, some employees define empowerment as doing what they want—when, where, how, why, and if they want.

Some managers fear that giving employees too much latitude is similar to letting the inmates run the asylum. They worry that freedom, untempered by a sense of responsibility and good judgment, will produce the wrong results.

One way organizations can help mitigate managers' fears about empowerment is to increase employee accountability. It is important to ensure that employee accountability is egalitarian: In other words, if employees are accountable to managers, then managers also should be accountable to employees. Some organizations try to break down "class distinctions" between job levels by using position-neutral terms—for example, they may refer to all employees as associates.

Specifically, employees should be held accountable for

- behaving responsibly toward others
- operating with a positive approach
- producing desired, agreed-upon results
- being responsible for their own credibility and for keeping their word
- giving their best.

The Glue

The glue that holds empowerment together is compassionate leadership. The four conditions for empowerment—participation, innovation, access to information, and accountability—are necessary, but they are insufficient without the right kind of leadership.

Compassionate leadership is characterized by openness, receptivity to new ideas, honesty, caring, and dignity and respect for people. Compassionate leadership acknowledges that a leader's main role is to create a vision for the future and to lead the way. Compassionate leaders create conditions that encourage employees to become involved.

Workers support the idea of compassionate leadership. In recent studies, employees describe effective leaders as compassionate and also as caring, honest, inspirational, forward looking, competent, open, and trustworthy.

Organizations in which leaders wield a lot of power create environments that are hostile to empowerment, through restricting the open exchange of information and limiting opportunities for innovation. Leaders need to create environments in which employees trust each other. Only then will people feel comfortable about experimenting with new ideas and safe enough to take reasonable risks.

Employees need to know that their leaders want them to participate. They need to know that their leaders are willing to listen to them, support them, and remove barriers to their ideas. In turn, leaders need to trust subordinates and other leaders. A high level of trust all around encourages innovation and risk taking.

The impetus for empowerment doesn't necessarily stem from a commitment to empowerment itself. It may be driven by a desire to put initiatives in place that can support continuous improvement and total quality—which can't be achieved unless employees are involved, committed, and empowered.

Organizations spend millions of dollars each year on total-quality training. For them to reap the benefits of such expense, they need to ensure that their employees are empowered as well.

The Internal Context of Human Resources Management

Just as the external environment has an impact upon what occurs in an organization, a number of internal factors have an impact upon the management of human resources. Internal factors range from the work environment to the individuals who make up that environment to work policies to work stress and health-related issues. Internal and external factors interact, in a relatively unpredictable fashion, and result in potentially unintended organizational consequences. The articles in Part 5 reflect the internal issues that may have an effect upon organizational outcomes.

Chapter 12 includes articles that address the issue of accountability. People in organizations need to be held accountable for their decisions and actions; when accountability is lacking, many problems result. As a group or organization gets larger, a diffusion of responsibility occurs. With broadening spans of control, accountability becomes especially important. The articles deal specifically with problems surrounding accountability in the context of a human resources program.

Various other issues that influence the internal environment of an organization are treated in the Chapter 13 articles. Sexual harassment is considered in relation to the organizational outcomes associated with this problem. One of the most serious concerns in the internal work environment is the incidence of stress-related problems. Sources of stress are investigated, as are employee assistance programs that are necessitated by the outcomes associated with excessive stress.

CHAPTER 12

Accountability in Human Resources Systems

Accountability is the management philosophy that all individuals are liable or accountable for how well they use the legitimate authority vested in them by an organization. Have people lived up to their responsibilities and their duties to perform the activities assigned to them? If individuals fail on the tasks for which they are accountable, some punitive action should result. By the same token, success should bring desired rewards.

In the context of human resources, accountability refers to the notion of responsibility for either effective or ineffective human resources programs. Where does this responsibility reside? The question is not necessarily straightforward. Can outcomes be dissociated from environments and attributed solely to those charged with implementation? Probably not! Accountability is a complex issue.

The articles in this chapter develop the emerging notion of accountability in human resources systems. First, Frink and Ferris outline its application in human resources management systems. They suggest ways in which accountability can be measured and discuss why this notion is becoming so important in human resources management.

In the second article Peach examines the issue of CEO compensation—how it is determined, how it is tied to incentives, how much CEOs are paid, and how and to whom a CEO is accountable. The author suggests a greater emphasis on the link between pay and performance as one way in which accountability can be achieved.

Suggestions for Further Reading

Adams, L. (1992, February). Securing your HRIS in a microcomputer environment. *HR Magazine,* pp. 56–61.

Barkley, W., Jr., & Green, T. (1992). Safe landings for outplaced employees at AT&T. *Personnel Journal, 71,* 144–147.

Brookes, D. (1993, February). Merit pay, the hoax. *HR Magazine,* pp. 117, 119.

Ceriello, V. (1992). How to sabotage HRMS planning. *Personnel Journal, 71,* 102–104.

Islam, N. (1993). Performance contract: Contractualization of the government–public enterprise interface. *Optimum, 23,* 53–59.

Klay, W. (1993). The temporal, social, and responsiveness dilemmas of public personnel administration. *International Journal of Public Administration, 16,* 945–967.

Ochsner, R. (1991). Newcomp: A glimpse of the future. *Compensation & Benefits Management, 7,* 79–80.

Osborne, J. (1993). The supervisor's role in managing change. *Supervisory Management, 38,* 3.

Rollins, T., & Fruge, M. (1992). Performance dimensions: Competencies with a twist. *Training, 29,* 47–51.

Winterle, M. (1993, January/February). Toward diversity, with carrots and sticks. *Across the Board,* p. 50.

Accountability in the Management of Human Resources

Dwight D. Frink and Gerald R. Ferris

"When the cat's away, the mice will play" states the old adage. In the late 1960s and early 1970s, President Richard Nixon was referred to as "King Richard" by some detractors. Many believe his administration's downfall was rooted in a belief among its members that they were an elite cadre, above the law, answerable to no one but themselves. In other words, there was no "cat"—they did not feel accountable to anyone, and their actions were unconstrained. On the other hand, some detractors of President Bill Clinton claim that he is pandering to all the "fringe" groups representing special interests and that he cannot keep his promises to all those groups no matter how good his intentions may be. In other words, he is acting as though he feels accountable to all ideologies: There are too many "cats," and thus he has been accused of being indecisive—his decisions have too many constraints.

In the business community there are claims that firms should be held accountable for everything associated with their operations and functions, even innocently intended but negative outcomes that may not become apparent for many years. Johns-Manville was almost bankrupted by asbestosis claims, and the federal government was forced to bear responsibility for the Love Canal cleanup because no firms capable of being held liable or bearing the cost were in existence. Another current topic of popular debate is the spiraling CEO salary ranges, accompanied by claims that CEOs should be held accountable for performance to justify their salaries.

Each of these examples describes a situation involving accountability to a different contingent or audience. In the case of the Nixon administration, the feelings of accountability were related to a legal system or structure, and because the administration was the head of that structure, its members were accountable to no one. In the Clinton example, accountability is perceived to be to the constituencies that exert political influence or apply pressures on the president. In the perspective regarding business firms, the focal group for accountability is the public, whereas the Love Canal situation exemplifies accountability to the community and the environment. Finally, the CEO salary question concerns accountability to business partners or coinvestors (i.e., stockholders and lenders) as well as to other members of the organization.

These examples illustrate how an individual or body can be accountable to any of several constituencies—or even to multiple constituencies. In this article we focus on accountability in human resources systems. First we discuss what is meant by accountability. Next, we examine the nature of constituencies in organizations, those to whom one is accountable, and consider some implications of contextual conditions. Then we look at ways accountability is enforced in organizational contexts. Finally, we discuss the policy and practical implications of accountability systems in human resources management.

Definition and Nature of Accountability

So, what is this thing called accountability, and how does it differ from responsibility? The situations mentioned earlier suggest a common theme. In each situation someone or some entity wanted the individual, group, or organization to answer for what was said or done and to bear the consequences of the statements or actions. Is this the same as responsibility? One could see accountability as the likelihood of being required to defend one's actions or decisions to some public or constituency. Responsibility could be seen in a more restrictive sense as being liable for the accomplishment of some task or outcome. Both of these notions can be discussed in terms of external conditions, which are the structural, operational, and normative standards in the workplace, or in terms of internal conditions, which are defined in terms of one's responses to external conditions. In other words, the external perspective deals with the context, or situation, and the constraints in that situation; the internal perspective deals with the ways individuals respond to the situational constraints. The internalized approaches can be termed "felt responsibility" and "felt accountability."

The external approach to the concept of accountability has to do with environmental characteristics, or structures, that provide some type of internal or external reward or sanction for actions or decisions. These structures include systems of written rules, pay systems, organizational structures and reporting systems, and social norms. The rewards and sanctions in these contexts include items ranging from disciplinary measures to take-home pay to feelings of social acceptance and approval.

Let us return to the "cats," or the audiences. Who are they? In the earlier examples, they included individuals and entities in structural positions, such as political constituencies, the general public, specific communities, and business partners and coinvestors. To this list could be added superiors, subordinates, peers and group members, and those in specialized areas, such as quality control, accounting, and legal affairs. Another question critical for organizations, and especially for human resources functions, concerns the motivation or authority underlying accountability in the organization. In other words, why should people feel accountable, and how are accountability systems instituted and en-

forced? The primary mechanism in most organizations is the performance evaluation and incentive system. People respond to accountability partly because of the direct benefit or cost that results from compliance or noncompliance. In other words, accountability systems are organizational control systems. Many firms have instituted management by objectives (MBO) or other goal-setting and review systems in efforts to link accountability and compensation to specific, measurable outcomes. Other systems of accountability include elections, feedback systems, and reward/sanction systems, both formal and informal. In the past it was popular to discuss a firm's lore and culture. One reason for the importance placed on these subjective standards was that rewards and sanctions could be meted out according to the extent to which one espoused, venerated, and adhered to corporate imagery or icons.

Accountability Issues at Different Levels in the Organization

This discussion of accountability has so far been very general. Within the general scope of organizational studies, we will narrow the focus by examining accountability at five different levels of analysis: organizational, leadership, group, individual behavior, and individual decisions. At each level there are both internal and external categories—that is, there are constituencies both within and outside the organization that may call the organization or its members to be accountable.

Accountability at the Organizational Level

A number of organizational issues can be viewed in terms of accountability. This level of analysis deals with issues that are relevant to the organization as an entity, to decisions and policies that are determined at the board level, to the operations and mission of the organization, and to organizational strategy and policy. Such issues may include environmental stewardship, legal compliance, community citizenship, human resources (HR) policy, quality and safety of outputs and operations, specific strategy and objective positions, and responsiveness to ownership (e.g., short- *and* long-term performance). It is not difficult to imagine the constituencies that would hold the organization accountable on these various issues. Organizations are expected by legal, business, and social constituencies to conform to norms of behavior and output. They are expected to be conscientious regarding their impact on the environment; their comportment as members of the community; their treatment of their employees; the nature, production, and application of their outputs; their future plans; and their handling of finances.

Monks and Minow (1991) observe that many organizations have replaced the goal of profitability with the goal of ensuring the status quo for their prerogatives, that they have replaced the "industrial purpose" with a myopic, short-term self-interest. They further suggest that these organizations will not be competitive against organizations with a larger purpose. They call for a means to make the organization accountable to some entity for the sake of the organization itself and of its ownership (i.e., stockholders), the business community, the public, and even the nation and the national economy.

Accountability for Leadership

The issues surrounding accountability for leadership are much the same as those just discussed, and some may argue that there is no distinction. We offer this separate category for convenience in discussion. Some of the additional issues this category includes are CEO compensation, culture, morale, management, and human resources practices, as well as the means by which all of the items in both this and the previous category are implemented. These are issues on which the organizational leadership, the management, may exert direct or indirect influence.

One example in this category concerns unionization. Unionization can be seen as a means to make management accountable. Historically, unions have emerged in response to perceptions of inadequate pay, inappropriate working conditions, and/or improper management policies and practices. Firms have been successful in resisting unionization when they have convinced workers that management could provide better conditions by dealing directly with the employees themselves, rather than through a union intermediary. Management's ability to make these assertions hinges on its ability to suggest that it is communicating honestly and will act in a manner consistent with the assertions. This in turn is consistent with the notion of management's being answerable for what it does. In other words, one may hold that firms would not be unionized if management were accountable to the workers and that avoiding unionization depends on management's ability to influence the workers to believe that it is accountable for its actions regarding the workers.

Accountability at the Subunit or Group Level

The use of team-based operations and empowerment programs is steadily increasing in all types of organizations. Such operations and programs emphasize accountability as relevant to the local unit or group. At this level, accountability issues include teamwork, quantity and quality of outputs, attendance, organizational control mechanisms (e.g., work rules and norms), justice systems, and individual and group development—issues related to daily operations and procedures. The issues are of the sort that surround interpersonal relationships and the interactions with organizational systems and technology. At this level the systems and policies are in place and generally accepted as given; thus the accountability issues involve how the subunit or group deals with those givens.

A notable example at this level concerns performance evaluations. Performance evaluation is usually designed to be as objective as possible so that an employee's performance can be assessed with accuracy. In spite of efforts to make the process objective, much of it is subjective and depends heavily on the way the evaluator feels about the employee, which can influence the ratings. As we will see in the following section, performance evaluation is an accountability mechanism for employee outputs at the individual level, but a system that helps the evaluator feel accountable for accurate evaluations may lead to increased accuracy if the associated accountability mechanisms are designed properly. The subunit or group can be held accountable for the evaluation system and its implementation because that system is an essential means for assessing and monitoring the group's outputs.

Accountability at the Individual Level

Individuals can be held accountable in organizations through many means, including both structural and normative means. Accountability issues at this level center chiefly on the ways the individual responds to the work environment, including the operational, social, and regulatory systems within the organization. Some issues at this level are organizational citizenship behaviors (i.e., behaviors that are not necessarily an explicit part of the employee's duties but that are desirable and functional for the organization, such as finding better ways to do the work or mentoring another employee), individual productivity, adherence to rules, effort and motivation, ethical behavior, and social interactions. All items at this level are explicitly concerned with employee behaviors, not with attitudes or thoughts.

An example of a situation where individual accountability may be at issue is when an employee performs an illegal act at the firm's place of business or while doing the work of the firm (e.g., driving carelessly). The illegal act in question may not be explicitly prohibited by organizational policy or rules. The way the firm requires accountability for such an act will have repercussions for other employees and the community beyond the immediate consequences for the misbehaving employee.

Accountability within the Individual

The previous category was concerned solely with employee behaviors. Accountability *within* the individual is different: The concern here is with the way the employee thinks about the workplace and related activities. Klimoski and Inks (1990) suggest that conditions of accountability affect not only what people think, but *how* they think as well. They hold that people's evaluative mental processes take into account the conditions of accountability and that people actually think differently when they are accountable for the outcomes of their thought processes (i.e., actions or decisions). Ultimately, an organization's best interests are served when desired behaviors are internalized, when they occur of the employee's own volition rather than because of external or organizational constraints. It is desirable that employees act in the best interest of the firm because they want to, not because the firm requires them to.

We have seen that accountability is relevant at each of several levels of analysis. It is important to keep these distinctions in mind when considering accountability in organizations. As we discuss accountability in the management of human resources, implications arise from the level of analysis that affect both the understanding of the issues and the means for dealing with them.

Accountability Issues for Human Resources Functions

To this point, we have discussed accountability in a general sense and only alluded to human resources functions. How does this concept of the likelihood of answerability manifest itself in human resources functions? First, we categorize some basic elements of human resources functions, and then we discuss how accountability plays out in these elements.

The systematic processing of human resources into, through, and out of organizations includes five basic functions. First, the selection function is intended to locate and place individuals whose knowledge, skills, and abilities match the needs of the organization.

Second, the performance evaluation function is designed to enhance organizational effectiveness by optimizing the organizationally relevant contributions of each individual. The promotion and succession functions have the dual objectives of facilitating career advancement for the employees and matching personnel needs and objectives within the firm. The fourth function concerns compensation policy and decisions, which can serve to attract, retain, motivate, and direct the efforts of an organization's members. The final human resources function, the outflow function, entails processing people out of the organization. Its purview includes retirement, layoffs, resignations, terminations, and deaths.

In the management of the human element in organizations, there is a need to reassess the use of a rational model. Where human resources are concerned, planners and managers cannot apply the simple methods of materials requisition, relying on standard suppliers with systematic warehousing and retrieval for use when needed. The social forces and interactions inherent in dealings with people (Ferris & Mitchell, 1987) require a different set of methods and rules. The people who constitute the organization's human element will not always have perspectives or agendas that are the same as, or even compatible with, those of the organization or its management. Because people perceive and process information individually, there is need for a way to bring these diverse individuals—as well as their perspectives and agendas—together to some common standard, preferably an ethical set. This necessity spawns a host of dilemmas that must be addressed in the staffing, evaluation, compensation, and outflow functions of human resources management.

Staffing

Judge and Ferris (1993) reviewed the staffing process from a perspective of organizational fit, which may be the perspective adopted by most organizations. Alternatively one may approach the staffing function, including internal mobility, from a rational perspective, using strictly job- and task-related criteria. In either case there must be some mechanisms that establish standards and support adherence to these standards before the decision criteria can be set forth effectively. Even if it were possible to minimize subjectivity in pursuit of a rational model, it seems unlikely that personal perceptions and biases could be addressed adequately if there were no way to hold the decision makers accountable for their decisions. Rynes and Boudreau (1986) found that college recruiters were not held accountable for their selection decisions. In the absence of some mechanism to ensure accountability, the selection process could become highly unconstrained because the decision maker would be unaccountable for the selection process, the selection decisions, or both. (An extreme example is Hollywood's notorious casting couch!)

In the selection process there are multiple sources of accountability, including organizational policy, supervisors of both the decision makers and the employees, industry standards, professional and certifying organizations, and the legal system. Arising from the legal system are three main sources of accountability: the body of corporate law and regulation, licensing and certifying agencies, and civil rights and fairness laws. Typically, these cast a very loose web of constraint on selection decisions, but that web may be tightening. Companies have been found liable for damages resulting from employees' illegal actions on the grounds that the employer should have known, through the selection process, the employees' propensities for such actions.

Because the staffing process is crucial in determining the makeup of an organization, it seems appropriate to scrutinize that process to enhance the effectiveness of staffing decisions for the organization. Accountability cannot be viewed as a universal solution for the problem of staffing decisions, however. Gordon, Rozelle, and Baxter (1988) found increased stereotyping among lab experiment subjects who felt accountable for staffing decisions.

Performance Evaluations

Performance evaluation comprises two fundamental elements: the definition of performance and the means of evaluating performance as defined. Accountability provides a means of linking these two elements as well as a basis for approaching them. Accountability for conduct is a universally accepted norm (Tetlock, 1992); it provides the basis for social structure as individuals are seen as agents of their own actions (Cummings & Anton, 1990; Inzerelli & Rosen, 1983) and therefore subject to evaluation for behavior. Thus, performance evaluation is an accountability mechanism intended basically as a means of organizational control (Eisenhardt, 1985; Ouchi & Maguire, 1975). So, for the ratee, performance evaluation both is based on and helps define performance; it also provides information about how well standards are being met. The closeness of the linkages between the evaluations and their outcomes determines the influence of accountability mechanisms within the evaluation system upon the behavior of the ratees (Cummings & Anton, 1990).

This defining process also forms a psychological contract between the ratee and the organization that becomes part of the basis for the employee's perceptions of organizational justice (Cummings & Anton, 1990). The rater, as a representative of the organization, as well as the organization itself as a social and legal entity, is responsible for fair evaluations, based on appropriate and useful performance criteria, and for the tightness of the linkage between the evaluation and any resulting outcomes. Therefore, it is appropriate to establish accountability mechanisms for the organization's performance evaluation system and methods.

The dual nature of organizational control and responsibility is exemplified in the area of performance monitoring. In a highly computerized environment, it is possible to monitor employees unobtrusively via their use of the computer network. It is relatively simple in this type of environment to impose very stringent behavioral controls and very tight evaluation-outcome linkages. However, this practice may negatively influence perceptions of justice and fairness within the organization, and it raises a series of ethical questions.

Accountability mechanisms seem even more important in light of the potentially ambiguous and political nature of performance evaluations (Ferris & Judge, 1991). Two potentially biasing conditions in the performance evaluation process are subjectivity and affectivity. Subjectivity permits individual rater discretion, and affectivity may mediate the evaluation decisions. Accountability mechanisms may counteract the biasing effects of these conditions by clarifying standards and evaluating the rater according to those standards. Two ways to hold the rater accountable are to include the rating process in the rater's own performance evaluation and to provide a feedback system to the ratee. Klimoski and Inks (1990) found raters modifying their ratings in the directions of the ratees' expected ratings. They suggested, however, that ratings may be distorted when face-to-face feedback is expected. They further proposed that ratings may be distorted in two different ways: by amount and by direction. Such modifications of ratings may actually be useful in that (1) raters' individual biases against certain types or persons may be reduced and (2) a restriction of range in ratings may result in a reduction in nontask considerations and, hence, greater validity. Of course, biases that are random, not monitored, or misunderstood could hardly be useful or appropriate. This particular point has two implications: We need to know much more about these issues, and accountability mechanisms need to be carefully selected and implemented to match the purpose and method of the evaluation system. For example, Martell and Borg (1993) found a restriction of range in ratings when a panel of evaluators conducted the ratings. Questions remain regarding the accuracy and validity of the restricted-range evaluations and their usefulness in the particular organizational context.

A third way to make raters and organizations accountable for performance evaluations is to ensure tight linkages between evaluations and any ensuing outcomes. If goals are set, do the participants follow up on them? How tightly are evaluations linked to compensation? Are promotion recommendations or other incentives realized?

Compensation

Perhaps no area of accountability in human resources management has received more press than CEO compensation. Crystal (1991) and Gomez-Mejia and Balkin (1992) suggest that the CEO compensation system is a prime example of what can happen when there are no constraints other than token self-justification to a board or committee, which has a vested interest in justifying the salary structure rather than monitoring it because the members are likely CEOs themselves. In a common method for establishing CEO salaries, the CEO hires a salary consultant, who makes a market-based recommendation to the CEO, who includes the recommendation in a report to the board of directors. The common rationale for the level of salary is that the firm, to be competitive, must have the very best leadership, and if the recommended (and inflated) salary is not paid, the CEO will leave for a better offer. Note that this rationale is very clearly separated from any performance or other measurable criteria. If the firm is doing poorly, it needs a "savior" and must pay a premium for that savior. If the firm is doing well, it needs to pay a premium in order to (1) reward the leader, (2) maintain the high image consonant with success, and (3) ensure continued success. Monks and Minow (1991) recommend that stockholder groups become active in the calling of both the CEOs and the corporate system to account for what some see as excessive and detrimental compensation practices.

Movements toward accountability are discernible in other aspects of compensation, as well. One such trend is, as mentioned earlier, a clear linkage between the performance evaluation and compensation systems. This linkage has the potential to impose accountability

for compensation decisions on individuals. Another trend is the increased emphasis on linking compensation systems to strategic organizational objectives. This linkage has the potential to impose accountability for the entire compensation system on the compensation policy decision makers. Underlying the notion of strategy-compensation accountability linkages is the concept of responsibility for firm performance.

Compensation analysis often focuses on either market forces or perceptions of equity from a general policy perspective. It sometimes identifies individual performance levels or specifies a particular level within a range that is set by the general policies. Increasingly, we see attempts to incorporate team or group concepts into the process. Seldom, however, do we find any constituency willing to assume responsibility for firm performance. Generally, this level of accountability is reserved for coaches of athletic teams and independent business people and entrepreneurs. The highest levels of compensation accountability would include linkages between performance and compensation. We cannot assume, however, that such practices are universally beneficial. As seen in both earlier and subsequent sections of this article, accountability can potentially have adverse effects.

Outflows

In the context of outflows, three general areas seem especially relevant to discussions of accountability: (1) the reasons or purposes behind outflow decisions, (2) the sources of those decisions, and (3) ethical and civic responsibility for outflow decisions and policies. There are three general types of outflows—resignations, layoffs, and terminations—which are in turn relevant to the purposes of outflow decisions.

Voluntary turnover (i.e., resignations) is often examined in the context of job satisfaction. Though accountability in this context seems useful, it would imply exit interviews to determine the reasons for resignations, and such interviews are not often feasible. Otherwise, supervisors can be held accountable for turnover if, in fact, this turnover may be indicative of managerial performance.

As organizations downsize, and as they monitor the performance of their employees, they frequently find it necessary to sever the employment relationship with particular individuals. The manner in which those decisions are made and the extent to which decision makers are held accountable represent a critical area of concern. These issues are examined in greater detail in the article by Ferris, Howard, and Bergin, which appears later in this book.

Status of Accountability in Organizations and Calls for Change

U.S. businesses continually receive calls to be accountable from various quarters, as discussed earlier. These calls are in response to perceptions of the status of business and its dealings with the environment in which it operates. Examples of the major areas of concern include CEO salaries, business policy, environmental stewardship, and internal affairs. We will discuss these examples in the context of the larger question of the status of accountability in organizations.

Salaries for CEOs of major corporations are spiraling, currently rising at an average of about 70 times the income of the average worker. Executives in the United States are the highest paid globally, while U.S. firms are losing ground in terms of profits and market share. In 1991, for example, profits slipped 21 percent while CEO compensation increased 5 to 10 percent. Perhaps the issue here is not the dollar value of these salaries but the unchecked power sought and wielded by these CEOs. A condition exists in which executives rigidly resist efforts to curb their discretion in establishing their own compensation packages, as such curbs represent an encroachment not only on their personal finances but on the prerogatives they enjoy in their positions. This condition has its roots in the independence and individualism inherent in American culture, but it is permitted—and even perhaps exacerbated—by the absence of accountability at the top.

As discussed earlier, the relationship between management and labor is an area where accountability proves to be an important issue. Historically, the prevailing paradigm was the old master-servant relationship, where the employer "owned" the employee for the amount of time for which that employee was paid. Although feelings of "belonging" to an organization are potentially useful to both parties, viewing employees as a commodity that management can purchase and discard without taking account of the differences between human resources and other resources is dysfunctional in general. One suggested reason for this dysfunctional view is the adoption of a short-term perspective regarding both the human resources and the indicators of success, such as profits. The Competitiveness Policy Council chastised U.S. business in general for its short-term emphasis, stating that "the first, and perhaps most fundamental, problem is America's proclivity to think and act with a short-term horizon." Although almost anyone would agree that a short-term view is myopic and ultimately damaging to an organization's future well-being, nevertheless the short-term perspective dominates American business decisions.

One suggested reason for this condition, as well as a prescription for addressing it, is related to the mechanisms of accountability under which the decision makers operate. Historically, management has been evaluated on quarterly performance by the requirements and publications of federal agencies, such as the Securities and Exchange Commission (SEC), and media such as financial publications. To receive evaluations that please investors, management is enticed to act according to short-term interests. These short-term pressures, as well as individuals' own tendencies to consider immediate results, tend to produce similar short-term approaches to dealing with human resources policy. As argued earlier, one of the fundamental objectives of the union movement has been to impose an accountability system regarding the organization's human resources. Additionally, Title VII of the Civil Rights Act, the Age Discrimination in Employment Act, and the Americans with Disabilities Act serve as examples of government efforts to impose accountability for employment practices in response to a lack of sclf-monitoring. Because businesses did not accept the society and the community as entities to which they were accountable, mechanisms were imposed via regulatory agencies to affect organizational policy regarding human resources.

Since the 1970s firms have been cited for environmental abuses, and the issue persists. Environmental activists claim, for example, that timber cutters are devastating timber resources in the Northwest beyond repair, indicating that the loggers are unaccountable to any viable entity with environmental interests. The timber producers, on the other hand, claim that they are planting more trees than they are harvesting and that the forests replacing those harvested are more productive and healthier; they imply that activist groups aiming to shut down logging operations are unaccountable for actions that not only hamper operations but may prove dangerous for the harvesting crews as well. Another controversial area is water resources: Despite dramatic efforts to restore and clean up some waterways, many are said to be still polluted and even dangerous for local residents. A chemical firm in Northwest Florida has repeatedly been accused by some local residents of polluting a stream used for discharge of waste water, a charge that the firm consistently denies. Local agencies were unable to find conclusive evidence that the plant was the sole culprit, and the plant found itself essentially unaccountable for waste water discharge. Even where organizations can be held accountable through the legal or regulatory system, the legendary sluggishness of bureaucracy has the effect of leaving them largely unaccountable, especially in the short term, for much of what may be questionable practice.

The increasing competitiveness of the global market provides major challenges for businesses accustomed to dominating their markets, and adjustments can be difficult but they are necessary. As firms make judgments and plans to deal with changing conditions, some efforts fail whereas others succeed. When a firm fails to make adjustments, it is usually the firm's financiers, especially its stockholders, who stand to lose the most. General Motors has seen its market share and profitability decline steadily over the past 20 years. In response to massive losses and lack of accountability at the top, the board of directors imposed dramatic changes in 1991. Two top executives were demoted, and CEO Stempel lost his position as chair of the board's executive committee while retaining his CEO status. Essentially, the change was designed to send a signal that the directors were holding top management accountable for performance as well as instituting a system whereby accountability for performance was expected of top executives.

Robert Monks and Nell Minow (1991), in *Power and Accountability,* suggest that the way to restore the corporate system to its originally intended design is to revive management accountability. These authors define accountability as political legitimacy. They maintain that this country's corporate structure should work exquisitely but that it does not because of the failure of accountability mechanisms. In their view the powerful must be accountable to those affected by that power. A problem arises because the corporate structure is splintered into a multitude of specialties, so that communication is incomplete and thus continuity in accountability does not exist. The fundamental issue here is the proper use of private power. Individuals in a corporate context have the opportunity to develop private power in that social context. The way an individual applies this power to his or her agenda, then, is a factor in the way accountability mechanisms will be called for by some constituency. Monks and Minow further suggest that the key to an organization's success as a form, or type of entity, lies in its "internal dynamic of accountability" (p. 7).

According to Michael Jacobs (1991), the major problem is the fact that the providers of capital (shareholders and lenders) are only distantly related to the users of capital (corporate managers). He claims that the relationship between the two is characterized by distrust and antagonism and is dysfunctional for the organization. Solutions to this problem must involve all parties because all are participants in the situation and contributors to its causes, and all may be well served by mechanisms of viable accountability, where the parties sense the likelihood that they will be held accountable for both policy and outcomes.

In one effort to impose accountability on business management, the SEC approved a rule permitting nonbinding, advisory votes on compensation plans. The commission further mandated that firms clear up the confusion regarding the structure of these often complex and difficult plans. This is one example of an increase in the government's willingness to join in responding to calls for accountability.

Increasing Accountability

So far we have made it sound as if being held accountable is a universally good thing: If we simply tell people what constitutes desired behavior and put in place appropriate monitoring devices with appropriate rewards and punishments, functional organizational behavior is sure to follow. Obviously, it is not that simple. People have conflicting interests, goals, and personal characteristics, and any one accountability system cannot elicit appropriate behavior from all people in all situations. Nor is the development of an accountability system necessarily straightforward.

It is not difficult to see that accountability mechanisms in any system (informal, organizational, social, and so forth) will likely meet with some resistance, both in implementation and in operation. After all, it is rare for individuals or groups to submit willingly to increased constraints upon the discretion they

enjoy. In this section we discuss this issue from three perspectives: structural implications for increased accountability, potential for resistance, and some basic application principles.

Structural Implications for Increased Accountability

The structural implications for accountability in organizations include issues arising from three areas: the means by which accountability mechanisms are supported or enforced (organizational reward systems and justice systems), assessment mechanisms (performance evaluation systems), and organizational contingencies (organizational structure).

Motivation theories propose that people are motivated to choose one course of action over another for the purpose of achieving desirable outcomes and avoiding undesirable outcomes. The ability of an accountability system to influence behavior is contingent on the perceived positive or negative impact of compliance or noncompliance. The difference between accountability systems and motivation systems is that accountability is broader and more abstract: Though accountability includes motivational implications, it is directly concerned not with motivating employees but with establishing a system of potential constraints on behavior through the requirement of answerability that should result in organizationally preferred behaviors. In principle, however, there is substantial overlap in the implications for design and implementation.

If a group of bank managers are rewarded for the number of accounts they have on the books, it is likely that they will find as many ways as possible to add to the list as well as to prevent deletions. This could result in practices such as keeping the accounts of deceased patrons on the list. Although this practice would result in a greater number of accounts on the books, it would probably not be an organizationally desired outcome: It would require extra work that did not generate income, and the objectives of the policy would not be served. Accountability systems and the accompanying reward and justice systems must be carefully thought out, and possibly even installed on a trial basis, for assurance that the mechanisms elicit the desired behavior and not an undesirable alternative.

This leads to another type of structural consideration: the evaluation mechanisms that provide the basis for holding people accountable for some type or standard of behavior. It is clearly desirable that the individual be assessed as accurately as possible if there are rewards and sanctions associated with accountability. One way to achieve accurate assessments is to use multiple sources of information, such as supervisors, peers, self, subordinates, and clientele. This multidimensional approach will improve accuracy in most cases. Another potential way to enhance the usefulness of accountability systems is to evaluate outcomes as well as behaviors. There are advantages to each approach. Evaluation of behavior helps address the criterion problem, yet it is not always satisfactory in supporting desired outcomes. Results-oriented evaluation tends to be less detailed, yet it is often less valid as a means of assessing an individual's contributions. Results-oriented evaluation eliminates alternative means of fulfilling obligations, as in the example concerning the bankers. Had the system incorporated a measure of the desired outcomes of the number of accounts, the practice of retaining accounts of deceased customers would have been counterproductive for the manager. A potential outcome from performance-based, or results-based, evaluations is an alternative type of job security. Labor organizations typically pursue job security as a primary objective. The concessions management may make on this issue may be very costly, with the job becoming an entitlement regardless of the individual's contributions. An alternative under an accountability system using a performance criterion is performance-based job security ("As long as you perform, you will have a job").

A third area of structural implications concerns the type of work engaged in and the technology used. Increasingly, firms are implementing team-based and "empowerment" initiatives. If the focus is on lifting tight individual-level controls in favor of group-level controls, how should the organization adjust accountability mechanisms (performance evaluations, reporting structures, discipline systems, quality control, goal-setting and management systems, etc.) to maintain accountability at the individual level while pursuing teamwork or autonomy? The previous comments regarding performance evaluations are relevant here as well. Performance-based evaluations permit integration of team outputs with individual evaluations and also allow evaluation of individuals' autonomous contributions without violating that autonomy via close behavioral monitoring or control. The use of multiple levels of goal setting may also promote accountability in these environments. If the firm uses MBO or some other goal-setting system, goals can be established for multiple levels of the organization; this method provides a means of accountability for actions and decisions that not only make the individual look good but have organizational benefits as well. Goal-setting systems provide for a unique type of accountability in that the objectives can be tailored explicitly to provide for the development of the individual as well as the organization, and a built-in follow-up, or accountability, mechanism allows measurement of performance against the standards set by the goals. This measurement against standards also provides a way to link compensation or incentives to performance.

Potential for Resistance to Accountability Systems

As mentioned earlier, people tend to resist encroachment on the areas in which they have discretion. It may also be argued that people generally attempt to enlarge the spheres in which they have discretion or autonomy. The feeling that one may be held accountable for actions or decisions limits one's perceived discretion. Further, people often tend to attempt to reduce uncertainty in their surroundings or environments, and one means to do this is to secure entitlements or claim rights. The most resistance to accountability mechanisms is likely to arise in those latter situations—specifically, situations involving entitlement, autonomy, or ambiguity. Examples of such environments include educational institutions, research and development departments, and entitlement positions, which are characterized by either unclear relationships between efforts and outcomes or weak linkages between outputs and rewards or sanctions. To impose accountability in these situations, management needs to pay special attention to ascertaining the appropriate means-ends relationships to include and deciding how to measure and standardize them. Alternatively, accountability mechanisms can reduce ambiguity if standards are clear and consistently applied. In such instances, the relationships between one's efforts and the outcomes from those efforts are clarified, and evaluation criteria are explicit or well understood; uncertainty is thus eliminated. The potential for alternative outcomes indicates that accountability systems are necessarily complex and must be considered as such. The following section discusses practical considerations in the implementation of accountability systems.

Basic Application Principles

The concept of accountability juxtaposes two very different types of organizational environments. One is rather loose and characterized by trust, flexibility, and autonomy. At the other extreme is an environment characterized by monitoring, verification, and accountability—a tightly controlled organization. Because either extreme is unlikely to be optimal, the best accountability systems should seek a balance between these two organizational paradigms. As President Ronald Reagan stated concerning the relationship between the United States and the former Soviet Union, "Trust, but verify." The balance point or area will not necessarily be similar from one situation to the next, but elements from both perspectives are useful.

A second consideration in the implementation of accountability systems concerns the fact that organizations are extremely complex, with oft-competing objectives. For that reason, all aspects of both organizational and normative reward systems should be analyzed to ensure commonality of purpose and reinforcement of appropriate means-end relationships. As in the banking example presented earlier, the organizational goals may differ from the individual goals, and a successful accountability system must recognize and address those differences.

People are information seekers, and often the information they seek concerns their performance in relation to some standard. Thus, feedback can be highly motivating. Incorporation of feedback mechanisms is an essential aspect of human resources development and an important consideration in the implementation of accountability systems.

Conclusion

Where Does the Buck Stop?

The United States spent $1.5 billion on the Hubble Space Telescope in eager anticipation of unlocking more secrets of the universe. The disappointment was global when it was discovered that the telescope could not work to standard because the 8-foot main mirror was made wrong and could not focus as well as hoped. How could this $350 million part, the heart of the telescope, be wrong? How was it possible for an error of that magnitude to slip through the host of engineers and craftspeople building the mirror, as well as the project administrators at NASA? This situation can be cast in terms of failed accountability mechanisms. The following discussion is based on the observations of Capers and Lipton (1993), who offer insights into the failure of the mirror project to meet standards.

First, the contractor, under intense competitive pressure and in response to information from NASA, "low-balled" the price, expecting additional funds to be available later. This put intense financial strain on the entire project, and individuals in different parts of the organization had competing accountabilities—that is, to the mirror quality and to the bottom line. In addition, intense time pressures for completion exacerbated the division of loyalties regarding accountability. The initial information from NASA had implied that additional funding would be available for unforeseen technological difficulties, but the agency later backed away from this commitment, and no agency personnel were accountable for the inferences that more money would be forthcoming.

The time and money pressures mounted as the project continued, and management's concerns were with these issues; thus, normal scientific rigor was de-emphasized in favor of management's concerns, another accountability failure. Accountability for the quality of the product was replaced with accountability for the schedule, and quality measures were overlooked.

In the midst of this confusion, people were contending with a shift in management style at the contracting firm. The firm had shifted to a matrix-type structure. Each worker had two or more bosses, the department supervisor and the project supervisor, and this type of dual accountability can have offsetting effects.

NASA had accountability problems as well. On the heels of the Challenger disaster, the agency was desperate to reestablish its credibility and viability. In the process, it seems that the emphasis may have shifted from substance to form, and the mirror was in the middle. The quality engineer sent by NASA to oversee the project was explicitly told to ignore mirror quality and focus on safety issues because another group was to handle the quality issues. Unfortunately, no one else was told to oversee quality. In fact, there were only three NASA engineers on site at the plant, as opposed to the twenty involved with the building of the Saturn V booster rockets some years earlier. It is notable that of the thousands of parts in the telescope, the mirror is the only one that has no NASA official's signature for quality; when later asked to sign off for quality, the NASA engineer refused.

The NASA headquarters at the Marshall Space Flight Center were headed by an individual who had a notorious dislike for bad news and so was given little; the same problem was criticized during the Challenger investigation. This circumstance highlights the fact that accountability can be normative, occurring in the context of social or informal systems, as well as structural, occurring in the context of the organization's formal systems. Stein and Kanter (1993) sum up their analysis of the situation by stating that "the culprit becomes a system under such pressure to perform that mistakes are encouraged, constructive actions undercut, and information withheld" (p. 59).

Who Are You Singing To?

This is the central issue in discussions of accountability systems. As discussed earlier, people process information differently, depending on the way they view accountability for their decisions or actions. In the Hubble example, there were multiple constituencies to which the players in the drama felt accountable. Unfortunately, they all overshadowed the most important audiences: the taxpayers, the scientific community, and themselves. The other issue of note in that example is that, even if you feel accountable to the right audience, what you feel accountable for is just as important in terms of end results. The issue of accountability permeates organizational, as well as social, concerns and is becoming seen as a critical element in the design and implementation of organizational systems, especially human resources systems.

References

Capers, R. A., & Lipton, E. (1993). Hubble error: Time, money, and millionths of an inch. *Academy of Management Executive, 7,* 41–57.

Crystal, G. S. (1991). *In search of excess: The overcompensation of American executives.* New York: Norton.

Cummings, L. L., & Anton, R. J. (1990). The logical and appreciative dimensions of accountability. In

S. Sivastva, D. Cooperrider, & Associates (Eds.), *Appreciative management and leadership* (pp. 257–286). San Francisco: Jossey-Bass.

Eisenhardt, K. M. (1985). Control: Organizational and economic approaches. *Management Science, 31,* 134–149.

Ferris, G. R., & Judge, T. A. (1991). Personnel/ human resources management: A political influence perspective. *Journal of Management, 17,* 447–488.

Ferris, G. R., & Mitchell, T. R. (1987). The components of social influence and their importance for human resources research. In K. M. Rowland & G. R. Ferris (Eds.), *Research in personnel and human resources management* (Vol. 5, pp. 103–128). Greenwich, CT: JAI Press.

Gomez-Mejia, L. R., & Balkin, D. B. (1992). *Compensation, organizational strategy, and firm performance.* Cincinnati, OH: South-Western.

Gordon, R. A., Rozelle, R. M., & Baxter, J. C. (1988). The effect of applicant age, job level and accountability on the evaluation of job applicants. *Organizational Behavior and Human Decision Processes, 41,* 20–33.

Inzerelli, G., & Rosen, M. (1983). Culture and organizational control. *Journal of Business Research, 11,* 281–292.

Jacobs, M. (1991). *Short-term America: The causes and cures of our business myopia.* Boston: Harvard Business School Press.

Judge, T. A., & Ferris, G. R. (1993). The elusive criterion of fit in human resources staffing decisions. *Human Resource Planning, 15,* 47–67.

Klimoski, R., & Inks, L. (1990). Accountability forces in performance appraisal. *Organizational Behavior and Human Decision Processes, 45,* 194–208.

Martell, R. F., & Borg, M. R. (1993). A comparison of the behavioral rating accuracy of groups and individuals. *Journal of Applied Psychology, 78,* 43–50.

Monks, R. A. G., & Minow, N. (1991). *Power and accountability.* New York: HarperCollins.

Ouchi, W. G., & Maguire, M. A. (1975). Organizational control: Two functions. *Administrative Science Quarterly, 20,* 559–569.

Rynes, S., & Boudreau, J. (1986). College recruiting in large organizations: Practice, evaluation, and research implications. *Personnel Psychology, 39,* 729–757.

Stein, B. A., & Kanter, R. M. (1993). Why good people do bad things: A retrospective on the Hubble fiasco. *Academy of Management Executive, 7(4),* 58–62.

Tetlock, P. E. (1992). The impact of accountability on judgment and choice: Toward a social contingency model. In M. P. Zanna (Ed.), *Advances in experimental social psychology* (Vol. 25, pp. 331–377). New York: Academic Press.

Chief Executive Officer Accountability and Compensation Concerns: Perceptions, Problems, and Proposals

E. Brian Peach

Introduction

As far back as the 1930s, Franklin D. Roosevelt publicly condemned the high salaries of chief executive officers (CEOs) and their "entrenched greed" (Brownstein & Panner, 1992), and the topic of CEO compensation has been an occasional media target ever since. However, beginning in the 1980s, and as we move through the 1990s, increasing media attention to CEO pay has steadily increased. Respected business periodicals such as *Fortune* and *Business Week* regularly rake CEOs across the hot coals of public opinion. *Fortune* magazine referred to CEO pay as "madness" (Loomis, 1982). In its 1992 annual review of executive pay, *Business Week* referred to CEO pay as an "excessive free-for-all, divorced from reality of corporate results" (Byrne, 1992, p. 52) and on the cover asked in large print, "Are CEOs paid too much?" The question seems especially valid as the once stratospheric sum of $10 million in annual compensation is now regularly achieved by a number of CEOs, and two CEOs have exceeded $100 million in a single year (Byrne, 1993).

In his book on executive pay, however, Ira Kay (1992) contends that much of the criticism of CEO pay is unfounded, as the average top CEO makes less than the average top entertainer or sports figure, and in constant dollars CEOs made less in the 1980s than they did in the 1930s. Other writers also defend the pay of CEOs (Brownstein & Panner, 1992; Murphy, 1986).

Certainly, CEO compensation is a complex issue with so many factors affecting it that a simplistic analysis will lead to incorrect conclusions (Deckop, 1987). Yet it seems useful to focus on the key question: Are CEOs worth their pay? To answer this question we will start with the somewhat emotional issue of how high CEO compensation is actually becoming. Next, we will look at a number of compensation theories underlying the establishment of CEO pay programs and follow with discussions of some theoretical and practical problems with establishing and administering CEO compensation. After reviewing research findings concerning CEO pay, we will conclude with suggestions for improving the ways CEOs are paid.

CEO Pay—How High Can It Go?

Comparative Rates of CEO Compensation Growth

In 1977 a McKinsey Consulting partner complained that executive pay had logged the largest single increase (14.3 percent) in McKinsey survey history and that it was time for a fundamental reexamination of executive compensation (McLaughlin, 1977). Such an increase is small potatoes today. In the 1980s CEO pay increased 212 percent, an average of 21 percent per year. The next highest job category increase was for teachers, who saw a 95 percent increase as school boards tried to make teachers' historically low pay more competitive. Engineers received a 73 percent raise over the decade, and factory workers trailed with 53 percent. In comparison, the Standard and Poor 500 stocks average increased 78 percent (Byrne, 1991). But it doesn't stop there.

With Clinton's election in 1992 and the threat of higher income taxes, CEOs cashed in their accumulated stock options, and average CEO pay jumped 56 percent in one year. Even in 1990, when corporate profits fell 7 percent, average CEO salary and bonus climbed 3.5 percent, and average total compensation increased 7 percent. Generally in the United States, CEO pay increases were comparable to those for other jobs from 1960 to 1980, but since 1980 CEO pay has increased more rapidly than inflation, corporate profits, corporate value, and all other workers' pay.

Relative Size of CEO Compensation

Two millennia ago Plato felt that the highest-paid worker should receive no more than 5 times the wage of the lowest-paid worker. More recently, management guru Peter Drucker commented that the top pay in an organization should be no more than 20 times the lowest pay. At the beginning of the 1980s, however, CEO pay was 42 times that of the lowest worker. By 1990 it was 85 times the lowest worker's pay, and the top tax rate had been reduced from 70 percent to 33 percent (Byrne, 1991). By 1992 it had jumped to 157 times the pay for the lowest worker, 5 times the pay for Japan's CEOs, who received 32 times the lowest Japanese worker's wage (Byrne, 1993).

Total Amounts of CEO Compensation

Tracking total compensation can be a little complicated as cash compensation consists of three components: salary, bonus, and long-term incentives. Long-term incentives can accrue over a period of time and be cashed in a single year. Steven J. Ross of Time Warner received a total of $280 million over 17 years, but $78 million of it came in 1990. Some critics say such high numbers are anomalies—not representative of true CEO pay. So we will start by looking at average CEO pay before returning to examine just how high CEO pay can go.

According to *Business Week*'s annual executive survey data, in 1960 the average CEO received $190,383. In 1970 CEO pay was over $300,000, by 1980 it was about $625,000, and in 1990 the average CEO pay was almost $2,000,000. In 1991, a year when corporate profits fell 18 percent, CEO salary and bonus dropped, but average total compensation increased 26 percent to almost $2,500,000. To avoid higher taxes in later years, in 1992 CEOs cashed in accumulated long-term options, pushing average total compensation to $3,842,247, and the top twenty CEOs all made over $22 million each (Byrne, 1993).

Four million dollars may seem impressive, but it pales in comparison with the earnings of the top achievers. Michael Eisner of Walt Disney raised eyebrows in 1988 when he netted over $40 million, but his salary and bonus (he cashed no options) were still $11 million in 1990. Also in 1990, Steven J. Ross of Time Warner received over $78 million, and Donald Pels of LIN Broadcasting received over $186 million when his company merged with McCaw Communications. Anthony O'Reilly of Heinz received over $75 million in 1991 and followed it with almost $37 million in 1992 for a 2-year total of $112 million. Leon Hirsch's $62 million in 1992 placed him fourth in total compensation, behind Charles Lazarus of Toys 'R' Us with $64 million, Sanford Weill of Primerica with $67 million, and Thomas Frisch of Hospital Corporation of America with a staggering $127 million. The 1993 leader appears to be Michael Eisner with $197 million. Where does it stop? Roberto Goizueta of Coca Cola had 1992 pay of over $15 million and 1990–1992 total compensation of over $100 million; he reportedly has stock options worth almost $400 million. What can justify a half billion dollars in compensation to a single CEO? To answer that, we will look at the rationales for CEO pay.

Paying CEOs—Rationales and Rhetoric

The free market relies on economic theory, and one of the tenets of economic theory is that the compensation of the CEO should be related to the performance of the organization (Conlon & Parks, 1990). We will look at a number of psychological, behavioral, and economic theories that support linking compensation to performance. We will also look briefly at other rationales that are used or proposed for compensating CEOs.

Expectancy Theory

Expectancy theory as a basis for work motivation was developed by Victor Vroom (1964). The theory argues that motivation for an individual to complete an act is based on the belief that performance will lead to a valued reward. Thus, if we want CEOs to increase organizational performance, we should base their compensation on organizational performance. A logical extension of this notion is that, for greater performance, we should provide greater incentives.

Equity Theory

Equity theory involves a social comparison of our inputs and outputs to those of some other individual (Adams, 1963, 1976). The comparison can be with others in similar or dissimilar jobs within and outside the organization, with the pay system structure, or with the self as perceived (Goodman, 1974). To be viewed as fair (equitable), rewards for effort in a social exchange should be distributed according to the level of individual contribution. Thus, higher levels of effort and organizational success should be rewarded with higher levels of compensation.

Agency Theory

Agency theory is currently the dominant economic control perspective (Eisenhardt, 1989). An agent is a manager without a significant equity position in a firm. Agency theory assumes that managers (agents) are utility maximizers who likely have different objectives than outside investors (principals) and who therefore are likely to make decisions inconsistent with their principals' wishes in order to maximize their personal utility or wealth (Jensen & Meckling, 1976). Historically, principals were in direct control of their organizations and could monitor their agents' ac-

tivities. As principals changed from owner-entrepreneurs to minority shareholders to absentee shareholders, direct monitoring became costly or impractical. In such situations, to ensure alignment between the objectives of principals and the behavior of agents, agency theory states that performance incentives for agents should be based on their achieving the principals' objectives.

Human Capital

In addition to incentives, a number of other rationales for paying CEOs have been advanced. Human capital theory (Becker, 1964) addresses differences between managers based on such variables as work experience, education, and job tenure. The logic here is that as jobs become more complex and demanding, CEOs must make greater personal investments in job-related skills and experience, and firms must pay more to attract qualified CEOs.

Corporate Size and Hierarchy

A number of reasons have been suggested to justify increases in pay related to organizational size. Research has found that organizations attribute different degrees of worth to different positions on the basis of organizational level, independent of the characteristics of those positions (Mahoney, 1979). Assuming that there are limitations on an individual's span of control, as the number of employees in an organization grows, the number of levels in the hierarchy would increase. Because typical expectations are for a 30 percent raise in pay with each level (Mahoney & Weitzel, 1978), increased hierarchical levels can lead to rapid increases in pay at the top.

Other suggested reasons include the increased ability to pay and the increased complexity that comes with size. A stronger argument concerns the effects on a CEO's marginal revenue product as resources controlled by the CEO increase. If a CEO is paid on marginal contribution to the firm, manipulation of larger resource bases will lead to larger marginal revenue products from the CEO and thus justify higher compensation levels (Finkelstein & Hambrick, 1988).

Tournament Theory

According to tournament theory, executive promotions can be equated with lotteries or tournaments. Winners at each level are allowed to advance to the next, with CEO representing the grand prize. In this context, contestants will be willing to forgo some compensation to remain in the contest (O'Reilly, Main, & Crystal, 1988). This theory would help to explain why there are such large differences between the pay of CEOs and of their immediate subordinates. Additionally, as the number of levels (tournaments) increases, and the difficulty of each tournament increases, the pay at the top must be correspondingly larger.

Summary

Each of these theories supports higher pay for CEOs under conditions of increased CEO performance or increased demands placed on the CEO. Whether the purpose is to stimulate the necessary action (expectancy), maintain a sense of fairness (equity), ensure that performance matches ownership interests (agency), reward preparation effort (human capital), or reward increased contribution (marginal revenue), each of these theories assumes that higher pay is somehow related to measurable differences in organizational performance. The question of how much a CEO is worth, then, becomes two questions: How much difference *can* CEOs make? and finally, How much difference *do* they make? We'll look next at the problems affecting whether CEOs can make a difference and then review research on how much difference CEOs do make.

Theoretical Problems with CEO Pay

Money as a Valued Reward

The application of the expectancy, equity, or agency theory assumes that money is a desired reward and that increasing the amount of the reward increases its attractiveness. We will look later at whether there is actual research support for a link between incentives and performance. The point here is that writers have challenged the concept of money as an incentive (Herzberg, 1968) or contended that money actually lowers motivation (Deci, 1972).

One argument is that incentives, as extrinsic motivators, do not change attitudes or behavior, and the more open-ended and cognitive the required behavior (i.e., CEO behavior), the worse people perform. Thus, incentive-based plans are inherently flawed and cannot work (Kohn, 1993). Another contention is that large rewards have a reverse-incentive effect: The larger the reward, the more likely it is that the task will be viewed as difficult, risky, tedious, or unpleasant (Freedman, Cunningham, & Krismer, 1992).

Incentives and Organizational Theory

A further criticism is that reliance on incentives violates principles of organizational theory and is inappropriate under conditions of uncertainty, interdependence, and complexity (Pearce, 1987). In an environment of uncertainty, providing a CEO with a set of specified performance measures restricts the CEO's ability to respond in a flexible manner. The reciprocal nature of interdependence (Thompson, 1967) among the CEO, subordinates, and the board of directors makes it difficult to fix responsibility or blame for organizational outcomes. Williamson (1975) contended that organizations exist because they are more efficient and transaction costs are lower in organizations than in the marketplace. Individual incentives inject the marketplace back into the organization, adding to complexity and reducing efficiency.

Incentives and Adverse Side Effects

Others levy the criticism that incentives work but that they have adverse side effects (Baker, Jensen, & Murphy, 1988). For example, incentives differentiate workers on the basis of performance, and failing to achieve objectives results in low CEO morale and reduced productivity.

Evidence Supporting Incentives

On the positive side, considerable evidence exists that pay is important relative to other extrinsic or intrinsic rewards and that it has the power to influence people's performance (Beer, Spector, Lawrence, Mills, & Walton, 1984). Although people in general are motivated by many things and pay is not equally important to everyone, those who have elected to be in the business world are likely to be motivated by money (Crystal, 1978; Ellig, 1982). In fact, the problem may not be that incentives are ineffective but rather that they are too effective. Because it is difficult to specify all outcomes, misspecification of outcomes can lead to gaming by CEOs who, in their zeal to maximize their personal rewards, optimize the specified performance measures rather than accomplishing activities leading to what they know to be the desired performance. Thus, the problem is not with incentives in theory but with incentives in practice—which we will cover next.

Practical Problems with CEO Pay

Despite general acceptance of the theoretical potential of incentives, the magnitude and nature of CEO compensation, as discussed earlier, have led to widespread concern that CEO pay is out of control (Baker, 1977; Crystal, 1991). Major concerns include determining who is in control of setting pay levels (i.e., the CEO or the board of directors), deciding how pay levels are established, selecting incentive measures, and selecting performance measures.

Boards of Directors and CEO Pay

Members of the board of directors are officially responsible for setting the CEO's pay. Their determination of an appropriate pay level and compensation package is influenced by individual members' assumptions and beliefs, the relative power and preferences of the board and the CEO, and market factors (Finkelstein & Hambrick, 1988).

In its ideal conception, a board of directors consists of inside and outside members. Inside members are officers of the firm and therefore are subject to considerable influence from the CEO. Outside directors, however, should have no economic ties to the firm and therefore should be able to provide frank and unbiased input. CEO pay is set by a compensation committee, which should consist only of outside members. Such a board is the ideal; according to many observers, reality is considerably different.

Board Independence

Most observers concede that inside members owe their allegiance to the CEO and therefore will not surface problems or oppose the CEO. In practice the CEO typically is also chairman of the board; therefore, the CEO selects who will serve on the board, as only the CEO's nominations are presented to the shareholders for a vote (Colvin, 1992). Another action CEOs take to influence their pay in a positive sense is to select for board membership active CEOs who make more than they do, knowing that such CEOs will likely be amenable to higher levels of compensation.

Both monetary and nonmonetary rewards for board members are linked more to strong relationships with the CEO than to organizational success. Monetary rewards can be significant. Pepsico directors received $78,000 each in 1990; the average director received $32,352 for 92 hours of work, plus fees for being on committees, reimbursement for expenses, and benefits such as retirement plans (Dobrzynski, 1991). Thus, board members are naturally reluctant to terminate or reduce the pay of CEOs because they bear a disproportionate share of nonmonetary costs (e.g., confrontation, loss of friendship, personal discomfort) for challenging the CEO, and they receive no real monetary benefits (Baker, Jensen, & Murphy, 1988). The establishment of benefits such as substantial pensions after 10 years of service on the board can add to the reluctance of a board member to take actions against a CEO (Crystal, 1992). Gaining power over the board allows the CEO to establish a preferred pay package, choose contingent versus non-contingent pay, and determine the height of hurdles that trigger incentive bonuses (Finkelstein & Hambrick, 1988).

Problems with the Compensation Committee

Typically, outside board members own trivial amounts of stock and are therefore less than perfect agents for the shareholder. Board member compensation is usually not structured to force alignment of board member interests with stockholder interests.

Members of the compensation committee sometimes have economic ties to the CEO. Roberto Goizueta of Coca Cola received $81 million worth of stock options the same year he paid a member of his compensation committee $24 million in fees (Byrne, 1992). Five percent of firms have CEOs who sit on each other's boards, and several have CEOs who sit on each other's compensation committees (Lissy, 1992). It is hard to picture a group making a dispassionate, unbiased decision knowing that any critical action is subject to retaliation and any generous act is likely to be reciprocated.

Market factors can affect CEO pay in a number of ways. CEOs are assumed to be competing in a marketplace for their jobs and compensation. This leads to the assumption of an informed seller (the CEO) and an informed buyer (the compensation committee). In fact, the CEO is a highly informed seller, who has access not only to the firm's compensation specialists but in many cases to outside compensation consultants. To make decisions, the compensation committee in most instances relies on information provided by the CEO. Even though the committee may have access to the CEO's consultant, the consultant has been hired by and is most loyal to the CEO (Crystal, 1992). Another market factor is wage surveys, which are discussed later.

Benefits and Limitations of Stock Options as an Incentive

From the perspective of the firm and the board of directors, stock options have a num-

ber of very real advantages. First, the projected value of the stock options does not have to be deducted from current profits or reported to stockholders in the proxy statement. Thus, regardless of the size of the stock option granted, its value is transparent to stockholders when it is granted. Second, when the stock option is exercised, the value may be used as a tax deduction against earnings, but there is no transfer of cash—just a transfer of shares resulting in a dilution of share value to the stockholders. Third, if the stock option is exercised after the CEO leaves the firm, the action does not have to be reported to stockholders in the proxy statement (Colvin, 1992).

In addition to the cash flow and profitability advantages, stock options were thought to fulfill agency theory's quest for alignment of the interests of CEOs and shareholders. A typical option gives the CEO the right, with no obligation, to purchase company shares for 10 years at the market price on the day the option was granted. The theory is straightforward: By raising share value, the CEO maximizes wealth by creating shareholder value.

Stock options, however, have increasingly been criticized as failing to achieve their objectives. There is a lack of downside risk for CEOs because if the stock price goes down, they simply do not exercise their options. Because many firms have experienced declines in stock price, compensation consultants have devised a number of remedies for CEOs and boards who want to maintain an illusion of performance-based pay. Some firms, such as Apple Computer, reprice a CEO's stock options when the stock price drops, allowing the CEO to exercise the option at a profit despite the evident lack of performance and loss of value to stockholders.

Market Wage Surveys

Market surveys supposedly help to maintain pay equity by ensuring that the CEO earns a competitive salary. One problem is that a typical board wants to be a top third or top quartile payer because of either institutional pride or CEO concerns. Over time this has the inevitable effect of ratcheting up pay, as all firms are chasing a moving target. Boards justify the above-average pay through a variety of mechanisms (Crystal, 1992). One is simply to announce that the firm uses a premium pay policy. A second approach is to find some organizational performance measure that is above average to justify above-average CEO pay. Another approach is to put the CEO temporarily on a pay raise diet—providing lower-than-market pay raises. A final approach, when confronted with average pay higher than desired, is to send the consultant back for a new survey with different reference companies. The consultant earns extra fees and eventually identifies a set of firms with the desired average CEO pay.

Pay Option Complexity

When the rising tide of American business was lifting the boats of most CEOs, tying pay to performance through stock options was almost a sure thing. But when the economy took a downturn, CEOs looked for alternative pay plans and found a lot of help from compensation consultants (Byrne, 1992; Crystal, 1992). Consultants convinced CEOs that the stock market was the wrong measure of performance, and as new and more complex varieties of stock options were introduced, the link between pay and performance became even weaker.

Pay Based on Firm Size

A problem with pay based on firm size is that when fixed relationships between pay and size are adopted, CEO performance is no longer a part of the equation. Primary causes for adoption of a mechanical link lie with compensation consultants and market surveys (Baker, Jensen, & Murphy, 1988). One consultant's wage handbook states, "The general rule is that as sales volume doubles, executive pay increases by one third" (Davidson, 1989, p. 75). If firms accept this guideline as policy, CEOs will seek to increase firm size even when it adversely affects other measures such as shareholder value.

Severance Pay

One type of compensation that has been criticized as hard to justify is severance pay as enjoyed by CEOs. Organizations commonly pay employees some form of severance pay, especially when termination is not for poor performance. The amount of severance usually ranges from several weeks' to several months' pay. A CEO, however, typically receives three to five times the annual salary as a base severance pay. In addition, there can be consulting contracts, accelerated stock options, and extended benefits (Dalton, Dailey, & Kesner, 1993).

The large severance pay package has been justified as a reward for outstanding service over an extended period and as a recruiting tool for failing firms or firms in bankruptcy, as they would have difficulty attracting talented CEOs without some guarantee. Another defense is that really well run companies are often takeover targets; to protect CEOs from takeovers, severance programs such as golden parachutes provide safety nets and encourage continued high performance.

The response to the first argument is that CEOs make a substantial amount of money, and outstanding performance is generally recognized during the CEO's tenure. On the other hand, many CEOs receive substantial severance pay packages where performance was clearly not outstanding. Frank Lorenzo, having led Eastern Airlines into bankruptcy, was essentially bought off by his board. He received over $30 million in severance pay, and his stock was repurchased for $14 a share when its market value was $5. Peter Cohen, who was subjected to severe criticism for his management of Shearson Lehman, received $10 million when he was ousted. Steven Ross, who received $78 million when his Warner Communications merged with Time, Inc., received another $44.5 million in severance pay when he was asked to leave by the Time Warner board. Regardless of whether CEO performance is high or low, it is not clear to many observers why a huge bonus is necessary when a CEO departs.

Concerning the problem of attracting CEOs to failing firms, critics concede that severance guarantees are useful to attract new CEOs but contend that they make no sense for those already employed and responsible for the crises.

Golden parachutes designed to protect high-performance CEOs from takeovers can actually encourage takeover attempts. A CEO guaranteed a large sum in the event of a takeover can put the firm into play, effectively inviting a takeover. F. Ross Johnson, as CEO of RJR Nabisco, attempted a leveraged buyout. Such a maneuver allows other bidders to compete, and Johnson's consortium lost. But Johnson received $53 million in severance pay.

The high cost of severance pay packages becomes even more questionable in the context of recent legislation passed by Congress. For severance payments that exceed three times the average annual earnings for the past 5 years, there is a nondeductible 20 percent excise tax. In response to the legislation, some boards engage in what is termed "grossing up," a tactic whereby they increase the total amount provided to an executive to compensate for the tax. When Gerald Tsai, CEO of Primerica, was ousted, the board gave him $19.2 million in severance pay but provided another $8.6 million to cover the taxes.

Summary

The preceding discussion highlights the marketplace breakdown in the application of theories of CEO compensation. Paying for non-performance-related criteria such as size, and using reward measures that pay off regardless of organizational performance, break the link between pay and performance. This calls into question the paying of huge sums under the guise of reward for performance. Agency theory requires structuring pay to align CEO objectives with shareholder objectives. If CEOs control the compensation structure through passive boards, their actions will likely be uninfluenced by the desires of the ownership.

True Reality: What Works, What Doesn't

CEO Pay and Organizational Size

Research has consistently found a positive relationship between organizational size and CEO pay (Lambert, Larcker, & Weigelt, 1991). A variety of measures of organizational size have been linked to CEO pay, including sales volume and number of employees (Mellow, 1982) and rate of change in size (Lambert, Larcker, & Weigelt, 1991). A study of the practice of increasing firm size through acquisition found that CEO compensation always increased with size (Schmidt & Fowler, 1990).

Data collected by the Conference Board documents that for a 10 percent increase in firm sales, CEO pay increases 3 percent and that the relationship between size and pay is consistent across time and industries (Baker, Jensen, & Murphy, 1988). Another study also found a 2 to 3 percent increase in pay for a 10 percent increase in sales (Murphy, 1985). Such results are disturbing to many researchers as they indicate that purposeful increase of organizational size will lead to increased pay for CEOs, irrespective of any adverse effect on shareholder value.

CEO Pay and Organizational Performance

Research results in this area have been mixed (Gerhart & Milkovich, 1990; Gomez-Mejia, Tosi, & Hinkin, 1987). Although some research has found no link between pay and performance (Benston, 1985; Kerr & Bettis, 1987), the lack of a significant relationship has been attributed by other researchers to inappropriate measures or techniques. A large body of research has linked pay to performance, and researchers generally believe that pay affects performance (Ehrenberg & Milkovich, 1987).

Current research efforts generally attempt to identify which factors affect the strength of the pay-performance relationship. One major factor is the degree of ownership, as researchers have found that managers behave differently when a single equity holder owns as little as 5 percent of outstanding stock. One study found that as outside ownership increased, boards had greater influence on pay, and incentive alignment with organizational performance measures was also greater, whereas insider-dominated firms had pay related more to firm size (Gomez-Mejia, Tosi, & Hinkin, 1987; Tosi & Gomez-Mejia, 1989).

Although the level of CEO pay has been found to influence performance, confirming predictions of expectancy theory, a concern is the relatively small influence that pay seems to have. There is no research evidence that astronomical pay packages lead to outstanding organizational performance. More research is necessary to identify the factors that strengthen and weaken the relationship.

Also of concern is the lack of power exhibited by boards unless there is significant outside control. A trend that may shift more power back to boards is the increasing activism of financial investors such as pension funds and mutual funds. As owners of substantial blocks of stock in large numbers of firms, fund managers can be effective guardians of shareholder interests.

Solutions and Suggestions

Not surprisingly, many solutions have been put forth to address the deficiencies identified in the two sections on problems with pay. Although the various lists differ in detail, they essentially agree on accomplishing a couple of critical items: tightening the link between pay and performance and shifting the power over CEO pay from the CEO to the board.

Tightening the Pay-Performance Linkage

Incentives are effective only if they are a significant part of the total pay package. Base salary and bonus should be reduced as a percentage of total pay. One writer suggested a maximum of $1 million in salary and bonus, with the remainder of any compensation paid in the form of long-term rewards tied directly to organizational success (Byrne, 1992).

Tying rewards to organizational success means using organizational performance measures that relate to creation of shareholder value. Accounting measures such as return on assets, quarterly profits, and return on equity are susceptible to manipulation by CEOs without value for shareholders being created.

The use of incentives such as stock options that have no downside risk for the CEO should be discontinued (Kay, 1992). One approach is to issue stock options at a high premium, such that stock price must increase significantly before it is profitable for the CEO to exercise the option, with no swapping or repricing of stock options if the stock price fails to go up. In general, larger stock holdings by CEOs are encouraged. This could be accomplished through payment of bonuses in stock and a requirement for CEOs to hold stock for a minimum period.

Reempowering the Board

The compensation committee needs to be housecleaned. Only outside members with no economic ties, interlocking directorships, or other linkages to the firm should be on the committee. The compensation committee should have a clear charter stating its policies in the proxy statement. Although compensation consultants should be used with care, if one is needed, the committee should hire its own consultant, who reports directly to the committee (Lear, 1992). Committees should discontinue their reliance on market surveys and stop automatically paying at above-average levels. Compensation comparisons should be based on value creation.

Other Recommendations

One reason for the decrease in active ownership of firms by financial institutions was the Glass-Steagull Act of 1933, which prohibited banks from owning stock. Japan and Germany have strong bank ownership, which results in a longer-term perspective for CEOs and a greater emphasis on creating shareholder value. Repeal of the Glass-Steagull Act would increase owner interest in long-term performance.

Downsizing for organizational survival may be a defensible strategy, but laying off workers while paying CEOs huge bonuses has led to calls for worker representation on boards (Wilhelm, 1993).

References

Adams, J. S. (1963). Toward an understanding of inequity. *Journal of Abnormal and Social Psychology, 67,* 422–436.

Adams, J. S., & Freedman, S. (1976). Equity theory revisited: Comments and annotated bibliography. In L. Berkowitz (Ed.), *Advances in Experimental and Social Psychology.* New York: Academic Press.

Baker, J. C. (1977, July–August). Special Report. Current executive compensation practices elicit critical opinions. *Harvard Business Review,* 54–66.

Baker, G. P., Jensen, M. C., & Murphy, K. J. (1988, July). Compensation and incentives: Practice vs. theory. *The Journal of Finance, 43(3),* 593–616.

Becker, G. S. (1964). *Human capital.* New York: National Bureau of Economic Research.

Beer, M., Spector, B., Lawrence, P. R., Mills, D. Q., & Walton, R. E. (1984). *Managing human assets.* New York: Free Press.

Benston, G. J. (1985). The self-serving management hypothesis: Some evidence. *Journal of Accounting and Economics, 7,* 67–84.

Brownstein, A. R., & Panner, M. J. (1992, May–June). Who should set CEO pay? The press? Congress? Shareholders? *Harvard Business Review,* pp. 28–38.

Byrne, J. A. (1991, May 6). The flap over executive pay. Investors, employees, and academics are asking, how much is enough? *Business Week,* 90–96.

Byrne, J. A. (1992, March 30). Executive Pay. Compensation at the top is out of control. Here's how to reform it. *Business Week,* pp. 52–58.

Byrne, J. A. (1993, April 26). Executive pay: The party ain't over yet. *Business Week,* pp. 56–64.

Crystal, G. S. (1992, July–August). CEO pay: How much is enough? *Harvard Business Review,* 130–139.

Colvin, G. (1992, April 6). Getting CEO pay right. *Fortune,* pp. 61–69.

Conlon, E. J., & Parks, J. M. (1990). Effects of monitoring and tradition on compensation arrangements: An experiment with principal-agent dyads. *Academy of Management Journal, 33(3),* 603–662.

Crystal, G. S. (1978). *Executive compensation: Money, motivation, and imagination.* New York: AMACOM.

Crystal, G. S. (1991, Fall). Why CEO compensation is so high. *California Management Review,* pp. 9–29.

Dalton, D. R., Dailey, C. M., & Kesner, I. F. (1993). Executive severance agreements: Benefit or burglary? *Academy of Management Executive, 7(4),* 69–76.

Davidson Consultants. (1989). *Wage and salary administration in a changing economy.* Chicago, IL: Dartell Press.

Deci, E. (1972). The effects of contingent and noncontingent rewards and controls on intrinsic motivation. *Organizational Behavior and Human Performance, 8.*

Deckop, J. R. (1987). Top executive compensation and the pay-for-performance issue. In D. B. Balkin & L. R. Gomez-Mejia (Eds.), *New perspectives on compensation* (pp. 285–293). Englewood Cliffs, NJ: Prentice Hall.

Dobrzynski, J. H. (1991, May 6). Directors' pay is becoming an issue, too. *Business Week,* p. 94.

Ehrenberg, R. G., & Milkovich, G. T. (1987). Compensation and firm performance. In M. Kleiner, R. N. Block, M. Roomkin, & S. W. Salsburg (Eds.), *Human resources and the performance of the firm* (pp. 87–122). Madison, WI: Industrial Relations Research Association.

Eisenhardt, K. (1989). Agency theory: An assessment and review. *Academy of Management Journal, 31,* 488–511.

Ellig, B. R. (1982). *Executive compensation—A total pay perspective.* New York: McGraw-Hill.

Finkelstein, S., & Hambrick, D. C. (1988). Chief executive compensation: A synthesis and reconciliation. *Strategic Management Journal, 9,* 543–558.

Finkelstein, S., & Hambrick, D. C. (1989). Chief executive compensation: A study of the intersection of markets and political processes. *Strategic Management Journal, 10,* 121–134.

Freedman, J. L., Cunningham, J. A., & Krismer, K. (1992). Inferred values and the reverse-incentive effect in induced compliance. *Journal of Personality and Social Psychology, 62(3),* 357–368.

Gerhart, B., & Milkovich, G. T. (1990). Organizational differences in managerial compensation and financial performance. *Academy of Management Journal, 33(4),* 663–691.

Gomez-Mejia, L. R., Tosi, H. L., & Hinkin, T. (1987). Managerial control, performance, and executive compensation. *Academy of Management Journal, 30(1),* 51–70.

Goodman, P. S. (1974). An examination of referents used in the evaluation of pay. *Organizational Behavior and Human Performance, 12,* 170–195.

Herzberg, F. (1968, January–February). One more time: How do you motivate employees? *Harvard Business Review,* pp. 53–62.

Jensen, M. C., & Meckling, W. H. (1976). Theory of the firm: Managerial behavior, agency costs and ownership structure. *Journal of Financial Economics, 3,* 305–360.

Kay, I. T. (1992). *Value at the top: Solutions to the executive compensation crisis.* New York: HarperCollins.

Kerr, J., & Bettis, R. A. (1987). Board of directors, top management compensation, and shareholder returns. *Academy of Management Journal, 30(4),* 645–664.

Kohn, A. (1993, September–October). Why incentive plans cannot work. *Harvard Business Review,* pp. 54–63.

Lambert, R. A., Larcker, D. F., & Weigelt, K. (1991). How sensitive is executive compensation to organizational size? *Strategic Management Journal, 12,* 395–402.

Lear, R. W. (1992, October). De-fanging CEO compensation. *Chief Executive, 80,* 14.

Lissy, W. E. (1992, November–December). Currents in compensation and benefits. *Compensation & Benefits Review,* 17–23.

Loomis, C. J. (1982, July 12). The madness of executive compensation. *Fortune, 106,* pp. 42–52.

Mahoney, T. A. (1979). Organizational hierarchy and position worth. *Academy of Management Journal, 22(4),* 726–737.

Mahoney, T. A., & Weitzel, W. (1978). Secrecy and managerial compensation. *Industrial Relations, 17,* 245–251.

McLaughlin, D. J. (1977, Autumn). Surging executive pay: Time to take stock. *McKinsey Quarterly,* 46–59.

Mellow, W. (1982). Employer size and wages. *Review of Economics and Statistics, 64,* 495–501.

Murphy, K. J. (1985, April). Corporate performance and managerial remuneration: An empirical analysis. *Journal of Accounting and Economics, 7,* 11–42.

Murphy, K. J. (1986, March–April). Top executives are worth every nickel they get. *Harvard Business Review,* pp. 125–132.

O'Reilly, C. A., III, Main, B. G., & Crystal, G. S. (1988). CEO compensation as tournament and social comparison: A tale of two theories. *Administrative Science Quarterly, 33,* 257–274.

Pearce, J. L. (1987). Why merit pay doesn't work: Implications from organization theory. In D. B. Balkin & L. R. Gomez-Mejia (Eds.), *New perspectives on compensation* (pp. 169–186). Englewood Cliffs, NJ: Prentice Hall.

Schmidt, D. R., & Fowler, K. L. (1990). Post-acquisition financial performance and executive compensation. *Strategic Management Journal, 11,* 559–569.

Thompson, J. D. (1967). *Organizations in action.* New York: McGraw Hill.

Tosi, H. L., & Gomez-Mejia, L. R. (1989). The decoupling of CEO pay and performance: An agency theory perspective. *Administrative Science Quarterly, 34(2),* 169–189.

Vroom, V. H. (1964). *Work and Motivation.* New York: Wiley.

Wilhelm, P. G. (1993). Application of distributive justice theory to the CEO pay problem: Recommendations for reform. *Journal of Business Ethics, 12,* 469–482.

Williamson, O. E. (1975). *Markets and hierarchies: Analysis and antitrust implications.* New York: Free Press.

CHAPTER 13

Work Environment Stressors, Support, and Health

Physical and psychological components of the work environment may result for some employees in excessive job stress, poor performance, and the breakdown of social relationships within and outside the workplace. Certain employees may experience even more serious outcomes, such as alcoholism, drug abuse, permanent handicap, or death. A major piece of federal legislation designed to remove or reduce such physical and psychological hazards is the Occupational Safety and Health Act (OSHA) of 1970. Although opinions regarding the effectiveness of OSHA are mixed, it certainly has increased awareness of the importance of protecting employees.

In addition to environmental stressors related to safety issues, other workplace issues contribute to stress. One example is sexual harassment. An individual experiencing sexual harassment at work is in, at least, a hostile working environment. Legal protection against sexual harassment is still evolving, with the Supreme Court taking up the issue of psychological damage to a person who claims harassment. The Court decided that the individual alleging harassment need not demonstrate psychological damage. According to this finding, sexual harassment has occurred if a hostile working environment has been created; the plaintiff does not have the burden of demonstrating that he or she has experienced psychological damage.

Many organizations have attempted to develop effective employee assistance programs to combat the stress associated with juggling work and personal concerns and to demonstrate their support for their workers. This is a controversial area: A number of experts think that organizations have no right to become involved with non-work-related concerns of employees. Organizations have become involved in employee assistance programs for other than altruistic reasons. Such programs have been shown to be related to the development of a more effectively functioning organization.

How far can organizations go? Where do their rights end and the rights of the employees begin? How much can an organization know about its employees? How much should an organization know about its employees? Should we all be concerned about these issues, or should we just leave the answers to the whims of our organizations? The articles in this chapter will provide food for thought concerning these questions.

In the first article, Beehr, Fenlason, and Gudanowski examine the problem of work-related stress. The authors define work stress, present a model that seeks to explain it, and discuss approaches for dealing with that stress and its consequences for the individual and the organization. They suggest ways in which managers can recognize and help manage individual stress.

Thacker, in the second article, analyzes an important concern for many organizations: sexual harassment. She writes from the perspective of the recipient of sexual harassment and attempts to explain the reactions of those who experience such harassment.

The third article, by Smith, alerts us to a rather frightening occurrence. The right to privacy in the workplace has come under increasing fire. Companies can legally infringe upon the privacy of employees in a number of different situations. Employers can, under certain circumstances, tap your phone, look at your e-mail, or photograph you performing personal functions.

In the last article, Stollak and Martocchio describe the stakes and stakeholders associated with employee assistance programs (EAPs). The benefits of EAPs are discussed in relation to each of the involved constituencies.

Suggestions for Further Reading

Aldrich, M. (1993). Ergonomics for managers. *Management Services, 37,* 20–22.

Braverman, M. (1993). Preventing stress-related losses in the workplace. *Compensation & Benefits Management, 9,* 51–57.

Cronin, M. (1993, July). One life to live. *Inc.,* pp. 56–57.

Knotts, R., & Johnson, J. (1993). AIDS in the workplace: The pandemic firms want to ignore. *Business Horizons, 36,* 5–9.

Laabs, J. (1993). Insurance coverage must be clearly defined. *Personnel Journal, 72,* 30–32.

Pasternak, C. (1993, February). HRM update. *HR Magazine,* pp. 22, 24.

Perkins, A. (1993). The costs of inflexible job arrangements. *Harvard Business Review, 71,* 9–10.

Solomon, C. (1993). HR is solving shift-work problems. *Personnel Journal, 72,* 36–48.

Stress-related illness "costs UK 1.5 million working days a year." (1993). *Personnel Management, 25,* 11.

Stuart, P. (1993). HR actions offer protection during takeovers. *Personnel Journal, 72,* 84–87+.

Work and Stress: Implications for Human Resource Management

Terry A. Beehr, Kristofer J. Fenlason, and David M. Gudanowski

It has become popular in recent years to blame all sorts of unusual and dramatic employee actions on the "stress" of the job. Newspaper articles have chronicled incidents across the country in which disgruntled employees or former employees shoot or otherwise attack their supervisors or co-workers, in which specific jobs are labeled stressful because they present occasional danger to life and limb, and in which employees commit suicide. Although these incidents may have resulted from work-related stress, there is usually little strong evidence that this is the case. Such dramatic examples are not the routine or most typical outcomes of occupational stress.

The more typical outcomes of occupational stress develop more slowly and result in less dramatic but still serious consequences for both employees and organizations. Employees have been reported to suffer from peptic ulcers and cardiovascular disease in addition to anxiety, depression, and job dissatisfaction, all resulting from work-related stress. These outcomes may be detrimental to the employees' health, and they may also affect the productivity or health of the organization. Recent reports indicate that organizations are facing an increasing number of court cases and workers' compensation claims based on charges of work-related stress. The cost of just two possibly stress-related illnesses, peptic ulcers and cardiovascular disease, has been estimated nationally at around $45 billion, and the cost of job stress for executives alone has been estimated in the billions of dollars. Many of these estimates are based on the direct costs of illnesses and therefore do not include hidden costs, such as the effects of employees' working at lowered levels of efficiency while still

on the job. Clearly, job-related stress is an issue that managers must address for their own health, the health of their subordinates, and the health of their companies.

A Description of Work-Related Stress: The Case of Carl Johnson

The following composite description of an employee experiencing the beginning stages of stress is drawn from almost two decades of research on work-related stress.

Carl Johnson, age 32, has a wife and two children and an M.B.A. from Central Michigan University. He has been working at General Manufacturing, Inc., for 8 years. Carl works in the personnel department, and, although he has had adequate pay raises over the years, his basic responsibilities have remained pretty much the same. At certain times of the year he travels a good deal to recruit new employees. The recruiting activity has become increasingly difficult and uncertain because General has decided to expand and because Carl feels pressure to include larger percentages of minorities and women among the new recruits needed for the expansion. While in the office Carl supervises four people; each does a variety of work, including performing job analysis with a system developed by Carl's supervisor, interviewing applicants, conducting orientation for new employees, providing training sessions for supervisors, and so forth.

In the last couple of years, slow but perceptible changes have occurred in Carl's behavior. When Carl started working at General, he was fresh from college, was newly married, and was considered a hard-driving, aggressive, ambitious, outgoing employee. Now he is often the last to arrive at work and the first to leave. At work Carl stays to himself, keeping his door closed most of the day. His supervisor and co-workers do not come around to talk to him the way they used to, and he does not seek them out. Even lunches, which he used to enjoy with others, are solitary occasions now. Carl has had trouble sleeping and finds that a drink or two before bedtime helps. He often feels ill and experiences a sense of dread on Sunday nights and on the nights before his recruiting trips. He has been having periodic stomach trouble, and although he has not yet seen a physician, he has taken quite a few sick days off from work in the last 6 months. He feels that his life is going nowhere and that the way he does his job makes no real difference.

Carl has been wanting to quit his job for several years, but he has taken no concrete actions. He has fantasized about making a career change, although he is not certain what direction to take. Lately he has been thinking that maybe he should return to school to become a psychologist.

Carl Johnson is a typical example of an employee who is just far enough into the stages of job stress that the effects are noticeable to people who know him well, including his supervisor (in Carl's case, the manager of personnel at General Manufacturing). As with many issues, employee health becomes important only when something has gone wrong; it is poor health that catches the manager's attention.

It is apparent that Carl Johnson is experiencing stress in his job—but what constitutes stress, and what causes it?

What Is Job Stress?

Use of the word *stress* typically implies negative effects for the individual, but this broad definition of stress can sometimes be confusing. In the workplace, work-related or job stress concerns the adverse effects of work situations on the health (both psychological and physical) of employees. The work situa-tions that affect employee health can have consequences for the employing organization as well. The consequences that take the form of ill health are referred to as *strains* on the individual employee. The aspects of the work environment that "cause" the individual strains and that may lead to organizational consequences are known as *stressors*.

Job stress is a difficult subject to master because of its complexity. Understanding it requires a combination of skills from the fields of management, medicine, psychology, and sociology. Also, knowledge of cause-and-effect sequences in job stress requires long-term study because some of the most serious consequences are slow to develop. Finally, organizations vary greatly in composition, orientation toward employees, and management style; this variation adds further complexity.

Because working conditions and organizations differ, there is a need to pinpoint which aspects of the job, the person, or the organization contribute to job stress. Many different models and theories have been proposed as ways to conceptualize stress in organizational settings. One model, put forward by Beehr, is useful for analyzing stress.

A Three-Part Model of Job Stress: Uncertainty, Importance, and Duration

Beehr's model defines stress as a cognitive (psychological) state in which an individual faces a particular decision-making or problem-solving situation. This situation is characterized by a great deal of uncertainty associated with obtaining important outcomes, and the uncertainty has a long duration. If this model is written out mathematically, it takes the following form:

$$\text{Stress} = (\text{Uncertainty} \times \text{Importance} \times \text{Duration})$$

Because the model is multiplicative, there will be no stress if any of the three terms is zero. That is, there will be no stress in a situation if no uncertainty is associated with obtaining the expected outcomes, if the outcomes are of no importance, or if the situation is very short term (duration close to zero). With this model the total amount of job stress will be the sum of all of the work situations that contain some measure of uncertainty, importance, and duration.

It seems obvious that stress is greater when important outcomes are involved and when the stress is of long duration, but what about uncertainty? It is intuitively appealing to think of uncertainty as stressful; of course, it can be uncomfortable and disruptive. Uncertainty, as used in this model, is present in two types of situations that are highly common in a wide range of work environments. In the first type of situation, the employee (manager or subordinate) is uncertain whether his or her efforts will culminate in a desired performance. For example, Carl Johnson may be uncertain whether his efforts to recruit minorities and females will result in enough hirings. The less certain he is that his efforts will have the desired effect, the more stress he feels. The second type of situation occurs when a person is uncertain whether his or her own performance (which may or may not be satisfactory) will lead to a desired outcome. For example, Carl Johnson may be performing his job adequately from day to day, but he may doubt whether this adequate performance will lead either to a sense of personal satisfaction or to more tangible outcomes such as promotions.

Different instances of uncertainty may be found in any job. The two just mentioned—that is, uncertainty that effort will result in performance ($E \rightarrow P$) and that performance will lead to a particular outcome ($P \rightarrow O$)—are associated with particular stressors.

Three Approaches to Job Stress

The Person-Centered Approach

One popular approach to understanding job stress starts with the assumption that stress is primarily a function of the person. For example, employees exhibiting certain personality traits or behaviors may be identified as those most likely to develop heart disease. Unfortunately, with this approach the chances for change are slim because the logical treatment would be to alter the employee's basic personality or behavior patterns—a very difficult task.

The Job-Centered Approach

A second approach is to identify stressful jobs. One can isolate a single job, such as air traffic controller, or rank order many jobs in terms of their stressfulness. This method will not eliminate the negative effects of stress, however. For example, if the job of air traffic controller is identified as stressful, the only apparent suggestion would be to do away with the job—obviously, an unacceptable solution.

The Job Characteristics Approach

The job characteristics approach entails the identification of the job's stressful characteristics. Many jobs can have similar characteristics: for example, an element of time pressure. The job characteristics approach focuses on more specific causes of stress than does the job-centered approach, and it is more likely to be useful in remedying the adverse effects of job stress. Although it may not be possible to eliminate a job, it may be possible to change some of its stressful characteristics.

In this approach, the causal elements (stressors) are the job characteristics themselves. Role conflict, role ambiguity, role overload, and underutilization of skills are four such stressors. Role conflict occurs when an employee is expected, as part of the job, to do something that would conflict with other job or nonjob demands or with his or her personal values. With role ambiguity, an employee is not sure what is expected on the job or how the reward system works. In role overload, the employee cannot complete the work that is expected because there is too little time or because he or she does not have the necessary skills. Underutilization of skills may occur when an employee has more skills than the job requires.

Carl Johnson may be experiencing some of these stressors. He may be experiencing role conflict if he has not met the expectations that he recruit an increased number of highly qualified employees and that many of these employees be females and minorities. Although Carl's usual recruiting efforts have led to an adequate number of highly qualified people, they may not simultaneously have resulted in increased percentages of females and minorities. He therefore might feel conflicting expectations. (Of course, one solution might be to change his usual recruiting tactics and become more successful.) Judging from the case description, Carl is probably not experiencing role ambiguity; his job appears to be well defined. In fact, it may be that he knows all too well what is expected of him and is feeling the third role stressor, role overload—not having enough time to do what is expected of him and experiencing great uncertainty about whether his recruiting efforts will succeed. Finally, Carl seems to be underutilizing his skills. His job has not changed in years, and if regular raises are proof, he is performing it adequately. This underutilization may result in uncertainty about job satisfaction and personal fulfillment in his career.

Although other stressors exist in the work environment, those mentioned here seem to occur frequently in many different jobs. Some of the stressors may be present in a job from time to time but not constantly. Role overload, for example, is worst at times of deadlines, such as the end of the tax year for many accountants. It is assumed that the more pervasive the stressors are, and the more they influence important outcomes, the more unsettling they will be to employees.

Another job characteristic deserves mention in relation to job stress: the degree of social support. Although some researchers have defined social support as the mere presence of others, most see it as a more "active" type of social influence: that is, something supportive done by someone for someone else. It appears that there are at least two types of social support, instrumental and emotional. Pro-

viding instrumental social support involves suggesting ways, or actually lending a hand, to complete the work or to deal with work stressors. Giving emotional social support may simply mean caring, listening sympathetically, and sharing a felt intimacy in the work relationship. Employees benefit from caring friends at work as well as off the job, particularly when stressors are highly evident.

The social influence of managers on their subordinates has long been deemed important in leadership and organizational dynamics. Similarly, the supportive activities of coworkers in general, and work groups in particular, have been recognized since the days of the Hawthorne studies as important aspects of the work environment. Consequently, it is logical to expect social influences on job stress, whether the social support comes from supervisors or from co-workers. Certain organization theories recommend supervisor and co-worker support for the sake of organizational effectiveness, but such support also may help to alleviate occupational stress.

The final job characteristic that seems important for the person experiencing potentially stressful situations at work is control. Control, participation in decision making, autonomy, and job decision latitude are all terms implying that people have considerable say in what happens as they do their jobs. People whose jobs have this characteristic of control generally tend to be more satisfied and to feel less psychological strain at work. This seems to be true even though the exact reason is not clear and explanations vary a bit from one organizational expert and theory to another. One way to look at this is to consider the job characteristic of *low* control as an additional stressor. On Carl Johnson's job, the fact that he and his staff use a job analysis method developed by his supervisor might be a clue that he is not enjoying a large amount of autonomy. One of his problems might be that he is only allowed to follow directions laid down by someone else.

Generally, of course, people in higher positions in an organization tend to have more say in how to do their jobs than people lower in the organization's hierarchy. In addition, organizations with broad spans of control are likely, on average, to contain jobs with more control. This is because supervisors who are responsible for the work of larger numbers of people simply have less time available, per person, to devote to controlling their subordinates. Therefore, if all else is equal, subordinates are freer to act on their own in such organizations than in organizations with narrow spans of control. As usual, however, things are not simple. Broader spans of control may create more role ambiguity if the job holders neither receive adequate direction from their supervisors nor take control of the situation themselves.

On the flip side of the control coin are personal characteristics that make people feel in control (aside from the presence of the job characteristics of autonomy, control, decision latitude, and so forth). Certain control-related personality characteristics that are relatively stable over time and across situations make people more or less likely to experience strains. One such characteristic concerns internal versus external locus of control. People who have internal locus of control orientations tend to believe that events in their lives (including events at work) are under their own control. Those with external control orientations tend to believe that their own efforts would not significantly control the events around them at work; instead they feel that both good and bad things just happen to them and that they can do nothing about it. Much like employees in jobs characterized by little control, those whose personalities lead them to believe in little internal control tend to have more strain-like symptoms. People who believe in their own internal control are at least more likely to try to deal effectively with the problematic situation, whether it involves role ambiguity, role conflict, or some other stressor.

Consequences of Job Stress

Consequences for the Employee

Job stress has three types of consequences that are especially relevant to the employee:

physical, psychological, and behavioral. Among the potential physical consequences are coronary disease, peptic ulcer, and other more general effects on physical health. It has been suggested that stress may increase susceptibility to a variety of physical problems. Psychological consequences include dissatisfaction with one's life, low self-esteem, psychological fatigue, boredom, emotional exhaustion, resentment toward the job, and generally poor mental health often manifested in depression. Examples of behavioral consequences are increased smoking or reduced ability to quit smoking (which may have long-term effects on physical health), excessive drinking, and even marital discord.

Interviews by Beehr for a study of occupational stress in employees netted the following remarks:

> [There is a] general uptightness—[I] cannot relax.

> [I drink enough coffee that] I get pretty wired by 5:00.

> I get pretty soused.

> I fear I'm going to forget to do something important or not be in tune, and something terrible will happen.

> I can't eat because of all the things that get brought up and nothing gets done.

Consequences for the Organization

Although most of the consequences of job stress are important to both the employee and the organization, several have traditionally been of particular interest as measures of organizational effectiveness. Organizations need to be concerned about very high levels of stress because it seems most likely that poor job performance (and therefore organizational ineffectiveness) will occur in high-stress situations. In general, the higher the level of stress on the employee, the lower the level of performance (though it is possible that job performance may actually improve with a limited increase in stress because the job becomes more challenging under such circumstances). Organizations may also suffer the effects of employee job stress through increased monetary burdens in workers' compensation and court judgments obtained by employees who believe their lives have been adversely affected. If the present legal trends continue, not only will companies pay more in compensation judgments and court costs, but corporate insurance rates will rise as well.

Other consequences for the organization can be classified under the rubric of withdrawal. Employees experiencing too much stress tend to be absent frequently and less involved with their work. This latter form of withdrawal is psychological: Employees too long under stress just seem to quit caring, a development that obviously also has implications for their behavior at work. Employees may also withdraw through turnover, changing jobs within the organization or going outside. One extreme form of withdrawal is occupational abandonment, where an employee leaves not only the organization but also the field. This type of withdrawal should be viewed as especially serious when the field is difficult to get into, requiring years of schooling or a great deal of sacrifice or dedication to enter. Withdrawal, whether physical or psychological, represents an attempt to cope with the stress. If work is an aversive experience, the employee is behaving rationally by trying to get away and stay away from it. Withdrawal from work may not be an effective coping mechanism, however. In fact, some forms of withdrawal may led to additional problems for the organization. The following quotes from people experiencing job stress indicate some of these organizational consequences:

My goal is to get a new job by September.

I wouldn't want to do this forever.

Sometimes I would like to get out of this business.

Getting no recognition for something leads to an "I don't care" attitude.

My needs sometimes get in the way of doing a good job.

I do not socialize with people I work with.

[Other people here are] touchy. I don't want to talk with them.

I don't want to know about decision making here anymore.

Consequences for Society as a Whole

The consequences of job stress are not limited to the employee and the employer. Our society has long cherished an ethic that expects hard work from its citizens. Some forms of withdrawal mentioned here are clearly inconsistent with that ethic and are therefore in conflict with a dominant society norm. In addition, if the incidence of ill health due to job stress is sufficiently widespread, society also incurs costs in terms of an increased burden on already overloaded medical and social welfare resources. Further, if negative effects of stress on performance were frequent, the result would be a diminished gross national product and a reduction in the products and services available for consumption. A broad perspective on the problem of job stress shows that it is important to more parties than just employee and employer.

How Managers Can Recognize Stress and What They Can Do about It

Because managers are in positions of responsibility, they can influence organizational situations more directly than can lower-level employees.

Stress on the Manager and How to Deal with It

The weight of responsibility, along with ambiguity, conflict, overload, and sometimes underutilization of skills, can make a manager's job very stressful. One obvious way for managers to determine whether they are experiencing job stress is to assess the stress potential of their jobs by looking for potential effects on themselves or their work. There are several diagnostic questions to ask: for example, "Is the quality of my work deteriorating?" Under conditions of overload the quality may decline even if the employee is highly productive. "Do I dread coming to work each day? Do I avoid co-workers while I'm at work? Do I dislike answering the telephone because it may mean more work or questions about the progress I'm making on current projects?" If these questions are answered affirmatively, the manager may be using withdrawal as a technique for avoiding job stress. "Has my health been declining? Do I seem to have more than the usual (for me) number of physical complaints? Am I frequently nervous and jumpy? Do I become tired easily? Am I feeling more depressed than usual?" These questions are aimed at the strains or personal consequences of the job stressors.

Finally, one may ask diagnostic questions directly about potential stressors in the job environment. "Do I have frequent deadlines? Is it clear exactly what I should do on my job? Has it been made clear how my work is evaluated and rewarded in my company? Are there conflicting expectations placed upon me by people in my work situation?" If the answer to these questions is yes, some potentially stressful situations are present, regardless of whether they have yet affected job performance or health. Employees who were beginning to recognize that they were in stressful work situations made these statements to interviewers:

This job does not allow me to use my talents.

[My superiors here] fail to recognize some of my better talents.

[There is] sometimes a lack of leadership, and some of us move in and take control. Ambiguity results. We are not really in command but feel we must do something.

[There is] too much work to do to get sick.

[I am] being told, "You have to do this. I don't know how the hell you're going to pull it off, but you have to do it."

If the answers to the questions indicate that the manager is in a stressful situation, there are three ways to ease the situation. A first set of strategies is aimed at the symptoms of job stress. One of the most important steps is to see a physician about one's current physical health. A thorough physical examination will often uncover physical symptoms before they become severe. Without early diagnosis, prevention is difficult.

Similarly, seeking help from a psychological counselor is an approach aimed at the psychological symptoms. Other approaches recommended by some psychologists include attempts at controlling physiological symptoms psychologically. The mind and body are interrelated, and certain methods by which the mind can control aspects of the physiology are becoming popular in the United States. Some examples are relaxation training, biofeedback, and transcendental meditation. Although scientific proof that these techniques can cure or prevent the ill effects of job stress is sparse and incomplete, it is clear that people can learn to control some of their physiological processes when they engage in these techniques. As with many decisions faced by management, however, it behooves us to take action before waiting for years of research; these techniques represent current possibilities for relieving the effects of job stress.

A second set of approaches for easing job stress is aimed more directly at the causes—the job stressors. If the problem is role conflict, the people sending the conflicting messages can often be informed about the problem. A joint session aimed at reducing the conflict can result in a new definition of the employee's role(s)—one that is more productive and satisfying. If the manager experiencing the conflict does not tell the people concerned that their messages are in conflict, they have no reason to change. When role ambiguity is the job stressor, asking for clarification of company policies, procedures, and job duties should help. If the responses to these questions are also unclear or indicate that nobody knows for sure what the particular manager's job entails, the manager could take the initiative by defining the job himself or herself—defining it clearly so that stress is reduced and defining it in a way that is productive for the organization. In most companies, a manager who chooses this approach and performs well in the redefined job is considered highly effective. Approaches aimed at reducing stress from role overload include delegating authority and seeking additional assistance, either temporarily or on a permanent basis. Most managers have at least some minor tasks that can be delegated to competent assistants; in fact, the assistants may find this rewarding. Delegation not only relieves the manager of the overload but also helps to develop the skills of other employees.

A final approach aimed directly at the stressor, one that may reduce all the stressors, is to seek a job in another company. If no other remedies are possible in the particular organization, it may be beyond the manager's ability to alleviate the situation. A more favorable situation may be necessary for the individual's welfare. This approach does little to help the organization, however. Often, many cases of turnover must be seen before any large-scale organization change is attempted to correct the problem.

The third set of strategies consists of approaches aimed at easing the effects of job stressors without changing them directly. If the stressors in the manager's job cannot be reduced directly, making some other changes can often reduce their ill effects. Some of Beehr's work has shown that employees can better withstand the effects of role ambiguity if they have job autonomy. If the manager can get more autonomy in day-to-day activities, he or she is less likely to suffer the ill effects of stress. Similarly, psychological support seems to help, whether it comes from people in the workplace or from friends and family after

work. When overload is the problem, the practice of queuing, or deciding the order in which to tackle one's many tasks, may help alleviate the stress. Obviously, the amount of work is still the same, but this orderly approach ensures that the most important things will get done, and the manager can derive a sense of accomplishment by progressing through the list.

Another strategy for reducing the harmful effects of stress involves off-the-job activities. One straightforward approach is to take time out to eat lunch away from the office. Too often managers feel they need to work every minute of the day, even during lunch. In fact, this may be a symptom of overload; there is probably too much to do in the time available. Taking a break may even improve the quality of the work that gets done. Managers can also try to take nonworking vacations. Overloaded managers tend to skip vacations or to take work with them when they do go away. But legitimate opportunities for time out should not be passed up. Many people are surprised to discover that they can take some time off and still get their work done.

Finally, physical activity is important in helping people withstand some of the effects of job stress. Vigorous exercise may do more to prevent coronary disease than milder activities such as walking or golf. Because vigorous activity can be detrimental to some people's health, one should always consult a physician before starting a challenging exercise program. Choosing an activity that is intrinsically interesting will make it easier to stick with the program.

Stress on the Subordinate and How to Deal with It

The symptoms of stress in a subordinate's job are the same as for the manager, but they are often difficult for the manager to observe. Withdrawal in the form of absenteeism is a potential sign of stress, but absenteeism may have many other causes. Ill health is another sign of job stress, but as with absenteeism, the causes are not always clear. However, if absenteeism and ill health combine with avoidance of other employees (including the manager) and with low-quality work, job stress may be the culprit.

In trying to discern job stress among employees, a manager may want to ask some of the same diagnostic questions that he or she asked regarding his or her own behavior. If it is apparent that an employee is experiencing job stress, the manager may want to intervene personally by trying to alleviate the stressor (such as role ambiguity), or he or she may refer the employee to an appropriate resource, such as a company employee assistance program. It is clear from the growing number of stress-related workers' compensation claims and court cases that the manager who is aware of employee stress should do something.

One important response that a manager can make is to be socially supportive. Because the characteristics of the workplace appear to contribute to job stress and because managers control some of these characteristics, they should consider themselves potential sources of support. For example, a manager may provide support in responding to a subordinate's requests for help. If it is at all possible, when the subordinate asks for an assistant, clerk, or secretary, the manager should try to supply one, if only on a temporary basis. This assistance can help the subordinate get through times of especially heavy stress, such as approaching deadlines. If ambiguity or conflict is the stressor, the manager may be one of the parties sending ambiguous or conflicting messages. A subordinate asking for clarification or resolution of such conflict deserves the manager's serious attention.

Another way social support can alleviate stress in the workplace is through direct impact on the strains. Researchers have found that social support almost always reduces a number of strains in work-related stress. This finding is especially important when managers are unwilling or unable to change the stressful characteristics of the job itself. Even though the job may remain the same, social support may still help to alleviate the harmful effects of stress. For example, socially sup-

portive co-workers can help to relieve boredom or dissatisfaction; a manager can help to relieve an employee's anxiety about a project by discussing the expectations and providing assurance that he or she will be supportive of the employee's efforts.

Three Management Styles and Their Relationships to Job Stress

If job stress is a relatively new concept for most managers, it will be helpful to highlight probable relationships between job stress and other more familiar concepts. In this section we look at the relationship between job stress and each of three management styles: traditional management, participative management, and contingency management.

Traditional Management

By the traditional management style we mean the use of bureaucratic and classical administrative approaches. Some of the key elements of the traditional style are hierarchy of authority, written job descriptions, unity of command, impersonality, and rational-legal authority, usually administered in a relatively authoritarian manner.

Role ambiguity is not supposed to occur in traditionally managed organizations because of the clearly written job descriptions. With one exception, the traditional management style should result in little ambiguity. The exception refers to unexpected situations; written job descriptions cannot anticipate all possible events. Unexpected developments can lead to widespread role ambiguity, especially if the organization's environment is changing so rapidly that new descriptions cannot be written quickly enough to keep up with the changes. Similarly, if the structure of the organization and all written job descriptions are initially adequate, there should be little role overload except in unexpected situations, such as those caused by a change in the work environment or a change to a different work environment. Likewise, conflicting demands from two or more people would not be expected in a traditional organization because of the unity-of-command principle (though other kinds of conflict may occur if an unexpected situation arises requiring an employee to accomplish a task in a manner that would break bureaucratic rules). On the other hand, underutilization of skills may well occur under the traditional style of management. Employees may become "trapped" in jobs that are overly routine and not challenging. In summary, although the traditional management style may allow underutilization of skills, it is not likely to generate the first three types of job stressors if (1) the organization's structure and all job descriptions are initially adequate and (2) the organization's environment does not change or changes only gradually.

Once job stress occurs in a traditionally managed organization, it can be difficult to alleviate. Any change in such an organization tends to be slow, and change aimed at alleviating stress would be no exception. Because traditionally managed organizations are supposed to be impersonal, there may be little opportunity for psychological support. Because of the hierarchy of authority and the traditional, authoritarian use of power, job autonomy will likely not be conferred on many people. Thus, two means (social support and autonomy) for alleviating the effects of stress are essentially eliminated. The ability of the traditional management style to deal with job stress, therefore, is low.

Participative Management

The participative management style emphasizes the sharing of authority with subordinates. Sometimes managers share authority with groups of subordinates; at other times they delegate authority to individuals. Participation can occur in many areas, such as goal setting, scheduling, determination of work methods, and evaluation. Participative management techniques attempt to use more of the employees' skills and abilities—their resources—than do most other management approaches.

The participative management style is likely to result in role clarity rather than ambiguity because employees have considerable say in defining their roles, and people who define their own roles should understand them more clearly. Similarly, there is likely to be little role conflict under participative management, particularly if group rather than individual decision making is encouraged. Group participation results in more interactions with the people who make demands upon the employee, and conflicting and ambiguous expectations are likely to be noticed and changed or clarified. The impact of the participative management style on role overload is less clear. Ideally, overload problems would also be addressed in group sessions, but this may not always occur. It is even possible that participative management could lead to more rather than less overload because employees would have more responsibility and more meetings to attend.

The psychological support that can help alleviate job stress is likely to be plentiful in participatively managed organizations because of the high degree of interaction among co-workers. Autonomy is also likely to be strong enough to help ease the effects of stress. This is less likely to be true where group participation prevails over individually oriented participation, however, because group influence may at times limit the individual's autonomy. Overall, the participative style is more likely than the traditional management style to engender lower-stress jobs.

Contingency Management

The contingency management style dispenses with the notion of one best organizational structure and one best management style for all situations. It allows for the use of different management styles at different times. For example, the traditional management style may be effective when employees have few skills and strong security needs and when the organization's technology and environment are relatively simple and stable. Participative management may be more effective when employees are highly skilled and have strong ego needs and when the organization's technology and environment are complex and rapidly changing.

The contingency management style offers the most promise for reducing job stress. Conflict and ambiguity are likely to be low in a traditionally managed organization as long as the environment is stable; if the environment is unpredictable, the participative style is recommended as helping to reduce the ambiguity and conflict caused by environmental changes. Role overload is likely to be low in a traditionally managed organization; under participative management it may be somewhat higher for the reasons cited earlier. Autonomy and support are likely to be low in a traditionally managed organization, but presumably they would be less necessary in such an organization because, given the stable environment, the amount of ambiguity and conflict would be minimal. Participatively managed organizations, on the other hand, are likely to have high levels of autonomy and support.

The Work-Nonwork Stress Interface

Employers have recently been growing more acutely aware of the potential for problems at the interface between people's work and nonwork lives. People who are under stress either in the workplace or outside of work experience problems that have repercussions in the other sphere. Thus, work-related stress can interfere with home life, and stress at home can affect work-related behaviors. Although this interface problem can occur for any employee, researchers have observed it most frequently in relation to working women's interrole conflicts—that is, conflicts between their work and nonwork roles. The clearest illustrations usually involve time: There often appears to be insufficient time available for a woman to function in both work and nonwork roles at the desired level. Another concern has been documented less often in research: It seems likely that stressors off the job may lead to strains that could affect job perfor-

mance or even attendance. After all, a strain is basically an illness, and a sick employee has difficulty performing optimally on the job.

Individual Welfare and Organizational Welfare: Conflict or Complement?

By definition, the primary focus in an examination of job stress is the welfare of the individual rather than the welfare of the organization. For humanitarian reasons, managers would like to help individual employees by reducing adverse stress. However, if reducing stress would mean undercutting the organization's effectiveness, the individual could be harmed anyway—by being employed in a floundering organization. Therefore, it is important to consider the approaches for reducing job stress in light of both individual and organizational welfare.

Approaches aimed at reducing the effects of stress are not likely to harm the organization; in fact, they may even improve organizational effectiveness. Medical treatment of employee illnesses, psychological counseling, and exercise programs will (1) make employees stronger and therefore more capable, (2) reduce absenteeism due to illness, and (3) result in employees with higher self-esteem and the desire to perform well to keep that self-esteem high.

Similarly, increasing social support and the degree of job autonomy is likely to benefit the organization as well as the individual. In fact, some organizational theories promote the use of support and autonomy (whether by these or other names) to increase organizational effectiveness.

With one possible exception, approaches designed to reduce job stress by attacking the causes, the job stressors themselves, are also likely to help the organization. Reduction in role ambiguity and role conflict will make employees more effective by clarifying how they should channel their efforts, and it will reduce absenteeism due to stress. Reduction of role overload may be the exception just mentioned. While improving organizational effectiveness by reducing absenteeism and increasing the effort expended toward high-quality job performance, reducing overload may reduce *quantity* of performance. It is not known, however, whether the benefit of increased quantity attributable to overload is enough to offset the cost of decreased quality of work and irregular attendance.

A radical technique for reducing stress on the individual, one that may hurt the organization, is the employee's search for a better job (one in which he or she can be productive with less stress) in a different organization. It seems especially likely that highly skilled workers will take this approach because they can find new jobs more easily than can less-skilled workers. This type of turnover may be especially costly for the organization (al-though the individual may benefit from it). One implication, of course, is that management should try to reduce stress so that employees will not make this choice.

Finally, it has been suggested that the use of contingency management would lower job stress for organization members. It seems that this technique for helping the individual could only benefit the organization; in fact, contingency management often is proposed primarily for the reason that it makes organizations more effective.

Overall, it is clear that alleviating job stress is nearly always likely to help rather than hinder the organization's functioning. Paying attention to job stress does not mean ignoring the organization's welfare.

Dealing with Sexual Harassment in the Workplace: Understanding the Behavior of Sexual Harassment Targets

Rebecca A. Thacker

The problem of sexual harassment in the workplace is one that requires an active response on the part of organizational managers. Following the Supreme Court's decision on sexual harassment in *Meritor Savings Bank, FSB v. Vinson* (1986), organizations were cautioned to define and communicate policies on sexual harassment.

Equal Employment Opportunity Commission defined sexual harassment as

> unwelcome sexual advances, requests for sexual favors and other verbal or physical conduct of a sexual nature when submission to such conduct is made either explicitly or implicitly a term or condition of an individual's employment . . . or such conduct has the purpose or effect of unreasonably interfering with an individual's work performance or creating an intimidating, hostile, or offensive working environment. (Equal Employment Opportunity Commission, 1980, p. 25024)

The Supreme Court's definition of sexual harassment in *Meritor v. Vinson* is similar and is also dual in nature: (1) the conditioning of benefits (e.g., promotions, pay raises) upon the receipt of sexual favors and (2) behaviors that create an offensive or hostile working environment (e.g., touching, sexual comments and jokes). As a result, organizations have been cautioned to explain the dual nature of sexual harassment in organizational policies.

In particular, organizations have been advised to set up complaint procedures for targets of sexual harassment and to inform employees that the organization no longer condones sexual harassment among its employees. The existence of sexual harassment policies, however, may not be as effective as policy makers might wish. Evidence suggests that targets of sexual harassment often are reluctant to invoke organizational complaint procedures (Livingston, 1982).

Unless targets are willing to use organizational policies designed to curb sexual harassment incidents, policies will be virtually useless. Thus, if organizations are to be effective in their efforts to eradicate sexual harassment, an understanding of the underlying dynamics of both sexual harassment and target response is necessary.

The Process of Sexual Harassment

Descriptive studies have indicated gender-based differences in sexual harassment complaints. The majority of accused harassers are male, and the majority of the targets of sexual harassment are female (Tangri, Burt, & Johnson, 1982; Terpstra & Cook, 1985; United States Merit Systems Protection Board, 1981, 1988). Males who exhibit sexually harassing behaviors are more likely to be perceived as sexual harassers than are women who exhibit the same behaviors (Gutek, Morasch, & Cohen, 1983; Reilly, Carpenter, Dull, & Bartlett, 1982). Also, females are more likely than males to view the same set of social-sexual behaviors as sexually harassing (Thacker & Gohmann, 1993). Consequently, sexual harassment is often characterized as a male-initiated phenomenon. Although cases of female harassers and same-gender harassers exist, sexual harassment targets are typically female.

Sexual harassment often carries with it an element of force and unwanted attention. Furthermore, sexual harassment frequently involves coercion (Thacker & Ferris, 1991); that is, the harasser often has the potential to inflict damage upon the target. Sexual harassment involves coercive behavior if the following conditions are met: (1) The harasser has the potential to inflict damage upon the target; (2) a threat to do damage to the target is implied, and the target recognizes the existence of the threat; and (3) the threat is enforced if the target does not comply.

A harasser may have coercive potential because of the harasser's control over promotions, raises, working conditions, or performance evaluations. The threat is either implied or explicitly stated (e.g., receipt of sexual favors in return for a raise, implying that the raise will not be given without the sexual favor). The harasser has not only the legitimate power to carry out the threat but also the power to follow through if the target refuses to comply. When the target is unwilling to challenge the harasser's power for fear of the consequences, the harasser's behavior is reinforced. If the target fails to file a complaint against the harasser, then the mere existence of a complaint procedure is useless as a deterrent.

In other instances the harasser may have no formal authority over the target, but the target is dependent upon the harasser in some way. For example, the harasser may have a specific body of knowledge, expertise, critical information, or necessary support for the target to do his or her job effectively. Although a formal reporting relationship does not exist, the target is nonetheless dependent upon the harasser. In effect, those with expertise or critical information can threaten to withhold information important to effective job performance if noncompliance or complaints about the harasser's behavior result. Again, fear of the consequences may prevent the target from reporting the harasser's behavior.

Hence, targets may be unwilling to challenge the harasser's attempts at domination and control for fear of the consequences. Fear of the consequences results in the target's ignoring the harasser and passively accepting the harasser's overtures or complying with the harasser. Targets frequently report job loss, increased psychological distress, and unpleasant working conditions for refusing to comply with harassers' demands (Terpstra & Cook, 1985; United States Merit Systems Protection Board, 1981, 1988).

The presence of organizational policies may do little to extinguish sexual harassment behaviors, even though policy statements explicitly detail the organization's lack of tolerance for such behaviors. Sexual harassment is more likely to occur if harassers believe that their actions have a high probability of success. To the extent that harassers believe that their behavior will go unchallenged, the frequency with which sexual harassment occurs can be expected to increase. Indeed, research evidence suggests that ignoring the sexual harassment or complying with it can have the result of reinforcing the harassment (Silverman, 1976). Of critical importance to coping with sexual harassment in the workplace, then, is an understanding of targets' responses to sexual harassment.

Target Responses to Sexual Harassment

Anecdotal evidence and Title VII case evidence (Thacker, 1992a) suggest two conceptual models to describe the behavior of targets of sexual harassment: (1) confrontation and (2) passive and acquiescent behavior. Confrontation is based on reactance theory, which suggests that individuals become motivationally aroused when behavioral freedom is threatened (Brehm, 1966, 1972). Passive and acquiescent behavior is based on learned helplessness (Seligman, 1974). Learned helplessness rests on the notion that, regardless of a person's actions or behaviors, unpleasant outcomes are unavoidable.

Typical organizational policies concerning sexual harassment may neglect to provide an effective relief mechanism for targets responding with passive, acquiescent behaviors. On the other hand, typical sexual harassment policies do provide a mechanism for targets who respond with confrontational behaviors. Therefore, an understanding of both forms of target response is critical to development of effective organizational sexual harassment policies.

The Confrontation Model

The confrontation model is based on reactance theory. Reactance is a "motivational state directed toward the reestablishment of the free behaviors which have been eliminated or threatened with elimination" (Brehm, 1966, p. 9). Sexual harassment is an infringement upon personal freedom because it limits individuals' freedom to act as they desire. In some cases individuals must comply with the sexual harassment to avoid a negative occurrence such as termination, demotion, distasteful remarks, and so forth. In other cases targets must comply with the sexual harassment to receive a positive outcome such as a promotion, raise, or favorable performance evaluation.

In effect, the issue is one of personal control. Attempts to regain lost control are forms of reactance. A variety of methods exist by which individuals can attempt to restore lost control; one of these is direct confrontation of the source of the problem (Brehm, 1966). For example, a target of sexual harassment may exhibit reactance behavior by actively (i.e., verbally) refusing to comply with the harasser. Similarly, another example of reactance behavior is threatening to complain about the sexual harasser's behavior to a supervisor or another person of higher authority.

To experience reactance, individuals must feel an increased amount of self-direction, perceiving that they can do what they want in directing their own actions and behaviors (Brehm, 1966; Wicklund, 1974). Refusing to comply with a sexual harasser's demands and threatening to complain about the harasser's behavior are indications that the target wants to control his or her working environment by removing obstacles that hamper his or her ability to do so.

Yet anecdotal and legal case evidence clearly suggest that some targets do not behave as if they have the capacity to direct their own behavior and control their workplace environments (e.g., Thacker, 1992a). Rather, the response to sexual harassment is more appropriately characterized as passive and acquiescent. Not only do some targets fail to complain, but they accept, either actively or passively, the harassers' behavior.

Learned helplessness is a conceptual model that explains this second form of target response. For these targets, merely communicating the organization's complaint procedure and strong opposition to sexual harassment will be ineffective as a relief mechanism. Targets with passive, acquiescent responses to harassers will be reluctant to rely upon the organization's verbal condemnation of sexual harassment as a mechanism for relief. Regardless of the organization's demonstrated opposition to sexual harassment, some targets are simply not comfortable with confrontational behavior. Therefore, critical to the development of *effective* sexual harassment policies is an understanding of this form of target response.

Passive, Acquiescent Responses to Sexual Harassment

Whereas reactance theory predicts direct confrontation of the individual infringing upon another's freedom, learned helplessness predicts a more passive response to sexual harassment. Individuals experiencing learned helplessness perceive that, despite their efforts, unpleasant or dissatisfying outcomes cannot be averted (Overmier & Seligman, 1967; Seligman, 1974). In effect, learned helplessness results from a perception that individuals have lost personal control over their ability to influence their environment.

Helplessness behavior, over time, tends to reinforce individuals' belief that they are helpless, thus reducing perceived control over their environment. Anecdotal accounts of sexual harassment incidents indicate that targets often go along with sexually harassing behavior. For example, some targets are subjected to unwanted touching, patting, or kissing in the workplace. Rather than threatening to complain, verbalizing disapproval, or stating their refusal to comply, targets submit to the harassers' behavior. Women in particular have been found more likely to accept power imbalances in organizations and to acquiesce to those possessing organizational power than have men (Mainiero, 1986).

Targets displaying passive, acquiescent behaviors are likely to fail to report or complain about incidents of harassment to appropriate authorities (Gutek, 1985; United States Merit Systems Protection Board, 1981). Furthermore, passive, acquiescent targets are also reluctant to invoke formal organizational policies (Livingston, 1982). Along with feeling uncomfortable about displaying active, confrontational behaviors, targets may simply feel that they are incapable of changing the harassers' behavior.

The perception that targets will be unable to control job-related outcomes because they cannot affect the behavior of harassers perhaps serves to induce helpless, passive behaviors. Perceptions that one is helpless to affect workplace outcomes such as whether one is harassed may also prevent a target from using an organization's complaint system.

Particularly when the harasser has authority over the target or when the harasser is at a higher level than the target, the target may experience feelings of helplessness. Ultimately, failure to take advantage of an organization's sexual harassment policy may revolve around an issue of power; that is, if the harasser has power or authority and the target does not, then the most enlightened organizational policy will not deal effectively with sexual harassment.

Gutek (1985) concluded that organizations provide little support for targets of sexual harassment; hence, for targets the "overall picture is one of resignation to such incidents" (p. 2). Organizations should be mindful of this possibility when designing sexual harassment policies. Although part of the organization's

policy should provide a mechanism for those comfortable with confrontational behaviors (i.e., refusing to comply with or complaining about the sexual harassment), steps should also be taken to ensure that targets uncomfortable with confrontational behaviors invoke the organization's sexual harassment policy.

To be effective, then, sexual harassment policies must attempt to make targets comfortable with displaying confrontation behaviors. Furthermore, sexual harassment policies must discipline sexual harassers without regard to organizational level. Such actions attempt to counteract the reluctance on the part of some targets to confront their harassers or to complain about the harassers' behavior.

Dealing with Sexual Harassment in the Workplace: A Three-Pronged Approach

Organizations might wish to consider a three-pronged approach to reduce the incidents of sexual harassment and to deal with sexual harassment complaints. One aspect of the approach involves organizational communication about sexual harassment. The second aspect entails actively involving employees as a means of preventing sexual harassment. The third aspect involves proactive organizational responses to sexual harassment complaints.

Organizational Communication

The organization should establish a policy with an explicit statement that sexual harassment will not be condoned. The policy should also indicate the organization's commitment to eradicating sexual harassment. Most important, the policy should be communicated to *all* levels of the organization.

Organizational communication about sexual harassment should further explain the types of behavior that can potentially constitute sexual harassment. The organization should alert employees to the two forms of sexual harassment: (1) the conditioning of benefits (e.g., promotions, pay raises) upon the receipt of sexual favors and (2) behaviors that create an offensive or hostile working environment (e.g., touching, sexual comments and jokes, questions about sexual preferences).

A step-by-step procedure for voicing a sexual harassment complaint should be set out in the organization's sexual harassment policy. Seventy-three percent of the respondents in the 1988 United States Merit Systems Protection Board (USMSPB) survey stated that they believed that publicizing complaint channels would reduce the occurrence of sexual harassment; however, only 55 percent of the respondents reported that the federal agencies for which they worked actually took such action.

A sexual harassment complaint procedure could follow the lines of traditional grievance procedures. Once the target is directed to the appropriate person for dealing with work-related complaints in the organization, the investigating party would be instructed to gather evidence from both the target and the accused harasser, with corroborating testimony from witnesses where feasible.

A time frame for investigation and resolution should be established. Dissatisfaction with resolution of the complaint, on the part of either the target or the accused harasser, should also have an outlet. That is, either party to the complaint should have recourse to some higher authority in the organization, such as the senior official in charge of labor relations or human resource management.

However, a sexual harassment complaint procedure should not name the employee's supervisor as the party with whom the complaint is initially registered. Supervisors are sometimes the very persons against whom sexual harassment complaints are filed. Complainants should, then, be referred initially to an objective third party, such as a human resource manager or an organizational ombudsman.

Although most of the federal agencies participating in the USMSPB study indicated that they had issued policy statements prohibiting sexual harassment, many respondents in the study felt that the policy statements needed to be more comprehensive and forceful. Some respondents indicated that the policy should state explicitly the penalties that would be imposed upon sexual harassers.

Such suggestions lay the necessary groundwork for responding to sexual harassment complaints. Yet such steps will not be effective in eradicating sexual harassment from the workplace, given the passive, acquiescent behaviors exhibited by some targets. Employees at all levels of the organization should be involved in training and education efforts in an attempt to overcome the reluctance of some targets to complain about offensive behavior.

Employee Involvement

Training employees at all levels of the organization concerning the behaviors that constitute sexual harassment is a necessary ingredient for sexual harassment prevention. Seventy-six percent of the respondents in the 1988 USMSPB survey indicated that training employees would lead to a reduction in the frequency with which sexual harassment occurred. Training employees not only has the advantage of alerting potential harassers to the type of behaviors that will not be condoned but also removes any confusion about the behaviors the organization will find problematic.

The 1988 USMSPB study indicated that the majority of the employees receiving training in sexual harassment were managerial and supervisory personnel rather than nonsupervisory personnel. Indeed, sexual harassment training fits nicely into traditional supervisory and management training and development programs.

However, nonmanagerial and nonadministrative personnel, as well as managers, supervisors, human resource managers, and EEO administrators, should be informed about the types of behavior that constitute sexual harassment. Moreover, training must go further than simply defining sexual harassment behaviors. Because some targets display passive, acquiescent behaviors, employee involvement should be targeted toward making potential targets comfortable with displaying confrontational behaviors such as refusal and complaint.

Role-playing may be one method of dealing with targets' reluctance to display confrontational behaviors (Thacker, 1992b). Providing employees the opportunity to act out responses to sexual harassment scenarios may remove some of the fear associated with confrontation in uncomfortable situations. Once employees have the opportunity to respond to various sexual harassment behaviors in a nonthreatening atmosphere, they may be more comfortable with exhibiting confrontational behaviors that were previously sources of discomfort.

In addition, counseling employees about feelings engendered by sexual harassment might also promote confrontational behaviors. Some targets report feelings of embarrassment and humiliation as a result of being sexually harassed (United States Merit Systems Protection Board, 1988). Such feelings are not conducive to displaying confrontational behaviors. Explaining that the root of such feelings probably lies in social conditioning may reduce a target's tendency to engage in passive, acquiescent behaviors.

Socialization and cultural norms serve to reinforce the perception that men are expected to pursue sexual relationships with females. Males are socialized to accept the role of initiator in sexual relationships, whereas females are socialized to accept sexual overtures initiated by males (LoPiccolo & Heiman, 1978).

Expressing anger or voicing a complaint against a harasser requires a female to violate norms or appropriate roles and behaviors. Not surprisingly, then, targets sometimes report feeling guilty about the sexual harassment, which further inhibits the target from taking action against the harasser (Jensen & Gutek, 1982).

Explaining the consequences of passive acceptance of sexual harassment might also help to induce confrontation behaviors, rather than passive acceptance or helplessness behaviors, on the part of targets. Research evidence suggests that ignoring the sexual harassment or complying with it can result in reinforcing the harassment (Silverman, 1976). Impressing upon employees the long-term consequences of failure to confront sexual harassers, not only for themselves but also for others, may help to induce reactance behaviors.

Proactive Response to Sexual Harassment Complaints

The organization should be explicit about the necessity for prompt objective investigation of sexual harassment complaints. Persons responsible for conducting the investigation should be named (e.g., human resources manager, labor relations specialist, staff ombudsman). The organization should stress the objectivity of the investigating parties, as disagreement over the behaviors that constitute sexual harassment is not uncommon (United States Merit Systems Protection Board, 1988). Because behaviors reported as sexually harassing are sometimes not intended as such by the individuals accused of the harassing, it is critical for the organization to provide an objective investigation process.

Communication should also be very explicit about penalties or disciplinary action that will be taken against proven sexual harassers. The organization could treat sexual harassment in the same way that other types of ineffective and unacceptable performance are treated. For example, disciplinary reports in the harasser's file, probation, suspension, and even termination are possible actions that could be taken against harassers.

Although 72 percent of the USMSPB survey respondents stated that enforcing penalties against harassers was an effective method of reducing sexual harassment, only 27 percent of the employees stated that such action had been taken by their agencies. Supporting the written policy with visible action seems to be critical to legitimizing the organization's stated intent to eradicate sexual harassment. Without such visible commitment to eradicating sexual harassment in the workplace, organizational policies may be ineffective. Not only will harassers perceive that they will suffer few, if any, adverse consequences, but current and future targets will also be reluctant to invoke a complaint policy that fails to achieve its desired result.

Summary

Organizational policies to deal with sexual harassment in the workplace must be designed to deal with two potential forms of target response to sexual harassment: (1) confrontation of the sexual harasser through either refusal or complaint and (2) passive, acquiescent responses to sexual harassment.

The mere existence of a policy that communicates the organization's lack of tolerance for sexual harassment and sets up a complaint procedure is an insufficient relief mechanism for targets uncomfortable with active, confrontational behaviors. Organizational policies must also be designed to facilitate active complaints by targets displaying passive, acquiescent responses to sexual harassment. Training and counseling, along with prompt investigation and active enforcement of penalties against sexual harassers, should provide deterrents to sexual harassment in the workplace.

References

Brehm, J. W. (1966). *A theory of psychological reactance.* New York: Academic Press.

Brehm, J. W. (1972). *Responses to loss of freedom: A theory of psychological reactance.* Morristown, NJ: General Learning Press.

Equal Employment Opportunity Commission. (1980). Discrimination because of sex under Title VII of the Civil Rights Act of 1964, as amended: Adoption of the interim interpretive guidelines. *Federal Register, 45,* 25024–25025.

Gutek, B. A. (1985). *Sex and the workplace.* San Francisco: Jossey-Bass.

Gutek, B. A., Morasch, B., & Cohen, A. (1983). Interpreting social-sexual behavior in a work setting. *Journal of Vocational Behavior, 22,* 30–48.

Jensen, I., & Gutek, B. (1982). Attributions and assignment of responsibility for sexual harassment. *Journal of Social Issues, 38,* 121–137.

Livingston, J. (1982). Responses to sexual harassment on the job: Legal, organizational, and individual actions. *Journal of Social Issues, 38,* 5–22.

LoPiccolo, J., & Heiman, J. (1978). Cultural values and the therapeutic definition of sexual function and dysfunction. *Journal of Social Issues, 16,* 171–194.

Mainiero, L. A. (1986). Coping with powerlessness: The relationship of gender and job dependency to empowerment-strategy usage. *Administrative Science Quarterly, 31,* 633–653.

Meritor Savings Bank, FSB v. Vinson (106 S.Ct. 2399, 1986).

Overmier, J. B., & Seligman, M. E. P. (1967). Effects of inescapable shock upon subsequent escape and avoidance learning. *Journal of Comparative and Physiological Psychology, 63,* 28–33.

Reilly, T., Carpenter, S., Dull, V., & Bartlett, K. (1982). The factorial survey technique: An approach to defining sexual harassment on campus. *Journal of Social Issues, 38,* 99–110.

Seligman, M. E. P. (1974). Depression and learned helplessness. In R. J. Friedman & M. M. Katz (Eds.), *The psychology of depression: Contemporary theory and research* (pp. 83–113). Washington, DC: Winston-Wiley.

Silverman, D. (1976). Sexual harassment: Working women's dilemma. *Quest: A Feminist Quarterly, 3,* 15–24.

Tangri, S., Burt, M., & Johnson, L. (1982). Sexual harassment at work: Three explanatory models. *Journal of Social Issues, 38,* 33–54.

Terpstra, D., & Cook, S. (1985). Complainant characteristics and reported behaviors and consequences associated with formal sexual harassment charges. *Personnel Psychology, 38,* 559–574.

Thacker, R. A. (1992a). A descriptive study of behavioral responses of sexual harassment targets: Implications for control theory. *Employee Responsibilities & Rights Journal, 5,* 155–171.

Thacker, R. A. (1992b). Preventing sexual harassment in the workplace. *Training and Development Journal, 46,* 50–53.

Thacker, R. A., & Ferris, G. R. (1991). Understanding sexual harassment in the workplace: The influence of power and politics within the dyadic interaction of harasser and target. *Human Resource Management Review, 1,* 23–17.

Thacker, R. A., & Gohmann, S. F. (1993). Male/female differences in perceptions and effects of hostile environment sexual harassment: "Reasonable" assumptions? *Public Personnel Management, 22,* 461–473.

United States Merit Systems Protection Board. (1981). *Sexual harassment in the Federal workplace: Is it a problem?* Washington, DC: U.S. Government Printing Office.

United States Merit Systems Protection Board. (1988). *Sexual harassment in the Federal government: An update.* Washington, DC: U.S. Government Printing Office.

What the Boss Knows about You

Lee Smith

Dear Dr. Confidentiality,
Can the boss look into my head?
> Sincerely,
> Quaking in my cubicle

Dear Q:
Not yet. But remember that indiscreet message you punched into the computer system and then deleted? Company engineers can retrieve those electronic musings. Also, the spigot overhead that looks like part of the sprinkler system could be a miniature video camera. And your supervisor may have equipped his phone with a voice stress analyzer that detects any suspicious warblings when you defend your expense account.
> Take precautions,
> Dr. C.

Privacy is under stress as never before. As business squeezes out more productivity, companies turn to electronic gadgets to track workers' moves. With health insurance costs soaring, employers offer incentives to workers for round-the-clock clean living. Home and office merge while work and private time blur. At the end of the workday, Mom and Dad ferry home more work on floppy disks. The next morning they drop off the kids at the company day care center.

Today the companies that employ us seem to know everything from our charities to our cholesterol counts, including how much we save, what our credit rating may be, whether our children are toilet trained (the day care center needs to know), who our heirs are, and what model of car we prefer to rent. That's okay. Maybe. Trouble is, it's becoming increasingly possible for outsiders to tap into that information as well. That's not nearly as okay.

Washington's interest in privacy issues is growing. Proposed legislation that would require credit bureaus to divulge to a consumer free of charge all the information it has collected about him will soon be considered by the House Consumer Credit and Insurance subcommittee. Also, Senator Paul Simon (D-Illinois) is promoting a bill that would restrict employers that eavesdrop on customer service operators.

In this article *Fortune* examines current concerns over privacy. The discomforting conclusion: Companies are intruding more deeply into the lives of employees, and even though corporate intentions may be benign, the risk of a backlash is growing. Worker anxiety is likely to rise right along with the surveillance level, possibly hurting performance.

Most companies have failed to take steps to ease that apprehension by explaining to employees how supervisors look and listen in on subordinates, why it's done, and what the limits are. Yes, says the boss, we will canvass all electronic mail if we suspect criminal activity, such as drug trafficking. But no, your supervisor won't be told you're seeing a psychotherapist twice a week.

Workplace privacy is an issue that reaches beyond employer and employee relations. Business is increasingly vulnerable to corporate espionage. The employee who uses a cellular telephone is operating a mobile radio station that may inadvertently be broadcasting confidential information to anyone within radio-wave earshot.

As more electronic routes intersect and as all data go digital, the information highway of computers and telecommunications probably will attract roving brigands, who will waylay the unwary and plunder their secrets—and money. Microsoft Chairman Bill Gates acknowledges that the electronic networks his software helps build are merely "a tool, and like a hammer they can be used to hit a nail or smash someone in the face." Gates and his kind may know how to protect themselves from highwaymen, but the "technically challenged" could get hurt.

Encroachment on employee privacy has strong traditions. Many nineteenth-century industrialists made sure their laborers went to church. Eighty or so years back, Ford Motor Co. sent social workers to employees' homes to determine whether their habits and finances were worthy of bonuses.

The 1950s added the fashion of psychological profiles to the job interview. Among the 566 questions an applicant had to answer on the Minnesota Multiphasic Personality Inventory were such disturbing and intrusive inquiries as whether the sentence "I deserve severe punishment for my sins" aptly described the candidate's thoughts. Although many companies continue to collect psycho-profiles of their new hires, enlightened employers dumped such tests in the late 1960s. Plumbers with beards and flowered bell-bottoms proved as able to install sinks as the clean-shaven. Says Alan F. Westin, a Columbia University law professor and authority on workplace privacy: "Whether you had an MBA *was* relevant. Your lifestyle was *not.*"

That golden age didn't last beyond the 1970s. In the 1980s victims of assault and other crimes began to target companies as deep pockets. Why didn't Consolidated Crayons know that the security guard it hired was a convicted rapist? So companies began to canvass job applicants about criminal records. The forces most responsible for renewed intrusions on privacy were concerns about safety and costs—mostly drugs and health care—as well as the spreading web of electronic devices that keep workers wired to the office.

Drug testing.   The goal of a drug-free workplace, set by President Reagan in September 1986, means that an increasing number of workers submit to urinalysis tests that can detect traces of amphetamines, cocaine, heroin, and other controlled substances. The American Management Association reports that of the 630 members that responded to a survey, 85% will conduct such tests on at least some employees, generally the new ones, in 1993, up from 52% in 1990. Of those tested so far this year, 2.5% showed signs of drug use.

The federal government requires that all contractors who do more than $20,000 worth of business with Washington conduct random tests on a cross section of workers. Some companies go beyond the requirements. Many examine all new hires. Motorola plans to test all employees every three years no matter how long they have been with the company.

But airlines want Washington to reduce requirements. Carriers must now test at random a number equal to 50% of all their pilots, flight attendants, mechanics, and dispatchers a year, at a cost of close to $100 per test. The debt-burdened airlines argue that a rate of 10% would be adequate.

Health care.   The average cost of providing health insurance has risen to about $4,000 per employee, up from just over $1,600 a decade ago. Only 10% of employees and their dependents account for about 70% of total medical costs. But the 1992 Americans with Disabilities Act, which protects the handicapped from job discrimination, has made it almost impossible for employers to screen out the riskiest cases.

So companies have switched tactics. If you can't jettison them, at least try to keep them healthy. For the most part, such company programs are logical and humane, such as reimbursing workers for Smoke-Enders or Weight Watchers classes. But carried too far, paternalism looks very much like tyranny.

Electronic tethers.   No phenomenon has more complicated the issue of workplace privacy than the profusion of notebook computers, modems, and similar gadgets in the executive portable office. At times, such devices enhance privacy. A financial analyst can simultaneously crunch numbers and press grapes in the happy isolation of a Napa Valley vineyard.

But the same machines make it close to impossible to remain private. The fax hums into Sunday morning silence as the boss raises a few more questions before Monday's meeting. Beepers and electronic pagers find managers on vacation, in cars, at meetings, at parties, on the golf course—anywhere. The office no longer has walls. Privacy watchers have paid little attention to the electronic monitoring of upscale workers, including production and sales managers. Westin points out that a CEO can tap into a database and find out the progress of a project at any point. But if people know top management is constantly judging their work, it can destroy creativity. Says Westin: "Teams assigned to new undertakings won't take chances because they will worry not about how the project will look in the end, but how it will look at 3 P.M. on Tuesday."

By and large, continues Westin, workers trust management to use information it collects about them fairly. This year he helped Lou Harris Associates survey 1,000 workers at 300 companies, some with as few as 25 employees, others with more than 1,000. As many as 70% think consumer credit bureaus are far too nosy. "But by overwhelming majorities of 90% or more," reports Westin, "they think employers collect only information that is relevant and necessary."

Employers who let themselves be lulled by such scores are surely shortsighted. What companies demand to know and what employees insist on keeping private are clearly on a collision course. Attitudes about workplace privacy may seem touchy-feely, but then so are the moods that add up to consumer confidence. And when that heads south, there goes the bottom line.

A Multiple Constituency View of Employee Assistance Programs

Matthew J. Stollak and Joseph J. Martocchio

Employee assistance programs (EAPs) have made significant inroads into the hearts and minds of American businesses and corporations. Nearly 100 percent of *Fortune* 500 companies and over 10,000 companies in general offer some form of aid to their workers. The significance of EAPs for business operation has not gone unnoticed as numerous journals (*EAP Digest, Employee Assistance Quarterly, Journal of Employee Assistance Research*) and textbooks (Dickman, Challenger, Emener, & Hutchison, *Employee Assistance Programs: A Basic Text,* 1988) have been published. Diversity in the sizes and types of EAPs, however, makes it difficult to establish the cost of operating an employee assistance program.

As the title of this book suggests, we are concerned with the perspectives, context, functions, and outcomes of human resources management (HRM). But with whose perspectives are we concerned? Under what context? What are the functions? What are the resulting outcomes? As with any organizational subunit, various constituents have varied needs. A given constituent group may have a unique "perspective" on what activities the organizational subunit performs and what the group wants from that subunit. The EAP, as one relevant organizational subunit of human resources management, has a number of constituents with whom it must interact.

This article will examine the different constituent perspectives on the EAP. First we will define the nature and design of EAPs. Then we will focus on the multiple constituency approach, with special emphasis on the constituents of the EAP. Finally we will present implications for managing human resources.

What Is an EAP?

Employee assistance programs have been broadly defined as "mechanisms that provide the workplace with systematic means for dealing with personal problems that affect employees' job performance" (Blum & Bennett, 1990, p. 143). *Personal problems* refers to "the abuse of alcohol and drugs, psychiatric disorders, marital and family problems, and, to a limited extent, financial and legal difficulties" (Blum & Roman, 1989, p. 259).

Employee assistance programs have become increasingly broad in the scope of services that they offer. Holosko and Feit (1988) identify four stages or "generations" of programs that have emerged in the short history of EAPs. The first stage of EAPs, known as occupational alcoholism programs, focused purely on the problems associated with alcohol. The second stage was marked by the expansion of EAP focus toward a broad range of behavioral problems that are related to job performance. In addition to addressing alcohol-related problems, program offerings expanded to cover all types of addiction counseling, marital and family intervention, and mental health services. Concurrent with expansion of EAP activities was expansion into more diverse organizational settings—for example, educational institutions and health care.

The third-generation programs are referred to as the "new wave" EAPs. Emphasis is on a more proactive and preventive approach that addresses issues relating to overall employee health, wellness, and lifestyle.

Finally, the fourth generation of programs may be called "case management" programs. While maintaining the types of services already described, the case management approach tailors services to meet the unique needs of individuals. In an effort to contain costs, employees are tracked and monitored as they are linked to specialized services both within and external to the work organization.

Employee assistance programs play a critical role in addressing workplace problems. A brief examination of these job performance problems confirms the importance of the EAP as a unit worthy of examination. It is estimated that 20 percent of any work force is affected by personal problems that impact job performance (Masi, 1992). A 1989 study by the National Institute on Drug Abuse indicates that 12 percent of individuals in the work force have alcohol- and drug-related problems, while 6 to 8 percent have emotional problems. The result is a 25 percent decrease in productivity and increased costs for a given organization. Such lost productivity costs are calculated to be $50.6 billion for alcohol and $26 billion for drugs (Masi, 1992). Table 1

Table 1.
Quantifiable and qualitative losses resulting from job performance problems

Quantifiable losses	Qualitative losses
• Absenteeism	• Friction among workers
• Utilization of health benefits	• Damage to public image
• Overtime pay	• Poor decision making
• Tardiness	• Threat to public safety
• Machine downtime	• Threat to corporate security
• Sick leave abuse	
• Workers' compensation claims	• Trust in employee
	• Trust in employer
• Disciplinary actions	
• Disability payments	
• Retraining	
• Personnel turnover	
• Productivity losses	

Adapted from Masi, D. A. 1992. Employee assistance programs. In D. A. Masi (Ed.), *The AMA handbook for developing employee assistance & counseling programs:* 3. New York: AMACOM.

outlines the types of losses that are attributed to job performance problems. Clearly, EAPs are an important weapon for combatting these workplace maladies.

The Multiple Constituency Approach

An organization wants to know whether or not it is effective. Is our product targeting the right audience? How can we improve our performance? Are our customers satisfied? These are some questions businesses have consistently tried to address. Researchers have adopted a number of approaches, such as the systems model (Katz & Kahn, 1966; Yuchtman & Seashore, 1967), in trying to provide organizations with answers to such questions. The multiple constituency approach arose out of a sense of dissatisfaction with the available organizational effectiveness models. The primary concern of multiple constituency models revolves around the question: "Whose preferences should be satisfied through the distribution of the outcomes of organizational performance?" (Zammuto, 1984, p. 606).

The multiple constituency model of evaluation has been most developed in the work of Tsui (1984, 1987, 1990) on personnel departments. "Effectiveness," Tsui argues, "is defined from the perspectives of the constituencies, who also define the subunit's activities and its evaluation criteria" (1984, p. 188). The model of evaluation focuses on three dimensions: the constituencies of an organization, the activities an organizational department performs, and the criteria on which the department and the organization are evaluated.

The constituencies.   Tsui refers to a constituency as "a group of individuals holding similar preferences or interests pertaining to the activities of a focal organizational unit" (1990, p. 461). A constituent, then, is a single individual within a constituency or stakeholder group. Each organization has a number of constituencies with which it must contend. Some are specific, such as unions in a unionized firm. Most often, though, organizations face similar constituents—owners, managers, employees, and customers.

The activities of a department.   For Tsui, the concern is with domain specification and taxonomy. What are the important activities that should be performed by a personnel department? Under what conditions will these activities change? What kinds of activities are perceived as effective? Are these activities affected by the types of personnel hired by an organization? How many activities should be performed?

The evaluation criteria.   How do we measure the performance of a personnel department and an organization? The multiple constituency model argues that constituents define the criteria by which the department is measured. Both process and outcome criteria affect personnel actions only when they are considered in relation to multiple constituencies who assign weight to and help measure the criteria. The criteria that are chosen may affect constituency satisfaction.

The employee assistance program can be seen as an important part of the human resources function. Tsui's (1987) conceptual analysis notes that the operating level of a firm is composed of organizational units involved in the actual design of products. As the definition of an EAP implies, it, too, is involved in the delivery of services.

Who Are the Constituents of the EAP?

Given our view of the multiple constituency model, who are the constituencies that influence EAP operation?

The steering committee.   The steering committee is responsible for planning the EAP in collaboration with management and other professional employees. Once the program is implemented, the steering committee assumes overall management of the program. Though it does not have case-by-case responsibility, the steering committee does offer input at the public policy level. Training and

orientation programs are additional responsibilities (Battle, 1988; Wright, 1985).

The EAP staff.   EAPs have integrated service delivery, with counselors, trainers, and occupational social workers who provide assistance. The counselor typically offers a broad-brush treatment service for a broad range of psychosocial problems. The counselor must stay abreast of company policies as well as advances in the field. Most of all, the counselor is the keeper of confidentiality of information.

The trainer collaborates with the counselor in providing orientation and training regarding the operation of the EAP. Although most of the training occurs during the implementation of the program, the trainer will often return to offer seminars in various areas of interest, such as AIDS, stress management, sexual harassment, and violence in the workplace.

Organizational management.   This constituency comprises what is typically referred to as "top management": human resources managers, department heads, and executives—those at the top of the organizational hierarchy. It is often argued that top management support is necessary for policy implementation.

Supervisors.   Through constructive confrontation, supervisors are responsible for referring employees with deteriorating job performance to the EAP for help. It is expected that supervisors will undergo yearly training to remain sensitive to the latest changes in EAP technology.

Users of the program.   Program users clearly influence the operation of the program because they are so closely tied to its performance. Some employees enter the EAP voluntarily, either through self-referral or at the suggestion of others. Other employees may be required, through disciplinary action, to enter the program or face job loss.

The medical department.   The medical department offers the program a number of supportive services, such as integrating EAP services into the overall health care delivery system.

Unions.   Within unionized firms, labor's endorsement is often perceived as critical to the success of the EAP. Before the establishment of EAPs, it was often the union that provided assistance to troubled employees. As Tramm (1985) argues, the role of the union is a complex one:

> Is the union's primary function to protect the chemically dependent, including the alcoholic, from disciplinary action by management? Is it to act as watchdog for the chemically dependent's job while the sick individual participates in treatment? Or is it to sanction the "human contract" of labor-management relations—the possibilities for a relationship of total human concern—while management is more interested in issues of economy and production? (p. 95)

Family members.   Although family members do not directly influence EAP and organizational operation, they are directly affected by the treatment given to the troubled employee as well as by organizational changes. An employee's drinking problem does not affect the employee alone, nor does organizational relocation or downsizing. Also, family members may encourage or discourage an employee's use of the program.

External constituents.   Numerous external constituents also affect the operation of EAPs. The government, through legislation, affects the types of services and programs offered by companies. For example, the Federal Comprehensive Alcohol Abuse and Alcoholism Treatment and Rehabilitation Act of 1970 recognized alcoholism as a handicap that must be treated like any other disease, and the Drug-Free Workplace Act of 1988 required certain federal contractors to certify that they provide and maintain a drug-free workplace.

Insurance companies, through third-party payment, affect the development of community resource network strategies. If employees are referred outside of the company's EAP service provider to other community resources, treatment is generally covered by the company's or the union's insurance.

The general public, in a limited way, affects organizational provision of services. Employers are rapidly moving toward corporate social responsibility, an approach that "focuses on assisting corporations and business to make a commitment to the social and economic well-being of the communities in which they operate" (Gould & Smith, 1988, p. 12). This approach recognizes the fact that corporations have an indelible impact on the communities in which they reside. Adoption and implementation of EAP services is one way for corporations to show commitment to their communities.

Program Design

Having identified the relevant constituencies, we turn now to the activities and guiding policies of the EAP. First we will consider six aspects of the EAP core technology. Next, we will discuss eleven ingredients for success. Finally, we will review four components of EAP programs.

The EAP Core Technology

In his important work on organizations, Thompson (1967) examines the role of the core technology. Thompson refers to the core technology as the central activities of an organization, which the organization tries to protect from environmental influences. Organizations must cope with uncertainty when dealing with both the internal and the external environments. Protecting one's technologies is key to reducing uncertainty. The concept of an organizational core technology has been extended to employee assistance programs. Roman and Blum (1985, 1988) have identified six aspects of an EAP core technology.

The first component of the EAP core technology is *the identification of employees' behavioral problems on the basis of job performance issues.* Emphasis is placed on the specific job-related stressors rather than the symptoms related to alcoholism or other problems. This component assumes that dysfunctional job-related behavior can be identified easily by supervisors.

The second component of an EAP core technology identified by Roman and Blum (1988) is *the provision of expert consultation to supervisors, managers, and union stewards on the appropriate steps to take in utilizing employee assistance policy and procedures.* Blum and Roman (1989) have delineated four functions of this type of assistance. First, assistance facilitates the first component by equipping supervisors to distinguish between job-based problems and symptomatic ones. A second function is information processing: The EAP specialist distributes information about the way the system operates. A third function is the creation of linkages to other organizational policies. The final function of this component serves to diminish the "troubled supervisor" syndrome. Supervisors may experience conflict between the duties of serving the organization and trying to aid their subordinates. Educating supervisors can alleviate the pressures that may give rise to conflict.

The third component of the EAP core technology is *the availability and appropriate use of constructive confrontation.* Typically, an employee is faced simultaneously with "proof" of job performance deterioration and an EAP referral for improvement. Through confrontation an organization can demonstrate its positive attitude toward helping employees.

A fourth component is *the development of microlinkages with counseling, treatment, and other community resources.* This component focuses on the individual, determining what "fit" of community resources is available. If outside referrals are made, the EAP can provide case management and can control costs by demanding that outside sources be accountable for the efficiency and quality of their services. The success of microlinkages clearly depends on the EAP specialist's awareness of community services.

The fifth core component of EAP technology is *the creation and maintenance of macrolinkages between the work organization and counseling, treatment, and other community resources.* Whereas the fourth component focuses on the individual, emphasis here is on the service providers. This core component operates as a gatekeeper, balancing the needs of the client, the service provider, and the organization. Quality, accessibility, and accountability of referral sources are emphasized. Again, one must assume that service providers are in sufficient quantity in the surrounding area. Further, it has been argued that 4,000 to 6,000 employees are needed to create one viable EAP position (Featherston & Bednarek, 1981). On the other hand, 15 to 20 percent of the work force needs some sort of help (Masi, 1992).

The sixth and final component of the core technology is *the centrality of the employee's substance abuse problems as the program focus with the most significant promise for producing recovery and genuine cost savings for the organization in terms of future performance and reduced benefit usage.* It is hoped that, through the adoption and implementation of employee assistance, the organization can effectively, successfully, and constructively address substance abuse problems (Blum & Bennett, 1990; Blum & Roman, 1989; Roman & Blum, 1985, 1988). However, this core component should be expanded to include the increasingly diverse number of services that EAPs are currently offering.

Ingredients for EAP Success

Given this core technology, researchers suggest that a number of elements must be present for an EAP to be effective (Balgopal & Patchner, 1988; Dickman, 1988). Eleven "ingredients" are seen as critical. First, endorsements must be present. Employees will not view the program as legitimate unless there is active involvement from the highest level of the corporate structure. Second, if an organization is unionized, endorsement must come from labor. Third, a policy statement is needed. The intentions and philosophy of the program must be clearly stated. A fourth crucial ingredient is confidentiality. Employees seeking assistance for their problems must be secure in the knowledge that their problems will be kept in the strictest confidence. Fifth, training must be given to supervisors as well as labor stewards. It is suggested that training occur at least once a year. Financial coverage is also critical to a successful EAP. "When employees are clear that participating in the EAP may cost them something but that it won't break them, they will be more apt to accept a referral or to refer themselves" (Balgopal & Patchner, p. 98). Professional personnel are a seventh element. The EAP coordinator as well as the EAP staff must have sufficient knowledge and expertise in employee assistance, as well as access to needed resources. Broad service components are an eighth element. The EAP must be able to respond to a wide variety of employee needs and problems. A ninth element is accessibility. Employees need to be able to gain access to EAP sites quickly and conveniently as well as in a confidential manner. Just as critical for EAP success is awareness. The EAP must market its attributes throughout the organization. Finally, the EAP must conduct program evaluation.

Components of the EAP

As EAPs have grown, so has knowledge concerning their operation. Certain common elements have arisen that typify the diverse programs that are offered. These elements have been outlined by the U.S. Department of Health and Human Services (1987) and can be grouped into four functions: policies and procedures, administrative functions, education and training, and evaluation.

First, most EAPs have written policy statements that make their purposes clear. The policy statement often reflects both management's and labor's attitudes toward the objectives of the program. Confidentiality rules are developed and laid out to specify how records are maintained, how long they are maintained, who has access to records, and what information is released to whom and

under what conditions. Further, written procedures outline the appropriate actions to take vis-à-vis individuals referred by management, the union, or co-workers. Procedures are also developed to govern use of the program by employees and their family members.

Second, a number of administrative functions concerning the EAP are established: its position in the organization, its physical location, its record-keeping system, the relationship of the EAP to medical and disability benefit plans, the appropriateness of malpractice/liability insurance, and the qualifications of EAP staff.

A third common function involves education and training. The focus is on communication about EAP services that are available to employees and their families, employee education concerning substance abuse and other recognized problem areas, training for supervisors and labor stewards in appropriate constructive confrontation, and orientation regarding the appropriate roles of management and union representatives.

A fourth function involves the development of files for use in reviewing outside programs and evaluating both the program and the progress of its clients. On an individual level, the EAP focuses on follow-up and aftercare to assess employee improvement. On a macro level, the company communicates with and rates external referral sources, as well as evaluating overall EAP effectiveness through any number of methods, such as cost-benefit analysis or cost-effectiveness analysis.

Referrals

As we have seen, there is considerable variety in the services offered by EAPs. Yet, how do users come in contact with the EAP to take advantage of those services? This section outlines particular routes to assistance and their impact on the various constituents.

Self-Referral

Employees (or, sometimes, members of their families) may use EAP services in confidentiality for personal problems. In deciding to utilize the EAP, an individual typically goes through three stages. First, the person recognizes, through either self-reflection or interaction with others, that he or she has a problem and tries to manage it so that it does not disrupt work or family relationships. Second, the person realizes that he or she can no longer contain the problem and must take action. Finally, the person decides to contact the EAP or some other community resource.

Defining what constitutes self-referral has been troubling for EAP researchers. Often, employees who are believed to self-refer have actually been pressured by family members, supervisors, or peers to seek help (Sonnenstuhl, Staudenmeier, & Trice, 1988).

Supervisor Referral

When we looked at the core technology of EAPs, we saw that supervisor recognition of deteriorating job performance and the ensuing constructive confrontation were critical. This job performance model, which arose from the Alcoholics Anonymous philosophy involving "hitting bottom" and the industrial and labor relations philosophy of fairness (Sonnenstuhl et al., 1988), defines emotional problems in the context of the workplace, offers employees the opportunity to change their behavior, and prevents them from being unnecessarily rushed into treatment. Trice and Beyer (1984a) found that employees who experienced constructive confrontation combined with counseling showed greater improvement than those who experienced either one alone.

Peer Referral

Peer referral is most often seen in union-based EAPs. Union leaders are critical of the job performance model, arguing that union solidarity should shelter employees from the demands of employers. Instead, the union helps its members and protects them from being forced into treatment. Whereas the job performance model focuses on constructive confrontation, proof of job impairment, and coercive motivation to use the EAP, the peer referral model re-

lies on intervention, deepening concern, and ongoing support (Molloy, 1985).

Medical Referral

Medical referrals constitute a small portion of the paths taken to employee assistance. A study of the Anheuser-Busch national EAP, for example, showed only 2 percent of referrals attributed to the medical department (Magruder, 1988). A medical referral is based on the identification of a medical symptom or group of symptoms related to a personal problem such as alcohol abuse. Referral to the EAP is viewed as part of the required treatment plan. The decision to utilize the EAP, however, is up to the employee.

Other Sources of Referral

As we have mentioned, other parties may push an employee toward assistance. Family members may want a troubled employee to seek help. A benefits or safety department may want an employee to visit the EAP. Even courts, especially in driving-under-the-influence (DUI) cases, may refer employees to the EAP.

Service Delivery System Options

Just as each organization has its own unique operation and culture, EAPs assume different forms. Phillips and Older (1985) have identified six distinct models for the delivery of employee assistance services. Differences in EAP services often arise from variations in organizational size, the amount of organizational slack available for EAP services, and the willingness of upper management to provide such slack in support of those services. In this section we will examine the various types of EAPs that constituents may encounter. Each subsection will first describe the nature and operation of a particular model and then outline the various benefits and disadvantages of the model for each constituency.

Model 1—Internal Program

Several types of internal programs exist. They can be categorized as (1) programs providing assessment and referral services; (2) programs providing assessment, referral, and counseling services; and (3) internal programs located off site. Coordination of client activity occurs within the context of the work environment. Follow-up and feedback are coordinated by the treatment resource and designated EAP personnel. EAP staffing varies with the kind of service provided: Programs that offer counseling need professional staff members with formal training.

Constituency perspectives. *Users of the program.* Users find the program advantageous in that it is visible and accessible. With the internal program commonly on site, employees may be more familiar with the program and the services that it offers. However, on-site programs encounter the problem of confidentiality. Users may be reluctant to visit the EAP if they may be observed by others. Further, an internal program is less likely to be perceived as a benefit by employees.

EAP staff. A number of advantages accrue for the EAP staff. An internal program offers a sense of ownership. Staff members believe they have greater say in what services are offered. As insiders, EAP staff feel they are better able to influence change within the organization. Being inside also improves knowledge of the organization and its culture. Internal EAPs can respond to and intervene in crises more rapidly than other types of programs. Finally, internal programs offer EAP staff the opportunity to improve communications within the organization.

Internal programs also have disadvantages for EAP staff. Only large organizations are able to front full-time staffs to oversee such programs. As a result, the staff may consist of a part-time person or persons, inadequately trained and with insufficient time to see all troubled employees when they need help. A limited staff is expected to fill numerous roles; skills and expertise will be limited as well. Burnout may result. Finally, staff members may experience conflict between provider and organizational roles: Whom is the EAP staff supposed to serve—the troubled employee or top management constraints?

Supervisors. Supervisors like internal programs for the improved communications with EAP staff that may occur, as well as the familiarity with EAP operations. Supervisors thus view internal programs as more credible than other types of programs.

Organizational management. Given the high cost of providing a full-time staff, management is reluctant to adopt this type of program, especially in mid-size and smaller organizations. However, internal programs do afford greater control over the types of services that are offered and the staff that is hired. Organizational control also means greater commitment on the part of management. Upper management must have the ability to evaluate the skills and performance of EAP staff, and this is not always the case.

Medical department. An internal program offers the medical department an opportunity to better integrate EAP services with the organization's overall health care delivery system. In fact, EAP resources exist at some stage of development within most medical departments.

Model 2—Service Center Program

The service center program is an external, or contracted, EAP. An outside agency is responsible for its major functions. Service centers fall into two categories. One type provides treatment through third-party reimbursement; the other is free-standing, referring employees to appropriate community treatment facilities. The service center also may offer assistance with organizational development and with the clinical functions of assessment, referral, follow-up, and feedback.

Constituency perspectives. *Users of the program.* The advantage of the service center program lies in its ability to protect the confidentiality of clients better than an internal program can. Because the program is off site, employees may be less reluctant to use it. Service center programs often have more diverse staffs than internal programs and thus can serve a broader range of employees. The service center also allows for better identification of community resources.

Despite these advantages, employees may not be as familiar with EAP services and operations. The service center may present an accessibility problem for employees who do not have their own transportation. Being located off site also limits the ability of EAP staff to respond immediately to crises. Also, treatment may be too narrow.

EAP staff. Because it needs to interact with a broad range of organizations, this type of EAP employs a more diverse staff. Staff members are better able to identify resources and maintain communication with professionals in the community.

Unfortunately, being external to an organization, staff may suffer from a lack of knowledge concerning the organizational environment and the work culture. Communication with the contracting organization may be difficult, and EAP staff may have trouble relating to the work issues within the organization.

Supervisors. Supervisors are less enthusiastic about service center programs. They are less accessible to EAP staff and are reluctant to deal with "outsiders." Without a meaningful EAP liaison, service center programs are likely to be contacted. This perspective can be seen as a product of "social distance"; the extent to which the supervisor felt there was someone in the service center program who knew the work organization.

Organizational management. The service center is more suitable for small organizations because of the lower costs involved and the diversity of resources that are made available. Some managers prefer service center programs because they fear the liability of medical malpractice that may arise if company clinicians treat employees. Contracting out provides the opportunity to shift medical liability (Sonnenstuhl, 1986).

Model 3—Internal Program with Service Center Support

This model adopts the service center approach but recognizes the ability of professionals within the work organization to publicize the EAP, assist employees, and motivate them to utilize the services. Options for assistance are thus available within or outside the workplace; the service center simply serves as a support for the internal EAP.

Constituency perspectives. *Users of the program.* For users the advantages of the program are similar to those of service center programs—assured confidentiality and greater staff expertise and skill. This approach, with accessibility, familiarity, and responsiveness to crises, does not share the disadvantages of the typical service center.

EAP staff. With service center support, EAP staff can call on a greater range of resources. However, the combination of in-house and external resources may engender communication difficulties around role definition.

Supervisors. This approach resolves some of the skepticism that supervisors feel toward service centers. EAP staff are more accessible, and supervisors are more familiar with EAP operation. However, if the approach is to be optimally utilized, an internal liaison must be present, or its advantages will be lost.

Organizational management. From management's standpoint the major drawback is cost. Combining the internal program with service center support increases the cost of operating the program. Also, given potential difficulties with role definition, organizational management may find it difficult to hold someone accountable if problems arise.

Model 4—EAP Located in a Treatment or Social Service Agency

This type of EAP is offered at no cost, or through a contractual arrangement, by a treatment or social service agency within the community. This approach is often adopted because the necessary assessment and referral services are not available within the organization and no free-standing service center can be established. The EAP staff consists primarily of internal coordinators who facilitate training and referral, but treatment takes place off site.

Constituency perspectives. *Users of the program.* For program users in small towns or rural areas, this type of approach may be the only one capable of providing the needed resources. Because counseling takes place off site, confidentiality is better protected.

EAP staff. As with other off-site approaches, understanding of and communication with the work organization are limited. However, staff members of local facilities may feel they have a vested interest in the success of the program; EAP staff will be more committed to making the program work.

Supervisors. Again, supervisors will be less familiar with the operation of the EAP and may be more reluctant to make referrals. An EAP coordinator from the agency must work to encourage supervisor acceptance.

Organizational management. In this model treatment can often be provided under the company's existing medical coverage. Although this approach is less costly, it still carries the price tag of questions about the validity of the assessment or diagnostic service as well as the validity of the referral.

Model 5—Union-Based EAP

In this model services are provided by the union at the union office or hiring hall. The impetus for providing assistance comes from union coordinators. Employees are referred to external treatment resources, and follow-up is coordinated by the company EAP. Depending on the contract, supervisors and management may refer union members to the EAP office.

Constituency perspectives. *Users of the program.* For users who are union members, the EAP is seen as much more credible. Given the union dislike of constructive confrontation, the union may provide a safer haven. Confidentiality is more likely to be protected.

EAP staff. In the union setting the EAP staff's skills and expertise may be limited. Staff may not have connections to community resources. However, in this setting there is no conflict between the duty to serve the organization and the duty to serve the employee. EAP staff can concentrate more fully on the employee without the concern for accountability to organizational management.

Supervisors. Beyer, Trice, and Hunt (1980) found that supervisors were more likely in unionized facilities than in nonunion installations to apply government policies concerning alcoholism. This phenomenon may be attributed to familiarity with those policies. Supervisors in unionized facilities were well informed about union support for those policies and were therefore more likely to invoke them.

Organizational management. Because the union bears the cost of implementing and administering the program, management incurs little cost. Given the adversarial relationship between management and labor, union-based EAPs are likely to be viewed with some suspicion. However, cooperation is more likely to be found between managers and lower-level union officers than between managers and higher-level officers; cooperation may be seen as political rather than empathetic (Trice & Beyer, 1982).

Model 6—Group Consortium

A consortium develops out of small organizations' need for service and typically constitutes the only source of assistance for members of those organizations in the realm of personal problems. Assistance is provided for members of a profession, such as lawyers or teachers. External treatment resources are utilized.

Constituency perspectives. *Users of the program.* Often, the consortium is the only source of assistance available to its users. The unique nature of the clientele also promotes flexibility in service delivery. Programs are designed to meet the particular needs of members. Confidentiality remains a problem, however, and there is no off-site screening and referral.

EAP staff. EAP staff are better able to coordinate treatment and monitor follow-up to meet the specialized needs of the clientele. As in model 1 (the internal program model), there are improved knowledge and communication within the organization, yet targeting a specific clientele limits the types of resources utilized. Available and useful community resources may be ignored.

Supervisors. As with model 1, the group consortium is internal and thus has more credibility with supervisors. Supervisors will be more familiar with the EAP process and staff.

Organizational management. The consortium approach is costly given the substantial staffing requirements. Further, a high degree of interorganization and cooperation is needed if the program is to be effective. The complexity of policy making increases, and there is less individual input into system operation.

Evaluation of EAPs

What problems does the researcher face in attempting to evaluate EAPs? A California State University survey on the current status of cost savings in evaluation of EAPs identified major obstacles that affected eighty-two organizations responding to the nationwide survey. Inavailability of data and lack of time were cited by 43 percent of the respondents as the two major obstacles they encountered in conducting evaluations of their programs. Cost constraints, confidentiality concerns, and difficulty in designing an evaluation strategy were the other difficulties that were reported as most prevalent (Burton & Houts, 1990).

Organizations that attempt to conduct thorough EAP evaluation often meet with roadblocks regarding the data required for such an undertaking. Many companies simply do not have useful, retrievable information available for program evaluation. Often, records that are supposed to be kept by program staff and supervisors are in reality not maintained consistently. Because of privacy concerns, qualitative data regarding clients' views of services and the impact of the program on their work environment are seldom collected systematically (Balgopal & Patchner, 1988). The main source for such data is anecdotal writings, which also may not be kept on a regular basis. Often, however, the evaluation effort itself leads the organization to organize, systematize, and update EAP data systems, to the benefit of future program planning and service delivery (Holosko, 1988).

The question of who should be responsible for collecting data for evaluation purposes is an issue in itself. Often the use of outside consultants only reinforces concerns about confidentiality and privacy. Moreover, there is no guarantee that the EAP staff will cooperate fully with the outside consultants in obtaining the necessary data, as their commitment to the program evaluation may be less than firm (Balgopal & Patchner, 1988). On the other hand, if data collection is the responsibility of EAP staff, their lack of research skills may complicate the project; a considerable time investment might be needed for them to acquire the necessary skills. Further, the EAP staff may be wary about the evaluation outcome and concerned about what the results may reveal about the program.

Another problem plaguing evaluation attempts is the lack of a shared database that would allow different EAPs to obtain comparison information on treatment results, utilization rates, and cost-benefit issues. The lack of such information makes it difficult for organizations to compare in-house and externally contracted programs, broad-brush and specialized EAPs, and job performance scales and to assess the general impact of these programs on the workplace (Bureau of National Affairs, 1987).

The issue of participant confidentiality is another major concern in EAP evaluation. The employee has already taken a difficult step in seeking assistance to deal with substance abuse, marital or family conflicts, or emotional problems. Compounding this difficulty with apprehensions about personal data being exposed in an evaluation process is likely to be extremely threatening. For their part, EAP staff may be extremely reluctant to share information that is protected under doctor-client privilege. All employees have the right to ask for help and to know that their problems will be kept in the strictest confidence.

For sound evaluation, certain elements of the research design must be in place; this has not always been the case in past evaluations. The preferred design is an experimental one incorporating random assignment to both treatment and control groups (Balgopal & Patchner, 1988), as in the testing of new therapeutic drugs. Random assignment serves to draw samples that are representative of a known population and comparable to one another within sampling error limits. The use of a control group rules out extraneous factors that may affect the course of an experiment (Cook & Campbell, 1979). In EAP evaluation, ideally one would sample the population to obtain representative numbers of program users and nonusers. Unfortunately, however, use of the design that would be sound research practice would be both difficult and unethical in the context of an EAP. One cannot randomly assign some people to a control group while others in an experimental group are receiving services. Clearly, assigning an alcoholic to a control group would be unsafe as well as unethical. Further, because of confidentiality concerns, even a comparison group of non–EAP users cannot be incorporated into a research design because an individual in the comparison group might erroneously be perceived by a supervisor, fellow worker, or researcher as an EAP client.

If the measurement tool is to be considered reliable, it must be possible to conclude that the behavioral changes of a person in treatment result from participation in the EAP and are not due to factors other than the treatment program itself. As discussed earlier, some EAP clients seek treatment voluntarily, whereas others are formally referred by supervisors because of poor job performance. The nature of the selection process may influence findings in an EAP evaluation as outcomes may reflect factors in addition to the EAP itself (Tompkins, 1990).

Tompkins (1990) also points out that sample size may well be a problem in EAP evaluations. An evaluation will be valid only if it is based on a sample that represents the target population in terms of employee demographic characteristics. In addition, the sample must be large enough to represent the various types of individuals for whom the program was designed (Kurtz, Googins, & Howard, 1984). Companies may need to compare their experiences, and they can accomplish this only through cooperative research efforts.

Conducting an EAP evaluation is very costly and time-consuming. Often companies feel that spending $500,000 to evaluate a program that costs only $300,000 to run is not a wise business decision (Walsh & Egdahl, 1989). Follow-up studies for EAP clients, recommended to last from 3 to 5 years, are likewise extremely costly and time-consuming, yet they are essential for an accurate assessment of sustained behavioral change brought about by an EAP (Kurtz et al., 1984).

The criteria that are ultimately chosen to evaluate the EAP must meet the needs of various constituencies within the organization. In addition, these measures must reflect the specific goals of the EAP being evaluated. Top management, the EAP staff, employees, and supervisors all have different points of view regarding the EAP and its evaluation. As Straussner (1988) points out in a discussion of a study of EAPs in New York, top management is often looking for ways to avoid unnecessary costs, whereas the EAP staff and employees are more concerned about the accessibility and confidentiality of the EAP. Supervisors can become an EAP's most important allies if positive experiences result from the referral of employees to the program (Googins, 1989).

It is fair to conclude that pressures to evaluate EAPs will continue as corporate decision making is driven by concern for the bottom line, the high costs of employee benefits, and increased competition in national and foreign markets. Currently, there are no firm answers concerning which methodologies should be used in company settings to assess employee assistance programs. Until such answers are available, many EAP managers will be under pressure to persuade senior managers as well as other constituents that their programs deserve ongoing company support and commitment.

Implications for
Human Resources Management

Strategic human resources management focuses on the best way to fit human resources policies and practices to an organization's business objectives and operational requirements. The employee assistance program is an important function of HRM that has both short- and long-term implications for organizational success. Personal problems, such as substance abuse, may be related to a decline in personal and co-worker safety and productivity or to an increase in absenteeism or even criminal behavior (Tompkins, 1990; Trice & Beyer, 1984b). Addressing personal problems through the offerings of an EAP can help shape a productive work force, which is clearly essential if an organization is to remain competitive.

The necessity of identifying the multiple needs of diverse constituencies also has strong implications for HRM. One potential use of the multiple constituency approach concerns the control of resources. For an EAP or any other organizational subunit, adequate funding and staffing are clearly necessary. Perceived EAP effectiveness may affect the amount of resources that the EAP can negotiate. The multiple constituency approach may provide avenues the EAP can take to secure a favorable assessment from those wielding power over resources. An understanding of the nature of the constituencies may also help EAP managers solicit resource assistance from other organizational units, assistance that could in turn help meet the needs of those constituencies.

According to Blum and Roman (1989), the EAP is viewed as a human resources tool with substantial potential for reducing uncertainty. But, as we have noted, the EAP alone will not have much impact on uncertainty. The absence of strong quantitative data makes it difficult to establish the relative effectiveness and success of EAPs. The multiple constituency approach, however, provides a useful framework to help EAP managers understand the conflicting constituent demands they encounter. By identifying the various services desired by the constituencies and the criteria by which the EAP is judged, managers can achieve a better fit with the organizational operation and culture.

Conclusion

We have examined the functions of the employee assistance program, the contexts in which it operates, the perspectives of its various constituencies, and the different outcomes that may occur with the use of the multiple constituency approach. Evaluation of EAPs has proven to be a daunting task. The continuing shifts in emphasis within EAPs, as well as the changing constraints both within and external to the organizational work environment, make the multiple constituency approach a critical tool for future human resources and EAP practices.

References

Balgopal, P. R., & Patchner, M. A. (1988). Evaluating employee assistance programs: Obstacles, issues and strategies. In M. Holosko & M. D. Feit (Eds.), *Evaluation of employee assistance programs* (pp. 95–106). New York: Haworth.

Battle, S. F. (1988). Issues to consider in planning employee assistance program evaluations. In M. Holosko & M. D. Feit (Eds.), *Evaluation of employee assistance programs* (pp. 79–94). New York: Haworth.

Beyer, J. M., Trice, H. M., & Hunt, R. (1980). Impact of federal sector unions on supervisory use of personnel policies. *Industrial and Labor Relations Review, 33,* 212–232.

Blum, T. C., & Bennett, N. (1990). Employee assistance programs: Utilization and referral data, performance management, and prevention concepts. In P. M. Roman (Ed.), *Alcohol problem intervention in the workplace* (pp. 143–162). New York: Quorum Books.

Blum, T. C., & Roman, P. M. (1989). Employee assistance programs and human resource management. In G. Ferris & K. Rowland (Eds.), *Research in personnel and human resources management* (Vol. 7, pp. 259–312). Greenwich, CT: JAI Press.

Bureau of National Affairs. (1987). *Employee assistance programs: Benefits, problems and prospects* (BNA Special Report). Rockville, MD: Author.

Burton, G., & Houts, L. (1990). *The current status of cost-savings evaluations in EAPs.* Internal paper, California State University, Fresno.

Cook, T. D., & Campbell, D. T. (1979). *Quasi-experimentation: Design & analysis issues for field settings.* Boston: Houghton Mifflin.

Dickman, J. F. (1988). Ingredients of an effective employee assistance program. In J. F. Dickman, B. R. Challenger, W. G. Emener, Jr., & W. S. Hutchison, Jr. (Eds.), *Employee assistance programs: A basic text* (pp. 110–121). Springfield, IL: Charles C Thomas.

Dickman, J. F., Challenger, B. R., Emener, W. G., Jr., & Hutchison, W. S., Jr. (Eds.) (1988). *Employee assistance programs: A basic text.* Springfield, IL: Charles C Thomas.

Featherston, H., & Bednarek, R. (1981). A positive demonstration of concern for employees. *Personnel Administrator, 26(9),* 43–47.

Googins, B. (1989). Revisiting the role of the supervisor in employee assistance programs. *Drugs in the workplace: Research and evaluation data* (NIDA Research Monograph 91). Washington, DC: National Institute on Drug Abuse.

Gould, G. M., & Smith, M. L. (1988). *Social work in the workplace.* New York: Springer.

Holosko, M. (1988). Prerequisites for EAP evaluations: A case for more thoughtful evaluation planning. In M. Holosko & M. D. Feit (Eds.), *Evalua-*

tion of employee assistance programs (pp. 59–67). New York: Haworth.

Holosko, M. J., & Feit, M. D. (1988). Onward and upward. In M. Holosko & M. D. Feit (Eds.), *Evaluation of employee assistance programs* (pp. 281–283). New York: Haworth.

Katz, D., & Kahn, R. L. (1966). *The social psychology of organizations.* New York: Wiley.

Kurtz, N. R., Googins, B., & Howard, W. C. (1984). Measuring the success of occupational alcoholism programs. *Journal of Studies on Alcohol, 45(1),* 33–45.

Magruder, D. W. (1988). A national employee assistance program: An example. In J. F. Dickman, B. R. Challenger, W. G. Emener, Jr., & W. S. Hutchison, Jr. (Eds.), *Employee assistance programs: A basic text* (pp. 139–148). Springfield, IL: Charles C Thomas.

Masi, D. A. (1992). Employee assistance programs. In D. A. Masi (Ed.), *The AMA handbook for developing employee assistance and counseling programs.* New York: AMACOM.

Molloy, D. J. (1985). Peer referral: A programmatic and administrative review. In S. H. Klarreich, J. L. Francek, & C. E. Moore (Eds.), *The human resources management handbook: Principles and practice of employee assistance programs* (pp. 102–110). New York: Praeger.

Phillips, D. A., & Older, H. J. (1988). Models of service delivery. In J. F. Dickman, B. R. Challenger, W. G. Emener, Jr., & W. S. Hutchison, Jr. (Eds.), *Employee assistance programs: A basic text* (pp. 133–138). Springfield, IL: Charles C Thomas.

Roman, P. M., & Blum, T. C. (1985). Modes and levels of data management affecting the EAP practitioner. In S. H. Klarreich, J. L. Francek, & C. E. Moore (Eds.), *The human resources management handbook: Principles and practice of employee assistance programs* (pp. 203–221). New York: Praeger.

Roman, P. M., & Blum, T. C. (1988). The core technology of employee assistance programs: A reaffirmation. *ALMACAN, 15,* 3–8.

Sonnenstuhl, W. J. (1986). *Inside an emotional health program: A field study of workplace assistance for troubled employees.* Ithaca, NY: ILR Press.

Sonnenstuhl, W. J., Staudenmeier, W. J., Jr., & Trice, H. M. (1988). Ideology and referral categories in employee assistance program research. *The Journal of Applied Behavioral Science, 24(4),* 383–396.

Straussner, S. L. A. (1988). A comparison of in-house and contractual employee assistance programs. In M. Holosko & M. D. Feit (Eds.), *Evaluation of employee assistance programs* (pp. 69–78). New York: Haworth.

Thompson, J. D. (1967). *Organizations in action.* New York: McGraw-Hill.

Tompkins, C. P. (1990). *Drug abuse among workers and employee assistance programs.* Paper presented at the NIDA Center for Drug Abuse Services Research Annual Advisory Committee Meeting.

Tramm, M. L. (1985). Union-based programs. In S. H. Klarreich, J. L. Francek, & C. E. Moore (Eds.), *The human resources management handbook: Principles and practice of employee assistance programs* (pp. 95–101). New York: Praeger.

Trice, H. M., & Beyer, J. M. (1982). A study of union-management cooperation in a long-standing alcoholism program. *Contemporary Drug Problems, 11,* 295–317.

Trice, H. M., & Beyer, J. M. (1984a). Work-related outcomes of constructive confrontation strategies in a job-based alcoholism program. *Journal of Studies on Alcohol, 45,* 393–404.

Trice, H. M., & Beyer, J. M. (1984b). Employee assistance programs: Blending performance-oriented and humanitarian ideologies to assist emotionally disturbed employees. In J. R. Greenley (Ed.), *Research in community and mental health* (Vol. 4, pp. 245–297). Greenwich, CT: JAI Press.

Tsui, A. S. (1984). Personnel department effectiveness: A tripartite approach. *Industrial Relations, 23(2),* 184–197.

Tsui, A. S. (1987). Defining the activities and effectiveness of the human resource department. *Human Resource Management, 26(1),* 35–69.

Tsui, A. S. (1990). A multiple constituency model of effectiveness: An empirical examination at the human resource subunit level. *Administrative Science Quarterly, 35,* 458–483.

U.S. Department of Health and Human Services. (1987). *Standards for employee alcoholism and/or assistance programs.* Public Health Service, Alcohol, Drug Abuse, and Mental Health Administration. Washington, DC: National Institution on Drug Abuse.

Walsh, D. C., & Egdahl, R. H. (1989). Corporate perspective on work site wellness programs: A report on the seventh PEW fellows conference. *Journal of Occupational Medicine, 31(6),* 551–556.

Wright, D. A. (1985). Policy and procedures: The essential elements in an EAP. In S. H. Klarreich, J. L. Francek, & C. E. Moore (Eds.), *The human resources management handbook: Principles and practice of employee assistance programs* (pp. 13–23). New York: Praeger.

Yuchtman, E., & Seashore, S. (1967). A system resource approach to organizational effectiveness. *American Sociological Review, 32,* 891–903.

Zammuto, R. F. (1984). A comparison of multiple constituency models of organizational effectiveness. *Academy of Management Review, 9(4),* 606–616.

Outcomes of Human Resources Management

Successful implementation of a quality human resources program will usually result in a number of positive organizational outcomes. It is, however, sometimes difficult to determine a priori which interventions will be successful. Our intention in Part 6 is to indicate those factors that will have significant effects upon the outcomes of human resources management programs—the bottom line. Human resources programs are costly. But, in a long-range view of the process, the costs will be returned in terms of effectiveness, productivity, and the satisfaction of individuals in an organization. Money can be wasted on human resources or invested in human resources. The implications are obvious: Preparing and implementing well-thought-out human resources programs will only improve the bottom line of organizational success.

The articles in Chapter 14 are concerned with employee attitudes. The way employees view their work, the way they are managed, and the organization itself all affect the way employees perform. Negative attitudes toward work-related factors or toward the organization can be quite dysfunctional. Have we as a society developed different work values from those of our predecessors? The articles in this chapter provide insight into this issue.

In some instances, the most effective decision is a separation decision. Employees may leave an organization voluntarily or involuntarily for a number of reasons. Chapter 15 concerns the separation process and emphasizes techniques for handling it in a legally defensible manner.

Chapter 16 is related to the assessment of the most important outcomes in human resources—performance and effectiveness. What must an organization do to maximize the effectiveness of the human resources management program? Much advice is offered pertaining to activities that are essential to human resources competitiveness from both a dollar cost perspective and a strategic perspective.

CHAPTER 14

Employee Attitudes

Work-related attitudes play an important role in organization performance. Many of individuals' work-related attitudes result from myriad interactions with factors related to human resources programs. Thus, human resources professionals are instrumental in determining, developing, and improving work-related attitudes. Those attitudes include attitudes toward the job itself; attitudes toward the context or setting in which the work is performed; and attitudes toward co-workers, subordinates, and supervisors. Although the ways in which attitudes affect performance are not easy to predict, they nonetheless do have some impact upon performance.

There have been many reports that work-related attitudes have become less positive over the last few decades. Two possibilities are associated with negative work attitudes: They may be a sign of significant underlying problems in an organization, and they may be a cause of some undesirable organizational outcomes in the future (absenteeism, poor performance). Because they are linked to a number of deleterious organizational outcomes, negative attitudes can be directly related to the organization's financial viability.

The first article in this chapter, by De Meuse and Tornow, suggests that the relationship between organizations and their employees has become tattered. There is much to do to rebuild this relationship. Mirvis and Kanter, in the second article, elaborate on the same notion. There has been a marked increase in the cynicism of American workers. They mistrust management and feel exploited. Because workers are influenced by their attitudes, work life will suffer. The authors recommend an overhaul in the relationship between organizations and employees.

Suggestions for Further Reading

Barks, J. (1993). Should you be more picky about warehouse pay? *Distribution, 92,* 71–75.

Bracken, D. (1992). Benchmarking employee attitudes. *Training & Development, 46,* 49–53.

Denton, D. (1992). Keeping employees: The Federal Express approach. *SAM Advanced Management Journal, 57,* 10–13.

Doyle, K. (1992). From babies to boardroom. *Incentive, 166,* 32–35, 132.

Hauser, R., Jr., & Hebert, F. (1992). Managerial issues in expert system implementation. *SAM Advanced Management Journal, 57,* 10–15.

Keep your internal customers happy. (1993, March). *HR Focus,* p. 7.

Kumar, S., Gupta, Y. (1993). Statistical process control at Motorola's Austin assembly plant. *Interfaces, 23,* 84–92.

Management at BBC and BA is "out of touch," staff survey shows. (1993). *Personnel Management, 25,* 5.

Schiemann, W. (1992, April). Why change fails. *Across the Board,* pp. 53–54.

Vargo, R., & McDonough, S. (1993). How to do more with less. *Financial Executive, 9,* 41–45.

The Tie That Binds—Has Become Very, Very Frayed!

Kenneth P. De Meuse and Walter W. Tornow

"I don't trust them. They have lied to me too many times."

A disgruntled employee

"My staff schedules Friday lunches together just like this will be the last Friday we'll be together. We do this every Friday—waiting to be terminated!"

A frustrated manager

In 1956, William H. Whyte wrote the book *The Organization Man*. It described a phenomenon in Corporate America in which an employee completely invested himself in *his* company—working 60- to 70-hour weeks, being on the road whenever and wherever needed, relocating on a dime's notice. In other words, he did whatever the company asked. In return, *his* employer would provide a "good job" with "good pay," offer plenty of advancement opportunities, and grant annual merit increases. In other words, the company offered financial security! It was a womb-to-tomb mentality.

Such an employer-employee relationship gave order, predictability, accountability. It reassured employees who had 30-year mortgages, monthly car payments, and plans for their children's education and retirement. On the other hand, it also permitted employers to develop 5- and 10-year strategic plans, because it guaranteed a stable work force for managerial succession and business continuity. It was a tidy, neatly wrapped, little world. The corporate knot between employer and employee was well tied.

During the 1990s, Whyte's book no longer applies. Obviously, now the book would be titled *The Organization Person* because more than half of the employees in America are women. But much more importantly, the phenomenon of such an "organization man" no longer exists. Nowadays, a new corporation-person bond is emerging, one that assumes each party is much less dependent on the other, one in which mutual loyalty is rapidly disappearing, and one in which mutual trust may be at an all-time low.

Public opinion polls clearly show employees are becoming less committed to their employers. For example, a 1986 *Business Week* poll of 600 mid-level managers indicated that 65% believed salaried employees were less loyal to their employers now than they were 10 years ago. A 1987 *Industry Week* readership poll revealed that 70% felt loyalty between employees and their companies was rapidly disappearing. Fully 60% admitted they were less loyal than they were five years ago.

Evidence reveals that, likewise, employers are less committed to their employees. In many companies, "RIFs" (reductions in force) have become a way of life. Approximately two million managers have lost their jobs since 1980 due to corporate takeovers. The *Wall Street Journal* estimated that in 1985 alone, 600,000 mid-level managers were squeezed out in corporate belt-tightening. Many of the pillars of American business have cut staffs in recent years: AT&T, Apple Computer, General Motors, Du Pont, CBS, Eastman Kodak, Dow Chemical, Control Data, Ford Motor Company, Kraft, Westinghouse, Honeywell—the list goes on and on.

Further, more and more top executives appear to be taking care of themselves via the

Reprinted with permission of The Human Resource Planning Society from *Human Resource Planning, 13:3* (1990): 203–213.

"golden parachute." For instance, when CBS was taken over by Sony, Thomas Wyman was booted out as CEO. He did not leave empty handed, however. He received $4.3 million up front plus $400,000 a year for the rest of his life; he was only 57 years old (Bell, 1988). When Brunswick Corporation bought Bayliner Boats, the Bayliner CEO retired. He retired with $400 million! We live in a time of golden parachutes, silver parachutes, tin parachutes, and no parachutes. What message do these executive cash bonanzas communicate to the average employee? PROTECT THYSELF FIRST—WE ARE!

Perhaps, the most disconcerting evidence that the "tie is fraying" can be found in a 1989 Louis Harris poll of 1041 office workers. Only 39% of these employees felt their company's management was honest and ethical when dealing with employees. Harris concluded, "Office workers plain just don't trust management to deal fairly with them" ("Office Workers Less Satisfied," 1989, p. 12A).

The Psychological Contract

Academic scholars frequently refer to the emotional bond between employer and employee as the "psychological contract" (Schein, 1980; Schermerhorn, Hunt, & Osborn, 1985; Tornow, 1988). It represents an implicit agreement that each party will treat the other fairly. It is unwritten and unofficial and therefore not legally binding. Assumptions and expectations about each other are only vaguely communicated. The motivation for compliance is based entirely on presumably shared beliefs and mutual trust. Consequently, if the "contract" is broken, deep, long-lasting feelings of betrayal and resentment result.

The psychological contract differs greatly from other employment contracts. Employment contracts (e.g., offer of employment letters, policies in employee handbooks, specific employee agreements) are explicit, written, and legally binding. These documents clearly spell out each party's responsibilities and duties. If the contract is broken, sanc-

tions occur. Whereas the motivation for compliance in the psychological contract is based on mutual trust, the motivation in the employment contract is based on fear of legal reprisal. Thus, with employment contracts one's vulnerability is lower and the rule enforcement is not dependent upon each party's sense of fair play.

As we begin the 1990s, the tie that binds in the case of employment contracts is a legal one that remains very strong. In contrast, the emotional tie (psychological contract) appears to be very frayed.

The Psychological Contract of Yesterday

Exhibit 1 depicts the employer-employee relationship during the 1950s and 1960s. It shows that the fundamental premise was a fair day's work for a fair day's pay. When that agreement was intact, the tie was strong. The company had an employee who was dependable, who would work hard, and who (above all) would be *loyal*. In turn, the employee had employment with a company who he/she could count on, who paid fairly, and who offered continuing fringe benefits. In short, a company who provided *job security*. Each party benefited.

The Psychological Contract of Today

The situation is vastly different today (see Exhibit 2). Today both parties are much more self-reliant. An "I will take care of myself" orientation pervades the relationship. The em-

Exhibit 1
The Psychological Contract of Yesterday

Employee's Responsibility	Employer's Responsibility
• "Fair" day's work	• "Fair" day's pay
• Sustained good work	• Continued employment
• Sustained good work	• Merit pay increases
• Extra hard work	• Advancement
• Quality work	• Recognition & acknowledgement
• LOYALTY	• JOB SECURITY

Exhibit 2
The Psychological Contract of Today

Employee's Responsibility	Employer's Responsibility
• Focus on personal needs	• Focus on corporate goals
• Career/self development	• Corporate growth
• Legal protection	• Legal protection
• SELF-RELIANCE	• SELF-RELIANCE

ployee plays a much more active role in monitoring job duties, supervisory practices, merit raises, and career development. The employer uses a more performance-based, impersonal, cost-conscious perspective when managing employees. Because of the need to be flexible and adaptive to change in the organizational environment, the employer-employee relationship frequently assumes a short-term posture, and immediate results are emphasized.

Why the Change?

Paul Hirsch, in his book *Pack Your Own Parachute* (1987), refers to an employment strategy in sports called "free agency." In such a strategy, professional athletes attempt to maximize their position by peddling their services to the ball club who offers the biggest paycheck. Their exclusive focus is their own welfare. Their sense of loyalty to teammates, ball club, community, and owner is deferred. Hirsch suggests American managers might want to adopt a similar strategy.

This employment orientation is a far cry from the "organization man" phenomenon of the 1950s. What could have caused such a drastic shift? The answer lies in two areas. First, tremendous changes have occurred in society in general. Second, significant changes have occurred in the work environment in particular.

The Changing American Landscape

America has changed greatly and continues to change. In many respects, we are becoming a society of individuals. Our sense of identity is to self, rather than to a group. There appears to be an eroding attachment to national heritages, religions, communities, families, and *corporations*.

A sense of permanence and continuity is being replaced in our relationships with temporariness. Even our marriage vows have transformed from "love, honor, and obey till death do us part" to "love, honor, and obey till love do us part." The average American moves every five years.

Moreover, there appears to be a growing need for instant gratification. Rather than expecting to work long and hard for things we value (new car, new house, college degree, job advancement), we want it immediately. If we do not have the money, we borrow it. If we do not have the patience or tenacity for earning a college degree, we purchase it. If our employer won't grant us an advancement, we go elsewhere.

Social controls are giving way to legal controls. The so-called "man-of-his-word" and "handshake" rituals are going the way of the dinosaur. Two-thirds of the world's lawyers practice in America. As a society, unwritten agreements are being replaced by written contracts. Should we expect our workplace to be anything different?

Perhaps related to this point is the apparent loss of mutual trust in our society. Burglar alarm systems, locked cars, and walking your child to school are some manifestations of a nontrusting world. Employment contracts, legal documents, and binding agreements are manifestations of a nontrusting workplace. Along with an erosion in mutual trust, there also appears to be a weakening of the norm of reciprocity. Returning favors and helping out friends is as uncommon today as quilting bees and barn raisings.

Finally, two societal factors directly tied to the work world are (a) the increasing number of highly educated professionals working in companies and (b) the plethora of corporate mergers and takeovers. In the case of professional employees, their allegiance most frequently is to their profession rather than the company. For example, she is an engineer first, an employee of IBM second; he is an accountant first, an employee of General Motors second.

The onslaught of mergers and acquisitions has precipitated an unprecedented number of corporate restructurings and concomitant employee layoffs. This is the first time in the history of business that employee termination may be completely independent of poor performance or incompetence—terminations frequently occur because the acquiring firm needs to reduce the debt load. A terminated engineer from a high-tech firm in California put it this way: "It took me nine months to realize they laid off the position, not me!"

The Changing Work Environment

The above societal changes have had a direct effect on the workplace in America. During the 1950s and 1960s, employees had stability, permanence, and predictability. During the 1970s and 1980s, employees experienced constant change, temporariness, and uncertainty. During the 1950s and 1960s, there was a relatively stable, full-time workforce. Today, there is "just-in-time" manufacturing and a "just-in-time" workforce. In 1980, there were 28 million part-time employees; six years later there were 34 million. Fully 85 to 95% of American corporations presently use temporary workers (Kanter, 1989). In some respects, Corporate America has moved from using employment agencies to secure employees to using outplacement firms to remove employees. Exhibit 3 displays some of the major trends that illustrate just how significantly the work environment has been changing (also see Marks, 1988).

In short, there is a new reality today. The implicit, psychological contract between employer and employee has been profoundly altered. The conditions of the 1950s and 1960s fostered:

1. reciprocal dependence,
2. within-company growth,

Exhibit 3
The Changing Work Environment

1950s and 1960s	vs.	1970s and 1980s
Stability		Constant change
Permanence		Temporariness
Predictability		Uncertainty
Stable work force		Shifting work force
Full-time employees		Part-time employees
Internal employees		External employees
Fixed work patterns		Flexible work patterns
Employment >>>Retirement		Gradual retirement
Employee retention		Targeted turnover (RIFs)
Develop employees		Buy employees
Value loyalty & tenure		Value performance & skills
Company-defined benefits		Company-defined contributions
Job security		Job tentativeness
Advancement opportunities		Limited opportunities (plateauing)
Creating value through slow growth		Buying value through rapid acquisition (M&As)

3. linear career development,
4. prescribed retirement at age 65,
5. corporate identity,
6. commitment to company, and
7. strong corporate loyalty.

Nowadays, the focus is on:

1. self-reliance and taking responsibility,
2. across-company growth,
3. multiple careers,
4. extended employment,
5. self (professional) identity,
6. commitment to self, and
7. weak corporate loyalty.

The Psychological Contract— A Period of Transition

Although these changes may leave one with a sense of disillusionment and frustration, they were necessary and adaptive. Such changes in the business environment have permitted companies to reduce cost and to become more market oriented, competitive, and flexible.

They have provided American corporations and employees alike opportunities to become more mature, independent, and successful.

Under the traditional (paternalistic) mode of management, where company loyalty was rewarded with lifetime employment, mutual complacency tended to creep in. Today, neither employer nor employee guarantees lifetime security. This situation does not mean that loyalty and commitment must die. Rather, it means they must be generated through different avenues.

To recapture employee loyalty and commitment, companies are realizing the need to share more with their employees when it comes to power. They must share risks as well as gains. This approach of Total Employee Involvement (TEI) includes providing important information about the business, delegating responsibility for performance management, sharing decision-making authority, and allocating rewards based on corporate success (Lawler & Mohrman, 1989).

Knowledge—a key source of power—gets shared. Employees throughout the company are informed of the organization's mission, goals, and strategy (vision), as well as the business conditions that represent threats and opportunities to the company's continued well-being. Greater self-management of performance is encouraged by providing employees with clear objectives and standards of performance, as well as the necessary feedback systems that allow employees to adjust performance accordingly. In addition, organizations gain employee commitment by creating more opportunities for employee involvement in decision making regarding their work and by linking rewards to employee contributions to the success of the business. Employers act "to make everyone an owner in the organization" (Hallett, 1988, p. 36).

In return for sharing more power and control with employees, organizations expect their employees to be more self-reliant and to take greater responsibility for their performance and career management. The result is that loyalty and commitment become more

focused on the employment relationship and what employer and employee must do to keep the relationship mutually beneficial.

Implications for Managing in the 1990s

The changing psychological contract has significant implications for effective human resource management (HRM) practices during the 1990s. The creation of a progressive organizational culture to capitalize on this newly evolving employer-employee relationship is needed. Issues pertaining to both these areas are presented in this section.

Initiating Effective HRM Practices

Staffing.   Successful organizations will develop a more flexible workforce through part-time and contract arrangements. Such an approach benefits both employers and employees. Employers (a) can hire for fluctuating needs, short-term projects, or crisis situations, (b) save money on medical and other employee benefits, and (c) retain valuable employees who cannot or choose not to work full time (Bergsman, 1989). Also, such a staffing strategy helps maintain an up-to-date skills mix and balance of experience to meet the needs of the business in a cost-effective way.

Employees, in turn, benefit from greater flexibility in work schedules and place. Further, the organization's core employees experience greater employment security by being buffered from the up-and-down vagaries of the typical business fluctuations.

Other staffing practices to consider include greater use of job rotation, job sharing, lateral transfers, and job enrichment as ways to counterbalance decreased opportunities for the traditional upward mobility track. Finally, more emphasis should be placed at the entry-level hiring stage to assure that applicants get realistic job previews and understand the expectations and responsibilities of working in this changing kind of environment.

Performance management.   Drawing on the Total Quality Management (TQM) precepts from Japanese management practices, employers need to redesign their performance appraisal systems so they act more as total and continuous performance management processes (Ishikawa, 1985). Such an approach allows employees to become more autonomous and take more responsibility for managing their performance. As a first step, performance "contracting" should take place with the employee's key customers/clients. This step assures a clear understanding of what products and services are expected and the standards for evaluating performance effectiveness. Secondly, performance feedback should be put into place that permit employees to monitor their own performance and make the needed adjustments when necessary. For this purpose, soliciting inputs from multiple sources can frequently be valuable to capture the multiple needs and perspectives of an employee's multiple clients.

In short, the emphasis needs to shift from managers *doing* performance appraisals—which all too frequently turn out to be treated as one-shot, once-a-year events that are not well liked by either manager or employee—to a continuous process of work-oriented communication that focuses on managing performance. In this approach, both manager and employee take responsibility.

Compensation.   Traditional systems of compensation have the effect of heavily rewarding tenure and position, rather than contribution and ability. Such compensation packages promulgate the "fair day's pay for fair day's work" and entitlement mentality. Successful employers of the 1990s will require employees to have a stake in departmental (company) profits and losses. Whereas job security once denoted life-long employment and retirement plans, today it means having a shared destiny in the success and failure of the business (Santora, 1989).

A key compensation strategy for getting there is for employers to begin switching from fixed to more variable forms of pay (Brown, 1989). The latter can better reflect the need for more risk sharing and incentive motivation. To assure that incentive compensation maintains its motivational effects, compensation designers need to differentiate when it is more appropriate to link rewards to the individual, team, or organizational level of performance (Sundstrom, De Meuse, & Futrell, 1990).

Finally, employers will need to take a more strategic look at their reward system by looking at *total* compensation. How does the design of the total system link to the overall business strategy of the organization?

Training.   In training and developing employees, the focus must shift to activities that favor life and career planning, as well as continuing education and retraining. These activities reduce the chance for skills obsolescence and organizational dependency on the part of the employee. They also tend to increase the employee's sense of autonomy and self-confidence. As a result, the employer is able to maintain a more up-to-date workforce. In addition to recognizing its value to the current employer, it also serves to enhance the perceived marketability of the employees outside the company. Marketability provides insurance in case of drastic action taken by the employer to reduce the workforce.

Termination.   Shorter product cycles, increased competition, globalization, and the merger environment are causing more and more companies to implement RIFs. How one manages the downsizing process greatly influences employee morale, productivity, and the likelihood of "wrongful discharge" suits (Robino & De Meuse, 1985). As a rule, companies should (a) inform affected employees as soon as possible, (b) provide job search and placement assistance (e.g., conducting resume writing and interview skills workshops; notifying other firms of impending layoff with listing of position titles), and (c) dispense equitable severance pay. Such practices communicate an openness and sensitivity that fosters trust. Mutual trust is an imperative for successful companies during the 1990s (De Pree, 1989).

Many companies are developing innovative programs that decrease the likelihood of massive layoffs and other drastic forms of employment swings. For example, Motorola weathered an economic slump in the semiconductor business without significant layoffs during the mid-1980s. Rather than laying off 10% of their workforce to match the weakened demand, employees began working a four-day week every other week. This strategy permitted Motorola to keep thousands of employees on the payroll who otherwise would have been laid off. Consequently, Motorola employees felt a sense of corporate commitment and unity (shared destiny). In contrast, Texas Instruments dealt with the semiconductor slump by instituting layoffs. These layoffs were accompanied by a loss of skilled employees, a reduction in morale among those who stayed on, a difficult transition back to full production, and problems of quality control while new employees learned their jobs (O'Toole, 1985).

Creating a Progressive Organizational Culture

HR as a strategic partner.   In the past, personnel departments all too frequently were administrative in scope and reactionary in nature. Their primary purpose appeared to be processing insurance forms, moving paper from one line manager to another, and establishing the bowling league. Personnel lacked clout, true corporate identity, and real purpose.

Today, there is tremendous complexity, diversity, and sophistication confronting human resources management. Society has changed; employees have changed; companies have changed. So must the recruiting, training, motivating, leading, communicating, and retaining of people change. It is critical that human resources become a strategic partner in the corporate hierarchy. The days when "everyone knows that anyone can do HR" are past.

To be a strategic partner, the HR function must be staffed by competent, professionally trained managers and representatives. The head of HR must have a fundamental understanding of other areas in the company, such as marketing, manufacturing, engineering, etc. (Coates, Jarratt, & Mahaffie, 1989). The senior HR manager must help other executives view the workforce as a valuable asset to be nurtured, rather than labor costs to be reduced. This individual will be able to document the HR function's value by establishing measurement systems that clearly show the financial impact HR contributes to the bottom line.

The HR function must be a role model and champion the way in facilitating the needed changes in the employment relationship. Human Resources must assure that the organization's HR systems and practices are aligned with and in support of the needs and strategies of the business. Also, the function should foster a climate that values growth and development and help define strategies for regaining employee commitment and loyalty.

Line managers as effective HRM practitioners.   Line managers need to change their role from one of planning, organizing, and controlling to one of leading, facilitating, and supporting. They must lead through visioning and gaining commitment, and emphasize the management of processes rather than people, since people now are more self-managing. Toward this end, managers need to assure that employees can and will do their jobs effectively. This requires giving them training, information, tools, and decision-making authority. Performance management must be a continuous process, as should be the search for opportunities to recognize employee contributions.

Employees empowered to be self-managing. Employees working under the new psychological contract must actively communicate and validate their expectations and assumptions about the employment relationship. They need to stay informed of organizational directions and business challenges and assume responsibility for managing their performance and development planning. In addition, employees must keep their skills updated and maintain a network that links them with others for support and coaching.

Employers, in turn, need to recognize and accept these changes. Management must empower employees to have more influence and control over their performance and work careers.

Conclusion

Is the workplace worse than before? Is it better than before? It depends on one's expectations and values. We can state with certainty that it is different! Management must recognize these differences and lead, communicate, motivate, select, train, and pay accordingly. What worked before will not necessarily work now! These are new times; they demand new management and new organizational practices. The psychological contract between employer and employee is just as important as it was 30 years ago. However, today's "contract" is one of shared destiny and mutual benefit rather than one of job security and corporate loyalty.

References

Bell, R. *Surviving the 10 Ordeals of the Takeover.* (New York: AMACOM. 1988).

Bergsman, S. "Part-time Professionals Make the Choice." *Personnel Administrator,* 1989, *34(9),* pp. 49–52; 105.

Brown, D. "The Corporate Times They are a' Changing." *Management Review,* 1989, *78(9),* pp. 7–9.

Coates, J. F., Jarratt, J., and Mahaffie, J. "Workplace Management 2000: Seven Themes Shaping the U.S. Work Force and its Structure." *Personnel Administrator,* 1989, *34(12),* pp. 51–55.

De Pree, M. *Leadership Is an Art.* (New York: Doubleday, 1989).

Hallett, J. "New Patterns in Working." *Personnel Administrator,* 1988, *33(12),* pp. 32–37.

Hirsch, P. *Pack Your Own Parachute.* (Reading, MA: Addison-Wesley, 1987).

Ishikawa, K. *What Is Total Quality Control? The Japanese Way.* (Englewood Cliffs, NJ: Prentice-Hall, 1985).

Kanter, R. M. "From Climbing to Hopping: The Contingent Job and the Post-Entrepreneurial Career." *Management Review,* 1989, *78(4),* pp. 22–27.

Lawler, E. E., III., and Mohrman, S. A. "High-Involvement Management." *Personnel,* 1989, *66(4),* pp. 26–31.

Marks, M. L. "The Disappearing Company Man." *Psychology Today,* 1988, *22(9),* pp. 34–39.

"Office Workers Less Satisfied—Survey Reports." *Huntsville Times,* June 1, 1989, p. 12A.

O'Toole, J. "Employee Practices at the Best Managed Companies." *California Management Review,* 1985, *28(1),* 35–66.

Robino, D. J., and De Meuse, K. P. "Corporate Mergers and Acquisitions: Their Impact on Human Resource Management." *Personnel Administrator,* 1985, *30(11),* pp. 33–44.

Santora, J. E. "Compensation: Du Pont Builds Stakeholders." *Personnel Administrator,* 1989, *34(9),* pp. 72–76.

Schein, E. H. *Organizational Psychology* 3rd Ed. (Englewood Cliffs, NJ: Prentice-Hall, 1980).

Schermerhorn, J. R., Jr., Hunt, J. G., and Osborn, R. N. *Managing Organizational Behavior* 2nd Ed. (New York: John Wiley & Sons, 1985).

Sundstrom, E., De Meuse, K. P., and Futrell, D. "Work Teams: Applications and Effectiveness." *American Psychologist,* 1990, *45,* pp. 120–133.

Tornow, W. W. "Contract Redesign." *Personnel Administrator,* 1988, *33(10),* pp. 97–101.

Whyte, W. H. *The Organization Man.* (New York: Simon & Schuster, 1956).

Beyond Demography: A Psychographic Profile of the Workforce

Philip H. Mirvis and Donald L. Kanter

What is on the minds and in the hearts of managers and workers today? When talking with executives about the challenges they face in managing their workforces and reviewing the results of national surveys about people's attitudes about life and their jobs, one theme emerges boldly and bluntly: Loyalty and *esprit de corps* have given way to mistrust and looking out for oneself. Cynicism is on the rise. Fellow feeling is on the wane.

Listen to some of the problems of people responsible for recruiting, assisting, and leading today's turned-off employees:

- A *recruiter* reports that there are two types of young people coming into her company. From colleges and MBA programs come erstwhile corporate climbers. They have studied the business, make comments about its strategy, but seem only to want to talk about how to get ahead. From high schools and trade schools come youngsters who don't seem to have any interest in the firm. They complain about entry-level salaries, yet don't profess to have any career ambitions. They *are* interested primarily in work hours and vacations.

- A *human resource representative* worries that plant and clerical employees are vulnerable to layoffs unless margins improve. Yet when he introduced a suggestion system, no one showed any enthusiasm. Plant workers wondered "What's in it for me?"

Clericals have adopted a 9-to-5 mentality and complain constantly about having to do too much work for too little payoff.

- A *production supervisor* finds employees resentful and bitter. They say management doesn't give a damn about them. Company "big shots" are seen as a "bunch of 'BSers'" who only care about profitability and their own inflated salaries. In turn, a *retail store manager* says her employees don't give a damn about customers. They prefer to gab with their co-workers rather than help shoppers find merchandise. And, when they do help, they make it plain how inconvenient it is and make the customer feel like a jerk.

Needless to say, young recruits, vulnerable plant and clerical personnel, and sour production and sales people have a different story to tell. It's rife with claims that they are routinely misled by management and taken advantage of by their companies. To their eyes, company life is a jungle. Hence, they conclude, it's only smart to look out for oneself.

What Have We Wrought?

There are many trends in the working world that feed this cynical mindset. Remember that America is going through "de-industrialization" with the loss of over 20 million jobs in heavy industry in the 1980s (Harrison & Bluestone, 1988). Older workers have been laid off or given early retirement en masse. And youth seeking blue-collar jobs don't find the opportunities or the recompense that were available to their parents.

Still, the best and brightest find attractive jobs in finance, real estate, and some high-profile personal services. High-technology work has its rewards, too, but high tech accounts for less than 10% of the jobs today. And service workers in general earn much less than those in industry, have fewer benefits, and have less job security (Reich, 1991).

Furthermore, companies are cutting back, downsizing, merging, and acquiring at a feverish pace. The fallout: Estimates are that *Fortune* 500 companies have reduced their ranks by 2.2 million in the 1980s (Buono & Bowditch, 1989). As a result, notions of cradle-to-grave security have given way to Paul Hirsch's (1987) counsel: "Pack your own parachute."

Finally, on a more everyday basis, surveys show that a majority of working people believe their firm's pay and promotion systems are unfair, say they aren't consulted sufficiently on decisions that affect them, and have concluded management doesn't really care about their welfare and well-being.

These broad economic developments, and perceived business practices, are shaping the attitudes of working people today. But as dispiriting as present day work attitudes may be, they simply reflect a trend that has taken shape over the past 20 years. Harris polls, for example, show that confidence in business has fallen from approximately a 70% level in the late 1960s to about 15% today (The Harris Survey, 1966, 73, 86). Opinion Research Corporation (1982) finds that ratings of management's competence, honesty, and integrity have dropped almost as dramatically among American workers in the same period.

For the past several years, we have been studying the rise of cynicism in America—what the ancient Greeks called "dog-like" contempt of human nature and the zealous pursuit of self-interest (Kanter & Mirvis,

1989). Our national surveys find that today nearly half of the American working populace have a cynical outlook on life and see selfishness and fakery at the core of human nature. What is more, these life attitudes color and distort people's work experience and give relations between employee and employer a cynical edge.

At issue here is how leaders in organizations—particularly line managers and human resource representatives—might think about the sources of cynicism in their workforces and how they might respond to it. A beginning point is to reconsider what influences people's attitudes about their jobs.

Ingredients in Work Attitudes

Most conceptions and studies of work attitudes consider three sets of "work-related" factors that influence people's job satisfaction, involvement, loyalty, effort-on-the-job, and intentions to leave their companies (see Figure 1):

1. Distal work stimuli. These are factors such as company size, shape, industry, and technology which, to an extent, define the formal organization and determine the mix of jobs, patterns of employment and promotion, and levels of compensation within firms. Company culture, in turn, is seen as influencing management practices and human relations as well as the beliefs, expectations, and conduct of organization members. All of these represent *contextual* factors for employees. And, although they have a bearing on how the organization operates, they are more distal stimuli than, say, everyday work experiences.

2. Focal work stimuli. The characteristics of jobs, work groups, and supervision, as well as working conditions, performance appraisals, pay practices, and the like constitute focal work stimuli for employees. These are usually the best predictors of their work attitudes and the most likely subjects of their praise or criticism. They represent the *content* of employment. These factors are also

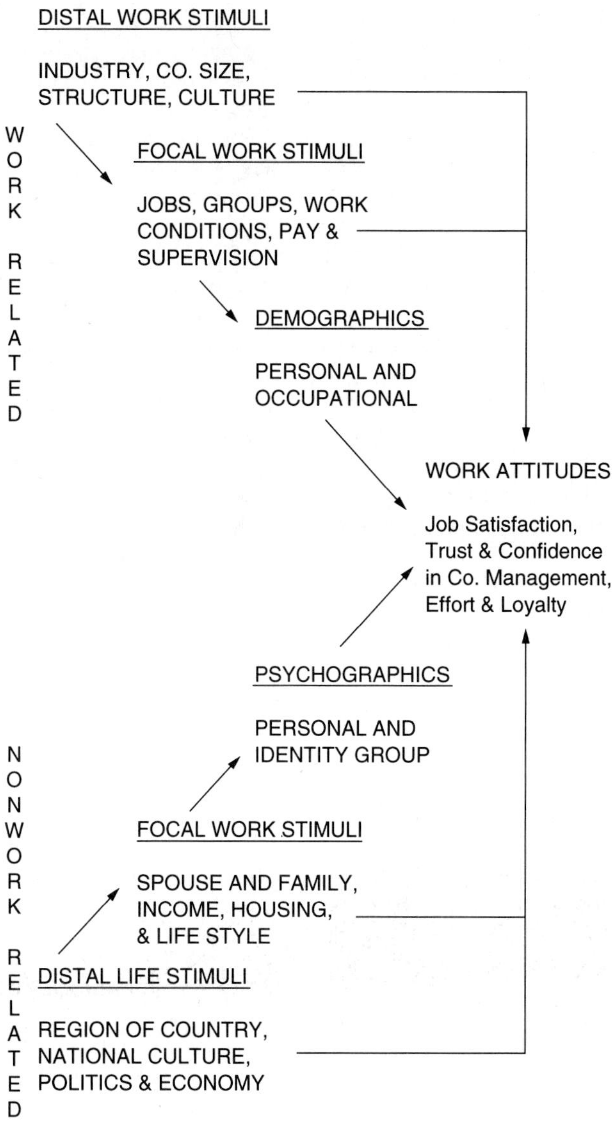

DISTAL WORK STIMULI

INDUSTRY, CO. SIZE,
STRUCTURE, CULTURE

W
O
R
K

R
E
L
A
T
E
D

FOCAL WORK STIMULI

JOBS, GROUPS, WORK
CONDITIONS, PAY &
SUPERVISION

DEMOGRAPHICS

PERSONAL AND
OCCUPATIONAL

WORK ATTITUDES

Job Satisfaction,
Trust & Confidence
in Co. Management,
Effort & Loyalty

PSYCHOGRAPHICS

PERSONAL AND
IDENTITY GROUP

N
O
N
W
O
R
K

R
E
L
A
T
E
D

FOCAL WORK STIMULI

SPOUSE AND FAMILY,
INCOME, HOUSING,
& LIFE STYLE

DISTAL LIFE STIMULI

REGION OF COUNTRY,
NATIONAL CULTURE,
POLITICS & ECONOMY

Figure 1. Work- and non-work-related factors influencing attitudes

most amenable to influence and enhancement by line managers and human resource experts. Indeed, the introduction of new job designs, more teamwork, and better pay-for-performance schemes have been linked to improved work attitudes (Seashore et al., 1983).

3. Demographics. Finally, work attitudes are influenced by the demographic make-up of an organization. The effects are twofold. First, demographics have a bearing on people's opportunities and experiences at work. For example, managers, clericals, and hourly employees have different types of jobs, gain distinct rewards from their companies, and, in general, have more and less favorable work experiences. In most companies, too, older workers have more seniority and thus better pay and jobs than younger ones, and there may be differences across occupations in the relative proportion of men versus women or whites versus minorities. All of this reflects the *structural* impact of demographics.

Second, there are *psychological* effects related to demography. Daniel Yankelovich (1979), for example, has found significant differences between the work ethic and values of young "new breed" workers and their forebears. He finds many of the new breed imbued with the "psychology of entitlement" and far more demanding of and less responsive to their employers than older workers. Other experts have found differences in expectations and values across income strata, gender, race, and so forth.

Although careful study of these three sets of "work-related" factors is useful in predicting and understanding work attitudes, many "non-work-related" factors also have a bearing on people's attitudes on the job. Here, too, three sets of factors invite attention:

4. Psychographics. A broad range of studies concerned with "values and lifestyles" confirm that people's psychological predispositions and outlooks have a bearing on their attitudes and behavior as consumers and as employees. Of immediate relevance are attitudes about life that are readily evoked in the work situation. For example, people's self-esteem and locus of control have been found to be important ingredients in estimations of the likelihood of succeeding on the job and gaining valued rewards (Lawler, 1973). Attitudes toward authority, trust in other people, and confidence in the future can, as we shall see, also impinge on attitudes about the job and one's company.

The psychological effect of these outlooks on work factors is evident. But here, too, structural effects can be deduced. Life attitudes are not randomly distributed through the population. Members of the same "identity groups"—say the same age, gender, race, and such—have had overlapping life experiences which may, in turn, predispose them toward more or less favorable attitudes about particular company practices and cultures. In this way, psychographics and demographics interact, and both need to be considered in interpreting the attitudes of "groups" of employees.

5. Focal life stimuli. Psychographic characteristics are, in turn, influenced by stimuli in the environment. The nonwork equivalent of the content of a job is the content of people's lives—their family structure, income, housing, and lifestyle. These factors, too, have a bearing on people's life transactions, including those involving their work, their company, their co-workers, and their working conditions. Urban workers, for example, seem less responsive than rural ones to enriched jobs, and married employees put different value on the flexibility of their work schedules than do single employees. These factors serve to modify the perceived content of work and its relative desirability.

6. Distal life stimuli. Finally, the general state of the economy, developments in politics and society, and other factors that affect living influence people's attitudes. These, too, are contextual forces, having an effect on how companies do business and generally shading employees' opinions of their employers and jobs (see Yankelovich & Immewahr, 1983). Region of the country is another variable to consider. It is strongly related to relative levels of exploration versus conservatism. Certainly nationality and differences in national culture also play a role in shaping life attitudes and those having to do with the workplace (Hofstede, 1980).

Our primary interest is with the relationship between life attitudes and attitudes about the job. Specifically, we are concerned with cynicism and its function in the formation of work attitudes. Certainly it can serve as a predisposition because people's prior assumptions about other people and institutions selectively focus their attention and heighten their vigilance to cues that others are taking advantage of them. In turn, a cynical outlook may also make people especially attentive to opportunities to gain advantage. This can translate into general mistrust of management, a readiness to disparage co-workers, and a predilection for naysaying. It can also lead to back-biting and politicking among the more expeditious, self-serving types.

Cynicism also influences people's attributions about what has happened at work and why. In this way, it provides justification for rumor mongering and finger pointing. And it can prompt self-promotion and flank-protection rather than productive problem solving and loyalty to the cause. These are familiar problems to executives, of course, and cause for concern in many companies. The best companies have, as a result, sought to enrich employees' jobs, build work teams, establish better pay systems, and even tried to enliven and humanize their company cultures. What is more, they have tried to tailor their policies and practices to changes in the demography of their companies and have taken into account the special needs of employee groups.

How have employees responded? Some have reciprocated in kind with more effort and loyalty. But, even in the best firms, there is often a generalized wariness over management's motives and suspicions over whose ends are best served by improvements in the workplace. We feel this is due to the corrosive effects of cynicism in the workforce. Let us see, then, how life attitudes compare with work attitudes among working people today.

Life versus Work Attitudes

Do you believe that most people will tell a lie if they can gain by it? Do you believe that most people claim to have standards of honesty and morality, but that few stick to them when money is at stake or that people pretend to care about one another more than they really do? Some 65% of a national sample of American workers agree (either strongly or slightly) that people will tell a lie if they can

gain by it. Many also agree that people pretend to care more than they really do (58%), and even more claim to be honest and moral but fall short when money is at stake (67%). A smaller proportion believe that people are just out for themselves and that most people are not really honest by nature (see Table I).

Based upon answers to these questions, we classify 48% of the American workforce as cynical, having adopted a cold, calculating outlook on life. Cynics agree that lying, putting on a false face, and taking advantage of others are fundamental to human character and conclude that, basically, people are just out for themselves. The remainder have either a somewhat wary or wholly upbeat opinion of human nature.

Such cynical attitudes about life are paralleled in attitudes about work. A first glance at Table I suggests that people's attitudes about life are even more jaundiced than those about their work. Note, however, that measures of life attitudes were taken on a 4-point scale (without the option of neither agreeing nor disagreeing with a statement), while work attitudes were measured on a 5-point scale (with the midpoint option). With that in mind, the table reveals strong correspondence between people's attitudes toward life and their jobs.

For example, suspicions about people's trustworthiness are seemingly carried over into the workplace, where 41% of the population doubt the truth of what management tells them, and 49% say that management will take advantage of them, given a chance. There is a widespread perception that, in society at large, a lot of people get ahead even though they don't deserve it. In turn, over one-quarter of the workforce says that getting ahead in his/her company depends on who you know, not on how good a job you do. Many (59%) say that "these days a person doesn't know whom he or she can count on." Many (56%) also say that a lot of people in their companies "do just enough to get by."

The parallels run deep: Many agree that the best way to handle people is to tell them what they want to hear. Likewise, they opine

Table I.

Americans' Attitudes about Life and Work

	% agreeing/ 4-pt. scale		% agreeing/ 5-pt. scale
TRUST			
Most people will tell a lie if they can gain by it.	66%	I often doubt the truth of what management tells me.	41%
If you aren't careful, people will take advantage of you.	81%	Management will take advantage of you if you give them a chance.	49%
FAIRNESS			
A lot of people seem to get ahead even though they don't deserve it.	54%	Getting ahead in my company depends on who your friends are, not on how good a job you do.	27%
The best way to handle people is to tell them what they want to hear.	39%	Management of my company never lets employees know the real reason behind decisions that affect them.	39%
FELLOW-FEELING			
People pretend to care about one another more than they really do.	58%	Management in my company isn't interested in what the average employee thinks or feels.	47%
These days a person doesn't know whom he or she can count on.	59%	A lot of people in my company do just enough to get by.	56%
COMMUNITY			
An unselfish person is taken advantage of in today's world.	55%	In my experience, it doesn't pay to work extra hard for my company.	26%
What I do or think doesn't really count for much.	26%	My job is not considered to be important by my employer.	18%
TIME PERSPECTIVE			
Nowadays, a person has to pretty much live for today and let tomorrow take care of itself.	46%	Management in my company is more interested in profits than in people.	36%

that management never lets employees know the real reasons behind decisions that affect them. Many say that unselfish people are taken advantage of in today's world. In turn, many also say that it doesn't pay to work extra hard in their companies. Finally, there is a perception among many today that, things being as they are, people should pretty much live for today and let tomorrow take care of itself. They also find that management is more interested in short-term profits than the longer-term benefits to people and the organization.

The connection between people's life and work attitudes is clearest when comparing selected job attitudes of the cynics versus more upbeat members of the sample (see Figure 2). The data show that cynics are more mistrustful of management and less inclined to trust co-workers, don't think they have a fair shot at advancement, and don't believe that management listens to them or values what they do on their jobs. Cynics are also much more apt to doubt the integrity of their management and are much less inclined to express loyalty or commitment to their firms. Overall, they have

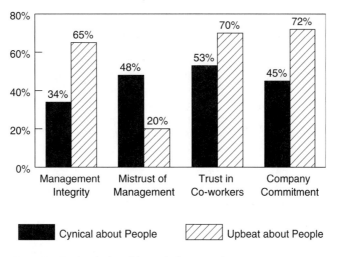

Figure 2. Work attitudes of the cynical versus upbeat

far more jaundiced attitudes about their work than do the rest of the workforce. How, then, did they get this way?

The Cynical Mindset

There are three key elements in the development of the cynical outlook. One is the formulation of unrealistically high expectations, of oneself and of other people, which generalize to expectations of society, institutions, authorities, and the future. At the same time, these heady aspirations are fed by the media, particularly television and its advertisers, which celebrate the opulent good life and make it seem as though success can be attained by buying the right products and cultivating the right image. In a sense, it doesn't matter that many Americans' material drives are unrealistic or that their needs for fulfillment are insatiable. What does matter is that expectations for having it all and attaining self-actualization along the way have set people up for disappointment.

A second ingredient in cynicism is the experience of disappointment, in oneself and in others, and consequent feelings of frustration and defeat. Here, too, the media has played a role in shaping the collective psyche. Elec-

tronic exposés of the failed promises of public officials provide people with a steady diet of disappointment. Constant exposure to media messages portending a wealthier, healthier, happier, or holier *you* all serve to raise hopes which, when dashed, lead to a sense of betrayal.

The third ingredient of cynicism is thus disillusionment, the sense of being let down or of letting oneself down, and more darkly the sense of being deceived or used by others. Cynics often trace their disappointment to the "system"—the politicians and business leaders, the bankers and brokers, the unions and management, the media and advertisers—all the powerful interests that take advantage of people like themselves. Many have concluded that it is a Darwinian world and that it is only prudent to look out for number one. To think otherwise is naive or dupish, and who wants to be taken for a sucker?

In sum, cynicism is one way people cope with an unfriendly, unstable, and insecure world. To anchor it in our model of work attitudes, we need to understand how it has been cultivated and spread through the workforce. We turn, first, to societal stimuli and their impact on today's workers.

Societal Stimuli:
Putting Work into a Context

Seymour Lipsett and William Schneider (1983) attribute widespread disaffection in the American public to an overarching and growing "confidence gap." For instance, 20 years ago, most people trusted their government, the press, and organized religion. Today, by comparison, the majority believe that politicians lie, that the press deceives, and that many preachers are hypocrites. Twenty years ago, saving for family and the future was a virtue. Nowadays, it looks foolish. Twenty years ago, most college students hoped to find work that was socially useful. Today they are looking for money and status—period (Harris Survey, 1966, 1973, 1986; Watts, 1981).[1]

What's behind the confidence gap? Our interpretation is that anxiety, frustration, and suspicion, engendered by duplicitous authorities, unresponsive institutions, and an uncertain future, have been working their way deeply into the American psyche over the past two decades to the point where they are having an effect on people's outlooks about themselves and their fellow man. Surely the political, economic, social, and media environment have all contributed to and reinforced cynicism in the population at large. Baby boomers, for instance, energized by new music, lifestyles, protest, and dreams in their youth, experienced high hopes for a better society. Then these utopian dreams were transformed into the "Big Chill" of the '70s. The boomers' anthem changed from "do it now" to "get it while you still can."

The high prosperity of the Reagan era led to "Morning in America" hopes in the '80s. The rich got richer. But America turned into a debtor nation, divided further along class and racial lines, and self-dealing brokers and politicians led a passing parade of unethical and illegal conduct through Wall Street and Washington. Amidst this cynical menage, avarice and amorality came into fashion, and gritty self-sufficiency characterized the national mood.

Even with success in the Gulf War and uplifting signs of a "gentler and kinder" nation to point to, cynicism remains pronounced in the '90s. Economic uncertainty, coupled with dog-eat-dog competition for good jobs and housing, has created unrest and led to invidious comparisons between the "haves" and "have nots." And there remains a strong belief that "anything goes" in society amidst the fallout of the S&L scandal, doubts about the motives of members of Congress, and a plethora of everyday scams and hustles in the news. All of this means that business, as a primary institution in society, will be influenced by the cynicism of its employees much as it also sows it.

Still, these broad societal stimuli have had a differential effect on today's workforce. People from different social groups have experienced either more or less frustration and are either more or less apt to cultivate the cynical outlook. To understand how cynicism works its way into organizations, then, we need also to understand its variability among groups in our society.

Cynicism and Life Experiences:
Factoring in Demographics

As a result of people's historical experiences, personal makeup, and current circumstances, cynicism has taken either a greater or lesser toll on different segments of our society. Table II provides a breakdown for various demographic groups.

Age Trends

To summarize trends by age, 54% of workers age 18 to 24, 48% of those age 25 to 34, and roughly 45% of those age 35 to 54 fit the profile of the cynic. Higher levels of cynicism are found for those 55 and older still in the workforce. What is behind these trends? Youth, for example, is supposed to be a time of idealism. However, there is considerable evidence that the expectations of today's young people, particularly with regard to money and financial success, far exceed society's ability to deliver. Time-honored routes to material betterment

Table II.
Profile of the Cynical versus Upbeat

	Cynical (%)	Upbeat (%)
AGE		
18–24	54	31
25–34	48	33
35–44	45	38
45–54	46	33
55 over	56	28
EDUCATION		
Some HS	68	23
HS Grad	55	25
Trade/College	50	32
College Grad +	35	49
INCOME		
Less $20k	60	27
20–29,999	55	29
30–39,999	47	37
40–49,999	38	38
50k more	36	47
RACE		
White	44	37
Black	70	21
GENDER		
Male	52	22
Female	45	35
COLLAR COLOR		
Blue Collar	58	24
Pink Collar	47	34
White Collar	39	43
UNION		
Member	47	31
Nonmember	48	35
ORGANIZATION TYPE		
Profit	51	31
Not-for-Profit	43	39
Government	45	38

oriented set of priorities. The character of Alex in TV's *Family Ties* is one example. Hard-driving young cynics like Alex seem to prosper in today's political, economic, and cultural environment. They value success and some want to attain it at any price. Youth who are less well off turn to the trappings of success—high-priced stereos and fashions—and say to hell with saving money.

Pundits call this the "me" generation. Surveys confirm that young people at every education and income level want more than their forebears and seem to be more dissatisfied with what they get. We suspect that many of the young conclude they have been cheated. Today's young also bear cynical scars that have desensitized them to signs of manipulation and deception by politicians, executives, and others in power. Many have lessened their expectations of the honesty and integrity of public figures. Statistics confirm the manifestations: Young people are not as inclined to vote or to volunteer for political campaigns as older Americans.

Baby boomers were raised in a time of "great expectations," as Landon Jones (1986) points out, and suffered great disillusionment from the world they encountered. The Vietnam veterans' slogan, "We are the unwilling, led by the unqualified, doing the unnecessary, for the ungrateful," exemplifies the gritty cynicism that some embraced to cope with their experiences. Many others have lived out their peer group's anthem "Tune in, turn on, drop out" and used cynicism to escape from the world around them.

In addition to the historical bases for their disillusionment, many boomers encounter contemporary sources of cynicism. Baby boomers grew up with the traditional birthright that their economic well-being would exceed that of their parents. Today they find it harder to buy homes and harder to find good-paying jobs than did their parents. Their numbers have swelled the job ranks and reduced their earning power. To many, the cancellation of this birthright is seen as an injustice or, more colloquially, a "rip-off."

and security are more precarious for the young in an increasingly service-based economy. Moreover, those with a high school or trade school degree will not find the opportunities to earn and advance that were available to their parents.

In turn, college graduates, beginning with their professional curricula, seem to have adopted a more personally pragmatic, career-

However, the data here show that boomers are not as cynical as young people. What has happened? One popular interpretation is that the boomers have simply grown up and become members of that "over 30" age group that could not be trusted. Ralph Whitehead's (1984–85) study of the "New Collar" workers summarizes the distinct inputs into the psychology of baby boomers today. The bad news, notes Whitehead, is that boomers are getting less in their lunch pail. This, we believe, has undermined their birthright and left many of them cynical and embittered. "The good news is baby boomers are getting more out of life," adds Whitehead. Indeed, those with socially oriented values and lifestyles have experienced the freedom to express them in their work and lives. This enables boomers to cope more optimistically with the world around them. Indeed, 38% of the boomers classify themselves as upbeat.

Several factors influence the higher levels of cynicism found in the over-55 age group. First, its members have less education and, for those over 60, lower incomes than those in other age groups. Second, a greater proportion of its members are blue-collar workers. There are, moreover, some genealogical reasons to expect higher levels of frustration among older people. As H. H. Munro notes, "The young have aspirations that never come to pass, the old have reminiscences of what never happened."[2]

Beyond this, specific social and economic factors have affected these age groups. The oldest members of the sample had direct experience with the Depression and all of the apprehension and disillusionment that it wrought. Moreover, there is evidence to suggest that older workers today are suffering disproportionately in the current economic restructuring. Plant shutdowns and corporate downsizing efforts have put the squeeze on workers over 50, forcing some into early retirement but many more into belt-tightening lifestyles. Frankly, there are signs that corporate America has forgotten the contributions of its more senior workers. Many have been callously labeled as deadwood and passed over for promotions and raises in order to meet the demands of the record numbers of baby boomers.

Social Class

Maxims from the popular culture make it plain enough that people of means as opposed to the less advantaged have different life experiences and outlooks on life. Manx poet Thomas Brown, for example, wrote, "A rich man's joke is always funny,"[3] while the French writer Anatole France opined, "It is only the poor who pay cash, and that not from virtue, but because they are refused credit."[4]

People's perceptions of "how the world works" are related to their own socioeconomic status and prospects. It is clear enough today that those with less education and those who earn less income have a far less comfortable lot and face a much less promising future than the better educated and better off. Some have, of course, adapted to their station in life and adjusted their expectations to current realities. Many others have turned to cynicism.

Some 68% of those lacking a high school degree hold a cynical outlook on life, as do a majority of those who are high school graduates. By contrast, only 35% of those who have graduated from college or attained more schooling are cynical. As to income, less than 40% of those who earn over $40,000 a year are cynical, whereas about 55 to 60% of those who earn less than $30,000 are cynics.

In the highly technical and more competitive economic environment of today, higher education, more so than ever before, is a prerequisite for success. The distinction between the haves and have nots increasingly lies between those who have earned a college degree and those who have not earned one. In the same fashion more money is now required to sustain a middle-class lifestyle.

The tragedy of polarized prosperity is that, in a phrase, it kills the American Dream that so long sustained optimism, the work ethic, and ambition. The consequences are expressed vividly in the selfish "where's mine" attitude of downwardly mobile cynics in the workforce and in the cold detachment of tough-minded realists who look out only for themselves.

Aspirations for the good life mark all social classes in America today. When queried as to what was "most important" to them on the job, people at all education levels place heavy emphasis upon good pay, of course, but polls also show that the lesser educated look for nearly as much stimulation and challenge out of their jobs as do college graduates (Quinn & Staines, 1979). However, the gap between what is important to people on the job and their satisfaction widens dramatically between the most and least educated.

Higher-paying and higher-status jobs simply are not available to as many workers as in the past. Not 20 years ago, over 75% seeking professional, technical, or managerial jobs could find them; today, that figure is less than 60% (Reich, 1983). Roughly 40% of the new jobs created in the country in the past several years pay less than $7,500. One psychological fallout of having overeducated workers in underpaying and understimulating jobs is cynicism.

We do not imply, of course, that higher education per se makes people less cynical. Indeed, in some respects, the current collegiate environment is a breeding ground for young, self-interested strivers, the erstwhile players in business. Our point is that those with college credentials have more opportunities to get ahead and put their education to work. Still, a substantial segment of the best educated have embraced the cynical life view.

Race

Some 70% of the minorities in our sample fit the profile of the cynic as compared with 44% of the whites. Of course, minorities are less well off than whites on nearly all indicators of educational attainment and economic well-being. Such factors, when coupled with the history of discrimination that many minority groups have faced in this country, contribute to their higher levels of cynicism.

Certainly a disproportionate percentage of members of minority groups copes with an objectively tougher, harder world by using cynicism to preserve self-respect. But their cynicism is not accounted for by class differences alone. Lower-income blacks, for example, are only somewhat more cynical than their white counterparts. Higher-income blacks, by comparison, are much more cynical than whites of equivalent status. Hence it would seem that vestiges of racism, with consequent mistrust and anger, also factor into blacks' life experiences.

Gender

Some 52% of the men express high levels of cynicism versus 45% of the women surveyed. What is more, women are much more inclined to have an upbeat outlook on other people. Certainly society's predominant image of the cynic is male. Cynical characters in the movies and television (as played by James Dean in *Giant* or Carroll O'Connor in *All in the Family*), in country-western ballads and pop music videos (sung by Merle Haggard and Elvis Costello), and in comic books and newspaper cartoons (the oafish Duffy or savvy P. J. McFey), come in all shapes and sizes, but they are mostly all male. Our point is that cynicism among men is a more visible and socially sanctioned orientation to life. Men are simply not discouraged from being cynics, particularly when their cynicism can be equated with a macho type of realism and worldliness.

By comparison, Sally Fields in *Norma Rae,* Jane Fonda in *The China Syndrome,* and Fonda, Lily Tomlin, and Dolly Parton in *9 to 5* all play potentially cynical characters. What is notable, however, is that these women are depicted initially as naive and innocent, seemingly victimized by their environment. Moreover, in the end, they triumph over their nemeses. This may not just be Hollywood's preference for a happy ending. Our culture, again in our opinion, simply insists that its women assume a sunnier outlook on life.

This cultural imperative, that men can be visible and vocal cynics and that women should appear to be sunnier and more generous minded, has roots in the distinct psychosocial makeup of each gender. For example, Carol Gilligan's (1982) studies, in which subjects are asked to make judgments about the motives of other people and describe their own processes of moral reasoning in real-life crises, suggest that women are less judgmental and emotionally distant than men. Studies by Redford Williams (1989), moreover, show that men who fit the cynical profile are more apt to be aggressive and hostile in their attitudes and behaviors.

Such interpretations are speculative, we acknowledge, and by no means apply to all men or women. We needn't be as speculative when it comes to differences in cynicism across occupational groups in our society.

Collar Color and Union Status

Based on the survey questions, the majority of the blue-collar respondents (58%) believe that most people are manipulators, will lie and pretend to care if it is to their advantage, and are basically out for themselves. By contrast, a smaller proportion of clerical (47%) and white-collar (39%) respondents see such attributes as fundamental to human nature.

To a large extent, the differences in cynicism between white- and blue-collar workers represent differences in people's education level and income. Blue-collar workers have less education and earn less money—key factors in the general profile of the cynic. A more in-depth look across occupations within the blue-collar rank shows cynicism to be most prominent among service, maintenance, and security personnel—cooks, gardeners, barbers, custodians, guards, and those in the fire and police service—among others. It is just as pronounced among technicians and tradesmen—computer operators, repairmen, mechanics, and plumbers. Factory workers, machine operators, and truck drivers are not quite as cynical as the other blue-collar workers.

It is notable that cynicism is highest among blue-collar service workers—those who are in the front line of commercial and public service. People who go into such jobs say that "working with people" is important to them. At the same time, they report that they are "underappreciated" by their employers and the public, and that they are "overworked" on their jobs. It may be that their initial high hopes of serving have been relinquished.

In turn, sales representatives, managers, and supervisors are less cynical than office workers. Their higher levels of education and income partially account for their relatively more upbeat outlook. It is also worth noting that a larger proportion of these people are self-employed or enjoy more autonomy and freedom on their jobs which, along with professional status, may be a mediating factor in their judgments about life.

Interestingly, our 1990 survey found no differences in cynicism among union members versus nonmembers. An earlier survey, in 1980, found union members to be more cynical. In the interim years, cynicism has increased among nonmembers, indicative, perhaps, of their vulnerability in the economy.

Organization Type

Our analysis showed some significant differences between the levels of cynicism reported by people working in the profit-making sector, government, and not-for-profits. Specifically, those in the profit-making sector had higher levels of cynicism.

There were, however, some significant differences in cynicism among people working within this sector. For example, cynicism was pronounced in transportation services, hotels and restaurants, and repair shops. Here we see the blue-collar service cynics—squeezed by the economy. Cynicism is high in entertainment and advertising concerns where hustlers are at work. Finally, cynicism is very high in public utilities and to some extent banking and financial concerns.

By comparison, cynicism was markedly lower in health services and education. The high number of professionals in these industries is one factor. Furthermore, studies of these white-collar workers show that they have many of the same commitments to service as those going into governmental work. However, they are not as frustrated by their jobs or as hampered by red tape and bureaucracy. They are also in the business of healing and teaching—causes bound to attract more idealists and, in our estimation, more upbeat types of people.

Building Credibility: Top-Level Leadership

We recognize that people in large measure bring cynicism with them to their jobs. However, we also believe that the cynical outlook is cultivated in *cynical companies*—those that embody expedient, self-serving values, that support managers who engage in deceptive and exploitative practices, and that communicate in a one-sided, hyped-up, and disingenuous fashion to their employees. Regaining trust and restoring confidence in the American workforce requires that companies cultivate more salutary values, manage people in a more even-handed and reciprocal fashion, and operate in a more honest and straightforward manner. The work of inculcating these values, in turn, has to start at the top of the corporate hierarchy.

Something to Believe In

Where society sends messages that life is a jungle and that looking out for number one is integral to getting ahead, it is incumbent on executives who want to counter the cynical mindset to communicate a more uplifting picture of company life. In their study of corporate cultures, Terry Deal and Alan Kennedy (1982) found that of 80 companies surveyed, 25 had, in the eyes of their employees, a clearly articulated philosophy. Eighteen of these firms espoused what the authors call "qualitative values" that bespoke human ideals.

Statements of philosophy define what a company stands for and what it expects of its members. Well thought out statements address, among other subjects, the company's beliefs about people, attitudes toward customers and aspirations for quality, standards of management and expectations of employees. A caution: Simply formulating a company credo will not necessarily capture people's imaginations or stir their idealism. Indeed, it has become fashionable for companies to develop philosophy statements, have them printed on glossy brochures, and then ignore them in everyday management practice. What is crucial is that companies "live" their corporate ideals.

Participation in Governance

Some of the cynicism found in companies today stems from people's frustration with their situations and powerlessness to change things. Caterpillar Tractor faced growing disillusionment among the younger segment of its workforce in the 1980s. Women and minorities also complained of being disenfranchised in the company. An economic downturn and two unexpected strikes by the local UAW pitted management against the worker and people against one another. A growing chorus intoned that Cat had lost touch with its people. Proposals for productivity improvement were met with chary resistance. The labor strike lingered—hung up on "noneconomic" issues. Plainly Cat had to make a new kind of deal with people—one that recognized and responded to growing mistrust in the ranks.

Accordingly the company undertook a worldwide effort to redefine Cat's employment culture. Several task forces staffed by management and employees surveyed blue-collar workers, clerical, professional, and managerial personnel, and dealers to delineate people's expectations and what Cat would have to do to meet them. Countless focus group meetings with minorities and women were held, and management got an earful. The Human Resource Strategy Conference, as it was known, involved 10,000 people in fact finding and resulted in a roster of the rights and responsibilities of both the company and its employees.

Recommendations to upgrade training, conduct and publish the results of attitude surveys, involve employees in more job-related decisions, and improve the communication skills of management were adopted and implemented. The UAW became a partner with management in formulating Cat's strategies for introducing new technology. Many in the company likened their efforts to a Constitutional Convention where people could get together, speak plainly and forthrightly, and find common ground. Slowly and surely Cat has regained its reputation as a model employer among its workforce (Mirvis, 1985).

Regular Reality Checks

Graphic Controls, an instrument manufacturer, tests its credibility with employees every two years. Results from employee surveys are published not only internally but also for stockholders and the public. GC's former Chairman, Will Clarkson, was not satisfied with saying "People are our most important asset." He published information so that all could adjudge whether that valued asset was being well managed.

Undoing Life Experiences

Companies that want to combat cynicism have to undo the cynical formula and meet their employees halfway or more in the search for common ground. This means instilling realistic expectations in new employees, attending to sources of satisfaction and disappointment, and redressing practices that sow disillusionment. A sampling of "best practices" illustrates how-to-do-its.

Recruiting with Realistic Expectations

New entrants to the workforce have high expectations of their jobs and themselves. Companies hype up their hopes further by promising the better educated a fast track to success and tantalizing more everyday recruits with pledges of outstanding pay, generous benefits, and bright opportunities. They give job applicants the "come-on" and when opportunities fail to materialize, they are left with an embittered and righteously ripped-off workforce.

To start things off in a more genuine manner, give recruits a realistic preview of their job horizons and their potential in the firm. Let them talk with peers to get the "inside dope" about what to expect from a job and to gain an honest picture of company life. That way self-selectivity operates among job applicants, enabling them to "select out" of jobs that do not match their aspirations.

Several companies also provide employees with regular information on job grading, salary schedules, and promotion rates. This information enables people to calibrate their own career potential. It helps when work group members have a say-so in hiring and promoting people. This allows the group members to select people whose aspirations and outlooks fit the job and to recommend the most able for advancement.

Role Models

Michael Lombardo and Morgan McCall (1984) conducted a study of the characteristics of the "intolerable boss." Bosses were faulted for being egotists, incompetents, and martinets, but the most faulted were "snakes in the grass." These managers lied, failed to honor commitments, used their authority to extort confidences, and generally could not be trusted. There is one way to solve the problems posed by cynical managers: fire them. Quite another option is to promote managers based upon their demonstrated trustworthiness and integrity. Senior managers in upbeat companies fill meaningful roles as mentors, teaching employees the ropes and promulgating higher-minded ideals. In these companies, managers are recognized and rewarded for producing results, but also for developing the right kind of talent. This includes inculcating civility and morality in the next generation of company leadership.

Delivering on the Basics

"Cynicism starts with the paycheck," one informant told us. In cynical companies, people believe that they do the work, and the company profits. Pay and promotion decisions are administered autocratically and shrouded in secrecy. It is via the "grapevine" that people come to the conclusion that they are being taken advantage of and exploited.

Cynics are convinced that "something" is being manipulated behind their backs. To counter this perception, compensation practices in upbeat companies are open and the reward systems are transparent. Research by Edward Lawler (1981) shows that people consistently overestimate what their peers are making when pay rates are kept secret. He counsels, therefore, that all rates, steps, and grades in a compensation program be made public to employees. Lawler has also conducted several studies wherein employees have been involved in conducting industry salary surveys and actually setting pay rates in a corporation. He has found that this participative process produces pay systems that are both credible and motivating for all concerned.

Trustworthy companies want people to know where the profits are going and are open about who is getting what; it's all part of acknowledging and rewarding results. They also find innovative ways to meet the distinct needs of segments of the workforce. If young blue-collar workers want to learn more and earn more, companies can adopt pay-for-skill programs wherein blue-collar workers gain more compensation as they master jobs. Clericals want their status and importance to be recognized and want to be part of a team. Employers can find ways wherein staff people earn a portion of cost savings that come from team accomplishments and productivity improvements. Many service employees see no future in their jobs. Companies can spend monies to train them and develop career paths that allow them to move ahead. For those who are productive but want more freedom and time for themselves, flexi-time or time-off provisions can be adopted in lieu of a bonus. All of these counter the cynic's perceptions that rewards are rigged and allow people to obtain rewards that "work" for them.

Practicing What Is Preached

Cynical companies may say "People are our most important asset," but they counterfeit that by paying top executives 100 to 500 times more than hourly workers. Ben & Jerry's Homemade, a Vermont ice cream manufacturer, turns this ratio on its head. There is a 7-to-1 salary ratio between the highest-paid managers and lowest-paid production workers. Want to raise top management salaries? Bring the bottom up!

Corporate social responsibility is a central pillar of this business, and there are hints its idealism is rubbing off on employees. Ben & Jerry's has gone on record with its commitment to social responsibility, and, as surveys of the company show, 85% of the employees strongly approve. Such practices can work in "New Age" companies, but what about old line firms? Many are taking steps to institute more egalitarian and communitarian management practices. Out are executive parking places, private dining rooms, and limited stock options. In are companywide gatherings, common eating rooms, and broad-based employee stock ownership. Firms such as Johnson & Johnson put corporate ideals into practice through health improvement programs that include physical exercise and paid check-ups for employees.

Dealing with Disillusionment

Good economic times can help to foster good management, but how about when times are tough? Firms undergoing merger or acquisition, or who are downsizing and cutting back, often engender cynicism in the way they handle their people. To counter this at the Unisys Corporation, created by the merger of Burroughs and Sperry, top management formulated new ideals bespeaking meritocracy and partnership and put them solidly into practice. That way people are at levels to become active participants in an effort to bring new corporate values focused on improving quality, teamwork, customer service, and human satisfaction to life (Mirvis & Marks, 1991). The success of such efforts provides solid evidence that companies can cope with competition and retain commitment even in the face of business challenges and downturns. But it requires management to "tell it like it is" in hard times, give people an honest and realistic picture of troubles, and ensure that everyone "shares the sacrifice" when costs must be reduced.

A National Problem, Local Remedies

These are only a few potential ways to redress the effects of cynicism in the workforce today. Plainly, cynicism has taken on the proportions of a national malady, and efforts to regain credibility will have to be taken throughout the society, not just in the workplace alone. Problems of the underclass, of which cynicism is part cause and part consequence, cry out for national attention. It is troubling that so many young people come into the workforce bearing a cynical edge. Educator John Holt (1980) has proposed that businesses place high school students in part-time jobs to help them see that work can be meaningful and that employers are not, in general, callous or exploitative. Proponents of national service for young people speak to the same ends.

It is worrisome that so many blue-collar operatives and sour service deliverers are experiencing dead-end dreams. This will neither make manufacturing more competitive nor will it bring customer service back up to world class standards. Lower-end manufacturing and service personnel not only want jobs, they want careers. Why can't career planning, so prominent among executives, be brought down the ranks? Why isn't career pathing, an important service of human resource departments, being put to work to help lesser-skilled employees prepare for their futures?

The efforts we describe will take time and cost money. They begin, in each and every company, by acknowledging the depth and breadth of the problems cynicism poses, and by engaging people in a dialogue concerning what to do about them. In our experiences, managers shy away from this conversation. What is important to recognize, as the statistics bear out, is that cynicism is to be found at every level of the company, among all age segments, social classes, and occupations. Cynical managers are just as reluctant to open this "can of worms" as are cynical workers. But having a straightforward, two-way dialogue on what is causing cynicism at work—diagnosing where and why expectations are out of line, identifying how companies and their people are failing to strike a fair compact, and pinpointing where practices are out of line with preachings—at least opens up communication channels. This kind of discussion can clear the air and give all concerned the breathing space they need to figure out how to rebuild trust and regain credibility in a straightforward, even-handed, noncynical manner.

The authors want to thank Diagnostic Research, Inc. for conducting the national survey and the Human Resource Policy Institute of the School of Management, Boston University for their financial support of the analyses.

References

Buono, A. F., & Bowditch, J. L. (1989). *The human side of mergers and acquisitions*. San Francisco: Jossey Bass.

Deal, T., & Kennedy, A. A. (1982). *Corporate cultures*. Reading, MA: Addison-Wesley.

Gilligan, C. (1982). *In a different voice*. Cambridge, MA: Harvard University Press.

Harris, L. & Associates. (1966: September 13–25, 1973: January 3–7, 1986: Nov. 26–Dec. 2). *The Harris Survey*.

Harrison, B., & Bluestone, B. (1988). *The great U-turn*. New York: Basic Books.

Hirsch, P. (1987). *Pack your own parachute*. Reading, MA: Addison-Wesley.

Hofstede, G. (1980). *Culture's consequences*. Newbury Park, CA: Sage.

Holt, J. (1980, July). Growing up engaged. *Psychology Today*, pp. 14–16, 23.

Jones, L. (1986). *Great expectations: America and the baby boom generation*. New York: Ballantine.

Kanter, D. L., & Mirvis, P. H. (1989). *The cynical Americans.* San Francisco: Jossey-Bass.

Lawler, E. E. (1973). *Motivation in work organizations.* Monterey, CA: Brooks/Cole.

Lawler, E. E. (1981). *Pay and organization development.* Reading, MA: Addison-Wesley.

Lipset, S. M., & Schneider, W. (1983). *The confidence gap: Business, labor and government in the public mind.* New York: Free Press.

Lombardo, M. M., & McCall, M. W. (1984, January). The intolerable boss. *Psychology Today,* pp. 45–48.

Mirvis, P. H. (1985). Formulating and implementing human resource strategy: A model of how to do it, two examples of how it's done. *Human Resource Management, 24(2),* 385–412.

Mirvis, P. H., & Marks, M. L. (1991). *Managing the merger.* Englewood Cliffs, NJ: Prentice-Hall.

Opinion Research Corporation. (1977). *Changing worker values: Myth or reality?* Princeton, NJ: ORC.

Quinn, R. P., & Staines, G. L. (1979). *The 1977 Quality of Employment Survey: Descriptive statistics with comparison data from the 1969–70 and the 1972–73 surveys.* Ann Arbor, MI: Survey Research Center, ISR, University of Michigan.

Reich, R. (1991). *The work of nations.* New York: Knopf.

Reich, R. (1983). *The next American frontier.* New York: Penguin.

Seashore, S. E., Lawler, E. E., Mirvis, P. H., & Cammann, C. (Eds.) (1983). *Assessing organizational change: A guide to methods, measures, & practices.* New York: Wiley Interscience.

Whitehead, R. (1984–85). *The new collar voter.* Amherst, MA: University of Massachusetts. Survey by The Gallup Organization and Yankelovich Clancy Schulman for *Time* magazine. Reported in The new collar class. (1985, September 16). *U.S. News & World Report;* and Whitehead, R. (1987, January 4). Courting the baby-boom vote. *Boston Globe.*

Williams, R. C. (1989). *The trusting heart.* New York: Times Books.

Yankelovich, D., & Immerwahr, J. (1983). *Putting the work ethic to work.* Public Agenda Report on Restoring America's Competitive Vitality, The Public Agenda Foundation.

Yankelovich, D. (1979). Work, values and the new breed. In C. Kerr & J. M. Rosow (Eds.), *Work in America: The decade ahead.* New York: Van Nostrand Reinhold.

Endnotes

1. Statistics on college students are from The Higher Education Research Institute, University of California, Los Angeles, 1967 through 1987.

2. Munro, H. H. (Saki). (1958). Reginald at the Carlton. In *Short stories of Saki.* New York: Modern Library.

3. Brown, T. quote cited by Green, J. (1984). *A cynic's lexicon.* New York: St. Martin's Press.

4. France, J. A. T. quote cited by Solly, J. R. (1925). *A cynic's breviary.*

CHAPTER 15

Organizational Exit

The final people-processing activity in personnel and human resources management is organizational exit, or the ways in which people voluntarily or involuntarily move out of organizations. The two most commonly discussed issues related to exit are absenteeism and turnover. They are among the most persistent problems in personnel management, and they represent major costs to many companies. However, a basic difference exists between the costs associated with these two phenomena. The costs and causes of absenteeism, whether personally or situationally determined, tend to remain with the organization. The costs and causes of turnover, on the other hand, sometimes leave the organization; this can prove to be advantageous, especially if the people who leave are poor performers and those who replace them bring new perspectives and talents. Decisions about absenteeism and turnover are ultimately made by employees and are, therefore, considered to be more voluntary than involuntary.

Other forms of organizational exit, in which representatives of the organization often directly initiate and control exit decisions and policies, are termination for cause (e.g., disobedience, insubordination), redundancy or incompatibility, and retirement. For the latter two forms of organizational exit, outplacement services are sometimes provided. An increase in the number of successful challenges to the common-law doctrine of employment at will (the need from time to time to terminate employees with loyal and productive service to the organization) and a realization of the difficulties inherent in the transition from work life to retirement have promoted additional interest in these forms of exit.

In the first article in this chapter, Ferris, Howard, and Bergin posit that a number of organizational exit decisions are surrounded by political behaviors. Politics infiltrates most activities in organizations, and exit decisions are no exception. All too often, rationality is superseded by politics.

Abelson, in the second article, examines the phenomenon of employee turnover. He summarizes current information about turnover, discusses turnover cultures and how they affect turnover decisions, and outlines a turnover audit process that will be helpful in the management of turnover.

The third article, by Kuzmits, focuses on the issue of long-term absenteeism. The author discusses factors that should be included in an absenteeism control program and makes a number of suggestions for implementing absenteeism programs.

Buckley and Weitzel, in the fifth article, address the issue of employment at will, a doctrine that protects the employer's right to discharge employees for no reason. They clearly articulate the rights and duties of both employers and employees, and they offer a number of suggestions to employers dealing with this important issue.

In the final article in the chapter, Simon deals with outplacement, an important issue for organizations faced with downsizing. The author examines the nature and objectives of outplacement programs and services. As he states, such programs are beneficial for both the organization and the employee.

Suggestions for Further Reading

Bedi, H. (1993). Letting people go gracefully. *Asian Business, 29,* 4.

Corbett, L., & Harrison, N. (Winter 1992–1993). Manufacturing performance and employee involvement: A study of factors influencing improvement. *International Studies of Management & Organization, 22,* 21–32.

De Vader, C., & Bateson, A. (1992). Employee job change: Effectively managing the transition. *SAM Advanced Management Journal, 57,* 30–35.

Finegan, J. (1993, July). People power. *Inc.,* pp. 61–63.

Hawkins, C. (1993, June 28). "We had to recognize that people have lives." *Business Week,* p. 88.

Kennedy, M. (1992, December). The black widow syndrome. *Across the Board,* pp. 9–10.

Lissy, W. (1993). Emotionally troubled employees. *Supervision, 54,* 20–21.

Overman, S. (1993, June). Myths hinder hiring of older workers. *HR Magazine,* pp. 51–52.

Scicolone, M. (1993, February). A documentation system worth viewing. *HR Magazine,* pp. 34–38.

Stuart, P. (1993). How to save your job. *Personnel Journal, 72,* 91.

Rationality and Politics in Organizational Exit Decisions

Gerald R. Ferris, Jack L. Howard, and T. Gregory Bergin

Organizational exit is a rather broad term encompassing the various ways in which employees leave an organization, both of their own free will and in response to decisions by the organization. Our interest here is the second type of exit, in which organizations make decisions to terminate the employment relationship with particular employees for a number of reasons, including poor performance or organizational downsizing efforts. Ideally, such exit decisions are made rationally—that is, all relevant information is gathered and processed, work-related criteria are used, and the decision makers are held accountable for their decisions. We suggest, however, that organizational exit decisions are not always made rationally but that politics or influence sometimes enters into the decision process and outcomes. In this article, we suggest specifically how employees may attempt to bolster their job security and ensure their retention in the organization through the use of impression management tactics and strategies.

Types of Exit Decisions

Individuals are terminated by organizations for a variety of reasons. When employees fail to perform to company standards, the company may find it necessary to terminate them for just cause (i.e., poor performance). Unfortunately, when businesses base termination decisions on poor performance, they usually rely on subjective performance ratings because for most jobs there are not objective performance measures, particularly as we move away from production jobs. When a termination decision is based on subjective performance measures, the opportunity exists for unintentional error as well as for

errors of commission, or intentional manipulation on the part of the individual being evaluated or of the rater.

Not all terminations are based solely on poor performance. Sometimes organizations are forced to downsize, and this structural change results in terminations for reasons other than poor performance. More and more companies in the United States have experienced downsizing. Cascio (1993) defines it as "the planned elimination of positions or jobs," with jobs representing groups of positions that are similar in their essential functions or their reasons for existing. In the 1980s and 1990s, organizations in the United States have been downsizing at an alarming rate. Manufacturing firms have cut their work forces by more than two million workers since 1980 (Cascio, 1993). Since 1987, six million permanent reductions have occurred in U.S. businesses, and the pace of reduction appears to be even faster in 1993 (Baumohl, 1993; Fuchsberg, 1993). These reductions have affected white-collar as well as blue-collar workers: From 1989 to 1992, more than two million middle managers were put out of work (Neikirk, 1993). Also, the most recent recession appears to have hit white-collar workers harder than in the past. Although middle managers constitute from 5 to 8 percent of the work force, they represented 17 percent of the dismissals from 1989 to 1991 and accounted for 32 percent of unemployed workers in 1992 (Cascio, 1993). These statistics indicate the magnitude of downsizing in the United States, which appears to be hitting workers at all organizational levels.

Downsizing in some instances is based on a decision rule driven by new technology and reflecting an effort to increase efficiency, profitability, or competitiveness (Neikirk, 1993). Adherence to the decision rule might result in the termination of an entire unit within an organization. Efficiency might underlie the decision rule when a company attempts to streamline operations through the reduction of work and the elimination of internal functions or levels (Cascio, 1993). Implementation of cost-containment strategies, such as the use of information systems and transaction processing, represents another way in which a company might try to become more efficient through streamlining. Attempts to increase organizational efficiency through the use of these methods results in a need for fewer employees.

Although companies that downsize may do so with the goal of becoming more efficient or effective, evidence indicates that a majority of these organizations fail to demonstrate an increase in profitability or efficiency; this result potentially limits their ability to compete (Baumohl, 1993). The reduced competitiveness might be due to a reduction in the number of employees available to perform a particular kind of work, but it might also be a result of the conditions under which the remaining employees are forced to operate. Those who stay are forced to work harder; the result is higher levels of stress and discontent and lower levels of creativity, loyalty, and morale (Baumohl, 1993; Rifkin, 1993).

When downsizing is not based on a decision rule, it is difficult to predict who will be eliminated, how many employees will be dismissed, and what skills or talents might be lost. It appears that top management in some firms has attempted to downsize in such a way as to preserve consistency and harmony; this might indicate that management was looking for a particular "fit" in the employees that remained (Cameron, Freeman, & Mishra, 1991). In such a case, employees might use political behaviors in efforts to remain with the organization; indeed, politics has been found to be a key factor in some cases of organizational downsizing (Hardy, 1985; Hardy & Pettigrew, 1985). Although a proper "fit" between the organization and the individual might be important to the organization, the employer still needs workers who are capable and competent. If businesses make downsizing decisions in such a way that employees retained are *not* the most talented or qualified ones, it is not surprising that they should operate less effectively. Thus, although effectiveness is the apparent goal of downsizing, the actual outcome of the process sometimes falls short of that goal.

The Importance of Effective Exit Decisions

There are two principal reasons why organizations need to make effective decisions regarding employee termination. First, such decisions should be functional. Consider, for instance, the termination decisions related to downsizing: If the decisions are functional, the workers who stay will be more qualified or talented than those dismissed, and the company's competitive position will be improved. Although this is the desired outcome of downsizing, the evidence discussed indicates that downsizing has not led to increased organizational effectiveness. This might indicate that the decisions regarding terminations were dysfunctional. To make functional decisions, the employer must be able to identify correctly the workers who should be dismissed.

A second reason for making effective termination decisions is that the legal ramifications of those decisions have increased. In the past, many of the court cases involving human resources staffing pertained to hiring. In 1990, however, over 60 percent of the bias charges filed were aimed at promotion and termination decisions, whereas fewer than 9 percent of these charges related to hiring decisions (Lublin, 1991). This trend indicates that the focus of anti-discrimination litigation may be shifting from entry-level selection to both promotion and termination and increases the importance of making defensible exit decisions.

The cost of making poor decisions regarding terminations increased with the passage of the Civil Rights Act of 1991. In termination cases related to sex, disability, or religion, punitive damages and jury trials are possible under that legislation. Not only has the legal focus shifted toward discharge decisions, but the punitive damages can be extremely high, as was demonstrated in a California court case when a Texaco manager passed over for promotion was awarded $17.7 million dollars, $15 million of it in punitive damages (Lublin, 1991).

Reasons for Ineffective Exit Decisions

The traditional assumption has been that decisions regarding the flow of individuals into or out of an organization are based on a rational model. If the rational model were followed, the people making decisions about human resources staffing would know the specific requirements of the jobs in question, and the job applicants or incumbents would have the necessary skills to perform the jobs effectively. It has been suggested, however, that staffing decisions do not follow the rational model and that elusive concepts such as the "fit" of an individual influence staffing decisions, which include outflow or exit decisions (Judge & Ferris, 1993).

Fit represents some level of match between the applicant and the organization in relation to the values or goals of each. It is thought that applicants having the necessary abilities to perform a job may not necessarily be successful unless there is some level of match between these individuals and the company. Match may indicate skills or abilities, or it might reflect the extent to which the decision maker likes one person more than another. Because the concept of fit is so vague, its use in organizational exit decisions could be problematic, but it clearly does serve as the criterion for many exit decisions.

Because fit is often not clearly defined, employees may be able to manage the images they present to the supervisors and evaluators responsible for making termination decisions, thus conveying the impression that they do fit

(Judge & Ferris, 1993). This possibility would indicate that organizational exit decisions may be based on the form that an individual presents, rather than on the substance that he or she has to offer the employer (Ferris & King, 1991). Moreover, those deciding who will stay and who will exit may be evaluating the incumbents with images of themselves or the organization in mind (Ferris, Frink, & Galang, 1993). If this is true, an objective decision rule is not being used, and the difficulty of distinguishing between people who are qualified from an objective standpoint and people who have constructed the image of competency is exacerbated (Judge & Ferris, 1993). Recognizing this problem is one matter; correctly identifying and analyzing it when it occurs is much more difficult.

The problem associated with people's appearing to fit is further compounded by the fact that, in many human resources staffing contexts, the employer places little or no accountability on the decision maker (Boudreau & Rynes, 1986). Lacking clear direction from the organization, the decision maker may believe that he or she has made a good selection decision when in reality the decision could prove ineffective in the long run. The use of the notion of an employee's fit in the company and the lack of accountability add up to a situation where ineffective decisions are highly possible.

Politics in Organizational Exit Decisions

Organizational exit decisions, whatever the reasons behind them, are surrounded with ambiguity. If a termination results from "poor performance," subjectivity may compromise the supervisor rating on which the decision was likely based. Although some downsizing decisions are driven by a particular decision rule (e.g., seniority-based decisions; certain jobs, not people, being cut), in many cases no such rule exists. Often the company only knows that labor costs must be cut by a certain percentage and that a certain number of people must therefore be eliminated. Even when a specific decision rule is in place, subjectivity continues to surround the decision of who is let go.

High levels of ambiguity create opportunities for employees to exercise influence over their own job security as they try to ensure that they are not the ones eliminated. These efforts may take the form of self-promotion behaviors whereby employees attempt to convince management of their value to the organization. For instance, an employee may enhance his or her role in the success of a group project; although the essence of the employee's message may not be incorrect, it may not be particularly accurate either. Or an employee might use ingratiating behavior to focus directly on the supervisor, who might be perceived as having considerable influence over the termination decision.

Employees might attempt to minimize a perceived threat or avoid unwanted consequences by using defensive behaviors (Ashforth & Lee, 1990). This subset of political behaviors differs from self-promotion behaviors in that defensive behaviors focus on protecting, as opposed to promoting, the employee's self-interest. The basic premise of these behaviors is the avoidance of blame, unwanted attention, and change. Individuals can evade unfavorable situations by playing safe, which may mean avoiding making controversial judgments or risky decisions. By taking safe courses of action, individuals can avoid offending anyone, thus staying on the good side of those around them in the company (Kanter, 1977; Kerr, 1975).

Employees can also stretch out their work to give the impression that they are busy. This behavior may also create the impression that the work is very time-consuming—and if work is time-consuming, it must be important to the organization. Although stretching out work may not be a sophisticated tactic, it can provide further protection for the workers.

When work activities do not yield the desired results, an employee may blame some external source, which serves as a scapegoat. By deflecting blame to external factors, the employee might imply that other parties are responsible or that the cause of the problem has been identified, further protecting his or her image. Closely resembling scapegoating is misrepresentation of information to others within the organization. A person may engage in misrepresentation by distorting information, embellishing the importance of oneself to the organization, or selectively presenting or withholding information. Although this tactic appears deceitful, its use may not always be conscious. For example, technical language has been known to mask the motives of experts (Edelman, 1977). Perhaps the experts do not always have motives, but because those with whom they are communicating do not fully understand what is being communicated, the result is miscommunication that was not intended to be deceitful.

The behaviors just discussed have been found to influence the way employees are perceived by superiors. Employees might also attempt to create situations in which the organization becomes dependent upon them (Pressey, 1993). They can do this in a number of ways. One way is to develop particular expertise that the company not only values but relies upon. The effectiveness of this type of tactic may increase as the number of workers in a company who are familiar with the technology decreases. For example, if several people in the organization know how to use the computer program responsible for effecting direct pay deposits into employees' bank accounts, the company may find it easy to terminate one of them. However, if only one employee is capable of performing the direct deposits, it may be difficult to terminate him or her. In other words, that specialized capability may make that employee indispensable.

Another way to create the image of indispensability is to become a critical linkage from one's own department to other parts of the organization. By working with individuals in other areas, an employee may become the only person in the department who understands the processes of the other units in the company. The employee's current department may become dependent on him or her for knowledge of the other departments and for the linkages themselves. The benefit of this tactic can be twofold. First, the employee may develop skills that will be transferable into another department in the event of downsizing; this is an important consideration as some departments may grow during organizational downsizing. Second, as the employee becomes the so-called communication link, with the background necessary to communicate effectively with other key units, he or she appears indispensable to the company and has achieved increased job security.

In the foregoing discussion, we have identified particular political tactics employees might use in trying to exercise influence over important human resources decisions and perhaps ensure their job security. However, the success of any of these tactics depends, to a great extent, upon an individual's political skill. The fact that an employee attempts to behave politically does not necessarily mean that such behavior will be effective and produce desired outcomes. Employees will differ in their political skills and in their abilities to diagnose situations and select the most effective political tactics or behaviors, given the situational constraints and knowledge of the target (i.e., supervisor, peer, etc.). We suggest that political skill might be a function not only of experience but also of personality. For example, an employee might possess just the right mix of intelligence, shrewdness, and social awareness to read people and social settings accurately and to adapt his or her behavior convincingly to the situation. The word *convincingly* is key to the success of political tactics. A major determinant of the effectiveness of political behavior is one's ability to demonstrate the behavior in a manner that appears genuine, well intentioned, and not self-serving.

We have described an alternative perspective on human resources outflow decisions; not the assumed rational model but rather a situation characterized by self-interest, political behavior and skill, ambiguity, and lack of accountability. Indeed, managers making outflow decisions may be pursuing their own agendas in efforts to maintain their own power bases. However, even when managers seek to make the most effective possible outflow decisions, the political skill of some employees may result in the best politicians being retained in the organization and the best performers being let go. To better understand the political dynamics of job security, let's take a closer look at the way employees attempted to manage impressions of their importance during an organizational downsizing at a high-technology firm we will call DTN Systems.

The Politics of Job Security at DTN Systems

DTN Systems is a fairly new entrant in the high-technology industry when compared to the likes of IBM, yet the firm has been very competitive. However, the competitiveness and volatility of the high-tech industry can force organizations within the industry to change rapidly. In recent years the competition has been so intense that many organizations within this industry, including DTN, have been forced to downsize.

DTN approached the challenge by attempting to evaluate its processes and determining which of them were the most critical for organizational success. Then the employees were evaluated. On the surface this appears to be a rational approach because processes are basic to an organization's functioning. However, it is very unlikely that an organization can evaluate its processes without the employees realizing that an evaluation is underway. This is what happened at DTN, and in efforts to save their jobs, employees attempted to enhance the importance of the processes they supported.

Employees became aware that all functions of the organization were under evaluation, and they realized that components that did not prove to be critical would more than likely be eliminated. Through their actions, employees tried to convince their supervisors that they were valuable to DTN. It did not matter whether they were important or not; what mattered was that they were perceived to be of value to the organization.

During the downsizing, information management and data processing professionals felt very vulnerable. Hoping to improve their chances of survival, each of these groups tried to manage the images they presented to their superiors. Employees manipulated their images along two dimensions, depending on how they perceived their managers. If a manager was results oriented, the workers would present themselves as deliverers of services; the manner in which the services were delivered was less important than the service delivery itself. If the manager was process oriented, the employees were in a different situation.

Although PC computing is very important at DTN, employees could deliver the results in nearly any format if they had results-oriented managers. However, most of the managers at DTN are more process oriented and feel committed to the power of new technology to raise the organization to a higher level of competitiveness. As a result, for programmers it was important to deliver their services in state-of-the-art packaging. Consequently, a premium was placed on opportunities to learn new technologies and acquire the latest skills. Of course, the personal challenge for each programmer was to continue to deliver new services and simultaneously to learn new skills. If a worker was fortunate, he or she was assigned to a development team to create the new technology. The reassigned employees were able to develop new skills while creating the impression that they were critical to the success of DTN. Unfortunately, the new processes were rarely deployed because of the volatility of the high-technology industry.

Acquiring the latest skills or learning the newest software package is of paramount importance in programming communities. If an employee was left on an old system that was not going to be upgraded or receive new revisions, while the industry was moving away from his or her system, personal growth and upward mobility would appear limited. Many programmers in that situation read the handwriting on the wall and chose to pursue their opportunities outside DTN.

Another strategy employees used was to align themselves with departments that were more results oriented. For example, finance/accounting departments and certain sales and marketing areas look at the same rows and columns of numbers (e.g., sales by product by area) as information management does to evaluate the success of their operations. In finance/accounting and sales and marketing, delivery of the numbers was of critical importance; less important was how the numbers were obtained. As a result, many programmers at DTN migrated from their information management departments to other, more results-oriented departments.

The second way in which employees could manage their images was by screening their behaviors, and employees in data processing units did just that. When data processors discovered which processes the evaluation had determined to be critical, they attempted to demonstrate to their supervisors how they actually supported the critical processes through their efforts or abilities. For example, an employee might demonstrate how she does something that relates remotely to the critical process and then focus on the way the process depends upon her input; this would enhance her value. Or an employee might try to portray his contribution to the company as being different because of the new technology, whereas in reality it is fundamentally no different than before that technology was adopted.

The data processing employees also tried to bring about changes in the perceptions of their supervisors, changes that could lead to dysfunction in organizational terms. For example, while attempting to demonstrate their importance to the company, employees could be hanging on to outdated processes. Better and more efficient ways of accomplishing the work may not be implemented because of the perceived worth of the current method. The employees become synonymous with the "critical process," which would be eliminated if it were examined from an objective viewpoint.

When DTN Systems was faced with downsizing, it attempted to evaluate the value of various processes to the organization. Although many might agree with this approach to decision making, the result was that employees did their best to shape perceptions of their value to DTN. The outcome was an environment in which objective evaluation was difficult at best. Rather than stating their intentions, employees were behaving politically by attempting to ensure their job security by demonstrating the importance of their jobs to the organization.

How We Can Improve Organizational Exit Decisions

When we make important employment decisions, such as those concerning termination, we need to feel that we are making these decisions as accurately as possible. We want to be confident that the employees we terminate really are the lower performers and that those we retain are indeed the more effective individuals in our organization. However, increasing legal challenges of such decisions by former employees who believe they were unjustly terminated point to problems with our decision-making processes. Furthermore, the disappointing results of downsizing—organizations that are no more effective, productive, or profitable than before downsizing occurred—provide additional evidence that exit decisions are not being made in the best possible way. Indications are that politics, not rationality, may be driving these decisions.

Although the evidence shows that organizations' decisions regarding downsizing have had disappointing results, these results can give us some insight into ways to make better decisions in the future. First of all, one significant problem for many companies facing the exit decisions associated with downsizing has been the presence of ambiguity. Employers have done little to eliminate the ambiguity. The first step in reducing the ambiguity is to specify clearly the criteria to be used by decision makers. Employers need to ensure that the decision makers understand specifically what they are evaluating and what method to use in evaluating processes or individuals.

Once we have made sure that the decision makers understand the criteria, we need to impress upon them that they will be held accountable for their decisions. With a sense of accountability, they might make these decisions more conscientiously and obtain better results. This is not to say that holding the decision makers accountable is the single factor that will do most to improve the decision making, but it should heighten their awareness that they need to act in the best interest of the company. If ambiguity can be reduced and decision makers held accountable, human resources outflow decisions should be improved.

Conclusion

Organizational exit decisions often have failed to produce the results they were intended to produce. Downsizing continues to occur at a very rapid rate, yet companies that downsize are typically less effective than they were before downsizing. We believe that this has occurred because decisions regarding organizational exit involved political behavior more than rational behavior. Employees manipulate information about their jobs in an effort to protect and secure their positions, a behavior that is understandable and probably natural. Individuals will attempt to enhance their personal value as well as their performance and their contributions to the organization. They will also attempt to align themselves with the critical processes of the company to increase the perception that they are indispensable. These behaviors are the result of employees' efforts to save their jobs.

As a result of all of this misinformation, decision makers in organizations may not always make the most effective decisions. Failure to improve the effectiveness of human resources outflow decisions may well result in less productive employees being the survivors of downsizing efforts, and increased litigation initiated by productive employees who were terminated without just cause. The costs of such outcomes are high.

However, effective decision making is not impossible. Because of the downturn in the economy and increased global competition, now more than ever organizations need to ensure that they are making effective decisions. The ambiguity surrounding the decision criteria need to be clarified and increased accountability placed upon the decision makers. If these steps are taken, organizational exit decisions should be improved considerably, and the resulting organization may become more effective.

References

Ashforth, B. E., & Lee, R. T. (1990). Defensive behavior in organizations: A preliminary model. *Human Relations, 43,* 621–648.

Baumohl, B. (1993, March 15). When downsizing becomes "dumbsizing." *Time,* p. 55.

Boudreau, J., & Rynes, S. (1987). Giving it the old college try. *Personnel Administrator, 32,* 78–85.

Cameron, K. S., Freeman, S. J., & Mishra, A. K. (1991). Best practices in white collar downsizing: Managing contradictions. *Academy of Management Executive, 5,* 57–73.

Cascio, W. F. (1993). Downsizing: What do we know? What have we learned? *Academy of Management Executive, 7,* 95–104.

Edelman, M. (1977). *Political language: Words that succeed and policies that fail.* New York: Academic Press.

Ferris, G. R., Frink, D. D., & Galang, M. C. (1993). Diversity in the workplace: The human resources management challenges. *Human Resource Planning, 16,* 41–51.

Ferris, G. R., & King, T. R. (1991). Politics in human resources decisions: A walk on the dark side. *Organizational Dynamics, 20,* 59–71.

Fuchsberg, G. (1993, October 1). Why shake-ups work for some, not for others. *The Wall Street Journal,* pp. B1, B10.

Hardy, C. (1985). Fighting cutbacks: Some issues for public sector administrators. *Canadian Public Administration, 28,* 531–549.

Hardy, C., & Pettigrew, A. M. (1985). The use of power in managerial strategies for change. In R. J. Rosenbloom (Ed.), *Research on technological innovation, management, and policy* (Vol. 2, pp. 11–45). Greenwich, CT: JAI Press.

Judge, T. A., & Ferris, G. R. (1993). The elusive criterion of fit in human resources staffing decisions. *Human Resource Planning, 15,* 47–67.

Kanter, R. M. (1977). *Men and women of the corporation.* New York: Basic Books.

Kerr, S. (1975). On the folly of rewarding A while hoping for B. *Academy of Management Journal, 18,* 769–783.

Lublin, J. S. (1991, December 30). Rights law to spur shifts in promotions. *The Wall Street Journal,* p. B1.

Neikirk, W. (1993, February 21). Big business thinks smaller: Profound changes affect job market. *Chicago Tribune,* Section 1, pp. 1, 10, 11.

Pressey, D. (1993, May 16). Shrinking firms swelling ranks of "dislocated." *The News-Gazette,* p. C1.

Rifkin, G. (1993, Jan. 3). The loneliness of the layoff survivor. *The New York Times,* Section 3, p. 25.

Turnover Cultures
and the Turnover Audit

Michael A. Abelson

Employee turnover is of great concern to organizations. One reason for this concern is that employee turnover is very costly to companies. The estimated cost of replacing an employee can run as high as 50% of that person's annual salary. This is not surprising, considering the costs of recruiting, orienting, and training a replacement. A second reason for the concern is that turnover can lead to personal tensions in other employees. This has the potential to further increase turnover and organizational ineffectiveness, because those who remain do additional work until the replacement performs at an acceptable level.

Scholars have examined employee turnover decisions to better understand them and to develop suggestions for effective coping in the workplace. This article summarizes much of what is known, describes how turnover cultures affect turnover decisions, and then develops a turnover audit process for better managing turnover decisions.

What We Know about Turnover Decisions

Knowledge of what is generally understood about turnover gives insight on how it can be better managed. Research has focused on aspects of the turnover decision and specific factors related to employee turnover.

Aspects of Turnover Decisions

Aspect 1. Defining turnover. Turnover has been examined as the activity that occurs when a person leaves a specific job as well as when he or she leaves a specific organization. We use the organizational approach in this article for two reasons: First, job-specific turnover can be a form of career development.

In this situation, the organization retains the person's services. This is much different than when a person leaves an organization and his or her services are no longer available. Second, research studies generally use an organizational turnover perspective. Confidence that past research is pertinent to the discussion here is enhanced if we use the same definition.

Aspect 2. The turnover decision follows a process. Several approaches to the process have been suggested, but the most researched and accepted approach is the one developed by Mobley (1977). He suggests that people follow a fairly complex process that has five steps. First, people evaluate their existing job and determine their level of personal satisfaction with it. If they are dissatisfied, they progress to the next step—thinking of quitting. During this step, they think about their present job circumstances and determine the personal benefits and costs of quitting. For example, how much time will the search require and what is the probability of finding an alternative job? The third step in the process includes the intent to search, the actual search, and the evaluation of alternatives. Work and nonwork factors now enter into the decision process. A spouse, moving costs, and other factors may be issues. New alternatives may be added and old ones withdrawn at this time. The present employer may enhance the current job or increase job benefits to persuade the employee to remain. In the fourth step, the employee compares alternatives to the present job and makes a decision. This decision is not always easy. The job incumbent may return to Step 3 and renegotiate alternatives. The fifth step is the actual staying or leaving behavior. Although the decision is made in Step 4, actual behavior may not always closely follow that decision. Other factors may enter into the decision process, suggesting that previous steps should be revisited.

Since turnover is a process that occurs over time, it can be interrupted at any time. The earlier in the process intervention occurs, the more likely the employee will remain at the same job. Satisfying a dissatisfied employee (the beginning of the process) is easier than changing someone's mind after they have searched for and found potential alternative employment that is attractive (Step 4). An effective strategy for managing turnover, then, is to be aware of current employees' tendencies toward remaining or leaving and taking appropriate action as soon as possible.

Aspect 3. Not all turnover is bad. Turnover of some employees can be very positive. A staff member may not be performing at the company's standards. If this person leaves, this is referred to as a functional turnover because it is positive for the organization. Only when high-performing staff members leave is the turnover deemed negative or dysfunctional (Dalton & Todor, 1979). Appropriate action therefore may be to allow or even promote a current employee to leave. Greater employee turnover in some organizations may even improve effectiveness. Organizations with very low turnover may find that increasing turnover results in new employees with different, more creative, or better ideas (Steers & Mowday, 1981).

One real challenge for organizations is to have an optimal level of turnover (Abelson & Baysinger, 1984). On an individual basis, this means that the cost of keeping people (e.g., compensation, interpersonal dilemmas) is equal to the benefit the organization receives from them. High performers may be allowed to leave if other organizations are willing to pay more than the current organization thinks they are worth. Some football players receive more than twice their annual pay from another team because that team values them more highly. Effectively managing turnover may mean allowing high performers to leave. The result is a more manageable budget and less disharmony, which is created by rewarding some people in the organization disproportionately.

Aspect 4. Certain types of turnover are neither controllable nor avoidable (Dalton, Krackhardt, & Porter, 1981). People leave organizations for many reasons. Reasons such as better pay, supervision, and advancement opportunities elsewhere are controllable by the organization. Pregnancy, a spouse's moving to take a job in a different location, or leaving to obtain an advanced degree are usually not controllable. As would be expected, employees who remained on the job reported the same levels of satisfaction and commitment to the organization as people who left for unavoidable reasons. Departed employees who left for unavoidable reasons reported less satisfaction and commitment than did either those who stayed or those who departed because they had no choice (Abelson, 1987).

Effective management of turnover is difficult. There is no need to attempt to affect behaviors that are outside our control. Effective management means identifying the step in the turnover process that a staff member is experiencing and taking appropriate action to change his or her behavior where possible.

Aspect 5. Turnover behavior can be planned or impulsive. A planned, five-step turnover process was presented previously. Research shows that many people follow this path in making a turnover decision. Others take a more abrupt approach. Mobley (1977) suggests that impulsive behavior can occur when a person begins and ends turnover with the decision to leave. In these situations, it appears that a sudden, unexpected decision is made.

What may also be occurring is that the employee has been thinking about leaving for some time, but the decision is made abruptly as the result of some small or single work or nonwork factor (Sheridan & Abelson, 1984). This particular factor pushes the person past the point of no return.

Managing a planned, progressive turnover process is difficult. Managing what appears to be impulsive behavior is even more demanding. Effective turnover management requires awareness of employee perceptions of the workplace and determining how people are responding to the numerous factors that contribute to turnover (we examine these in the next section). The key is to intervene after the first symptoms appear. This helps in dealing with both planned and seemingly impulsive decisions to leave the company. Truly impulsive turnover decisions require patience as well as the realization that some turnovers are unavoidable.

Aspect 6. The expected turnover rate for any organization or organizational subunit is not known. Staff members and managers know salary levels and performance goals throughout the year. These figures add certainty and assist in planning, organizing, and performing. Who will leave during the year and what the total turnover is expected to be for a work group are rarely known. This contributes to uncertainty in the workplace.

Specific Factors Related to Turnover Decisions

Many factors in the individual, organization, and environment affect turnover decisions. The personnel function has a direct impact on many of these through the recruitment/ selection process, training/development activities, and the appraisal/reward structure. Management decisions affect turnover through various organizational issues, such as how jobs and the organization itself are structured. Economic cycles and geographic location are environmental factors that affect turnover decisions. All of these affect the individual's perception of the workplace and staff movement through the turnover process.

Personnel function effect.   The process of recruitment and selection influences turnover through its effects on who enters the organization. The effect of employee demographics has been extensively studied because these factors can be controlled to some extent. The only consistent finding in this regard is that

older people leave less frequently and that greater tenure in the organization lowers the probability of turnover. The tenure research is not helpful in selecting new employees from outside the organization, but it is useful when considering people for higher-level positions in the same organization. Gender, education, family responsibility, and personality have sometimes been related to turnover, but these relationships are very complex and the evidence about them is inconclusive.

The process used for hiring people has been more strongly related to turnover than have many individual demographic factors. Effective matching of the person's aptitude and abilities for the job is important (Mobley, 1982). Their personal potential satisfaction with the job and organization also affect turnover decisions (Lofquist & Dawes, 1969). A great deal of research has demonstrated that a realistic job preview, in which the person is given accurate information about the job and the organization before they accept the position, also decreases turnover (Wanous, 1980; McElvoy & Cascio, 1985).

The practices a person experiences upon entering the organization, such as orientation and training/development, also influence turnover decisions. Orienting and socializing new staff members regarding the written and unwritten norms and rules of the organization allow them to interact more effectively. Orientation also helps employees feel that they are a part of the organization more quickly. Training and development programs, in which staff members learn to perform desired organization and job-specific actions, further enhance an appropriate match between staff and job needs. Furthermore, the more specific the training, the less transferable it is to other organizations and the less the expected turnover (Abelson, Ferris, & Urban, 1988). Both orientation and training/ development lead to a more comfortable fit between the person and the organization and build upon the matching process that is so effective in the recruiting and selection process.

The process used to appraise and reward individuals is related to turnover even more than is pay. A fair and honest appraisal process that effectively evaluates work outcomes contributes to less frequent turnover (Cotton & Tuttle, 1986). Furthermore, the reward system itself must be viewed as fair and equitable (Hulin, 1966: Kerr & Slocum, 1987; Mobley, 1982). Staff members view systems as inequitable if different levels within the organization or other individuals are overly rewarded financially or nonfinancially. The actual pay is not an issue if it is perceived by employees as an equitable amount (Mobley, Griffith, Hand, & Meglino, 1979). Some absolute level usually does need to be attained, however. Two or three percent raises may be comparatively fair and equitable within an organization, but if other organizations have vastly higher pay scales, turnover levels will increase.

Management decisions effect. Turnover decreases when management allows employees to become actively involved and participate in various aspects of the job. Job design research has demonstrated that if the work is meaningful to the employee, the employee experiences an ability to make decisions regarding the work, and the employee obtains feedback from the job itself, positive outcomes, such as decreased turnover, occur (McEvoy & Cascio, 1985). Furthermore, higher turnover can be expected when the task is routine or repetitious (Mobley, 1982).

Management decisions regarding organizational design issues also influence turnover decisions. When decisions are made and actions directed from a central administration or low levels of communication within the organization occur, higher levels of turnover can be expected (Price, 1977; Price & Mueller, 1986). Administrations that are considerate of employees, on the other hand, have lower levels of turnover (Mobley, 1982). Furthermore, some studies found that smaller organizations (less than 250 people) have greater turnover because of the inability for internal transfer, but most research demonstrates that there is no consistent relationship between size and turnover levels (Mobley, 1982; Terberg & Lee, 1984).

When management promotes staff involvement in work and work-related decisions, lower turnover rates result. This can be implemented through effective use of job design or by having less autocratic administrations that keep staff members informed and are more responsive to staff needs.

Environmental factors effect. Employee perceptions that acceptable employment is available elsewhere affect decisions to proceed through the turnover process. However, few studies have examined the effect of environmental factors on individual turnover decisions. The results of studies examining this relationship, however, are consistent and strong. Healthy economic cycles with low unemployment rates enhance perceptions that opportunities exist elsewhere and result in higher turnover rates (March & Simon, 1958; Mobley, 1982; Price, 1977). Pay levels also affect turnover decisions (Armknecht & Early, 1972). Employees may be more likely to move to a different geographic area with a lower unemployment rate or higher salaries. Furthermore, people may consider leaving one organization in a relatively depressed industry for employment in another industry if their skills are transferable.

Population size and change in size have also been related to turnover decisions. The larger the geographic area, the greater the turnover (Terberg & Lee, 1984), while the greater the change in population, the greater the turnover (Harrington & Abelson, 1988). Both of these relationships seem appropriate in that each allows the individual greater opportunity to find employment elsewhere. Therefore, the greater the perceived opportunities in the environment because of a healthy economy or the size of the labor pool, the more the environment promotes decisions to change jobs.

Individual perceptions. The personnel function, management decisions, and economic factors affect turnover decisions. Individuals combine the information they receive from these areas and develop an overall impression that helps guide them through the turnover process. As previously stated, the turnover process begins when an employee begins to feel dissatisfied. Levels of satisfaction, commitment, and uncertainty in the job all affect dissatisfaction and how an employee feels about remaining.

Overall satisfaction and satisfaction with the job itself are two factors that affect the turnover process. Satisfaction with pay, supervision, promotion opportunities, and coworkers sometimes affect that decision, but not consistently.

Employee commitment to organizational values and goals also affects turnover process decisions. The relationship between commitment and turnover is even stronger than the relationship between satisfaction and turnover. As with satisfaction, greater commitment inhibits movement through the turnover process (Bluedorn, 1982). Commitment or loyalty may be effective because they sometimes promote employees to ignore problems they believe exist. Loyalty to the organization displaces this other information in our decision process.

Uncertainty surrounding the job environment also affects perceptions about the decision to leave. The more uncertainty people experience, the more uncomfortable the situation. Certain levels of uncertainty or ambiguity are expected. Some jobs and professions are more ambiguous than others. Dissatisfaction occurs when this level becomes too high or is prolonged over an extended period of time. Realistic job previews may be effective because they reduce the level of uncertainty. Job enrichment or allowing staff members to take more responsibility in the work may also decrease turnover because it allows people to make decisions that decrease uncertainty levels.

These three variables—satisfaction, uncertainty, and commitment—are consistently related to movement through the turnover process. Any organization can therefore expect increased turnover when these factors occur in the work environment. Another key

to managing turnover, then, is the effective management of these factors.

Summary

Effective management of turnover requires an awareness that turnover is a process, that not all turnover is bad or uncontrollable, and that turnover can be planned or seem impulsive. It is also important for management to be aware that numerous factors contribute to turnover decisions. These factors arise from personnel practices, management decisions, and environmental factors.

Effective management of turnover requires that management take appropriate actions after they become aware of factors that contribute to employee decisions to leave. Since turnover is a complex process, intervention should occur as soon as symptoms appear. Dissatisfaction, lack of commitment to the organization, and stress caused by role or job ambiguities are the most readily apparent causes of the symptoms. Organizations can control these problems through being aware of and managing turnover cultures and by developing turnover audit procedures.

Turnover Cultures

Turnover culture is the history, reputation, and perception people have of activities that affect employee turnover decisions and ultimately the unit turnover rate (percentage of staff leaving per year compared to the total number of staff members). Turnover cultures can result in very low or very high turnover rates. IBM has a turnover culture that promotes a low turnover rate (3.1% a year during 1980–1985). 7-Eleven has a turnover culture that promotes a very high turnover rate (over 100% per year for a similar time period).

Cultures evolve from two distinct components. First, there are meanings contained in the culture's norms, ideologies, and values, namely, staff interpretations of what they experience in the workplace. Second, these meanings are expressed, affirmed, and communicated to members through several channels (Trice & Beyer, 1984). The practices pertinent to our discussion are those discussed previously: personnel practices, managerial decisions, and methods the organization uses in dealing with environmental factors.

Staff members develop meanings from their interpretation of these practices. Recruitment and selection practices directly affect perceptions of turnover culture. An organization hiring the best people irrespective of age demonstrates an emphasis on quality. If some of those hired are older, they will typically remain employed longer. Since they are more qualified, they are also better performers. Both of these actions reduce the stress and tension experienced by existing staff members. Remaining staff members are therefore more committed to an organization taking actions that reduce their stress and promote their personal goals. The outcome is potentially lower turnover rates.

Realistic job previews and an effective orientation program suggest a better match between new employees and job requirements. This match increases personal levels of satisfaction. This honest approach to hiring and effective orientation promotes commitment to the organization and its values. The outcome for both is the same—less desire by the employee to begin thinking about quitting.

Organizations that have poor performance-appraisal processes and inequitable pay distribution have the opposite effect. They promote dissatisfaction and movement through the employee turnover-decision process that most likely results in a decision to leave.

Managerial decisions also affect perceptions of the turnover culture. Jobs that possess meaningfulness, allow people the opportunity to take responsibility, and give feedback from the job itself promote satisfaction in those who value such opportunities. If staff members value and receive these, they perceive the culture favorably and tend to remain. If staff members do not value these aspects in the job and are required to have them, they will be dissatisfied and will probably progress through the turnover process. Organizations

can optimize their turnover culture strategy by deciding which type of employee they wish to retain. Organizations can structure the job to retain a specific group of employees. Organizations can also structure jobs flexibly so that those who want added components in their job can obtain them and those who do not want the additional components can work in positions in which those components are limited or not available. The organization's practices will be perceived by the staff and acted upon by loyalty and retention or dissatisfaction and turnover.

Managerial decisions regarding organizational structures also affect turnover decisions. Management can centralize decisions, reduce communications, and show little consideration for staff. Staff members who perceive this negatively will become dissatisfied and demonstrate little consideration for the organization by beginning the turnover process.

Environmental factors also affect turnover cultures. Low unemployment rates in a particular geographic area and rapid population growth may lead to less commitment of staff because of numerous positive opportunities in the area. These factors are less controllable by the organization. If the organization has developed a positive turnover culture, demonstrating most practices that enhance satisfaction and commitment, staff members are less likely to leave. The other opportunities may have hidden costs. Staff members are not willing to risk the uncertainty of these hidden costs because they have positive expectations of the organization. Furthermore, large organizations may have the ability to transfer staff members to other locations that have the additional opportunities made available by competing organizations. This further promotes a positive turnover culture in that the organization gains a reputation for supporting and working to enhance the goals of its staff members even when relocation and losing a valued employee at the current location is required.

Organizational strategies for managing turnover cultures can be described along two continua. First, organizations manage turnover cultures at different levels of *consistency* across the various personnel function areas, management decision areas, and environmental factor areas. This can also be referred to as the *intensity* of areas promoting a similar turnover culture. Stated differently, consistency is the extent to which organizational activities in different areas promote a common perception of turnover culture. Staff members either feel satisfied and committed and have clarity in their job or role, or they do not. Second, the management of turnover cultures occurs at some level of *deliberateness.* Deliberateness ranges from highly planned to not at all planned.

Organizations such as Ross Perot's Electronic Data Systems (EDS) deliberately managed turnover cultures and did so consistently across numerous areas. The culture in EDS before it was purchased by General Motors had a reputation of strongly supporting and being loyal to staff members. These attributes were consistently demonstrated across personnel functional areas (hiring the best people and using realistic job previews), management decision areas (allowing staff much responsibility in decision making), and environmental factor areas (staff members being extremely loyal and not taking opportunities at other firms unless they were extremely appealing). Staff members perceived that these norms, ideologies, and values were deliberate as well as consistent.

Organizations such as Texaco promote the opposite approach to managing turnover cultures. During the several years Texaco and Pennzoil were entangled in litigation regarding ownership of another oil company, management of employee turnover cultures seemed to lack both deliberateness of planning and consistency across areas. Texaco seemed preoccupied with litigation to the point of declaring bankruptcy and allowing the courts to make crucial decisions that frequently affected personnel satisfaction, commitment, and role and job ambiguity. Some of those actions promoted positive turnover cultures while others promoted negative turnover

cultures. Litigation-related decisions were made to promote organizational needs irrespective of planning or deliberateness in support of most personnel.

During the 1980s, Apple Computer, with apparently little general planning but high consistency across areas, under the direction of Steve Jobs, and General Motors (GM), with much planning but limited intensity across areas, are organizations exemplifying the other two approaches.

Effective management of turnover cultures can assist organizations in hiring and developing staff they desire. EDS's reputation of a strong management team and staff compared to Texaco's negative reputation attest to the value effective management of turnover cultures can have on organizations.

Turnover Audit

Another approach to manage turnover is to develop a turnover audit. This is a record of staff turnover that can be used to diagnose whether turnover problems exist, and if so, what actions are needed. Turnover audits require a four-step process.

Keep Records

The first step is for the organization to keep records of everyone who leaves. This information is used to better identify the extent to which the six aspects of the turnover decision discussed, at the beginning of this article, can be used to diagnose turnover deficiencies and their causes.

Information on all staff members who leave the organization should be collected. First, the reason for leaving and their performance level should be included. This assists in determining the extent to which the turnover was controllable and whether it was functional for the organization. Second, a record of the job or activity and organization the employees are going to give additional insight on the controllability of the turnover and the specific actions the organization can take to better manage turnover. Third, the level of planning or impulsivity of the turnover decision should be documented. This information can be used to determine the extent supervisors are focusing on turnover-intervention strategies. Fourth, the departing employees' job titles and positions are needed. This allows diagnosing whether a particular role in the organization is disproportionately contributing to turnover. Fifth, the work unit and immediate supervision should be entered. This allows determining whether particular managers need education on better managing staff turnover. Finally, the dates the employees began and left are needed. These give information on tenure lengths. They also are useful in developing more effective recruitment strategies that prepare the organization for expected vacancies.

Determine Whether Turnover Is an Issue Needing Further Attention

Many organizations assume that certain levels of turnover signal the need for additional intervention and costly actions. The second step in the turnover audit is to determine the extent turnover is an issue needing further attention.

It is important to determine the *adjusted* turnover rate before making this determination. First, obtain the actual number of those who have left. Second, subtract the number of people who left for uncontrollable or unavoidable reasons. Third, subtract those people whose leaving was positive or functional for the organization. They may have been poor performers or caused tremendous negative tension in others. Fourth, divide this number by the total number of people. This number is the adjusted turnover rate and a better indication of whether turnover is an issue needing additional attention. Calculating the adjusted turnover rate for different units, supervisors, and the total organization gives additional insight on where action may be needed.

Determine Patterns

This step requires that staff members examine and analyze information obtained in previous steps. Patterns or trends in the data should be noted. Determining adjusted turnover rates for different units, jobs, and supervisors allows the organization to compare organization statistics and diagnose trouble spots. Determining the adjusted turnover rate for the entire organization helps focus the level of concern needed for the entire organization.

Patterns should also be examined to determine whether certain leader styles, personnel function activities, and management decisions are contributing to turnover decisions. The organization can use this information to determine what costs are associated with employee turnover and what actions should be taken, as well as where intervention would most effectively manage turnover.

Take Action

The fourth and last step in the turnover audit is to take action. After diagnosing the situation, it may be decided that no action is needed. The adjusted turnover rate may be much lower than management expected. Employee turnover may therefore no longer be an issue.

Examining patterns and trends gives insight into where action may be needed and appropriate. Organizational actions are usually costly, so accurate diagnosis and appropriate action identification are important.

One supervisor or a small group of supervisors may be responsible for high levels of adjusted turnover. Training how to diagnose individual progression through the turnover process and appropriate intervention strategies may assist in more effective management of turnover. Also, one or several positions may contribute to much of the adjusted turnover. Redesigning these jobs or hiring people who more appropriately match the needs of the position may reduce turnover in these areas. Furthermore, high adjusted organizational-level turnover rates may require examining turnover culture issues and attempting to develop a more consistent and planned approach to managing turnover.

Numerous strategies can be taken to more effectively manage turnover. Only a few are mentioned. Obtaining the appropriate data and analyzing it in a manner that allows for accurate diagnosis followed by planned actions promote more effective management of employee turnover decisions within organizations. The turnover audit is a cost-effective strategy to use to assist organizations in meeting this goal.

Conclusion

Employee turnover is a much-researched area of behavioral science. An overview of what is currently known about the turnover process and the particular individual, organizational, and environmental factors contributing to turnover decisions was presented. Two different approaches to managing turnover decisions were also examined.

Employee turnover is very costly for the organization and for the individual. Identifying and managing turnover cultures allows organizations to better cope with employee turnover decisions. Developing turnover audits determines the extent turnover needs attention and where that attention is needed. Using knowledge of both turnover cultures and turnover audits assists management in more effectively managing one of its scarcest resources: human capital.

References

Abelson, M. A. (1987). Examination of avoidable and unavoidable turnover. *Journal of Applied Psychology, 72,* 382–386.

Abelson, M. A., & Baysinger, B. D. (1984). Optimal and dysfunctional turnover: Toward an organizational level model. *Academy of Management Review, 9,* 331–341.

Abelson, M. A., Ferris, G. R., & Urban, T. F. (1988). Human resource development and employee mobility. In R. S. Schuler, S. A. Youngblood, & V. Huber (Eds.), *Readings in personnel and human resource management.* St. Paul, MN: West.

Armknecht, P. A., & Early, J. F. (1972). Quits in manufacturing: A study of their causes. *Monthly Labor Review, 95,* 32–37.

Bluedorn, A. C. (1982). The theories of turnover. In S. Bacharach (Ed.), *Research in the sociology of organizations* (Vol. 2). Greenwich, CT: JAI, 75–128.

Cotton, J. L., & Tuttle, J. M. (1986). Employee turnover: A meta-analysis and review with implications for research. *Academy of Management Review, 11,* 55–70.

Dalton, D. R., & Todor, W. D. (1979). Turnover turned over: An expanded and positive perspective. *Academy of Management Review, 4,* 225–235.

Dalton, D. R., Krackhardt, D. M., & Porter, L. W. (1981). Functional turnover. An empirical assessment. *Journal of Applied Psychology, 66,* 716–721.

Harrington, K. V., & Abelson, M. A. (1988). *An empirical examination of an organizational level turnover model for hospitals.* Presented at the Academy of Management's 48th Meeting, Anaheim, CA.

Hulin, C. L. (1966). Job satisfaction and turnover in a female clerical population. *Journal of Applied Psychology, 50,* 280–285.

Kerr, J., & Slocum, J. M. (1987). Managing corporate culture through reward systems. *Academy of Management Executive, 1,* 99–108.

Lofquist, L. H., & Dawes, R. V. (1969). *Adjustment to work—A psychological view of man's problems in a work-oriented society.* New York: Appleton-Century.

McEvoy, G. M., & Cascio, W. F. (1985). Strategies for reducing employee turnover: A meta-analysis. *Journal of Applied Psychology, 70,* 342–353.

March, J. G., & Simon, H. A. (1958). *Organizations.* New York: Wiley.

Mobley, W. H. (1977). Intermediate linkages in the relationships between job satisfaction and employee turnover. *Journal of Applied Psychology, 62,* 237–240.

Mobley, W. H. (1982). *Employee turnover: Causes, consequences, and control.* Reading, MA: Addison-Wesley.

Mobley, W. H., Griffith, R. W., Hand, H. H., & Meglino, B. M. (1979). Review and conceptual analysis of the employee turnover process. *Psychological Bulletin, 86,* 493–522.

Price, J. L. (1977). *The study of turnover.* Ames, IA: Iowa State University Press.

Price, J. L., & Mueller, C. W. (1986). *Absenteeism and turnover of hospital employees.* Greenwich, CT: JAI.

Sheridan, J. E., & Abelson, M. A. (1984). Cusp-catastrophe model of employee turnover. *Academy of Management Journal, 26,* 418–436.

Steers, R. M., & Mowday, R. T. (1981). Employee turnover and post-decision accommodation processes. In L. L. Cummings & B. Staw (Eds.), *Research in organizational behavior* (Vol. 4, pp. 127–172). Greenwich, CT: JAI.

Terborg, J. R., & Lee, T. W. (1984). A predictive study of organizational turnover rates. *Academy of Management Journal, 27,* 793–810.

Trice, H. M., & Beyer, J. M. (1984). Studying organizational cultures through rites and ceremonials. *Academy of Management Review, 9,* 653–669.

Wanous, J. P. (1980). *Organizational entry: Recruitment, selection and socialization of newcomers.* Reading, MA: Addison-Wesley.

What to Do about Long-Term Absenteeism

Frank E. Kuzmits

John Bradley, a press operator for a large metropolitan newspaper, was absent from work last Friday. Over the past four months, he has been absent a total of 11 times; each absence was a single-day episode on either a Friday or a Monday.

Mary Green, a claims adjustor for a large insurance company, was absent 83 days last year and 129 days the previous year. Her absenteeism stems from a work-related injury suffered in a fall from a ladder at work. She is scheduled for surgery in three days, and is expected to be recuperating at home for several weeks.

These hypothetical cases demonstrate that most organizations have two kinds of absenteeism problems. One kind is the frequent offender, the employee whose numerous one-day absences often fall on a Friday or Monday. This kind of employee collects a high number of so-called "attitudinal" absences, temporary respites from work which generally reflect a preference to do something other than spend eight hours in the office or plant. The absence is deliberate, planned and surreptitious. The employee may feign illness or claim an emergency in order to avoid disciplinary action for unexcused absenteeism.

The second form of absenteeism—long-term absenteeism—is very different. First, it is not deliberate or planned. Long-term absenteeism results from a work or nonwork injury which generally has nothing to do with the employee's work ethic or personal value system. Second, the chronic single-day offender may hold a different set of values and attitudes about work. The behavioral practices of high-frequency absentees place their work ethic in question—in that they deliberately avoid going to work on a regular basis. Third, the organizational consequences of the two forms of absenteeism are much different. Single-day absences may cause supervisors to shift employees around in order to fill vacant positions, often requiring immediate on-the-job training followed by close supervision to ensure that productivity and quality standards are met. Single-day offenders may also be subjected to frequent counseling and discipline, and therefore further consume supervisors' time.

It is precisely for these reasons that management may not believe that long-term absenteeism is really that much of a problem and that absenteeism control efforts should be directed primarily at the chronic high-frequency absentee. Unfortunately, this belief fails to recognize that long-term absenteeism can be very costly indeed.

The High Cost of Long-Term Absenteeism

What are the costs of long-term absenteeism? Elements of labor overhead which are affected by long-term absenteeism include:

1. *Benefits.* Most organizations continue to provide benefits for employees who are absent on a long-term basis, for a stipulated number of days. It is common for a firm to provide benefits up to 120 or 180 days or more for employees on long-term leave. With the average cost of benefits estimated at $3.65 per hour, an employee who is absent for a 60-day period (480 hours) costs the firm $1,752.00 in bene-

Reprinted with the permission of *HRMagazine,* published by the Society for Human Resource Management, Alexandria, VA.

fits alone.[1] (In addition, the firm also may be required to absorb the cost of replacing the employee's benefits, in effect doubling the cost of benefits for a single position).

2. *Workers' compensation premiums.* Employers who use a private carrier for workers' compensation are likely to face a premium increase as a result of work-related long-term absenteeism. With a private insurer, a firm's premiums are usually determined in part by comparing their three-year loss record to a three-year industry standard. Premiums increase for a firm whose loss experience is above the industry standard.

3. *Lost productivity.* As is the case with short-term absenteeism, the time and effort associated with recruiting, orienting and training replacement employees also exists for the long-term absentee. The productivity of the new or transferred employee will suffer until a standard level of competence is achieved—perhaps days or weeks after assignment.

Long-term absenteeism is expensive and often disrupts the normal functioning of an organization. For these reasons, firms must take long-term absenteeism seriously and create mechanisms to minimize and control the problem.

One Company's Experience

One company which has successfully managed the problem of long-term absenteeism is the H. J. Scheirich Co., a medium-sized cabinet manufacturer located in Louisville, Kentucky. The firm employs approximately 400 skilled and semiskilled employees who are represented by an AFL-CIO union.

Several years ago, the firm's management realized that frequent one-day absences and long-term absenteeism were both having a negative impact on labor costs and worker productivity, due primarily to the factors cited above. To combat these problems, the company formulated absenteeism policies in 1979 to control both incidental and long-term absenteeism. The policies were negotiated be-

tween Scheirich and the union, and were included in the firm's labor agreement. To combat the problem of incidental absenteeism, the firm enacted a no-fault absenteeism policy that places conservative limits on the number of occasions an employee may be absent without disciplinary action being taken.[2]

To control the long-term absenteeism problem, the absenteeism policy included a statement that enabled the firm to take action when excessive long-term absenteeism occurred. The statement read: "Action may be taken when cumulative time lost from work for any reason substantially reduces the employee's services to the company." This statement was included in the absenteeism policy to enable management to take necessary action when an employee's long-term absenteeism becomes detrimental to the operation of the business. As a rule of thumb, Scheirich industrial relations personnel determined that any employee whose absenteeism record was three percentage points above the plant average was excessive, and their absenteeism record would be closely monitored. Because of the need for a flexible policy, management stressed that this was only a guide and not a hard and fast rule.

Although the union asked management for a specific percentage that would result in an automatic discharge for unavailability for work, management had several reasons for believing that this would create undue hardships in administering the policy. First, establishing a set percentage of absenteeism would not permit evaluation on a case-by-case basis. A defined percentage might be disastrous for employees who may have had excellent attendance records but, due to one serious illness, may miss a considerable amount of time over a period of a year or two. Second, should a set percentage of absenteeism subject an employee to discharge, an employee may be tempted to return to work too soon, and perhaps aggravate an injury or illness. Third, a defined percentage may serve as an open invitation to be absent for that amount of time. Nonetheless, several arbitrators have held that the company does not have to establish a set of percentage of absenteeism.

Between 1979 and 1985, the company terminated 11 employees for "unavailability for work." In each case, the employee's absence record was far in excess of Scheirich's rule of thumb, and it was determined that the services of the employee to the company were reduced to the point where termination was the only reasonable option for the company. Of the 11 employees, three employees did not grieve the termination; three employees (with the union) grieved the termination through the third step of the grievance procedure; and five employees grieved the termination through arbitration. Although minor differences among the five arbitrated cases existed, the positions of the company, the union and the arbitrators were very similar. Their positions are summarized below.

The Company's Position

The text of the arbitration records shows that the company offered the following evidence to support the discharges.[3]

1. "The company's absenteeism policy has two parts. The more frequently utilized provision is aimed at discouraging frequent absenteeism. It deals with employees who are chronically absent. However, arbitrators unanimously recognize an employer's right to release employees who, in the judgment of the employer are unavailable for work to such an extent and over such a time that their value as an employee ceases to justify retaining them. This view is consistently applied even when the excessive absenteeism is for legitimate reasons. This is particularly valid when there is no evidence that the employee's attendance can ever become acceptable. The last paragraph of the company's attendance control rules explicitly states the company's intent to utilize this doctrine when the need arises.

2. "The basis for the employee's termination was 'unavailability for work.' The terminations were not processed under the progressive disciplinary procedure for excessive short-term absenteeism. The company did not question the legitimacy of the absences. The employees were discharged because the company believed that their unavailability for work was such that their value to the company was reduced to the point where their continued employment could not be justified.

3. "The employee's absence over a period of five years averaged well over twice the plant average (the plant average was five to seven percent a year with little fluctuation from year to year). Unavailability for work becomes a factor only after it extends over a two to three year period.

4. "In each case, the company determined that it was unreasonable to expect the physical condition of the employees to improve. Therefore, the company also believed it to be unreasonable to expect their attendance to improve."

The Union's Position

In each arbitration hearing, the union argued that the employee was improperly discharged. The union's reasons for requesting that the discharges be overturned included:

1. "The grievant was improperly terminated without contractual just cause. Just cause does not exist when an employee's absences are a result of genuine occupational injury. The grievant's disabilities were not incurred in an intentional manner, and without proof of intentional or reckless misconduct on the part of the grievant, no discipline whatsoever could appropriately be imposed.

2. "The company has promised that it would not take disciplinary action against any worker who is absent because of hospital confinement and work-incurred injury. The labor agreement specifically states that these forms of absenteeism will not be recorded as occurrences of absence for purposes of disciplinary action; therefore, the company has imposed discipline for excused absences.

3. "Other employees have accumulated worse records than the discharged employees and have not been discharged.

4. "The company has not established a fixed percentage of attendance which must be

maintained by employees even though the union has asked for this."

The Arbitrators' Positions

As in the case of both management and labor, the position and opinions of the arbitrators in all five cases were very similar. The following opinions are included in the discussions of the arbitrators:

1. "The employer has the right to determine that it is going to operate its business with full-time employees and if an employee is hired to be a full-time employee he or she has no right to expect an arbitrator to grant part-time status. If the employee cannot remain a full-time employee, then it is not unreasonable that the employment relationship cease.

2. "It would be unreasonable to expect the company to set a percentage cut-off point as the benchmark for determining whether an employee has become a part-time employee. The case-by-case method currently used by the company is a reasonable method for making a difficult determination required in cases of this sort.

3. "The company has a legitimate need to maintain its right to terminate employees for nondisciplinary reasons because it has a substantial interest in maintaining a reliable and efficient workforce. Chronic absenteeism is an obstacle to an efficient operation.

4. "It is well established that a company may terminate an employee who is excessively absent for legitimate reasons without any indication that the condition giving rise to the absence will improve. Where an employee cannot produce some evidence that he will eventually be able to return to full-time work or where the evidence indicates no realistic hope that the employee will be able to resume his job on a regular basis, the arbitrator has held that management is entitled to release the individual and reassign the work.

5. "If an employee is off for medical reasons often and for lengthy periods of time, the individual in reality becomes a part-time employee. No company can compete when it cannot count on the regular and continued attendance of its employees . . . when over a period of several years the employee is out for lengths of time for one or more medical reasons, the company cannot nor should be required to continue such an individual as an employee."

Interestingly, two arbitrators quoted Frank and Edna Elkouri's widely read *How Arbitration Works* (Washington, D.C.: Bureau of National Affairs, 1981) in regard to the issue of long-term absence as a legitimate reason for discharge. The following quote is included in the discussion of two arbitration proceedings: "The right to terminate employees for excessive absences even when they are due to illness is generally recognized by arbitrators."[4]

Arbitrators' Awards

The arbitrators supported the company's position and upheld the discharges in four of five cases. In one case, the award was given to the employee only because management failed to notify her before discharge. The arbitrator stated, "If there had been sufficient warnings to the grievant, I would have had no hesitancy in sustaining the termination but under the circumstances it is my intention to return the grievant to work."[5] The employee declined to return to work.

Caveats for Management

A review of the arbitration cases discussed above underscores the fact that something can be done to control long-term absenteeism. However, management must be prepared to carefully plan and enact a strategy to ensure that long-term absenteeism is kept at minimum levels. Elements of a plan to control long-term absenteeism should include:

1. *Dual-purpose absenteeism policies.* One of the primary elements in the strategy to control long-term absenteeism is an absenteeism control policy that focuses on both short-term and long-term absenteeism. Each form of absenteeism represents a unique form of employee behavior and therefore must be addressed with individual and specific policy statements.

2. *Guidelines for "excessive" absenteeism.* A second issue deals with the problems of determining when long-term absenteeism becomes "excessive." Although the definition of "excessive" is management's responsibility, it must be perceived as fair by employees, unions and—should a grievance reach arbitration in the union firm—arbitrators. If the policy is not fairly written and enforced, employees will reject and grieve the policy and arbitrators may invalidate it. It is important to develop a rule of thumb for defining excessive absenteeism such as the guidelines of the firm discussed in this study; it's also important to recognize that the guidelines must be flexible to enable management to consider each case on its individual merits.[6]

3. *Likelihood of improvement.* Evidence must strongly suggest that the employee's long-term absenteeism is not likely to abate. In particular, arbitrators will seek medical evidence from health care professionals that pertains to the employee's ability to return to full-time work. If the employee cannot produce evidence of an ability to resume the job on a full-time basis, an arbitrator is likely to support management's right to release the employee and reassign the work.

4. *Documentation.* Employees whose absenteeism labels them as potential candidates for dismissal should be notified in writing that their behavior is being monitored and that their attendance must improve to avoid further action. (The importance of this procedure is underscored by one arbitrator's decision to give the award to the employee solely because of management's failure to properly warn the employee.)

5. *Communication.* It is important that management's attitudes, policies, practices and procedures concerning long-term absenteeism be communicated and explained to employees. Although the events which lead to long-term absenteeism—accidents, injuries and serious illnesses—are not the deliberate choice of the employee, knowing that management takes the issue of long-term absenteeism seriously may motivate employees to return to work as soon as possible.

Preventive Measures

The focus of the discussion so far has been directed towards solving a problem once it has occurred. In closing, it seems appropriate to note that organizations should also take specific measure to *prevent* long-term absenteeism from taking place. Some important measures include:

1. *Thorough physical examinations.* Medical examinations by health care professionals will uncover many existing health problems, such as back and other musculoskeletal problems. Some firms require applicants applying for heavy-labor jobs to undergo two independent examinations.

2. *Pre-employment checks.* The investigation of applicants' work histories should include inquiries into their accident and injury records in addition to their absenteeism behavior.[7]

3. *Safety program.* Although job-related illness accounts for only a portion of long-term absenteeism, a successful safety program in industrial settings will no doubt keep on-the-job accidents and injuries—and thus long-term absenteeism—at a minimum.

Reducing and controlling long-term absenteeism is a formidable challenge to human resource managers. It may require new systems and procedures to define, monitor and control absenteeism; and in the unionized firm, certain policy and procedural decisions will likely be subject to negotiation. However, the investment in time and effort in developing a strategy to control long-term absenteeism will help maintain a productive labor force and minimize labor overhead.

References

1. J. R. Morris, "Benefits Growth: Back to the Days of Yore," *Nation's Business,* February 1985, p. 22.
2. See F. E. Kuzmits, "Is Your Organization Ready for No-Fault Absenteeism?" *Personnel Administrator,* December 1984, pp. 119–127.

3. The quotes reflecting the opinions of the company, union, and arbitrators are taken from the following arbitration proceedings: H. J. Scheirich Co. (S. E. Alexander, November 9, 1981); H. J. Scheirich Co. (W. G. Seinsheimer, November 17, 1981); H. J. Scheirich Co. (E. R. Render, July 9, 1982); H. J. Scheirich Co. (E. R. Render, November 6, 1984); H. J. Scheirich Co. (W. G. Seinsheimer, November 20, 1985). Information concerning the arbitration proceedings may be obtained from the author, School of Business, University of Louisville, Louisville, KY 40292.

4. F. Elkouri and E. Elkouri, *How Arbitration Works,* Washington, DC: Bureau of National Affairs, 1981, p. 545. Arbitrators are in general agreement that management may discharge employees for excessive absenteeism even where the absences are caused by legitimate illness. See *Kimberly-Clark Corp.,* 62 LA 1119 (1974); *Pennsylvania Tire and Rubber Company,* 59 LA 1078 (1972); *Westinghouse Air Brake Company,* 53 LA 762 (1969); *Husky Oil Co.,* 65 LA 47 (1975); *General Electric Company,* 39 LA 979 (1962); *Celanese Corporation,* 9 LA 143 (1947); *Coca-Cola Bottling Co.,* 65 LA 357 (1975); and *Hawaii Transfer Company,* LTD, 74 LA 531 (1980).

5. H. J. Scheirich Co. (W. G. Seinsheimer, November 17, 1981, p. 13).

6. One arbitration case not included in this article dealt with chronic absenteeism that was not related to long-term disability, but to a high degree of occasional absences which put the employee's absence percentage over twice the plant average (H. J. Scheirich Co., D. L. Beckman, September 24, 1984). The employee was terminated for unavailability for work and, with the union, grieved the termination to arbitration. The arbitrator gave the award to the company, primarily because the employee's absence exceeded the long-term absence guidelines created by the company. Thus, this case points out that guidelines for excessive absenteeism pertain not only to sickness and disability but a large accumulation of occasional absenteeism as well.

7. Pre-employment checks which include medical history inquiries or physical examinations should be based on an applicant's current ability to do the job for which he or she is applying. Check your state employment statutes if you have any question regarding your legal rights and responsibilities regarding your screening procedures.

Employing at Will

M. Ronald Buckley and William Weitzel

Employment, one of the most cherished and instrumental activities in American society, remains at the discretion of the employer even though Title VII of the Civil Rights Act of 1964 and the Age Discrimination Act of 1967 have constrained the conditions under which employment can occur or be terminated. Employment is considered a contract between the employer and employee. Both parties are considered free to enter and to break the relationship at will if there is no end to the relationship specified in the employment contract.[1]

Today there seems to be much confusion concerning the rights and duties of the employer and the employee with respect to the employment relationship.

Individual Job Rights vs. Employer's Prerogatives

Approximately 70 percent of the United States labor force is employed without the benefit of a stated contract. These employees can be released from employment with little or no notice. Recent developments within the court system indicate some change from a "hands off" employment posture to one which restricts an employer in the employment relationship.[2]

Employees protected from at-will managerial prerogatives include union members covered by collective bargaining agreements, civil service employees and those covered by expressed and implied employment contracts. Further, all employees are protected from arbitrary discharge by constitutional provisions of due process. Therefore, the issue of employment-at-will is essentially one of an individual's job rights contrasted

with an employer's right to employ whomever he or she wishes.

In the past, English Common Law allowed employers to exercise almost total control of the employment relationship, enabling them to make decisions concerning the management of their personnel at will. Growing out of the precedent of master-servant, the master had the right to discharge the servant for good, bad or no reason.[3] The ideas about freedom of contract developed during the industrial revolution in the late 1880s and gave rise to what is now known as employment-at-will. Employment-at-will gave employees the right to quit whenever they chose and allowed employers to employ or discharge in a similar fashion. Until this period, the length of employment contracts were believed to be for a single year.

Limitation by Statute and Employer Actions

In the 1900s, a number of restraints were placed upon employers regarding their right to discharge employees. The National Labor Relations Act of 1935 provided employees with the right to form labor unions and to engage in collective bargaining without fear of being discharged for these actions. Through collective bargaining, terms of employment and procedures for arbitration of grievances further limited the employer in the employment relationship.

Title VII of the 1964 Civil Rights Act and the Age Discrimination Act of 1967 added additional considerations to the employment relationship. Employers' discharge decisions had to be "blind" with respect to employees of protected subgroups. Through these acts, it became illegal to discharge employees merely because they were females, part of racial minorities, religious groups, national origin minorities and those within the ages of 40 and 70 years.[4]

To comply with these laws, employers created internal documents, manuals, policy statements and practices for assuring that internal decisions were "blind" to these protected groups. By putting into writing the terms and conditions under which personnel actions including termination can occur, employers have produced statements about employment which the courts can and have interpreted as contracts for all employees.

Conversations between employer's representatives and employees about employment conditions constitute an oral agreement or contract. If an oral agreement can be proven, it defines the conditions under which an employee can continue employment.

The employer has a right to do whatever must be done to assure that the enterprise is successful. Herein lies the basis for disagreement. If the employee questions whether his or her discharge was necessary in order to assure the successful continuation of the enterprise, it will be left for the court to make the final decision.

Limitation by Precedent and Legal Rulings

In a landmark case, *Peterman v. International Brotherhood of Teamsters Inc.,* 344 p. 2d 25 (1959), Peterman refused to commit perjury under oath in support of the teamsters and was fired by them. The court held in favor of Peterman, who sued to return to his job. An employer cannot fire an employee for failing to support the employer in immoral actions, because such action would run counter to the "intentions of public policy."

Other actions by the courts at the state and federal level have left many managers wary of what actions they can safely engage in. Some feel that their prerogatives have been severely limited, with the power shifting toward protection of employees and away from a concern with organizational well-being.

David Ewing has argued that the basis of all managerial authority is the right to hire and fire.[5] To some extent, the courts seem to agree with this notion. Discharge which is based upon economic necessity has not been overturned by the courts.[6] As long as it can be demonstrated that employment-related decisions are not unfairly discriminatory, the courts reject the idea that employers have to show cause for terminations.

State and federal court rulings vary in judicial philosophy. Alabama, Georgia, Illinois, Indiana, Texas and Wisconsin appear to hold to the common law view that a manager's right to discharge an employee is virtually beyond questioning.[8] Other states have taken on a case-by-case approach, assessing the relative merits of the arguments made by each party.

The federal courts seem to follow the situational approach, weighing the value of managerial prerogatives in comparison to the value of employment security. Federal courts have tended to lean toward employees' rights unless the termination is based upon managerial decisions which are aimed at ensuring the financial well-being of the organization.

Employment-at-will cases will be heard in state courts unless the company is engaged in interstate commerce or the issues in dispute involve federal law. If one of these criteria is met, then the case may be heard in either state or federal court. The following are a number of synthesized principles based upon the legislative decisions concerning employment-at-will:

Principle 1: Economic Reasons. Employers' rights to dismiss employees for economic reasons have been consistently upheld. In *Clutterman v. Coachman Industrial Inc.,* the court upheld Coachman's right to release Clutterman for economic reasons, stating, "Courts must take care not to interfere with a legitimate exercise of managerial discretion."

A district court granted a summary judgment in *Sorosky v. Burroughs Corp.* against the employee who claimed that the firm which released him as part of a decision to streamline operations had violated an implied contract. The court said it would not interfere in the "legitimate, non-pretextual exercise of managerial discretion."[9]

Principle 2: Good Cause. Employers may release employees for "good cause." The court definition of good cause [from *Crosier v. United Parcel Service Inc.,* 150 Cal. App, 3d 1132 (1983)] says ". . . the court must balance the employer's interest in operating his business efficiently and profitably with the interest of the employee in maintaining his employment and the interest of the public in maintaining the balance between the two." Virtually all courts have supported employers' rights to terminate an employee who is demonstrably unacceptable (incompetent, lazy, uncooperative, or abusive to other employees).

Principle 3: Limitations on Managerial Prerogatives. The specific limitations set by the courts to managerial prerogatives to hire and fire at will fall into three categories:

Provisions of federal or state law. Although there are discrepancies between the interpretations made by federal and state courts, the states seem to adopt what the federal courts have decided. The courts seem to be willing to allow an organization to set any truly business-related goal and to follow it in all of their practices, including the ways in which they handle personnel issues. The courts then weigh employer rights in contrast with employee civil rights as discussed before (e.g., race, religion, sex, etc.).

Before the courts will hear any complaint, employees must establish a *prima facie* case. This case must state that the employee is a member of a protected class, a victim of an unfair employment practice, qualified to be placed in another position at the time of discharge or demotion, and prove the employer did not act neutrally in regard to race or sex or any of the other protected classes.

The clear intentions of public policy. The primary issues of public policy protect employees from arbitrary dismissal for:

- filing a legitimate workman's compensation claim[10]
- exercising a legal duty such as jury duty[11]
- refusing to violate the law[12]
- having the right to certain benefits such as a pension[13]
- refusing to take a polygraph test
- reporting illegal conduct by the employer
- refusing to violate a professional code of ethics
- refusing to lobby for a law or political candidate favored by the employer.[14]

Implied contracts and covenants of good faith and fair dealing. The limitations of managerial prerogatives in relation to good faith and fair dealing means that each party agrees to deal with the other in good faith. This is similar to the Uniform Commercial Code which states, "Every contract or duty within this Act imposes an obligation of good faith in its performance or enforcement."[15]

Two somewhat different illustrations of this point follow. In *Pugh v. See's Candies Inc.* [171 Cal. Rptr. 917 (1981)], the court determined that an implied contract existed between the employer and Pugh. Pugh had a long-term employment history with See's Candies, which included raises and promotions. The court ruled that the implied contract from these prior actions removed the employer's ordinary discretion to terminate the employee at will.

A New Hampshire court upheld a decision that a female employee had been dismissed in bad faith following her refusal to date and "be nice" to her foreman. The court held that ". . . a termination by the employer of a contract of employment-at-will that is motivated by bad faith or malice or based on retaliation is not in the best interest of the economic system or the public good, and constitutes a breach of the employment contract."[16]

Oral promises have been interpreted as implied contracts by some state courts. For example, during a pre-employment interview with McGraw-Hill, an employee was told that

McGraw-Hill would not terminate an employee without "just cause." When the employee was summarily terminated eight years later, the court held that McGraw-Hill had broken its contract with the employee.[17]

Discharging Risks

Employers have not been successful in firing employees for refusing to submit to polygraph tests because this is deemed an unnecessary invasion of employees' privacy rights. There is further risk to an employer whose representatives may say something which can be considered libelous or slanderous during the discharge process. Employers have lost lawsuits for inflicting emotional distress on an employee at the time of termination of employment. Actions by employers that have been determined to be grounds for punitive damages include:

- negligence
- intentional infliction of emotional distress

Suggested Guidelines for Employers

To avoid a lawsuit when handling employee discharge, managers must consider these issues:

1. The courts are quite clear on the issue of implied and expressed contracts.

2. Employers should carefully make promises to their employees. Supervisors should know the legal implications of verbal promises which are made. Personnel management should review written work policies and employee handbooks for any implied contracts. When implied contracts are found, management practice needs to be consistent. Policy writers in organizations must ensure that future personnel policy statements do not create unintentional agreements which will be enforced by courts.

3. Job applications should clearly state that employment is at will. Similarly, employee handbooks and information should be revised to remove any implications that employment is other than at will.

4. New employees should be given realistic job previews which include realistic, achievable opportunities for them to reach higher levels of employment. Recruits should be shown both the positive and negative sides of organizational membership. Employees should be given detailed job descriptions which include both personal, professional and developmental objectives.

5. Performance appraisals must be conducted honestly and accurately to truly reflect negative as well as positive aspects of an employee's performance. If any employee is summarily discharged but has only received positive evaluations, this can be effectively used to blunt the personnel decision. Dissatisfaction/satisfaction with an employee's performance should be recorded and communicated with the employee.

6. A procedure should be established for both the airing and resolution of complaints and grievances. If an employee's grievance is denied by a fair hearing panel, this is admissible evidence in court and will potentially tip the scales in the employer's favor.

7. It makes good sense to handle the termination process humanely. An employee who feels abused or unfairly treated is more likely to bring a wrongful dismissal suit against his or her former company. In order to engender more positive feeling, organizations should choose to provide outplacement services and/or counseling, if possible, for terminated employees. Additionally, exit interviews provide the employee with a chance to express feelings about the work environment and his or her termination. The information gathered in an exit interview may be helpful from a human resources standpoint. It may also be of use in litigation concerning employee termination.

- impairment of economic opportunity or growth (such as firing to avoid payment of pensions)
- discharge to avoid paying bonuses on sales
- making incorrect statements upon firing (slander)
- hiring a person to do a job but making it impossible for the person to do that job.[18]

The most legally defensible reasons for releasing an employee from service are economic necessity on the organization's part, or failure to adequately perform required work on the individual's part. The right to fire should never be used arbitrarily, as a retaliatory measure or as an expression of prejudice. There is surely a need for a clear code of ethics to prevent employees from being placed into positions which compromise public policy. Cases involving issues such as law violations, price fixing, perjury, jury duty, workmen's compensation claims and product safety are symptoms of the larger problem which is the lack of business ethics in an organization.[19]

Notes

1. Daniel J. Koys, Steven Briggs and Jay Grenig, "State Court Disparity on Employment at Will," *Personnel Psychology,* 40 (1987), 565.

2. Stephen A. Ploscowe and Marvin M. Goldstein, "Trouble on the Firing Line," *Nation's Business,* (March 1987), 36.

3. "The Erosion of Employment at Will," *Personnel,* (July–August 1981), 46.

4. James A. Bryant and Michael C. Giallourakis, "Employment at Will: Where Is it Going and What Can Be Done?" *S.A.M. Advanced Management Journal,* (Summer 1986), 13–14.

5. David W. Ewing, "Your Right to Fire," *Harvard Business Review,* (March–April 1983), 32.

6. Stephen R. Carley, "At-Will Employees Still Vulnerable," *ABA Journal,* (October 1, 1987), 66.

7. *Ibid.*

8. Ewing, *loc. cit.,* 33.

9. Carley, *op. cit.,* 68.

10. In *Reuther v. Fowler & William Inc.,* where the court decided in favor of an employee who was released from his job for filing against his employer for workmen's compensation.

11. In *Ness v. Hocks,* 536 p. 2d 512 (1975), the court ruled in favor of an employee who was terminated for serving on a jury against her employer's will.

12. The court decided in favor of an employee who was fired for refusing to participate in a price-fixing scheme in *Tameny v. Atlantic Richfield Co.,* 610 2d 1330 (1980).

13. A company lost a court battle when it fired an employee in order to avoid paying him a pension, i.e., *Savodnik v. Korvette Inc.,* 488 E. Supp. 822 (1980).

14. William H. Holley and Roger S. Wolters, "Labor Relations—An Employment-At-Will Vulnerability Audit," *Personnel Journal,* April, 1987, 132.

15. Bryant, *loc. cit.,* 16.

16. *Monge v. Beebe Rubber Co.* as cited in Bryant, *loc. cit.,* 17.

17. Bryant, *op. cit.,* 18.

18. Koys, *loc. cit.,* 572.

19. William N. Bockanic and J. Benjamin Forbes, "The Erosion of Employment at Will: Managerial Implications," *S.A.M. Advanced Management Journal,* (Summer 1986), 19.

Outplacement: Meeting Needs, Matching Services

Donald R. Simon

Henry Ford once said of the Model T, "You can have any color you want, just as long as it is black." For years, consultants spoke of a variety of outplacement programs, but they delivered only two models: a Cadillac and a stripped-down compact. More recently, competition has brought out the complete line, and there's now an outplacement model to fit every need and budget.

The Cadillac is the full-service, individualized outplacement program priced at $5,000 to $15,000 per person. This model began as an executive service where price was not the main concern. The lower-priced models are group programs that run from $50 to $500 per person. The wide gap between service levels originally developed because of different market forces. Corporations felt that high-end service wasn't necessary for everyone. They seldom had a group laid off at the same time and place, so for mid-level employees they usually did nothing at all. And once people were terminated, they were "out of sight, out of mind." But when outplacement entered the era of downsizing and large-scale layoffs from the assembly line to the vice-presidential suite, a good price *and* good service became critical.

Some outplacement consultants still resist offering high-quality yet moderately priced programs because they erode profits on the more expensive models. Yet a July 1987 survey by the American Management Association showed that 48 percent of major U.S. corporations provide some outplacement services as a standard company benefit. "Doing our best for displaced people" rated first among the reasons for providing outplacement, followed by improved image in the community, increased productivity among remaining workers, fewer lawsuits, and less unemployment compensation liability and benefit extensions.

Each of the following players has a role in outplacement services:

- Consultants, who must be willing to deliver service based on need, not on how much they can get the client to pay.
- Corporate executives, who should plan ahead for terminations and layoff, allowing ample time and money to take care of their people.
- Human resource people, who must select and monitor transition programs with care and be able to demonstrate to top management why outplacement assistance is good business.
- All employees affected by the layoff—those who are let go *and* those who remain. Guaranteed lifetime employment is a myth, and everyone should take advantage of any services offered.

The Case for Outplacement Programs

The continually changing U.S. economy *requires* effective outplacement programs. Former "smokestack industry" employees such as steel mill and mine workers are seeking jobs in the service sector. Unemployed people in all industries are turning to self-employment or are going back to school instead of relocating. *Monthly Labor Review* reports that only 6 to 20 percent of employees affected by a plant closing are willing to relocate. And, although career workshops have been available for years, outplacement firms need to offer more than that. Effective outplacement training must address the need for services and information such as

- financial and career counseling;
- connections with established training programs and resources in the community;
- workshops and seminars to teach business start-up skills.

In the latter case, professionals and executives who have successfully started small businesses could be tapped for advice and follow-up services.

Studies showing correlations between layoffs and child abuse, alcoholism, and other ills have prompted civic intervention with some outplacement services. A handful of states and cities continue to lobby—although with little success under the Reagan administration—for plant-closing legislation that will guarantee employees and job employment agencies the right to be told of a layoff 30 to 90 days in advance. Lobbyists contend that people deserve greater employment protection against employers who hire and fire "at will" and that before anyone can apply for state unemployment benefits they must receive basic skills training. Similar movements at the federal level reflect a growing concern that laid-off people have access to substantial resources during the transition period.

A number of corporations report success with contemporary approaches to outplacement. Volkswagen of America worked collectively with the state of Illinois and its labor union to run two-week workshops for soon-to-be-laid-off employees. Groups of 25 to 50 alternately worked half days and attended workshops the other half. At a plant in California, Ford Motor Company opted against having one major, disruptive layoff and, instead, gradually phased out employees by reducing a three-shift workday to two shifts. The company invested in job-search training packages and hired its labor union to deliver the training—an innovative and increasingly popular delivery method.

In Maryland, General Electric designed a comprehensive resource center to benefit displaced workers at one of its facilities. The frequently updated resource center stocks employer lists, secretarial support, telephones, job-placement directories, and more. And in Colombia, South America, Exxon Corp. used training videos and workbooks to help put laid-off expatriates back on their feet. Workers and their spouses received job-skills training before returning to the United States plus ongoing counseling once they got back. Corporate programs such as these make layoffs much less painful.

Outplacement Strategies

The original outplacement efforts were theoretical and packaged. Management's frequent reply to calls for outplacement assistance was "Give 'em a book." But consider this: Would you learn to play golf by reading a book? By hearing someone tell you about it? Or even by practicing your swing in a classroom and receiving feedback just once?

No—you need hands-on practice plus ongoing feedback and support. Similarly, outplaced employees who just learned they're out of a job also need feedback and support as well as counseling and new learning opportunities. Some may experience learning difficulties that stem from feelings of stress, fear, and rejection, and consultants should be sensitive to these difficulties.

As HRD practitioners face a broader variety of transition services as well as a broader range of people, some crucial management decisions are at stake. Practitioners are responsible for recommending *what* transition services to offer, depending on the needs of the people affected and the willingness of the organization to foot the bill, and *who* will deliver the services. Whether internal or external, public or private, this decision also depends on the organization's needs and budget and on the availability of experienced people to deliver the services.

When evaluating the appropriate level of job assistance to give terminated employees, consider the following points:

- The higher the level of the employee, the more time it will take that person to find a position and the more sophisticated will be the techniques he or she must use. Also, middle-level managers and executives *expect* a good outplacement package and are likely to create problems if not offered a full-service program.

- Employees with many years of service have a tougher time. Older people who haven't been in the job market for a while may experience more stress, lack current skills, and face interview bias when competing with younger applicants.

- The tighter the job market, the longer the job search will take. As some industries grow, others decline. Some job functions, such as computer positions, are transferable, but many technical jobs are not. Factors such as relocation or a possible salary cut also influence the level of outplacement support needed.

- When deciding on the level of service to offer, management should consider the emotional needs of individuals. One way to handle special needs is to offer a supplement to a standard package for hardship cases.

To establish a standard policy, many corporations simply consider the average needs of most people. Companies that work out a formula in advance sometimes can avoid negotiating a package for each individual. Most major corporations provide a full package of outplacement services for executives—generally people who earn $50,000 or more per year—and a group program for hourly workers. Figure 1 summarizes a full-service, a middle-level, and a group program—everything from the Cadillac outplacement program to the stripped-down compact model.

Full service means highly personalized and complete outplacement services for a year or as long as is necessary. The middle-level program includes individual counseling and some follow-up to get people back on solid ground. The group format gives an overview of the job market, helps people develop a solid resumé, and sends them on their way with "call if you have questions."

The Impact on Image and Productivity

Corporations spend considerable time and money trying to convey a positive human resource philosophy to employees and the community. These messages are often taken for granted or are viewed with suspicion. Yet employees do notice how people are treated—in good times and bad.

While the purpose of a layoff is usually to save money by reducing staff, low morale and fear among those who remain can have a far more devastating effect on the productivity of the company. Usually management hopes that people will drag themselves back to work and that the discontent will blow over. A better strategy is to have a transition program in place and to use layoffs and terminations as prime opportunities for the public to see how effective an organization is at retaining productivity and at treating everyone humanely.

Helping former employees has a direct impact on the productivity of remaining workers in several ways. First, former employees will pass on the word to remaining employees, many of whom will identify closely with laid-off employees and feel that but for fate, they too would be without a job. For them the stress of a layoff or a reorganization may be just as great as it is for those who leave.

Helping former employees also provides a groundwork for positive leadership of those

Figure 1
Summary of Outplacement Levels

	Full-Service	Middle-Level	Group Program
Immediate Counseling	Yes	Seldom	No
Spouse and Family Support	Individual and private	Some, as a group	Seldom
Assessment	Full package of career and psychological tests with in-depth feedback	Career tests with some feedback	Limited and self directed
Career Planning	Personalized and based on assessment	Small, group sessions with some counseling	Briefly mentioned in the workshop
Resumé and Letters	Custom resumés written and cover letters produced	Resumés typed and copies made	Training and critiquing provided
Job-Hunting Tips and Techniques	Individual strategies developed	Training with some follow-up	Concepts presented in the workshop
Contact Lists	Custom-researched lists with contacts identified	Computerized list provided	Access to reference materials
Office	Private office through transition period	Office for 30 days	May have access to a resource center
Support Services	Typing, copying, postage, answering service	Limited after first month	None or very limited
Ongoing Counseling	One-on-one (initiated by consultant)	Several sessions by appointment	None or very limited
Usually Provided for	Middle managers to senior executives	Low-level exempts to middle managers	Nonexempts to low-level exempts
Typical Cost per Person	12 to 15% of salary, plus expenses	$2,000 to $5,000, plus expenses	$100 to $1,000, plus expenses

who remain. Executives need to look these people in the eye and ask them to keep up the good work. Executives who feel apologetic about the treatment of former employees often avoid such a direct challenge.

The need for transition services extends to current as well as former employees. Spouse relocation assistance, preretirement planning, and internal job transfers are among the services that a proactive human resource department can offer.

Planning for a Smooth Transition

A transition program alone cannot guarantee smooth sailing when people learn they are losing their jobs, but advance planning can help. Allow time to compute severance pay and handle benefits paperwork for terminated employees. Train managers on how to conduct a termination meeting and how to deal with employees' stress. Counsel executives on how to deal with the people who don't leave.

Lawsuits, negative public exposure, personal tragedies, and lost productivity can be avoided or reduced with good planning. Even full outplacement services are less costly than lawyers and lost time. Planning ahead also minimizes the negative impact on remaining workers, directly benefiting the corporation. Executives generally support outplacement because it demonstrates positive corporate citizenship.

Other important planning hints include:

- Convince top management of the benefits of sufficient planning time.

- Engage outside consultants in advance. They may be helpful during the planning stage.

- Provide advance notice to employees of an upcoming layoff.

- Publish a detailed explanation of the layoff. In a properly prepared layoff, employees learn of the reasons for the upcoming layoff or plant closing, who will be affected, and how much time they'll have to get started on new job campaigns.

- Offer training sessions on interviewing, resumé writing, and other techniques to prepare people for job hunting. Preparation increases a sense of control and confidence and almost always results in a reciprocal commitment to be productive: "The company is treating me fairly and I will be fair with it."

- Evaluate internal programs. Making the transition program available isn't enough. A solid program effectively presented by staff with the time to provide counseling is essential. To get a rough idea of how much service can be delivered, divide the number of participants by the number of human resource hours available.

Cost-Effective Programs

While the need for outplacement services is clear, the willingness of organizations to pay for them sometimes is not. Management may argue, "We can't afford outplacement. We need to conserve money—that's why we're having the layoff." When the bottom line is at stake, management wants a good business reason to invest in former employees.

Yet the cost of helping people in transition is usually small compared to the total cost of a layoff. Add up the costs for extension of benefits, severance pay, lease cancellations, relocations, business interruption, capital cost write-offs, and refitting the remaining people to reorganized jobs. In such a perspective, outplacement costs are relatively minimal.

The key to improving transition programs is to deliver top-notch services at a reasonable cost. This means considering new delivery methods such as video-based training. Well-designed training also can lessen the need for expensive personal counseling.

Companies should make certain that the outplacement service they purchase matches the fee they are charged. A customer paying for a full program deserves to get one.

Choosing a Consultant and a Program

When hiring a consultant, ask for references. Find out past results and track records. An advance meeting of those who will be assigned to the project is a good idea. Good and bad consultants can charge equally, so pick a good one. Make a tentative decision based on quality and a general review of prices, then negotiate a specific contract that meets your needs. This approach avoids the problem of comparing the apples and oranges of competing proposals and lets you start cooperating early on with the selected firm.

To get a feel for the depth of an internal or external outplacement program and the competency of its provider, ask the questions listed in Figure 2. Thoughtful answers to these questions and evidence of well-constructed materials indicate a high-quality program.

Once a program is underway, get direct feedback from the participants. Check back after the first few days. You can expect to hear

Figure 2

Questions to Ask Potential Outplacement Providers

1. What management training do you provide to reduce the possibility of a lawsuit?
2. How do you handle the first "ventilation" meeting with the individual?
3. What assessment instruments do you use, and how do you gather feedback?
4. What materials and program outlines are available for the person who wants to seek self-employment?
5. How do you train people to use the telephone?
6. What booster workshops do you offer?
7. How does the program involve the spouse and family?
8. What materials explaining the available services do individuals receive?
9. Are videos available for follow-up or specialized training?
10. What reference materials and contact lists do people receive?
11. Are full-time consultants or contractors used?
12. What kind of reports do you send to the company?
13. How do you rebuild company morale following a layoff?

good reports the first couple of weeks when the activity and structure is high. Touch base three weeks after the start of the program and monthly thereafter.

A few outplacement participants may want more service than is provided. They'll project their difficulties onto the company or pro-gram regardless of how good it is. A poor or limited program has the following telltale signs:

- poorly attended workshops;
- unused or underused resource facilities and supplemental services;
- complaints consistently raising the same issues;
- no results—that is, job seekers don't find jobs.

Some companies avoid evaluating and selecting an outplacement firm themselves and instead let employees choose from several firms. Studies show—and common sense dictates—that people under stress often cannot investigate objectively and may lack perspective on the true difficulty of the transition process. Unemployed people may be vulnerable to persuasive firms and may not necessarily make the best decision. For the same reason, it's not wise to give people a choice between cash and outplacement.

The benefits of providing assistance at a sociological level are compelling. Helping former employees get a job is similar to the Chinese proverb, "Give a man a fish and you feed him for a day; teach a man to fish and you feed him for a lifetime."

CHAPTER 16

Performance and Effectiveness

Productivity in work organizations has become a prominent concern in this country. A growing of number of organizations have become interested in determining what conditions in the work environment might contribute to their overall effectiveness. The key phrase in the discussion is "developing and maintaining competitiveness." Companies need to define and develop those factors that contribute to strategic competitiveness. We compete in a world economy; thus, we need to be aware of cutting-edge ideas for achieving and maintaining competitiveness.

Commensurate with the growing desire to enhance performance is the need to improve fiscal soundness through effective human resources programs. In these days of diminishing budgets, the functional areas of organizations, one of which is human resources management, are often required to justify their existence. This justification is frequently related to overall contribution to the bottom line. The administration of human resources certainly has an impact on organizational competitiveness and on the bottom line. With the increase in influence of the human resources department comes more responsibility for the overall effectiveness of the organization. We believe that human resources programs are up to the challenge. They can and do make a difference.

The first article in this chapter, by Galang and Ferris, highlights the factors influenced by the human resources department. Human resources do not stand alone. They affect and are affected by many of the other functional areas of the organization. Human resources effectiveness is an important issue that organizations need to evaluate.

Schneier, Shaw, and Beatty, in the second article, take up one of the fundamental challenges of human resources, the improvement of performance within a cost-containment strategy. This is a considerable challenge and, as the authors indicate, should be attempted only if the organization can shift to a long-term perspective. Performance improvement takes time, patience, and commitment.

Suggestions for Further Reading

Barnett, T., & Cochran, D. (1991, January). Making room for the whistleblower. *HR Magazine*, pp. 58–61.

Ciampa, D. (1989, October). The human resource challenge. *Manufacturing Systems*, pp. 74, 76.

Eyes, P. (1993). Realignment ties pay to performance. *Personnel Journal, 72*, 74–77.

Gauch, R. (1992). The changing environment in management information systems: New roles for computer professionals and users. *Public Personnel Management, 21*, 371–382.

Lawrence, S. (1989). Voices of HR experience. *Personnel Journal, 68*, 64–75.

Payson, M., & Rosen, P. (1991, April). Playing by fair rules. *HR Magazine*, pp. 42–43.

Recardo, R. (1990, December). Appropriate reward systems for JIT processes. *Journal for Quality & Participation*, 30–36.

Reingold, J. (1993, September 28). Prudential Insurance. *Financial World*, p. 60.

Steinburg, C. (1993). The downfall of teams. *Training & Development, 47*, 9–10.

The Human Resources Department: Its Influence and Effectiveness

Maria Carmen Galang and Gerald R. Ferris

The growing importance of human resource management (HRM) in the American workplace has been recognized and acknowledged for its meaningful impact on organizational competitiveness (e.g., Kochan, Katz, & McKersie, 1986). Although many arguments have been made with respect to the positive effect of HRM in organizations, little has been done to focus on the role of the human resources (HR) department in these developments. This article investigates the influence of the HR department and argues that without influence, the HR department is unlikely to be effective and that the benefits that the organization derives from HRM will be diminished as a result.

We first explore the meaning of effectiveness of the HR department and then discuss the determinants of HRM in organizations. We argue that the influence of the HR department is key to the existence and nature of HRM systems in the organization and thus indirectly determines outcomes from HRM. Finally, we examine the determinants of the HR department's influence, including the means to acquire influence.

The importance of influence is underscored by the existence within organizations of groups with competing interests. Because of the competition, organizational decisions are made on the basis of the relative power and influence of these various groups (Pfeffer, 1981). The most influential group then is able to affect organizational decisions in a way that favors its own particular interests. The HR department is obviously one such interest group with respect to the way the organization's human resources are managed. Thus, with influence, it is able to determine

the HRM systems that are adopted by the organization. The HR department's influence, then, becomes a key element in the outcomes of HRM for the organization.

Effectiveness of the HR Department

Like other members of the organization, the HR department needs influence to have its programs and projects carried out. The effectiveness of the HR department can, however, be viewed in two different ways. A narrow view of the department's effectiveness concerns its ability to get its programs implemented. A broader view, and a more important one from the organization's perspective, is of the effectiveness of the programs it proposes and manages in obtaining results desired by the organization.

Frost (1989) delineates two power conditions that present the HR department with differing dilemmas. In the first condition the department lacks power and hence faces the problem of acquiring the power it needs to effectively influence the way the organization's human resources are managed. The second condition is a situation in which the organization values human resources and the HR department has power—that is, HR has been given the responsibility to manage the organization's human resources. The question faced in this high-power condition is whether the HR department is able to deliver the expected results—in other words, whether the programs it implements contribute to organizational performance.

The distinction between *department* and *function* is an important one (Legge, 1978; Schuler, 1993). Legge clarifies the distinction, explaining that *function* more appropriately refers to an activity, whereas *department* means the "institutionalized presence" that is normally given responsibility for the activity. However, the HRM *function* may or may not be carried out by an HR *department.* Schuler illustrates this distinction by pointing out international differences in the importance given to each one. In North America both the department and the function have grown in importance, whereas in Japan the function has long been recognized as important, with the department having only a modest role. Neither department nor function enjoys importance in Western Europe and Australia.

Our view is that effectiveness of the HR department refers to its ability not only to have its programs implemented successfully (Schein, 1983) but also to have the programs that contribute to the organization's performance carried out. Thus, without an influential HR department, the organization is unlikely to take full advantage of the potential benefits offered by various HRM practices (McDonough, 1986). Tsui and Gomez-Mejia (1988) proposed an integrative model that distinguishes between two types of HR effectiveness. The first type is *functional HR effectiveness,* or the ability of the HR department to contribute to the organization's optimum use of its human resources. The second type is *organizational HR effectiveness,* seen as resulting from both the HR department's actions and the actions of line managers in collaboration with the HR department.

The contributions of HRM to the organization have been both suggested and demonstrated. Peters and Waterman's (1982) *In Search of Excellence* points out that the key distinguishing factor in excellent organizations is the way they manage their human resources. Schuler (1993; Schuler & MacMillan, 1984) maintains that the "effective acquisition, deployment and utilization of human resources" provide the firm with competitive edge because they contribute to profitability, product quality, and employee motivation. Trice, Belasco, and Alutto (1969) argue that

the value of various personnel practices lies in their ceremonial roles but that such ceremonial roles provide the organization with the legitimacy needed to gain the support and resources not only from external sources but from its members as well.

These provocative ideas have received research support. Huselid (1993a, b) reviews studies that have looked at the effects of specific HRM practices, such as job enrichment, training programs, profit sharing, compensation and recruiting systems, and other workplace innovations. In general, such practices result in positive outcomes for the firm, such as reduced turnover, higher productivity, and improved financial performance.

The effects of HRM as a system on organizational outcomes have also been investigated (Huselid, 1993a, b; Ichniowski, 1990; Kravetz, 1988; Schuster, 1986). Kravetz, for example, surveying 150 *Fortune* 500 companies from thirty-six different industry groups, concluded that companies with progressive human resource management performed better financially in terms of sales growth, profit growth, equity growth, and growth in earnings per share within a 5-year period and in terms of the previous year's profit margin. Human resource progressiveness was measured by a questionnaire of fifty-one items pertaining to the nine aspects listed in Table 1.

Table 1
Human Resource Progressiveness, as Defined by Kravetz (1988)

Communication progressiveness
Degree of emphasis on people in the company culture
Degree to which management is participative
Emphasis on creativity and excellence in the workplace
Extensiveness of career development and training
Effectiveness in maximizing employee job satisfaction
Degree of recognition and reward for good performance
Usage of flextime, work at home, and part-time employment
Degree of centralization and flattened management hierarchy

Conducting two studies designed to address the shortcomings of previous studies like Kravetz's, Huselid (1993a, b) still found support for the positive impact of HRM. His findings, again based on a survey of organizations from a broad range of industries, showed higher profits, higher market value, lower employee turnover, and higher productivity with the use of a sophisticated system of HRM practices (see Table 2).

These studies provide one way of measuring the HR department's effectiveness: looking at the attainment of organizational outcomes. Tsui (1984) points to one other means that has been used, the process-oriented approach, which focuses on the activities of the HR department. She offers a third alternative, assessments of various constituencies who have a stake either as suppliers of the HR department's resources or as recipients of its efforts. Effectiveness of the HR department is determined on the basis of the satisfaction of

Table 2

Sophisticated HRM Practices, as Defined by Huselid (1993a, b)

Proportion of the work force administered an employment test prior to hiring

Proportion of the work force receiving formal performance appraisals

Proportion of the work force whose performance appraisals are used to determine their compensation

Proportion of the work force who have access to company incentive plans, profit-sharing plans, and/or gainsharing plans

Proportion of the work force whose jobs have been subjected to a formal job analysis

Proportion of non-entry-level jobs filled from within in recent years

Proportion of the work force who have access to a formal grievance procedure and/or complaint resolution system

Proportion of the work force who are included in a formal information-sharing program (e.g., newsletter)

Proportion of the work force who are administered attitude surveys on a regular basis

Proportion of the work force who participate in Quality of Work Life (QWL) programs, Quality Circles (QC), and/or labor-management participation teams

---

the interests and expectations of multiple constituencies, which include top executives, other departments, employees, unions, government agencies, and external interest groups. Tsui's (1984, 1987, 1990; Tsui & Milkovich, 1987) multiple constituency approach suggests that satisfaction of constituency expectations is one relevant determinant of the HR department's influence. In fact, Tsui's 1990 study showed a positive relationship between the satisfaction of executives and the HR department's budget, and budgetary resources have been shown to be a basis of HR departments' power in organizations (Salancik & Pfeffer, 1974).

One conclusion that we can draw from these studies is that it matters what kinds of HRM programs are adopted. It is not merely the presence of HRM but the types of HRM programs that are implemented that bring benefits to the organization. However, there are two views on this matter. One is the best-practice approach, as illustrated by the studies just cited and the numerous prescriptions that have been offered by both practitioners and academics. The other is the contingency approach, such as Meshoulam and Baird's (1987) notion of external and internal fit of HRM, which argues that the appropriate HRM system (i.e., orientation, programs, methods, activities) depends on the organization's stage of development and the congruence of the various components of the HRM system. Buller's (1989) study of eight high-performing firms also concludes that the level of integration of HRM with the firm's strategic planning should depend on the nature of the environment faced by the firm. This is in contrast to the advocating of strategic human resource management (e.g., Butler, Ferris, & Smith-Cook, 1988) and the study by Smith-Cook and Ferris (1986), for example, which showed that HRM in high-performing firms in declining industries is more strategically oriented and more horizontally integrated than it is in low-performing firms.

To recapitulate, we have argued thus far that without influence, the HR department is unlikely to see the acceptance and successful implementation of HRM programs that benefit the organization. Thus, the HR department is seen as key factor for the existence and nature of HRM in the organization.

Determinants of HRM

The existence of an HR department is not the only factor that influences the way an organization's human resources are managed. Different perspectives have been offered to explain the variations in HRM practices found in organizations. Jackson, Schuler, and Rivero (1989) identify five different perspectives; behavioral, institutional, economic, control, and political. Taking the behavioral perspective, which focuses on the patterns of employee behavior required by organizational characteristics as determining the nature of personnel practices, Jackson and colleagues' study of 267 organizations shows the influence of industry sector, competitive strategy, technology, and organizational structure on various aspects of performance appraisal, compensation, and training practices.

External factors, such as government intervention and unionism, have also been specifically identified as reasons for the rise in influence of HRM in U.S. organizations (Baron, Dobbin, & Jennings, 1986; Kochan & Cappelli, 1994). Saha (1989) reviewed research concerning the sources of variation in organizations' personnel practices and found that organizational size, type of ownership, industry and technology, union presence, resource slack, top management philosophy, and the personnel manager's education and training were frequently reported factors. Fifteen theoretical studies classified the sources of variation into external and internal factors. Unions, government, competitors, and technical innovation were the frequently mentioned external factors, and work force demographics and values were the internal factor most often mentioned.

Tsui and Milkovich (1987) classified these internal and external factors more generally according to three different perspectives. The structural functionalism perspective emphasizes internal factors such as organizational size and growth. External factors are stressed by the strategic contingency view, which sees HRM as responses to critical contingencies arising from the organization's environment. The third perspective, strategic human resource management, considers both external and internal influences in that external factors are filtered through the organization's business strategy. Tsui and Milkovich, however, criticize the failure of these perspectives to take account of political pressures that influence personnel activities, proposing the multiple constituency approach to address this shortcoming.

An early study by Dimick and Murray (1978) integrated and compared the political perspective and the more traditional argument of technical rationality. On the basis of their findings, they proposed a model of organizational influences on personnel policy choices, asserting that technical rationality is a major basis for policy choices. Hence, such variables as organizational size and resource slack are important determinants. However, Dimick and Murray also argued that where technical rationality is constrained, political influences become the predominant factor explaining personnel policies.

The various determinants of HRM in organizations that have been indicated by these studies are schematized in Figure 1. In this simplified portrayal, the influence of the HR department is segregated, that department being the focus of this article. Thus, although various organizational and environmental factors determine the organization's HRM system, the HR department is also shown as a key factor. The department's effectiveness in influencing the HRM systems adopted by the organization ultimately affects the outcomes that the organization is able to derive from HRM and hence the effectiveness of HRM.

Empirical studies have shown that the HR department's presence is significantly and positively related to certain HRM policies and

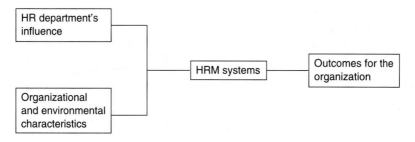

Figure 1. Determinants and Consequences of HRM

practices (Pfeffer, 1989), such as selectivity in hiring standards (Cohen & Pfeffer, 1986); to promotion from within and external hiring for only a few, limited positions (Pfeffer & Cohen, 1984); and to proliferation of job titles (Baron & Bielby, 1986). These studies also indicate the presence of other interest groups—in particular, unions—that exert a negative influence on these practices. Other studies have pointed to other interest groups that have implications for HRM in organizations—for example, professional, technical, and managerial groups (Baron, Davis-Blake, & Bielby, 1986); other organizational subunits or departments (Moore & Pfeffer, 1980; Pfeffer & Davis-Blake, 1987); and shareholders (Dimick & Murray, 1978). In fact, Tsui's multiple constituency approach deals with empirically identifying these various groups (Tsui, 1990) and their preferences and expectations (Tsui, 1987; Tsui & Milkovich, 1987).

The presence of various other interest groups leads to the question of the extent of their influence and to the question of their ability to become the dominant influence in organizational decisions. Consistent with this article's focus, the subsequent discussion centers on the HR department's influence and the means by which it is able to gain and maintain influence. Thus, although organizational and environmental characteristics may provide some advantages, the need for the HR department to play an active role and exert influence is underscored by the presence of other interest groups.

The HR Department's Influence

Baron and colleagues (1986) provided a historical account of the increased influence of personnel management in organizations, which they attributed largely to government interventions to address labor shortages during World War II and secondarily to the efforts of personnel specialists, who saw a potential loss of power with the end of the war and its corresponding problems, which had given them importance in organizations.

More recently, a 1984 survey by McDonough (1986) among senior HR executives in companies ranging in size from 100 to 40,000 employees and representing all major industrial classifications found that, in general, HR departments had become more powerful and influential in the preceding 5 years. Observations to the contrary have also been made. McDonough's survey in fact revealed significant differences in the power of HR departments across organizations. Follow-up interviews of twelve HR executives and line managers revealed four obstacles:

1. line managers' unfavorable perceptions of the HR staff;
2. line managers' apprehension about losing power to an expanded HR function;
3. top management's perceptions of the HR staff's incompetence to deal with crucial company concerns;
4. HR executives' apprehension to take on a new, expanded role. (pp. 22–23)

Legge (1978) and Frost (1989) pointed to the possibility of a self-perpetuating low-power condition for the HR department. Because the HR department lacks power and influence, actions are taken within the organization that inadvertently lead to human resource problems, which are then left to the HR department to resolve. However, the solutions are inevitably inappropriate and under the pressures of time and work demands, a crisis mode sets in, resulting in line management's poor perceptions of the HR department as summarized in the following themes:

1. Line management tends to have a confused, hazy, and/or stereotyped perception of the potential nature and scope of a personnel department's activities.
2. Middle and junior line management in particular tend to consider that personnel departments are "out of touch" with the kind of problems and constraints which face them. (Legge, 1978, p. 52)

Legge (1978; Legge & Exley, 1975) attributes this lack of power to the difficulty of demonstrating the effectiveness of personnel management. This difficulty is seen to stem from the difficulty of ascertaining cause-and-effect relations for the function. Many of the outcomes, such as absenteeism or productivity, are also determined in large part by a host of factors other than the way human resources are managed or the efforts of the department tasked with that management function (Tsui, 1984). It is for this reason that Tsui has proposed an alternative that takes into consideration assessments made by the personnel department's multiple constituencies.

Another reason proposed by Legge (1978; Legge & Exley, 1975) for the difficulty of evaluating the effectiveness of personnel management is its "omnipresent" nature. Other management functions are involved in personnel work, and personnel programs are implemented through other departments; the ensuing results are a lack of direct control by the personnel department and an impression that personnel management is not a truly specialized activity requiring unique knowledge and skills. The personnel department thus experiences a reduction in "nonsubstitutability," which is one source of power in organizations (Hickson, Hinings, Lee, Schneck, & Pennings, 1971). Schuler (1993) has suggested that HR departments may be facing demise with the renewed interest among line managers in exercising more control over HR activities. This trend toward decentralization could mean a loss of power for HR departments unless they "could seize the opportunity to be vital members of the management team" (Schuler, 1993, p. 12).

Gaining and Maintaining Influence

Because of the existence of interest groups that may have competing preferences and beliefs, the influence of the HR department cannot be taken for granted. To be effective, it needs to be actively engaged in gaining and maintaining influence. The research reporting significant relations between various interest groups and HRM practices, however, does not explain how and why these groups are able to influence the nature of HRM in the organization. This gap in our knowledge leads to the question of what determines one's influence—in other words, to the sources of power and the use of power.

There are two dominant theories of subunit power. The strategic contingencies theory (Hickson et al., 1971) states that an organizational subunit derives power by controlling strategic contingencies faced by the organization. This control is determined by the subunit's ability to cope with uncertainties, its centrality in the work flow, and the nonsubstitutability of its activities. The resource dependence theory (Pfeffer, 1981; Salancik & Pfeffer, 1974) attributes power to the control over critical resources that are difficult to acquire.

Although these dominant theories do not directly address the ways in which these strategic contingencies and critical resources are determined, Hambrick (1981) has suggested that they are determined by the requirements of the organization and the environment it faces. Thus, certain organizational and environmental factors create a potentially favorable situation for the HR department to have power. Beer, Spector, Lawrence, Mills, and Walton (1985) list some characteristics that make HRM a crucial concern for organizations: increased international competition, increasing complexity and size of the organization, slower growth, greater government involvement, increasing education of the work force, changing values of the work force, more concern with career and life satisfaction, and changes in work force demography.

On the other hand, however, the notion of socially constructed reality (Berger & Luckmann, 1966) suggests the potential for political skill as an additional source of power. By managing meanings through the use of language and symbols, organizational actors can define these strategic contingencies or critical resources and thus claim power despite the absence of favorable organizational and environmental characteristics (Pfeffer, 1981; Pondy, 1977; Watson, 1977). The possibility of being able to shape and define reality also suggests the necessity for organizational actors to engage actively in influence behaviors that enable them to gain and maintain power, lest competing interest groups define that reality in their own favor. One must use power in order not to lose power.

Other means of claiming power despite the absence of a favorable situation have also been indicated. For example, Hambrick's (1981) study suggests that by engaging in environmental scanning behaviors, an executive can acquire influence even when his or her functional responsibility does not concern critical contingencies as defined by the requirements of the organization and its environment. This notion supports the model of "discovered threat" proposed by Russ (1987), which argues that boundary spanners whose functions no longer represent critical contingencies for the organization discover new threats to the organization that they could

control and cope with. For personnel specialists in particular, professionalization was also identified as one means for maintaining power when the end of World War II portended a potential loss of power (Baron et al., 1986).

Legge (1978; Legge & Exley, 1975) further identified two strategies personnel specialists used in gaining more influence: namely, conformist innovation and deviant innovation, which differ in terms of the values pursued or espoused. Conformist innovation accepts and emphasizes organizational values such as cost-effectiveness, efficiency, and productivity. The deviant innovation strategy attempts to redefine the goals and values the organization must pursue and against which the personnel function must be evaluated. Legge argues that both strategies are potentially effective, depending on the economic condition of the organization. Where resources are scarce, conformist innovation is more effective. Deviant innovation, on the other hand, can be effective when slack allows more experimentation in the organization. This argument is reflected in the current prescriptions for HRM to be more management or business oriented because of the highly competitive environment facing organizations at present (e.g., Schuler, 1993). In fact, focusing on the bottom line is one way for the HR department to position itself strategically in the organization.

Others hold a different view with respect to values and intraorganizational power. Enz (1988), for example, demonstrated that top management's perceptions of value similarity related to a department's power. Watson (1977) also argues that the power of any department within an organization is constrained by the congruence of its activities with the interests of those who control the organization. However, Enz and Watson do not address the question of whether this relation between value congruity and power is contingent on other factors such as economic conditions.

In discussing the role of power and politics in HRM, Frost (1989) likewise identifies the importance in strategy decisions of values, one of three significant issues faced by managers. The involvement of HR personnel in the question of "what is right" ensures the contribution of HRM to organizational performance. Frost also criticizes the emphasis the HR department places on "doing things right" without giving corresponding attention to "doing the right things," which is of major concern to line managers.

Although the aforementioned studies represent arguments concerning what strategies and tactics are available and effective, only one study so far may be viewed as dealing with the HR department's strategies to gain influence. Tsui (1990) examined factors influencing effectiveness assessments made by multiple constituencies of the HR department; these factors included the department's adaptive responses such as co-optation, responsiveness, and outcomes satisfying the expectations of various constituencies. By obtaining favorable assessments, the HR department is likely to acquire resources and support and thus be able to gain influence. Tsui's multiple constituency approach is also able to address the issue of demonstrating effectiveness, which is problematic for the HR department.

Co-optation is only one possible influence tactic. Asking personnel practitioners, "In what ways do you get your way in your relationships with other managers outside the personnel department, either in policy matters or in day-to-day managing?" Watson (1977) obtained responses classified in Table 3. Of course, the literature on influence behaviors provides a more comprehensive repertory of tactics from which HR professionals can draw (e.g., Kipnis, Schmidt, & Wilkinson, 1980).

Aside from influence skills, Tsui's (1990) study also pointed out the need for technical competence in order to be able to perform the activities expected by multiple constituencies and deliver the desired outcomes. Even where the function of the HR department is defined as dealing with critical concerns of the organization, the department still needs to be able to claim that it has the sole and requisite expertise to address these concerns (Hickson et al., 1971; Watson, 1977) and deliver expected results (Frost, 1989). Competence, therefore, refers to both technical expertise and political skills, which are important sources of influence for the HR department.

Table 3

Influence Tactics Used by Personnel Practitioners in Survey by Watson (1977)*

Persuasion/argument/convincing people, etc. (49)

Cultivating contacts/working on relationships/winning people's confidence, etc. (23)

Authority/direct orders/telling/pulling rank/getting authority from the top, etc. (19)

Planting ideas in the minds of others, etc. (15)

Threats/bullying/blackmailing/cajoling, etc. (12)

Use of expertise/knowledge (8)

Name dropping (8)

---

*Numbers in parenthesis represent numbers of approaches mentioned.

Conclusion: The HR Department's Influence and Effectiveness

There is as yet no direct empirical evidence linking the influence of the HR department to the effect of HRM on organizational performance. However, studies have shown a relationship between the presence of an HR department and HRM practices. Studies have also documented the favorable outcomes of HRM for organizations. Given both kinds of evidence, it is likely that a positive relationship between the HR department's influence and organizational performance can be found. The underlying argument is that the HR department possesses expertise and knowledge with regard to the effective management of human resources, which ultimately results in organizational competitiveness. With the influence to get its programs accepted and successfully implemented, the HR department will be able to utilize its expertise and bring about the organizational outcomes desired from HRM. The organization thus will derive the potential benefits that HRM has to offer.

References

Baron, J. N., & Bielby, W. T. (1986). The proliferation of job titles in organizations. *Administrative Science Quarterly, 31,* 561–586.

Baron, J. N., Davis-Blake, A., & Bielby, W. T. (1986). The structure of opportunity: How promotion ladders vary within and among organizations. *Administrative Science Quarterly, 31,* 248–273.

Baron, J., Dobbin, F., & Jennings, P. D. (1986). War and peace: The evolution of modern personnel administration in US industry. *American Journal of Sociology, 92,* 350–383.

Beer, M., Spector, B., Lawrence, P. R., Mills, D. Q., & Walton, R. E. (1985). *Human resource management: A general manager's perspective.* New York: Free Press.

Berger, P. L., & Luckmann, T. (1966). *The social construction of reality.* New York: Doubleday.

Buller, P. F. (1989). Successful partnerships: HR and strategic planning at eight top firms. *Organizational Dynamics, 17,* 27–43.

Butler, J. E., Ferris, G. R., & Smith-Cook, D. S. (1988). Exploring some critical dimensions of strategic human resource management. In R. S. Schuler, S. A. Youngblood, & V. L. Huber (Eds.), *Readings in personnel/human resource management* (pp. 3–13). St. Paul, MN: West.

Cohen, Y., & Pfeffer, J. (1986). Organizational hiring standards. *Administrative Science Quarterly, 31,* 1–24.

Dimick, D. E., & Murray, V. V. (1978). Correlates of substantive policy decisions in organizations: The case of human resource management. *Academy of Management Journal, 21,* 611–623.

Enz, C. A. (1988). The role of value congruity in intraorganizational power. *Administrative Science Quarterly, 33,* 284–304.

Frost, P. J. (1989). The role of organizational power and politics in human resource management. In A. N. B. Nedd, G. R. Ferris, & K. M. Rowland (Eds.), *Research in personnel and human resources management* (Supplement 1, pp. 1–21). Greenwich, CT: JAI Press.

Hambrick, D. C. (1981). Environment, strategy, and power within top management teams. *Administrative Science Quarterly, 26,* 253–276.

Hickson, D. J., Hinings, C. R., Lee, C. A., Schneck, R. E., & Pennings, J. M. (1971). A strategic contingencies theory of intraorganizational power. *Administrative Science Quarterly, 16,* 216–229.

Huselid, M. A. (1993a). Human resource management practices and firm performance. *Industrial and Labor Relations Review,* manuscript under review.

Huselid, M. A. (1993b). The impact of human resource management practices on turnover and productivity. *Academy of Management Journal,* manuscript under review.

Ichiniowski, C. (1990). *Human resource management systems and the performance of U.S. manufacturing businesses.* (NBER Working Paper Series No. 3449.) Cambridge, MA: National Bureau of Economic Research.

Jackson, S. E., Schuler, R. S., & Rivero, J. C. (1989). Organizational characteristics as predictors of personnel practices. *Personnel Psychology, 42,* 727–786.

Kipnis, D., Schmidt, S. M., & Wilkinson, I. (1980). Intraorganizational influence tactics: Explorations in getting one's way. *Journal of Applied Psychology, 65,* 440–452.

Kochan, T. A., & Capelli, P. (1984). The transformation of the industrial relations and personnel function. In P. Osterman (Ed.), *Internal labor markets* (pp. 133–161). Cambridge, MA: MIT Press.

Kochan, T. A., Katz, H. C., & McKersie, R. B. (1986). *The transformation of American industrial relations.* New York: Basic Books.

Kravetz, D. J. (1988). *The human resources revolution: Implementing progressive management practices for bottom-line success.* San Francisco: Jossey-Bass.

Legge, K. (1978). *Power, innovation and problem-solving in personnel management.* London: McGraw-Hill.

Legge, K., & Exley, M. (1975). Authority, ambiguity and adaptation: The personnel specialists' dilemma. *Industrial Relations Journal, 6,* 51–65.

McDonough, E. F. (1986). How much power does HR have, and what can it do to win more? *Personnel, 63,* 18–25.

Meshoulam, I., & Baird, L. (1987). Proactive human resource management. *Human Resource Management, 26,* 483–502.

Moore, W. L., & Pfeffer, J. (1980). The relationship between departmental power and faculty careers on two campuses: The case for structural effects on faculty salaries. *Research in Higher Education, 13,* 291–306.

Peters, T. J., & Waterman, R. H., Jr. (1982). *In search of excellence: Lessons from America's best-run companies.* New York: Warner.

Pfeffer, J. (1981). *Power in organizations.* Marshfield, MA: Pitman.

Pfeffer, J. (1989). A political perspective on careers: Interests, networks, and environments. In M. G. Arthur, D. T. Hall, & B. S. Lawrence (Eds.), *Handbook of career theory.* New York: Cambridge University Press.

Pfeffer, J., & Cohen, Y. (1984). Determinants of internal labor markets in organizations. *Administrative Science Quarterly, 29,* 550–572.

Pfeffer, J., & Davis-Blake, A. (1987). Understanding organizational wage structures: A resource dependence approach. *Academy of Management Journal, 30,* 437–455.

Pondy, L. R. (1977). The other hand clapping: An information-processing approach to organizational power. In T. H. Hammer & S. B. Bacharach (Eds.), *Reward systems and power distribution in organizations: Searching for solutions* (pp. 56–91). Ithaca: New York State School of Industrial and Labor Relations.

Russ, G. (1987). *Boundary spanning: What comes after controlling critical linkages?* Working paper, department of management, Texas A&M University, College Station.

Saha, S. K. (1989). Variations in the practice of human resource management: A review. *Canadian Journal of Administrative Science, September,* 37–45.

Salancik, G. R., & Pfeffer, J. (1974). The bases and use of power in organizational decision making: The case of a university. *Administrative Science Quarterly, 19,* 453–473.

Schein, V. E. (1983, October). Strategic management and the politics of power. *Personnel Administrator,* pp. 55–58.

Schuler, R. S. (1993). World class HR departments: Six critical issues. *The Singapore Accounting and Business Review,* forthcoming.

Schuler, R. S., & MacMillan, I. C. (1984). Gaining competitive advantage through human resource management practices. *Human Resource Management, 23,* 241–256.

Schuster, F. E. (1986). *The Schuster report: The proven connection between people and profits.* New York: Wiley.

Smith-Cook, D., & Ferris, G. R. (1986). Strategic human resource management and firm effectiveness in industries experiencing decline. *Human Resource Management, 25,* 441–458.

Trice, H. N., Belasco, J., & Alutto, J. A. (1969). The role of ceremonials in organizational behavior. *Industrial and Labor Relations Review, 23,* 40–51.

Tsui, A. S. (1984). Personnel department effectiveness: A tripartite approach. *Industrial Relations, 23,* 184–197.

Tsui, A. S. (1987). Defining the activities and effectiveness of the HR department: A multiple constituency approach. *Human Resource Management, 26,* 35–69.

Tsui, A. S. (1990). A multiple-constituency model of effectiveness: An empirical examination at the human resource subunit level. *Administrative Science Quarterly, 35,* 458–483.

Tsui, A. S., & Gomez-Mejia, L. R. (1988). Evaluating human resource effectiveness. In L. Dyer & G. W. Holder (Eds.), *Human resource management: Evolving roles and responsibilities.* Washington, DC: Bureau of National Affairs.

Tsui, A. S., & Milkovich, G. T. (1987). Personnel department activities: Constituency perspectives and preferences. *Personnel Psychology, 40,* 519–537.

Watson, T. J. (1977). *The personnel managers.* London: Routledge and Kegan Paul.

Companies' Attempts to Improve Performance While Containing Costs: Quick Fix versus Lasting Change

Craig Eric Schneier, Douglas G. Shaw, and Richard W. Beatty

American corporations' generally poor record at increasing their productivity has been well documented and frequently discussed in the popular press. We are constantly reminded how growth in U.S. productivity has slowed relative to other leading nations. As significant growth opportunities for many U.S. companies diminish due to increased global competition, these companies face pressure to increase their productivity in order to continue to sustain the earnings increases that afford them to invest in their future.

U.S. productivity grew at an annual rate of only 0.7% during most of the 1980s. Blue-collar workers' productivity grew at an annual rate of 2.8%, while white-collar workers' productivity decreased significantly (Thurow, 1986). More recent statistics (see e.g., O'Reilly, 1992) reveal that these trends have continued. These data are especially disquieting since the number of U.S. white-collar workers has grown to about twice the size of the blue-collar work force. In service companies, which employ about 95% of white-collar workers, productivity improvements have been negligible (Henkoff, 1991).

The Downsizing Response to Productivity Problems Has Not Worked

U.S. corporations' typical response to declining white-collar productivity and competitive cost pressures has been to cut the size of its work force, including its white-collar work force. Hundreds of companies have "restruc-

tured," "downsized," or "rightsized" over the last decade. These include such household names as Kodak, General Motors, Chrysler, Pratt & Whitney, General Electric, Unisys, Digital, and even venerable IBM.

The news is not that most companies are downsizing. The news is that downsizing typically does not work. Surviving managers in companies that have experienced white-collar layoffs say they have not seen the desired boost in productivity. One such example is a downsized *Fortune* 100 company that saw its expenditures for external consultants and contractors obliterate the savings realized from their headcount reduction. Many of the downsized former managers returned to do the same work—as higher-paid external contractors rather than employees. In another well-known company, too many experienced, highly skilled engineers opted for the rich early retirement package, not only requiring a multimillion-dollar charge against earnings, but also leaving a gaping hole in critical knowledge.

Empirical research reinforces the anecdotes. A recent survey of 1,468 downsized companies conducted by the Society of Human Resource Management (SHRM) found that in 50% of the companies, productivity either stayed the same or worsened (Henkoff, 1990). Research sponsored by the American Productivity and Quality Center concluded that only half the companies surveyed were satisfied with the results of their cost-reduction and restructuring efforts (Koretz, 1991). Additional

Reprinted with permission of The Human Resource Planning Society from *Human Resource Planning, 15:3* (1992): 1–25.

dismal results of downsizing come from a survey of 1,005 companies that have either downsized, reorganized, or restructured through a merger or organization (cited in Bennett, 1991). Most of these companies did not achieve their objectives of reduced expenses, increased profits, or increased productivity. Less than half reduced expenses, less than a third increased their profits, and only one-fifth increased their productivity.

The purpose of this article is to review and assess the approaches companies are taking to improve productivity, particularly in white-collar positions. A case is made for an approach described as *work effectiveness,* which more and more companies are using successfully. Its distinguishing feature is a focus on eliminating and streamlining the *work* performed, as opposed to eliminating only the *people* who perform the work, in order to attain lasting productivity improvement. Only when the source of the cost—the work people perform—is removed, will costs decrease. As Peter Drucker (1991) has observed:

> . . . In manufacturing, working smarter is only one key to increased productivity. In knowledge and service work, working smarter is the only key. (p. 72)

The Vicious Cycle of Downsizing

In their zeal to remain competitive, many U.S. companies are led into a vicious cycle of cost cutting. The vicious cycle works this way: Due to, for example, increased competition which hurts revenue and results in a cash flow squeeze, companies reduce costs dramatically and quickly. For most, the large visible cost they initially turn to first is their people: The work force is downsized.

But companies too often take out the people, not the work. The same amount of work exists but there are fewer people to do it. The result is frustration, stress, insecurity, and disloyalty. Perhaps too few people now exist to identify and prevent the underlying problems. Instead, they must spend time "putting out fires." The cash squeeze severely limits research and development efforts. There may be too little cash available to invest in efforts to identify root causes of, for example, poor quality or noncompetitive technology.

Hence, the costs persist. The following are all potential sources of high costs: poor quality (perhaps from raw materials bought on price versus quality), unnecessary reports (perhaps due to lack of trust of subordinates) that soak up scarce resources, performance measures that track in great detail actions that are only marginally important (or even counterproductive) to customers, computer programs with a patchwork of "fixes" that slow operations, decisions that must weave their way through review layer after review layer, or reward systems that say "cover your tracks, don't innovate." As Exhibit 1 notes, these conditions lead to further erosion in customer satisfaction, and hence revenue. A "solution" is to hire people back. But by increasing costs, this path often restarts the vicious cycle. Even if this path is resisted, due to hiring freezes and headcount ceilings, fundamental problems of quality, satisfaction, or cost-competitiveness remain unsolved, and worsen. Hence short-term pressures to cut costs again become even more intense and the vicious cycle repeats.

Points on a vicious cycle become amplifying feedback processes. Senge (1990) calls them "engines of growth," which generate an "accelerating decline" (p. 79). That is, once downsizing occurs but the work to be done is not reduced, the remaining work force perceives even more pressure to perform, yet is now insecure and hence does not take necessary risks which lead to innovation, innovations which could recapture cost advantage or market share. But insecure people rarely innovate. Productivity, revenue, or quality may soon suffer, further weakening market position. Now management becomes convinced even more strongly of the need to reduce costs, and will downsize again.

Consider Kodak, a company with enormous strengths in technology—a powerful global brand name. When Colby Chandler

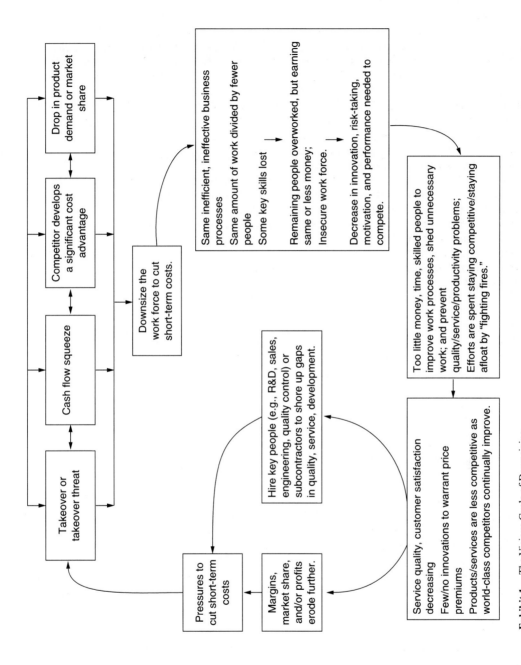

Exhibit 1. The Vicious Cycle of Downsizing

became CEO of Kodak in 1983, he downsized to reduce bureaucracy and enhance cost competitiveness. Profits increased 63% the following year. In 1985 and 1986, losses occurred for six straight quarters. Kodak downsized again. Profits tripled the following year. In early 1989, profits fell; Kodak downsized again. A new CEO, Kay Whitmore, took over and ordered 4,500 people cut. For Kodak, like many other companies, numerous complex forces (e.g., an acquisition, a rise in the value of the dollar) were at work during this period (Bardwick, 1991). As one Kodak manager put it: "Costs exist for a reason, if you don't take the reasons away, the costs will return" (Henkoff, 1990, p. 41). The vicious cycle of downsizing was probably at work at Kodak.

Downsizers Play a Game of Catch Up

Companies with repeated downsizings have made the mistake of getting caught in a game of catch up. As they attempt round after round of cost cutting, predominantly via downsizing, in order to catch their leading competitors, these competitors are continually moving ahead, usually not by downsizing but by fundamentally changing their work processes.

Even though they face difficult economic times, the performance and strategies of automobile manufacturers are instructive. Ford and GM have improved their cost positions and their products' quality; however, Honda still builds its Civic with only 11 hours of direct labor. Ford requires 16 for its comparable Escort model. GM averages over 30 hours of direct labor (Taylor, 1991), and has recently announced plant closings and downsizing.

The efficiency game in the auto industry is not played solely at the low end of the price scale. Toyota averages 13 direct labor hours per car and Toyota's Lexus competes head on (and very favorably) in this country with Mercedes, but does so with one-sixth the labor hours. Toyota has now overtaken Chrysler as the third largest automobile producer in the world. The U.S. auto industry is slowly realizing that downsizing alone will not enable it

even to catch, let alone surpass, Honda's or Toyota's levels of productivity and quality. Fundamental changes in work processes are needed. As one Toyota executive has explained: "Our current success is the best reason to change things" (Taylor, 1990).

Alternative Approaches to the Search for Productivity

Although downsizing is popular, and receives considerable press, companies actually use a number of different approaches to enhance productivity, some focusing on people and expenses, and some on work and processes. A look at the options companies use puts them in perspective. (See Exhibit 2.)

Hiring freezes are often a first step in trying to manage headcount. Since they do not directly affect the organization's current employees, they are relatively painless. Although a manager needing a critical skill available only from outside the organization might disagree, hiring freezes do not cause enormous organizational upheavals.

Financial separation incentives also typically cause relatively minor disruptions. The most common form of financial separation incentive is an early retirement program, whereby employees that meet age and service criteria are encouraged to leave with an enhanced retirement package. AT&T recently separated 12,000 managers through such a program. Despite a program cost of $160 million, AT&T claims to be saving $450 million annually on overhead (Dichter and Trank, 1991).

A second, less common form of financial separation incentives are programs that are open to all employees. Under such a program, special severance packages are offered to employees with a certain amount of tenure, regardless of how close they are to retirement. Digital Equipment, recently faced with troubled times following years of prosperity, offered employees severance packages tied to years of service: from 40 weeks of pay for those with up to two years of service to 104 weeks of pay for those with 20 years of ser-

Exhibit 2
Approaches to Improve Productivity*

APPROACH	DESCRIPTION
People and Expense Focus:	
1. Hiring Freeze	Company ceases hiring, with very few exceptions
2. Financial Separation Incentives	Certain employees offered financial incentives to leave or retire early
3. Budgetary Controls	Strict controls are placed on increasing overhead expenses; detailed substantiation required for expenditures
4. "Mandated" Layoffs	Work force reduced by specific percentage or number, across entire company, or within division or unit
Work and Process Focus:	
5. Time and Motion Studies	Studies aimed at analyzing and then streamlining worker activities to increase efficiency/speed (most typically conducted with production workers)
6. Task Analysis	Emphasis on analysis of work, often by external party; outputs of white-collar (overhead) jobs and units analyzed to assess their costs and their "value" to customers; redundant or low-value tasks that can be eliminated, reduced, or improved are identified; often a target overhead reduction (e.g., 30–40 percent) is provided
7. Work Effectiveness	Emphasis on data gathering and implementation; internal "customer-supplier" teams identify improvement opportunities and implement solutions; work processes mapped, identifying underlying causes of problems, reducing the amount of work, improving processes and related systems (e.g., measurement; reward)

Each approach has numerous variations and specific titles; those descriptors chosen here are meant to be illustrative and representative.

vice (Edelman, 1990). Digital's program achieved its desired result, but in some cases these strategies are too successful and critical skills are lost. Recently, SouthWestern Bell had twice as many people as it intended opt for early retirement, leaving quite a deficit in its skill bank (Hwang, 1991).

Budgetary controls are a useful means of controlling the growth of overhead expenses. Peter Grace of W.R. Grace and Harold Geneen of ITT were CEOs noted for imposing tough controls on managers' budgets. Recently, CEO David Johnson of Campbell Soup has used budget control effectively to begin to turn around the company. Many companies are beyond the stage of needing to *control* costs, though; they must embark on a journey to *decrease* costs significantly, and do so every year. Emerson Electric, one of the most successful U.S. corporations over the last 30 years, requires every employee to have an ongoing cost reduction initiative (Knight, 1992).

Ulrich and Lake (1990) expand the list of variations to budgetary controls in their excellent discussion on "alternatives to layoffs." Budgetary controls related to reduction in compensation costs include:

- Job sharing
- Leave of absence
- Work sharing
- Less paid time off
- Pay cuts
- Demotions.

As Ulrich and Lake (1990) note, however, the above strategies have some disadvantages. In addition to potential morale issues, the net economic effect of the strategies can be small unless the organization (or unit) affected is large. The signal these actions send, however, about the urgency of the need to cut costs, may be as important as their economic benefit.

"Mandated" layoffs (downsizing) are one of the most common approaches to improving productivity in the U.S. Facing the largest car and truck sales slump in almost ten years, Ford laid off salaried workers as part of a cost-cutting program to save over $1 billion in early 1991. GM, as noted above, has followed suit. Layoffs may improve a company's productivity in the short term by cutting inputs (i.e., cost) in the typical "inputs divided by outputs" productivity ratio.

In *time and motion studies,* the targeted processes are typically performed by hourly production, warehouse, or distribution employees, rather than white-collar employees. Studies are conducted by a team of engineers or analysts who assess repetitive tasks and develop the most efficient way of conducting the targeted work process. The focus here is often not on a task's effectiveness (e.g., quality), but rather on its efficiency (e.g., speed).

Task analysis refers to a group of techniques used to document the various activities that "overhead" (or white-collar) workers are engaged in. These can be analyzed to identify and then eliminate, or substantially reduce, redundant and low-value tasks. Task analysis approaches are based on the accurate premise that although organizational changes (e.g., reorganizations) occur regularly, companies rarely replace tasks with the new work needed to accommodate the changes; they simply add to the tasks already being performed. As a result, individual employees, and entire groups of employees, may be engaged in a task, such as producing a specific management report, that is no longer valued by its "customer." Productivity improvements are made by focusing employees on higher-value tasks. McKinsey and Company popularized this approach in the 1970s and 1980s with their "overhead value analysis" (OVA) approach.

Work effectiveness is related to task analysis approaches to improve productivity and is closely aligned with continuous improvement, process improvement, and work re-engineering (Hammer, 1990). It often relies on groups of internal and external customers and suppliers to identify opportunities for improving the effectiveness and efficiency of various organizational processes; however, rather than focusing only on specific tasks and outputs of work units, the work effectiveness approach analyzes the entire chain of tasks that comprise the processes housing all organizational work. It not only focuses on eliminating and reducing work that has low value to customers, but also focuses on improving the effectiveness of any specific process (e.g., invoicing, manufacturing changes, sourcing, or administering pay increases). The approach is structured but highly participative, leading to results that have a high probability of being implemented, since those who do the work diagnose the problems and formulate the recommendations (Beer et al., 1991).

Work effectiveness, described more fully below, requires empowered people or teams, a forum where candid (upward) communication can take place, and a structure to identify and solve problems. Those that are closest to the work process—contributors (suppliers), process "operators," and beneficiaries (customers)—identify opportunities for improvement and generate practical solutions. They "own" the modification to the process. General Electric is an example of a company that has had such an effort underway since 1989, as part of their Work-Out initiative (Stewart, 1991).

Selecting an Approach to Productivity Improvement

A company's productivity objectives help it determine which approaches are most suitable. Typical objectives and their implications are:

1. *Curtail or stop the increase in overhead expenses.* Budgetary controls and hiring freezes have been useful to achieve this objective.
2. *Reduce low-value, redundant work.* Task analysis and time and motion studies are specifically aimed at this objective. Time

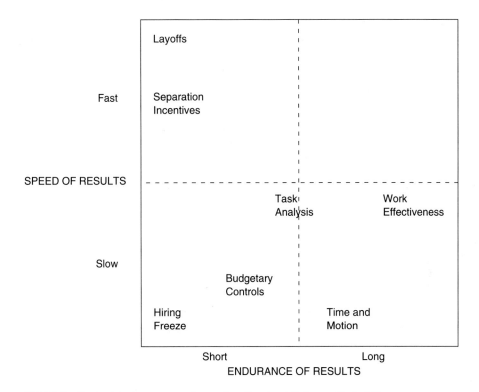

Exhibit 3.   Productivity Improvement Approaches: Speed and Endurance Trade-Offs

and motion studies are more appropriate if an organization is targeting specific types of repetitive work. If the objective is focused on a whole organization, all staff units, or a large single unit, some form of task analysis may be more appropriate.

3. *Reduce overhead expenses quickly.* Layoffs can be a fast way to reduce overhead expenses in the short term.

4. *Reorient the organization to consistently improving productivity in an enduring way.* This objective is considerably different than the others since it implies not only attaining specific productivity improvements, but instilling in the company's culture an analytical framework for continually questioning the value (both efficiency and effectiveness) of work to its customers, eliminating low-

value work, and precluding its return. Work effectiveness has been useful, given the approach's scope, structure, and degree of participation of workers and managers (see e.g., Hammer, 1990; Henkoff, 1990).

Most organizations want the best of both worlds: *enduring* productivity gains obtained *quickly*. However, they typically face a trade-off. Exhibit 3 shows that approaches with the most enduring results tend not to produce quick results. As the vice-chairman of a leading consumer products company that had repeatedly downsized recently noted: "Crash diets may help you lose a few pounds quickly, but they don't make you more fit; you have to change your eating habits and lifestyle to improve fitness, and to stay fit."

An organization could consider the various advantages and disadvantages associated with each productivity improvement approach (summarized in Exhibit 4). For example, one unit may not want to take the chance of losing some of its best performers, in which case using voluntary financial separation incentives may not be appropriate. Imposing a hiring freeze may unnecessarily restrict some units if they demand special talents that are in short supply.

Exhibit 4
Advantages and Disadvantages to Alternative White-Collar Productivity Improvement Approaches

APPROACH	POTENTIAL ADVANTAGES*	POTENTIAL DISADVANTAGES*
1. Hiring Freeze	a. Can be done at no cost to company b. Simple to implement c. May have minimal negative impact on morale of employees	a. May not have a significant impact on productivity b. May preclude opportunities to obtain needed skills, fresh perspective
2. Financial Separation Incentives	a. All terminations are voluntary b. May be relatively painless way of reducing white-collar employees	a. May lead to loss of valued employees b. May be expensive c. May not have a significant impact on productivity
3. Budgetary Controls	a. Good "preventive maintenance" approach keeps expenses under control b. May instill strong sense of fiscal management	a. May not provide enough impact for companies with currently excessive overhead b. May inappropriately restrict some high-value, high-leverage, high-potential units if applied uniformly across the company
4. Mandated Layoffs	a. May be quick way to achieve expense reduction b. May target those with performance problems, if done carefully	a. May not have lasting impact on productivity (or on costs or profits) b. May not address root causes of decreased white-collar productivity c. May have negative effects on employee morale
5. Time and Motion Studies	a. Analyzes workers' actions and processes, identifying causes of problems (e.g., delays, inaccuracies) b. May lead to lasting change	a. Scope is generally confined to a few organizational processes b. May not have a significant impact on organization's overall productivity
6. Task Analysis	a. Utilizes data-based process to identify redundant, low-value work b. Focuses on reducing work and, if appropriate, reducing number of white-collar employees	a. Some improvements may be difficult to implement b. The organization's key processes (potential causes for low production) may remain unchanged c. Can take a relatively long time
7. Work Effectiveness	a. Solutions are developed by those involved in the process, making them more easily implementable b. May address barriers (e.g., structure, systems, skills) to lasting effectiveness/productivity	a. May be slow to implement b. Requires organizational leadership, commit- and discipline

*Illustrative, not exhaustive

Improving Productivity with Work Effectiveness

Most companies have numerous examples of work that is not productive or of low value to its customers:

- In one of the world's largest oil companies, field geologists, who must locate the reserves around the world that are the key to future revenues, spend 40% of their time in their offices in committee meetings.

- One national insurance company took 25 days to process an approved claim from its receipt to its payment; in that entire period, the claim was worked on for an average total of 17 minutes.

- A worldwide automobile maker had 500 people in accounts payable; only 100 did accounts payable work; the other 400 were administrative, technical, accounting, and HR personnel, and clerical staff.

- A *Fortune* 500 electronics company spent $20 million to manage its field inventory, which was valued at $10 million.

- U.S. automakers recall 75% of all cars sold to correct defects (at their expense of course).

One recent study (cited in Kaydos, 1991) found that white-collar work can be categorized as follows:

- Correcting errors and solving problems (e.g., computer programs with "bugs"; invoices with erroneous totals; automobile "recalls"):   **40%**
- Ineffective, unnecessary, and/or optional work (e.g., reports no one reads):   **10%**
- Necessary, accurate, useful work: **50%**

Low-value work, and inefficient or ineffective work processes, not merely headcount, are the primary targets of the work effectiveness approach.

Companies' Experience with Work Effectiveness

Numerous companies have successfully used various forms of the work effectiveness approach to target specific work processes. For example, in examining the information it provided to the IRS, Corning discovered that it could eliminate a detailed financial summary, saving it 400 work hours a year. Xerox used a cross-functional team of middle managers to examine and change the distribution process for its copiers, boosting their customer satisfaction index from 70% to 90%. Other Xerox teams focused on analyzing high inventories, resulting in $200 million a year in inventory cost savings.

In Oryx Energy Company, formerly a Sun Company subsidiary, "natural" work teams were given the power to devise and implement solutions to business problems, as opposed to the hierarchical decision-making approach. The teams were cross-functional in composition. They surveyed the corporate culture to obtain baseline data and found that performance measurement, rewards, and other systems were not compatible with innovation and problem solving, but reinforced the status quo. They implemented a mechanism to link key company goals to rewards and gathered input on managerial performance from subordinates. The teams cut $75 million in overhead costs, eliminated over 1,500 unnecessary reports, and ultimately operated their units with 1,000 fewer people.

Participation: A Basic Premise of Work Effectiveness

Two foundation beliefs of the work effectiveness approaches are that most employees are capable of identifying productivity improvement opportunities, and that they desire to make their organization more effective. Companies that limit improvement efforts to managers are not leveraging their employees to achieve desired productivity gains. In fact, case studies demonstrate that without widespread organizational involvement, significant change is unlikely (see Lawler, 1992, for a review). As Schaeffer and Thomson (1992) have noted, too many change or improvement initiatives are merely programs that focus on activities, not results, and are led by staff units or consultants, not operating managers. Schaeffer and Thomson (1992) summarize this problem as follows:

> They design training courses, they launch self-directed teams, they create new quality-measurement systems, they organize campaigns to win the Baldrige Award. Senior managers plunge wholeheartedly into these activities, relieving themselves, momentarily at least, of the burden of actually having to improve performance. (p. 85)

Top executives create many change *programs* that fade as their interest wanes, replaced by the next program. Workers and managers at all levels, working together, can create *change* (see Beer et al., 1991).

Appropriate Organizational Context and Circumstance for Work Effectiveness

Comparing work effectiveness to the numerous forms of task analysis, work effectiveness is typically:

- Applied more broadly—to work processes and units engaged in service, and operational, technical, administrative, professional, and managerial work at all hierarchical levels
- More participative, resulting in more ideas to improve work effectiveness, typically leading to a greater commitment to change, and better chance of lasting implementation
- More likely to address the fundamental questions—whether work (or a work process) should be completed in the first place, and if it must be done, whether it should be done inside or outside the organization
- More likely to tackle directly the underlying infrastructure—for example, organizational structure, such as number of levels, and management systems (such as planning, budgeting, or performance measurement and reward) that often support the inefficient way work may currently be done and thus inhibit lasting change.

The Anatomy of a Work Effectiveness Effort

Communicating need to change and providing tools. Most work effectiveness approaches utilize a methodology[1] that relies on employee groups to work with their suppliers (i.e., those that provide a service or "product" to them) and customers (i.e., the recipients of their services or products) to discuss examples of work and processes that could be improved. (Companies have successfully applied this approach to working with both internal and external suppliers and customers [see Jick, 1990].) Exhibit 5 provides a broad summary of the principal steps, but there are, of course, innumerable specific varieties of work effectiveness in practice (see Henkoff, 1990; Kaplan and Murdock, 1991). Once improvement opportunities have been specified and defined, small teams focus on determining appropriate analyses to conduct. After communication by line managers of the compelling need to change, teams typically receive basic instruction on specific analytical tools (e.g., flow charts or cause and effect diagrams) and are provided sufficient time to adequately conduct the analyses.

Data gathering and analyses. As noted in Exhibit 5, two key steps in a typical work effectiveness approach are focused data gathering and analysis. The importance of focusing efforts on key issues, describing the current state, and analyzing data in order to achieve successful change is consistently advocated by those discussing lasting change efforts (e.g., Beer et al., 1991; Walker, 1992). There must be a clear view of the present, and a compelling need to change. Data, not casual perceptions, are often compelling to decision makers. A four-step data gathering process is usually recommended:

Exhibit 5
Work Effectiveness: Basic Steps

BASIC STEPS*	PROCESS	ILLUSTRATIVE TOOLS
1. Identify improvement opportunities, low-value work	Internal and/or external, cross-functional customer and supplier teams discuss, brainstorm	Process mapping; survey of customers on value of work, quality of work; costing of work processes
2. Prioritize opportunities	Internal and/or external customer and supplier teams determine specific priorities	Prioritization criteria (e.g., speed, cost, quality) established, with relative importance set
3. Analyze the current work processes of high-priority opportunities	Small-team work and individual work, with inputs from relevant parties; "benchmark"** best practices (internal and external)	Cost/benefit analyses; Pareto analysis
4. Develop recommendations for process improvement work elimination	Small teams develop improvement recommendations and action plans and submit for approval	Action planning/resource allocation/ scheduling; flowcharting; "force-field" analysis
5. Obtain approval to implement	Leadership decision making	Cost/benefit analysis review; policy review
6. Implement	Small teams change the process, as well as systems, structure, skills as required	New performance measures; new spending authority levels; elimination of work products, work steps; outsourcing
7. Follow up; continuously improve	Involve specific task forces and all managers	Surveys of customers, suppliers, subordinates, team members, peers

Does not include choice of unit, team, and leader; setting objectives for initiative, communication of initiative's objectives, and orientation of participants.
**See e.g., Camp (1989).*

1. Obtain data from customers, suppliers, process operators, and relevant others on: current practice, symptoms, problems, causes, solutions, priorities, barriers.
2. Develop "critical workflow" maps that sketch out, in sequence, the broad, major steps of a process.
3. Develop a detailed "process map," usually describing each step via a flow chart, attach time to perform each step and elapsed time to perform all steps.
4. Identify all key decisions and describe the decision-making process, including roles

(e.g., who "decides," who "provides input," etc.) of key participants.

Once the above noted data is obtained, teams are able to analyze current work processes to identify and prioritize potential improvements. In addition, the detailed snapshot of "what is" uncovers potential problems (e.g., inappropriate managerial style, measures of performance, or skills) that can block implementation and lasting change (Walker, 1990).

Candor and decision making.   When work effectiveness teams have finished their analyses and developed recommended improvements and action plans, they present them to the appropriate managers for decision. This forum must be conducive to candor. (Often an open dialogue with managers/officers about real problems precedes discussion of specific recommendations.) One work effectiveness principle is prompt decision making, which speeds up desirable organizational changes and motivates teams to continue applying the concepts after their defined "project" is implemented. One of GE's sessions to eliminate unnecessary work has been described as follows (capturing the candor and the bias for action noted above) (Stewart, 1991):

> A group of 40 to 100 people, picked by management from all ranks and several functions, goes to a conference center or hotel. The three-day sessions begin with a talk by the boss, who roughs out an agenda. . . . For a day and a half they go at it, listing complaints, debating solutions. . . . The boss . . . comes back and takes a place at the front of the room. Often senior executives come to watch. One by one, team spokesmen rise to make their proposals. By the rules of the game, the boss can make only three responses: He can agree on the spot; he can say no; or he can ask for more information. . . . (pp. 42–43)

Follow-up and monitoring.   Multiple customer-supplier groups often work simultaneously throughout the organization to provide additional leverage for improving productivity. Analyses needing more work are completed. The team's progress is tracked and coordinated, perhaps initially by an individual or group with such a charter, but later by the managers and subordinates themselves. The objective is to eliminate, not create, bureaucracy. Hence coordinators, managers, and trainers are to be kept at a minimum.

Work Effectiveness:
Necessary Conditions for Success

Where successful, the work effectiveness approach has been based on a number of necessary conditions, summarized in Exhibit 6. For

Exhibit 6
Work Effectiveness: Necessary Conditions for Success

1. CEO and/or other top executives lead the effort.
2. Key managers of units, functions are actively involved, are not merely supportive bystanders.
3. A compelling business need to improve exists and is communicated; efforts are focused on specific problems and clear results/outcomes are determined.
4. Relevant parties, representing different hierarchical levels, job groups, and functions, participate in identifying areas of improvement and developing and implementing solutions.
5. Participants frequently and candidly communicate (vertically and horizontally) business needs, issues, solutions, and progress.
6. Thorough descriptions of work processes and data-based analyses of identified issues are conducted prior to reaching solutions.
7. No "sacred cows" (e.g., reporting relationships, staff size, incentive pay plan) exist which are "off limits."
8. Leaders make prompt decisions and changes are implemented quickly.
9. Those who contribute to process improvements are recognized and rewarded.
10. Appropriate changes in systems (e.g., performance measures), skills (e.g., managerial vs. coaching), structure (e.g., reporting relationships), and behaviors/style of managers (e.g., candid communication, listening) are made to reinforce the improvements identified and facilitate implementation.

example, it is critical that senior-level managers be involved, not only by participating in customer-supplier sessions (discussed below), but also by recognizing and reinforcing results achieved. This is not a responsibility that can be delegated. In addition, it is important to make the process analytically based by, for example, documenting or mapping current processes (see e.g., Robson, 1991). This ensures that only well-thought-out changes are made, and provides an analytical framework for employees to work with in their day-to-day responsibilities.

Finally, there should be no "sacred cows"; no organizational processes can be off-limits. For example, a key characteristic of the executives' incentive pay system in one large consumer goods company had recently been revised at great cost and with considerable political infighting during the process. A work effectiveness team's analysis, however, found that the incentive pay system's performance measures inhibited some of the "right" behaviors (e.g., partnering with suppliers to attain quality improvement, not just lower costs), and encouraged some of the "wrong" behaviors (e.g., protecting one's functional "turf," slowing decision making). The system was scrapped and replaced.

Critical to the success of work effectiveness is moving it from being a program or event to becoming an organizational habit. Although these approaches have relied on individuals and specific groups to make numerous organizational improvements, the organization must cement the changes and the approach into its ongoing activities and values. This can be aided by changing relevant systems (e.g., rewards and performance management systems), organizational structure (e.g., reporting relationships), management style (e.g., participation in decision making), and by developing and rewarding appropriate skills (e.g., problem solving or initiative) among all employees.

The alteration of systems, structure, and skills to assure that change lasts is often advanced (see e.g., Beer et al., 1991). What types of structures, skills, and systems support and sustain work effectiveness improvements? Studying such companies as GE, Corning, Citicorp, Northern Telecom, Wal-Mart, and Merck, among others, provides consistent clues:

- *Structure:* Organizations supporting change have flat, horizontal, process-based versus functional structures, and an integrated, fluid network of relationships relying on teams, not bosses (see e.g., Charan, 1991; Ostroff and Smith, 1992).

- *Skills:* For managers in adaptive companies, the preferred style for managers is that of a coach; for all workers, broader discretion requires strong interpersonal, group process, communication, and leadership skills; deep functional expertise may be the "price of admission" for those in customer- and process-based companies, but the rewards will go to those who are results oriented and to both leaders and collaborators (see e.g., Kotter, 1990; Senge, 1991; Whitely, 1991).

- *Systems:* Compensation systems that reinforce work effectiveness are based on performance, not seniority, and emphasize providing rewards via variable pay rather than merely base pay; appraisal systems emphasize ongoing management and development of performance and the execution of business strategy rather than merely rating; broad career "bands," rather than numerous, narrow job classes, are used to stimulate lateral, developmental moves (see e.g., Schneier, 1991, et al.; Ulrich and Lake, 1990; Lawler, 1992).

Structural, skill, and system changes allow work effectiveness efforts to go beyond activities and events to lasting change. But these changes strike at the heart of an organization's culture, as they address, for example, the amount of authority resting in positions and in relationships, the measurements, and the rewards. They are often necessary but extremely difficult changes to make (see Exhibit 6).

Breaking the Vicious Cycle of Downsizing

The pattern of successive downsizings that Kodak has suffered through, noted earlier, has

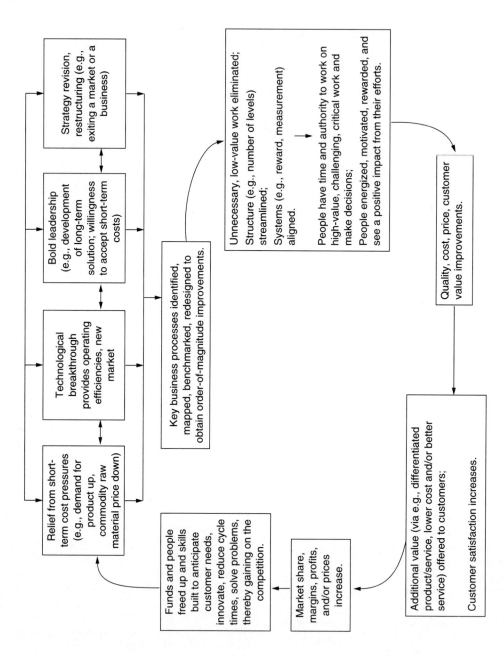

Exhibit 7. Breaking the Vicious Cycle of Downsizing

been repeated over the last few years by many historically successful companies. The evidence is compelling that downsizing too often leads to little more than further downsizing: a vicious cycle (see Exhibit 1) that treats symptoms but does not cure the diseases. While it is difficult medicine to take, work effectiveness approaches have offered many companies one way out of the vicious cycle. As discussed above and noted in Exhibit 7, work process improvements have eliminated low-value work and its associated costs in terms of people, time, and materials. When time is freed up and people are empowered, they are able to focus their energies on high-value-added tasks, such as preventing problems, versus putting out fires. People can develop new technologies or products via innovation, ultimately increasing customer satisfaction, and hence revenues and profits. An improved financial position takes the pressure off the crisis that led to the need for short-term cost cutting and the cycle can repeat itself, leading to further improvements.

There are certainly numerous complexities (e.g., recessionary economic conditions, deregulation, cost of and availability of capital) that today's companies must realistically manage in order to break a vicious cycle of downsizing. Further, work effectiveness approaches require several necessary conditions for success (see Exhibit 6). Yet, companies such as Texas Instruments, Corning, British Petroleum, Ford, Harley Davidson, and numerous others have broken the vicious cycle of downsizing and developed alternatives to short-term "fixes" applied to underlying problems.

Kotter and Heskett (1992) present data to support this relationship between "performance-enhancing cultures" and financial performance (described in Exhibit 7). Companies with performance-enhancing cultures have broken the vicious cycle of poor performance and downsizing via strong leadership, a customers focus, and effective communication. These "adaptive" cultures, as Kotter and Heskett (1992) characterize them,

are able to sustain and build on their success. And like the cycle seen in Exhibit 7, successful performance provides the resources and hence the springboard to regenerate.

Work Effectiveness at Northwest Equipment: A Case Study

In the 1980s, Northwest Equipment (not the company's real name), a durable goods manufacturer, came close to extinction. It was the largest, with over one billion dollars in revenue, and the leading competitor in its industry. Productivity and product quality had slipped badly, though, while costs continued escalating at an unacceptable rate. As its orders dropped, Northwest believed it had little choice but to lay off a large proportion of its 8,000-person hourly work force and slash its exempt work force by 50%, removing several layers of management, consolidating responsibilities, and eliminating numerous positions. After these radical tactics, the company survived, in time to face another crisis.

Competitive Pressures

While Northwest was busy restructuring itself, it was frantically trying to meet its delivery schedules with its reduced work force in order to hold its best customers. Customers' expectations were increasing significantly. Customers began to document the negative financial impact that the poor reliability of Northwest's (and their chief competitor's) products had on their own companies' costs. Total cost over the life of equipment purchased from Northwest became a major concern to customers as they continually searched for ways of reducing their own costs. Northwest's downsizing cut costs, enabling it to lower prices and win back market share; however, little was done in the downsizing effort to improve product reliability. Customers' expectations now outpaced Northwest's ability to provide products at the desired level of reliability. During this period, Northwest's competitors had invested in improvement programs and were beginning to sell products that more closely met the customers' expectations.

Too Much Work

Northwest employees complained that they did not have enough time to focus on their customers' main concerns. Much of their time was spent correcting errors in assembly or servicing products returned under warranty due to quality problems. They were merely reacting to problems, not preventing them, and falling further behind. The vicious cycle had Northwest firmly in its grasp. Employees were already working extremely long hours, and had been doing so since the dramatic layoffs a few years before. When asked, they could point to numerous examples of low-value work that drained their time: too many approvals that slowed decision making, procedures and policies that no longer seemed relevant, and meetings that were unproductive. Rather than changing the processes or procedures, they lived with them—they and their managers had developed a high but unhealthy tolerance for enormous effort expended on low-value work.

With too many ineffective work processes, as well as an increasing competitive threat as a backdrop, Northwest sought an approach to improve productivity and quality. It had tried the quick fixes. Now it was looking for a solution, one that would reorient them to improving the value of the work to their external customers. Northwest knew it needed to involve all, or at least most, of its employees in order to change the culture, eliminate the tolerance for low-value work, and free people up to create long-term solutions.

Northwest's Approach

This particular work effectiveness approach had participation at the top from its inception. The CEO was constantly involved to get the effort underway and keep it going. He personally attended and led many of the sessions in which internal customers and suppliers identified underlying problems and began developing solutions. The organization's top managers were exposed to basic work effectiveness methods and tools, conducted sessions for themselves, and then helped cascade the process to the rest of the organization. During sessions led by either the CEO or one of his direct reports, cross-functional, internal customer-supplier teams were formed to identify issues, analyze relevant work processes, and develop recommended solutions. Each team had performance targets and accountability for results. Work effectiveness was not merely a set of activities; specific outcomes were expected from each session.

The CEO insisted that those examining issues conduct thorough analyses as an integral part of developing solutions. Despite its world-class engineering skills, Northwest was notorious for coming up with solutions without proper analyses. Rewards and recognition were given for extraordinary efforts at "fire fighting" and "crisis management" (correcting errors that should not have been made), not for basic improvement in work processes. The teams made recommendations based on their data gathering and analyses to the CEO and other executives. The executives would typically decide at a team's presentation whether or not to implement a recommended improvement.

In some cases, different teams identified organization-wide structures or systems that had to be analyzed in greater depth. For example, the rewards system was labeled a block to increasing the company's effectiveness. As noted above, it too often measured and rewarded effort, not results, and short-term fixes, not solutions. It pitted functions against each other with cost-cutting goals. To address rewards, Northwest formed a multifunctional, line management team to examine both performance measurement and reward processes. Basic, major work processes, such as manufacturing, maintenance, warehousing, and invoicing, were also mapped (described in detail) and analyzed to identify problems. Candid communication, accountability for solutions, active top management involvement, and data-based problem solving were the keys to Northwest's approach.

Results of Work Effectiveness at Northwest

Northwest can point to a number of successes tied to their work effectiveness effort, including:

1. Thousands of person-hours were saved by eliminating or *streamlining numerous administrative procedures and reports.* This was an important step, since after their massive restructuring earlier in the decade, little work had been eliminated. Some examples included:
   — Streamlining approvals by increasing approval authorities at lower organization levels by as much as 50 times their original level;
   — Rewriting procedures and reducing the time to replace and dispose of equipment from almost a year to one month;
   — Eliminating numerous management reports.

2. *Customer service warehouse activities* were improved in a number of ways: order-to-ship cycle was made nine times faster; over 80% of spare parts were shipped in two days (down from 14 days).

3. *Inventory costs* were decreased by 500%, saving tens of millions of dollars, by completely redesigning the raw material sourcing process, working more closely with fewer suppliers, and concentrating on quality, not just cost, with vendors.

4. The *rejection rate* due to poor quality of a key product component decreased from 35% to 5% once a team of employees (including hourly workers) analyzed the issues, redesigned manufacturing processes, and implemented solutions.

5. *Environmental cleanup* costs were reduced from $1250.00 per ton to $1.00 per ton by training plant personnel to repackage waste material for disposal.

Why Northwest Succeeded

Regardless of the specific approach, the keys to lasting change in organizations are beginning to emerge, and, as noted above, they are strikingly similar across settings (see Bolman and Deal, 1991; Hammer, 1990; Kaplan and Murdock, 1991; Beer et al., 1991; Waterman, 1987). Northwest was no exception. While not all of the items listed in Exhibit 6 were present in the Northwest case, the majority were.

Do Work Effectiveness, Total Quality, and Continuous Improvement Initiatives Differ?

Many organizations now have visible "total quality" initiatives (see Crosby, 1979; Deming, 1986; Juran, 1989). In addition, a significant percentage of organizations have taken a look at how they perform their work and made improvements in workflow or processes, enhancing cost, quality, speed, or customer service via continuous improvement (e.g., Robson, 1991). Are these efforts essentially incompatible or compatible with what has been summarized here as work effectiveness approaches?

Successful performance and productivity improvement approaches, whether they rely on work effectiveness, quality management, continuous improvement, administrative (overhead) value analysis, or even separation incentives, share several characteristics (e.g., "over-"communication, involvement at the top, link to business goals). When executed effectively, however, work effectiveness, as described here, contains differences from other approaches. Exhibit 8 notes some potential (depending on how each is applied) differences between work effectiveness approaches, total quality management approaches, and total quality. One key difference is the emphasis that work effectiveness places, at the outset, on designing a series of forums where managers and employees can communicate candidly, as opposed to classroom training events (see Schaeffer and Thomson, 1992). Work effectiveness improvements are sustained more by changed work processes than by the training events quite common in quality programs. But work effectiveness, like quality management, comes in many varieties, some no doubt less distinguishable from quality efforts than others; *effective* change initiatives are compatible; many cohabit the same company and reinforce each other.

Improving Performance and Productivity: "Treat the Symptoms" or "Cure the Diseases"?

If significant reductions in expenses are needed, for example, because of a drastic reduction in actual or anticipated demand, companies may have to resort to approaches such

Exhibit 8
Comparing Total Quality (TQ) and Work Effectiveness (WE)*

POSSIBLE SIMILARITIES	POSSIBLE DIFFERENCES	POTENTIAL COMMON PROBLEMS**
1. Cost reduction, quality improvement, performance improvement, and/or culture change are objectives	1. WE takes a "zero-based" approach to processes (i.e., first asks if the process should be eliminated); TQ may seek to improve existing processes	1. Emphasis on process and activity, versus results
2. Top management support is advocated as necessary	2. TQ typically emphasizes and may begin with use of a specific set of tools (e.g., SPC, cause and effect diagrams); WE uses any and all tools (including TQ tools) as a means for improvement	2. Event-driven, versus integrated into culture/fabric/daily operations of organization
3. Workflow focus		3. Staff- or consultant-, versus user-driven
4. Empowerment advocated	3. WE advocates attacking "head-on" any cultural or systemic "sacred cows" (e.g., organization reporting relationships, performance measures, rewards) that may block implementation; TQ usually operates within a function or department, hence some barriers to improvements are outside of the function's or department's control	4. Initiative broad, versus obtaining early success to build credibility
5. Logical, data-based approach utilized		
6. Continuous improvement advocated		
7. Determining and meeting customer expectations advocated		
8. Teams typically relied upon to produce significant improvements	4. TQ may (initially) be focused on skill building via classroom training; WE is focused on designing and conducting forums where candid communication takes place, followed up with actions on the job; training may be used but not necessarily as a critical or initial activity	
9. Follow-up advocated		
	5. WE has often begun in white-collar work; TQ has often begun in operations/manufacturing	

TQ and WE can be compatible and even interdependent performance improvement approaches.

*The lists are generalizations; both TQ and WE may be conceived and implemented differently from the above in any given setting.

**Applicable to most large-scale change initiatives.

as layoffs or early retirements. But a growing body of research and numerous companies' experiences, cited here, has shown that these methods typically do not provide lasting improvements. They treat symptoms that often lead to a repeatable cycle of actions with short-term payoffs. Organizations seeking sustained change and improvement are now looking to approaches that focus on streamlining work processes and eliminating low-value work, not merely reducing the number of people in the organization.

Endnote

1. As noted above, there are numerous variations of the work effectiveness approach. An example would be Hammer's "work reengineering" (Hammer, 1990).

References

Bardwick, J. Stemming the Entitlement Tide in American Business. *Management Review,* October, 1991, 57.

Beer, M., Eisenstat, R. A., and Spector, B. Why Change Programs Don't Produce Change. *Harvard Business Review,* November-December, 1990, pp. 158–166.

Beer, M., Eisenstat, R., and Spector, B. *The Critical Path to Corporate Renewal* (Harvard Business School Press: Cambridge, 1991).

Bennett A. "Downsizing Doesn't Necessarily Bring an Upswing in Corporate Profitability." *Wall Street Journal,* June 6, 1991.

Bolman, L. G. and Deal, T. E. *Reframing Organizations* (Jossey-Bass: San Francisco, 1991).

Charan, R. "How Networks Reshape Organizations for Results." *Harvard Business Review,* September-October, 1991, pp. 104–115.

Comp, R. C. *Benchmarking* (Quality Press: Milwaukee, 1989).

Crosby, P. B. *Quality Is Free* (McGraw Hill: New York, 1979).

Deming, W. E. *Out of the Crisis* (MIT Press: Cambridge, 1986).

Dichter, M. and Trank, M. Learning to Manage Reductions in Force. *Management Review,* March, 1991, pp. 40–46.

Drucker, P. "The New Productivity Challenge." *Harvard Business Review,* November-December, 1991, p. 72.

Edelman, L. "Analysts: Digital Taking a Risk with Severance Plan." *The Boston Globe,* March 12, 1990, p. 8.

Hammer, M. "Reengineering Work: Don't Automate, Obliterate." *Harvard Business Review,* July-August, 1990, pp. 104–112.

Henkoff, R. "Cost Cutting: How to Do it Right." *Fortune,* April 9, 1990, pp. 40–50.

Henkoff, R. "Make Your Office More Productive." *Fortune,* February 25, 1991, pp. 72–84.

Hwang, S. L. "SouthWestern Bell Says Many Apply to Retire Early." *Wall Street Journal,* December 9, 1991.

Jick, T. D. "Customer-Supplier Partnerships: Human Resources as Bridge Builders." *Human Resource Management,* 1990, 29(4), pp. 411–434.

Juran, J. M. *Juran on Leadership for Quality* (Free Press: New York, 1989).

Kaplan, R. B. and Murdock, L. "Core Process Redesign." *The McKinsey Quarterly,* 1991, pp. 27–43.

Kaydos, W. *Measuring, Managing, and Maximizing Performance* (Productivity Press: Cambridge, MA, 1991).

Knight, C. F. "Emerson Electric: Consistent Profits, Consistently." *Harvard Business Review,* January-February, 1992, pp. 57–70.

Koretz, G. "Layoffs Aren't Working the Way They're Supposed To." *Business Week,* October, 1991.

Kotter, J. P. and Heskett, J. L. *Corporate Culture and Performance* (Free Press: New York, 1992).

Kotter, J. P. *The Leadership Factor* (Free Press: New York, 1990).

Lawler, E. E. *The Ultimate Advantage* (Jossey-Bass: San Francisco, 1992).

O'Reilly, B. "Preparing for Leaner Times." *Fortune,* January 27, 1992, pp. 40–47.

Ostroff, F. and Smith, D. "The Horizontal Organization." *The McKinsey Quarterly,* 1992, pp. 148–168.

Robson, G. D. *Continuous Process Improvement* (Free Press: New York, 1991).

Schaeffer, R. J. and Thomson, H. A. "Successful Change Programs Begin with Results." *Harvard Business Review,* January-February, 1992, pp. 80–89.

Schneier, C. E., Shaw, D. G., and Beatty, R. W. "Performance Measurement and Management: A Tool for Strategy Execution." *Human Resource Management,* 1992, in press.

Senge, P. M. *The Fifth Discipline* (Doubleday: New York, 1990).

Stalk, G. and Hout, T. M. *Competing against Time* (Free Press: New York, 1990).

Stewart, T. A. "GE Keeps Those Ideas Coming." *Fortune,* August 12, 1991, pp. 41–49.

Taylor, A. A "U.S. Style Shakeup at Honda." *Fortune,* December 30, 1991, pp. 115–120.

Taylor, A. "Why Toyota Keeps Getting Better and Better and Better." *Fortune,* November 19, 1990, pp. 66–79.

Thurow, L. C. "White-Collar Overhead." *Across the Board,* November 1986, pp. 25–37.

Ulrich, D. and Lake, D. *Organizational Capability* (Wiley: New York, 1990).

Walker, J. W. "Human Resource Planning, 1990s Style." *Human Resource Planning,* 1990, 13(4), pp. 229–240.

Walker, J. W. *Human Resource Strategy* (McGraw-Hill: New York, 1992).

Waterman, R. H. *The Renewal Factor* (Bantam: Toronto, 1987).

Whiteley, R. C. *The Customer-Driven Company* (Addison Wesley: Reading, MA, 1991).

Index